WITHDRAWN

opposing viewpoints SOURCES

foreign policy

opposing viewpoints

foreign policy

vol. 1

David L. Bender, *Publisher*
Bruno Leone, *Executive Editor*
M. Teresa O'Neill, *Senior Editor*
Claudia Debner, *Editor*
Bonnie Szumski, *Editor*
Lynn Hall, *Editorial Assistant*
Pat Jordan, *Editorial Assistant*

David Owen Kieft, Ph.D., *Consulting Editor*
Associate Professor of History
University of Minnesota, Minneapolis

greenhaven press, inc.

577 Shoreview Park Road
St. Paul, MN 55126

ISBN 0-89908-516-4
ISSN 0748-2841

"Congress shall make no law. . .abridging the freedom of speech, or of the press."

first amendment to the US Constitution

contents

foreword

"It is better to debate a question without settling it than to settle a question without debating it."

Joseph Joubert (1754-1824)

The purpose of Opposing Viewpoints SOURCES is to present balanced, and often difficult to find, opposing points of view on complex and sensitive issues.

Probably the best way to become informed is to analyze the positions of those who are regarded as experts and well studied on issues. It is important to consider every variety of opinion in an attempt to determine the truth. Opinions from the mainstream of society should be examined. But also important are opinions that are considered radical, reactionary, or minority as well as those stigmatized by some other uncomplimentary label. An important lesson of history is the eventual acceptance of many unpopular and even despised opinions. The ideas of Socrates, Jesus, and Galileo are good examples of this.

Readers will approach this anthology with their own opinions on the issues debated within it. However, to have a good grasp of one's own viewpoint, it is necessary to understand the arguments of those with whom one disagrees. It can be said that those who do not completely understand their adversary's point of view do not fully understand their own.

A persuasive case for considering opposing viewpoints has been presented by John Stuart Mill in his work *On Liberty*. When examining controversial issues it may be helpful to reflect on his suggestion:

> The only way in which a human being can make some approach to knowing the whole of a subject, is by hearing what can be said about it by persons of every variety of opinion, and studying all modes in which it can be looked at by every character of mind. No wise man ever acquired his wisdom in any mode but this.

Analyzing Sources of Information
Opposing Viewpoints SOURCES includes diverse materials taken from magazines, journals, books, and newspapers, as well as statements and position papers from a wide range of individuals, organiza-

tions and governments. This broad spectrum of sources helps to develop patterns of thinking which are open to the consideration of a variety of opinions.

Pitfalls to Avoid
A pitfall to avoid in considering opposing points of view is that of regarding one's own opinion as being common sense and the most rational stance and the point of view of others as being only opinion and naturally wrong. It may be that another's opinion is correct and one's own is in error.

Another pitfall to avoid is that of closing one's mind to the opinions of those with whom one disagrees. The best way to approach a dialogue is to make one's primary purpose that of understanding the mind and arguments of the other person and not that of enlightening him or her with one's own solutions. More can be learned by listening than speaking.

It is my hope that after reading this anthology the reader will have a deeper understanding of the issues debated and will appreciate the complexity of even seemingly simple issues on which good and honest people disagree. This awareness is particularly important in a democratic society such as ours where people enter into public debate to determine the common good. Those with whom one disagrees should not necessarily be regarded as enemies, but perhaps simply as people who suggest different paths to a common goal.

The Format of SOURCES
In this anthology, carefully chosen opposing viewpoints are purposely placed back to back to create a running debate; each viewpoint is preceded by a short quotation that best expresses the author's main argument. This format instantly plunges the reader into the midst of a controversial issue and greatly aids that reader in mastering the basic skill of

recognizing an author's point of view. In addition, the table of contents gives a brief description of each viewpoint, allowing the reader to identify quickly the point of view for which he or she is searching.

Each section of this anthology debates an issue, and the sections build on one another so that the anthology as a whole debates a larger issue. By using this step-by-step, section-by-section approach to understanding separate facets of a topic, the reader will have a solid background upon which to base his or her opinions. Each year a supplement of twenty opposing viewpoints will be added to this anthology, enabling the reader to keep abreast of annual developments.

This volume of Opposing Viewpoints SOURCES does not advocate a particular point of view. Quite the contrary! The very nature of the anthology leaves it to the reader to formulate the opinions he or she finds most suitable. My purpose as publisher is to see that this is made possible by offering a wide range of viewpoints that are fairly presented.

David L. Bender
Publisher

introduction

"A nation that rejects national interests as the mainspring of its policy cannot survive."

Arthur Schlesinger Jr., August 1971

An important axiom held by most modern international strategists is that the foreign policy of a nation must be consistent with what is believed to be that nation's best interests. However, seldom do the leaders of a democratic nation determine that nation's best interests without extensive debate and without an occasional compromise of ideals. As a world-leading democratic power, America is especially shadowed by this predicament. Is it in the best interests of the United States to acquire territory, to contain communism, to do what seems morally right as opposed to what is expedient, or to engage in trade protectionism? If the US acts upon one of these overriding interests, will the impact on the others be adverse or beneficial? The annexation of the Philippine Islands by the United States in 1898 following the defeat of Spain in the Spanish-American War is a telling illustration of this dilemma of national policy as it applies to the international arena.

On January 9, 1900, Albert J. Beveridge, an influential Republican senator from Indiana, delivered a speech before the US Senate calling for support of the recent annexation of the Philippines by the United States. He reminded his Senate colleagues that the Philippines are a "territory belonging to the United States... [from which] we will not retreat." His emotional plea concluded with this warning, namely that if America wavers in its determination to maintain possession of the Pacific islands, "every other progressive nation stands ready to relieve us."

Although the acquisition of the Philippines profaned America's professed constitutional principles of freedom, equality and self-determination, many political leaders and important citizens believed that America needed colonies in order to enhance its strength, security, and credibility in the global community of nations. The economic and military advantages of a colonial empire were obvious. Colonies provided a ready market for the sale and distribution of surplus goods produced in the mother country.

Many were rich in valuable resources which were unavailable at home. Finally, colonies could serve as naval bases in the event of war and as stepping-stones from which further colonization would be possible.

There were many groups and individuals who opposed the colonial ambitions of Beveridge and other like-minded politicians. On October 17, 1899, one such group met in Chicago and formed the American Anti-Imperialist League. The League's avowed purpose was to oppose all persons seeking political office who supported the "forcible subjugation of any people." At about the same time, the Democratic party formally stated its opposition to colonialism. In fact, the party's 1900 presidential platfrom prominently displayed these words: "No nation can long endure half republic and half empire." And Carl Schurz, one of America's most authoritative 19th century statesmen, decried colonialism as "the very thing against which the Declaration of Independence remonstrated, and against which the fathers rose in revolution." At the core of all opposition to the Philippine enterprise stood the belief that any imperialistic adventure would ultimately prove fatal to the American democratic tradition.

However, the forces of expansionism won the day. It was a time in American history when appeals to the ethical sensibilities of the nation were of small consequence against the weightier arguments of national wealth and international status. In the 19th century, most of the major European powers, led by England, were hungrily creating extensive colonial empires throughout much of the world. As a member of the Western family of nations, the architects of US foreign policy were convinced that America's best interest lay in implementing similar policies. Whether the annexation of the Philippines did or did not actually serve America's best interests continues to be debated.

While today there is no question of the United

States annexing another country, the problem of what policies best serve America in our complex, problem-ridden world remains. America cannot avoid making difficult judgments about how much and what kind of aid to give developing countries. It cannot avoid policy decisions regarding trade and alliances with countries whose internal policies may be considered morally repugnant. It cannot avoid the question of what degree of involvement in the affairs of other nations is necessary to counteract a perceived communist threat to its own security. As was the case with the Philippines, the pivotal question is unchanged: What policy course best serves America's interests?

This anthology of *Opposing Viewpoints SOURCES* attempts to approach American foreign policy in the broadest possible way. It begins with a comprehensive series of opinions debating the basis and goals of foreign policy and their relationship to defense, trade, foreign aid, human rights, interventionism, covert operations, and terrorism. It continues by presenting discussions on the nature and scope of US global strategy specifically relating to Europe, Asia, Central America, the Third World, Africa, and the Middle East. The viewpoints are drawn from a wide spectrum of authoritative sources. They include the ideas of politicians, journalists, academics, clergy, diplomats, and revolutionary leaders. Moreover, the editors have endeavored to incorporate such relevant materials as documents and position papers from governmental agencies (both foreign and American) and privately funded organizations. If falls upon the reader to evaluate these sources and finally decide: By what course of action can America best serve its national interests?

"The fundamental problems of politics, in the modern world as in the ancient one, have been and inevitably will be moral."

Morality Must Guide Foreign Policy

Henry Steele Commager

The fundamental problems of politics, in the modern world as in the ancient one, have been and inevitably will be moral. To the ancients the maxim that no state could long flourish without virtue was clear. Equally clear was the conclusion that no state had ever conducted itself virtuously over a long span of years. We are all familiar with the philosophical and the practical debate over this problem, one that has perplexed statesmen and philosophers from the beginnings of history. We need only think of the New Testament account of Herod's massacre of the Innocents—an issue that conjured up, or *seemed* to conjure up, Reasons of State.

This issue is very much with us today, and with greater urgency than at any previous era of history. For the first time the issue of Reasons of State directly concerns not just one people or one nation but the whole of mankind—indeed, the fate of the earth. And it is one that, historically and philosophically, American experience may illuminate.

A New Paradise

From the beginning of their independent history Americans assumed that they could somehow escape the fate history had meted out to all other peoples; that, protected as they were by a wide ocean, aloof from the quarrels that had afflicted nations "who feel power and forget right," and with land enough for their descendants "to the thousandth and thousandth generation," they might indeed confound history and "advance to destinies beyond the reach of mortal eye." Thus Tom Paine asserted that the American "was a new Adam in a new Paradise." So too the "poet of the Revolution," Philip Freneau, boasted that "Paradise anew shall flourish/By no second Adam lost."

Henry Steele Commager, "Machiavelli in the New World," *Worldview*, August 1983. Reprinted with permission.

Washington's favorite poet, David Humphreys, wrote more elaborately:

All former empires rose, the work of guilt,
On conquest, blood, or usurpation built
But we, taught wisdom by their woes and crimes
Fraught with their lore, and born in better times
Our constitutions form'd on freedom's base....

In his first inaugural address Washington made it official:

The foundation of our national policy will be laid in the pure and immutable principles of private morality. . . .(For) there is no truth more thoroughly established than that there exists in the economy and course of nature an indissoluble union between virtue and happiness, between duty and advantage, between the genuine maxims of an honest and magnanimous policy and the solid rewards of public prosperity and felicity.

Though there are antecedents in the ancient and even in the early modern world, it was Machiavelli who first used the term Reason of State in the sense in which it has since been accepted and who first propounded the arguments that have ever since been used to vindicate it. With his writing—chiefly *The Discourses on Livy*—he gave it not only dignity and authority but almost official status. Machiavelli's concern was not with morals but with power, and his philosophy was secular. His logic was that embraced by most modern nations, certainly since the eighteenth century, and embraced alike by princes, aristocracies (this notwithstanding Montesquieu's conclusion that the principle of an aristocracy is *honor*), and, in modern times, by both republican-democratic and Communist-totalitarian states alike—namely, that the claims of the state take precedence over *all* competing claims and that the survival, the prosperity, and the glory of the state (or the crown, or the republic, or the soviet) is the ultimate good.

Reason of State

Machiavelli did not regard himself as an enemy of morality, and quite rightly by his own logic. For that logic was a secularization of religion. As formal religion insisted that the triumph of the true Church justified any conduct, including warfare, banishment, torture, or death, it followed that a secular religion could invoke the same sanctions to achieve *its* ends.

It was to the prosperity, power, and glory of France that Machiavelli addressed himself. That goal was a moral one because it contributed to the triumph of the House of Medici and opened the way to the absorption of lesser states and, ultimately, a unification of Italy. This, in turn, would bring peace and prosperity. Thus, on behalf not only of Florence but of Italy, the prince must be exalted, must have absolute power over his subjects.

In all this, Machiavelli anticipated the ultimate rationale for the ultimate victory of political, military, and economic nationalism—a nationalism still prepared to project its own code of ethics and morality on its own people and on other peoples and nations.

"In his first inaugural address Washington made it official: 'The foundation of our national policy will be laid in the pure and immutable principles of private morality.'"

Few chapters in the history of civilization are more instructive, or sobering, than that which recounts the emergence of modern nationalism in the eighteenth century and recalls the brief hope that an enlightenment, associated with both science and morality, could somehow impose itself upon that nationalism. That chapter is particularly interesting to us because it was in the New World that that goal was realized, however briefly. But it was an ideal and a hope that flickered on the horizons of the *philosophes* of every Western nation—the hope that morals and science both followed laws of nature and that these laws would somehow win the allegiance of rulers and philosophers alike.

The evidence here is as elaborate as the *Grand Encyclopédie* that is perhaps the most appropriate monument to the Enlightenment. Thus Joseph Banks, for forty-one years president of the Royal Society, was the patron and guardian of science everywhere. He sponsored Captain Cook, and rejoiced when Benjamin Franklin and French statesman Jacques Necker promulgated an order to their joint navies not to disturb the great captain as he was engaged in activities beneficial to mankind. It was an age when Rousseau could pay tribute to "those great cosmopolitan minds that make light of the barriers that sunder nation from nation, and embrace all mankind within their benevolence." It was an age when George III could cherish the Philadelphia-born

Benjamin West as his court artist and when all through the war West could welcome American students to his atelier—students whose paintings celebrated American victories over the British.

Enlightened Policies

Much of this was the expression of individuals; much of it too was an expression of enlightened academic and governmental policy.

How illuminating is the history of the Royal Society, founded in 1642 by Charles II under the auspices of such "natural philosophers and moral philosophers" as Sir Isaac Newton and John Locke and embracing in its fold men of letters as well as men of science. It was Christopher Wren, then doubling as professor of astronomy at Oxford University and architect of St. Paul's Cathedral, who drafted the charter: "The way to so happy a government...is in no manner more facilitated than by the promoting of useful arts which...are found to be the basis of civil communities and free government, and which gather multitudes, *by an orpheus charm,* into cities and companies...."

A century later the American Philosophical Society (of which Jefferson was to be the third president) wrote a similar provision into its charter: "Whereas nations truly civilized will never wage war with the arts and sciences and the common interests of mankind, the Society should retain cordial relations with learned societies everywhere in the world, regardless of politics and war."

Some of the Enlightenment philosophers had already gone so far as to propose learned academies, not merely to advance knowledge but to guide the destinies of nations. That was the essence of Condorcet's ambitious plan in *The New Atlantis,* which proposed an international society of natural philosophers, whose members would be concerned not with practical investigations but with "pure" research. It was to be sponsored by crowned heads of nations and supported by contributions from several governments, the aristocracy, and, prophetically enough, by the business and commercial community. "All the scientists," Condorcet asserted somewhat wildly, would "be animated by a passion for truth," and governments, eager to contribute "to the happiness of the human species," would follow its recommendations.

Platonic Republic

The philosophy that animated all these individuals was the Platonic concept of a Republic: Kings would be philosophers and philosophers would be kings. Alas, that did not work out—except in America. There alone it was the philosophers, natural and moral alike, who were in fact chosen by the people to guide the affairs of state: Franklin, president of Pennsylvania; John Adams, chief justice of Massachusetts and author of its first constitution;

Jefferson, governor of Virginia and vice-president and president of the new nation; John Jay, governor of New York and the first chief justice of the new nation; James Madison, who drafted the national Bill of Rights; and, in the same company, those two English-born philosophers who found refuge in America and helped create and mold the new nation, Thomas Paine and Joseph Priestly.

The superiority of the claims of science and philosophy over those of politics was as much part of the American Enlightenment tradition as was the supremacy of the Constitution over legislation or executive conduct.

The drama of morality in America was to be played out against two competing or alternating backgrounds—the background of nationalism (we were, after all, the first nation to be "made") and the background of modern science. The animating drive of the first was the wealth and glory of the state; the animating impulse of the second, enlightenment and cosmopolitanism. The seminal principle of the first was power, that of the second, "the illimitable freedom of the human mind."

Americans have never been willing to acknowledge formally the principle of "Reasons of State." Here as elsewhere they have preferred to find more exalted arguments for justifying their conduct: that they are "God's children" or his "chosen people" or that their country is "the promised land" and their government "the last best hope of earth." These are not only euphemisms but substitutes for reason. And however nature and history may have conspired to provide supporting evidence for these terms, the rationale has commonly been that which has animated all other modern states.

Manifest Destiny

The American version of Reason of State was, from the start, based on religious and cultural grounds. This combined speedily to conjure up the fancy (perhaps the conceit) of "Manifest Destiny"—a destiny more manifest to the Americans who profited from it than to the native inhabitants who were its victims. The philosophy of Manifest Destiny was not, in fact, very different from that elaborated by Machiavelli: first, that God had presided over the migration from the Old World to the New; second, that God could not have intended that so vast and rich a territory be confined to a few scattered tribes but looked with favor on its occupation by an enlightened Christian people; and third—and closely connected with the second—that the native peoples were, after all, heathens and, unless prepared to be converted, destined for eternal damnation.

This philosophy had the immense advantage of being impossible to refute and readily refurbished for almost any new circumstance. It applied to the territories controlled by the Spanish as well as by Indians, thus justifying the annexation of two Floridas, the Mexican War, and the acquisition of Texas and California as well as all the land between. If the Spaniards were not heathens, they were Catholics, and that was almost as bad. Manifest Destiny rationalized (and still does) American hegemony over the Caribbean—this for strategic purposes, which can always be found and were found to apply to Hawaii and the Philippines.

"How revealing it is . . . that Americans already have put out of their minds and consciences responsibility for inaugurating the age of atomic warfare."

This philosophy could be stretched, if necessary, to justify slavery as well as conquest. The story is too familiar for repetition. Suffice it to recall that generations of civilized and virtuous Christians persuaded themselves that slavery, far from being a "necessary evil," became quickly a positive good. And a blessing alike to slaves and to masters. It rescued millions of Africans from "certain damnation" and, by conferring on them the blessings of Christianity, assured them eternal salvation. It provided the basis for a high civilization in the South; it was essential to national and world prosperity.

We should take this long and painful chapter of our history to heart, for better than anything else in our own experience it makes clear how a highly civilized and Christian people could, for over two hundred years, persist in practicing and justifying what most of us now find inexplicable and immoral.

The Task of Empire

Some features of this American Reason of State persisted long after formal slavery was abolished and long after manifestations of racial prejudice were outlawed through constitutional amendment. Not only did that prejudice persist and flourish, but it emerged, thirty years after the Civil War, in a new form of imperialism. As the *Washington Post* put it: "The taste of empire is in the mouth of the people even as the taste of blood in the jungle. It means an Imperial policy, the Republic, renascent, taking her place with the armed nations." It was the "imperial policy" that dictated the three-year war against the Filipinos fighting for their independence, a war characterized by moral arrogance, the illusion of the white man's burden, and brutality. We have forgotten (but perhaps the Filipinos have not) the once-popular soldiers' song:

Damm, damm, damn the Filipinos
Slant-eyed kakiack ladrones
And beneath the starry flag
Civilize them with a krag
And return us to our own beloved homes.

Reason of State in the U.S. was a curious amalgam of imperialism, commercial interest, the white man's burden, and religion—all bundled together in President McKinley's famous explanation of how God directed him to rule the Philippines. It was a rationalization that the poet William Vaughn Moody lamented in his "Ode in Time of Hesitation":

> Lies, lies, it cannot be! The wars we wage
> Are noble, and our battles still are won
> By justice for us, ere we lift the gage
> We have not sold our loftiest heritage.
> The proud Republic hath not stooped to cheat
> And scramble in the market place of war
> Ah, no! We have not fallen so
> Tempt not our weakness, our cupidity!...
> O ye who lead, take heed
> Blindness we may forgive but baseness we will smite.

Where now is our William Vaughn Moody?

"Machiavelli . . . first used the term Reason of State in the sense in which it has since been accepted: . . . That the claims of the state take precedence over all competing claims."

It is scarcely necessary to illustrate the American propensity for justifying by Reason of State what is surely the most fateful series of decisions made in recorded history: the decision to drop the atomic bomb on Hiroshima and Nagasaki in August, 1945, and the decision (Truman's also) to go ahead with the nuclear race in 1953. Neither the military nor the larger international justifications that have been proferred will, I think, be accepted by later generations—if any. But how revealing it is, in this connection, that Americans already have put out of their minds and consciences responsibility for inaugurating the age of atomic warfare. Indeed, by a process of self-induced amnesia they still talk of the threat of a "first strike" and of how such a strike is to be prevented—as if we had not already made the first strike almost forty years ago, and this though there was no danger of a counterstrike that had to be deterred.

No More Arrogant Decisions

As we contemplate this long record, we may still conclude that we are indeed God's "chosen people," but there is considerable evidence to the contrary. Today, every major problem has international and often worldwide ramifications, and global cooperation has become necessary to survival. It is the imperative nature of this requirement that offers gound for hope.

Certainly no nation may continue to harbor that notion which partakes of the "unpardonable sin"—that it has the right to decide on the survival of the human race and the fate of the earth. It is an arrogance that makes that of Milton's Lucifer seem moderate.

Henry Steele Commager is a distinguished historian who has written numerous books. He is John Woodruff Simpson Lecturer at Amherst College.

"A case can be made that there is already more morality in American foreign policy than we can survive."

Moralizing Can Be Detrimental to Foreign Policy

Paul Craig Roberts

The complaints we hear today about the absence of morality in American foreign policy may be deceptive. A case can be made that there is already more morality in American foreign policy than we can survive. This case has never been presented, and I want to present it for consideration. There is an inconsistency in the modern frame of mind that almost precludes positive interpretations of Western experience. A result is that the considerable demands for progress are expressed in terms of accusations against ourselves. In short, our morality is inverted into a form of self-condemnation. Michael Polanyi has written about how the modern frame of mind has been shaped by an inconsistency in the intellectual foundations of Western civilization, an inconsistency that may work itself out in the destruction of our civilization. The inconsistency stems from the secularization of Christian moral fervor, which produced demands for the moral perfection of society, and from the impact of modern science on our concept of knowledge, which produced a critical philosophical positivism that is sceptical of the reality of moral motives.

The result of the former is a social and political dynamism that is committed to the moral perfection of human society. But the result of the latter is a sceptical sophistication that tends to see morality in terms of high sounding rationales for lowly but truer motives. We are all used to moral motives being unmasked as rationalizations for class and individual interests or explained as expressions of social, economic, psychological or political needs.

This unmasking does not prevent moral expression or demands for progress, but does make it easier for moral expression to take a denunciatory rather than an affirmatory form. A morally affirmatory

statement, especially if it is in defense of existing society or its achievements, arouses the suspicion of dishonesty and is subject to being unmasked. It encounters objections both from the advocates of social change, who see it as a defense of the status quo, and from sceptics who look for the real motive that is operating behind the moral guise.

Scepticism and Moral Indignation

On the other hand, a morally denunciatory statement, especially if it is an accusation against existing society, is seen as an expression of the indignation of the morally honest reformer. In this way moral motives can be asserted backhandedly in praise of social dissenters easier than they can be asserted straightforwardly in praise of society's achievements. Scepticism and moral indignation are complementary in the critique of society. Together they support the social and political dynamism that is committed to achieving progress by remaking society.

The combination of scepticism with moral denunciation has led to many reforms that have humanized Western society and also to outbreaks of revolutionary violence, because the way they combine against existing society preempts its moral defense while at the same time focusing moral indignation against it. In the intellectual world this has made it difficult for affirmative accounts of Western experience, whether in the interpretation of Western history, or in the explanation of social and political reform, or in the defense of an anti-communist foreign policy. Any scholar, intellectual, or student who attempts to establish that good will has been an effective force in Western civilization runs a risk of being dismissed as naive and unscientific or even as intellectually dishonest, because any reform attributed to the efficacy of good will can also be explained in terms, for example, of the triumph of class interests. As would be expected, affirmative interpretations of Western achievements

Paul Craig Roberts, "Alienation and US Foreign Policy," *Modern Age*, Spring 1977. Reprinted by permission of the author.

drop out of contention, leaving the field to cynical accounts that further undermine the moral confidence of the West in its past experience and future direction.

The Untenability of Affirmation

The untenability of affirmation has rendered ineffective, and even impossible, any moral defense of the West. Affirmations of Western achievements or institutions are likely to provoke stiff and strident protests against jingoistic justifications of imperialism and neo-colonialism and, at best, to be chided for complacency. This poses a serious problem for the continued existence of Western civilization, but it is not the most serious. The inconsistency in the modern frame of mind presents an even more serious problem. The restraint scepticism places on moral expression means that moral feelings, which have been secularized and given social purpose, have no legitimate positive form of expression. Since moral affirmations receive a sceptical response, moral expression has a safe outlet only in accusations of immorality against existing society.

"Any scholar, intellectual, or student who attempts to establish that good will has been an effective force in Western civilization runs a risk of being dismissed as naive and unscientific or even as intellectually dishonest."

This means, unfortunately, that a society in which this frame of mind is prevalent will express its desire for progress mainly in an attack on itself, and it will rely on self-criticism as its means for achieving progress. At the same time, however, attacks on alternative institutions will tend to be dismissed as defenses of the status quo, and scepticism about the policies and motives of an opposing society will be given short shrift as an expression of jingoism. An attack on an opposing society's practices and motives implies a defense of one's own—and that is taken as indifference to existing evils. Among many intellectuals such an attack will be more effective in eliciting resentment rather than support, because it focuses attention away from the domestic imperfections which are seen as the real barrier to progress.

The further a society is outside the Western framework, the less it will provoke the West's moral indignation. The "double standard," to which (primarily) conservatives have objected, is merely a reflection of the modern frame of mind. It is only to be expected that within this frame of mind denunciatory rhetoric will rise to new heights over

the execution of 5 terrorists in Spain but not over the execution of tens of hundreds of thousands of ordinary people by communists in Cambodia.

Modern Alienation

We are all by now familiar with the modern alienated intellectual whose alienation amounts to a moral hatred of existing society. He has a passion for moral improvement of his society, but he has worked out the doctrine of doubt to its logical conclusion. Since he cannot find moral motives safe from the suspicion of mere conformity, self-interest, or hypocrisy, he can find no safe grounds for moral affirmation. His moral passions, being thus denied legitimate expression, are satisfied by turning his scepticism against his own society. He denounces its institutions and policies as masks for the material profit of vested interests. Michael Polanyi has shown that this inconsistent combination of moral scepticism with moral indignation is held together by their joint attack on society.

Of course, everyone is not equally affected by this frame of mind to the extent that an alienated intellectual is, and all critics of society are not alienated intellectuals. Nevertheless, its impact is pervasive. Today we grow up in this frame of mind in the way we grow up in our language. But whereas the structure of our language has been extensively studied, the structure of our frame of mind has not. That something is amiss has not escaped notice, but the usual appellations of "double-standard," "death-wish," "guilt," etc., are too feeble to give us a handle on our dilemma.

Take a typical American liberal intellectual. His commitment to his society is usually conditional upon institutional and policy changes. Therefore, his allegiance at any point in time is weak, because to satisfy his desire for moral honesty he must forever remain an opponent of existing society. His program will not emphasize building on the past achievements and successes of the society, but correcting past failures and righting past wrongs. He will not see his country's gifts of foreign aid as attesting to its moral sense, but the insufficient amount will be evidence of an immoral foreign policy. He will justify foreign nationalization of his fellow citizens' property as a necessary remedy for neo-colonial exploitation. He will not see lack of progress in arms limitations as a reflection on the opponent's intentions but, instead, on his own country's lack of good faith. He will not see a strong defense posture as a justifiable response to an external threat, but as "provocative" and the cause of an arms race. On the domestic scene he will champion the failure as victims of society, and he will explain the successful in terms of ill-gotten gains. He will not even be a Marxist, but just an ordinary member of the verbalist institution.

The fusion of moral scepticism with the demand for moral perfection means that the West's morality becomes immanent in attacks on itself. Readers of the *Washington Post* and *New York Times,* and university students, are all accustomed to the use of moral scepticism to unmask the alleged immorality of existing society. To note this is not to attack the press and the universities, but to observe that this frame of mind is so endemic that the challenge it presents to foreign and defense policies necessary to the survival of the West and to protect its interests must be realized.

West's Attacks on Self

The West has relied for so long on a self-critical posture as its means of achieving improvement that it naturally and unthinkingly adopts this stance in its relations with external enemies. . . .

The communists do not share our dilemma. In their doctrine the morality of Marxism is immanent in its historical inevitability. Marxism does not rely on self-scepticism as a means of achieving progress. The destruction of the West by Soviet communism poses no moral dilemma to them, because they see it as the inevitable consequence of historical progression.

"The fusion of moral scepticism with the demand for moral perfection means that the West's morality becomes immanent in attacks on itself."

However, our own defense poses a considerable moral dilemma to us because of the frame of mind I have analyzed. In any realistic assessment of the strategic balance, this disadvantage must be included.

Paul Craig Roberts holds the William E. Simon Chair in political economy at the Center for Strategic and International Studies at Georgetown University.

"What lies at the root of America's foreign policy problem...has been a confusion of values."

Foreign Policy Must Be Based on Ideology

John Lenczowski

The seeds of totalitarian regimes are nurtured by misery and want. They spread and grow in the evil and soil of poverty and strife. They reach their full growth when the hope of a people for a better life has died. We must keep that hope alive.

—President Harry S. Truman
(Truman Doctrine Speech
March 12, 1947)

With these words, President Truman revealed an understanding of a basic truth that has too often been forgotten: that there are inextricable links and similarities between domestic and foreign policies. In both cases policy-makers are concerned with similar problems: the satisfaction of basic human needs, the creation of wealth, the attraction of constituencies, the protection of human rights, and the attenuation of threats to the public order.

One can observe, for example, that American foreign policy has treated the Third World much in the same way as we treat in the inner-city ghetto: We send food stamps and welfare (foreign aid) for the poor, and when the natives get restless, we send in the police. And just like the ghetto, the Third World continues to stagnate.

Aimless Drift

But, in the last decade U.S. policy has suffered from an aimless drift. It has been reactive and defensive rather than active and positive. We have had to *cope* with events seemingly beyond our control rather than try to *create* international conditions favorable to us. We no longer send in the police; we simply fence off the area and issue proclamations about the counterproductiveness of rioting. In short,

"A Foreign Policy for Reaganauts," by John Lenczowski, is reprinted by permission from *Policy Review*, Issue No. 18 (or Fall 1982). *Policy Review* is a publication of The Heritage Foundation, 214 Massachusetts Ave. NE, Washington DC, 20002.

it has been typically lamented that America had no strategy. The problem here, of course, is that a strategy is nothing more than a means to an end. You cannot have a strategy without goals, nor goals without values. What lies at the root of America's foreign policy problem, therefore, has been a confusion of values, the absence of a guiding philosophy, a conceptual framework, a positive vision toward which policy-makers can strive.

Since so much of the conduct of foreign policy simply consists of staving off trouble, the absence of such a guiding philosophy means that foreign policy success is often measured against a standard of much lower expectations than those focused on domestic concerns. Thus, the very act of staying out of war may be considered a foreign policy success, notwithstanding the fact that the world may be in political, economic, and revolutionary upheaval to the ultimate detriment of vital national interests. This can be so since foreign policy-makers are usually less immediately accountable to their domestic constituents than domestic policy-makers are. The effects of foreign policy failures are less visible to the domestic public and are often likely to have longer periods of gestation. In other words, it is easier for our foreign policy-makers to get away with either mistakes or even betrayals of the public trust.

But the values that govern our domestic policies can also serve as a guide to our foreign policy and as a standard of its success. These are the values enshrined in the Constitution, the Bill of Rights and the Declaration of Independence, which have made possible both political pluralism and the conduct of orderly and peaceful political change. To divorce foreign policy from these values is to set it adrift and to make it, quite literally, aimless.

Crucial Similar Ideologies

The links between our values, the national interest, and political conditions abroad are inescapable. To guarantee our national security, our most vital interest, we need unimpeded access to sea lanes, energy supplies, raw materials, and if necessary, foreign military bases. Such access depends upon the cooperation of as many friendly countries as possible. Whether or not a country will be friendly depends largely upon how much it shares common values with us. It is a matter of common observation that those governments which respect human rights and the independence of their neighbors tend to be friendly; and those which systematically violate human rights and enslave other countries tend to view us as enemies and as a threat to their legitimacy. It is here that distinctions between the different ideologies of nations are so crucial (including such distinctions as that between totalitarianism and authoritarianism). To disregard these is to pretend that the world is enjoying true peace and is not disturbed by a serious moral conflict. It is to deny the fact that ideas, even ostensibly strange, irrational, and non-pragmatic ones, influence the minds and actions of foreign leaders. It is to ignore the basic truth that moral conflicts between nations translate into political and strategic conflicts.

"To divorce foreign policy from (national) values is to set it adrift and to make it, quite literally, aimless."

In the course of our philosophical vertigo of the past decade, we have failed to understand many of the ideological underpinnings of contemporary international problems. For reasons peculiar to the dominant rationalistic and secular ideological tendencies of our intellectual elites, we continually refuse to accept the possibility that others may entertain, in an equally rational fashion, different ideological or religious beliefs. Thus, Islam as an influence on politics was systematically ignored. We have also failed to take seriously the ideological influence on Soviet foreign policy. The ideology of Marxism—Leninism is said to be a moribund ideology, an atavism from revolutionary days that has more ceremonial quality than true contemporary meaning, at most a convenient rationale for various policy actions. It is said that when the ideology clashes with the interests of the state, it is dumped for the natural, pragmatic course.

But the pragmatic tactics must have a purpose, which can only be defined by values. The survival of the state, of course, is a purpose. But the preservation of a certain political order within that state requires a deeper purpose. Further, in foreign policy, some criteria must define who are allies and who are

enemies. These criteria must be ideological. They cannot permanently conflict with the values which underpin the power of the ruling elite and which determine the legitimacy of the regime.

Legitimacy of Government

We in America, so accustomed to freedom and democracy, take the question of legitimacy for granted. We assume, almost without thinking, that our popularly elected governments are unimpeachably legitimate. Meanwhile, however, we fail to comprehend how much legitimacy is the burning concern of everyone from IRA hunger strikers to regimes which need for their continued hold on power such things as: Berlin Walls, hundreds of thousands of border guards, pervasive secret police systems, total control of all information and educational media, political infiltration of all social organizations, hundreds of millions of dollars worth of radio jammers to keep foreign broadcasts from poisoning the minds of their citizens, and "psychiatric clinics" and slave labor camps for vocal objectors. The engine propelling such institutions of repression and enslavement is the suspicion by the ruling elite that their people might not voluntarily choose either them or their political order if they had the free opportunity to do so. They suspect that, according to democractic principles, theirs is an illegitimate government. So how do they legitimize themselves beyond pursuing the tyrannical measures of the doctrine of "might makes right"? They justify themselves according to Marxist-Leninist ideology. They behave according to its tenets since to deviate noticeably from this ideology would be to undermine their sole basis for power.

In present circumstances, the greatest national security threat to communist leaders is an ideological one. The Soviets, for example, know that the United States and the West have no domestic constituency in favor of military action against them. Even in the days of anti-communist fervor and military superiority, there was scarcely any support for even the dispatch of military equipment to the Hungarian freedom fighters, much less to any separatist groups within the Soviet colonial empire itself. There is even less now. Nor do the Soviets perceive an economic threat: their consistent course since the days of Lenin's New Economic Policy has been to trade with the West to get the new technology that they cannot produce themselves. So where is the threat? It is an ideological one—the threat of democratic ideas, the threat of the truth penetrating information barriers and puncturing the fictions erected to prevent an upsurge of popular outrage by the Soviet people themselves. The threat is the threat of being perceived as illegitimate by their own citizens. The external security threat is thus, paradoxically, an internal security threat. That is why the Soviets have invented the Brezhnev Doctrine, and why they are an aggressively imperialist and anti-democratic-capitalist power. To maintain internal security, they must eliminate the sources of ideological contagion and help install foreign regimes that share their own concept of legitimacy.

To say that this ideology is moribund is to be blind to the real political impact it continues to have. Not only is it the indispensable vehicle of legitimacy, but it also serves as a set of ideals and as a distinct set of strategies and tactics for discontented intellectuals and revolutionaries around the world. Who can deny that the primary centers of revolutionary thought and action in Latin America are the Marxist-imbued national universities? Are the Marxist ideals and Leninist tactics of these revolutionaries moribund? What indeed is the so-called ''theology of liberation'' that has arisen in some parts of Latin America? Is it not a form of Marxism? The fact is that just as the ideology of democracy is alive in the minds of men, such ideologies as Marxism-Leninism are alive, are believed, and are taken seriously by many.

The East-West Conflict

The result of such conflicting ideologies is the East-West conflict. This has at its roots what have proven to be irreconcilable differences of an ideological nature about the nature of man, governmental legitimacy, human rights, economic systems, and concepts of good and evil in general. There is one difference between East and West that is especially relevant to their systemic conflict. This is the difference in conceptions of the normal state of international relations. The communist view is that relations between nations will always be in a state of conflict until the entire world becomes communist and participates in relations of proletarian internationalism. Conflicts will in the meantime include ''interimperialist'' conflicts among the capitalist nations, the ''anti-imperialist'' struggle of the Third world, as well as the struggle between the two social systems. According to explicit pronouncements of communist authorities, ''peaceful coexistence'' is a form of struggle against imperialism, allowing all forms of conflict but all-out war. Military means, of course, are justified to protect the gains of socialism anywhere in the world. Thus, associations among socialist nations no longer are voluntary: it is inadmissible to escape the fold. Communist foreign policy can in consequence never be a *status quo* policy. Since conflict is the norm, struggle to shift the correlation of forces must continue until ''peace'' is achieved.

The western conception of international relations, in contrast, sees peaceful relations as the norm. The West is inclined, therefore, to pursue *status quo* foreign policies as a general rule. Where the communist system asserts the irreversibility of its conquests, the West has so far accommmodated. Thus, as communist theory has divided the world

into ''war-zone'' (the non-communist world) and a ''peace-zone'' (the communist world), both East and West have concerned themselves only with international problems in the war-zone: the peace-zone, being at ''peace,'' is out of bounds. The upshot is a conflict between the people and the elites, between democracy and totalitarianism, or, to put it in economic terms, between theories of growth and redistribution. . . .

A New Doctrine?

What is therefore needed is a change in foreign policy comparable to the recent intellectual and politcal revolution in our domestic policy. Military preparedness, is, of course, a *sine qua non* of a new foreign policy; but it should be accompanied by appropriate foreign economic and political initiatives. It should be plain that it is not sufficient to protect U.S. interests by military power alone in places abroad where people see the United States as indifferent or hostile to their economic and political concerns. What is needed is a positive vision, *consistent* with traditional American values, that can be exported to the rest of the world. What is needed, literally, is a new, yet traditional, foreign policy ''doctrine,'' with all the ideological connotations that the word implies.

''Whether or not a country will be friendly depends largely upon how much it shares common values with us.''

The centerpiece of such a doctrine must be those values which have made America a revolutionary political success. These offer a vision of a world in which as many countries as possible can enjoy genuine legitimacy, political pluralism, democratic free market economies, civic freedoms, economic growth, prospect of upward mobility, and a rising standard of living for all people in society. It is doubtful, of course, that the world will ever fully realize such a dream. But that does not mean that real progress cannot be achieved. In comparison with the entire history of the human condition, we in America have succeeded. Such Third World countries as Taiwan, Singapore, and South Korea have also taken enormous strides. And such countries as Sri Lanka and Ivory Coast, which are trying some of the recipes of American economic success, are beginning to move in the same positive direction.

Success, of course, will only come in degrees. Hence the importance of being able to make those distinctions—such as between totalitarianism and authoritarianism, or between socialist and capitalist economic orders—which are relevant to assessing the varying degrees of progress. One maxim here especially should not be forgotten; that although capitalism may not be a fully sufficient condition for a truly liberal society, it is, from all historical experience, an essential component. It is because the capitalist free market is fundamentally a democratic institution that it has historically expedited the kind of political evolution that results in liberal democracy. To borrow a phrase that Marxists employ when introducing a coincidence, it is no coincidence that Ivory Coast, after twenty years of capitalist growth, has been able to hold its first free parliamentary elections since its independence.

Reaffirm Moral Values

The means toward these ends are several; the first of such means is moral argument. No politician or statesman ever succeeded in sustaining popular support unless he credibly explained his program in moral terms. America needs a campaign to reaffirm the goodness and essential justice of our system. After all, it is toward the American system that the emigrants of this world continue to flock. "Voting with your feet" remains one of the only democratic institutions in the non-democratic world. By this judgment, the American ideology wins all "elections" hands down.

"We have failed to understand many of the ideological underpinnings of contemporary international problems."

As I have shown elsewhere, The Soviets consider the moral strength (or "ideological strength") of a nation to be the key criterion in their assessment of the strengths and weakness (or "correlatin of forces") within that nation. Something, after all—and not advanced weaponry—has prevented (or, at this writing, at least delayed) a Soviet invasion of Poland. Something, and not economic power, compelled the Soviets to banish Aleksandr Solzhenitsyn rather than execute him. As it happens, the Soviets saw "ideological weakness" as the greatest weakness of America during the period of so-called "detente." This was based fundamentally on their perception of the ideologically-rooted breakdown in the traditional American foreign policy consensus. If there was any reason for our defeat in Vietnam, it was our demoralization, partly inspired by a vigorous propaganda campaign conducted by the communists. Where they appropriated for themselves all the anti-colonial, nationalist, and liberation slogans, and asserted the legitimacy of their political-economic order, we balked morally, only to splutter some half-hearted notions about how we would introduce some new political-economic order that would be "more

appropriate" for Vietnam: a "Third Force," a combination of capitalism and socialism complete with redistributionist "land reform."

But the moral means must be connected to an economic means. And here there is no "Third Force"—or other alternative with legitimacy if we go by the American conceptions of human rights. The economic means, therefore, must be to export to the world the original (and currently revived) recipe of American economic success; free market growth, freedom to earn and dispose of the fruits of one's labors, and production and distribution priorities guided by prices set by the democratic free market and not by an authoritarian elite.

Remove Barriers to Production

We should thus encourage the removal of all those barriers to production such as excessive taxes and tariffs that destroy incentives; government regulations that foster uncertainty and increase production costs; and abuse of the creation of money that destroys its utility as a reliable unit of account and store of value. We should encourage common markets, common currencies, free trade areas, enterprise zones with tax holidays of the kind enjoyed in Taiwan and Sri Lanka, and private, as opposed to government-authoritarian, enterprise. Since so much of the world is involved in agriculture, yet remains hungry, we should encourage agricultural reforms such as: adoption of private systems of rural credit; elimination of transportation restrictions, goverment-set food prices, and requirements that produce be sold to the government (which forces farmers to subsidize government-run industrialization schemes); and the elimination or reduction of a myriad of taxes on land, marketing, income, exports, and so on. People should be reminded that any place where "14 families" control all the private wealth is a place *without* real free markets and competition, places where *government* is used to protect monopolies, privileges, and corrupt relationships. Finally, foreign aid should be used as both a carrot and stick to encourage free market institutions. For example, if a country's production incentives were being crushed by excessivley high marginal tax rates, the U.S. government could propose that it significantly lower these rates, offering in return to pay for any revenue lost as a result of tax reduction. Since the budgets of such countries tend to be small, the sum would be negligible. Besides, in most countries where tax rates are prohibitive, revenue increases from tax reduction would vitiate the necessity of such payment.

The principal mechanisms of exporting the American Idea are public diplomacy and foreign information. Every weapon in this non-military arsenal must be deployed: international broadcasting, American libraries abroad, international educational, cultural and visitors' exchanges, the distribution of books, pamphlets, television programs and films, the hiring of more foreign service information officers as well as foreign nationals (such as journalists) to work in U.S. information posts abroad, and the increased, vocal use of international forums such as the U.N. for ideological offensives. These functions are a necessary complement to traditional diplomacy in the age of mass media. Indeed a new symbiotic relation must be developed between traditional and public diplomacy. For too long, our voices of public information have been muted and sometimes even censored for fear of offending the foreign governments we were trying to accommodate.

"Pragmatic tactics must have a purpose, which can only be defined by values."

Accommodation is surely a vital tool of diplomacy. But it never should still the voice of freedom. What is needed is a capacity to conduct a "two-track" foreign policy, where both the publics and governments of foreign countries may be independently addressed. The Soviets are very skillful at such a policy: they blast American imperialism over Radio Moscow while simultaneously calling for arms control negotiations. The British can do it too: when a foreign government complains to the British ambassador about an offensive broadcast of the BBC, the ambassador issues a polite disclaimer: "I sympathize with you, but our foreign office has no control over BBC programs." American ambassadors, on the contrary, will send home complaining cables which end up muzzling Voice of America broadcasts.

Two-Track Foreign Policy

The blunt truth is that a two-track foreign policy is the only way we can avoid diluting the strength of our political-philosophical message while simultaneously making necessary diplomatic compromises. We would otherwise dilute our national will and morale while negotiating with adversaries. For example, arms control negotiations involve diplomacy, compromise, linkage, the avoidance of actions that would worsen relations with the Soviet Union. Under traditional non-ideological diplomacy, this requires doing anything to avoid offending the Soviets, such as not inviting Solzhenitsyn to the White House. But the United States thus runs the risk of demoralization: the tendency is to oversell detente and the benefits of arms control as steps toward peace. The result is a false sense of security and the obscuring of those ideological factors that make the East-West conflict philosophically irreconcilable. Public and political opinion, as we well remember from the heyday of

detente, then tends to ask the question: if the East-West conflict is subsiding; why need we spend large sums of money on defense? It is for this reason, among others, that those who are conscious of Soviet political strategy tend to be skeptical of the arms control process.

The Soviets, of course, fully realize this danger of ideological backsliding. This is why they never cease to stir the morale of their troops—both military and civilian. Indeed, the essence of Soviet internal debates over military doctrine centers around the moral factor. Colonel Rybkin's famous quotation on the winnability of nuclear war is based precisely on this: "The *a priori* rejection of the possibility of victory is bad because it leads to moral disarmament, to disbelief in victory, to fatalism and passivity." The difference between Soviet and American moral strength, however, is that the Soviets fundamentally suffer from illegitimacy and must artificially bolster their moral strength through total control and manipulation of all information media and propaganda. We in America, however, derive our strength from our legitimacy, and need to be prodded only when we take the blessings of our system for granted.

A final element of a morally self-confident foreign policy must be the politico-military-economic support of pro-Western forces struggling for freedom around the world. It is true that we have had a tradition of offering such support. Sometimes, circumstances dictate that it must be done covertly. But as a rule, the United States should conduct such support *openly*. This supplies the key ingredient in any political struggle: moral support. There is nothing that can help such a struggle better than our vigorous declaration of the justice of the cause in question.

In short, what is needed is an ideological offensive by the United States, an offensive for our ideals of freedom, growth, social mobility, and popularly based legitimacy. In a dangerous world, it is a non-military weapon which we can use to prevent ever having to use our military weapons. It is the weapon offering that hope of a better life that people crave around the world. Mere defense, as defensiveness, is no longer enough against the enemies of our values. In diplomacy even more than in war, as Napoleon observed, attack is the best form of defense.

John Lenczowski has taught government and politics at the University of Maryland. He has also worked as a US House of Representatives staff member. This viewpoint is excerpted from Policy Review, *the quarterly journal published by The Heritage Foundation.*

"Ideology is the curse of public affairs because it converts politics into a branch of theology and sacrifices human beings on the altar of abstractions."

Ideology Is Detrimental to Foreign Policy

Arthur Schlesinger Jr.

Foreign policy is the face a nation wears to the world. The minimal motive is the same for all states—the protection of national integrity and interest. But the manner in which a state practices foreign policy is greatly affected by national peculiarities.

The United States is not exempt from these unimpeachable generalities. As Henry James, an early American specialist in international relations, once put it, "It's a complex fate, being an American." The American character is indeed filled with contradiction and paradox. So, in consequence, is American foreign policy. No paradox is more persistent than the historic tension in the American soul between an addiction to experiment and a susceptibility to ideology.

On the one hand, Americans are famous for being a practical people, preferring fact to theory, finding the meaning of propositions in results, regarding trial and error, not deductive logic, as the path to truth. "In no country in the civilized world," wrote Tocqueville, "is less attention paid to philosophy than in the United States." And, when Americans developed a distinctive philosophy, it was of course the pragmatism of William James. James perceived a pluralist universe where men can discover partial and limited truths—truths that work for them—but where no one can gain an absolute grip on ultimate truth. He stood against monism—the notion that the world can be understood from a single point of view. He stood against the assumption that all virtuous principles are in the end reconcilable; against faith in a single body of unified dogma; in short, against the delusions of ideology.

Yet at the same time that Americans live by experiment, they also show a recurrent vulnerability to spacious generalities. This is not altogether surprising. The American colonists, after all, were nurtured on one of the most profound and exacting ideologies ever devised—the theology of Calvin—and they passed on to their descendants a certain relish in system and abstraction. The ideas of the Americans, as Tocqueville found in the 1830s, "are all either extremely minute and clear or extremely general and vague." The Calvinist cast of mind saw America as the redeemer nation. It expressed itself in the eighteenth century in Jonathan Edwards' theology of Providence, in the nineteenth century in John Calhoun's theology of slavery, in the twentieth century in Woodrow Wilson's vision of world order and in John Foster Dulles' summons to a holy war against godless communism. The propensity to ideology explains too why the theory of American internal society as expounded by some Americans—the theory of America as the triumph of immaculate and sanctified private enterprise—differs so sharply from the reality of continual government intervention in economic life.

Realism vs. Ideology

This tension between experiment and ideology offers one way of looking at the American experience in the world affairs....Two strains have competed for the control of American foreign policy: one empirical, the other dogmatic; one viewing the world in the perspective of history, the other in the perspective of ideology; one supposing that the United States is not entirely immune to the imperfections, weaknesses and evils incident to all societies, the other regarding the United States as indeed the happy empire of perfect wisdom and perfect virtue, commissioned to save all mankind.

This schematic account does not do justice to the obvious fact that any American President, in order to command assent for his policies, must appeal to both reality and ideology—and that, to do this effectively, Presidents must combine the two strains not only in

Arthur Schlesinger Jr., "Foreign Policy and the American Character," *Foreign Affairs*, Fall 1983. Reprinted by permission of the author.

their speeches but in their souls. Franklin Roosevelt, the disciple at once of Admiral Mahan and of President Wilson, was supreme in marrying national interest to idealistic hope, though in the crunch interest always came first. Most postwar Presidents—Truman, Eisenhower, Kennedy, even Nixon—shared a recognition, alert or grudging, of the priority of power politics over ideology.

"No paradox is more persistent than the historic tension in the American soul between an addiction to experiment and a susceptibility to ideology."

The competition between realism and ideology was complicated, however, by two developments: by the fact that the United States in the twentieth century became a great power, and by the fact that balance of power in the twentieth century faced the gravest possible threats. There was in 1940 a very real monster to destroy and after 1945 another very real monster to contain. These threats demanded U.S. intervention abroad and brought the tradition of isolationism to a permanent end. But the growth of American power also confirmed the messianism of those who believed in America's divine appointment. And the fact that there were a couple of real monsters roaming the world encouraged a fearful tendency to look everywhere for new monsters to destroy.

Messianic Approach

The present Administraiton represents a mighty comeback of the messianic approach to foreign policy. "I have always believed," President Reagan said last November, "that this anointed land was set apart in an uncommon way, that a divine plan placed this great continent here between the oceans to be found by people from every corner of the earth who had a special love of faith and freedom." The Reagan Administration sees the world through the prism not of history but of ideology. The convictions that presently guide American foreign policy are twofold: that the United States is infinitely virtuous and that the Soviet Union is infinitely wicked.

The Soviet Union, Mr. Reagan has proclaimed, as an "evil empire," the focus of evil in the modern world." Everything follows by deductive logic from this premise. The world struggle is "between right and wrong and good and evil." When there is evil loose in the world, "we are enjoined by scripture and the Lord Jesus to oppose it with all our might." Negotiation with evil is futile if not dangerous. The Soviet Union is forever deceitful and treacherous. The Soviet leaders erect lying and cheating into a

philosophy and are personally responsible for the world's manifold ills. "Let us not delude ourselves," Mr. Reagan has said. "The Soviet Union underlies all the unrest that is going on. If they weren't engaged in this game of dominos, there wouldn't be any hot spots in the world." Not content with the orchestration of crisis in the Third World, the Soviet Union, once it acquires a certain margin of numerical superiority in warheads, can well be expected to launch a surprise nuclear attack on American targets. Safety lies only in the establishment of unequivocal military dominance by the United States, including a first-strike capability. If this means a nuclear arms race, that is Moscow's fault, not Washington's, because America's heart is pure. In any event nuclear weapons are usable and nuclear wars are winnable. We shall prevail.

The seizure of foreign policy by a boarding-party of ideologues invites a host of dangers. Most of all you tend to get things wrong. Where the empirical approach sees the present as emerging from the past and preparing for the future, ideology is counter-historical. Its besetting sin is to substitute models for reality. No doubt the construction of models—logically reticulated, general principles leading inexorably to particular outcomes—is an exercise that may help in the delineation of problems—but not when artificial constructs are mistaken for descriptions of the real world. This is what Alfred North Whitehead called "the fallacy of misplaced concreteness," and it explains why ideology infallibly gets statesmen into trouble, later if not sooner. The error of ideology is to prefer essence to existence, and the result, however gratifying logically and psychologically, undermines the reality principle itself.

Splendid Abstraction

Ideology withdraws problems from the turbulent stream of change and treats them in splendid abstraction from the whirl and contingency of life. So ideology portrays the Soviet Union as an unalterable monolith, immune to historical vicissitude and permutation, its behavior determined by immutable logic, the same yesterday, today and tommorow; Sunday, Monday and always. We are forever in 1950, with a crazed Stalin reigning in the Kremlin and commanding an obedient network of communist parties and agents around the planet. In the light of ideology, the Soviet Union becomes a fanatic state carrying out with implacable zeal and cunning a master plan of world dominion.

Perhaps this is all so. But others may see rather a weary, dreary country filled with cynicism and corruption, beset by insuperable problems at home and abroad, lurching uncertainly from crisis to crisis. The Soviet leadership, three quarters of a century after the glorious Bolshevik revolution, cannot provide the people with elementary items of consumer goods. It cannot rely on the honesty of bureaucrats or the loyalty of scientists and writers. It confronts difficult ethnic challenges as the non-Russians in the Soviet Union, so miserably underrepresented in the organs of power, begin to outnumber the Russians. Every second child born this year in the Soviet Union will be a Muslim. Abroad, the Soviet Union faces hostile Chinese on its eastern frontier and restless satellites on the west, while to the south the great Red Army after three and a half years still cannot defeat ragged tribesmen fighting bravely in the hills of Afghanistan.

I don't want to overdo the picture of weakness. The Soviet Union remains a powerful state, with great and cruel capacity to repress consumption and punish dissent and with an apparent ability to do at least one thing pretty well, which is to build nuclear missiles. But there is enough to the reality of Soviet troubles to lead even the ideologues in Washington to conceive Soviet Russia as a nation at once so robust that it threatens the world and so frail that a couple of small pushes will shove its ramshackle economy into collapse.

Soviet Ideology

The Soviet Union of course is ideological too, even if its ideology has got a little shopworn and ritualistic over the long years. It too sees the enemy as unchanging and unchangeable, a permanently evil empire vitiated through eternity by the original sin of private property. Each regime, reading its adversary ideologically rather than historically, deduces act from imputed essence and attributes purpose, premeditation and plan where less besotted analysts would raise a hand for improvisation, accident, chance, ignorance, negligence and even sheer stupidity. We arrive at the predicament excellently described by Henry Kissinger: "The superpowers often behave like two heavily armed blind men feeling their way around a room, each believing himself in mortal peril from the other whom he assumes to have perfect vision . . . Each tends to ascribe to the other a consistency, foresight, and coherence that its own experience belies. Of course, over time, even two blind men can do enormous damage to each other, not to speak of the room."

By construing every local mess as a test of global will, ideology raises stakes in situations that cannot be easily controlled and threatens to transmute limited into unlimited conflicts. Moreover, ideology, if pursued to the end, excludes the thought of accommodation or coexistence. Mr. Reagan has instructed us that we must oppose evil "with all our might." How now can we compromise with evil without losing our immortal soul? Ideology summons the true believer to a *jihad*, a crusade of extermination against the infidel.

The Russians are in no position to complain about such language. It has been more or less their own line since 1917. Reagan is simply paraphrasing Khrushchev: "We will bury you." Still the holy war has always represented a rather drastic approach to human affairs. It seems singularly unpromising in the epoch of nuclear weaons. And the irony is that, while Soviet ideology has grown tired, cynical and venal, the New American crusade is fresh and militant; and the Washington ideologues thereby present the Kremlin with an unearned and undeserved opportunity to appear reasonable and prudent. In particular, the American dash into ideology promotes a major Soviet objective, the turning away of Western Europe from the alliance with the United States.

"The convictions that presently guide American foreign policy are twofold: that the United States is infinitely virtuous and that the Soviet Union is infinitely wicked."

Having suggested the current domination of American foreign policy by ideology, let me add that this domination is far from complete. Mr. Reagan's world view is not necessarily shared even by all members of his own Administration. It is definitely not shared by the Republican leadership in Congress. In general, it has been more vigorously translated into rhetoric than into policy. The suspicion has even arisen that Mr. Reagan's more impassioned ideological flights are only, in Wendell Wilkie's old phrase, "campaign oratory," pap for right-wing zealots to conceal the Administration's covert creep to the center in domestic affairs. And the prospect of a presidential election next year creates a compelling political need for the Administration to attend to public opinion—a concern that may be a force for restraint in Central America and that could conceivably drive the Administration into arms control negotiations well before November 1984. Still, Mr. Reagan is not a cynical man, and, whatever the tactical function of his speeches, they must also in some sense express sincere convictions.

Rhetoric vs. Policy

The greater restraint on ideology comes from the nature of foreign policy itself. The realism of the Founding Fathers sprang from the ineluctable character of international relations. National interest in the end must set limits on messianic passions. This fact explains the Administration's tendency to march up the ideological hill and then march down again, as in the case of the pipeline embargo. For the United States does not have the power, even if it had the wisdom, to achieve great objectives in the world by itself. Because this is so, a responsible foreign policy requires the cooperation of allies, and allies therefore have it within their power to rein in American messianism.

The pipeline embargo is only one example of the modification of ideology by interest. Ideology favors a blank check for Menachem Begin in Israel, but interest argues for the comprehensive approach to a Middle Eastern settlement that Reagan set forth on September 1, 1982, in the most impressive speech of his presidency. Ideology calls for the support of Taiwan at the expense of mainland China. Interest argues against policies tending to unite Chinese and Soviet communism. Ideology argues against a course that leaves black Africa no friends but the Soviet Union. Ideology calls for the excommunication of socialist regimes. Interest sees benefits in cheerful relations with France, Spain, Italy, Portugal, Greece and Sweden. Ideology calls for chastisement of the debtor nations in the Third World. Interest leads to an additional $8.4-billion contribution to the International Monetary Fund.

Ideology and Central America

Yet there remain sectors of policy where ideology still holds sway. One, for the season at least, is Central America. No one can be too sure over the longer run because the Administration has marched up and down this particular hill more than once in the last two years. During the vicariate of General Haig, insurgency in Central America was deemed a major Soviet challenge demanding a mighty American response. Then, in the first tranquilizing days of Secretary Schultz, the impression was allowed to spread that perhaps the troubles had ample local origins and, despite allegations of extracontinental instigation, might be amenable to local remedies. Subsequently Secretary Schultz caught the ideological flu, and by mid-1983 we were back at the global test of will.

"National interest in the end must set limits on messianic passions."

Unquestionably the United States is facing tough problems in Central America. Nor does it meet the problems to observe that they are, in some part, of American creation. Twenty years ago the Alliance for Progress set out to deal with poverty and oligarchy in Central America. But the Alliance changed its character after the death of President Kennedy, and American policy abandoned concern with social change. When revolution predictably erupted in Central America, ideology rejected the notion of local origins and decreed that the Russians were back at their old game of dominos.

Ideology, it should be noted, offers a field day for

self-fulfilling prophecies. If you shape rhetoric and policy to what you regard as a predestined result, chances are that you will get the result you predestine. Having decided a priori that the Nicaraguan revolution was a Soviet-Cuban conspiracy, Washington gave the Sandinistas little alternative but to seek support from the Cubans and Russians. The French wanted to sell Nicaragua arms and send in a military mission. Washington, instead of welcoming a democratic presence that would have been reliably alert to Soviet deviltry, exploded in indignation. When the CIA does its best to overthrow the government in Managua, we express unseemly shock that this government dare take measures to defend itself. Maybe it would have happened anyway, but the ideological policy makes insurgent anti-Americanism inevitable.

The present Washington disposition is to raise the stakes and to militarize the remedy. We are trying to provide the government of El Salvador with sufficient military aid to defeat the insurgency and to provide the insurgency in Nicaragua with sufficient military aid to defeat the government. If we don't act to stop Marxism in Central America, the argument runs, dominos will topple, and the Soviet Union will establish a bridgehead in the center of the Western Hemisphere. "Our credibility would collapse," Mr. Reagan has said, "our alliances would crumble, and the safety of our homeland would be in jeopardy." In April 1983 he denied any "thought of sending American combat troops to Central America." By June the thought had occurred, and he now cautioned, "Presidents never say never."

Understanding Others' Interests

Other views are possible. The historian is bound to note that unilateral military action by the United States in Latin America is nearly always a mistake. Another by-product of ideology, along with the self-fulfilling prophecy, is the conviction that the anointed country, whether the United States these days or the Soviet Union in all days, understands the interests of other countries better than they understand their own interests. So in 1967 President Johnson sent Clark Clifford on an Asian tour, charging him to get the states of the South East Asia Treaty Organization to increase their contributions to the forces fighting communism in Vietnam. Clifford was astonished to discover that other Asian countries, though considerably more exposed to the danger, took it less tragically than the United States did and saw no need to increase their contributions. When he thereafter became Secretary of Defense, Clifford did his best to wind down American participation in the war.

If a Marxist Nicaragua (population 2.7 million) or El Salvador (population 4.5 million) is a threat to the Hemisphere, it is a more dire threat to Mexico, to Costa Rica, to Panama, to Venezuela, to Colombia than it is to the United States. These nations are closer to the scene and more knowledgeable about it; they are a good deal more vulnerable politically, economically and militarily than the United States; and they are governed by men just as determined as those in Washington to resist their own overthrow. When Latin American countries don't see the threat as apocalyptically as we do, only ideology can conclude with divine assurance that they are wrong and we are right. Are we really so certain that we understand *their* world better than they do?

In any event, ideology is a sure formula for hypocrisy, if not for disaster. Mr. Reagan says righteously that we will not "protect the Nicaraguan government from the anger of its own people." A fine sentiment—but why does it not apply equally to the government of El Salvador? Why do we condemn Nicaragua for postponing elections until 1985 while we condone Chile, which postpones elections till 1989? Would the Administration display the same solicitude for elections and rights in Nicaragua if the Somozas were still running things?

Ideology insists on the inflation of local troubles into global crises. National interest would emphasize the indispensability of working with Latin Americans who know the territory far better than we do and without whose support we cannot succeed. Let Mexico, Venezuela, Colombia and Panama—the so-called Contadora Group—take the lead, and back them to the hilt. Only if all agree on the nature of the response will intervention do the United States more good than harm in the Hemisphere. If it is too late for a negotiated settlement and our Latin friends reject military intervention, then we may have to resign ourselves to turmoil in Central America for some time to come—turmoil beyond our power to correct and beyond our wisdom to cure. . . .

Deliverance from Ideology

What the world needs is above all deliverance from ideology. This is not to suggest for a moment any symmetry between the United States and the Soviet Union. In the United States, ideology is a lurking susceptibility, a periodic fling, fooling some of the people some of the time but profoundly alien to the Constitution and to the national spirit. Washington's current ideological commotion is the result, not of popular demand or mandate, but of the superficial fact that in 1980 the voters, unable to abide the thought of four more years of what they had, had Reagan as the only practical alternative.

In the Soviet Union ideology remains the heart of the matter. It is not a susceptibility but a compulsion, inscribed in sacred texts and enforced by all the brutal machinery of a still vicious police state. Yet even in the Soviet Union one senses an erosion of the old ideological intensity until a good deal of what remains is simply a vocabulary in which Soviet leaders are accustomed to speak. Let not a spurt of American ideologizing breathe new life into the decadent Soviety ideology, especially by legitimizing the Russian fear of an American crusade aimed at the destruction of Russian society.

Antidote for Ideology

In the end, ideology runs against the grain of American democracy. Popular elections, as the Founding Fathers saw long ago, supply the antidote to the fanaticism of abstract propositions. High-minded Americans have recently taken to calling for a single six-year presidential term on the ground that Presidents, not having to worry about reelection, would thereby be liberated to make decisions for the good of the republic. This assumes that the less a President takes public opinion into account, the better a President he will be—on reflection, a rather anti-democractic assumption. In the instant case, the best things Mr. Reagan has done—his belated concern about racial justice, about the environment and natural resources, about hunger, about women, about arms control—have all been under the pressure of the 1984 election. He might never have cared if he had had a single six-year term. It may well be that Presidents do a better job when politics requires them to respond to popular needs and concerns than they would if constitutionally empowered to ignore popular needs and concerns for the sake of ideological gratification.

"The error of ideology is to prefer essence to existence, and the result, however gratifying logically and psychologically, undermines the reality principle itself."

Ideology is the curse of public affairs because it converts politics into a branch of theology and sacrifices human beings on the altar of abstractions. "To serene Providence," Winston Churchill wrote an American politician nearly 90 years ago, "a couple of generations of trouble and distress may seem an insignificant thing. . . .Earthly Governments, however, are unable to approach questions from the same standpoint. Which brings me to the conclusion that the duty of governments is to be first of all practical. I am for makeshifts and expediency. I would like to make the people who live on this world at the same time as I do better fed and happier generally. If incidentally I benefit posterity—so much the better—but I would not sacrifice my own generation to a principle—however high—or a truth however great."

Arthur Schlesinger Jr. is a historian and Albert Schweitzer Professor in the Humanities at the City University of New York.

"In our two-party democracy, an effective foreign policy must begin with bipartisanship, and the sharing of responsibility for a safer and more humane world."

Foreign Policy Must Be Bipartisan

Ronald Reagan

I'd like to address your theme of bipartisanship with a view toward America's foreign policy challenges for the 1980s.

All Americans share two great goals for foreign policy: a safer world and a world in which individual rights can be respected and precious values may flourish.

These goals are at the heart of America's traditional idealism and our aspirations for world peace. Yet, while cherished by us, they do not belong exclusively to us. They're not "made in America." They're shared by people everywhere.

Tragically, the world in which these fundamental goals are so widely shared is a very troubled world. While we and our allies may enjoy peace and prosperity, many citizens of the industrial world continue to live in fear of conflict and the threat of nuclear war. And all around the globe, terrorists threaten innocent people and civilized values. And in developing countries, the dreams of human progress have, too often, been lost to violent revolution and dictatorship.

Quite obviously, the widespread desire for a safer and more humane world is—by itself—not enough to create such a world. In pursuing our worthy goals, we must go beyond honorable intentions and good will to practical means.

Key Principles

We must be guided by these key principles.

Realism. The world is not as we wish it would be. Reality is often harsh. We will not make it less so if we do not first see it for what it is.

Strength. We know that strength alone is not enough, but without it there can be no effective diplomacy and negotiations; no secure democracy and

peace. Conversely, weakness or hopeful passivity are only self-defeating. They invite the very aggression and instability that they would seek to avoid.

New Economic Growth. This is the underlying base that ensures our strength and permits human potential to flourish. Neither strength nor creativity can be achieved or sustained without economic growth—both at home and abroad.

Intelligence. Our policies cannot be effective unless the information on which they're based is accurate, timely, and complete.

Shared Responsibility With Allies. Our friends and allies share the heavy responsibility for the protection of freedom. We seek and need their partnership, sharing burdens in pursuit of our common goals.

Nonaggression. We have no territorial ambitions. We occupy no foreign lands. We build our strength only to assure deterrence and to secure our interests if deterrence fails.

Dialogue With Adversaries. Though we must be honest in recognizing fundamental differences with our adversaries, we must always be willing to resolve these differences by peaceful means.

Bipartisanship at Home. In our two-party democracy, an effective foreign policy must begin with bipartisanship, and the sharing of responsibility for a safer and more humane world must begin at home.

Rebuilding America's Leadership

During the past 3 years, we've been steadily rebuilding America's capacity to advance our foreign policy goals through renewed attention to these vital principles. Many threats remain, and peace may still seem precarious. But America is safer and more secure today because the people of this great nation have restored the foundation of its strength....

Much as been accomplished, but much remains to be done. If Republicans and Democrats will join

Ronald Reagan, address before the Center for Strategic Studies, Washington DC, April 6, 1984.

together to confront four great challenges to American foreign policy in the 1980s, then we can and will make great strides toward a safer and more humane world.

Challenge number one is to reduce the risk of nuclear war and to reduce the levels of nuclear armaments in a way that also reduces the risk they will ever be used. . . .

Our safety and security depend on more than credible deterrence and nuclear arms reductions. Constructive regional development is also essential. Therefore, our second great challenge is strengthening the basis for stability in troubled and strategically sensitive regions. . . .

Expanding opportunities for economic development and personal freedom is our third great challenge. The American concept of peace is more than absence of war. We favor the flowering of economic growth and individual liberty in a world of peace. And this, too, is a goal to which most Americans subscribe. . . .

Trust the people, this is the crucial lesson of history and America's message to the world. We must be staunch in our conviction that freedom is not the sole possession of a chosen few, but the universal right of men and women everywhere. President Truman said, "If we should pay merely lip service to inspiring ideals, and later do violence to simple justice, we would draw down upon us the bitter wrath of generations yet unborn." Let us go forward together, faithful friends of democracy and democratic values, confident in our conviction that the tide of the future is a freedom tide. But let us go forward with practical means.

Restore Bipartisan Consensus

This brings me to our fourth great challenge: we must restore bipartisan consensus in support of U.S. foreign policy. We must restore America's honorable tradition of partisan politics stopping at the water's edge. Republicans and Democrats standing united in patriotism and speaking with one voice as responsible trustees for peace, democracy, individual liberty, and the rule of law.

In the 1970s we saw a rash of congressional initiatives to limit the president's authority in the areas of trade, human rights, arms sales, foreign assistance, intelligence operations, and the dispatch of troops in time of crisis. Over 100 separate prohibitions and restrictions on executive branch authority to formulate and implement foreign policy were enacted.

The most far-reaching consequence of the past decade's congressional activism is this: bipartisan consensus building has become a central responsibility of congressional leadership as well as of executive leadership. If we're to have a sustainable foreign policy, the Congress must support the practical details of policy, not just the general goals.

We have demonstrated the capacity for such jointly responsible leadership in certain areas. But we have seen setbacks for bipartisanship, too. I believe that once we established bipartisan agreement on our course in Lebanon, the subsequent second guessing about whether to keep our men there severely undermined our policy. It hindered the ability of our diplomats to negotiate, encouraged more intransigence from the Syrians, and prolonged the violence. Similarly, congressional wavering on support for the Jackson plan, which reflects the recommendations of the national Bipartisan Commission on Central America, can only encourage the enemies of democracy who are determined to wear us down.

Strong President and Congress

To understand and solve this problem of joint responsibility, we have to go beyond the familiar questions as to who should be stronger, the president or the Congress. The more basic problem is: in this "post-Vietnam era," Congress has not yet developed capacities for coherent, responsible action needed to carry out the new foreign policy powers it has taken for itself. To meet the challenges of this decade, we need a strong president and a strong Congress.

Unfortunately, many in the Congress seem to believe they're still in the troubled Vietnam era, with their only task to be vocal critics and not responsible partners in developing positive, practical programs to solve real problems.

"We must restore America's honorable tradition of. . . . Republicans and Democrats standing united in patriotism."

Much was learned from Vietnam—lessons ranging from increased appreciation of the need for careful discrimination in the use of U.S. force or military assistance to increased appreciation of the need for domestic support for any such military element of policy. Military force, either direct or indirect, must remain an available part of America's foreign policy. But, clearly, the Congress is less than wholly comfortable with both the need for a military element in foreign policy and its own responsibility to deal with that element.

Presidents must recognize Congress as a more significant partner in foreign policymaking, and, as we have tried to do, seek new means to reach bipartisan executive-legislative consensus. But legislators must realize that they, too, are partners. They have a responsibility to go beyond mere criticism to consensus building that will produce positive, practical, and effective action.

Bipartisan consensus is not an end in itself. Sound and experienced U.S. foreign policy leadership must always reflect a deep understanding of fundamental American interests, values, and principles.

Achieving Progress

Consensus on the broad goals of a safer and more humane world is easy to achieve. The harder part is making progress in developing concrete, realistic means to reach these goals. We've made some progress. But there is still a congressional reluctance to assume responsibility for positive, bipartisan action to go with their newly claimed powers.

We've set excellent examples with the bipartisan Scowcroft commission, bipartisan support for IMF funding, and the bipartisan work of the Kissinger commission. But it's time to lift our efforts to a higher level of cooperation; time to meet together, with realism and idealism, America's great challenges for the 1980s.

We have the right to dream great dreams, the opportunity to strive for a world at peace enriched by human dignity, and the responsibility to work as partners, so that we might leave these blessed gifts to our children and to our children's children.

We might remember the example of a legislator who lived in a particularly turbulent era, Henry Clay. Abraham Lincoln called him "my beau ideal of a statesman." He knew Clay's loftiness of spirit and vision never lost sight of his country's interest, and that, election year or not, Clay would set love of country above all political considerations.

The stakes for America for peace and for freedom demand every bit as much from us in 1984 and beyond—this is our challenge.

Ronald Reagan was elected president of the United States in 1980. This viewpoint is taken from an address before the Center for Strategic Studies in Washington, D.C. on April 6, 1984.

viewpoint 6

Bipartisanship Harms Foreign Policy

Richard Falk

American foreign policy remains compulsively bipartisan on the most basic issues of principle and practice. Whether the issue is the controversial deployment of Pershing II and cruise missiles in Europe, the application of the War Powers Act to American military operations in Lebanon, the exclusion of the PLO from the Mideast peace process, or even the costly pursuit of interventionary goals in Central America, disputes between leading Democrats and Republicans are generally restricted to tactics and nuances. Underlying assumptions are rarely questioned, and genuine alternatives of policy are almost never advocated when representatives of the two main political parties debate foreign policy. As a result, U.S. foreign policy is essentially frozen at a time when the pressures for fundamental adjustments are becoming ever more intense....

The American foreign policy process itself reinforces bipartisanship. Intelligence services process vital information through the White House and national security bureaucracies, which are staffed by large and influential corps of civil servants whose careers have been shaped by the bipartisan consensus regarding the proper role of the United States in the world. This consensus is informally "enforced" by the media and by special interests. Political figures believed to challenge the consensus or even to raise fundamental doubts about it are discredited. Henry Wallace, Barry Goldwater, Eugene McCarthy, Fred Harris, George McGovern, George Wallace and Jerry Brown have lost "credibility," that is, political relevance, because they stood for views or constituencies that challenged the prevailing foreign policy consensus. Each story, of course, is different, but the pattern confirms the assertion that it is politically costly, if not suicidal, to swim against

the bipartisan current....

Other Factors

There are other factors at work. The monolithic character of the Soviet Union, especially its ability to speak with a single, unwavering voice on world issues, exerts pressure on Americans to sustain a consistent foreign policy. America's role as alliance leader imposes additional pressures for policy continuity; even as it is, the United States is criticized abroad for its frequent subtle shifts of tone and emphasis. Experts in and out of government often are able to use supposedly dispassionate knowledge to make the public believe that genuine alternatives to current policies are "unreasable" or "extreme," and lie outside the orbit of "responsible discussion."...

Against such formidable obstacles, it may seem foolhardy to question the current bipartisan foundations of American foreign policy. Yet, unless this consensus is challenged, American foreign policy will be unable to bridge the widening gap between the content of the bipartisan consensus and the world situations to which it is being applied. Bipartisanship has virtually nullified the electoral process as a means of reforming foreign policy. We proceed from Vietnam to El Salvador without any serious debate as to whether it is necessary or serves American interest to intervene in foreign societies to control the outcome of largely internal struggles. We continue to build nuclear weapons systems without pausing to question the postulates of the arms race, or even to inquire whether there might be cheaper and saner forms of deterrence. A decade ago there was unquestioning support at the top echelons of the political process for placing multiple warheads (MIRVing) on missile systems. Now there is comparable bipartisan enthusiasm for the alleged stabilizing virtues of single-warhead missiles. Aside from keeping weapons-makers happy, such policy gyrations reveal more about the bipartisan strictures

Richard Falk, "Lifting the Curse of Bipartisanship," *World Policy Journal*, Fall 1983. Reprinted by permission of the World Policy Institute, 777 United Nations Plaza, New York, NY 10017.

on the political process than they do about the merits of the various weapons choices.

The current bipartisanship is an outgrowth of America's dominance in the non-communist world after World War II. This leadership role rested firmly on American military and economic power, but even more so on the diplomatic and ideological preeminence the United States enjoyed in the years after 1945....

Postwar Concensus

The postwar consensus that emerged did represent a reasonable fit between means and ends, and was seemingly vindicated for at least the first fifteen years by an impressive record of accomplishments: Europe and Japan staged remarkable economic recoveries and built their futures around American-style political institutions; the world economic system entered a period of rapid and sustained growth; and, outside of Eastern Europe, the Soviet Union was confined to its borders and substantially isolated as an ideological force without provoking World War III. At critical points, Washington was able to mobilize widespread international support, as it did when it obtained United Nations support for its defense of South Korea in 1950-52. It was also able to use its position of nuclear predominance to force a humiliating Soviet retreat in the Cuban missile crisis of 1962.

"How can the United States adapt to a new global setting if the American people are not given a genuine choice?"

All along, contradictory forces were at work eroding the effectiveness of the postwar consensus. The decolonization process produced new outlooks among the nations of Asia, Africa, and Latin America that challenged the premises of U.S. diplomatic leadership. The success of the economic recovery facilitated by the United States, especially the performance of Germany and Japan, the main losers in World War II, produced a more plural and competitive world economic order that reshaped the hierarchy of relations upon which Washington's control had earlier rested. U.S. resistance to political radicalism in the Third World often aligned the United States with reactionary forces which often proved to be "losers" in the competition for state power, perhaps most notably in the case of China. In the 1970s, these difficulties reached a dramatic climax with the American defeat in Vietnam, the rapid rise of oil prices, the militancy of Third World diplomacy, an Indian nuclear explosion, a series of anti-Western national revolutions, the end of easy economic growth, the emergence of high

unemployment and inflation in the West, and the deteriorating position of the United States economically.

The postwar consensus, while challenged by these shifts, failed to make suitable basic adjustments. Instead, the United States insisted on proceeding as if its overall dominance remained undiminished....

Bipartisanship has persisted despite substantial indications by the American people that they would be receptive to major changes in foreign policy, provided these were explained and endorsed by respected national leaders and backed by a leading political party. Substantial support exists, for instance, to end the arms race and to get out of the intervention business. But the government and the two political parties remain wedded to past assumptions about foreign policy goals. As a result, national policy discussion tends to focus on tactical disputes over narrow choices and controversies over styles of leadership....

The persistence of this unsuccessful and increasingly unpopular bipartisan stance on foreign policy poses a serious challenge for political democracy. How can the United States adapt to a new global setting if the American people are not given a genuine choice and if the governing process is resolved to cling to old policies, however discredited by experience? The stakes could not be higher— peace, economic vitality, a participatory democracy, and the possibility that international tensions can be handled without courting disaster. The failure of the current bipartisan foreign policy is partly a reflection of how the two-party system operates. If opposition is not mounted by the party out of power, then it does not enter into the formal political process. Only a far more intense popular campaign for foreign policy reform can lessen the constraints of bipartisanship and allow the electoral process and the institutions of representative government to be revitalized.

Richard Falk is Albert G. Milbank Professor of International Law and Practice at Princeton University and a senior fellow of the World Policy Institute. He is the author of The End of World Order.

"The absense of a global strategy. . .has been the hallmark of the Republican Administration."

The US Has a Weak Foreign Policy

Walter Laqueur and Charles Krauthammer

One can hardly speak of a Reagan foreign policy. The Reagan Administration's haphazard ventures into international affairs have consisted almost exclusively of harsh rhetoric, indiscriminate arms sales, irresponsible talk about limited nuclear war, and a bending of American national interest to the requirements of big business. Its call for a U.S. military build-up, without clearly explaining to the American people what foreign policy objectives such a build-up would serve, has radically eroded the consensus that had been developing during the last Democratic Administration in favor of strengthening our defenses. It will be the taks of the next Democratic Administration to rebuild this consensus by clearly delineating the foreign policy objectives of the United States and demonstrating that they are grounded in a desire to support freedom, preserve peace, and promote justice and human rights wherever possible.

The absence of a global strategy, of a basic concept of how to pursue American ideas and interests, has been the hallmark of the Republican Administration. Its excessive rhetoric has been accompanied by weakness and inconsistency of action. It has operated on the simple-minded belief that increasing military strength would somehow solve problems which are essentially political in nature. Military strength is vital. In its absence, America's voice cannot be heard, and, far from enhancing the cause of peace, this would encourage the drift toward world anarchy. But strength is not a policy. It is only the prerequisite for a policy. As a result, we have had only empty threats, vacillation, lack of political initiative, and, on various occasions, virtual paralysis in the foreign political field. It has been a sad performance, one that has caused confusion among our friends and left the

initiative to our adversaries.

(1) *U.S.-Soviet Relations.* We have long suffered from a basic failure to understand what can and cannot be achieved in relations with the Kremlin. The pendulum has swung between unrealistic optimism and unjustified despair. The present Soviet leadership does not want war with America, nor does it want to create major crises which could escalate into major war. But neither does it want peace, peaceful coexistence, or detente—as most Americans understand these concepts. It is not a revolutionary power; indeed, it is one of the most conservative regimes in the world. But it is still basically hostile to America and all its stands for. Soviet leaders believe that their influence has to be maintained at all cost in Eastern Europe against the wishes of the overwhelming majority of the population (the Brezhnev Doctrine). The have also used every opportunity to weaken America and the West in general, avoiding a direct collision but taking advantage of every vulnerability.

It follows that unilateral American concessions to the Soviet Union would be accepted without gratitude. They would be interpreted as a sign either of weakness or stupidity. Lowering American defenses would endanger world peace by encouraging the otherwise cautious Soviet leaders to engage in a more forward, aggressive policy in various parts of the world. They will be more willing to take risks if the risks are smaller.

Reciprocal Relations

The basic principle of U.S.-Soviet relations has to be reciprocity. The response to pressure has to be counter-pressure, the response to positive moves and initiatives has to be made in a similar spirit. This the present Administration has utterly failed to do. After a year of harsh rhetoric and purely symbolic anti-Soviet gestures, the Administration acquiesced in the re-Stalinization of Poland. The crushing of freedom in

Walter Laqueur and Charles Krauthammer, March 31, 1982. *The New Republic.* Reprinted by permission of THE NEW REPUBLIC, © 1982, The New Republic, Inc.

Poland should have been met with the strongest possible American economic countermeasures, including declaring Poland in default and cutting off credit, to make the Soviets pay the full price for empire. On the other hand, the Administration's obsession with the Soviet role in such conflicts as the civil war in El Salvador has bred cynicism and suspicion, and jeopardized domestic support for a firm anti-Soviet policy. The vacillation over Poland and the fixation on El Salvador as an East-West conflict have contributed to the perception of an America afraid to respond to real examples of Soviet imperialism and given to overreaction in cases with only the remotest Soviet involvement.

"Strength is not a policy. It is only the prerequisite for a policy."

It is unrealistic to pretend that between the U.S. and the Soviet Union there is anything other than a political struggle—a real conflict that cannot be wished away. As seen from the Soviet Union, the cold war has not ceased; only the atmosphere has changed at times. But it is equally foolish, and defeatist as well, to conclude that no agreement is possible with the Soviets. Like us, they want to avoid the unimaginable destruction of war and thus they too have a vested interest in crisis management and arms reduction. The Administration's single initiative thus far in office—the zero option for reduction of intermediate nuclear weapons in Europe—is to be welcomed. But there should also be an immediate resumption of strategic arms reduction talks. The fears and uncertainties created by the Reagan Administratin's perceived indifference to this issue have given rise to the concurrent spate of calls for an immediate bilateral freeze on nuclear weapons. But the "freeze" is a slogan, not a plan; and even if it were practical, it would cancel the zero option offer in Europe. That offer, by correcting the massive inequality that has resulted from the Soviet installation of SS-20 missiles in Europe, would help stabilize the European frontier, and thus make nuclear war in Europe far less likely. On strategic weapons, Democrats should support immediate negotiations for drastic and balanced reductions in concurrent arsenals, a goal that would be delayed, and perhaps prevented, by interminable debates over the meaning and enforcement of any bilateral "freeze."

(2) *America and Its Allies.* NATO came into being in a specific historical constellation that no longer exist. The need today for a defensive alliance is as strong as ever, but it has become imperative to reconsider and renegotiate the scope of the alliance and the rights and duties of its members. The failure to do so has weakened NATO; further delay may be fatal. The initiative ought to come from America as the senior and most powerful partner.

NATO Reform

It should be U.S. policy to encourage greater European political and military unity inside NATO, even if as a result American political preferences are not always accepted. Such an arrangement will be in America's long-term interest. In 1950 Europe (and Japan) were still in ruins. Today they are industrial giants, and they do not lack the manpower needed for their conventional defense. They should have a part in the alliance commensurate with their economic strength and their contribution to the defense of Europe.

NATO reform will cause some temporary upheaval. Americans have become accustomed to making the important decisions alone, and Europeans are used to taking a back seat—and acting like backseat drivers. Both will have to change their attitudes: NATO will have to become a joint venture.

What if it should appear that Europe, or substantial segments of Europe, lack the will to coordinate their defense efforts among themselves, to take greater responsibility for the conduct of NATO affairs? Or if it should appear that the interests among the segments of the alliance diverge more widely than hitherto assumed? These are possibilities, though remote ones. Although nations do not necessarily always act in their own best intersts, they do not usually act against them for any length of time. Located close to the superpower with the greater ambitions, they know (like most of the countries of the Middle East) that they need the help of the other superpower to restore the geopolitical balance. The alternative is not neutrality, but Soviet hegemony in Europe and the Middle East. There is a danger that American help is taken for granted, not only by our friends but especially by those who wish to follow an independent line. It is the duty of U.S. foreign policy makers to disabuse them of such misconceptions. It has to be made clear that the U.S. will be ready to defend Europe as in the past, but that such a relationship can no longer be a unilateral guarantee as it was in 1950. Europe's part in the alliance, its greater rights and greater duties, will have to be redefined.

(3) *The Third World.* One of the most regrettable features of U.S. foreign policy is its lack of success in third world countries. To a certain extent this is the result of objective difficulties. Many of these countries have attained independence only in recent decades; they lack political and social stability, and they confront major economic problems. It would have been a miracle if in this short time they had developed stable, democratic institutions. With some notable exceptions, rapid and violent change rather

than continuity has been the norm. This is unlikely to change in the foreseeable future.

US as Disinterested Friend

America can be a disinterested friend of the third world. Unlike the Soviet Union, the U.S. does not want to convert anyone to a specific political, social, or economic system. Our main long-term interest is that third world countries remain independent, free to make their own choices. We must recognize that although we regard parliamentary democracy as the best form of government, it is futile to pursue a foreign policy which seeks to impose our model on newly independent countries.

We should be willing to lend economic and development aid to a wide variety of third world countries, but only on two conditions: (1) that they demonstrate a decent respect for elementary human rights, and (2) that they demonstrate a decent respect for the United States and its interests. Those who make it a practice to vilify the U.S. and to act systematically against its interests cannot expect its assistance.

These principles apply not only to nations but to international organizations as well. The United Nations and its specialized agencies were established to promote human rights and the peaceful solution of conflicts between nations. Democrats have always supported these international ideals and helped establish the U.N. to realize them. To say that the U.N. has fallen short of these ideals is wrong. It has betrayed them. It systematically ignores violations of human rights and threats to peace; instead, it diverts its energies and resources to fanning the flames of selected regional conflicts, and assaulting Western values and interests. The United States must steadfastly resist these pressures in the U.N. If an automatic majority persists in subverting the noble aims of the U.N., we should seriously consider withdrawing the vast American contribution that makes U.N. activities possible in the first place.

Nonintervention as Policy

America's policy toward foreign conflicts should, as a rule, be one of nonintervention; military intervention always involves great risk. But no responsible American statesman could or should promise that the U.S. will refrain in any and all circumstances from intervention. There may be situations in which the consequences of passivity are worse. It is impossible to delineate precisely how the U.S. should respond to every contingency. However, it should be clear to potential aggressors that the U.S. will not tolerate a Soviet takeover of the Persian Gulf, nor the establishment of foreign military bases in this hemisphere. Intervention should be exercised only with the greatest circumspection, but to deny policy makers this option is tantamount to abdicating America's role in world affairs, with incalculable

consequences for the survival of Western societies and the cause of freedom.

(4) *The Middle East.* The Democrats must continue to work for peace between Israel and her Arab neighbors. The basis for such a search must be U.N. Security Council Resolution 242 and the Camp David agreements, which are the proudest accomplishments of the last Democratic Administration. The peace process must attempt to: (1) maintain and broaden the normalization of relations between Egypt and Israel; (2) achieve autonomy for the Palestinians in the West Bank and Gaza; and (3) expand the Camp David framework to bring in Israel's other neighbors.

It is important, however, to recognize that the Arab-Israeli conflict may not be susceptible to a quick or comprehensive solution in the near future. It is a deep-rooted dispute between conflicting nationalisms.

"The basic principle of US-Soviet relations has to be reciprocity."

There is no magic formula, and Washington must abandon the delusion that it can invent one. The absence of peace between Israel and her neighbors to the east is not the result of misperception. It results from the too accurate perception in Israel that the Arab states, except Egypt, consider Israel—all of Israel—"occupied territory" and intend, by a variety of means, to destroy it. Some of the means at their disposal have been demonstrated recently in Syria during the brutal suppression of the Hama uprising and in Lebanon by the endless death toll of its internecine terror and warfare. The U.S. must not add more means to the disposal of those—including Jordan—who refuse the path of recognition and negotiation. We must be steadfast in maintaining Israel's qualitative military superiority, because of our solemn commitment to her security, and because a strong Israel is the best deterrent to renewed war.

Seek Allies' Support

The U.S. has a special interest in the Persian Gulf because of the West's dependence on its oil supplies. U.S. foreign policy should make it absolutely clear that any intervention from the outside, directly or by proxies, would have incalculable consequences for world peace. The U.S. should seek the support of its Western allies in opposing foreign intervention in the Persian Gulf. But the indiscriminate sale of arms to unstable and unpredictable regimes in the area, particularly those that have consistently opposed military cooperation with the U.S., must cease. It can only be a source of more instability. Those nations which seek our protection should at least be willing to cooperate with us in common defense.

(5) *Africa.* The Democratic Party should pledge

itself to improve U.S. relations with all African nations, to strive for economic development and justice, to help the African peoples in their endeavor to raise standards of living and create conditions for a better life. It should give such support to all nations, regardless of their domestic political orientation, provided they do not serve as military bases for foreign powers. We support self-determination for Namibia and the movement to end apartheid—which, because of America's own long struggle for racial justice, has special meaning for us.

(6) *The Far East and Southeast Asia.* A Democratic Administration should aim at further improvement in relations with its partners—the non-Communist countries of the Far East and the ASEAN countries. Transient economic differences must not be permitted to deteriorate into trade wars. The issues involved must be negotiated in a spirit of good will. A Democratic Administration should favor the normalization of relations with Vietnam, provided it desists from military intervention in the affairs of its neighbors and ceases to threaten them.

(7) *China.* Progress in U.S.-Chinese relations must continue. Much headway has been made during the last decade, and there must be no reversal in this process. Certain areas of contention exist, but the common interests between the two countries are broader than the differences of interest and opinion between them. A determined effort must be made to overcome these difficulties.

"It should be US policy to encourage greater European political and military unity inside NATO, even if as a result American political preferences are not always accepted."

(8) *Latin America.* . . . We should make it clear that the U.S. will not tolerate the establishment of Soviet offensive bases in this hemisphere. While the resolution of the Cuban missile crisis of 1962 guaranteed that the U.S. would not invade Cuba, that agreement does not permit Cuba to engage in aggressive military adventures. Cuba can choose by its behavior whether it wishes normal or hostile relations with the U.S. If it pursues a genuinely independent policy, we should be prepared to reconcile our differences with Cuba.

We should give our support to forces pursuing liberty, independence, and economic and social progress throughout the hemisphere. We must recognize that these forces are historically weak in much of Latin America, that there has been a polarization between the antidemocratic forces of the left and the right. In these cases, U.S. foreign policy

faces unpleasant choices. Occasionally we will be forced to accept undemocratic regimes. In doing so, the level of our support must depend on the respect they show for human rights as well as their determination not to make common cause with the enemies of the United States and its allies.

Walter Laqueur is chairman of the International Research Council of the Center for Strategic and International Studies at Georgetown University. Charles Krauthammer is a senior editor of The New Republic.

"Realism and a readiness to work long and hard for fair and freely agreed solutions—that is our recipe for optimism."

The US Has a Strong Foreign Policy

George Shultz

Americans are, by history and by inclination, a practical and pragmatic people—yet a people with a vision. It is the vision—usually simple and sometimes naive—that has so often led us to dare and to achieve. President Reagan's approach to foreign policy is grounded squarely on standards drawn from the pragmatic American experience. As de Tocqueville pointed out, "To achieve its objective, America relies on personal interest, and gives full reign to the strength and reason of the individual." That is as true now as when it was said 150 years ago. Our principal instrument, now as then, is freedom. Our adversaries are the oppressors, the totalitarians, the tacticians of fear and pressure.

On this foundation, President Reagan's ideas and the structure of his foreign policy are so straight forward that those of us enmeshed in day-to-day details may easily lose sight of them. The President never does; he consistently brings us back to fundamentals. Today, I will talk about those fundamentals. They consist of four ideas that guide our actions.

• We will start from realism.

• We will act from strength, both in power and purpose.

• We will stress the indispensable need to generate consent, build agreements, and negotiate on key issues.

• We will conduct ourselves in the belief that progress is possible, even though the road to achievement is long and hard.

Reality

If we are to change the world we must first understand it. We must face reality—with all its anguish and all its opportunities. Our era needs those who, as Pericles said, have the clearest vision of what

George Shultz, speech delivered before the United Nations, September 30, 1983.

is before them, glory and danger alike, and, notwithstanding, go out to meet it.

Reality is not an illusion nor a sleight of hand, though many would have us believe otherwise. The enormous, grinding machinery of Soviet propaganda daily seeks to distort reality, to bend truth for its own purposes. Our world is occupied by far too many governments which seek to conceal truth from their own people. They wish to imprison reality by controlling what can be read or spoken or heard. They would have us believe that black is white and up is down.

Unpleasant Reality

Much of present day reality is unpleasant. To describe conditions as we see them, as I do today and as President Reagan has over the course of his presidency, is not to seek confrontation. Far from it. Our purpose is to avoid misunderstanding and to create the necessary preconditions for change. And so, when we see aggression, we will call it aggression. When we see subversion, we will call it subversion. When we see repression, we will call it repression.

• Events in Poland, for example, cannot be ignored or explained away. The Polish people want to be their own master. Years of systematic tyranny could not repress this desire, and neither will martial law. But in Poland today, truth must hide in corners.

• Nor can we simply turn our heads and look the other way as Soviet divisions brutalize an entire population in Afghanistan. The resistance of the Afghan people is a valiant saga of our times. We demean that valor if we do not recognize its source.

• And Soviet surrogates intervene in many countries, creating a new era of colonialism at the moment in history when peoples around the globe had lifted that burden from their backs.

• Nor will we shy away from speaking of other problems affecting the free and developing worlds.

Much of the developing world is threatened by a crisis of confidence in financial institutions and the stultifying effects of state-controlled economies. The naturally vibrant economies of many Western nations and trade between the world's major trading partners are threatened by recession and rising protectionism.

The great alliances that shore up world stability and growth—our hemispheric partnership and NATO, and the Western and Japanese industrial democracies—are challenged by new as well as chronic strains.

• Finally, the shadow of war still darkens the future of us all. There is no ultimate safety in a nuclear balance of terror constantly contested. There is no peace of mind at a time when increasing numbers of nations appear willing to launch their armies into battles for causes which seem local but have ramifications for regional and even global harmony.

Reality of Hope

The list of troubles is long; the danger of despair great. But there is another side to the present reality; it is a reality of hope. We are living in a fantastic time of opportunity.

"If we are to change the world we must first understand it."

Historians in the future will surely marvel over the accomplishments achieved by human beings in the last half of this century. We have expanded the frontiers of thought—in science, biology, and engineering; in painting, music, and mathematics; in technology and architecture—far beyond the point anyone could have dared predict, much less hoped for. We know much today about the oceans and forests and the geological strata that lock in the story of our past. We know more about a baby—or the brain—than was accumulatd in 10 millenia before our time. We are learning to produce food for all of us; we are no longer helpless before the threat of disease; we explore our universe as a matter of course. We are confronting the nature of nature itself. The opportunities are grand. This, too, is a clear reality.

Thus, realism shows us a world deeply troubled, yet with reason for hope. There is one necessary condition: The only way we can enhance and amplify the human potential is by preserving, defending, and extending those most precious of conditions—freedom and peace.

Strength

America's yearning for peace does not lead us to be hesitant in developing our strength or in using it when necessary. Indeed, clarity about the magnitude of the problems we face leads inevitably to a realistic appreciation of the importance of American strength. The strength of the free world imposes restraint, invites accommodation, and reassures those who would share in the creative work that is the wonderful consequence of liberty.

Strength means military forces to insure that no other nation can threaten us, our interests, or our friends. But when I speak of strength, I do not mean military power alone. To Americans, strength derives as well from a solid economic base and social vitality at home and with our partners. And, most fundamentally, the true wellspring of strength lies in America's moral commitment.

Military Strength

The bulwark of America's strength is military power for peace. The American people have never accepted weakness, nor hesitancy, nor abdication. We will not put our destiny into the hands of the ruthless. Americans today are emphatically united on the necessity of a strong defense. This year's defense budget will insure that the United States will help its friends and allies defend themselves—to make sure that peace is seen clearly by all to be the only feasible course in world affairs.

Along with military readiness and capability must come the willingness to employ it in the cause of peace, justice, and security. Today in Beirut the U.S. Marines—together with our allies Italy and France—are helping the Lebanese Government and Armed Forces assure the safety of the peoples of that tormented capital. Our Marines represent an extension of American power, not for war but to secure the peace. They are there to speed the moment when all foreign forces depart from Lebanon. There must be early agreement on a timetable for the full application of Lebanon's independence, sovereignty, and territorial integrity. Lebanon deserves the world's help—to secure peace and to rebuild a thriving society.

America will continue to use its strength with prudence, firmness, and balance. We intend to command the respect of adversaries and to deserve the confidence of allies and partners.

Economic Strength

The engine of America's strength is a sound economy. In a time of recession, industrialized and less developed nations alike are bedeviled by excessive inflation, restricted markets, unused capacity, stagnating trade, growing pressure for protectionism, and the most potent enemy of expansion—pervasive uncertainty.

The United States, with its vast human and scientific resources, can survive an era of economic strife and decay. But our moral commitment and our self-interest require us to use our technological and productive abilities to build lasting prosperity at home and to contribute to a sound economic situation abroad.

President Reagan has instituted a bold program to get the American economy moving. Our rate of inflation is down markedly, and we will keep it down. This will add stability to the value of the dollar and give greater confidence to international financial markets.

The recent drop in U.S. interest rates will stimulate new investments within and beyond our shores. Conservation through market pricing of energy has reduced U.S. demand for world energy supplies. We are putting the recession behind us. A growing and open American economy will provide new markets for goods and services produced elsewhere and new opportunities for foreign investment. Just as we have a stake in worldwide recovery, others will prosper as our recovery develops.

International Issues

For wider prosperity to take hold, we must cooperatively attend these international issues.

• The lure of protectionist trade policies must be resisted—whether in the form of overt import restrictions and export subsidies or by more subtle domestic programs. These can only distort world trade and impair growth everywhere. Let us determine to make the November ministerial meeting of the GATT (General Agreement on Tariffs and Trade) a time to stem these protectionist pressures and reinvigorate positive efforts for a more open trading system.

• The implications of the external debt of many nations must be understood. Immediate debt problems are manageable if we use good sense and avoid destablizing actions. But the magnitude of external debt will almost inevitably reduce resources available for future lending for development purposes. Economic adjustment is imperative. The International Monetary Fund can provide critical help and guidance in any country's efforts to smooth the adjustment process. The new borrowing arrangement proposed by the United States can be crucial to this effort.

• And the necessity of reducing government interference in the market must be recognized. Every nation has the right to organize society as its inhabitants wish, but economic facts cannot be ignored. Those facts clearly demonstrate that the world's command economies have failed abysmally to meet the needs of their peoples. The newly prosperous industrialized nations are those with the most free and open markets.

Moral Strength

The bedrock of our strength is our moral and spiritual character. The sources of true strength lie deeper than economic or military power—in the dedication of a free people which knows its responsibility. America's institutions are those of freedom accessible to every person and of government as the accountable servant of the people. Equal opportunity; due process of law; open trial by jury; freedom of belief, speech, and assembly—our Bill of Rights, our guarantees of liberty and limited government—were hammered out in centuries of ordeal. Because we care about these human values for ourselves, so must we then be concerned, and legitimately so, with abuses of freedom, justice, and humanitarian principles beyond our borders. This is why we will speak and act for prisoners of conscience, against terrorism, and against the brutal silencing of the Soviet Helsinki Watch Committee. This is why we are anxious to participate in periodic reviews of the human rights performance of ourselves as well as others. We welcome scrutiny of our own system. We are not perfect, and we know it, but we have nothing to hide.

"The only way we can enhance and amplify the human potential is by preserving, defending, and extending those most precious of conditions— freedom and peace."

Our belief in liberty guides our policies here in the United Nations as elsewhere. Therefore, in this forum the United States will continue to insist upon fairness, balance, and truth. We take the debate on human rights seriously. We insist upon honesty in the use of language; we will point out inconsistencies, double standards, and lies. We will not compromise our commitment to truth.

Readiness to Solve Problems

The world has work to do for the realists, the pragmatists, and the free. With a clear understanding of the troubled circumstances of the hour and with a strengthened ability to act, we need, as well, the vision to see beyond the immediate present.

All of us here represent nations which must understand and accept the imperative of fair engagement on the issues before us and, beyond that, of common effort toward shared goals. Whether we are seeking to bring peace to regional conflict or a resolution of commercial differences, the time of imposed solutions has passed. Conquest, pressure, acquiescence under duress were common in decades not long past, but not today. Not everybody who wants his concerns addressed will find us automatically receptive. But when negotiations are in order, America is prepared to go to work on the global agenda and to do so in a way that all may emerge better off and more secure than before.

We manage our problems more intelligently, and with greater mutual understanding, when we can bring ourselves to recognize them as expressions of mankind's basic dilemma. We are seldom confronted with simple issues of right and wrong, between good and evil. Only those who do not bear the direct burden of responsibility for decision and action can indulge themselves in the denial of that reality. The task of statesmanship is to mediate between two—or several—causes, each of which often has a legitimate claim.

"America will continue to use its strength with prudence, firmness and balance."

It is on this foundation that the United States stands ready to try to solve the problems of our time—to overcome chaos, deprivation, and the heightened dangers of an era in which ideas and cultures too often tend to clash and technologies threaten to outpace our institutions of control.

We are engaged in negotiations and efforts to find answers to issues affecting every part of the globe and every aspect of our lives upon it.

The Middle East

The agony of the Middle East now exceeds the ability of news bulletins or speeches to express; it is a searing wound on our consciousness. The region is in constant ferment. Unrest flares into violence, terror, insurrection, and civil strive. War follows war. It is clear to everyone in this hall that international peace, security, and cooperative progress cannot be truly achieved until this terrible regional conflict is settled.

All of us have witnessed in the past several months a graphic reminder of the need for practical peace negotiations in the Middle East. Of the nations in the world which need and deserve peace, Israel surely holds a preeminent place. Of the peoples of the world who need and deserve a place with which they can truly identify, the Palestinian claim is undeniable.

But Israel can only have permanent peace in a context in which the Palestinian people also realize their legitimate rights. Similarly, the Palestinian people will be able to achieve their legitimate rights only in a context which gives to Israel what it so clearly has a right to demand—to exist, and to exist in peace and security.

Necessity of Hard Work

This most complex of international conflicts cannot be resolved by force. Neither the might of armies nor the violence of terrorists can succeed in imposing the will of the strong upon the weak. Nor can it be settled simply by the rhetoric of even the most

carefully worded document. It can only be resolved through the give and take of direct negotiations leading to the establishment of practical arrangements on the ground.

In other words, it can only be resolved through hard work. For those who believe that there is no contradiction between permanent peace for Israel and the legitimate rights of the Palestinian people— and for those who believe that both are essential for peace and that neither can be achieved without the other—the task can truly be a labor of love.

On September 1, President Reagan challenged the parties to the Arab-Israeli conflict to make a fresh start on the road to peace in the Middle East. The Camp David agreements, resting squarely on U.S. Security Council Resolution 242, with its formula of peace for territory, remain available to those who would accept the challenge to make this journey with us. The road will not be easy, but in his statement, President Reagan made a number of proposals which, for those who are willing to join the effort, make the journey safer and easier. I call on all concerned to accept President Reagan's challenge and hasten the realization of true peace in the Middle East.

Arms Control

In addition to the imperative need to resolve regional problems, there is an equally significant global imperative: to halt, and reverse, the global arms buildup. As an American, I am aware that arms control and disarmament are a special responsibility of the world's most powerful nations—the United States and the Soviet Union. And as an American, I can report that we are fulfilling our responsibility to seek to limit and reduce conventional and nuclear arms to the lowest possible levels.

With this goal in mind, President Reagan has initiated a comprehensive program for negotiated arms reductions. In Central Europe, the most heavily armed region on this planet, the Western allies are seeking substantial reductions in NATO and Warsaw Pact troops to equal levels. To achieve this goal, we have recently introduced a new proposal designed to revitalize the talks in Vienna on mutual and balanced reductions in military manpower.

In the area of strategic arms, the United States has also taken the initiative by calling for a one-third reduction in the number of nuclear warheads that American and Soviet ballistic missiles can deliver. And in the talks in Geneva on intermediate-range nuclear forces, the United States has gone even further, by asking the Soviet Union to agree to a bold proposal for eliminating an entire category of weapons from the arsenals of the two sides. ·

But as important as these negotiations are, the problem of arms control cannot be left to the two superpowers. The threat of nuclear proliferation extends to every region in the world and demands the attention and energy of every government. This is not solely, or even primarily, a concern of the superpowers. The nonnuclear countries will not be safer if nuclear intimidation is added to already deadly regional conflicts. The developing nations will not be more prosperous if scarce resources and scientific talent are diverted to nuclear weapons and delivery systems.

Unfortunately, as the task becomes more important, it also becomes more difficult. Greater quantities of dangerous materials are produced, and new suppliers emerge who lack a clear commitment to nonproliferation. But the technology that helped to create the problems can supply answers as well. Vigorous action to strengthen the barriers to aggression and to resolve disputes peacefully can remove the insecurities that are the root of the problem. The United States, for its part, will work to tighten export controls, to promote broader acceptance of safeguards, to urge meaningful actions when agreements are violated, and to strengthen the International Atomic Energy Agency. We will not accept attempts to politicize—and, therefore, emasculate—such vital institutions.

Progress

Perhaps the most common phrase spoken by the American people in our more than two centuries of national life has been: "You can't stop progress." Our people have always been imbued with the conviction that the future of a free people would be good.

America continues to offer that vision to the world. With that vision and with the freedom to act creatively, there is nothing that people of goodwill need fear.

I am not here to assert, however, that the way is easy, quick, or that the future is bound to be bright. There is a poem by Carl Sandburg in which a traveler asks the sphinx to speak and reveal the distilled wisdom of all the ages. The sphinx does speak. Its words are: "Don't expect too much."

That is good counsel for all of us here. It does not mean that great accomplishments are beyond our reach. We can help shape more constructive international relations and give our children a better chance at life. It does mean, however, that risk, pain, expense, and above all endurance are needed to bring those achievements into our grasp.

Advances

We must recognize the complex and vexing character of this world. We should not indulge ourselves in fantasies of perfection or unfulfillable plans or solutions gained by pressure. It is the responsibility of leaders not to feed the growing appetite for easy promises and grand assurances. The plain truth is this: We face the prospect of all too few decisive or dramatic breakthroughs; we face the necessity of dedicating our energies and creativity to a protracted struggle toward eventual success.

That is the approach of my country—because we see not only the necessity, but the possibility, of making important progress on a broad front.

• Despite deep-seated differences between us and the Soviet Union, negotiators of both sides are now at work in a serious, businesslike effort at arms control.

• President Reagan has issued an important call for an international conference on military expenditure. The achievement of a common system for accounting and reporting is the prerequisite for subsequent agreements to limit or curtail defense budgets.

• The Caribbean Basin initiative establishes the crucial bond between economic development and economic freedom. It can be a model for fair and productive cooperation between economies vastly different in size and character.

• And the diplomatic way is open to build stability and progress in southern Africa through independence for Namibia under internationally acceptable terms.

Realism and a readiness to work long and hard for fair and freely agreed solutions—that is our recipe for optimism. That is the message and the offer which my government brings to you today.

"Perhaps the most common phrase spoken by the American people in our more than two centuries of national life has been: 'You can't stop progress.'"

I began my remarks here today with an informal personal word. Let me end in the same spirit. We must be determined and confident. We must be prepared for trouble but always optimistic. In this way the vast bounties produced by the human mind and imagination can be shared by all the races and nations we represent here in this hall.

A predecessor of mine as Secretary of State, whose portrait hangs in my office, conveyed the essence of America's approach to the world's dangers and dilemmas. He said we would act with "a stout heart and a clear conscience, and never despair."

That is what John Quincy Adams said nearly a century and a half ago. I give you my personal pledge today that we will continue in that spirit, with that determination, and with that confidence in the future.

George Shultz is the secretary of state under the Reagan administration.

*"Stability through strength is a lesson
we learned only after a disastrous
surprise attack and a costly world war."*

The Best US Defense Is Military Strength

James A. McClure

General Douglas MacArthur, on the eve of the capture of the Philippines by the Japanese, sadly noted that the history of failure in war could be summed up in the words "too late." Four decades later, as Western democracies find their peace and freedom threatened by another totalitarian aggressor—the Soviet Union—we ponder aloud whether our efforts to prevent war this time are also "too late."

Since the end of World War II, the peace of the world has depended upon a stable balance of power. Throughout the 1950's and 1960's, the U.S. and her allies continued to maintain and improve enough military force to make a Soviet attack unthinkable. However, during the post-Vietnam 1970's, U.S. advantages in conventional and strategic military forces were largely lost through neglect and naivete.

While the Soviets were engaged in a full-scale build-up of their armed forces, deploying ever more sophisticated weapons systems, the U.S. permitted its defenses to deteriorate dangerously. Negotiations, meanwhile, were touted as the only possible road to peace with the Soviets—despite the repeated warnings of our defense experts that the Soviet Union was well on the way to achieving decisive military superiority. A dangerous instability in the military balance was permitted to grow and, after a decade of negotiations for negotiations' sake, the "unthinkable" Soviet attack has become a realistic possibility.

Strategic Weapons Imbalance

The gravity of our predicament is apparent from a survey of U.S.-Soviet conventional and strategic nuclear forces. By far the most serious imbalance facing the U.S. is the overwhelming Soviet preponderance in strategic nuclear weapons. Unlike

James A. McClure, "Rebuilding America's Defenses—Before It's Too Late," *USA Today*, January 1982. Reprinted from *USA Today*, January 1980. Copyright 1980 by Society for the Advancement of Education.

our own defense strategists, Soviet military planners believe that a nuclear war can be fought and won. To insure that they will be the winners in the event of such a war, the Soviets have developed a number of new weapons systems and have undertaken an ambitious program of civil defense to insure that their vital industry, and enough of their population, survive any counter-strike.

The Soviet Union now possesses 344 more land-based ICBM's than the U.S. Their advantage in nuclear warheads is 4,306 to 2,154, more than two-to-one. This means that the Soviets already have four times as many warheads as the U.S. has missile silos. This Soviet potential is often described by defense analysts as a "window of vulnerability."

On the U.S. side of the ledger, our land-based ICBM force stands at 1,054—unchanged since 1967. Although the U.S. once enjoyed a considerable advantage in multiple warheads, we are now well behind. Moreover, U.S. missiles are much less powerful than their Soviet counterparts.

Soviet Submarine Threat

Besides its advantage in land-based nuclear forces, the Soviets have significantly strengthened their submarine-launched missile capabilities. Since 1970, they have added 49 new nuclear submarines to their rapidly expanding navy. Although Soviet subs do not at present match the quality of their American counterparts, the new Soviet Kiev-class submarines may well outmatch the best U.S. subs within a decade. Soviet submarines already threaten U.S. cities and defense sites and the threat can be expected to grow.

A major component of Soviet nuclear strategy is the new Backfire bomber. While the U.S. was abandoning plans for a manned bomber to replace our aging B-52's, the Soviets were busy deploying 60 of the supersonic Backfires. The Backfire capability is a major threat to Europe and the Middle East and a potential threat to the continental U.S.

U.S. air defense technology is now over 20 years old and, in the fast-paced world of technological innovation, experts say it could no longer provide even adequate warning and response.

A final and significant factor in the Soviet nuclear equation is civil defense. U.S. defense posture rests on the theory that both the American and Soviet peoples will be held as "nuclear hostages" in order to prevent war. However, the Soviets have never accepted the notion that their population must be sacrificed in a nuclear exchange, so they have undertaken a rigorous program of civil defense. Soviet citizens are drilled regularly in civil defense procedures, plans for evacuating entire Soviet cities have been fully prepared, and Soviet industries are designed and located with civil defense taken into full consideration.

Virtually No Civil Defense

The U.S., by contrast, has virtually no civil defense. Millions of lives that could be saved would now be lost in the event of war, simply because the most elementary preparations have not been made.

Soviet civil defense preparations are the clearest possible signal that Moscow is seriously weighing the possibilities of nuclear confrontation with the U.S.

Soviet advantages in strategic nuclear missiles, in manned bombers, and in civil defense represent a dangerous instability in the U.S.-Soviet military balance.

Stability can only be restored by making our own strategic forces a credible threat to the Soviets. This would require insuring the survivability of our missiles, maintaining strategic air forces capable of penetrating Soviet air defenses, and adequately protecting U.S. cities from a Soviet surprise attack.

Conventional Forces

As frightening as the strategic imbalance is, the inequity in U.S.-Soviet conventional forces is even worse. The latest available figures put U.S. ground forces at 910,000 men and women; Soviet ground forces number some 2,452,000.

In combat equipment, we are overmatched in almost every category. The Soviets possess 47,000 tanks to our 10,000. They have 60,000 armored carriers to our 14,000, giving Soviet troops a decided edge in tactical mobility. In artillery, the Soviet lead is 24,000 field pieces to our 4,925. Finally, in such critical weapons as anti-tank guided missile launchers and heavy mortars, the Soviets are, again, way out in front.

It should be further noted that, besides their advantage in sheer numbers, Soviet forces have a clear advantage in the quality and sophistication of their weapons and equipment.

The continuous Soviet upgrading of arms and equipment is contrasted by persistent U.S. reliance on obsolete weapons and vehicles. In the area of combat aircraft, for example, more than half of Soviet attack/fighters are new models, introduced since 1972; 62% of USAF attack/fighters, by comparison, are made up of aircraft deployed in 1963. Since control of the air determines control of the ground, the consequences of neglecting tactical air force needs are as awesome as they are obvious.

Chemical Weapons

In the field of chemical weapons, the Soviets also have gained a tremendous lead over U.S. and NATO forces. Given the lack of readiness of Western alliance armies to meet a Soviet lethal gas bombardment, many defense analysts fear that the Soviet advantage could be decisive in conventional warfare.

The Soviets have, in place, sophisticated decontamination units—units designed to keep Soviet forces in action while disorganizing and destroying U.S. ground forces. Our own chemical warfare capabilities, on the other hand, are nearly nonexistent, despite the fact that no formula for military stability that leaves out the problem of Soviet chemical weapons capability can possibly be considered workable.

As serious as the vulnerability of our land forces is, America's growing vulnerability at sea is a matter of the gravest concern to U.S. defense planners. Because America is a maritime nation and because it must supply and sustain its armies far from its own shores, naval superiority is vital to a U.S.-Soviet balance of power. The Soviet Union need not dominate the seas, providing it can deny them to U.S. and allied shipping in time of war.

Failure to Replace the Obsolete

Because of our purposeful failure to replace obsolete vessels with modern ships on a one-to-one basis, the once tremendous naval superiority of the U.S. has been dangerously diminished in the past decade. Meanwhile, the Kremlin has dramatically strengthened its power at sea with four brand new Kiev-class aircraft carriers, several classes of missile-firing cruisers and destroyers, and a new class of large, amphibious assault ships.

Since 1965, U.S. naval air capability has been cut in half, from 25 to 13 carriers. Of this number, only four are permanently deployed in front-line areas and one of the remaining nine has no air wing. The drastic decline in carriers and planes has cost the Navy the two-ocean capability it possessed in the pre-Vietnam era.

Apart from its decline in carrier strength, the U.S. Navy went from 267 to 189 surface warships between 1970 and 1979. During the same period, however, Soviet surface combatants soared in numbers from 215 to 279.

Although the U.S. has the lead in nuclear powered

vessels, Soviet warships are faster, possess more firepower and greater destructive range, and U.S. superiority in minelaying and mine sweeping has been yielded entirely to the Soviet navy.

America's advantage in attack submarines remains significant, but Soviet planners are rising to the challenge with an increasingly sophisticated anti-submarine warfare program.

All in all, the U.S.-Soviet naval comparison reflects a serious imbalance in the global military picture. Because of the large lead time required for new weapons systems, it is already too late to restore stability in this area before the end of the 1980's.

"With prevailing trends against us, we have little choice but to immediately begin rebuilding our defenses."

The quantitative and qualitative Soviet advantages in almost every category of conventional and strategic weaponry present the greatest threat in history to the peace and security of the U.S.—and any treaty or agreement that merely preserves the *status quo* only serves to perpetuate the threat.

Countermeasures

With prevailing trends against us, we have little choice but to immediately begin rebuilding our defenses. A number of countermeasures are available in the strategic and conventional arms area, and the time has come to employ them at once.
• To insure the survivability of our land-based missiles, we should deploy, as soon as possible, the MX ICBM in a land-mobile basing mode.
• A new strategic manned bomber, capable of delivering cruise missiles, should phase out our antiquated B-52 fleet.
• The 1972 Anti-Ballistic Missile Treaty should be carefully reconsidered and new ABM technologies studied as a possible deterrent to a successful Soviet first strike.
• The strategic doctrine of the U.S. should include a realistic program of civil defense. The needless loss of millions of American lives as a matter of policy is neither rational nor humane.

Even the immediate improvement of our strategic capabilities, however, is still not enough to restore balance to U.S.-Soviet relations. Our long-neglected conventional forces must, also, be brought up to strength.

Basic weapons such as tanks, mortars, fighter aircraft, and artillery must be modernized and produced in sufficient numbers to deter a conventional attack. Troops must have adequate supplies of ammunition and essential support

vehicles—all of which are presently lacking. Troop strength itself must be increased, by voluntary enlistment programs if possible, or universal military training if necessary. Finally, U.S. conventional forces must be fully trained and equipped to meet the hazards of Soviet chemical warfare advances. We should go forward with our own chemical warfare development, until and unless a verifiable agreement can be concluded with Moscow.

U.S. naval superiority, essential to our survival as a world power, must be secured. This will require a dramatic increase in the number of U.S. warships, aircraft carriers, and submarines.

Short-run expedients, such as the recommissioning of mothballed battleships, should not and can not be a substitute for much-needed modern naval weapons systems. The Navy should proceed with development of the Trident nuclear submarine, naval cruise missiles should be widely deployed, and American anti-submarine warfare research and development must be accelerated at once. All this is vitally necessary if the Navy is to perform its assigned task of guarding our overseas supply lines.

While a general build-up of our armed forces is necessary for the foreseeable future, it should be stressed that Americans still want a meaningful arms limitations agreement with the Soviets. American leaders are willing to negotiate for as long as necessary to achieve nuclear and conventional mutual force reductions. However, so long as the Kremlin wages aggressive war in Afghanistan and elsewhere; so long as they seek an overwhelming military advantage over the U.S.; so long as they maintain a war machine far beyond any reasonable or legitimate defense need, negotiation will be difficult, if not impossible. Persistent Soviet cheating and bad faith in past treaties and agreements make it extremely unwise to gamble our security on the strength of Moscow's promises.

Stability through strength is a lesson we learned only after a disastrous surprise attack and a costly world war. It is a lesson we seem to have forgotten in the aftermath of Vietnam. We can not afford to wait until history teaches us this lesson again. A new world war, and its attendant thermonuclear horror, would be a lesson learned "too late" for the survival of our country and, perhaps, mankind itself.

James A. McClure is a Republican senator from Idaho. He is a member of the Defense Appropriations Subcommittee.

"It is about time Americans started doing to the Soviets precisely what they have been trying to do to us, employing a strategy of quid pro quo in subversion and propaganda."

viewpoint **10**

The Best US Defense Is Subversive Activities

Jack Wheeler

Since the founding of the Grand Duchy of Muscovy in 1462, the Russian state has on the average increased its territory by the Size of Denmark every single year, or by the size of the entire country of Italy every seven years. Today, the Soviet Union contains over 100 separate ethnic groups and cultures. Since 1917 it has swallowed several entire nations, bit off large chunks of others, and violently subjugated into colonies 8 of the 13 countries on its border, as well as numerous others around the world.

Within the past decade, the Kremlin has added more than a dozen other nations to its sphere of influence. What was once French Indochina should now be considered Soviet Indochina—Laos, Kampuchea (Cambodia), and Vietnam. The USSR and its clients are now in control in Angola, Mozambique, Ethiopia, South Yemen, Benin, the Congo Republic, Grenada, and Nicaragua. The latest addition is Suriname. The genocide and chemical warfare being conducted in Afghanistan is only a dramatic variant of the ubiquitous hunger, bloodshed, and brutal dictatorship that always accompany Soviet colonization.

In the turmoil of the Bolshevik counterrevolution (which fascistically overthrew the *real* revolution of Kerensky, who had replaced the Czar's autocracy with a parliamentary democracy), enormous portions of the Russian empire declared themselves independent of Great Russian rule. In 1920, Finland, Latvia, Estonia, Lithuania, Belorussia, the Ukraine, Georgia, and Azerbaijan were all independent sovereign nations. All were subsequently conquered by Soviet military force, their borders subsumed within the borders of the USSR. Only Finland managed finally to escape.

Appeal to Patriotism

When Hitler's troops marched victoriously into Kiev, the capital of the Ukraine, in September 1941, the Ukrainian people welcomed them as liberators, deluging them with flowers. Millions of people in the Soviet Union joined the Nazis to fight against Stalin. It was only after Hitler began butchering and enslaving them as much as did Stalin that the latter was able to appeal to patriotism and launch a counteroffensive.

The history of Russia and the Soviet Union is filled with the Great Russians' subjugation of other peoples and cultures—the Little Russians, or Ukrainians; the White Russians, or Belorussians; the Georgians, Balts, Moravians, Poles, Ruthenians, Slovaks, Bessarabians, Crimea Tatars, Volga Germans, Tadzhiks, Turkmen, Armenians, Mongols, Azerbaijani, Uzbeks, Kazakhs, Kirghiz, and Afghans. The Kremlin has been occupied since 1917 by men obsessed with missionary Marxism and imbued with the ancient Great Russian desire for empire.

Because of the virulent synergy of missionary Marxism providing a religion-like justification for Great Russian imperialism, the principal purpose of the Soviet economy is the manufacture of weapons. It is correctly noted that while the United States *has* a military-industrial complex, the Soviet Union *is* one. Engaging in the most massive military build-up in history, the Soviets have achieved strategic superiority over the United States. The Soviet Navy is now acknowledged to be our equal in many areas, and a vast outpouring of tanks and conventional arms from Soviet munitions factories continues unabated.

Apocalyptic Threats

Wherever in the world—particularly now in our very backyard in Central America—there is a chance to destabilize America and the West using terrorists, guerrilla war, subversion, propaganda, or whatever, the Soviets are there with guns and money.

Moreover, the United States faces nuclear extinction at the hands of a state that has issued apocalyptic threats.

It is thus with good reason that the Reagan administration wishes the United States to take action. Its solution, however, is that the government vastly increase US military spending. This is quite curious, because "conservatives" constantly condemn "liberals" for always wanting to solve social problems by the government throwing billions of tax dollars at them.

What neither the conservatives nor the liberals see is that the Soviet Union is in reality utterly weak and vulnerable. It is this failure that, ironically, assures the Soviets a continued existence. Once the world recognizes the powerlessness of the Soviet Union— that the emperor has no clothes—the Soviets are through, the game is up.

Satellites and Inner Colonies

Everyone knows of the outer colonies of the Soviet empire—the "satellites" of Eastern Europe, Outer Mongolia, Cuba, etc. But it is less well recognized that the Soviet Union is itself a collection of *inner colonies*—the Ukraine; the Baltic countries of Latvia, Lithuania, and Estonia; the Transcaucasian countries of Georgia, Azerbaijan, and Armenia; and the Islamic-Turkic countries of central Asia. Soviet imperialism is practiced first and foremost on its own people within its own borders. And, like Humpty Dumpty in the children's rhyme, if the Soviet Union is ever broken up in any way, it can never be put back together again.

One of the most potent forces for political change in this century, especially since World War II, has been anti-imperialist nationalism. Accordingly, we should not seek to promote individual freedom in the Soviet Union so much as tribal freedom, that is, anti-Soviet, anti-Great Russian ethnic nationalism.

The best defense is a good offense. America and the West are under attack by the most dangerous imperialist power in history. It is about time Americans started doing to the Soviets precisely what they have been trying to do to us, employing a strategy of quid pro quo in subversion and propaganda. For the Kremlin is far more vulnerable to its own medicine than we are.

National Liberation Movement

And the way to do it for real entails, interestingly enough, no massive arms race or increases in the defense budget. It means spending money with a great deal more effectiveness, such as on developing and supporting a number of national liberation movements within the Soviet Union itself.

The goal of such a strategy would be either to establish a genuine peace with the Soviet Union such as America enjoys with former enemies like Japan, West Germany, Spain, and England, or to render the

Soviet Union incapable of being any sort of real threat to the United States, up to and including by dissolution of the USSR as a political entity.

The Kremlin must be driven to the conclusion that it cannot conduct a war with the West—nuclear or conventional—without a civil war breaking out among the USSR's inner colonies. The risk of war must be made so great for Moscow that this equation becomes inescapable: war with the West = dismemberment of the Soviet Union.

To achieve this, the US government must define a foreign policy whose goal is to secure from Moscow the realization that there is no exit from this equation: that the USSR's only alternative to political extinction as a nation-state is to abandon its strategy of global domination and its support of terrorist and subversive groups around the world, concentrating instead on developing the Soviet economy.

Disarmament or Dismemberment

Such an alternative entails major, radical disarmament. The message to Moscow must be clear: *disarmament or dismemberment.*

When we look at a Mercator projection world map on which the globe's curved lines have been straightened out on a flat surface, the USSR appears as a vast, seamless, monochrome blob, dwarfing the the rest of Europe and Asia. But this is an illusion. Africa, for example, which looks smaller than the USSR, is much bigger: the entire Soviet Union *plus* the entire continental United States could be fit into Africa with room to spare.

"Workers would be encouraged to demand independent unions; students, less ideology and an end to compulsory courses on Marxism."

Moreover, private mapmakers should be encouraged and government cartographers should be mandated to depict the Soviet inner colonies in separate colors with each designated "Soviet occupied." It is vital that the world change its perspective on the Soviet Union: it is not a monolithic, impregnable giant but a glued-together, imperialist empire that must some day come apart at its many seams.

The greatest potential weapon we have at our disposal against the Soviets is not the MIRVed ICBM, the Trident nuclear submarine, or even the incredible cruise missile. It is the CIA and a multitude of private, voluntary organizations. The most cost-effective move we could make in defense spending would be to shift the focus of CIA operations, giving this agency the directive to make trouble for the

Soviet Union. At the same time, the government should make it clear that the neutrality laws will not be interpreted in such a way as to prevent private organizations from playing an active role in such activities.

A program to undermine the Soviet empire should not waste time on grandstand plays like assassinations and coups d'etat. It should instead concentrate on taking tiny bites, causing small, irritating problems all over the place—worker unrest, ethnic unrest, complaints and moanings in three dozen places. In other words, make the Kremlin suffer, as the Mongols say, the death of a thousand cuts. Here are a few examples of what could be done.

Islamic Revival

There are over 47 million Moslems in the Soviet Union. While the elite of the Moslem clergy have been accorded power and privileges, the Moslem laity and the rank-and-file clergy have little freedom to practice their religion. In czarist Russia there were over 26,000 mosques; today there are only 200 in the entire USSR. With the resurgence of fire-breathing Islam throughout the Middle East it should not be difficult to stimulate an Islamic revival among Soviet Moslems.

Such a revival would encourge the already-proliferating secret Moslem brotherhoods that have led recent large-scale anti-Soviet riots in Tashkent, Dushanbe, and Chimkent. It would spark a resurgence of the famed "Basmachi" guerrilla movement among the Kazakhs and Kirghiz in the '20s and '30s. It would help bring to Soviet Moslems the true story of Soviet genocide being perpetrated upon their fellow Moslems in Afghanistan. And it would spark demands for greater religious freedom, the construction of more mosques, and most especially the freedom to make a *hadj*, a pilgrimage to Mecca. (To make a *hadj* is one of the five "commandments" of Islam, but only the political hacks among the Moslem clergy in the USSR are allowed out of the country. A hue and cry should be raised throughout all of Soviet Central Asia demanding equal rights for Soviet Moslems.) . . .

Sabotage and Harassment

Militant resistance groups could be organized in the European inner colonies—Latvia, Lithuania, Estonia, Belorussia, and the Ukraine. These would be similar to the French Resistance during World War II but updated for the '80s, trained to commit sophisticated acts of political sabotage against government and military facilities, records, and equipment. The publicly announced goal of these inner-colony national liberation movements would be outright national sovereignty and political independence a la Finland.

The Soviet Union, for example, is dependent for its functioning on computers, just as the West is. But Soviet computers are primitive compared to ours and are thus more vulnerable to sabotage.

America is home to many talented computer experts who are from Soviet-bloc countries and could be recruited to disrupt the functioning of Soviet computers. They could indulge, say, in "the entropy defense," adding extraneous, made-up data to important records. Adding millions of fake names to the government's lists of dissidents, workers under suspicion, and so on, would make such lists useless.

Scrambling citizens' identification numbers on computer files would generate awe-inspiring chaos in virtually every government agency. Computer "virus" programs could be introduced into a system; these eat and destroy other files in the entire system.

> *"Scrambling citizens' identification numbers on computer files would generate awe-inspiring chaos in virtually every government agency."*

Military phone networks in the USSR are connected to the military computer systems and to the public phone system as well. An ingenious computer manipulator could figure out how to gain access via public phones to the military's own computers. Of course, the cooperation of inside informants and accomplices is necessary, but given this, the possibilities for the most delightfully catastrophic computer sabotage are endless.

Handbooks on harassment techniques should be prepared and distributed, describing how to squirt epoxy glue into door locks, make antigovernment stickers with adhesives that etch the message into glass and can't be removed, get government officials to think their phones are tapped by other officials, and make homemade napalm from soap suds, egg whites, and gasoline. All such techniques of sabotage and harassment should be directed to impairing the government's ability to intimidate and control, while avoiding endangering the lives of private citizens.

Ethnic Unrest

Agents provocateurs could be used within all the inner colonies to foment worker, student, and ethnic unrest: complaints, demands, small strikes and demonstrations, in dozens of factories and universities. Workers would be encouraged to demand independent unions; students, less ideology and an end to compulsory courses on Marxism; ethnic groups, more autonomy and a return to their own cultural and legal traditions; and people everywhere, an end to the hated "internal passport," so they could travel throughout the country as they please. . . .

Carrots on Sticks

All of these offensive strategies are the sticks, designed to take advantage of the Achilles heel of the Soviet Union, to take it out of the game. But where there is a stick, there should also be a carrot, an enticement to play the game on our side. Diplomatic strategy should provide the carrot.

The Russian people and their leaders are not some crazed, bloodthirsty horde like the Mongols under Genghis Khan. Russians have made great contributions to Western civilization. Cultural greats, for example, include such Russians as Tchaikovsky, Rimski-Korsakov, Dostoyevsky, and Tolstoy.

The Russians have clearly demonstrated their capacity to behave barbarically, as have the Germans. Nonetheless, today there is an affinity between Germany and the other cultures of the West, certainly including America—and reasonably so. Russia and the Russian people also can become an ally of America's, and not as in World War II, when there was a marriage of cynical convenience to fight a common enemy, but on the basis of cultural affinity, trust, and friendship.

There do not have to be adversaries in the world, as the Marxist, fixed-pie view of reality suggests. The nations of the world can grow and prosper together.

So why does the Soviet Union look upon the United States as an adversary? It certainly isn't because we are capitalists rather than socialists or communists. After all, the Soviet Union's greatest adversary is China, yet China's government spouts nearly the same Marxist-Leninist line as the Kremlin does.

"A hue and cry should be raised throughout all of Soviet Central Asia demanding equal rights for Soviet Moslems."

Let's face it: America really isn't a belligerent, warlike country. There is more compassion, honest concern, and actual cash on the barrelhead given away by Americans for the well-being of mankind than by any other nation on earth. America simply isn't an imperialist power. It gave back Cuba and the Philippines and Okinawa and isn't trying savagely to colonize all over the world.

America's diplomatic attitude and operating principle toward the Soviets should be: don't attack us, and we won't attack you—morally, ideologically, subversively, economically, or militarily. Stop acting like an imperialist power, stop trying to foment disruptions and rebellions, *stop trying to make trouble.* Get the Cubans and East Germans out of Angola and

Ethiopia and South Yemen and Nicaragua, and get yourselves out of Afghanistan. Cease the constant outpouring of lies and childish propaganda about us. If you do, we'll leave you alone. If you don't, we'll dismantle you as a political entity....

China and USSR

China poses little threat to us. Its government is not aggressively imperialist and isn't voraciously colonizing all over the world. With the insanity of the Cultural Revolution behind them, the Chinese are concentrating instead on developing their own economy—without going on a credit binge and with a panoply of semicapitalist, private-incentive measures.

The Soviet Union should be in the same boat. At the very least, the Soviets must concentrate on keeping theirs afloat and must refrain from trying to sink ours. If they do not, the task of our diplomacy should be to explain to them that we can no longer refrain from simply pulling their plug.

We live in a risky world, perhaps the riskiest ever. All military graveyards are full of dead heroes. This is no time or place for rash moves, for a political charge of the light brigade leading us all into a nuclear Balaklava.

Yet America is in a fight for its life. Either we give up, lie down, and culturally die, or we figure a way to win, a way to take the bastards out.

Of course "the Commies" have enough nuclear weapons to blow us all off the map many times over. But we do not need to immobilize ourselves with panic over the prospect of *nuclear* war any more than, say, *germ* war. All-out biological germ warfare, for which the Kremlin is actually better prepared than we, would wreak just as much of a holocaust. It is fully as frightening as a nuclear war, and yet we single out the latter in which to wallow in fear-stricken anguish.

The Bomb as Suicide

The Soviets do have immense military power, unimaginably horrible power. But they also have a problem. They can't use it. For them to use the bomb would be an act of suicide—not because of the physical destruction that would be wrought by a retaliatory attack, but because of the political devastation that would result.

The Soviet Union really is Humpty-Dumpty. The "union" is not voluntary: the strong centrifugal forces within its borders are kept in check only by constant oppressive force. Today, with major demographic shifts, economic decline, disillusionment with Marxism, and the Polish situation, these centrifugal forces are coming into sharper and sharper focus—making the present a most propitious time for programs and policies that heighten the USSR's mortal ethnic problem.

A major purpose of such programs is to ensure that no matter what futile and hypocritical appeals to a nonexistent patriotism the Great Russians make to the other nations and cultures under their sway, no matter what precautions the Soviets take for a nuclear attack upon them, the vast destruction of such an attack would chaotically disrupt and break lines of communication and control between the Kremlin and a great many places throughout its empire. And once that empire is literally broken up into isolated, separate pieces, it can never be put back together again.

When the Kremlin Loses Control

Once the Kremlin loses control—even if only for a matter of days—of several portions of what previously was the USSR and its outer colonies, it will be unable to regain that control. The centrifugal forces will be unleashed; the inner colonies as well as the outer will say, "Do svidanya, Yuri!" The Soviet Union will simply vanish as an intact political entity; and whatever political structures arise in its place, there will be many of them, and they won't be taking orders from the Kremlin.

This is why, for example, the Warsaw Pact, and the possibility of its being a coordinated offensive threat to Western Europe, is such a fraud. NATO needs to develop its capacity for *subversion,* not its capacity to repel hypothetical attack by Eastern Europeans eager to conquer or die for the glory of Great Russia.

None of this means that anyone should consider for a pico-second calling the Soviets' bluff or a preemptive first strike against them. It means, rather, that the US government should be doing hardball negotiating with the Kremlin.

We *can* decisively put the Kremlin on the defensive in such negotiations. The particular techniques I've suggested for a subversive strategy of promoting ethnic nationalism within the Soviet Union are illustrative examples only. The employment or rejection of any one of them is not in itself important. What is vitally important is that the United States and the rest of the West go on a quid-pro-quo offensive against the Soviet Union and begin at least to exploit resolutely and confidently the USSR's mortal weaknesses.

There is enormous risk to us and the world no matter what we do. The Soviet Union is a society in a serious state of decay. There may well be more risk, however, in a policy of apprehensive, apologetic timidity than in trying to hasten and control to our benefit the Red empire's dissolution.

The course suggested here—to go for the USSR's jugular, to take advantage of the Soviet Union's Humpty-Dumpty vulnerability—is no more inherently risky than any other. It will require liberal doses of courage, caution, patience, skill, cool nerves, conviction, and self-confidence. But these are requirements for success and survival, both for individuals and entire cultures, in the first place.

America need have no fear of the Soviet Union. The state whose leaders have promised to bury us can be made to suffer the death of a thousand cuts—unless it chooses peace.

Jack Wheeler has a Ph.D. in philosophy and is an investigative journalist.

"We recognize arms transfers as a legitimate and sometimes necessary instrument of foreign and national security policy."

US Arms Sales Increase World Security

James L. Buckley

Sales and deliveries of major conventional arms—tanks, warplanes, artillery, and naval ships—to the developing nations have led to rising arms inventories and growing military capabilities in the Third World. Some of these have been stabilizing, some destabilizing; some in the U.S. national interest, and some not. Many nations, large and small, engage in the transfer of arms as part of their foreign policies, but the U.S.S.R., the United States, France, the United Kingdom, Italy, West Germany, and the East European Communist nations are by far the most significant suppliers.

The United States, however, is not, by any reasonable measure, the leading supplier of weaponry to the Third World that many people believe it is. If they illustrate anything, trends in the Third World arms trade illustrate the degree of U.S. restraint. In the first half of the decade covered by this report, which included the last years of the Vietnam war, the United States delivered larger quantities than other exporting nations or groups of nations in 7 of the 12 categories of major conventional weapons used in this report. In the second half-decade, however, the United States did not lead in any category and in one category (missile-equipped patrol boats) during these years did not export anything at all. The Soviets, by contrast, led in four categories between 1972 and 1976 and in the last half-decade led in seven. Similarly, the major West European arms exporters as a group were first in only one category of arms between 1972 and 1976 but between 1977 and 1981 led in five categories.

We ourselves are partly to blame for the misconceptions that abound on this subject. First of all, nowhere else in the world are arms transfers the subject of so much governmental disclosure, of such

intensive legislative scrutiny, or so extensive a public debate. This is as it should be, because we are a free society and because decisions to supply or not to supply weapons to states not firmly linked to us by shared history, values, and security alliances must be made only after the most serious deliberation. Secondly, our reports of "military sales" include a large proportion of transactions having little directly to do with the transfer of arms. For example, military sales, as normally reported, include construction (sometimes of hospitals), training, and various management services, along with weapons systems and their spare parts and support equipment. But one result of this way of doing business, as contrasted with that of other nations, is the impression of the United States as the Third World's leading armorer. That impression, as the following report makes clear, is significantly off the mark.

Legitimate Sales

We recognize arms transfers as a legitimate and sometimes necessary instrument of foreign and national security policy. To suggest, however, that the U.S. Government in this or in past Administrations has sought indiscriminately to press arms upon Third World nations is not supported by the facts. Other nations do not disclose the nature and levels of their foreign military sales or assistance to the same extent. Our knowledge of their activities, particularly those of the Communist states, is not complete. The data on their arms transfers contained in this report must, therefore, be regarded as the best minimum, but nonetheless reliable, estimate we can make.

Few activities are as difficult to measure as arms transfers. Data are incomplete, and estimates in monetary terms, the most commonly used measure, are fraught with many problems. These difficulties include the large differences in the composition of arms sales and security assistance programs from one

James L. Buckley, "Conventional Arms Transfers in the Third World," *Department of State Bulletin*, October 1982.

arms-exporting nation to another, down to such technical problems as accurate foreign exchange conversion and varying prices charged in different situations for any given foreign weapons system, particularly the more expensive ones....

The estimated constant-dollar value and quantities of conventional weapons sold and delivered to countries other than members of the major military alliances or states closely associated with them have remained fairly constant from year to year throughout the past decade. At the same time, patterns of supply have changed significantly. There has been a net growth in the military inventories of Third World countries; however, this report does not take into account reductions caused by combat losses, obsolete equipment scrapped, or weaponry not usable for lack of spare parts and support.

"The United States... is not, by any reasonable measure, the leading supplier of weaponry to the Third World"

As the term is used here, the "Third World" includes all nations except members of NATO and the Warsaw Pact; other European countries not belonging to either alliance; and Japan, Australia, and New Zealand. Other definitions of "Third World" could significantly affect summaries of this sort, but this one is broad enough to encompass most parts of the world where limited, conventional military conflicts have been occurring and in which the buying of weaponry may have a social and economic impact disproportionate to the size of the purchases....

Delivery Speed

The speed with which weapons, once ordered, can be delivered is an important factor in the Third World arms trade. As a consequence of the industrial capacity created to support the huge Soviet conventional force modernization program, Moscow has important advantages over all other arms-exporting nations. The U.S.S.R. can deliver significant amounts of weaponry very quickly, as it showed recently in Ethiopia and Vietnam and is now doing in Cuba. Moscow also can offer much more attractive loans than can Western suppliers. For nations not desiring the latest equipment, the U.S.S.R. has kept open the production lines for selected arms, such as the MiG-21 fighter, which is no longer in first-line Soviet units; it also maintains large quantities of older, refurbished weaponry. The Soviets have developed variations of many first-line weapons specifically for export. Other suppliers, in contrast, often must choose between providing new equipment

to their own forces or risk losing a sale by being unable to deliver until the weaponry comes off the line 2-4 years later. Moreover, most suppliers do not have large pools of used but still effective arms—as the United States once had—which can be provided quickly to their security assistance partners without adversely affecting the capability of their own front-line or reserve forces.

There are also differences among the programs of the major West European arms suppliers.

Compared to France

France, the third largest exporter to the Third World, follows a policy of developing on its own the full range of military hardware, usually of totally French design and of a quality and sophistication equal to that produced elsewhere. French forces, however, constitute too small a market to provide the economies of scale needed to produce sophisticated weaponry at reasonable unit cost. For this reason, France pursues arms exports and, because its products span the entire range of sophisticated weaponry, offers potential Third World buyers desiring this level of armament an alternative to buying U.S. or Soviet weapons.

Compared to West Germany

West Germany has for many years followed a restrictive arms export policy which eschews the sale of major lethal weapons to areas of tension. Bonn may now be moving toward a somewhat less stringent policy in which potential sales may be considered individually in the light of West Germany's broader world interest. Most of West Germany's arms exports, however, have been to European nations and are outside the scope of this report. Bonn's largest Third World market is in Latin America. West Germany does not produce a complete range of weapons—Bonn's primary combat aircraft, for example, are built under foreign license or within European consortia. Although other members of these consortia export arms containing West German components, in this report the dollar values of such sales are attributed to the selling nation.

Italian and U.K. arms exports are significantly smaller than those of the United States, U.S.S.R., and France. Although both nations can manufacture the full range of weaponry, each has limited the types of arms it produces, probably for financial reasons.

Two important supplier groups will be shown separately: the smaller West European nations and those of Eastern Europe. The smaller Western arms exporters compete against the United States, the major West European suppliers, and one another in the Third World within the limited range of high technology arms they can afford to develop. To a degree not found in the West, weapons design and production in the Warsaw Pact are standardized under the aegis of the Soviet Union. Pact members are allocated specific major systems to produce for the entire organization's forces and for re-export. This further broadens Moscow's arms production and supply base. The U.S.S.R., like any other licensor but to a far greater degree than any Western one, can orchestrate the arms exports of its allies. The latter often can provide weaponry, spares, and ammunition compatible with Soviet equipment in cases, such as the Iran-Iraq war, where Moscow for political reasons does not wish to be seen as a supplier. Within the Warsaw Pact, only Romania appears to act with some independence from Moscow. Yugoslavia is not a Warsaw Pact member but for convenience is included in the category "Other European Communist." Belgrade produces many weapons of Soviet design but pursues a much more independent arms export policy than other countries in this category. . . .

Small Dealers

In any given year, 60 or more countries sell some weaponry. Many, if not most, of the major weapons systems transferred by these "other" arms suppliers are actually re-exports of older weapons acquired elsewhere. A few Third World countries, however, are beginning to emerge as suppliers of new, domestically produced weaponry. Brazil, Israel, and China are noteworthy lesser exporters of new arms, although China is unique in that it supplies a wide range of 1960s-vintage, Soviet-designed arms.

"The rising cost of modern military equipment may well serve to restrain aggregate transfers to the poorer countries."

Private arms dealers, ranging from legitimate merchants to outright confidence tricksters, probably account for a far smaller share of the Third World's arms trade than is generally supposed. Although these dealers can probably furnish, licitly or otherwise, significant quantities of small arms, mortars, automatic weapons, ammunition, and the like, they generally cannot supply or support major systems. The con men, however, frequently allege that they can provide—given money in advance—such systems, complete with apparently legitimate end-user certification. Most, however, do not control the weaponry they are offering; rather, they solicit sales of used arms (which they often describe as new or of the latest model) that they only hope to acquire later, through middlemen and ultimately from governmental arms disposal programs. . . .

Outlook

It is virtually impossible to predict what will occur in such a complex and sometimes contradictory mixture of political, economic, social, and emotional factors as is the Third World arms trade. The composition of the weaponry sold may change; although some of the wealthier Third World nations may continue to buy the latest weapons regardless of cost, the poorer states may increasingly seek less complex or secondhand weaponry. Both major and emerging suppliers may strive to tailor a still larger variety of weaponry to Third World requirements.

James L. Buckley is the undersecretary for security assistance, science and technology.

"Instead of deterring war, the highly sophisticated weaponry may embolden the recipient to undertake military operations it would not otherwise have considered."

US Arms Sales Increase World Conflict

Gene R. LaRocque and Stephen D. Goose

Often ignored in the flurry of contradictory facts and figures, charges and countercharges about the nuclear arms race between the U.S. and the USSR and the conventional arms race between NATO and the Warsaw Pact is the degree to which Third World nations have been building large and increasingly potent armed forces. During the 1970s, Third World nations—some 130 of the world's 161 nations—spent more than $800 billion on military forces and munitions. Currently, these same countries are spending over $130 billion per year for weapons and to maintain about sixteen million men under arms. Military expenditures account for roughly 5.5 per cent of their gross national product and nearly a fourth of their central government expenditures. At the same time, many continue to have trouble meeting the basic needs of their citizens.

By traditional measurements some Third World countries rank high on the lists of military power:

• China ranks third in world military spending, Saudi Arabia fifth, Israel tenth, Egypt eleventh, and India thirteenth. Other Third World countries, including Iraq, Iran, Libya, South Korea, and Argentina, each spend over $4 billion annually on their militaries, which is equal to or more than all but a half-dozen NATO and Warsaw Pact members. Twenty-eight Third World nations spend over $1 billion per year on their military forces.

• The top seven countries in the world in terms of per capita military spending are developing nations: Qatar, Saudi Arabia, Oman, Israel, United Arab Emirates, Brunei, and Kuwait. In contrast, no Third World nation ranks in the top thirteen in per capita expenditure on health.

• In total number of armed forces, Third World nations hold nine of the top thirteen spots: China is number one; India, four; North Korea, five; South Korea, six; Turkey, seven; Taiwan, ten; Pakistan, eleven; Mexico, twelve; Egypt, thirteen.

• At least several dozen Third World countries have very powerful military forces in terms of their manpower and the quantity and quality of weapons and training.

Acquiring Arsenals

Third World nations have acquired large military arsenals primarily through two means. By far the most important is the purchase of weapons from other nations. The other is domestic production.

In the great debate over who is the number one arms merchant to the Third World, the U.S. and the USSR accuse each other, yet each seems to try hard to catch up. In an attempt to divert attention from the fact that fiscal year 1982 actually will be a record year for U.S. arms transfers, the administration is working hard to convince the American public that it is the Soviets who are the largest arms peddlers to the Third World.

Available data is sketchy and contradictory, but a compilation of data from a wide variety of sources shows that the Soviets, after lagging far behind the U.S., began to catch up in the mid-to-late 1970s and surpassed the U.S. in many, but not all, measures of arms exports to the Third World in the past few years. However, the administration is voicing concern over what appears to be at most a two or three-year phenomenon. Soviet arms exports are not likely to come close to matching the record U.S. level of $30 billion in 1982. If one looks at more than the past year or two, the supposed Soviet "advantage" disappears. From 1973, when world arms trade exploded, until 1980, the U.S. signed $75 billion in arms agreements with the Third World, the Soviets $56 billion.

Gene R. LaRocque and Stephen D. Goose, "Arming the Third World," *Worldview*, October 1982. Reprinted by permission.

US Allies Ship Arms

Moreover, if the objective is to prevent the USSR from gaining influence in Third World nations by denying them arms export markets and relationships, then the U.S. can rest assured that its allies are doing their part. France is the world's number three supplier, Britain number four, West Germany number five, and Italy number seven. In 1980 all non-Communist nations combined accounted for 61 per cent of arms agreements with the Third World; all Communist nations combined (including the Soviet enemy China) accounted for 31 per cent.

In all, about 75 per cent of the world's arms exports go to Third World nations. Total arms sales agreements with the Third World in 1980 were $41 billion, up 41 per cent from the $29 billion of 1979.

Much more is on the way. For example, as of 1980 the U.S. had delivered only half of the arms it had sold under the Foreign Military Sales program. This left a backlog of $55 billion of weapons in the pipeline. If the Reagan adminstration never sold another weapon, deliveries on existing contracts would stretch throughout most of this decade.

Three of the most notable aspects of weapons exports to the Third World are (1) the role of the United States, (2) the concentration of weapons in the Middle East/Persian Gulf/Southwest Asia region, and (3) the increasing sophistication of the weaponry provided.

The US Role

Prior to 1946 the U.S. had not provided military aid to any foreign country in peacetime. Throughout the post-World War II period, however, the U.S. has been the largest supplier of weapons to foreign nations. In the 1950s and 1960s, as part of the containment strategy, the U.S. shipped huge quantities of weapons overseas, usually on a grant or giveaway basis. While European nations were important recipients (especially France, West Germany, Britain, and Turkey), three Third World nations that were perceived to be acutely threatened by communism received huge amounts of grant military aid: South Vietnam ($6.4 billion), South Korea ($3.7 billion), and Taiwan ($2.7 billion).

It was not until the 1970s, and particularly the 1973 oil crisis, which created new financial powers, that U.S. and worldwide arms transfers took on gargantuan dimensions. U.S. weapons exports rose from an annual level of less than $5 billion to nearly $18 billion. For the decade, U.S. arms agreements totaled over $123 billion and included sales to about 130 nations.

President Carter came to office pledging to reduce the quantity and quality of U.S. arms sold to Third World nations. His administration turned down about $1 billion in requests for arms from more than sixty nations and cut off or significantly reduced U.S.

military assistance to over a dozen regimes recognized as consistent and gross violators of human rights. Nevertheless, during his tenure arms transfers rose to the near-record level of $17.4 billion in 1980. About $40 billion in arms were sold to Third World nations during the Carter administration, including controversial sales to Iran and Saudi Arabia.

Despite this, the Reagan administration has criticized Carter for failure to sell enough weapons overseas and has eliminated nearly all restraints on U.S. weapon exports. Under Secretary of State for Security Assistance James Buckley has called weapons exports "an increasingly important component of our global security posture and a key instrument of our foreign policy"; he has called Carter's human rights restrictions "self-inflicted injuries."

"Arms transfers of any sort lead to an increase in the destructive capabilities of the recipient and in the level of violence in the region."

U.S. weapons exports for the current fiscal year may reach $30 billion, far exceeding any previous year. In his first year in office, President Reagan:
• convinced Congress to increase U.S. military aid to Third World governments at the very time cuts were being made in U.S. domestic social programs;
• convinced Congress to repeal prohibitions on military aid, based on human rights records, to Pakistan, Argentina, and Chile;
• approved a $1.1 billion deal with Pakistan for forty F-16 fighter aircraft (another $1.6 billion in military loans is planned for the next five years);
• approved a $615 million sale to Venezuela of twenty-four F-16s (the first sale by the U.S. of highly advanced jet aircraft to any Latin American country);
• approved for the first time the sale of lethal military equipment to the People's Republic of China;
• passed the largest arms sale ever through a reluctant Congress, an $8.5 billion deal with Saudi Arabia, including AWACS aircraft and Sidewinder missiles.

The Middle East

Roughly two-thirds of all arms transfers to Third World nations have gone to the region which is now referred to as Southwest Asia (including the nations of the Middle East, Persian Gulf, and part of North Africa and South Asia). Over the past decade this region has accumulated about 70 per cent of all the tanks sent to Third World nations (22,000), 71 per cent of the light armor (27,000), 49 per cent of the artillery (27,000), 70 per cent of the supersonic aircraft (4,600), and 84 per cent of the surface-to-air missiles (30,000).

"Smarter" Weapons

The United States, Soviet Union, France, and other major suppliers are increasingly providing Third World nations with more advanced and destructive weapons. Some particularly favored customers are receiving the latest and best weapons that the suppliers have in their own inventories, sometimes before their own forces receive their full allotment.

The major Third World recipients of sophisticated U.S. arms are Israel, Saudi Arabia, Egypt, and South Korea, closely followed by Pakistan, Venezuela, and Morocco. These nations have received such items as F-15 and F-16 fighter aircraft, AWACS reconnaissance/command and control aircraft, a variety of advanced missiles, high-speed vessels, electronic radar and countermeasure devices, M-60A tanks, AH-1S attack helicopters, and self-propelled howitzers and artillery. These are front-line weapons being used by the U.S. armed services.

The major Third World recipients of Soviet arms are Syria, Iraq, and Libya, followed closely by Cuba, Ethiopia, South Yemen, and Vietnam. These nations have received MiG-23 and MiG-25 aircraft, Mi-8 and Mi-24 attack helicopters, several advanced missiles, Osa-II fast patrol craft, T-62 and T-72 tanks, and self-propelled howitzers and artillery.

There are many objections to be raised about the transfer of such high-technology weapons to foreign countries. Arms transfers of any sort lead to an increase in the destructive capabilities of the recipient and in the level of violence in the region. This is particularly true of more advanced weapons. Conflicts will be more destructive, both to the civilian population and to property. This can be seen in the current war between Iraq and Iran, where fighting is heavier than in any battle since World War II, and in the recent war in Lebanon.

Instead of deterring war, the highly sophisticated weaponry may embolden the recipient to undertake military operations it would not otherwise have considered. The weapons may even be turned against the supplier, or its close allies, in the future. Argentina sank three British ships with French-supplied Exocet missiles during the Falklands war.

Another complication arises from the fact that advanced weapons delivered by the U.S. are usually accompanied by a large contingent of U.S. military and civilian technicians to train indigenous personnel and to help mtaintain and operate the weapons systems. These technicians become so active in the day-to-day operation of the foreign military establishment that the danger of their becoming involved in any attack on the host nation, whether the U.S. desires to be involved or not, is great. The number of U.S. technicians overseas implementing arms sales has risen 25 per cent in the past two years.

Domestic Production

A growing number of Third World nations are developing their own armaments industries: At least twenty-four produce weapons of some type. Foremost among these are China, India, Brazil, Israel, South Korea, Taiwan, and South Africa. Others include Argentina, Chile, Venezuela, Egypt, Indonesia, and Malaysia. Most of these nations have developed their military industries in an attempt to lessen dependence on outside sources and to increase their prestige and political clout within their region. Economic benefits seldom have been the primary rationale for indigenous production of arms in the Third World.

Third World nations often begin by developing the ability to maintain and repair the weapons provided by other nations, then progress to the assembly of weapons components provided from abroad, then to the important step of producing entire weapons under license (or co-production), and finally to the ability to research, develop, and design weapons at home.

"Weapons may even be turned against the supplier, or its close allies, in the future."

Many Third World nations export arms. Brazil and Israel account for approximately two-thirds of all Third World arms exports, but most of the nations mentioned above sell weapons abroad. And there are several other nations that do not have a domestic production capability but re-export weapons previously purchased. Libya and Saudi Arabia are the main "re-exporters." The Third World share of arms exports remains small, less than 3 per cent, but it is growing and includes everything from small arms to major conventional armaments.

Brazil sells about $2 billion in weapons abroad per year. It produces a popular armored car, the Cascavel, and light transport aircraft, the Xingu, which it has sold to the French Air Force. Brazil also manufactures rifles, machine guns, air-to-surface missiles, jet trainers, and counterinsurgency aircraft.

Israel sells about $1 billion in weapons to foreign nations each year. It produces a wide range of infantry, naval, and air weapons. Israeli defense electronics, small arms, and ammunition are especially popular export items. The Israeli defense industry is apparently sophisticated enough to make improvements and modifications in U.S.-supplied equipment. Reports from Lebanon indicate that Israel has made changes in the avionics of F-16s and has put a new warhead on U.S. TOW antitank missiles.

China produces virtually all of its weapons, but they are considered relatively crude. Most are adaptations of Soviet weapons several generations old.

South Korea started its armaments industry in the early 1970s and is now considered capable of supplying roughly 70 per cent of its own military equipment. It needs the United States primarily for aircraft and electronic equipment. Most South Korean armaments are copies of U.S. weapons that are locally assembled or produced under license. South Korea manufactures bombs, howitzers, mortars, ammunition, missiles, tanks, naval vessels, helicopters, rocket and grenade launchers, recoilless rifles, and submachine guns. Among other things, it produced the M-48A5 diesel-fuel tank, Vulcan air-defense system, and Hughes 500MD assault helicopter under license. Its fast patrol boats, armored personnel carriers, and other military vehicles are considered to have good export potential.

The ever-growing domestic production capability of Third World nations increases the likelihood of future conflicts, since the developing nations will not be as heavily dependent upon the industrialized nations for spare parts and replacements for war losses. It will also make it harder to establish multilateral restraints on arms transfers.

World at War

In discussing all these weapons, it is important not to lose sight of their ultimate purpose: to conduct war. The wars in Lebanon, the Falklands, Iraq-Iran, El Salvador, and Afghanistan have focused public attention on conflict as Americans are again watching artillery fire and air bombardments on the evening news and reading of body counts in the morning paper.

Today there are about forty wars going on in the world. All but three (guerrilla activity in Spain, Italy, and Northern Ireland) are being waged in the Third World. Most are guerrilla wars and campaigns of urban terrorism, but there are also significant border wars, civil wars, and full-scale conventional conflicts. In the past several years only two wars have come to peaceful conclusions, and in both cases—Zimbabwe and the Falklands—fighting could resume.

Weapons provided mainly by the Soviet Union and the United States have permitted these wars to continue, perhaps encouraged their escalation, and certainly increased dramatically the power of small nations to kill and destroy. Surely it is time for big powers and Third World nations alike to realize that huge military establishments are of declining utility in achieving international objectives.

Gene R. LaRocque is a retired admiral in the US Navy and is director of the Center for Defense Information (CDI). Stephen D. Goose is a senior research analyst at the CDI.

Food Exports Should Be Used as a Weapon

Lowell Ponte

On January 4, 1980, the United States used food as a weapon against the Soviet Union for the first time. Less than two weeks before, Soviet troops had invaded neighboring Afghanistan. Such aggression against an independent nation would not be allowed "with impunity," declared President Jimmy Carter. The President's response: an embargo on grain sales to the Soviet Union.

Farmers and other Americans at first supported the President's firm policy, even though the embargo created a sudden surplus of grain that briefly sent prices spiraling downward. But it soon became evident that, because other nations were eager to sell grain, the United States and its farmers were suffering from the embargo just as much as the Soviet Union. On April 24, 1981, the new President, Ronald Reagan, lifted the embargo.

"From the farmer's point of view, the Soviet embargo was an utter disaster," says Secretary of Agriculture John R. Block. Yet Block does believe that the United States should be ready and willing to use food as a weapon. "Over the next twenty years," he has said, "food can be the greatest weapon we have."

Is Block right? Can we effectively use food exports as a diplomatic sword?

Leaky Embargo

The United States, with control over 57 percent of the world's exportable grain, is the Saudi Arabia of food. Only 8 of the world's 173 nations—the United States, Canada, Australia, New Zealand, Argentina, South Africa, France and Thailand—consistently produce significantly more food than they consume. And among these eight food-producing nations, the United States alone has a larger monopoly over food

exports than all the nations of OPEC combined have over world oil exports. In theory, if the United States chose to beat its plowshares into swords, its "food weapon" should be awesome.

What, then, went wrong with President Carter's grain embargo? The answers are complex, but the lessons we must learn from them are crucial to our rethinking of America's food aid-and-trade policies.

For any embargo to be effective, it must not leak. Yet leaks were legion in the Carter embargo. Consider:

• The President honored earlier agreements for the transfer of grain to the Soviet Union. As a result, of the 30 million tons of grain the Soviets bought worldwide during the 1979-1980 marketing year, *fully half*—15 million tons—came directly from the United States (much of it before the embargo was in place).

• Before the embargo, nations in Eastern Europe had ordered 16 million tons of American grains. When the embargo began, they suddenly increased their orders to more than 18 million tons, and the grain was sold to them without delay. "You'd have to be pretty naive to believe that increased exports to that area would not find their way to Russia," said the President of the Saskatchewan Wheat Pool in Canada in spring 1980.

• Although food-producing nations friendly to the United States agreed to hold their exports to the Soviet Union to "normal, historic" levels, these nations in fact sold to the Soviets more than *twice* as much grain as in the previous year.

Certain Facts

World population has been growing rapidly in recent decades, as doomsayers have warned. But so has food production; indeed, the amount of food available per person has actually been *increasing* during the past two decades. According to the U.N.'s Food and Agriculture Organization, even during recent years when famine seemed close at hand more than three of every four people on earth "lived in countries that were 95-percent or more self-sufficient in food energy." In many instances the poorest nations have harvests with yields per acre only half those of the United States. This fact, combined with the existence of large expanses of unused or underutilized arable land in underdeveloped nations, gives hope that these are the very places with the greatest prospect of increased food production during the next several years.

Those who argue that the United States can by itself wield a "food weapon" much like OPEC's "oil weapon" tend to forget certain facts. Few nations of the world can simply plant an oil derrick and hit oil. But virtually all nations can plant seeds and produce more food. It sounds impressive to say that the United States controls 57 percent of the world's exportable grain—until one learns that only one of eight bushels of the world's grain is imported or exported at all. Which means that the United States really controls only 8 percent of the total global grain supply.

"The United States controls 57 percent of the world's exportable grain."

OPEC, by comparison, controls more than half the global supply of oil used each year. Yet even OPEC, faced with conservation and a shift to alternative fuels in developed nations, is finding it hard to wield its oil weapon. The real price of oil in world markets, adjusted for inflation, is now dropping—and, barring a major disruption of supplies from the Persian Gulf, it is unlikely to rise again in the near future.

Feeding the Bear

But if many countries could move toward self-sufficiency in food if they chose to, there is one major developed nation that seems chronically unable to do so no matter how hard it tries: the Soviet Union. Despite investments sometimes topping $50 billion per year—more than five times what the U.S. government spends directly on agriculture—the Soviet Union has been unable to feed itself.

One problem is nature. With two-thirds of the country's prime crop land lying in the colder region north of the 49th Parallel, Soviet harvests are plagued with some of the world's worst weather. But weather is only one problem for the Russians. Politics is another. The Soviets' socialist system provides bad planning and few incentives. In recent years President Leonid Brezhnev has reluctantly admitted as much by quietly giving freer rein to rural citizens willing to grow their own back-yard gardens and sell their produce at profit. Such "free enterprise" inside the Soviet Union uses only about one percent of the

land under cultivation, but according to the Russian economics journal *Ekonomicheskaya Gazeta*, these entrepreneurs in 1980 contributed *31 percent* of Russia's meat production, *30 percent* of milk, *32 percent* of eggs, *35 percent* of vegetables, *64 percent* of potatoes, and *58 percent* of fruits and berries!

In the United States, some six million farmers grow enough food to feed the country and a goodly share of the world besides. By contrast, 26.4 million Soviet citizens work the land and yet their government must import food. The average Soviet agricultural worker grows enough to feed 9 other people—the same level of productivity U.S. farmers had in 1900, before the advent of modern machinery. Today, the average U.S. farm worker produces enough to feed about 50 other people.

A New Notion

But this very abundance has produced its own problems. Our farms have traditionally grown too much, and the resulting grain surpluses for years kept prices disastrously low for millions of farmers. During World War II, however, we discovered a way to deal with chronic food surpluses. Rather than destroy unwanted food, we would give it away to other nations or sell it at rock-bottom prices. This policy led in 1954 to Public Law 480, also known as Food for Peace.

Begun with the most practical and humanitarian of intentions, P.L. 480 is now beginning to find severe critics among liberals and conservatives alike. While this global welfare program did feed the hungry, it also often caused populations in poor nations to grow rapidly as food was turned into babies. The availablity of free or cheap food meant that farmers in these nations often could not earn enough from home-grown crops to improve their methods or their lives. This led millions to abandon farming, leaving their countries even less able to feed themselves without outside help.

Only in recent years have such nations begun to discover that higher prices for food mean that more food will be produced. This realization has already helped lead India toward food self-sufficiency. And last year higher prices for farmers produced a record harvest in the new African nation of Zimbabwe. Even the People's Republic of China has found that the free-enterprise incentives now offered on 40 percent of its collective farms encourage food production. If this notion—that a fair return for farm labor brings more food—should spread, then the world could be on the way to solving its food problems.

But the Soviet Union, often beset with severe crop failures, has taken another path to food, a path that has disrupted the world grain economy.

In 1972 Soviet buyers entered the U.S. marketplace and, through a series of quiet orders with separate companies, bought up more than *one-quarter* of the U.S. export grain crop. The Soviets acted quietly because news of their massive purchases would have indicated that Soviet demand was outrunning supply, and prices would have gone up suddenly and dramatically. Soviet agents elsewhere were also purchasing large shares of other nations' harvests—in all, about 30 million metric tons of the world's food supply that year.

Sudden Famine

For American consumers the repercussions of this Soviet buccaneering were painful. Poor U.S. crops in the inflationary years immediately after the Soviet purchases meant that the price of bread skyrocketed, as did the prices of meat, eggs, milk, poultry and other things derived from grain-fed livestock and poultry. Between 1972 and 1975, total U.S. food bills rose by an astounding *$54 billion.*

But what was painful for Americans was fatal elsewhere in the world. With grain suddenly in short supply, famine loomed. During 1972 and 1973, writes Lester R. Brown, president of the Worldwatch Institute in Washington, D.C., "the Indian government discovered that the Soviet Union had tied up most of the world's exportable wheat supplies." In the three poorest parts of India alone, writes Brown, "there were an additional 829,000 deaths compared with those of previous years." Between 1971 and 1975, nearly 760,000 deaths from famine occurred in Bangladesh, the world's eighth-most-populous country. In Ethiopia 200,000 died from starvation, and a like number died from the famine that swept the poor nations on the southern edge of the Sahara. In all, almost two million innocent men, women and children in the poorer nations of the world died of starvation.

Grain for Oil

But the shock waves set off by the 1972 Soviet grain raid did not end with famine. The Soviet purchases, exacerbated by poor crops worldwide, triggered a dizzying rise in world grain prices as nations scrambled for whatever food they could get at whatever price. As grain prices soared in August 1973, *The Wall Street Journal* noted that the United States could "now buy a barrel of foreign crude oil with less than a bushel of wheat, and a year ago it took almost 2½ bushels to get that barrel." The oil-producing nations were painfully aware that, relative to the food they needed to import, the value of their oil was sinking through the floor. This, the late Shah of Iran would say, was the real impetus behind the 1973 oil embargo, whose inflation and chaos echo in the world nine years later.

When oil prices quadrupled in world markets as OPEC's oil weapon made itself felt, the United States needed some way to offset the huge amount of money now required to buy foreign oil. It found a big part of the necessary capital in food. In 1973 with grain prices already higher than ever before, the

United States sold $9 billion in food to other nations. In 1974, in the wake of the oil embargo, the United States sold $21 billion in food abroad. By 1981 the United States was selling roughly $46 billion worth of food abroad, and the revenue from those sales offset half of the cost of imported oil.

Thus did America's surplus food, long a nuisance to be given away overseas, suddenly become the most profitable export item the country possessed—and an essential factor in slowing down the bleeding away of American dollars to foreign oil producers. Our golden grain had become the one commodity that ensured our supply of black gold—oil.

Diminishing Deposits

In pondering whether America can wield a food weapon as the OPEC nations do their oil weapon, analysts have begun to discover important similarities between food and oil.

Once upon a time oil was cheap. Vast natural ponds lay only a few feet under the sands of Saudi Arabia, and it cost less than ten cents to pump a barrel of oil from beneath the ground. To the Saudis, $1 per barrel seemed a profitable price. But it soon became apparent that however large their natural deposits of oil were, someday they would run out. When that day came, oil would be immensely valuable. Thus it seemed less than wise to sell off their finite supply cheaply.

"Higher prices for food mean that more food will be produced."

Most Americans fail to see a similarity between the amber waves of grain stretching across their nation's heartland and the oil flowing from Saudi wells. We tend to think of food as a perpetually renewable resource. We are wrong.

Our food, like the Saudis' oil, could someday run out. Both are the product of limited and priceless natural deposits that, once exhausted, will be gone for good.

For what happens when a stalk of wheat grows? Or a stalk of corn? What composes those precious grains we send overseas? The answer is that they are made from soil and water. And prime soil and water are diminishing resources.

Depleting Soil

It takes Mother Nature from 100 to 1000 years to create one inch of topsoil, the rich mulch of nutrients from which growing plants take nourishment. But in our present frenzy to squeeze food from farm lands, we are destroying on average an inch of topsoil every 45 years.

Where is this topsoil going? The answer: we are

exporting it to places like the Soviet Union. Yes, when we sell vast quantities of grain, we are literally exporting our topsoil, just as surely as Saudi Arabia is exporting its oil.

Once upon a time farmers could preserve their soil against such depletion. Their harvests were modest and, after a few years of taxing the soil with grain planting, they would let a field lie fallow or plant it with alfalfa or other cover crops that would restore nitrogen and other key nutrients to the land. But now American farmers tend to crop fields continually, producing one lucrative harvest of grain after another as they force-feed the land with fertilizers—an average of 200 pounds of nutrients per acre of crop land every year (or about 378 pounds *per citizen*).

One Department of Agriculture survey estimates that loss of topsoil at present rates, combined with other factors, will reduce American farm yields by eight percent in 50 years unless measures are taken to restore and conserve topsoil. Most farmers know this. But at present income, writes Lester Brown, it would cost the average farmer three times more to conserve his topsoil than he could recover in enhanced harvests by taking those measures. His choice, says Brown, is between going broke now, by expending huge sums to restore his topsoil, or going broke years from now when his topsoil is depleted and can no longer grow food.

"Most Americans fail to see a similarity between amber waves of grain stretching across their nation's heartland and the oil flowing from Saudi wells."

But if our present harvests depend heavily on fossil fuels to make the fertilizer that props up our eroding soil, so to a surprising degree do they depend on fossil water.

Fossil water? Yes, just as our topsoil took thousands of years in the making, so too did huge underground water reservoirs like the Ogallala Aquifer that stretches from South Dakota to Texas and New Mexico. Of every 100 gallons of water used in the United States, 81 go to irrigate crops. And 40 percent of this irrigation water comes from wells siphoning underground water deposits.

The trouble is, for every four gallons of water pumped from the Ogallala Aquifer, nature replaces only three gallons. The level in this underground reservoir is dropping by one to three feet per year, and it is possible that within 20 years it may no longer be able to support irrigation. Like Saudi oil, this precious natural deposit of water could soon run dry.

These facts point to a surprising conclusion: the United States is selling its grain at less than its real long-term cost. We are expending finite natural deposits in order to pump grain from our crop lands as fast as possible, without figuring the cost of these deposits into the price we get.

We are not alone in this predicament. All the grain growing nations are depleting their topsoil for immediate short-term benefit. And all feel compelled to squeeze a maximum harvest from their soil in order to help pay for oil imports.

But what if the major food-producing nations could be persuaded to imitate OPEC with a vengance—to sit down together and form a FOPEC, and organization of Food Producing and Exporting Countries that would agree to demand more dollars for fewer bushels of grain, thereby preserving the fertility of their crop lands?

Like OPEC, FOPEC could perform a major long-term service to the world. Like *OPEC?* Yes, indeed. In its odd way, OPEC has done America a lot of good. It has forced us (and other oil-importing countries) to conserve fuel as never before, to decontrol the fixed prices that helped keep our fuel artificially cheap and hence discouraged efficiency, and to assert our national independence through alternative energy sources.

Just as OPEC now finds itself diminished by a world increasingly independent of imported oil, a FOPEC would provide a powerful stimulus to other nations to grow more of their own food, and eventually to assert their food independence.

At the Third World Summit in Cancun, Mexico, last year, President Reagan offered to send U.S. agriculture experts to any nation eager to improve its own food production. But he made clear his belief that until nations took responsibility for their own development, no real progress toward ending the threat of famine could be made. As the earth's population grows, even the vast food-growing potential of the United States would be unable to assume the burden of feeding billions of hungry people. As one of President Reagan's favorite aphorism's says, "If you give a man a fish, you will feed him for a day. If you teach a man *how* to fish, you feed him for a lifetime."

Should we consider using food as a weapon? It is a power that destiny has put in our hands. Rather than reject it, we must consider the best and wisest ways to use this power to prompt development in other nations, to encourage cooperation, to discourage aggression. As Thomas Jefferson envisioned, by wise use of the power to trade what we have been blessed with, we may yet find in food a substitute for the sword and a means to keep peace in the world.

Lowell Ponte is a journalist. His articles are published frequently in Reader's Digest.

"Food is for eating and not for waging even the noblest political and ideological crusades."

viewpoint 14

Food Exports Should Not Be Used as a Weapon

Center for Philosophy and Public Policy

The United States produces and exports more food than any other nation, in a world where over a billion people are chronically malnourished and half a billion eke out an existence on the edge of starvation. Only a handful of nations produce more food than they consume, and the United States is chief among these, dominating the world's food supply to a greater extent than all the nations of OPEC combined dominate the world's oil. Such a vast productive capacity set against the rest of the world's desperate need places the United States in a position of awesome power to determine whether its neighbors eat adequately or go hungry.

In recent years, the United States has freely wielded its "food weapon" to further both its own security and economic interests and the broader goals of world prosperity and peace. Presidents from Eisenhower through Carter and Reagan have used American food aid and sales to achieve their own foreign policy objectives, whether rewarding anti-Communist regimes for capitalist solidarity or punishing repressive regimes for human rights violations. Food exports have been manipulated to stifle criticism of the American military intervention in Vietnam, to chasten the Soviet Union for its military intervention in Afghanistan, and to forge peace accords for the embattled Mideast. The frankly political use of food aid is sanctioned by American law: Title I of Public Law 480 authorizes the use of food aid to develop foreign markets for American agricultural commodities and to complement U.S. foreign policy objectives; Title III links food aid to development programs (in contrast to Title II, which grants aid almost exclusively on humanitarian grounds). And Section 116 of the Foreign Assistance Act provides for cessation of aid to nations whose

"Plowshares into Swords: The Political Uses of Food," published in *QQ: Report from the Center for Philosophy and Public Policy*, vol. 2, no. 4, Fall 1982. Reprinted by permission.

governments engage in gross violations of human rights. Thus the use of food as a policy instrument has received legislative legitimation.

Some observers urge that food exports should become still more politicized, recommending that the United States join with other food producing and exporting nations to form a "FOPEC" (Food Producing and Exporting Countries) cartel on the analogy of OPEC. The lead article in the May 1982 *Readers' Digest* hails the use of food as "America's secret weapon," quoting Secretary of Agriculture John R. Block's assessment that "Over the next twenty years, food can be the greatest weapon we have." But others recoil from using food as a weapon, insisting that the starvation of millions of innocent persons—half of them children—must not be ignored or exploited to achieve political or economic ends.

Is the political use of food a legitimate means to promote our military security and increase the export profits of our producers? Is it an acceptable tool for pursuing social, economic, and political justice and a stable world peace? Or is it wrong to use as a weapon or bargaining chip something which is the object of so central and universal a human need?

Food as National Property

The most extreme advocates of the politicization of food exports take the view that food is fully the property of the nation whose soil it is grown upon, just as oil is fully the property of the nation whose territory it lies beneath. America's abundant harvests were grown on American soil; therefore they are ours, to distribute as we choose. On this view, it is both our right and our obligation to use the power that food represents; to reject or ignore the possibilities of using food to enhance our own position in the world and to increase the world's peace and justice is to squander a valuable opportunity bequeathed to us. Just as individuals are given talents and abilities which they are expected to use wisely and well both for self-improvement and for bettering the world around them, so are nations given natural resources which they are to exploit both in their own national interest and in the interest of the global community. Thus, Lowell Ponte, defending the political uses of food in the *Readers' Digest*, writes, "Should we consider food as a weapon? It is a power that destiny has put in our hands. Rather than reject it, we must consider the best and wisest ways to use this power to prompt development in other nations, to encourage cooperation, to discourage aggression."

Against this view it can be argued, however, that the fertile soil and long growing season that make possible America's agricultural bounty are not gifts of "destiny," but benefits arbitrarily parceled out by nature, to which their beneficiaries have no special moral entitlement. That oil lies beneath the sand of Saudi Arabia and wheat grows well in the soil of Kansas are arbitrary facts of nature, to which no moral significance should be imputed. As political philosopher Charles R. Beitz argues in *Political Theory and International Relations*, "The fact that someone happens to be located advantageously with respect to natural resources does not provide a reason why he or she should be entitled to exclude others from the benefits that might be derived from them." The accidents of nature do not provide a secure foundation for morally decisive ownership claims.

"The fertile soil and long growing season that make possible America's agricultural bounty are not gifts of 'destiny.'"

Of course, a great deal of our agricultural productivity can be attributed to American technology, to our free enterprise system, and to the hard work of American farmers. These considerations do establish a special American claim to the fruits of our own labor. But this claim must always be set in the context of the original natural endowments which allowed technology, free enterprise, and hard work to be as spectacularly successful as they have been.

Food as Human Right

Furthermore, food is not just one commodity among others, some random stuff that the United States has a lot of. Food is an essential requirement of every human being on earth. As such, it is the object of a basic and widely recognized human right. Even were America's claim to the surplus produce of its farms more secure, it would still have to be weighed against the urgency of this universal human right,

which is at present so tragically unfulfilled.

The view that food is national property to be disposed of as we please, then, is unsatisfactory. At the very least this means that America is not free to use food as a weapon for promoting just any of our own national interests, at the expense of the more pressing needs of others. Nor are we free to use food to multiply the profits of American producers and distributors, at least not while millions suffer from chronic malnutrition.

It may be difficult to separate out cases in which food aid or sales are used merely to promote our own national interest from cases in which a broader set of goals is furthered: even highly politicized Title I food aid is directed only to countries with an evident use for imported food. Daniel E. Shaughnessy, former Deputy Coordinator of the A.I.D. Office of Food for Peace, points out, "Even the most humanitarian program has a political element to it, and conversely even the most political program has its humanitarian aspects."

But we are nonetheless able to identify certain political or economic uses of food that are ruled out once we reject the view that American-grown food is simply *ours*. Clearly, food aid that harms its recipients while benefitting American agricultural concerns is illegitimate. It would be impermissible to encourage a taste for American wheat in foreign rice eaters, with the goal of creating a dependency on American exports. Such an economic program has no redeeming humanitarian benefits. Nor would it be permissible to cut off badly needed food exports simply to curb expressions of anti-American sentiment in receiving countries. These are kinds of political and economic uses of food that must be rejected as unacceptable.

Politics-Blind Food Aid

These considerations may suggest that *all* political uses of food are illegitimate, that food *aid*, at least, should be awarded strictly on nonpolitical grounds, directed soley to those most in need. Food should be allocated to the hungry, period, not to hungry anti-Communists, or hungry consumers of American exports, or even to hungry human rights activists. Philosopher Thomas Nagel writes that truly humanitarian aid "should be directed at the impoverished purely in virtue of their humanity....Aid which simply lifts people off the absolute bottom and helps them to a minimally adequate diet addresses a need so general and basic that it is an inappropriate vehicle for the expression of political preference....A humanitarian food aid policy would therefore base allocation solely on nutritional needs."

In at least two ways, however, all food aid is and must be inherently political. In the first place, it is individual persons who suffer from hunger, while food aid is often awarded on a national level.

Problems thus arise in making sure that the neediest individuals in any country are indeed those who benefit from food aid granted to their government. Political and economic considerations are relevant here in ensuring that food aid accomplishes what it sets out to do—that it relieves the hunger of the hungriest. Second, all major food sales and grants have political, economic, and social consequences that go beyond the immediate relief of hunger. "No aid," Nagel recognizes, "can be entirely nonpolitical in its *effects*," and no responsible food export policy can refuse to take these into account.

Food Improperly Channeled

Food policies that are directed toward national governments must pay attention not only to a recipient nation's aggregate wealth or food supply, but to how wealth and food are internally distributed. In countries where wealth is greatly concentrated, as it is in much of the Third World, food and development aid may do little or nothing to relieve the misery of the poorest people, and may even aggravate distributional inequities by channeling additional income and influence to the already better off. Likewise, food aid directed impartially toward the hungry of all countries, regardless of their political systems or the human rights records of their governments, may serve only to prop up tyrannical regimes or stave off revolutionary reforms. Thus, politics-blind food aid can work against the welfare of those it is designed to help most.

Among the most important ancillary consequences of food aid are its impact on Third World development and population growth. Food aid may work either to encourage or discourage development, and development may be either beneficial or harmful to the worst-off in an underdeveloped country. Food aid may perpetuate dependency, stalling programs to boost domestic production and to achieve self-sufficiency; food aid directed at stimulating development may disrupt local patterns of subsistence and undermine traditional cultures. Anthropologist Norge Jerome calls attention to the "tragic and costly effects of public and private economic development programs on millions of individuals throughout the world. The demands of economic development programs have often triggered rapid changes in the traditional system of food production, processing, distribution, and consumption, and a decline in...nutritional status." There is currently a great deal of debate among economists and anthropologists over what sorts of development our food aid should be targeted to stimulate or avoid. Food aid cannot be given without some sensitivity to these debated consequences.

Pitting Poor Against Poor

Food aid also has complicated and disputed implications for a nation's population growth.

Opponents of food aid often claim that it pits the present poor against the future poor, by allowing the current generation of parents to continue to produce too many future children. On their scenarios, food aid averts a smaller famine today only at the price of creating a larger famine tomorrow. These critics recommend that food aid be channeled only to those countries which are making a good faith effort to control their rate of population growth, by linking food aid to contraceptive practice.

"Food is....the object of a basic and widely recognized human right."

But such linkage might well be counterproductive. In the developed industrialized countries population curves have fallen off only *after* a certain level of prosperity was achieved. Population control seems to be itself dependent on the availability of adequate supplies of food. One leading explanation of this phenomenon is that parents limit family size once child mortality rates have lowered sufficiently to assure them that what children they do have are likely to survive. As explained by Michael F. Brewer, former president of the Population Reference Bureau, this "child survival hypothesis...suggests significant changes in the content and staging of U.S. aid programs," with family-planning efforts carefully coordinated to follow programs of food aid and development. If aid levels are too low, or family planning programs ineffective, food aid may exacerbate the very problems it aims to alleviate. Once again, food aid cannot be parceled out with an oblivious eye to its other implications.

Food for Peace and Prosperity

The use of food aid to control population growth raises the question of the moral legitimacy of using the promise of food or the threat of its withdrawal to manipulate the behavior of individuals and nations. To make population control a condition of receiving food may seem a coercive interference in the internal affairs of sovereign nations, as well as in the very private and personal decisions individuals make about the size of their families. Shaughnessy dismisses efforts to link food aid with population control by asking, "Would the United States accept any foreign proposal that carried with it the caveat that we would have to meet birth control criteria?"

In the case of population control, food is used as an incentive to behavior that will end up reducing future hunger. Food is used, at least indirectly, to ensure the adequacy of future supplies of food. The same might be said of food programs designed to encourage or discourage various development patterns: the end goal of the manipulative pressures is to establish a solid agricultural base to feed future generations.

In other cases, however, food has been used manipulatively to achieve ends much less clearly related to the reduction of world hunger. President Carter, for example, cut off PL 480 food aid to Pinochet's Chile and Somoza's Nicaragua as part of his campaign against human rights violations. Both Kissinger and Carter used promises of increased food aid to bring about an Egyptian/Israeli peace settlement, dramatically increasing food aid to Egypt after Sadat's signing of both the Sinai peace agreement and the later Camp David accord. Recently Lester R. Brown of the Worldwatch Institute has suggested that U.S. grain sales to the Soviet Union might operate as a possible deterrent to any future nuclear exchange.

Diplomatic Tool

Is food an appropriate diplomatic tool for protesting human rights violations and giving peace its best chance? Despite the worthiness of the goals in these instances, it may still seem that food is a singularly inappropriate instrument of behavior modification— that, although the consequences of food aid and sales must be carefully weighed and assessed, it is wrong to use food to apply deliberate manipulative pressure on the governments of hungry people. The offer of food or the threat of its withdrawal can have an irresistible coercive force. It may seem unfair to use food as a diplomatic lever, however high the stakes.

"Food should be allocated to the hungry, period."

It seems overly fastidious, however, to refuse to make any distinctions among the ends for which food aid or sales may or may not be manipulated. To use food exports as a tool for ultimately improving world nutrition levels, or to dampen the nuclear arms race, is very different from using them to punish developing countries for trade with Cuba or the Soviet Union. That food is a central human need and the object of a basic human right does not make food exports sacredly immune from diplomacy and negotiations that may even work to ensure greater satisfaction of that need and protection of that right. Nor is the right to food the only right we care about protecting. Rights not to be tortured and rights not to be killed are very weighty as well, and manipulation of food to secure these rights may be fully justified.

How, then, do we sort out acceptable from unacceptable table uses of food? One first try at a principle is this: food exports may be used politically with the objective of reducing world hunger or preventing conditions that are equally grave and distressing, such as imminent war and widespread

and egregious violations of human rights. It is not wrong to withdraw food aid or sales from repressive regimes to punish their systematic violation of international human rights; it is not wrong to promise food aid or sales to belligerent regimes on the condition that they abstain from the horrors of war.

Withholding Food

Two caveats are in order, however. The first is that the political use of food carries with it the ever-present danger of self-deception and outright dishonesty. It is all to easy to convince ourselves that U.S. economic and security interests just happen to coincide with the needs of the hungry. Those who believe, or pretend to believe, that the menace of spreading Communism is an evil on a par with mass starvation will feel justified in diverting food from those who may need it most. Thus shipments of food to famine-stricken Bangladesh were delayed in 1974 when the United States discovered that that nation had sold jute to Cuba. There may well be good practical reasons for a near-universal ban on such overtly political manipulations of food. Otherwise we may find ourselves covertly filtering food aid and sales through the blinders of our own self-interest.

Second, even the most sincere efforts at making the world better may tragically misfire. Thus Jerome points to the dangers of well-intentioned development programs that work only to increase the poor's poverty and powerlessness; Brewer warns that the child-survival hypothesis is only weakly supported by available evidence, so that inadequate food aid programs may contribute to inadvertent population crises. Perhaps in the face of such widespread uncertainty we should harbor no grand schemes for using food to bring about any major international improvements. Our only sure truth seems to be that a quarter of the world's people are severely malnourished, and half of these are young children, innocent if anyone in this world ever is. Thus all we can do is to act, as sensitively and sanely as possible, minimizing whatever inevitable damage we unwittingly cause, remembering that in the final analysis, food is for eating and not for waging even the noblest political and ideological crusades.

The Center for Philosophy and Public Policy is an educational and research center engaged in the investigation of ethics in public policy formulation and debate.

"If we are not willing to utilize timely and effective economic measures to punish aggression...the ultimate cost in defense spending may be infinitely larger."

Soviet Trade Sanctions Are Effective

James L. Buckley

Thank you for the opportunity to discuss the President's decision of June 18 to expand sanctions to prevent the export of oil and gas equipment and technology to the Soviet Union. I intend to address the basis of the President's decision, the effect of the decision, and the reaction of our Western European allies.

The President's Decision

On December 29, 1981, the President imposed selected economic sanctions against the Soviet Union because of its role in the imposition of martial law and suppression of human rights in Poland. Those sanctions included the expansion of export controls on the sale of U.S. origin oil and gas equipment and technology and the suspension of all licensing of controlled exports to the Soviet Union. At that time, the President made it clear that if the repression in Poland continued, the United States would take further concrete economic and political actions affecting our relationship. Now, some 7 months later, martial law remains in effect, political detainees continue to be held, and the free trade union movement is still suppressed.

As a consequence, the President decided on June 18 to take the further concrete steps he had warned the Soviets about last December. Therefore, he expanded the December sanctions covering oil and gas equipment and technology to foreign subsidiaries and licensees of American firms. This is an area of crucial importance to the economy of the Soviet Union because of its dependence on exports of petroleum and natural gas for hard currency earnings, as well as the significance it places on development of a vastly expanded internal gas delivery system.

The June 18 decision to expand controls to U.S.

James L. Buckley, statement before the Subcommittee on International Economic Policy, the Senate Foreign Relations Committee, July 30, 1982.

foreign subsidiaries and licensees was based on the authority granted the President, under the Export Administration Act of 1979, to prohibit exports where necessary to further, significantly, U.S. foreign policy. The act gives the President the power to prohibit exports of goods or technology that are subject to U.S. jurisdiction or exported by any person subject to the jurisdiction of the United States.

We have taken note of the subsequent announcement of a slight relaxation of repression in Poland, as announced last week by the Polish regime. This does not meet our minimun requirements. We are, however, consulting with our allies on the implications of the Polish announcement.

Effect of the Decision

The actions taken last December had immediate effect on manufacturers and workers in the United States. U.S. firms have lost at least $800 million worth of potential business with the Soviet Union— the impact being spread across a variety of industries supplying parts for the Yamal pipeline, as well as heavy machinery and technology for other construction projects.

However, by only reaching U.S.-manufactured equipment, the December controls left open an important loophole which allowed the Soviet Union to obtain U.S.-designed equipment from foreign subsidiaries and licensees of American companies which were subject to the December sanctions. Thus, the recent expansion of those sanctions not only makes them more effective but equitable as well.

The obvious focus of the expanded sanctions has been on exports destined for the pipeline project. Clearly, the U.S. export control actions of December 29 and June 18 have had a major impact on equipment and the construction timetable for the Siberian gas pipeline to Europe. The U.S. position on the project is well known: We believe European participation in this project is ill-advised and potentially harmful to our joint security interests.

Soviet Pipeline

Upon completion, the pipeline will allow the Soviets to earn, through gas sales, some $8-$10 billion a year in hard currency. Such earnings will allow the Soviets to continue purchasing large amounts of critical Western technology for the modernization of the industrial base on which its military power depends, as well as continue to engage in foreign adventurism. It will roughly double European gas dependence on the Soviet Union, and gas is a particularly difficult fuel to replace on short notice.

As you know, the Administration, over the last year, has encouraged the allies to develop alternatives to Soviet gas to avoid any undue dependence which could make them vulnerable to Soviet pressures. The President's decision will clearly impede the construction of the pipeline, which is already behind schedule, and it will increase its cost, as well as delay the Soviet Union's plans for a dramatic expansion of its internal gas distribution system.

But let me emphasize that this impact on the Soviet economy was not, in and of itself, our primary goal. We are not engaged in economic warfare with the Soviet Union.

Above all, we seek an end to the repression of the Polish people. The sanctions imposed against the sale of oil and gas equipment increase the internal costs to the Soviet Union of the project and cause an additional strain on already thinly stretched Soviet resources. The President wants to make clear that the Soviets will bear those costs until there is real progress toward restoration of basic human rights in Poland.

Reaction of Our Western Allies

The extension of the sanctions obviously concerns our allies and affects our relationships with them. When the President made his decision to expand the controls, it was clear that it would not be welcomed by key allied governments. Since their expansion, our European allies have voiced their concerns individually and through the commission of the European Community. The gist of their complaints has centered around their contention that our sanctions will not produce the desired changes in Poland, that our actions exceed our legal jurisdiction, and that we have failed to consult with them on the sanctions.

Our allies, of course, attach greater significance to trade with the Soviet Union than we do. In addition, all of Europe has felt the pinch of the current recession. Jobs and investment related to the pipeline project were expected to provide a significant boost for hard-hit, heavy industry firms.

The President took those considerations into account in coming to his decision. He clearly

recognized the effect of the economic sanctions both in Europe and in the United States. Nevertheless, the President decided that, in the face of the continuing Soviet support of the repression of the Polish people, the costs of U.S. inaction simply outweighed the sacrifices that we would have to make to bring home to the Soviets our seriousness of purpose. The President had clearly stated that he would be forced to take additional measures if the situation in Poland did not improve. It did not, and he kept his word.

Sanctions Are Legal

Our allies have questioned the legal basis of our actions. We believe, however, that our sanctions are proper under international law. We believe that the United States can properly prescribe and enforce controls over exports and re-exports of U.S. goods and technology and over the actions of foreign subsidiaries of U.S. firms. The provisions in private licensing contracts regarding compliance with U.S. controls demonstrate that these controls are a familiar and accepted part of international commerce.

"Above all, we seek an end to the repression of the Polish people."

With respect to our relations with our allies, many have cited the pipeline decision as the proverbial straw that will break the camel's back and lead to a damaging policy of retaliation through higher tariffs or other measures. We disagree and believe that our difference with our allies can be resolved through continued constructive consultations. We intend to work hard toward that end. I would also stress that, despite our much publicized differences, we still share a community of interests much more substantial than the issues which are in dispute at the moment. We certainly share the common goals of helping Poland achieve an end to martial law, the release of all detainees, and a re-establishment of the dialogue among the government, Solidarity, and the church.

Deliberate Response

I hope this overview has provided some useful background regarding the context and effect of the President's decision to expand the sanctions against the Soviet Union for their role in the repression of the Polish people. I would also like to make a few observations. There was nothing capricious about the imposition of sanctions against the Soviet Union. They were a deliberate and measured response to Soviet actions that violate the most basic norms of international behavior. Therefore, any totaling up of economic gains and losses misses a major point, and that is the political importance of dramatizing, in a tangible way, the depth of Western disapproval and condemnation of Soviet behavior in invading, tyrannizing, and subverting other societies. In my own view, this factor alone would justify sanctions even if, in pure economic terms, the dollar costs to the West outweighed those to the Soviets.

"Our sanctions are proper under international law."

Nor should we be suprised that our European allies have a different perspective on the utility of the sanctions we have announced. Their security concerns center on Europe and have a narrower focus than ours. We hope that the costs imposed on the Soviet Union will influence that country's attitude toward Poland; but whether they do or not, they represent a severity of response that can help discourage Soviet adventurism elsewhere in the world, a point of great interest to the United States in view of our broader responsibilities for Western security interests.

Finally, if we are not willing to utilize timely and effective economic measures to punish aggression and thereby deter future adventurism, the ultimate cost in defense spending may be infinitely larger than the losses we are discussing today.

James L. Buckley is the undersecretary for security assistance, science and technology.

"Sanctions not only fail to keep the specified products from the targeted government, they are likely to harden its attitudes."

viewpoint 16

Soviet Trade Sanctions Are Not Effective

Sheldon Richman

Have you heard the story about the Soviet pipeline that an American president tried to scuttle with economic sanctions? No, not President Reagan's failed attempt last year to stop the Yamal natural-gas pipeline from Siberia to Western Europe. This other episode took place twenty years earlier. The Soviets had contracted with West German steel mills for the sale of wide-diameter pipe, and the Kennedy administration, succeeding where Reagan failed, pressured the German government into canceling the contracts.

But the Soviet project went ahead anyway, despite President Kennedy's policy. How? The answer was given to George Ball, an undersecretary of state at the time, when he later met Anatoly Dobrynin, Soviet ambassador to Washington. According to Ball, Dobrynin "told me with a sardonic grin, 'I wish to thank you on behalf of my government. When you got the Germans to renege on their contracts, you forced my country to do what we should have done long before—build facilities to make wide-diameter pipe. So we're grateful to you.'"

This was not the only time that U.S. trade sanctions had unintendend consequences. Reagan's failure to thwart a Soviet enterprise was merely the latest demonstration that trade sanctions (1) fail to achieve their stated objectives, and (2) often bring results that are undesirable in the view of the policy makers. It should be expected that when trade, the tool of peaceful cooperation, is twisted into a *weapon*, the consequences will be perverse.

The subject of economic sanctions has been much on the minds of the political, industrial, agricultural, and scientific communities in recent years. With memories of the Carter-imposed Soviet grain embargo and Reagan's attempt to stop the Soviet pipeline still

fresh, presidential power over exports is much discussed because of the expiration (September 30) of the Export Administration Act, the chief source of authority for licensing and restricting export activity. This act allows the president to ban certain products from export for reasons of national security (military equipment, for example), foreign policy (punishment, say, for human-rights violations), and short domestic supplies.

Each time the act has come up for reauthorization, Congress has become a battleground for the advocates and opponents of East-West trade. The battle is mirrored within the administration in the turf struggle between Commerce and Defense Departments. Anti-Soviet hard-liners favor more discretion for the president, while the pro-trade side, pointing to lost business, asks that his power be more limited.

Other considerations in the current fight over export controls include the concerns of the scientific community that the "anti-red-trade" movement under Reagan will extend to research and international contact among scientists. And there is a group of strategists who believe that unilateral trade restrictions hurt America's present system of alliances. They point to the friction generated by Reagan's attempted pipeline sanctions, especially the prohibition on exports by foreign firms using American technology under contract.

The fact is that Western Europe and Japan have long been more comfortable with Soviet-bloc trade than the United States. In 1979 U.S. high-technology exports to the Soviet Union totaled $183 million, only one-tenth the level of similar exports from West Germany, France, and Japan combined. The U.S. Commerce and Defense Departments' lists of restricted products and technologies are much longer than the list kept by the Coordinating Committee for Multilateral Export (COCOM), the informal organization comprising the United States, the NATO

Sheldon Richman, "What's Wrong with Red Trade?" *Inquiry*, October 1983. Reprinted by permission of the author.

countries (minus Iceland), and Japan. While America's colleagues on COCOM are willing to expand the list on the high-technology end in deference to the United States, they want lower-level technology and energy-related items removed.

The U.S. government has always claimed the authority to regulate exports for national-security reasons, but had rarely used it in peacetime until the onset of the Cold War. The Export Control Act of 1949 banned the sale of commodities that would "significantly contribute to the economic potential" of nations in a way that would prove "detrimental" to the United States.

This policy took an important turn in the era of detente. The Export Administration Act of 1969 sought to restrict only those things that "would make a significant contribution to the *military* potential" of such nations. (Emphasis added.) Though this wording has been carried over to later versions of the act, the Reagan administration appears to think in 1949 terms.

"When trade, the tool of peaceful cooperation, is twisted into a weapon, the consequences will be perverse."

Most of the current anti-trade sentiment comes directly from the belief that the East-West exchanges of the detente period were harmful, because they benefited the Soviets at America's expense, and second, because Soviet behavior was not moderated. The first belief is patently untrue. Though government subsidies of East-West exchange are objectionable, the Soviets have technologies and information worth obtaining. In a report to Congress last June *(Scientific Exchange Activities with the Soviet Union)*, the State Department outlined recent benefits from a variety of scientific and technical exchange programs established during detente. Valuable data was obtained in such fields as medicine, electrometalurgy, physics, microbiology, atomic energy, space research, air traffic control, and agriculture. For example, the report states, "U.S.-Soviet cooperation in physics...was undoubtedly among the best examples of the benefits of well-matched and carefully designed international scientific cooperation....In every project area, activities under the cooperative program have resulted in significant achievements, advancing U.S. scientific understanding of the field and providing valuable insight, which would otherwise not have been possible, into Soviet activities, approaches, and accomplishments in this area."

As for the second complaint, that the Soviets did not abandon their geopolitical objectives under

detente, the United States' continued intervention in Southeast Asia, Latin America (especially Chile), Africa, and the Middle East (especially Iran) hardly set a good example.

No one should have expected the Soviets to fundamentally change their system or world view just because trade expanded. Trade is a necessary, but not a sufficient, condition for civil relations.

This anti-detente lobby's alternative to East-West cooperation, boldly put, is economic warfare. Justifications for this policy are usually divided between foreign-policy and national-security considerations, and that division will be maintained here for purposes of analysis. But it should be recognized that there is no sharp divide between the categories. Buying nonmilitary products can release resources for the production of military equipment. Wheat, which Reagan is perfectly willing to sell the Russians, can feed troops. Nikita Khrushchev once quipped that buttons are the most strategic of products because they keep soldiers from having to hold up their trousers and fight with one hand.

In general, foreign-policy sanctions aim to punish a foreign government for conduct deemed undesirable. Nicaragua, for example, is banned from selling sugar here because President Reagan disapproves of the Sandinistas' treatment of their people and neighbors. But sanctions hold the seeds of their own failure. Governments, being jealous territorial monopolies, don't take humiliation well. So they find ways around the sanctions by locating other trading partners, setting up dummy corporations in third countries, or becoming more self-sufficient. And sometimes they retaliate.

There is a hard lesson in this for the United States. As economic potency becomes more decentralized, the United States will dominate fewer industrialized fields (if it dominates any today). Thus, eluding American sanctions will become progressively easier. Effective sanctions will depend on the U.S. government's ability to marshal loyalty from allies and neutrals. But this in itself will become more difficult as other governments and private groups develop interests and objectives independent of those of the United States. The prospects are not attractive: For the United States to persist in its penchant for international economic regulation, it will have to take actions that will further cultivate the image of a demanding, meddling, suspicious, and presumptuous power—only to find that these traits drive friends further away.

Despite some recent concessions, Reagan has done his part to cultivate this image and to open himself to charges of hypocrisy. The Europeans were disturbed by his banning their pipeline exports, while ending the grain embargo. Reagan's explanation, which should have embarrassed any self-styled free-trader, was that grain imports cost the Soviets hard currency, but energy exports procure them hard currency. How ironic that the Russian central planners grasped trade theory better than an American president. The Soviets buy grain from abroad only because it is cheaper than producing it themselves; moreover, how can the Soviets be expected to continue buying American wheat, if they can't get hard currency from energy sales?

There is further hypocrisy in Reagan's claim that it is foolish for Western Europe to buy natural gas from the Soviet Union. For years, the United States has imported from the Soviets such critical materials as gold, chromium, platinum-group metals, and titanium, as well as militarily useful technology. The Soviets have never interrupted this trade, not even during the Vietnam War or while U.S. sanctions were in effect.

Sanctions not only fail to keep the specified products from the targeted governments, they are likely to harden its attitudes. In 1974 Congress passed the Jackson-Vanik Amendment, which linked Soviet-American trade to the liberalization of Jewish emigration. It didn't prevent Jewish emigration from dropping by more than a third.

Retaliation against sanctions can take not only an economic form, but also a military form. The most dramatic example is the Japanese attack on Pearl Harbor, which followed the imposition of U.S. economic sanctions. While those sanctions were promoted as a nonmilitary method of thwarting Japan, the American leaders, realizing how provocative they were, in fact saw them as a "backdoor to war."

American experience with sanctions did not improve later. When communist revolutions succeeded in China (1949) and Cuba (1959), the United States denied diplomatic recognition and imposed trade embargoes. Neither regime was undermined. As Robert Wesson of the Hoover Institution writes, "Economic isolation of a communist regime hardens and intensifies it, giving it an excuse for failures and a reason to demand sacrifices and override rights. Boycott of Cuba has, of course, hurt the Cubans, but its most obvious effect has been to make the Cuban government dependent on the Soviet Union."

"Embargoes won't free captive people."

The ultimate justification for foreign-policy-related sanctions is a moral consideration, namely, that it is wrong for an American to do business with a government that mistreats its people. Well, what government doesn't, to some extent? When is a government too evil to trade with, and what government's hands are clean enough to enforce the sanctions?

It might be said that trading with the Russians is trading in the product of slave labor. Though undoubtedly true in many cases, embargoes won't free captive people, who might well end up worse off. And it will not do to argue that the deprivation of an embargo is likely to spark a revolution. As the late economist G. Warren Nutter pointed out, revolutions occur "in rapidly growing economies just emerging from poverty, not in poor stagnant economies." If Nutter is right, those wishing for revolutions behind the Iron Curtain should support open exchange of all kinds.

Sheldon Richman is associate editor of Inquiry, *a monthly publication of the Liberation Review Foundation in Washington, D.C.*

"Our nation is currently being targeted by Soviet weapons at least partially developed by Americans."

US Must Restrict High-Technology Exports

James D. Watkins

I had the pleasure of being one of ten thousand plus witnesses for a great Navy event last week, recommissioning for the fourth time of the modernized battleship New Jersey. During President Reagan's remarks, he told an assembled multitude that the New Jersey is a shining example of a navy which has capitalized on "cost effective application of high technology to existing assets" in order to help fill the defense void left in the wake of the tragically confused 70's. Nine 16-inch guns, twelve 5-inch guns, 32 of the newest long-range Tomahawk cruise missiles, 16 of the newest medium range cruise missiles, and an invulnerability to any conventional missile in the world. . . .Not a bad deal at the price of our cheapest low-mix frigate today.

But, the U.S. Navy has consistently been a leader in applying the best of America's modern technology.

Since the Civil War where armored warships—equipped with heavy cannon and propelled by steam—were first combat tested, the Navy has always integrated modern technology into our national force structure. For example, in 1955, with the words "Underway on nuclear power," USS Nautilus proved to a watchful world that we were a leader in nuclear propulsion and could effectively use technology in our modern submarine force, constantly applying new concepts so as to stay qualitatively well ahead of Soviet counterparts.

This recurrent theme continues—Today's Navy is heavily involved in using the latest American technology across the naval warfighting spectrum.

No sea is a safe harbor or protected lake. A survivable navy in the modern world must possess the latest surveillance techniques, information processing capabilities and platforms that can effectively deliver weapons in the incredible environments realistically projected in this decade.

James D. Watkins, speech before the Navy League, Pasadena, CA, January 3, 1983.

We are into modern technology in its most practical forms. From micro-miniature electronic components to the awesome 90,000 ton nuclear powered Nimitz class carriers and their sophisticated air wings. Tomorrow's navy will continue to strive to be the best possible expression of American technology and its practical utilization. Selected, critical technology is among our few remaining superiors in the existing, fragile military balance. This narrow edge makes up the extremely important difference which separates us from the Soviets. . .a difference we rely upon to attempt to hold a margin of American fighting superiority. . .a difference unfortunately evaporating even while I speak.

Practical Technology

Would any sensible nation accede to a policy which would allow the clear technological lead of its military to erode intentionally? Of course not! But unwittingly, accidentally? Possibly. For monetary gain? Unfortunately, yes. . . .

America has always prided itself in its ability to research, develop and effectively employ new concepts, being in the forefront of applied scientific advancement. This has been a national strength and has helped maintain us as leader of the western world and defender of freedom. The Soviets are not blind to this. They have seen that much of our strength, militarily and as a nation, lies in our steady flow of technological developments, a stream they have tapped in the past with alarming success.

Transfer of Concepts

We are certainly not endangered by the transfer of technological *concepts*. In fact, free exchange of scientific ideas is also one of our hallmarks of world leadership. Technological concepts can be transferred in the nations best interests, forging new diplomatic ties, helping needy nations and peoples. We would not wish to impede or prohibit the ebb and flow of knowledge. On the other hand, our goal should be to protect those few selected blue chips of U.S. military superiority which remain, what I like to call applied militarily-critical technology. Our concern is that no sooner do we develop, test and field new high technology systems aboard our ships and aircraft, than the Soviets easily and cheaply acquire this applied technology for their own use. In fact, it appears on the scene shortly after initial employment in our fleet. . .demanding we develop, test and field a technological leap-frog once again.

The Soviet Union and its surrogates are embarked upon the most impressive, systematic, calculated effort the world has ever known—using both legal and illegal means—to raid the free world's technological base. This effort has provided them with big dividends, in some critical instances shrinking our once eight-to-ten-year technology lead to a mere two to three years. As a result, I'm talking about the virtual elimination of the "comfort zone" once enjoyed between the time *we* develop it and *they* start to use it.

A Clandestine Sale

Technology transfer is too often thought of in terms of clandestine sale or transfer of specific goods or equipments, like a computer or a new missile system; or again in terms of stolen secret defense documents like the famous U.S. photo-satellite handbook sold by an American traitor only a few years ago. But no; the large body of transfer is subtle, harder to detect and deter. In fact, technology transfer largely occurs in our open marketing literature pushed by well-meaning breast-beaters of competitive industries who are too quick to publicize their highest technology achievements often derived from nuggets of military critical technology. An unrelenting, well-orchestrated and financed Soviet process is quick to collect scraps of information from these unwitting salesmen until all essential elements of the latest U.S. military capability are in Soviet hands.

"No sooner do we develop, test and field new high technology systems. . . .than the Soviets easily and cheaply acquire this applied technology."

How do the Soviets get away with this? Most of their efforts take place right before our very eyes; only a small effort continues to employ more traditional "hand-in-the-safe" techniques. Let us look at a few examples:

Published material. It is amazing what is openly published in magazines, journals and reports in this country. The Soviets are the world's largest producer of scientific and technical abstracts, employing over 100,000 full-time people to translate, review and catalogue information generated from "free societies."

In this country you can easily find full-color photographs with detailed layouts of our weapons, display consoles and interiors of aircraft and ships published in various defense, scientific and company journals. Conversely, you would have to be James Bond to see the inside of an equivalent military system in the Soviet Union.

Student exchanges is another seemingly innocent method of technology transfer.

Unfortunately, this exchange is hardly reciprocal. Where Americans in the Soviet Union typically study subjects such as history of czarist Russia and sociology, Soviets and Eastern bloc scholars in this country usually conduct research in scientific and engineering areas where their nations have critical technology shortfalls.

Scientific exchanges are another area of technology transfer abused by the Soviets. Since 1972 this nation has signed 10 bilateral agreements with the Soviet Union on scientific and technical subjects. At one time there were as many as 250 different ongoing projects in these 10 areas of agreement with over eleven hundred people engaged in this exchange.

Unwanted Transfer

One example of unwanted technology transfer is the case of a Hungarian who attended scientific conferences and studied magnetic bubble memory technology in the U.S., which incidentally represents a major leap forward in computer development. Later, in a Hungarian publication, some of his study's military and commercial implications became apparent when the Hungarians proudly claimed that they had provided the Soviets with new magnetic bubble memory capabilities. Fortunately almost all of these bilateral agreements have been terminated by the present administration.

But the most important and self-defeating of all areas of technology transfer is Soviet *importation of sophisticated manufacturing technology*, unwittingly delivered to them by our nation's finest manufacturers within the military-industrial complex. Must of this has, in the past, been carried out openly and legally in trade agreements between this country, other west nations, and the USSR.

Even in peaceful ventures the Soviets have proved themselves to be untrustworthy trading partners, taking the most innocent technological exchange and turning it into a military advantage. In a country where a toaster is a luxury item because not enough of them are manufactured it should be no surprise that our best technology, when transferred to the Soviets, goes not for improving the lot of the average Muscovite, but directly into a military apparatus which continues to grow at unprecedented rates.

A significant example is the Kama River Truck Factory in the Soviet Union, largest single truck factory in the world, and built exclusively with western technology.

The "Truck" Factory

Over 50 U.S. contractors and subcontractors were involved, providing automated foundry equipment, production lines and a computer system to run the entire plant...techniques in applied technology quite natural to us, but revolutionary to the Russian process. Now, while these trucks can be found on the streets of Moscow, they are predominantly in military colors in Afghanistan, and, the day before the 1981 communist party congress met in Moscow, the first fully militarized, all-wheel-drive and all-terrain Kama truck rolled off the American-built assembly line. Unfortunately, potential release of classified defense information precludes my exposure here today of facts related to the similar transfer of sophisticated technology far more significant to our nation's defense than trucks. Appropriate administration offices and congressional committees have been made aware of the details of this situation and are equally appalled.

And I have not even mentioned any of the illegal means of technology acquisition engaged in by Soviets and Eastern bloc nations.

Bribery, extortion, blackmail, agents who pose as businessmen and diplomats are all weapons in the Soviet clandestine effort to get our technology for themselves.

It is estimated than 5,000 Soviet and Eastern block agents are in this country ferreting out information to feed the sophisticated Soviet data base.

"Purchasing Agents"

Until recently there was a rapid growth in the number of Soviets permanently stationed in this country as "purchasing agents." The FBI estimated that about 40 percent of these people are full-time members of Soviet intelligence communities. They are infiltrating *your* business, *your* company, *your* defense industry.

Melodramatic? Not in the slightest. The problem is serious and is finally starting to get the attention it deserves in the White House, Congress and national agencies.

But this is not just your Government's problem. It's a problem for all who are concerned for the security of this nation. We must learn to discipline ourselves, to hold high technology cards close to our chest, carefully watching those with whom we deal to determine intentions.

Before this initiative to control transfer of critical technology runs its course, it will entail new legislation and policy direction at the national level. But laws and regulations are inadequate in themselves. What is required is a grass-roots effort

with combined support of American industry, academia *and* Government. And while there is no need for national paranoia, a clarion call is urgently needed for our free society to protect what should be, at least for a time, held as *our own*. There must be an educational program within industry itself to understand and accept that a significant problem exists, and then find a solution which is largely theirs to find. Once this is done, then perhaps industry can work successfully with defense and other national agencies toward establishing reasonable and practical guidelines for stemming the flow of selected, militarily-critical technology to the Soviet Union.

Benefits to Soviets

What are the benefits to the Soviet Union of this massive technology theft? Acquisition and application of our technology by the Soviets allows them to remain state-of-the-art without expenditure of massive amounts of time and money for research, development and testing. It means that each of their rubles spent on military hardware goes further and is multiplied by dollars *we* spend on research and development of systems and technologies which they can pick up from us and our allies nearly free of charge. Isn't it ironic that our nation is currently being targeted by Soviet weapons at least partially developed by Americans, partially financed by our tax dollars? We must do whatever is necessary to avoid being drawn into any arms race against ourselves, where we must counter our own advancement because it has been bought, given away or stolen off the shelf, and then integrated into the Soviet military machine.

"The Soviets have proved themselves to be untrustworthy trading partners."

America is a great nation with a great navy. Let no one question that. If we were not the best the Soviets would not try so hard to get what we already have. Our goal of a 600 ship navy before decade's end, build around 15 carrier battle groups, 4 modernized battleship-centered surface action groups, 100 attack nuclear submarines, increased lift for the marines, and the D5 missile abroad Trident submarines is many steps closer to reality with full funding of two nuclear carriers just authorized by Congress and the modernized New Jersey in commission.

But to reach this mark and keep our deterrent of warfighting capability we must ensure our nation's militarily-critical technology remains *our* technology. We cannot allow the Soviets to take *ours* for *theirs* and at such a bargain basement price. Too often in the past we have casually written off these costly losses as the price of a free and open society. I

contend we can have the latter without the burden of
the former if we put our minds to it. And if we can
do so, we would make as important a contribution to
the defense of our country as in effecting any other
of our major defense programs. In fact, if we can get
our national act together on this issue we would not
only enhance our warfighting capabilities vis-a-vis the
Soviet forces by limiting technology loss, but do so at
reduced defense spending levels as well. The time is
right for *all* of us, as American partners, to join hands
in an effort to keep what remains of our sparse
technological leads from slipping further through our
collective fingers. I can assure you of the Navy's
intense dedication to this end. Only by beginning *now*
can we hope to stem this flow by decade's end. So,
let us sound the national call to protect the best of
our arms from those who would use them against us.

*Admiral James D. Watkins is chief of naval operations
for the United States Navy.*

"Losing markets...is more detrimental to American business interests than losing technology is to American security interests."

viewpoint **18**

Technology Restrictions Threaten US Interests

Jon Zonderman

It would seem that America's greatest strength—open flow of information—is also one of its potentially greatest weaknesses, indiscriminately providing allies and adversaries with access to the same information at the same time. How to stop that flow of information, and of the technology that depends on it, is the fundamental question underlying the current legislative stalemate over the Export Administration Act's reauthorization. The hard-liners want to lengthen the list of items that may not be sold to Eastern bloc countries and to step up the effort to halt the unlicensed exporting of all such technologically sophisticated products. The pragmatists argue that a better way to secure American technology is to reduce the number of restricted items to those that are of the utmost military significance, then clamp down tightly on them.

Many business executives believe that even if American companies do not sell to the Eastern bloc, the companies of our allies will. Losing markets, these executives argue, is more detrimental to American business interests than losing technology is to American security interests.

Cooperation among the allies is a slippery facet of a slippery problem. It is also one with a history. As early as 1949 the Western nations had formed the Coordinating Committee for Export Controls (Cocom) to determine what technologies should be kept out of the hands of the Eastern bloc. Today, with the addition of the Federal Republic of Germany and Japan, among others, to Cocom, the committee's restrictions reflect the consensus of Western views on what are—and what are not—sensitive product categories. Unfortunately, Cocom is a voluntary organization, and enforcing its bans is left to the discretion of the member nations.

Jon Zonderman, "Policy High-Tech Exports," *The New York Times Magazine*, November 27, 1983. Copyright © 1983 by The New York Times Company. Reprinted by permission.

The export-control process breeds ironies. Senator Paul E. Tsongas, Democrat of Massachusetts, used to tell the story of how the Ethiopian national airline, seeking to buy the latest model Boeing 767, was thwarted by the United States Government. If Ethiopia were allowed to purchase the plane, with its sophisticated laser gyroscope, the Government's reasoning went, that gyroscope could fall into the hands of the Soviet Union, currently Ethiopia's great friend. So the Ethiopians turned to the French for a new Air-Bus. The punch line: The American company that manufactures the gyroscope had already sold it to France, an ally, for incorporation into the Air-Bus. "We lose the technology, we lose the foreign business and we become known as an unreliable supplier," Senator Tsongas argued. Ultimately, in this instance, such arguments prevailed: The Commerce Department granted Boeing its license in December 1982.

Export Irony

This October, the American Committee on East-West Accord, a privately funded nonpartisan group based in Washington, came to a conclusion similar to Senator Tsonga's. In the foreward to the group's book-length study, Robert D. Schmidt, vice chairman of the Minneapolis-based Control Data Corporation, wrote, "One reality we all should recognize is that there is no advantage in not doing business. Another is that we are not going to insure peace by trade alone....But the strategic relationship is such that we must either live with the Soviets on this planet or die with them. There is no point in aggravating our relations by punitive trade policies which are politically ineffective and economically self-destructive."

Many industry leaders have suggested that the Reagan Administration cease trying to regulate the flow of sophisticated products already on the world market and instead search for ways to control the next generation of technology. Rather than order Customs to stop, say, every meat scale with a microprocessor embedded in it, they argue, the Administration should be keeping a closer eye on companies in the business of developing such items as lasers and semiconductor-manufacturing equipment.

Operation Exodus

Despite such suggestions, the Reagan Administration has given highest priority to Operation Exodus, the Customs Service program of spot-checking advanced-technology exports to make sure they are duly licensed. From its inception in October of 1981, through October of this year, Operation Exodus detained 4,275 foreign-bound shipments, resulting in 2,330 seizures of goods valued at $148.8 million. Those seizures, each followed by an investigation, resulted in turn in 221 indictments. In a sense, however, even that figure is deceptive: Only 28 of the indictments were gained in cases involving so-called "dual-use" items; the rest concerned overseas munitions shipments in violation of the Arms Export Control Act or other Federal statutes—a State Department matter and one long under Customs' surveillance.

"There is no point in aggravating our relations by punitive trade policies which are politically ineffective and economically self-destructive."

At the same time Customs was receiving its mandate to run Operation Exodus, the Commerce Department was beefing up its own enforcement effort. It hired Theodore W. Wu, a former assistant United States attorney who had prosecuted export-control cases in Los Angeles, in the new post of Deputy Assistant Secretary for Export Enforcement. In fiscal 1983, Mr. Wu's Office of Export Enforcement referred 37 dual-use cases to the Justice Department, more than twice the number of referrals Commerce had generated in the preceding three fiscal years. Unfortunately, this has led to a situation that William N. Rudman, Customs' director of strategic investigations, describes as "two scorpions in a bottle, two agencies with precisely the same mission in a very limited area, tripping over each other."

Mr. Rudman says Customs has lately shifted the emphasis of its effort from the inspection of outgoing cargo, its traditional beat, to the investigation of technology-diversion schemes—such as the Bulgaria-bound computer equipment—which is the same kind of investigation Commerce initiates. Even so,

businessmen are still rankled by the amount of their export product that sits on docks while Commerce determines whether it is properly licensed or not.

Curbing Freedom

As American business men complain that the economy is being seriously eroded by the limitations placed on advanced-technology sales, American scientists have begun to protest what they see as efforts to curb the free flow of ideas. The scientists argue not only that the Administration's actions will infringe upon scientific freedoms, but also that diminished communication among colleagues will stifle scientific progress itself.

In the most dramatic example to date of scientific-research censorship by the Reagan Administration, more than 100 papers scheduled to be delivered at the 26th annual symposium of the Society of Photo-Optical Instrumentation Engineers (SPIE), held in San Diego in August 1982, were withdrawn after Defense Department officials suggested that their authors, most of whom were working under Government grants, could, by presenting those papers publicly, be in violation of the technical-data sections of the Arms Export Control Act or the Export Administration Act. Notification came just five days before the start of the conference and caused a number of seminars to be canceled or drastically narrowed in scope.

A spokesman in the office of Dr. Stephen D. Bryen, the Deputy Assistant Secretary of Defense for International Economic Trade and Security Policy, the office that applied the information clamp, asserted that the new directive was simply "the most current revision of security review procedures." Scientists, however, including SPIE's then-president Richard J. Wollensak, a vice president of ITEK Corp., in Lexington, Mass., see it as representative of the curtailment of scientific interchange. "At SPIE, we've been doing the same thing in the same way with pretty much the same topics for 25 years," Mr. Wollensak says. "The industrial people are fairly sensitive to the security problems of working with front-end technology. But the academics are very upset."

Concerned Academics

The academics are very upset indeed. In January 1982, a gathering of the American Association for the Advancement of Science was told by Adm. Bobby R. Inman, then deputy director of Central Intelligence, that scientists were letting a lot of valuable information go to the Russians. Admiral Inman suggested that the academics and industrial researchers think twice about publishing sensitive information in such areas as computers, lasers and crop projections and that they even consider setting up a system by which Government officials could review research results to determine whether they ought to be made public. The implied threat was: If you don't do it voluntarily, we may pass a law that makes you do it.

The response from the scientific community was swift, forceful and—for a community that had always been isolated in its laboratories—surprisingly unified. The A.A.A.S.'s Committee on Scientific Freedom and Responsibility began a newsletter in September 1982 aimed at keeping members up to date on information-control policy. The same month, the National Academy of Science issued a report entitled "Scientific Communication and National Security." The report's authors, who had received a number of classified briefings from intelligence officers, concluded that the problem of siphoned technology was both "substantial and serious," but found "no specific evidence of damage to U.S. national security caused by information obtained from U.S. academic sources." "To attempt to restrict access to basic research," the report went on, "would require casting a new set of controls over wide areas of science that could be extremely damaging to overall scientific and economic advance as well as to military progress."

Difficult Distinction

Although the United States Government has always restricted the sale of patently military technology to the Russians, the 1970's were the decade of the semiconductor, when the lines between commercial and military electronic products became hopelessly blurred. The same basic semiconductors and integrated circuits that go into video games also go into missile-guidance systems. The same small computer that can be used by an American moving company to make sure a vanload of household goods gets from Cleveland to Boston can also be used by a Russian commander to make sure a division of soldiers gets from Odessa to Prague. Military planners envision the day when the laser technology that now is able to fuse detached retinas will also be capable of disabling enemy communications satellites.

Similarly, cryptography used to be the exclusive purview of the military and intelligence communities. With the dawning of the computer-banking age and the proliferation of commercial data banks, cryptography has become increasingly important in the protection of financial privacy. Such "dual-use" technologies further smudge the boundary between commercial and scientific interests on the one hand, and those of national security on the other.

The 1979 Export Administration Act is a hodgepodge statute, formulated in the wake of a series of dramatic shifts in America's relations with the Soviet Union, but before the hard-line anti-Russian sentiment of the Reagan Administration had made itself felt on Capitol Hill. As Dr. Thane Gustafson, a RAND Corporation researcher, wrote in a 1981 Defense Department report, "Selling the Russians the Rope? Soviet Technology Policy and U.S. Export Controls," "For the past 10 years, the successive versions of the Export Administration Act...have been uneasy compromises between two objectives, that of protecting national security and that of promoting exports. The matter is complicated by the fact that...just about any export, including feed grain or drilling technology, can be considered a 'significant contribution' to Soviet military potential, provided one adopts sufficiently broad definitions."

Technological Choke Point

For the last six years many of the same panels, commissions and study groups that have pointed out how the Soviet Union is acquiring our most sensitive technology have also noted that overly broad definitions of what must be controlled and what constitutes national security are among the main reasons for the technology hemorrhage. They have urged policy makers to find the technological choke point, that point at which research crystallizes into product, then try to control that.

"Just about any export, including feed grain or drilling technology, can be considered a 'significant contribution' to Soviet military potential."

This argument first appeared in a 1976 report by a Defense Science Board task force. Known as the "Bucy Report," after the task force's chairman, J. Fred Bucy, then vice president and now president of Texas Instruments, based in Dallas, it concluded that the United States should control as tightly as possible "arrays of design and manufacturing equipment" and "keystone equipment," the precision instruments that can forge a critical industrial link—that can, for example turn a silicon chip into a semiconductor. The committee constructed a chart ranking the "effectiveness" of "technology-transfer mechanisms." Turnkey factories, designed and built under contract by Western companies, then turned over to their Eastern owners, and joint ventures, in which Western and Eastern firms share ownership and responsibility, rank as highly effective "mechanisms" of technology transfer, and hence ought to be licensed and monitored closely. Trade exhibits and simple product sales, by contrast, were seen as relatively low in effectiveness and therefore could be decontrolled.

The 1981 RAND report made many of the same points, then argued that, in addition, the Soviet Union lacks the management and innovation necessary to use even imported technology to full advantage. "If the Soviets fail to gain (an innovative) capacity," Dr. Gustafson wrote, "then imported technology will in many ways only perpetuate their backwardness and dependence, since by the time it is installed and functioning it is already out of date."

Trade License

Mr. Bucy and Dr. Gustafson called for the same thing, a serious reduction in the range of technology that is controlled, both unilaterally and through the Cocom agreements. Today, for an American company to be able to sell its products to Eastern Europe, it must secure a license from the Commerce Department. If they are advanced-technology products, Commerce generally consults with the Departments of State, Defense and Energy and the intelligence agencies. If there are no objections in Washington, it then refers the matter to the permanent United States delegate to Cocom, which is headquartered in Paris. He in turn consults with his fellow delegates, any one of whom can veto the American company's request.

"The complexity and the overbreadth of the regulations get to the point where people say, 'This is crazy. I can't deal with this.'"

If there is no veto, as is usually the case, Commerce grants the license—as it did 7,000 times in fiscal 1982. But so much red tape means that obtaining permission to sell to the Eastern bloc can take as long as two years and almost always requires between three and six months.

"Free world" licenses, by contrast, are handled with a minimum of fuss. According to Archie M. Andrews, director of exporters' services for Commerce, 98 percent of the 70,000 free-world applications submitted in fiscal 1982 were acted on within six weeks of submission and almost all of them were approved. When the Reagan Administration took office, there was a backlog of some 2,000 applications, which was reduced to a handful by year's end. Ironically, Operation Exodus has increased the backlog because more exporters are now taking the time to apply for licenses and because Customs Service personnel are requesting license determinations for all detained goods.

Limited Russian Access

Despite warnings like Mr. Bucy's and Dr. Gustafson's, the Reagan Administration has defined national security very broadly. But as yet, its efforts to limited Russian access to technical products and information have been viewed by many experts as heavy-handed and haphazard, of little value except

perhaps as a public-relations device for soothing American taxpayers and national-security hawks. One former Commerce Department official, now practicing as an exports lawyer, says, "It is impossible to enforce the Export Administration Act without having a cop on every corner....The complexity and the overbreadth of the regulations get to the point where people say, 'This is crazy. I can't deal with this.'"

"People should go back to the Bucy Report," advises Dr. Roland W. Schmitt, senior vice president for corporate research and development at the General Electric Co. in Schenectady, N.Y. "What it did especially well was look at the mechanisms of technology transfer."

Dr. Schmitt describes the Military Critical Technologies List, a 700-page compilation of technologies—products, product groupings and product designs—the Defense Department thinks should be controlled, as "a case of regulatory overkill. Instead of being a list of critical technologies, it's a list of all relevant technologies. It'd make more sense to say, 'Let's write down the 20 or 50 most critical items, the ones that would help the Soviet Union the most, and try to control them.' Ninety-nine percent of the problem would be solved with 1 percent of the effort."

Dr. Gustafson writes, in a similar vein, that the "critical weakness" of the Military Critical Technologies List "is that it is simply a listing of techniques that, if exported to a military competitor, *could* be harmful to us; it does not contain any clear conception of how or why technology tranfer actually takes place. It implicitly assumes that advanced technology is like virulent disease: It is enough for the recipient to be exposed for him to catch it."

Customs Service

While the Customs Service continues to spot-check hundreds of outgoing parcels each day and R. Bryen's office at the Pentagon pushes for greater control over information, other Government groups are trying to work *with* the business and scientific communities. One of these is the Commerce Department, where the feeling has always been that the majority of business people will abide by export laws if those laws are fair, can be easily dealt with and do not cause pointless delays.

"Voluntary compliance among the private sector is the first line of defense," Theodore Wu argues. "Prosecution, no matter how successful, does not get back lost technology." Compliance, he asserts, does not just mean completing the paperwork, but informing the Government of suspicious activities. "If someone else is sacrificing the national interest for short-term gain, the industry must be willing to inform the Government of it."

Mr. Wu tries to downplay the battle for turf that Commerce and Customs are waging. He stresses the interagency nature of groups he has headed, groups that have met with export-control personnel from other countries, whose members are drawn from the Departments of State and Defense, the F.B.I., and the intelligence agencies, as well as Customs and Commerce. Still, there is a great deal of friction. "We have terrible problems with the Commerce Department," says Customs' William Rudman. "They are precisely duplicating our effort, looking for the same sources of information. If those sources gives the information to Customs, Commerce is upset. If they give it to Commerce, Customs is angry."

Meanwhile, in the legislature, Congressmen and Senators fight to award the export-control pie to their preferred agency. The House, which passed its version of the new Export Administration Act during the last week of October, without seeking to terminate Operation Exodus gives the powers of enforcement to Commerce. The Senate version, which the Administration supports and which has been under consideration for several months, gives the powers to Customs. A conference committee will probably be established to resolve the differences; if not, the issue could still be in limbo come spring. Whatever the timetable, it is expected that some kind of shared enforcement role will ultimately be worked out.

The move to strip Commerce of its powers of enforcement and turn them over to Customs dates from May 1982, following the Senate hearings conducted by Senator Nunn, during which personnel from a number of Government agencies testified that Commerce, with a mere 10 enforcement officers at the time, was unable to do the necessary job. A larger issue was whether Commerce should even attempt, as the then Assistant Secretary for Trade Administration put it, to "wear two hats," promoting and policing exports at the same time.

"I believe the Senate is laboring under the burden of outdated facts," Mr. Wu says, defending his office's investigative function. Mr. Rudman, for his part, points out that Customs is already charged with enforcing the Arms Export Control Act, and is therefore in an ideal position to investigate "dual-use" violations.

Mr. Rudman and Mr. Wu also disagree about what Congress should do. "If (the legislators) compromise on this we'll be left with the status quo," says Mr. Rudman, who calls the current situation "an embarrassment." Mr. Wu believes that only a coordinated interagency effort is going to get the job done. Others believe that the battle for primacy need not be fought, that the two units are complementary, and that having enforcement aligned with licensing is entirely desirable.

Business seems willing to go along. "Trying to cooperate is an awareness issue," says Richard T. Guilmette, manager of corporate security and safety for Prime Computer, Inc., in Natick, Mass., and outgoing chairman of the Boston chapter of the American Society for Industrial Security, whose 900 members he has tried to make aware of export-control problems. A former military intelligence officer, Mr. Guilmette believes "we have to educate ourselves as to what in the industrial area has spinoff military value. Defense research takes place under extreme security. But high-technology companies that don't compete for Government contracts are ripe for the picking."

Workable Controls

Even at the Pentagon, an effort is being made to work with industry and academia in formulating a workable export-control policy. "We've got to be very careful we don't constrict the flow of technological development and the flow of technological cross-talk both at home and with our allies," cautions Dr. Francis B. Kapper, Assistant Deputy Under-Secretary for Technology Transfer at the Defense Department. "If you do not impose realistic and mutually agreed-upon controls, you can very quickly cut down that flow to a dribble."

"The Government's moves toward information control here at home have frightened some of our own scientists into silence."

Since early 1981, Mr. Kapper has been involved in discussions with academics about how to balance national security with intellectual freedom. The subject first arose that February, when the presidents of Stanford University, the California Institute of Technology, the Massachusetts Institute of Technology, Cornell University and the University of California wrote to Secretary of Commerce Malcolm Baldrige, Secretary of Defense Caspar Weinberger and then Secretary of State Alexander M. Haig Jr. It is at these five campuses that much of the research into the Very High Speed Integrated Circuit—or V.H.S.I.C.—which will vastly increase the speed of computers and other electronic instrumentation, is being carried on, funded in part by the Defense Advanced Research Projects Agency. The five presidents were voicing their shock at the V.H.S.I.C. program office's attempts to bar foreign scientists from participating in V.H.S.I.C. research. The college presidents questioned why Federal regulations were suddenly being enforced, arguing that the regulations would restrict publication and "discourse among scholars," as well as force them to discriminate on the basis of nationality in faculty hiring and student admission. The group concluded that before the Government extended the restrictions it should think seriously about their necessity and effectiveness, about the degree to which they would disrupt the university role and raise serious constitutional questions.

Unresolved Issues

The issue is still unresolved. Mr. Kapper is holding wide-ranging discussions with a number of academics and is heartened by the fact that, at least, the Defense Department and academics are talking.

It is obvious the problem is not going to go away. The halting of legal transfers of advanced technology to the Russians and the successful prosecution of a number of advanced-technology smugglers have pinched the flow of products, **thus raising the stakes** both for those seeking to "transfer" technology and for the Russians themselves. Moreover, the Government's moves toward the information control here at home have frightened some of our own scientists into silence while distracting others from their work.

That it is necessary and proper for the Government to seek to protect our vital technology, especially given today's shortened laboratory-to-market lead time, is not, for all but the most laissez-faire of scientists, businessmen and Government leaders, in question. What is in question are the mechanisms that the Government has deemed most effective in providing that protection. Increasingly, many of the same scientists, businessmen and Government leaders have begun to view them as both ill-conceived and doomed to failure. What is worse, some of them argue, such mechanisms—by freighting innovation with secrecy and constricting intercourse among colleagues—may ultimately prove destructive to the very interests they seek to preserve.

Jon Zonderman is a contributing writer to The Boston Business Journal.

"We need the Third World as much as it needs us."

The Case for Foreign Aid

Terence L. Day

Foreign aid is a popular whipping boy, especially during times of fiscal austerity.

At such times, citizens, public administrators and legislators often ask why "we" are wasting all that money overseas when we have problems at home that need attention.

Similar questions, even criticisms, were voiced about the space program. "Why are we wasting all that money on space?" as if we simply bundled up billions of dollar bills, placed them in rockets and fired them into outer space!

There seems to be a similar misconception about foreign aid, that we simply package up bundles of dollar bills and export them to foreign countries.

Land-grant universities that are experiencing growing international dimensions, sometimes face these kinds of questions, too. To help answer them, one such institution, Washington State University, put together the following case history from records in its controller's office, and of the firms with which it contracted.

Case History

On June 14, 1979, a white George S. Bush Co. truck pulled up to VWR Scientific in Seattle and loaded 14 cartons of scientific instruments which were delivered to Seattle-Tacoma International Airport.

The shipment left Sea-Tac on June 27 in the belly of Pan American Flight 122, a Boeing 747, destined for London's Heathrow International Airport to make connections for eventual delivery on July 17 to the University of Jordan in Amman.

The transaction was one of the final details of completing a four year contract to help the University of Jordan establish a college of agriculture.

The transaction was one of the final details of completing a four year contract to help the University of Jordan establish a college of agriculture.

It is but one small example of how U.S. Agency for International Development contracts benefit local, state and national economies, as well as the Third World nations.

This one contract involved $21,224.74 of business within Washington state—$19,944.70 to VWR for the instruments and $1,280.04 to Bush, of which Bush paid $1,164.32 to Pan Am for freight and $62.94 to Royal Globe Insurance Cos., a Seattle firm, for insurance. The remaining $42.78 Bush kept for local cartage, documentation and forwarding fees.

The entire sum came from AID and was part of several million dollars worth of non-agricultural goods and services bought in Washington state each year for shipment overseas as part of AID's economic development programs.

State Benefits

For the fiscal year ending Sept. 30, 1979, AID records show that Washington state sold more than $34 million worth of goods, services and agricultural products as a direct result of foreign aid programs and that an additional $5.5 million worth of technical service contracts were in effect with universities and individual experts for research or supervision of AID field projects.

Of that, more than $30 million was paid to the state's farmers and food processors for grain and other agricultural commodities sent to developing countries under the Food for Peace Program.

More than $4 million was paid to Washington manufacturers and other firms for goods and services used in overseas economic development programs administered by AID.

Sharing the business were 23 Washington firms that sold goods and 10 businesses, institutions and individuals that sold services. Nearly all of the money

Terence L. Day, "Foreign Aid No Bundle of Cash," *Agenda*, November 1981. Reprinted by permission.

went to companies and institutions in the highly urbanized Puget Sound Region.

John S. Robins, dean of the WSU College of Agriculture, says the university has been involved in international programs for nearly 30 years. That involvement has been increasing since the early 1970s, when it finished a project to help develop a university in Faisalabad (formerly Lahor), Pakistan. Since then it has been involved in a similar project in Jordan, and in others in Indonesia, Lesotho and Sudan.

Development contracts held by WSU total $36 million over a period of several years. Robins says WSU doesn't spend any state funds on the projects, and that wherever possible, all goods purchased for them are bought from Washington businesses. Federal law requires all purchases be from United States firms if they sell the items, and that transportation be on American carriers as far as possible.

Economic Stimulus

Besides the economic stimulus that these development programs create in our own economy, Robins cites a vital national interest.

"A half billion people are affected by the nutrition gap. Half to two-thirds of the children in developing countries are undernourished. The United Nations estimates that 12 million children under the age of five died of malnutrition last year. It would take 88 million tons of grain a year to fill the gap between food production and minimum nutritional needs in food-deficit countries.

"Americans cannot divorce the future of less-developed countries from the future of America."

"But developing nations import only about 44 million tons of grain, which leaves them still 44 million tons short of what they absolutely need. And the situation is getting worse," Robins says. "The projected shortfall in 1990 is between 132 million tons and 160 million tons.

"To put this in perspective, consider that Washington state produces only 3.5 million tons of wheat each year on its vast, rich wheatlands, and the entire United States produces only about 63 million tons.

Humanitarian Aspect

"The humanitarian aspects of helping solve world food and economic problems are obvious and compelling. But less obvious is the fact that we must help these people for our own protection."

Americans cannot divorce the future of less-

developed countries from the future of America, according to the dean. First, we have an economic self-interest. Some 1.2 million American jobs depend on exports to the Third World. Last year American farmers exported a fourth of all that they produced—commodities valued at $41 billion.

Indirectly that permits Americans to buy foreign-made consumer goods, including vehicles, television sets, radios and clothing, all of which contribute to the American way of life.

Foreign Aid Connection

And, Robins points out, exports are especially important to Washington state's economy although the average citizen may not realize it. Even farmers, whose livelihoods depend on exports, sometimes fail to make the connection between improved economics abroad and increased sales of our agricultural products.

Washington farmers export virtually all of their lentils, 90% of their dry peas, 80 to 85% of their wheat and substantial amounts of other crops such as apples, flower bulbs and hay. In addition, Washington seaports regularly ship grain from Montana and the Dakotas.

Creating Demand

"The ability of the United States, and of the state of Washington, to sell agricultural and other products on the world market is partly dependent upon the developing countries having the economic ability to purchase U.S. exports, and to have advanced sufficiently to have developed a demand for them," Robins says.

Since territorial days, Washington's farmers have depended on export markets as a "home" for much that they produce, but during the past 20 years the export market has soared. Exports of wheat to Asia have tripled. Taiwan's imports of wheat from the U.S. Northwest are up 228%. Hong Kong once bought less than 2% of its wheat from the United States. Today it buys 74% from us. Korea, which buys all of its wheat from the United States, has increased per capita consumption from 14 pounds in 1959 to 100 pounds today. Indonesia, which imported 42,900 tons of American wheat in the early 1960s, now imports more than 600,000 tons.

Prevents Revolution

"But," Robins says, "stimulation of our exports ultimately may prove to be one of the smaller benefits from America's commitment to developing nations. We saw what happened in Africa's Sahel in the early 1970s when drought devastated millions of acres of rangeland and millions of people were caught up in famine. Thousands died, we know that, but not many people realize that another significant consequence was that every single nation in the drought region changed governments as a direct or indirect result of that disaster.

"Most changed from generally democratic forms of government to generally totalitarian forms. The long-term implication of malnutrition is discontent, and from discontent flow things not good for humankind."

Robins warns: "We may be approaching a time when the Sahelian problem of the 1970s may be dwarfed by even larger problems in Africa. Climatic trends, if they continue, could result in a repeat of the Sahel—perhaps over a much larger area."

"The long-term implication of malnutrition is discontent."

The importance to the United States of the type of government in developing countries should be obvious in the wake of the dramatically rising prices demanded by OPEC nations for the fuel that provides the foundation of our technological society. Indonesia, which WSU will serve on a five-year development contract, supplies 15 to 20% of the oil imported by the United States.

"Our industrial society is dependent on other countries—many of them lesser-developed countries—for raw materials that are essential to our economy," Robins notes.

"To put it bluntly, we need the Third World as much as it needs us."

Terence L. Day is an agricultural research writer with Washington State University in Spokane.

"It is plainly not true that aid is indispensable for development."

The Case Against Foreign Aid

Peter T. Bauer and John O'Sullivan

Foreign aid is perhaps the only item of public expenditure in the West which is never criticized in principle. It is, of course, often said to be insufficient. Past aid programs, too, are sometimes denounced as inappropriate—in particular, aid which has financed obviously wasteful investment, or aid to oil-rich countries with a high per capita income. But this criticism is itself merely the basis for advocating that aid should be directed to more appropriate targets as well as increased.

The most familiar rationalizations for aid are that it is indispensable for development; that it is necessary for the relief of poverty; that it is an instrument for international redistribution of income; that it represents restitution for past wrongs; and that it serves the political and economic interests of the donors.

Third World Development

It used to be argued in the early days of foreign aid that it was indispensable for the development of poor countries. Without aid, incomes would be too low to generate the capital required for investment and thus for higher incomes. This argument was popularized as "the vicious circle of poverty."

Yet we know that all the present developed societies began poor and subsequently progressed without external aid. Large areas of what are now less developed countries (LDCs) also progressed rapidly long before foreign aid.

Moreover, Western societies made great progress in the past under conditions far more difficult than those which face LDCs today. These latter can draw on vast external markets, on an abundant supply of capital, and on a wide range of technologies which were not available in the early stages of Western

development. It is plainly not true that aid is indispensable for development.

Importance of Attitude

Economic achievement depends principally on people's attitudes, motivations, mores, and government policies. People in LDCs may place a high value on factors that obstruct material progress. They may be reluctant to take animal life, they may prefer the contemplative life over an active one, they may oppose paid work by women, or they may simply be fatalistic.

If, on account of such factors, they are uncongenial to material progress, then external doles will not promote development. For if the conditions for development, other than capital, are present, the capital required will either be generated locally or be available commercially from abroad. If the required conditions are not present, aid will be ineffective and wasteful.

Unrealistic Aim

To reduce poverty and distress is an irreproachable and unambiguous aim. That is perhaps one reason why this justification has come to loom large in aid propaganda. But there are certain moral and practical anomalies concealed here.

Aid to relieve poverty is not merely unconnected logically with aid as a spur to development; it is largely at variance with it. These two objectives differ in much the same way as alms to a beggar differs from scholarships to promising students, or assistance to an invalid from loans to establish young people in business.

The poorest people in any society are unlikely to have, to the same extent as the better off, the aptitudes and motivations that encourage economic achievement. Aid based upon the criterion of poverty, therefore, will have little impact on the economic progress of the recipient society as a whole.

Peter T. Bauer and John O'Sullivan, "The Case Against Foreign Aid." Reprinted from *Commentary*, April 1979, by permission; all rights reserved.

This confronts donors with a dilemma familiar to nineteenth-century social reformers. Are they simply to dispense aid and do nothing more? If so, they run the risk of transforming poor people into paupers permanently dependent on the dole. But the alternative is hardly more attractive. It is that donors should intervene extensively to instill in the recipient poor those qualities conducive to economic success.

Godlike Intervention

In many Asian and African societies, such godlike intervention would require wholesale reform of local social institutions and cultural values and therefore large-scale coercion of the alleged beneficiaries.

This stern necessity is recognized, indeed almost welcomed, by some of the more clear-sighted supporters of development aid, for example Professor Gunnar Myrdal. In his vast tome *Asian Drama* (1968), he specifies what would be required in India if "the government were really determined to change the prevailing attitudes and institutions and had the courage to take the necessary steps and accept their consequences." His proposed measures include the abolition of caste, a rational policy for husbandry, including the killing of cows, and "in general, enactment and enforcement, not only of fiscal, but also of all other obligations on people that are required for development."

"They run the risk of transforming poor people into paupers permanently dependent on the dole."

But as Professor Myrdal tentatively admits elsewhere in the book, ". . . institutions can ordinarily be changed only by resort to what in the region is called compulsion—putting obligations on people and supporting them by force." Is such social upheaval justified by the aim of relieving poverty? And even if it is, would aid be accepted by the recipients if they understood the terms? And would such measures even relieve poverty—or would they intensify it, by transforming a living society into a dejected, inert, apathetic mass?

Redistribution of Wealth

Since the UN General Assembly declared its support for a new international economic order in 1974, the redistribution of world income has become a leading aim of foreign aid. But this is a misleading phrase. When "world income" is "redistributed," what happens is that a proportion of incomes in developed countries is confiscated and handed over to the governments of recipient countries and the administrators of aid agencies.

Aid is a transaction between governments. Unlike progressive taxation, it cannot be even imperfectly adjusted to the personal and family circumstances of payers and recipients. Indeed, many people in donor countries are far poorer than many in recipient countries, especially those in recipient countries who actually benefit from aid. Hence, in the now familiar formulation, aid takes money from the poor in rich countries and gives it to the rich in poor countries.

Another argument for international "redistribution" is the need to contain an allegedly widening gap between the rich and poor countries. Yet the concept of such a widening gap is arbitrary, and the evidence for it is nebulous. It is based on faulty statistics and comparisons which overlook differences of physical and social context.

Restitution to Colonies

When other arguments fail, appeals are addressed to the West's guilty conscience and foreign aid is urged as restitution for past wrongs inflicted on the Third World.

In fact, some of the poorest Third World countries were never colonies. And such victims of colonialism as there were (people killed or maimed in colonial wars, tribal farmers dispossessed by colonists, slaves, etc.) are now dead and beyond the reach even of the World Bank. Their descendants have gained greatly from being born into the modern colonial and postcolonial world rather than into the circumstances of precolonial Africa and Asia.

Indeed, millions of people who would otherwise have died have survived because of Western techniques and ideas, notably medicine and public security, imported by colonial governments. Would the rest really have preferred a low life expectancy, continued poverty, disease, slavery and incessant wars in order to retain undisturbed control of mineral resources they were unable to develop adequately?

Even if it could be established that colonialism was, on balance, harmful to the colonized, any theory of restitution would still fail because of the obvious impossibility of righting historical wrongs. What date would we fix after which crimes might be considered for compensation? Any choice would be arbitrary and therefore unjust. How would we identify the victims and the beneficiaries? Not, surely, on racial grounds alone, with their primitive implication of collective guilt ("his blood be on us, and on our children"). And would all historical crimes be brought to book (Arab slave trading, precolonial wars of aggression in Asia and Africa) or only Western and colonial crimes? A statute of limitations on historical wrongs is more than just; it is unavoidable.

Political Self-interest

Finally, there is the suggestion—frequently put forward by aid advocates with Machiavellian pretensions—that aid serves the political strategy of the donors and that it promotes exports.

Yet to serve Western interests, aid would need to have clear conditions attached to it and to be adjusted to the conduct of the recipients. Such criteria have been notably absent from its operation. (Only recently the European Economic Commission assured the Marxist government of Angola that EEC aid would be free of political conditions.) Multinational aid, a large and increasing proportion of the total, is specifically supported on the grounds that it does not lend itself to arm-twisting or blackmail—a curious use of the concept, in which it is the payers and not the recipients who engage in blackmail.

But in practice, Western interests are also largely ignored in bilateral aid. Many, possibly most, recipients of aid, especially in Asia and Africa, have confiscated Western enterprises and yet have continued to receive aid. Examples include Algeria, Ghana, India, Mozambique, Sri Lanka, Tanzania, Zaire and Zambia. The hostility of many aid recipients to Western donors and their friendliness toward the Soviet bloc are also a familiar feature of the international scene.

If aid were like manna which simply descended from heaven, both costless and enriching everyone equally, producing no unlooked for and damaging consequences, then it could only be beneficial. But mundane aid is not at all like manna. It unleashes a host of repercussions, damaging to economic performance and development, which can easily outweigh the marginal effect on an inflow of subsidized resources.

Errors in Foreign Aid?

Aid promotes the widespread politicization of life in the Third World. This is because it goes to governments, not to the people at large—a distinction obscured by conventional terminology, which identifies a government with the people. Aid therefore necessarily increases the power, resources, and patronage of government in the society. This result is reinforced by preferential treatment of governments which try to establish state-controlled economies—a preference supported by the spurious argument that comprehensive state planning is necessary for material progress.

The beneficiaries are politically effective groups, especially politicians, but also the military, civil servants and politically acceptable businessmen. The victims are such unpopular groups as landowners, small traders, or members of particular tribes like the Ibo in Nigeria.

Large sections of the rural population are often severely harmed, sometimes directly, more often because measures against minorities disrupt the trading system on which their livelihood largely depends. Ethnic minorities are often the worst affected; in the Third World, economic controls are used widely and sometimes explicitly against the Indians in Burma, or against the Chinese in Malaysia.

In a politicized society, economic success or survival, and often even the physical survival of large numbers of people, come to depend on political developments and administrative decisions. This diverts the energies and activities of ambitious and resourceful men from economic life to politics, to the civil service and the politicized military—to the detriment of economic prosperity and progress. All this inevitably raises the political temperature and provokes acute political tension, especially in multiracial, multicultural, and multitribal societies—that is, practically all LDCs.

"Aid takes money from the poor in rich countries and gives it to the rich in the poor countries."

Aid also often supports projects so wasteful that they not only incur losses year after year, but absorb more domestic resources than the value of their output. Yet they are continued for such political reasons as the reluctance of the government to lose prestige at home or contacts with the donors, especially when these are politically congenial, or a desire to appear technologically up-to-date.

To mention but one of many examples, some years ago Tanzania received bush-clearing equipment under a Yugoslavian aid scheme. This was designed for use in temperate climates. Much labor and scarce water were necessary for cooling, to keep it going somehow in the tropics. It was only after protracted pressure from external advisers that the Tanzanian government agreed to abandon the equipment.

Aid Is Biased

Aid often biases social and economic policies toward inappropriate Western models. In many Asian and African countries, Western-style universities have been financed with aid when there is neither adequate personnel to staff them nor suitable jobs for their graduates, who become a discontented intellectual proletariat.

Western-inspired trade unions are another instance of inappropriate external models in aid-recipient LDCs; if they are effective, they inflate costs and thus impair both competitiveness and local employment opportunities.

But the most familiar and most inappropriate external prototypes are prestige industries and activities, such as engineering complexes, steel works and airlines. Even Laos and Ethiopia have, or at least had, their own national airlines (operated for them by foreign airlines who supplied personnel, organization and equipment).

Major psychological repercussions of aid also

deserve notice. Aid encourages the delusion that a society can progress from indigence to prosperity without the intermediate stage of economic effort and achievement. Insistence on the need for external donations obscures the necessity for the people of poor countries themselves to develop the faculties and attitudes and to adopt the conduct and the mores required for sustained material progress—if this is what they wish to do. (Of course, they may reasonably prefer to remain poor and to hold on to their traditional ways.)

Repercussions

Aid also subtly confirms and perpetuates ideas and modes of conduct which obstruct economic development—notably the idea that an improvement in one's fortunes depends on other people, the state, the rich, one's superiors, local rulers, or foreigners.

How did it happen, then, that such a far-reaching and momentous policy was advanced on the slender basis of negligible rationalizations; that it was nonetheless supported by public men and prominent academics with a notable lack of caution or skepticism; and that, despite plentiful evidence of its perverse and harmful consequences, it finally achieved the status of an undeniable axiom?

Benefits of Foreign Aid?

"In the beginning was the word." The concept of a less developed world, eventually to become the Third World, was forged after World War II, largely under U.S. auspices, to denote the whole of Asia other than Japan; Africa, except occasionally South Africa and Rhodesia; and Latin America. The less developed world, or Third World, is thus in effect the whole world outside the West and Japan, and it includes some two-thirds of mankind.

"Economic achievement depends principally on people's attitudes."

But "the word" was less a description of reality than an attempt to change it. Phrases like "the less developed world" served to provide a spurious veneer of unity to a vast aggregate of radically different, deeply divided, and often mutually antagonistic or bitterly hostile components.

What is there in common between, say, Papua New Guinea and Algeria, or between Malaysia and Argentina, or between Thailand and Botswana, or between Sri Lanka and Ecuador, or between Chad and Peru? In most LDCs, even today, the majority of people do not even know of the existence of other less developed countries, let alone feel a common solidarity.

Some are in a state of uneasy truce with their neighbors, as for instance India and Pakistan, as well as many African states. Others, like Algeria and Morocco, are in a state of intermittent hostilities; yet others are engaged in deadly combat, as are Ethiopia and Somalia.

Opposition to West

In one respect only are these various countries at all united—in distinction to and, as time has progressed, in their opposition to the West (from which they nevertheless demand and receive aid). But this invented and theoretical unity has served an important practical purpose. For Third World governments, agencies, and certain groups within the West, it has become a source of ideological and even financial advantage.

Ideologically, the invention of the Third World both reflects and promotes the radical-equalitarian belief that economic and social differences perform no useful function and are therefore abnormal and reprehensible. By this standard, the West stands condemned both for its internal arrangements, which permit of such differences, and also because it is more prosperous than most of the Third World. Removing resources from or otherwise undermining the position of this corrupt metropolis thus becomes an instrument for promoting international equality, reducing the power of the West, and encouraging state-controlled economies in Asia, Africa and Latin America.

In giving practical effect to these ideas, international ogranizations, notably the UN and its affiliates, have been a major force. Prominent staff members within these bodies—occupying highly paid and prestigious positions—have discarded even the appearance of neutrality to become, in effect, union organizers for the Third World. Thus, Dr. Mahbub ul Haq, director of the Policy Planning Department of the World Bank, an influential speech writer for Robert McNamara, wrote in his book, *The Poverty Curtain: Choices for the Third World:*

> A major part of the bargaining strengh of the Third World lies in its political unity. This unity is going to be even more important in the struggle ahead. One of the essential tactics of the Third World should be to proceed through the process of collective bargaining so that whatever bargaining strength its individual members possess is pooled together.

Such distinguished *apparatchiks* have done much to popularize the idea of a homogeneous less developed world with a common interest, and to organize concerted action by the most diverse countries against the West.

Proliferation of Politicians

Social scientists and academic economists form another pressure group which advocates—and benefits from—official aid. Before World War II, indeed, development economics did not exist as a well-defined academic subject. It owes its birth very largely to the emergence of foreign aid, which led to a proliferation of posts in universities and foundations. Those who toil in the vineyard of development economics can aspire to well-paid and prestigious posts with aid agencies and international bodies or in organizations supported by them.

But there are more subtle advantages to be gained from the extension of aid. For if we try to see the world as aid advocates would wish us to do, it appears to be divided into two sharply distinct categories.

One category is that of the people of the Third World, sunk in poverty, helpless and at the mercy of their environment, exploited by the West, caught in a vicious circle of poverty, unable to control their own fertility, devoid of will and with little capacity for individual action. In short, they are like paupers or children.

On the other side of a vast gulf are the prosperous people in the West, partly conditioned by their environment but with a will of their own; active but villainous; responsible for the plight of the world's poor, but refusing to take the actions required to improve it.

Condescending Attitude

There is no doubt which is the superior in this scenario. We emerged from poverty; they cannot. Their poverty is the result of our past exploitation; their chance of a better future rests with us. Whatever happens to the people of the Third World is determined by us.

In short, what poses as compassion comprises much condescension. And this condescension readily leads to coercion by enlightened guardians who will act in everyone's best long-term interests. Thus, writes Dr. ul Haq (Kings College, Cambridge; Yale; Pakistan Planning Commission; the World Bank):

> The Third World can help its cause a great deal by establishing a substantive secretariat to serve the needs of its own forums . . . manned by the best people from the Third World and its main task should be to produce well-researched, well-documented, specific proposals which harmonize the political and economic interests of the Third World.

Can anyone doubt that the ''best people'' will be drawn from such institutions as Cambridge, Yale, the Pakistan Planning Commission, the World Bank, and their surrogates in the Third World? And is it therefore any wonder that such people are fervent believers in aid and in the kind of future it contributes to creating?

Peter T. Bauer is professor of economics at the London School of Economics, Fellow of Gonville and Caius College, Cambridge, and Fellow of the British Academy. John O'Sullivan is parliamentary correspondent and editorial writer for the Daily Telegraph *(London).*

"Their social and economic advance will be crippled unless they are assisted."

US Foreign Aid Helps the Impoverished

An interview with Robert McNamara in *U.S. News & World Report*

Question: Mr. McNamara, you've been pleading with the U.S. and other industrialized nations to provide more money to poor nations—and rapidly. What's so urgent about this need?

Answer: The fundamental point is this: All of us are living in an increasingly interdependent world—interdependent both economically and politically. And that combination offers many opportunities for actions from which everyone will benefit. This is why it's urgent that the U.S.—in it's own national interest—act now to deal more effectively with the plight of the poorer nations.

Yes, I am pleading—to use your word—for a more realistic understanding of this basic point, and pleading for additional economic support for the less developed countries, not only through the transfer of resources but through expanded trading opportunities as well.

And I'm pleading for two reasons: It is very much in the interest of the developed countries themselves to do this, and it is very much in the interest of the developing countries that it should happen. The developing countries require economic support so that they can buy what they need from the rest of the world—an expense that is exacerbated by recent increases in oil prices. Those increases alone have more than doubled the current-account deficits these countries are facing in their trade and financial dealings with other nations.

A Plea for Aid

Their social and economic advance will be crippled unless they are assisted. If they are to make a reasonable rate of progress, they will need additional external financing. That's why I am pleading for them.

Robert McNamara, "A Plea for Aid to '800 Million on Margin of Life'," *U.S. News & World Report*, December 22, 1980. Excerpted from *U.S. News & World Report* issue of December 22, 1980. Copyright, 1980, U.S. News & World Report, Inc.

Question: Why is it in the national interest of the U.S., as you put it, for us to provide such help?

Answer: For the U.S., the fastest-growing markets for exports—and the greatest potential stimulus to U.S. employment and trade—are in these oil-importing developing countries. So it is a plus-sum game. If the U.S. does not act intelligently, there will be a deflationary impact on the world, and the U.S. will be hurt as a result.

Question: What's the source of opposition? Is it ignorance, or is it a feeling of irritation that some of these Third World countries ganged up on us in the United Nations?

Answer: It's both, but basically it's ignorance. You can put up with some of the irritations if you understand where your fundamental interests lie.

Serving US Interests

If we in the U.S.—I'm speaking now as a U.S. citizen, not as the president of the World Bank—really believed that our fundamental interests would be served by additional assistance, whether it be in the form of trading opportunities or financial assistance, we'd be very shortsighted to let our irritations guide our behavior.

Question: On the negative side, what can happen if we aren't forthcoming in the Third World? Political turmoil? Collapse?

Answer: In simple terms, one would expect a greater degree of economic disorder, lower rates of economic and social advance, which in turn would lead to political disorder.

The truth is that the U.S. can no longer isolate itself from political disorder in other parts of the world as easily as it could in the past. We see ample evidence of that today in the Middle East. And I think we'll see evidence of it in many other parts of the world.

Beyond that, there are the humanitarian and moral considerations. They are very important. They move me; I hope they'll move others.

Question: Can you elaborate on the humanitarian stakes involved?

Answer: The World Bank today serves roughly 100 developing countries, containing some 2.25 billion people, excluding China. Of those 2.25 billion people, roughly 800 million are literally living on the margin of life—just bordering between life and death. If these countries do not advance economically, the number of people who are trapped in poverty will increase. It's a disgrace to the human race that we tolerate such a situation.

A Humanitarian Gesture

So one has these two considerations: Very narrow national considerations of economic and political interests, and then the much broader humanitarian and moral considerations.

Question: You're talking about a role that obviously is bigger than the World Bank's role. What should the industrialized countries be doing beyond what the bank does?

Answer: The World Bank can play three very important roles: One is the narrow one of being a major source of funds. We have expanded our financial commitments roughly tenfold in the last 12 years.

Second, we can also play a role as adviser to the developing countries' governments. We have been increasingly active in that field.

For example, the oil-importing developing countries must ultimately pay for the higher-priced oil. There's no way to finance that indefinitely simply by piling up debt. In the end, the only way they can pay for it is by expanding their exports or reducing their imports—or by some reasonable combination of the two. But it's going to take time for them to make those policy changes, and we can be helpful on that process.

"The US—in its own national interest—acts now to deal more effectively with the plight of the poorer nations."

And, third, we can serve as a focal point for discussion of key development issues and of the actions required to deal with them—issues, for example, such as absolute poverty, the population problem and the energy situation. Over the past decade, we've sought to stimulate more thoughtful and practical discussion of these and other critical issues.

Question: Who are these 800 million people on the margin of life that you refer to? What countries do they live in?

Answer: They are what we have termed the absolute poor. One can divide the approximately 100 developing countries into two broad groups: One group comprises the low-income countries, with roughly 1.25 billion people. These include countries such as India, Bangladesh, Kenya and most of sub-Sahara Africa. And the other group comprises the middle-income countries, with roughly a billion people: Countries such as Brazil, Korea and Turkey.

The Absolute Poor

There are absolute poor in each of these two groups of nations—some 600 to 625 million in the low-income countries and some 150 to 175 million in the middle-income group.

Question: Many of these countries have been getting aid for years. Why haven't they been able to make it on their own? Why haven't many been able to feed themselves?

Answer: If you mean why haven't they been able to get along without external capital, I don't believe that historically any of today's developed nations did, either. At a comparable stage of development, for example, the U.S. was a borrower on a tremendous scale. Our railroads were financed by external capital. Much of our industry was financed by external capital. That's typical of a certain stage of economic development.

Question: But beyond that, why aren't the developing nations able to grow faster than they have? Why can't some feed their people?

Answer: On balance, they have learned to feed their own people. Take India. The World Bank is very active in agriculture there. Compare the years 1966 and 1980, for example. Both were drought periods. In 1966, India produced 72 million tons of cereal grain. In this past year, it produced 116 million tons. That is a 60 percent increase in 14 years, and India did not have to import grain this time.

Great Progress

What I am saying is that there has been great progress in these countries. Life expectancy increased on the order of 40 percent, on average, between 1950 and 1975. Never before in the history of the world has life expectancy of any large number of people increased 40 percent in a quarter-century.

Question: The more people there are, the bigger the problem becomes, doesn't it?

Answer: It does in one sense but not in another. Almost 12 years ago, I began to talk about the problem of population. We were absolutely right in recognizing it as an extremely important problem. But we were wrong in believing in too simplistic a solution, which was that if you supplied the world with contraceptives, the problem would be taken care of. But that is not the case.

It's a supply-and-demand problem. In terms of supply, you've got to have appropriate contraceptive services if fertility is going to be reduced on any broad scale. But you must also have a demand for their use, or not much is going to happen.

Reducing Population

One of the things that research has revealed is that there is a direct correlation between the percentage of females that have passed through primary school and the desire for small families. And there is also a direct correlation between fertility rates and life expectancy.

In India, for example, in order to be fairly sure that a male child would survive into his parents' old age, you needed statistically 6.7 births per woman throughout her reproductive years. And actual births were around 6.8. Obviously, the number of births was at least partly a function of parents' desire to have a male child to help take care of them in their later years.

"I am... pleading for additional economic support for the less developed countries."

If you can reduce infant mortality and increase life expectancy, there will be a marked change in the desire for large families. So the improvement of life expectancy—immensely desirable in itself—also has a beneficial effect on fertility reduction.

Question: You're saying aid is working—

Answer: Yes. Now, having said that, I want to emphasize that one has to insist on good management of scarce aid resources. We're proud of our efficiency in the World Bank. And one of the things I think we have proved is that you can be a hardheaded investor. You can demand efficiency in the investment of capital while at the same time being sensitive to social advance and social objectives and social values.

Question: Americans, as a whole, probably believe that they have given more aid than others and ask why they should do more—

Answer: Yes, they do believe that, but they're not fully correct. They're wrong to believe that they have done more over the last decade and that they shouldn't do more now.

No other industrial nation today, with the single exception of Italy, is doing as little in relation to the size of its population and the level of its income as the United States. Official development assistance by the U.S. amounted to 0.19 percent of gross national product in 1979. That is on the order of $20 per capita. Now, that's very little out of a GNP of about $10,000 per capita. A substantial portion of that, by the way, is really directed to security purposes—to Israel and other countries that do not fall in the category of low-income countries.

Giving More Aid

The average of all other industrialized nations, excluding the U.S., is 0.42 percent—more than double what we do. Yet our income per capita is higher, on average, than the others. In a speech at Harvard a few months ago, former Secretary of State Vance called the U.S. effort disgraceful. And Secretary of State Muskie has made the same point. I certainly believe they're right.

Question: Do Americans confuse our military assistance with development assistance?

Answer: Absolutely. And it's a confusion that contributes in part to the belief that we're doing more than we should. In every single poll I've ever seen on this subject, people invariably say we're doing five or 10 times more than we are. The other part of the problem is that they also believe that in a time of inflation, at a time of high unemployment and at a time when the federal government is—and should be—operating under substantial fiscal constraints, the U.S. should simply not try to do more.

Time to Do More

I contend that's wrong. It is a time to do more. If we don't do more, we are going to be in worse shape economically than we are. And we're going to have to face all of those social and political problems in the developing world I mentioned earlier.

Question: Why do you say that?

Answer: Consider the deflationary impact of our doing less. Today, there exists in the capital-surplus oil-exporting countries—members of the Organization of Petroleum Exporting Countries—roughly 100 billion dollars more in surplus capital than existed two years ago. Those surpluses aren't going to be buried in the sand. They're going to move into the money markets of the world.

If they do not move into productive investment in the developed or developing countries, the surpluses will have a deflationary impact on the whole world. I'ts absolutely essential to the developed economies that those surpluses be put to work. One way to put them to work is to use a modest portion of them for development assistance.

Question: What's the answer to this complaint: Why should we send millions of dollars to a country that I've never heard of when hundreds of thousands of people in the U.S. are in deep poverty?

Answer: My response is this: If the U.S. as a nation restricts this market of 2.25 billion people in the developing world—3.25 billion, if China is included—if it holds back their advance, it is going to sell fewer goods and have fewer jobs in this country. There's just no question about it. One out of every 7 manufacturing jobs in the U.S. depends on foreign trade. One out of every 3 farm acres is producing for export. More than 25 percent of U.S. exports are going to these oil-importing developing countries.

Hundreds of thousands of U.S. jobs depend on their growing markets.

Growing Markets

Manufacturers like Caterpillar or Ford know this. They know where their markets are. The markets that are growing the fastest are the markets in these 100 developing countries with 2.25 billion people.

Question: No farmer in Bangladesh is going to buy a Caterpillar tractor, is he?

Answer: Well, the farmer in Bangladesh is beginning to produce more. Henry Kissinger called Bangladesh a basket case. It's not a basket case today.

It's still in great difficulty. There are 90 million people in Bangladesh in 50,000 square miles—which is the size of the state of Florida—and two thirds of Bangladesh is alternately flooded or arid. There is high infant mortality, high illiteracy, high malnutrition and low life expectancy. But that economy is growing.

We believe that in the next five years Bangladesh will increase its food output by roughly a third. When they do that, they will be able to buy more from the U.S. Their imports are rising substantially every year. Where do those imports come from? They come from the developed world.

Question: What is the World Bank doing to recycle oil money?

Answer: In the simplest of terms, the World Bank is recycling it by increasing its lending. Those surplus funds flow into the world's money markets, and the World Bank borrows them for relending. In the year that ended June 30, the total financial commitments of the World Bank group were 12 billion dollars. In 1985, they're planned for 20 billion—an 8-billion-dollar-per-year increase in commitments in these five years. That is a major contribution to the recycling.

Question: Haven't the Arabs been reluctant to go along with that?

Answer: The Arabs are very anxious to see these funds recycled. They understand it is in their broader interests. They have played a growing role in what I'll call "direct recycling"—providing direct aid themselves to the developing countries—but there are some who would like them to do even more.

Question: Some critics contend that countries get excessively dependent upon foreign aid—

Answer: If aid sources—whether it be the World Bank, the U.S. or others—permit that, they should be severely criticized. I don't believe the World Bank has. One bit of evidence that it hasn't is that in 35 years the Bank hasn't lost a single dollar on either its soft or hard loans.

Countries do recognize that they must use World Bank loans productively and that they must repay them—and repay them on time. We insist on it.

Question: Are there any prospects that the Communist countries will give more aid to the very poor countries?

Answer: You'd have to address that question to them. Today, aid by the Soviet bloc is so small it's virtually not measurable. It's roughly 0.04 percent of their GNP.

Robert McNamara headed the World Bank from 1968 to 1980. He was secretary of defense during the Vietnam era under Presidents Kennedy and Johnson.

"As long as [oppressive] governments receive outside support in the form of economic and military aid and trade, they can more effectively resist reforms."

US Foreign Aid Hinders the Impoverished

Frances Moore Lappe, Joseph Collins, and David Kinley

Question: Doesn't our economic aid have a moderating influence on a repressive foreign government? A cutoff of U.S. aid would appear to doubly punish the poor who live under a repressive regime.

Answer: Unfortunately, history teaches us that this rationale for continuing aid is based on a fallacy—that U.S. official aid can promote economic advances for the poor where political rights are systematically denied. It cannot.

The plight of the poor majority in a country like Indonesia, a major recipient of U.S. aid, confirms this fact. Even the *Wall Street Journal* notes that an economic advance for Indonesia's poor depends on a "realignment of power in the villages." This is unlikely to happen, notes the *Journal*, as long as "the government won't even allow the landless to organize pressure groups." Political rights and economic rights cannot be seen as distinct.

Moreover, we must never lose sight of the fact that the very government that denies people both economic assets and political rights and violates their human rights is also the government that aid officials *must* collaborate with if they want to operate in that country. As well as giving material support, official aid gives that government credibility. As noted development economist Gunnar Myrdal comments, "It is with the people in this elite that all business has to be concluded. Even aid has to be negotiated through them." The effect, says Myrdal, is that "the power of the ruling elite...is then backed up." In part for this reason he concludes that aid from the industrial countries has "undoubtedly strengthened the inegalitarian economic and social power structure in the underdeveloped countries that stands as the main impediment to institutional reforms."

Aid Interfere with Reform

As long as such governments receive outside support in the form of economic and military aid and trade, they can more effectively resist reforms essential to equitable development, rather than inducing positive changes. In Nicaragua, for example, $300 million in U.S. aid to Somoza's narrowly based, oppressive government set the stage for an even more bloody and destructive confrontation. In 1978-1979, Somoza's National Guard, armed principally by the United States, leveled so much of the country in genocidal combat against the overwhelming majority of the Nicaraguan people that decades are needed to rebuild.

In 1980, in El Salvador, we are seeing a tragic repetition. While every report from that country describes the bloody repression, President Carter is trying to increase economic and military aid to the ruling junta. The Carter administration's rationale is that aid is needed to prevent chaos and to carry out the announced land reform. In 1980, however, Amnesty International issued a report accusing the Salvadoran government of using its land reform as a pretext for attacking the peasants, especially those involved in grassroots peasant organizations. While the Salvadoran government claims to have sent troops to the countryside to occupy the plantations it is expropriating, Amnesty International has charged that the troops are brutally murdering peasants and children. In February 1980, Archbishop Oscar A. Romero, El Salvador's leading church figure, widely known as a conservative, pleaded for a withholding of all U.S. aid until reforms were enacted. "The United States should understand the armed forces' position is in favor of the oligarchy. It is brutally repressive and while it does not change, the aid should not be given." Only weeks after this statement, Archbishop Romero was murdered.

Frances Moore Lappe, Joseph Collins and David Kinley. *Aid As Obstacle*, a Food First Book published by the Institute for Food and Development Policy, 1885 Mission St., San Francisco, CA 94103. Reprinted by permission.

When Aid Is Suspended

The U.S. government clings to regimes that favor U.S. corporate and military interests—no matter how brutally those regimes repress their own people—until they appear on the verge of collapse. Only then, perhaps, is aid suspended in an effort to promote a "moderate" solution that protects the structural status quo.

Ever since the U.S. Marines helped to install the Somoza family in state power in 1933, the Nicaraguan government has been known as one of the world's most notorious human rights violators. Yet in fiscal 1978, the Carter administration tripled what AID calls its "resource flow" to Somoza's Nicaragua. Even after popular armed uprisings began in early 1978, the Carter administration fought to maintain the level of funding for fiscal year 1979, and also sponsored a $32 million Inter-American Development Bank loan.

"The same multinational corporations that collaborate with aid institutions to develop electric power also manufacture electric appliances."

Only in the fall of 1978, following prolonged strikes of workers and business owners in a near-successful popular insurrection led by the Sandinista National Liberation Front, did President Carter finally suspend aid to Somoza. The suspension merely interrupted the planning of new projects. It allowed all AID project funds "in the pipeline," as well as the 11-member U.S. military advisory group, to continue. As Somoza's prospects for remaining in power dimmed during the liberation struggle which lasted more than one year, Carter administration officials tried in vain to identify an alternative group of leaders who could maintain "somozismo" without Somoza.

On Whose Side?

So far we have discussed the U.S. government's persistent support of repressive regimes. Further evidence that the U.S. government puts its weight against genuine reform can be compiled from a review of recent cases in which the United States has cut off aid just when meaningful structural reforms are under way.

Thailand. From 1973 to 1976, a civilian Thai government allowed peasants to organize for land and other agrarian reforms. The Farmers Federation of Thailand, founded in 1974, united one and one-half million farmers in a movement with great potential strength. Workers' organizations succeeded in doubling the minimum wage. During this period, AID sharply curtailed economic assistance and even

prepared to eliminate it. Under the civilian regimes, only U.S. *military* assistance to Thailand grew, expanding threefold.

In 1976, a military coup brought to power a government that brutally repressed workers, peasants, students, and religious groups who had been pressuring for progressive reforms. Many Americans remember the moving television and news magazine coverage of the ruthless police attacks on those resisting the military coup. Few Americans know, however, that the weapons used were supplied under the U.S.-funded Narcotics Control Program. After the military coup, AID's program in Thailand suddenly expanded sevenfold. While visiting Thailand in early 1978, we discovered AID's programs concentrated in the provinces which the military regime has designated "sensitive" due to ongoing resistance.

Chile. Economic aid was denied to the civilian government, elected in 1970, which sought to implement in an electoral and democratic manner the very reforms U.S. aid agencies *talk* about. U.S. aid was immediately restored in 1973, after a military junta overthrew the elected and increasingly popular government. Since that time, the military junta has ruthlessly taken millions of acres of land from peasants and sought to wipe out any dissent against its policies.

Nicaragua today. In early 1980, as the Nicaraguan government began to carry out an ambitious literacy campaign—to re-orient basic social services such as health care toward the needs of the majority and to deliberate on the most just and effective type of agrarian reform—the U.S. Congress debated whether or not to give aid to Nicaragua. After lengthy debate, aid was finally approved by five votes but at this date still hangs in limbo because of a general freeze on new appropriations. At one stage, the legislation included a stipulation that aid would be cut off unless democratic elections were held. In the final version of the bill, the President was instructed to "encourage" elections in Nicaragua. Few Americans are prepared to ask why Congress agonized over aid to Nicaragua today when aid to Nicaragua was hardly questioned while Somoza was in power. And why does massive aid flow without reservation to autocrats such as Marcos in the Philippines?

Unspoken but Understood

The truth is that however abhorrent such regimes are to most Americans, they share common interests with U.S. corporate lobbyists and foreign policy decisionmakers.

Governments in the Philippines, South Korea, Indonesia and similar regimes provide a "favorable climate" for multinational corporate investments which provides few, if any, restrictions on import, export, pricing and profit-repatriation activities. Countries with such governments have become sources of raw materials and low-paid, unorganized labor upon which ever-expanding corporate profits depend. Such regimes also welcome U.S. foreign military installations, partly as a guarantor of their own police states. To refuse to support repressive regimes such as those we have been describing would be to risk supporting democratic economic alternatives. Initiatives such as those in Nicaragua today pose a threat to powerful interests in the United States, both directly in terms of corporate investments and indirectly in terms of a potential example of people actively engaged in redistribution of economic and political power.

Question: If more of U.S. development aid were channeled through multilateral lending institutions such as the World Bank, wouldn't that solve the problem of our aid dollars being used for narrow foreign policy and corporate purposes?

Answer: International agencies are often seen as neutral since they are supposedly not beholden to any single government. The World Bank goes to considerable lengths to publicize its "professional" (implying "apolitical") stance. A brief examination of country loan allocations by the World Bank, however, suggests that it is no more partial to the resource, investment and security interests of multinational corporations and the governments they strongly influence than are the U.S. bilateral programs.

While 75 countries received loans from the World Bank in FY 1979, a mere 10 of them received over 56 percent of the total. Five governments among the 10 top recipients of U.S. bilateral economic aid are also among the 10 top World Bank recipients. They are Egypt, Indonesia, India, the Philippines, and Turkey. Only *two* of the Bank's 10 top loan recipients were countries the Bank classifies as "low income."

The majority of the Bank's leading recipients, governments such as those of Indonesia, Brazil, Mexico, South Korea, the Philippines and Colombia, are notorious for their neglect of policies helpful to the poor. In Africa south of the Sahara, the Bank's most favored country has been Nigeria—one of the higher-income African nations—where substantial revenues from its 1970s oil boom were squandered on the military, elite-oriented education, imports of luxury consumer goods, and prestige building projects of no benefit to the poor.

Human Rights

The World Bank also shows no to 14 countries on human rights grounds while approving 35 loans *to the very same countries.* The approved loans were said to meet basic needs or were granted because human rights conditions were said to be improving. The U.S. negative votes were meaningless anyway because all the loans to the 14 named human rights violators were ultimately approved.

Sometimes the U.S. voting pattern seems quite arbitrary. In the case of Boukassa's Central African Empire, the U.S. director at the African Development Bank thought a roads project deserved approval on "basic needs" grounds, despite acknowledged gross human rights violations. At the same time, the U.S. director at the Inter-American Development Bank voted not to fund roads in rights-violators Chile and Uruguay. Roads for the Chung Hee Park martial law government in South Korea were approved by the U.S. director at the Asian Development Bank. A program for irrigation in the Philippines was awarded by the U.S. director at the Asian Development Bank on basic needs grounds; he was directed to vote against the same type of program for Vietnam.

At other times it is clear that the political interests of the major western powers controlling the World Bank hold sway. To insure congressional passage of new appropriations for the Bank, Robert McNamara promised Vietnam's adversaries in the U.S. Congress that no new loans would be extended to Vietnam during fiscal year 1980. McNamara rationalized his move by declaring that the Vietnamese government was not capable of carrying out development programs. Yet it was clear to all that he was bowing to the interests of those wanting to punish the Vietnamese for their role in overthrowing the Pol Pot regime in neighboring Cambodia. By contrast, neither members of the U.S. Congress nor McNamara ever suggested that a similar cutoff should be applied to Tanzania after it invaded Uganda.

The World Bank does not operate fundamentally differently than U.S. bilateral assistance programs. Its loan decisions, including human rights restrictions, are manipulated to reward or to punish regimes according to narrowly defined policy interests of the U.S. (and other economically dominant governments). By "narrowly defined" we mean shaped by the interests of multinational corporations, Cold War rivalry, and hostility to any potentially threatening contrast to the concentrated power structure that has taken hold of the United States.

Question: Doesn't U.S. foreign aid go predominantly to agriculture and rural development?

Answer: Listening to top policymakers of Aid and the World Bank, one would certainly think so. In statements to Congress and to the public, they stress that since the early 1970s significantly greater portions of their program funds have been earmarked for agriculture, nutrition and rural development projects.

Appropriate Terminology

Rather than a redirection of development programs, we have discovered renamed development programs. With the American public increasingly concerned about hunger and some members of Congress questioning AID critically, AID has been careful to develop an "appropriate terminology." In recent AID presentations to Congress, for instance, an ever-wider range of projects is included under the program heading "Food and Nutrition." Many AID officials boast that over half of the agency's project funds now go for "Food and Nutrition." What we have discovered is that AID has turned "Food and Nutrition" into a catch-all category to include almost anything it finances outside the boundaries of major urban areas: electrification, roads, agricultural institutions and even "satellite application and training."

Electrification as "Food and Nutrition"

AID now lists electrification projects under the "Food and Nutrition" funding category. Rural electrification projects account for 40 percent of AID's "Food and Nutrition" lending in Asia.

Does rural electrification benefit the poor? According to AID's own studies the rural poor themselves generally rank electrification very low on their list of priorities. One useful report prepared, in fact, for AID, draws upon studies carried out in Central America, Colombia and the Philippines. The author, Judith Tendler, reaches this conclusion: "Impact studies of rural electrification consistently find that the *household users of rural electricity are the better off among the rural population.* This is not surprising, since household electricity usage requires expenditures for hookups, wiring, monthly consumption, and for the purchase of appliances." (emphasis added.) Tendler notes that the only way for a rural electric utility to be financially viable may well be by targeting appliance-using customers. Since rural electrification is more costly than urban, "...a rural utility will have to promote electricity consumption even more aggressively than the urban utility." If such is the case, "then rural electrification may not be conducive to having its impact directed to the rural poor," concluded Tendler.

Tendler also questions AID's promotion of central system supply as opposed to rural electrification through independent diesel generators. She stresses that central systems require management skills that are scarce in underdeveloped countries and that the impact of inevitable periodic breakdown is greatly magnified in a central system. "Unfortunately," observes Tendler, "the biggest argument against autogeneration [independent diesel units] is that it is easier for AID to finance a big capital project than lots of little ones."

Because of the evidence that household electrification schemes fail to help the poor, Tendler suggests that priority might be given to nonhousehold uses; i.e., rural light industries, but she doubts that AID should subsidize it. She notes that employment-generating effects may not be what they are often assumed to be and that the return to the entrepreneur is so great that no subsidies are needed to induce such use of electricity. Our own interviews with AID officials in Asia give substance to these doubts.

Rather than providing jobs to the poor, rural electrification appears to be threatening jobs.

Indonesia

One $36 million project that draws on funds earmarked for "Food and Nutrition" is Rural Electrification I. The U.S. Congress is told that "all" of the two million people in the area will benefit from "increased economic activity." This claim strongly contrasts with the assessment made by the chief of the AID agricultural office in Indonesia when we interviewed him about the likely impact. He predicted that the better-off landholders and shopowners would use the electricity to mill rice mechanically. When asked about the impact it would have on the millions of landless laborers, especially women, who depend on milling work for survival income, he stated that the project's net impact would be fewer jobs for the poor. (The conversion from the hand pounding to mechanical hulling of rice is already well under way on the island of Java. According to the *Wall Street Journal,* new techniques have already eliminated 133 million work days and $50 million in income per year for the landless women of the island.)

"Roads can facilitate the exploitation of an area's natural resources—not for the benefit of the local inhabitants, but for local elites and foreign corporate interests."

Without jobs, people go hungry. Electrification categorized as "Food and Nutrition" may be cruel irony indeed.

Who are the beneficiaries of rural electrification in Indonesia? One clue is that AID has suggested to the state power authority that it use monies in the housewiring fund, once rolled over, to finance consumer purchases of electric appliances. The same multinational corporations that collaborate with aid institutions to develop electric power also manufacture electric appliances.

Bangladesh

AID is lending $50 million to Bangladesh for rural electrification. This makes rural electrification its second largest program in the country. One of its main uses will be to power irrigation pumps. Who will benefit? Those who own pumps. Who owns the pumps? A small, already better-off group of farmers. The pumps will increase their income, making it possible, indeed probable, that they will expand their holdings and mechanize to the detriment of the small landholders and landless job seekers.

Moreover, as in Indonesia, rural electricity will rapidly lead to the displacement of the hand milling of rice by centralized power-operated mills. At present, 80 percent of all rice produced in Bangladesh is processed in a way that provides about 50 days employment for rural women between the ages of 10 and 49, according to a study by the Bangladeshi government. The same study reveals that most of those so employed are in families in the bottom socio-economic third of the rural population.

AID's own evaluations of rural electrification schemes in Costa Rica and Colombia reveal a clear pattern: benefits accrue to the already better-off who are owners of land, mills and dairy operations, not to the poor.

The AID rationale for such large lending for electrification in Bangladesh and other countries—and for the use of such a large part of the local "counterpart" funds—is that electrification will stimulate the development of rural industries. It is presumed in project plans that textile and food processing plants will be built and provide jobs for the rural poor, 40 percent of whom are now jobless. Since these plants, however, could not compete with other Asian-based factories in the production of export goods and since most of the people in the countryside are too poor even to buy adequate food, who will constitute a profitable market for consumer goods the plants would produce? Rural industry cannot prosper when the distribution of wealth and, therefore, income is skewed as it is in Bangladesh, Indonesia, and Pakistan where AID is pushing ahead with sizable new rural electrification projects. Only with reasonably equitable participation in the economy—primarily made possible through a genuine sharing of control over agricultural resources—can rural electrification serve to build rural industries integrated into the rhythms of agricultural work and oriented toward improved agricultural equipment as well as basic consumer goods for rural people.

In our experience, AID officials, when questioned, concede that a focus on rural electrification as a way to help the poor and hungry is illogical. They then grasp for straws that might justify their huge commitment of funds. One frustrated AID official proffered that rural electrification in Bangladesh would provide the amenities which could "induce government bureaucrats to go out into the countryside."

Rural Roads

AID's "Food and Nutrition" category also covers road projects. Here are just a few road projects AID classifies under "Food and Nutrition":

• Pakistan, "Rural Roads Phase II." $100 million in "Food and Nutrition" funds. The project will build or rehabilitate 1,600 miles of roads. The construction cost per mile is $62,500, a sure signal that construction is big on machinery and short on jobs.

Each advisor will cost $7,500 per month. AID notes that its longer-term plan is to assist in constructing or rehabilitating a total of 120,000 miles of rural roads in Pakistan. Based on the cost of its present program, this would mean over $7 billion of AID "Food and Nutrition" funds going to roads in Pakistan! AID describes the beneficiaries of this roads project: "Rural families of all income strata will benefit from the project, but the selection criteria for the roads will ensure that the majority of the beneficaries will be low-income farmers and the rural poor."

• Haiti, "Road Maintenance II." $8.6 million in "Food and Nutrition" funds "to expand and strengthen the Government of Haiti's National Highway Maintenance Service."

• Liberia, "Rural Roads Phase III." $5.2 million in "Food and Nutrition" funds.[19] According to two investigators from the University of Washington, this new interregional highway "will make it more convenient for Firestone (a massive rubber plantation operator) vehicles to traverse the country, but its relationship to the small farmers' economic and social benefits, the avowed goal, is non-existent."

• Bangladesh. Rural roads will cost an incredible $133,000 per mile, roughly 10 times more than the lowet cost rural roads project in comparable countries. Again, it is a "Food and Nutrition" project.

Building rural roads certainly sounds neutral, even beneficial. Yet we have come to understand in country after country that new roads in the context of sharp rural inequalities and a repressive government can harm the poor. Those who benefit most from rural roads are the larger commercial growers for whom better roads help in getting their crops to the cities and ports more efficiently. The middleman who buys from the poor and is fortunate enough to own some kind of truck can also make his operation more lucrative with the help of better roads. (In most rural areas the middleman already profits more on each unit than the peasant who produces the crop.) Moreover, in countries such as the Philippines, Zaire, Thailand and Guatemala where dictatorships attempt to quell rural resistance, rural roads make it easier to move troops and maintain control. Rural roads also open the countryside to those selling factory-made consumer items and processed foods, especially bottled soft drinks and beer. A boom in such novelties can destroy the market for more nutritious local food as well as the livelihood of village craftspeople. Finally, in countries controlled in the interests of a few, roads can facilitate the exploitation of an area's natural resources—not for the benefit of the local inhabitants, but for local elites and foreign corporate interests.

Frances Moore Lappe, Joseph Collins, and David Kinley are members of the Institute for Food and Development Policy.

"The administration's adoption of democracy as a substitute for personal rights. . .can only be interpreted as a cynical artifice to. . .leave the victims of oppression to their fate."

viewpoint **23**

Human Rights Must Be a US Priority

Charles Maechling Jr.

Human rights are in trouble. So obsessed is the Reagan administration with left-wing insurgencies in Latin America and the machinations of the Soviet Union and Cuba that it has not hesitated to twist through redefinition the traditional meaning of human rights and to ignore violations by so-called friendly regimes that flout both internationally recognized standards of behavior and the specific priorities of U.S. law. In El Salvador and Guatemala the administration's acquiescence in practices of torture and mass murder by client governments comes perilously close to endorsement of offenses condemned at the Nuremberg War Crimes Tribunals —specifically, the indiscriminate killing, torture, and secret detention of unarmed civilians for their political sympathies or support of resistance movements.

To understand this phenomenon one must first understand the problem the Reagan administration faced when it took office. Legislation on the books since 1973, as well as a whole range of international agreements, condemned internationally recognized human rights violations and raised formidable moral and legal barriers against assistance to precisely the dictatorial regimes the new administration wished to befriend. Section 116(a) of the Foreign Assistance Act of 1961, as amended, states: "No assistance may be provided. . .to the government of any country which engages in a consistent pattern of gross violations of internationally recognized human rights. . .unless such assistance will directly benefit the needy people of such country."

Section 502B requires the termination or reduction of security assistance and military sales to "any country, the government of which engages in a consistent pattern of gross violations of

internationally recognized human rights." Section 701 of the International Financial Institutions Act of 1977 subjects recipients of loans from the World Bank (International Bank for Reconstruction and Development) and other international financial institutions to virtually the same requirements. Beyond this, Congress has at various times enacted country-specific legislation embargoing or severely restricting security assistance to notorious violators.

Legislation Straightforward

The legislation is unequivocal in definitional intent. Section 116(a) of the Foreign Assistance Act defines gross violations of internationally recognized human rights as follows:

> . . .torture or cruel, inhuman, or degrading treatment or punishment, prolonged detention without charges, causing the disappearance of persons by the abduction and clandestine detention of those persons, or other flagrant denial of the right to life, liberty, and the security of the person. . . .

Section 502B repeats the definition of Section 116(a). Substantially the same definition appears in Section 112, covering agricultural sales, and in Section 701 and 703 of the International Financial Institutions Act. This language is unaffected by the recent Supreme Court decision abolishing the legislative veto.

In contrast to flagrant disregard of this legislation by the Nixon and Ford administrations, the Carter administration made human rights a key ingredient in its foreign policy and tried to apply the law's provisions as evenhandedly as competing considerations would permit. Its record was far from satisfactory, however. During four years in office—a period covering the worst excesses in Argentina, and among the worst in Guatemala and the former Portuguese colony of East Timor—a relatively small number of governments were viewed as having been "engaged in a consistent pattern of gross violations." Security assistance was cut off to even fewer countries—eight in Latin America: Argentina, Bolivia, El Salvador, Guatemala, Haiti, Nicaragua, Paraguay, and Uruguay. Moreover, the Carter rhetoric was so enthusiastic about the full range of human rights as to display no sense of priorities. Statements of administration spokesmen, including the president himself, tended to treat all rights as equal and all violations as equally repugnant, putting censorship and economic privation in the same class as torture and murder. Nevertheless, the Carter administration at least made an effort to enforce the law and did so publicly and vocally when private diplomacy failed.

The New Bench Mark

Even the inconsistent approach of the Carter administration, however, put the foreign-policy agenda of the Reagan administration at risk, especially in Latin America. The reason was obvious: Taken literally, U.S. human rights legislation would render indefensible the Reagan program for mending fences with notorious violators, such as the military dictators of Argentina, Chile, and Guatemala. If the definitional priorities of the Foreign Assistance Act were allowed to stand, Marxist governments with repressive but by no means murderous human rights records, such as Poland or Czechoslovakia, would show up as no worse than nominal democracies, such as South Korea or the Philippines; and Nicaragua's Sandinistas would certainly compare favorably with the murderous regimes of Guatemala or El Salvador. Moreover, primary focus on security of the person would make it difficult to pursue another political objective: identifying the Soviet Union as the supreme malefactor in the field of human rights.

"The authoritarian-totalitarian distinction soon collapsed under the weight of its insensitivity to right-wing atrocities."

Thus even before the Reagan administration took office, its more zealous ideologues were groping for a formula to emasculate the law while at the same time satisfying American political idealism. A first try was made by U.S. Ambassador to the United Nations Jeane Kirkpatrick and Ernest Lefever, President Ronald Reagan's initial choice to head the State Department's human rights bureau. They proposed a distinction between "traditional authoritarian" regimes and "totalitarian" regimes: The totality of regimentation in a socialist state, even if nonviolent in the conventional sense, was worse than the kidnapping, torture, mutilation, and murder of unarmed men, women, and children at the hands of the government death squads in a traditional authoritarian state. Kirkpatrick's article on human

rights in the November 1979 issue of *Commentary* magazine omitted all reference to the shocking crimes habitually perpetrated by Latin American dictators and military juntas. "Traditional autocrats," she contended, ignoring the daily abductions and murders in Argentina, "do not disturb the habitual rhythms of work and leisure, habitual places of residence, habitual patterns of family and personal relations."

Insensitive Distinctions

The authoritarian-totalitarian distinction soon collapsed under the weight of its insensitivity to right-wing atrocities. With public and congressional attention increasingly focused on the horrors in El Salvador, a new formulation surfaces when then Under Secretary of State Richard Kennedy sent an "eyes only," six-page memorandum to the secretary of state in October 1981. "Congressional belief that we have no consistent human rights policy," wrote Kennedy, "threatens to disrupt important foreign-policy initiatives.... Human rights has become one of the main avenues for domestic attack on the administration's foreign policy." The administration, argued Kennedy, should take the offensive and make human rights "the core of our foreign policy" by redefining them as "political rights." Human rights— meaning political rights and civil liberties," he contended, "conveys what is ultimately at issue in our contest with the Soviet bloc." He urged the State Department to "draw this distinction and to persuade others of it."...

The first year of the Reagan administration saw a concentrated campaign by Kirkpatrick and others to set the turmoil in Latin America in an East-West matrix and to whitewash the human rights violations of right-wing dictatorships. In a January 1981 article in *Commentary*, Kirkpatrick described the insurgents in El Salvador as "revolutionaries trained, armed, and advised by Cuba." In a later speech she asserted: "(R)evolutions in our times are caused not by social injustice." Michael Novak, the administration's delegate to the 37th and 38th sessions of the U.N. Human Rights Commission in Geneva, Switzerland, cast the sole vote to exonerate the military government of Argentina for its role in effecting the "disappearances" of thousands of civilians, including nuns, schoolgirls, and small children, who were abducted, tortured, and murdered by government death squads.

Human Rights Violations

The new assistant secretary of state for human rights and humanitarian affairs, Elliott Abrams, followed suit. When asked in a tape-recorded interview, "Which do you consider higher on the scale of human rights violations—torture, murder, and the destruction of innocent human life, or a regimented society?" he replied: "The first group of human rights violations are the personal rights, which would include torture, murder, detention, that kind of thing, ones that are done to your body." But in passing judgment on violators he stated that much would depend on their political progress. "What are the chances that we could move to a really Western-style, laudable democracy in Country X quickly. . . . For example, what portion of the population in Country X, a Third World country, a Latin American country, if you will, is killed or tortured? It will vary, of course, it is not 100 per cent; whereas, in a communist country the portion of the population whose political and civil rights are destroyed of course is 100 per cent because it is a dictatorship."

The administration also changed the basis of its reports to Congress. U.S. human rights legislation requires preparation of an annual State Department publication entitled Country Reports on Human Rights Practices, which is supposed to summarize the Department's evaluation of the human rights record of each actual or prospective recipient of military and economic assistance. The introduction to the 1982 volume, which covers calendar year 1981 and is therefore the first prepared by the Reagan administration, does conform to the definitional priorities of Section 116 in listing: ". . .first, the right to be free from governmental violations of the integrity of the person." But having said this, the introduction artfully shifts the focus. The rights themselves are declared to originate in democratic political institutions. "Political participation is not only an important right in itself, but also the best guarantee that other rights will be observed." Another section of the introduction keys violations exclusively to the rise of totalitarian regimes. Since two of the three examples listed—Nazi Germany and Fascist Italy—are defunct, only the Soviet Union remains as a target.

No Compassion for Victims

More recent pronouncements by Abrams and Kirkpatrick follow the guidelines of the Country Reports and the Kennedy memorandum. One looks in vain for any vestige of outrage over atrocities or compassion for victims in Kirkpatrick's speeches on human rights. Filled with turgid philosophizing about the nature of freedom, larded with pedantic references to Edmund Burke and Georg Wilhelm Friedrich Hegel, they ignore the appalling catalogue of contemporary abuses and treat all violations as a function of political rights. Asked by a reporter what the words "human rights" meant to her, Kirkpatrick replied: "Basically I think about fundamental political freedoms—free speech, free press, rule of law, due process." Abrams took the same line in the tape-recorded interview: "That's the thing. You could make the argument that there aren't many countries where there are gross and consistent human rights violations except the communist countries because

they have the system itself. It is certainly a plausible way of reading the statute."

The administration's strategy of insisting that political rights are the key to personal rights is reflected in its emphasis on "free elections." Kirkpatrick's praise for the elections in El Salvador in her November 4, 1982, speech on the subject failed to mention the absence of opposition candidates and voters' fears that the use of registration techniques might reveal their choice. Abrams added: "But free elections are not simply a human rights goal. They are also the means which will guarantee that other human rights are also respected. . . .This is why free elections should be the very heart of the human rights movement."

Definitional Confusion

Neither the language nor the legislative history of U.S. human rights legislation indicates any congressional intent to redefine human rights in political terms. Nevertheless, the administration's campaign to de-emphasize security of the person in favor of visionary political goals has achieved some success. The administration has been able to get away with such a distortion of legislative purpose largely because of definitional confusion, the recent origins of human rights as a constituent of foreign policy, and congressional laxity.

> *"Congress has been unbelievably indulgent in allowing the executive branch to evade the law by interpreting human rights to suit its own convenience."*

The term "human rights" is itself a flabby and in precise euphemism, embracing such a wide range of claims as to be almost meaningless. Americans instictively think of human rights in terms of civil liberties within a time-honored constitution and secure rule of law. In their personal experience the worst violations are likely to be police brutality, detention without bail, and denial of voting rights. The average American is unaware of the cheapness of human life in other societies, of the arbitrary powers over life and death enjoyed by security forces, and of the abduction, torture, and mass murder to which governments of other societies so frequently resort in internal conflicts . . . .

Revelation of the Holocaust

It took the Nazi Holocaust, the revelations of Joseph Stalin's purges, and expanding media coverage of horror in other corners of the world to give human rights a permanent niche in the foreign-policy agendas of civilized states. Since 1946 the decisions of the Nuremberg War Crimes Tribunals, insofar as they applied to crimes against humanity, have had the force of international law. The Universal Declaration of Human Rights was adopted by the United Nations in 1948 and was followed by the Genocide Convention, the International Covenant on Civil and Political Rights, the International Covenant on Economic, Social, and Cultural Rights, and a convention on racial discrimination, as well as African, European, and inter-American conventions on human rights. These instruments, together with the rulings and decisions of international and regional courts and commmissions, spell out in detail the internationally recognized human rights acknowledged by U.S. legislation. While it is technically true that within the instruments themselves no single right takes priority over the rest, the order in which they are listed in the universal declaration and in the civil and political convenant accords precedence to rights involving human life and security of the person. U.S. legislation and the external human rights policies of advanced democracies such as Canada, Great Britain, the Scandinavian countries, and Switzerland mirror this common-sense approach.

"The connection between human rights and the outward forms of democracy has been misleading most of all in Latin America."

Congress was at first slow to enforce the humanitarian standards of its own legislation. The original version of Section 502B enacted in 1974, covering security assistance, did no more than express "the sense of Congress." Technically, that wording made the legislation advisory rather than binding, and as such it was contemptuously disregarded by then Secretary of State Henry Kissinger. Only after he submitted a report of compliance in November 1975, while at the same time having a spokesman testify that in no case during the preceding year had the executive branch denied military aid on human rights grounds, did Congress move to tighten the requirement. It first amended Section 502B by making termination of security assistance "the policy of the United States." When that language had no effect, Congress made it a flat requirement in 1978.

But enforcement of the law continues to be weak. Congress has been unbelievably indulgent in allowing the executive branch to evade the law by interpreting human rights to suit its own convenience. In addition, the recent Supreme Court decision on the legislative veto has now almost certainly invalidated Section 617 of the Foreign Assistance Act, which empowers Congress to revoke foreign aid to violators in mid-stream. Apparently the decision does not affect country-specific legislation, which is couched in conditional terms.

A Diplomacy Leading Nowhere

As the Reagan administration enters its third year, where does human rights stand in U.S. foreign policy? From the beginning the administration has insisted that effectiveness is what counts. According to the introduction to the 1982 *Country Reports*, the object is "not to isolate them (friendly countries) for their injustice and thereby render ourselves ineffective, but to use our influence to effect desirable change." An effective "silent diplomacy" is what is supposed to distinguish the Reagan human rights program from that of its predecessor—which, according to Kirkpatrick, alienated "friendly nations" and "enabled anti-Western opposition groups to come to power in Iran and Nicaragua."

The argument sounds plausible, but does the record support it? During the Nixon and Carter administrations, quiet pressure on the Soviet Union did, in fact, lead to a more liberal emigration policy for dissidents and Jews—but this victory was achieved during an era of detente. Under Reagan, silent diplomacy seems to have been instrumental in releasing from prison South Korean opposition leader Kim Dae Jung. Otherwise, the administration has produced no evidence that its human rights policies have been effective. Silent diplomacy conducted with Latin American military juntas—assuming that it has actually been tried—has led nowhere.

A recent Americas Watch report, based on extensive interviews with refugees in southern Mexico by American lawyers and reporters and published in both the *Wall Street Journal* and the *New York Review of Books*, confirms press reports that the regime of former Guatemalan President Efrain Rios Montt undertook a systematic campaign to slaughter Indian villagers viewed as sympathetic to the guerillas, singling out women and children for especially bestial forms of killing. Even Abrams was forced to acknowledge that the situation in Guatemala is "terrible." In El Salvador an investigatory commmission of the Association of the Bar of the City of New York recently reported after an extensive on-site visit: "It is widely acknowledged, both within and without the government, that Salvadoran security forces engage in the practice of abducting civilians from their homes (and, on occasion, places of work or public gathering places), that such persons may expect to be severely tortured and thereafter murdered and that some thirty to forty thousand civilians have been murdered (exclusive of military operations) by security forces over the past three years." Since six leading left-wing politicians were abducted from a press conference and murdered in 1980, virtually the entire Salvadoran left-wing opposition has been killed or driven into exile. To judge from recent massacres in Lebanon and Uganda and from an upsurge of repression in Chile and Uruguay, silent diplomacy does not seem to be working in other corners of the world either.

Carter's Policies Successful

By comparison, the public diplomacy of the Carter administration, with all its imperfections, still wins praise from those with reason to know. Robert Cox, the exiled editor of the *Buenos Aires Herald*, has written that the Carter administration's condemnation of Argentine atrocities, together with then Assistant Secretary of State for Human Rights and Humanitarian Affairs Patricia Derian's private interventions, unquestionably saved lives. Cox's fellow journalist, Jacobo Timerman, after a Senate Foreign Relations Committee hearing on May 19, 1981, made perhaps the ultimate comment: "A silent diplomacy is silence; a quiet diplomacy is surrender."

In the face of such evidence, the administration has resorted to a variety of defensive tactics to justify requests to Congress for military and security assistance to violators. Its standard practice has been to scratch about for signs of progress toward democracy, especially through the panacea of free elections. Unfortunately, in the Third World and particularly Latin America, elections continue to be so riddled with fraud that, with a few honorable exceptions, a formal commitment to elections proves little. Nor is such a commitment or even the temporary existence of constitutional government in itself, a guarantee of fundamental rights. In most of these countries armies and security forces enjoy virtual autonomy and are allowed, even encouraged, to deal ruthlessly with nonviolent political protest— witness the gunning down of 100 demonstrating students in Mexico City before the 1968 Olympics and the virtual genocide of minorities in East Timor and in Bangladesh.

An even more reprehensible tactic has been the administration's campaign to discredit reports of human rights abuses by casting aspersions on victims or questioning the credibility of survivors. The most well-publicized example was Kirkpatrick's insinuation that the American churchwomen who were murdered by Salvadoran security forces deserved their fate because of their alleged political sympathies. Less flagrant, but equally insidious, has been the constant stream of official innuendoes to discredit the reports of the Roman Catholic church, Amnesty International, and other human rights organizations by impugning their political motives. Amnesty International has been a particular target for official denigration despite its inclusion as one of the three humanitarian organizations specifically commended in the Foreign Assistance Act as having special credibility.

Contradicting Testimony

Disparaging the testimony of refugees has been especially vicious. The reaction of Abrams to interviews by lawyers and human rights organizations with refugees that fled government massacres in El Salvador and Guatemala was: "The refugees there are not a representative proportion of the population. Although some are not guerrilla sympathizers, others may be." The suggestion that to establish credibility, refugees must be representative of the population and enamored of their persecutors would come as a surprise to the survivors of Auschwitz.

"Human rights have a way of coming in the back door when shut out from the front."

Superficially more telling has been the administration's contention that human rights organizations concentrate their fire exclusively on governments and ignore atrocities committed by guerrillas and terrorists. In this century, however, the state, with its army and security forces, holds a monopoly of violence in law and in fact. Deaths at the hands of guerrillas and terrorists have been statistically insignificant compared with the mass atrocities perpetrated by governments. The total number of deaths inflicted by resistance or partisan operations in Nazi-occupied Europe was small compared to the 15 million innocent civilians killed by the Gestapo and SS. Virtually all of the countless millions of unnatural deaths during the Stalin era can be attributed to the Soviet state. The civilian toll taken by the Khmer Rouge regime of Cambodia was between 1 and 3 million; by the Indonesian Army in the 1965-1966 massacres of communists, opposition groups, and ethnic Chinese, up to 500,000; by Idi Amin Dada in the small African country of Uganda, up to 300,000....

Misleading Policies in Latin America

The connection between human rights and the outward forms of democracy has been misleading most of all in Latin America. Its most bloodthirsty tyrants—Juan Manuel de Rosas of Argentina (1793-1877), Porfirio Diaz of Mexico (1830-1915), and Juan Vicente Gomez of Venezuela (1857-1935)—each governed under a constitution loaded with guarantees of the rights of man; their successors make a similar parody of democracy today. Thus Article 18 of the Argentine constitution declares that no inhabitant of the country can be punished without trial or arrested without written order, that the residence is inviolate, and that torture and the death penalty for political offenses are forever abolished. Articles 46 through 57 of the Guatemalan constitution spell out elaborate safeguards regarding conditions of interrogation and detention; immunity from arbitrary punishment; exemption from the death penalty for women, minors, and persons guilty of political crimes; and the personal liability of government personnel for violations of civil liberties. Article 7 of the most recent constitution of El Salvador (1962) actually recognizes "the right of the people to insurrection."

The administration's adoption of democracy as a substitute for personal rights not only has no sanction in the express language of the Foreign Assistance Act or its legislative history, but in view of the record can only be interpreted as a cynical artifice to pervert the intent of Congress and leave the victims of oppression to their fate. In a few notorious cases—the Guatemalan army, the Salvadoran National Guard and Treasury Police, the Phalangists in Lebanon—the administration has actually sought to reward the perpetrators of massacre by direct or indirect supply of more up-to-date weaponry, a policy not unlike furnishing gas chambers to Adolf Hitler. To the extent that the United States still stands for human rights at all, the nation is indebted to Congress and especially to the Foreign Operations Subcommittee of the House Appropriations Committee chaired by Representative Clarence Long (D.-Maryland).

The Power of Public Opinion

Still, the crucial question of where human rights fits into American foreign policy remains troublesome. How can commitment to human rights be reconciled with the overriding importance of strategic and geopolitical factors? Man's inhumanity to man has been a constant in human history. Countries cannot tailor their vital interests to reflect the imperfections of other societies. But certain points stand out.

First, the United States has been a beacon of freedom for the oppressed and a leader of humanitarian causes for too long a time to have this asset sacrificed for transitory and perhaps illusory victories over revolutionary movements rooted in circumstances beyond U.S. control. Any association of the United States with despotic regimes and barbaric methods of repression will not only tarnish America's image abroad; in the long run it will be corrosive of its political and humanitarian standards at home.

Second, in all but the rarest cases, the so-called hard choice between human rights and strategic imperatives is a fiction, a transparent scare tactic designed to provoke a paranoiac public reaction. The issue is not whether the United States should play Don Quixote and sally forth to redress the wrongs of the world. It is whether the United States should

comply with its own legislation and humanitarian traditions by refusing to countenance the inhuman practices of its more unsavory friends and clients. Why the United States, the only democratic superpower, should demean itself by catering to the sensibilities of the vicious tyrants who cling to its skirts is a mystery. Such a betrayal of U.S. traditions is a sign of weakness, not strength. There may not be much that the United States can do about distant cases like Argentina, Chile, and Indonesia, but clients closer to home can certainly be told in tough and unambiguous language that unless they conform to civilized standards, U.S. support will not only cease forthwith—it may well be shifted to the other side.

Human Rights an Inconvenience

Achieving such a reversal of approach in the face of a determined administration effort to circumvent the law will not be easy. The State Department is too fixated on relationships with governments to regard human rights as anything but an inconvenience. Congress cannot easily engineer policy changes in a field so clearly the constitutional prerogative of the executive branch. Yet as long as Congress holds the purse strings, it can always set parameters and enforce the law by threatening to cut off funds. Moreover, human rights is one area where the power of public opinion counts.

"Man's inhumanity to man has been a constant in human history."

The Senate Foreign Relations Committee should appoint a subcommittee dedicated solely to human rights and allocate funds for counsel and research staff. Along with the existing House Foreign Affairs Subcommittee on Human Rights and International Organization, this new subcommittee should be given a mandate to investigate and relentlessly expose abuses through open hearings. The focus should be on crimes against humanity and on enforcing present law. If both houses insist on rigorous compliance with their own standards and refuse to authorize assistance to violators, an aroused public can be counted on to support them. Human rights have a way of coming in the back door when shut out from the front.

Charles Maechling Jr. was an international lawyer and State Department advisor for political-military affairs during the Kennedy and Johnson administrations, and is a senior associate of the Carnegie Endowment.

"Attempts to make the world safe for human rights seem to be rooted in the naive view that the rest of the world is malleable, responsive to our wishes, and vulnerable to our threats."

viewpoint **24**

Human Rights Should Not Be a US Priority

Ernest W. Lefever

In the complex arena of world politics there is a widespread tendency to want or even demand more than is possible. Many people have not learned the truth of Otto von Bismarck's words: "Politics is the art of the possible." I am reminded of the insistent lady who said "I'd give my right arm to be ambidextrous." Today, I am addressing the relationship between human rights and foreign policy, a subject that has had more than its share of confusion and conflicting demands.

Three Concepts of Human Rights

Human rights and security are what politics is all about. Fifteen centuries ago Saint Augustine said that if it were not for government, men would devour one another as fishes. But governments often become corrupt, cruel, or tyrannical. When this happens, they are the most monstrous fish of all. Depending on its character, government can be the most effective protector of human rights or the most vicious violator of them. Hence, the struggle for viable and humane government is the heart of politics and ethics.

But there are no human rights without security. Order is the necessary but not sufficient precondition for justice and respect for human dignity. Chaos is the enemy of justice and freedom because it invites the law of the jungle, the survival of the fittest in the most brutal sense of that term.

My hypothesis is that there is no fundamental contradiction between human rights and security, if both of these concerns are properly understood. And neither can be advanced of fulfilled without freedom.

We should distinguish between three frequently confused concepts of human rights. The *first* has more immediate and universal application because it is rooted in the religion and ethics of virtually all

cultures and calls for sanctions against political authorities and others guilty of genocide, brutalizing innocent people, and similar atrocities.

The *second* and more precise concept of human rights is the fruit of the recent Western democratic experience and embraces a wide range of substantive and procedural rights and safeguards. Rights so defined are fully respected in perhaps fewer than a score of states. They include freedom of movement, speech, assembly, press and religion; equality before the law; periodic elections; being considered innocent until proved guilty; a judicial system independent from executive authority; and a variety of safeguards for accused persons. Many of these Western democratic rights are unknown and unattainable in large parts of the world where both history and culture preclude the development of Western-type democratic institutions, and they are often violated in the West itself. There are, however, significant differences in the extent to which human rights, more generally defined, are honored in non-democratic states.

The *third*, are so-called economic and social rights, such as the right to a job or health care. These are really objectives and aspirations, not rights, because they cannot be guaranteed by any government unless it is totalitarian. The price of gaining these "rights" is the sacrifice of freedom itself.

In our global system of sovereign states, there is a profound difference between the domestic and foreign policy of any government. Each government is sovereign only within its territory. In domestic terms, the first task of government is to *govern*, to wield effective control over the territory and to exercise a monopoly over the legitimate use of force within the state. The second task of government is to *govern legitimately*, to exercise power in accordance with the constitution and other laws, including those in effect under a state of emergency. The third task of government is to *govern justly*. Justice, said

Ernest W. Lefever, speech before the World Affairs Council, February 9, 1982.

Aristotle, is giving every man his due, adding that to treat all people equally is to treat some of them injustly. In moral terms, the highest object of government is justice. There are different stages and qualities of justice which define the range of human rights that can be guaranteed by a government.

Government and Foreign Policy

Foreign policy is also an essential task of government, but in sharp contrast to domestic policy, the government is severely constrained by the power and legitimate interests of other states. The external policy of all governments must be concerned primarily with external threats. Its chief object is to defend the territorial and political integrity of the state.

The foreign policy of smaller states seeks to mitigate threats from immediate neighbors by transforming enemies into neutrals and neutrals into allies. To this end, the government uses military, economic, diplomatic, intelligence, and informational instruments.

The foreign policy of large states, particuarly a superpower like the United States or the Soviet Union, is also concerned with national defense, but it has a larger role commensurate with the state's power and influence. It seeks to create an international "order" conducive to its larger purposes. If its purpose is to adust and change the status quo by peaceful means, it will pursue peace and stability.

If it is a revolutionary state, whether Hitler's Germany or Brezhnev's Russia, it will attempt to destabilize "unfriendly regimes" and thus prepare the way for expansion and the imposition of its will on alien peoples.

Hence, foreign policy is concerned about the external environment and its impact on the interest of the state, and domestic policy is concerned about the distribution of authority and freedom, control and consent within the state.

For the United States and all other democratic governments, the principal objective of foreign policy, therefore, is peace, and the principal objective of domestic policy is justice.

Human Rights and National Security

The present world crisis is characterized by a particular manifestation of the ancient struggle between tyranny and freedom, between coercion and consent. The Soviet Union is probably the greatest tyranny of all time. Its leaders are a conspiracy masquerading as a government. Moscow is motivated by utopian and messianic dreams, and is attempting to build a world order in its own image. It employs all "necessary" means—raw military power, threat, propaganda, disinformation, economic measures, subversion, and terrorism. In its view, the objective of a socialist paradise justifies any means that work.

In the face of this totalitarian challenge the United States has a responsibility to maintain interstate stability, to undergird the forces for peaceful change, and to conduct a policy designed to protect the interests and independence of allied and friendly states in Europe and the Third World. In undertaking this complex task, Washington must be concerned simultaneously with its national security, with international stability, and with human rights.

"Authoritarian regimes permit a significantly greater degree of freedom and diversity than totalitarian ones in all spheres—political, cultural, economic and religious."

The Soviet Union and its clients are the major threat to peace, security, and freedom in the world today. Moscow is the greatest violator of fundamental human rights at home and the greatest exporter of human rights abuses abroad. The Kremlin not only oppresses its own citizens but imposes its brutal system on other peoples as in Eastern Europe. It exports that system by direct aggression as in Afghanistan, by proxy forces as in Southeast Asia, Ethiopia, and Angola; by subversion as in Central America; and by terrorism as in the Middle East.

Consequently, in the name of both security and human rights, the United States must develop a military capability sufficient to deter nuclear war and capitulation to nuclear blackmail. In the name of human rights, I support the present Administration's emphasis on upgrading our strategic and conventional military forces, including defensive chemical weapons. This military strength must be buttressed by that of U.S. allies in Europe, Asia, and Latin America.

The foreign policy debate has been confused by a persistent failure to recognize the profound differences between a totalitarian state and an authoritarian state. In terms of political rights, moral freedom, and cultural vitality, there is a great difference between the two types of regimes. Most Asian, African, and Latin American countries are ruled by small elites supported by varying degrees of popular consent. Some are run by brutal tyrants, others by one-party cliques, military juntas, or civilian-military coalitions. Authoritarian regimes permit a significantly greater degree of freedom and diversity than totalitarian ones in all spheres—political, cultural, economic, and religious. Authoritarian rulers often allow opposition parties to operate and a restrained press to publish. Foreign correspondents can usually move about freely and send out uncensored dispatches. These regimes often permit relatively free economic activity and freedom of movement for their citizens.

There is far more freedom of choice, diversity of opinion and activity, and respect for human rights in authoritarian South Korea than in totalitarian North Korea. There is also far more freedom and cultural vitality in Chile than in Cuba.

Another crucial difference is the capacity of authoritarian rule to evolve into democratic rule. This has happened recently in Spain, Portugal, and Greece. In sharp contrast, a Communist dictatorship has never made a peaceful transition to more representative and responsive government.

To put it in its starkest and yet more precise terms, the prison walls in a totalitarian state are coextensive with the borders of the state. Every subject is a prisoner. We need only note the denial of emigration for the Soviet Union and the "wall of shame" in Berlin to dramatize this point.

As the leader of the Free World, the United States should pursue a vigorous and humane foreign policy designed to maintain its own security and that of its allies and to help create a world community that respects diversity and is safe for peaceful development and change. Human rights are an inescapable concern in all our foreign policy decisions because we Americans believe in freedom, justice, and dignity for all peoples.

One Moral Yardstick

Torture, exile under brutal conditions, harsh emigration restrictions, summary executions, and other abuses are reprehensible whether committed by *friend, foe* or *neutral*. There must be only *one* moral yardstick.

"Misguided U.S. policies have helped deliver the people of Iran and Nicaragua into the hands of regimes that show less respect for basic human rights than their less-than-perfect predecessors."

Saying this, we must recognize the limitations of American power and influence and the moral dangers of attempting to reform other peoples or to reshape their institutions. We should not indulge in what Denis Brogan once called "the illusion of American omnipotence," the tendency to overestimate the capacity of our government to mold the external world, particularly domestic developments in other countries. America is powerful, but it is not all-powerful. Our considerable leverage of the 1950s was diminished during the 1960s and has been further eroded by OPEC oil cartel, a weakened economy, the great leap forward in Soviet military might, and our

abandonment of Vietnam.

Quite apart from our limited capacity to influence intractable realities abroad, there is and should be a profound moral constraint on efforts designed to alter domestic practices, institutions, and policies within other states. Neo—Wilsonian attempts to make the world safe for human rights seem to be rooted in the naive view that the rest of the world is malleable, responsive to our wishes, and vulnerable to our threats.

Limited American Influence

The sometimes crusading and paternalistic rhetoric of a Jimmy Carter or a Woodrow Wilson drew upon an idealistic stream in the America character. But there is another and quieter stream, equally honorable, but less pushy and perhaps more persuasive—symbolized by the Biblical parable of a candle upon a stand or a city set upon a hill.

A former Secretary of State, John Quincy Adams, expressed this more modest understanding of American responsibility in 1821, appropriately on the Fourth of July: "Wherever the standard of freedom and independence has been or shall be unfurled, there will be America's heart, her benedictions, and her prayers. But she goes not abroad in search of monsters to destroy. She is the well-wisher to the freedom and independence of all. She is the champion and vindicator only of her own." (Quoted by George Kennan before the Senate Foreign Relations Committee, February 10, 1966.)

The impulse to impose our standards or practices on other societies supported by policies of reward and punishment, leads inevitably to a kind of reform intervention. We Americans have no moral mandate to transform other societies, and we rightly resent such efforts on the part of the totalitarians. There is more than a touch of arrogance in any efforts to alter the domestic behavior of allies, or even of adversaries.

Other states may request assistance from friendly governments on mutually agreed terms. But external forces, however nobly motivated, cannot impose justice, human rights, or freedom on other states without resorting to direct or indirect conquest. It may be possible to "export revolution" as the phrase goes—but we cannot export human rights or respect for the rule of law. Freedom and justice are the fruit of long organic growth nurtured by religious values, personal courage, social restraint, and respect for law. The majesty of law is little understood in traditional societies where ethnic identity or class tends to supersede all other claims on loyalty and obedience.

The United States should also avoid the peril of selective concern for human rights abroad. There are human rights zealots who are more upset about relatively small specific abuses against prisoners in a friendly authoritarian state than they are about massive abuses against the entire population of a hostile totalitarian state. Favorite targets of their moral outrage are countries like Argentina, South Korea, Taiwan, Chile and El Salvador, each an ally of the United States, each pursuing a constructive foreign policy that serves the cause of stability, and each under siege by a totalitarian adversary by direct threat, subversion, or both.

Many human rights activists tend to underestimate the totalitarian threat to the West and the totalitarian temptation in the Third World. Hence, they neglect or trivialize the fundamental political and moral struggle of our time—the protracted conflict between forces of total government based on coercion and the proponents of limited government based on popular consent and humane law.

Four Ways to Serve Freedom

We start with the premise that the United States has a reponsibility equal to its capacity to act and to influence external events, and consistent with the principle of sovereign equality among states. Recognizing our limitations and working in the spirit of John Quincy Adams, there are four appropriate ways the U.S. government and the American people can serve the larger cause of freedom and dignity in the world.

1. First, we can be worthy custodians of the freedom bequeathed us by the Founding Fathers and thus continue to give heart to the aspirations of peoples everywhere. We can give hope to those in bondage by demonstrating what the late Reinhold Niebuhr has called "the relevance of the impossible idea." We can never fully realize our own ideals, but we can strive toward them. In most other cultural settings, full respect for human rights cannot be expected in the foreseeable future. A quick change of regime will not enshrine liberty or justice. The message of our example may be clouded, but is not without influence. The struggle for a bit more freedom of choice or a better chance for justice is a never-ending one, and after small gains have been made, eternal vigilance is vital to avoid sliding back into bondage. Serving as an example of decency may be our most effective way to nudge forward the cause of human dignity.

2. Second, our government can advance human rights abroad by strengthening our resolve and our resources to defend our allies who are threatened by totalitarian aggression or subversion. This may require security guarantees, military assistance, and in some cases the presence of U.S. troops on foreign soil. Our combined effort to maintain a favorable balance of power has succeeded thus far in preserving the independence of Western Europe, Japan, and South Korea.

Misguided U.S. policies have helped deliver the people of Iran and Nicaragua into the hands of regimes that show less respect for basic human rights than their less-than-perfect predecessors. Human experience demonstrates that the best is often the enemy of the good. A fastidious opposition to an authoritarian regime may hasten the advent of a totalitarian one. To withold economic or military aid to a besieged ally whose human rights record is not blameless may help assure a far more repressive successor. This would be tragic.

"By the discreet use of quiet (not silent) diplomacy we can encourage friendly regimes to observe the rule of law."

3. By the discreet use of quiet (not silent) diplomacy we can encourage friendly regimes to observe the rule of law. We should never condone the violation of basic rights anywhere, but we should recognize the severe limitations of public preaching and punitive measures directed against our friends and allies. An attitude of mutual respect supported by material assistance provides a more favorable atmosphere for encouraging them to correct abuses, such as arbitrary arrest, prolonged detention without charges, and torture, and to observe international covenants they have signed.

4. Returning to the interdependence of human rights and national security, it is clear that the United States cannot fulfill its responsibilities to peace and freedom if it is militarily weak or if it lacks the will to use its power and influence. We need military strength great enough to deter a nuclear or conventional attack, to resist nuclear blackmail, to support our Free World allies, and to undergird a worldwide coalition to counter conquest, subversion, and terrorism.

We are being severely tested in South Korea, Taiwan, southeast Asia, Central America, and southern Africa. The stakes are high—the freedom, independence, and security of the scores of countries involved and a world in which freedom will have a chance to flourish.

If the Soviet Union and its allies succeed, the world will enter a new dark age from which it may take hundreds of years to emerge. But I believe there is still enough courage and will in the Free World to stave off this apocalypse.

Ernest W. Lefever is the president of the Ethics and Public Policy Center. He has taught political science at the University of Maryland, American University, and Georgetown University.

Human Rights Can Interfere with US National Interests

George Shultz

I would like to speak to you today about human rights and the moral dimension of U.S. foreign policy.

Americans have always been an introspective people. Most other nations do not go through the endless exercise of trying to analyze themselves as we do. We are always asking what kind of people we are. This is probably a result of our history. Unlike most other nations, we are not defined by an ancient common tradition or heritage or by ethnic homogeneity. Unlike most other countries, America is a nation consciously created and made up of men and women from many different cultures and origins. What unifies us is not a common origin but a common set of ideals: freedom, constitutional democracy, racial and religious tolerance. We Americans thus define ourselves not by where we come from but by where we are headed: our goals, our values, our principles, which mark the kind of society we strive to create.

This accounts in good part, I believe, for the extraordinary vitality of this country. Democracy is a great liberator of the human spirit, giving free rein to the talents and aspirations of individuals, offering every man and woman the opportunity to realize his or her fullest potential. This ideal of freedom has been a beacon to immigrants from many lands.

We are a people that never felt bound by the past but always had confidence that we could shape our future. We also set high standards for ourselves. In our own society, from Jefferson to Lincoln to the modern day, there have always been keepers of our conscience who measured our performance against our ideals and insisted that we do better. The revolution in civil rights is perhaps the most dramatic recent example, and it has given impetus to other revolutions, such as in women's rights. We are

blessed with a society that is constantly renewing and improving itself by virtue of the standards it has set.

In foreign affairs, we do the same. In the 19th century, when we had the luxury of not being actively involved in world politics, we, nevertheless, saw ourselves as a moral example to others. We were proud when liberators like Simon Bolivar in Latin America or Polish patriots in Europe invoked the ideals of the American Revolution. In the 20th century, since Woodrow Wilson, we have defined our role in the world in terms of moral principles that we were determined to uphold and advance. We have never been comfortable with the bare concept of maintaining the balance of power, even though this is clearly part of our responsibility.

Americans can be proud of the good we have accomplished in foreign affairs.

• We have fought and sacrificed for the freedom of others.

• We helped Europe and Japan rebuild after World War II.

• We have given generously to promote economic development.

• We have been a haven for refugees.

Thus, moral values and a commitment to human dignity have been not an appendage to our foreign policy but an essential part of it, and a powerful impulse driving it. These values are the very bonds that unite us with our closest allies, and they are the very issues that divide us from our adversaries. The fundamental difference between East and West is not in economic or social policy, though those policies differ radically, but in the moral principles on which they are based. It is the difference between tyranny and freedom—an age-old struggle in which the United States never could, and cannot today, remain neutral.

But there has always been tension between our ideals and the messy realities of the world. Any foreign policy must weave together diverse strands of

George Shultz, speech before the Creve Coeur Club, Peoria, IL, February 2, 1984.

national interest: political objectives, military security, economic management. All these other goals are important to people's lives and well-being. They all have moral validity, and they often confront us with real choices to make. As the strongest free nation, the United States has a complex responsibility to help maintain international peace and security and the global economic system.

At the same time, as one nation among many, we do not have the power to remake the planet. An awareness of our limits is said to be one of the lessons we learned from Vietnam. In any case, Americans are also a practical people and are interested in producing results. Foreign policy thus often presents us with moral issues that are not easy to resolve. Moral questions are more difficult to answer than other kinds of questions, not easier. How we respond to these dilemmas is a real test of our maturity and also of our commitment.

Approaches to Human Rights Policy

There are several different ways of approaching human rights issues, and some are better than others. One thing should be clear. Human rights policy should not be a formula for escapism or a set of excuses for evading problems. Human rights policy cannot mean simply dissociating or distancing ourselves from regimes whose practices we find deficient. Too much of what passes for human rights policy has taken the form of shunning those we find do not live up to internationally accepted standards. But this to me is a ''cop-out''; it seems more concerned with making us feel better than with having an impact on the situation we deplore. It is really a form of isolationism. If some liberals advocate cutting off relationships with right-wing regimes—and some conservatives seek to cut off dealings with left-wing regimes—we could be left with practically no foreign policy at all. This is not my idea of how to advance the cause of human rights.

One unattractive example of this approach derives from theories of American guilt, originating in our domestic debate over Vietnam. There are those eager to limit or restrain American power because they concluded from Vietnam that any exercise of American power overseas was bound to end in disaster or that America was itself a supporter or purveyor of evil in the world. Human rights policy was seen by some as a way of restricting American engagement abroad. Perversely, in this way of thinking, a government friendly to us is subjected to more exacting scrutiny than others; our security ties with it are attacked; once such a government faces an internal or external threat, its moral defects are spotlighted as an excuse to desert it. This is not my view of human rights policy either.

At issue here is not so much a tactical disagreement over human rights policy but fundamentally different conceptions of America and its impact on the world. What gives passion to this human rights debate is that it is a surrogate for a more significant underlying contest over the future of American foreign policy.

There should be no doubt of President Reagan's approach—not isolationism or guilt or paralysis but, on the contrary, a commitment to active engagement, confidently working for our values as well as our interests in the real world, acting proudly as the champion of freedom. The President has said that ''human rights means working at problems, not walking away from them.'' If we truly care about our values, we must be engaged in their defense— whether in Afghanistan and Poland, the Philippines and El Salvador, or Grenada. This is the President's philosophy: We are proud of our country and of what it stands for. We have confidence in our ability to do good. We draw our inspiration from the fundamental decency of the American people. We find in our ideals a star to steer by, as we try to move our ship of state through the troubled waters of a complex world.

''We must be staunch in our conviction that freedom is not the sole prerogative of a lucky few but the inalienable and universal right of all human beings.''

So we consider ourselves activists in the struggle for human rights. As the President declared to the British Parliament on June 8, 1982: ''We must be staunch in our conviction that freedom is not the sole prerogative of a lucky few but the inalienable and universal right of all human beings.''

Goals and Techniques

That was philosophy. But on a daily basis, we face practical issues and problems of human rights policy. On one level, human rights policy aims at specific goals. We try, for example, to use our influence to improve judicial or police practices in many countries—to stop murders, to eliminate torture or brutality, to obtain the release of dissidents or political prisoners, to end persecution on racial or other grounds, to permit free emigration, and so forth. Many American officials, including Vice President Bush and myself, have gone to El Salvador and denounced the death squads not only privately but publicly—all of which is having a positive effect. We have sought to promote an honest and thorough investigation of the murder of Philippine opposition leader Benigno Aquino.

President Reagan, during his visit to the Republic of Korea, . . . publicly stated his belief in the importance of political liberalization. But we have also made our thoughts on specific cases known privately, and several of these approaches have been successful. In our contacts with the Soviets, we have pressed for the release of human rights activists and for freedom of emigration. There are literally hundreds of such examples of American action. Sometimes we make progress; sometimes we do not—proving only that we still have much to do. In this context, I must pay tribute to your distinguished Senator, Chuck Percy [Sen. Charles H. Percy, R.-Ill.]. No one in the Senate has played a more important role than Chuck Percy in the struggle for the right of emigration for Soviet Jewry and other oppressed peoples, for religious freedoms, and for the release of prisoners of conscience.

The techniques of exerting our influence are well known. We try, without letup, to sensitize other governments to human rights concerns. Every year we put on the public record a large volume of country reports examining the practices of other countries in thorough and candid detail—the rights of citizens to be free from violations of the integrity of the person and the rights of citizens to enjoy basic civil and political liberties. The 1984 report has just been published—nearly 1,500 pages of facts about human rights around the world, something no other country undertakes. Twice each year, we also send the congressional Helsinki commission a public report thoroughly reviewing the record of Soviet and East European compliance with the human rights provisions of the Helsinki Final Act.

"How we reconcile political and moral interests are questions that call not for dogmatic conclusions but for painstaking, sober analysis."

Wherever feasible, we try to ameliorate abuses through the kind of frank diplomatic exchanges often referred to as "quiet diplomacy." But where our positive influence is minimal, or where other approaches are unavailing, we may have no choice but to use other, more concrete kinds of leverage with regimes whose practices we cannot accept.

We may deny economic and military assistance, withhold diplomatic support, vote against multilateral loans, refuse licenses for crime control equipment, or take other punitive steps. Where appropriate, we resort to public pressures and public statements denouncing such actions as we have done in the case of the Salvadoran death squads, Iranian persecution of the Bahais, South African apartheid, and Soviet repression in Afghanistan.

Multilateral organizations are another instrument of our human rights policy. In the UN Commission on Human Rights, we supported a resolution criticizing martial law in Poland—the first resolution there against a Communist country. The United States has been active and vigorous in regional conferences and organizations, such as the Helsinki process and the Inter-American Commission on Human Rights. We regret that some multilateral organizations have distorted the purposes they were designed to serve—such as UNESCO [UN Educational, Scientific, and Cultural Organization], which has not been living up to its responsibility to defend freedom of speech, intellectual freedom, and human rights in general.

Friendly governments are often more amenable to traditional diplomacy than to open challenge, and we therefore prefer persuasion over public denunciations. But if we were never seriously concerned about human rights abuses in friendly countries, our policy would be one-sided and cynical.

Thus, while the Soviet Union and its proxies present the most profound and farreaching danger to human rights, we cannot let it appear—falsely—that this is our only human rights concern. It is not.

Human Rights Dilemmas

Clearly, there are limits to our ability to remake the world. In the end, sovereign governments will make their own decisions, despite external pressure. Where a system of government is built on repression, human rights will inevitably be subordinated to the perceived requirements of political survival. The sheer diversity and complexity of other nations' internal situations, and the problem of coping with them in a dangerous world, are additional limits. How we use our influence and how we reconcile political and moral interests are questions that call not for dogmatic conclusions but for painstaking, sober analysis—and no little humility.

The dilemmas we face are many. What, for instance, is the relationship between human rights concerns and the considerations of regional or international security on which the independence and freedom of so many nations directly depend? This issue recurs in a variety of forms.

There are countries whose internal practices we sometimes question but which face genuine security threats from outside—like South Korea—or whose cooperation with us helps protect the security of scores of other nations—like the Philippines. But it is also true that in many cases a concern for human rights on our part may be the best guarantee of a long-term friendly relationship with that country. There are countries whose long-term security will probably be enhanced if they have a more solid base of popular support and domestic unity. Yet there are also cases where regional insecurity weakens the chances for liberalization and where American assurance of security support provides a better climate for an evolution to democracy. Human rights issues occur in a context, and there is no simple answer.

The Middle East

In the Middle East, to take a very different example, we have no doubt of Israel's commitment to human rights and democratic values. It is those very values we appeal to when we express our concern for the human rights and quality of life of the Palestinian people in the West Bank and Gaza—a concern that exists side by side with our understanding of Israel's security needs and our conviction that the basic problem can only be resolved through negotiation.

Another question that arises is: Do we know enough about the culture and internal dynamics of other societies to be sure of the consequence of pressures we might bring? If we distance ourselves from a friendly but repressive government, in a fluid situation, will this help strengthen forces of moderation, or might it make things worse? Pressures on human rights grounds against the Shah, Somoza, or South Vietnam had justification but may also have accelerated a powerful trend of events over which we had little influence, ending up with regimes that pose a far greater menace not only to human rights in their own country but also to the safety and freedom of all their neighbors.

In some countries, harsh measures of repression have been caused—indeed, deliberately provoked—by terrorists, who waged deliberate warfare not only against the institutions of society—political leaders, judges, administrators, newspaper editors, as well as against police and military officials—but against ordinary citizens. Terrorism itself is a threat to human rights and to the basic right to civil peace and security which a society owes its citizens. We deplore all governmental abuses of rights, whatever the excuse. But we cannot be blind to the extremist forces that pose such a monumental and increasing threat to free government precisely because democracies are not well equipped to meet this threat. We must find lawful and legitimate means to protect civilized life itself from the growing problem of terrorism.

The role of Congress is another question. There is no doubt that congressional concerns and pressures have played a very positive role in giving impetus and backing to our efforts to influence other governments' behavior. This congressional pressure can strengthen the hand of the executive branch in its efforts of diplomacy. At the same time, there can be complications if the legislative instrument is too inflexible or heavy-handed, or, even more, if Congress attempts to take on the administrative responsibility for executing policy. Legislation requires that we withhold aid in extreme circumstances. If narrowly interpreted, this can lead us rapidly to a "stop-go" policy of fits and starts, all or nothing—making it very difficult to structure incentives in a way that will really fulfill the law's own wider mandate: to "promote and encourage increased respect for human rights and fundamental freedoms...."

Impact on El Salvador

In the case of El Salvador, the positive impact the Administration has had in its recent pressures against death squads should be a reminder that certification in its previous form is not the only, or even the most effective, procedure for giving expression to our objectives. Sometimes a change in approach is the most worthwhile course. We are ready to work cooperatively with the Congress on this issue, but it should be clear that the answers are not simple.

Finally, the phenomenon of totalitarianism poses special problems. Sociologists and political theorists have recognized for decades that there is a difference between traditional, indigenous dictatorships and the more pervasively repressive totalitarian states, fortified by modern technology, mass parties, and messianic ideology. Certainly, both are alien to our democratic ideals. But in this year of George Orwell, 1984, we cannot be oblivious to the new 20th century phenomenon.

Suppression of religion because it represents an autonomous force in a society; abuse of psychiatric institutions as instruments of repression; the use of prison labor on a mass scale for industrial construction—these and other practices are typical of the modern Marxist-Leninist state. Totalitarian regimes pose special problems not only because of their more systematic and thorough repression but also because of their permanence and their global ambitions. In the last decade we have seen several military regimes and dictatorships of the right evolve into democracies—from Portugal, Spain, and Greece to Turkey and Argentina. No Communist state has evolved in such a manner—though Poland attempted to.

And the Soviet Union, most importantly and uniquely, is driven not only by Russian history and Soviet state interest but also by what remains of its revolutionary ideology to spread its system by force, backed up by the greatest military power of any tyranny in history.

I raise these issues not to assert answers but to pose questions. These are complexities that a truly moral nation must face up to if its goal is to help make the world a better place.

Human Rights and Democracy

The Reagan Administration approaches the human rights question on a deeper level. Responding to specific juridical abuses and individual cases, as they happen, is important, but they are really the surface of the problem we are dealing with. The essence of the problem is the kind of political structure that makes human rights abuses possible. We have a duty not only to react to specific cases but also to understand, and seek to shape, the basic structural conditions in which human rights are more likely to flourish.

This is why President Reagan has placed so much emphasis on democracy: on encouraging the building of pluralistic institutions that will lead a society to evolve toward free and democratic forms of government. This is long-term, positive, active strategy for human rights policy.

It is not a utopian idea at all. For decades, the American labor movement has worked hard in many countries assisting the growth and strengthening of free labor unions—giving support and advice, teaching the skills of organizing and operating. In Western Europe after World War II, it was the free labor unions, helped in may cases by free unions here, that prevented Communist parties from taking over in several countries. Today, free political parties in Western Europe give similar fraternal assistance to budding parties and political groups in developing countries, helping these institutions survive or grow in societies where democratic procedures are not as firmly entrenched as in our own.

"The cause of human rights is at the core of American foreign policy because it is central to America's conception of itself."

The new National Endowment for Democracy, proposed by President Reagan and now funded with the bipartisan support of the Congress, represents an imaginative and practical American effort to help develop the tools of democracy. Just as our traditional aid programs try to teach economic and agricultural skills, so our new programs will try to transfer skills in organizing elections, in campaigning, in legal reform, and other skills which we take for granted but which are basic to free, pluralistic societies.

Through the endowment, our two major political parties, along with labor, business, and other private groups, will assist countries and groups that seek to develop democratic institutions and practices in their own societies. The President is also directing AID (Agency for International Development), USIA (U.S. Information Agency), and other agencies to strengthen their programs for democracy, such as support for free labor movements, training of journalists, and strengthening judicial institutions and procedures. Sen. Percy also deserves particular credit here for his cosponsorship of the Kassebaum-Percy Human Rights Fund for South Africa, which will channel $1.5 million to private and community organizations in South Africa working for human rights.

It may not seem romantic or heroic to train African magistrates in Zimbabwe, provide technical help to the Liberian Constitution Commission, help publish a revised penal code in Zaire, help finance the education and research program of the Inter-American Institute of Human Rights in Costa Rica, or help provide international observers for free elections in El Salvador—but these programs help create the institutional preconditions for democracy. Democracy and the rule of law are the only enduring guarantee of human rights.

We should never lose faith in the power of the democratic idea. Democracies may be a minority in the world at large, but it is not true that they must always be so. Freedom is not a culture-bound Western invention but an aspiration of peoples everywhere—from Barbados to Botswana, from India to Japan.

In Latin America, for example, where the news is so much dominated by conflict, there is, in fact, an extraordinary trend toward democracy. Twenty-seven nations of Latin America and the Caribbean are either democratic or are formally embarked on a transition to democracy—representing almost 90% of the region's population, as compared with some 50% less than 10 years ago. And the trend has been accelerating.

Between 1976 and 1980, two Latin American nations, Ecuador and Peru, elected civilian presidents who successfully replaced military presidents. Since 1981, however, El Salvador, Honduras, Bolivia, and most recently Argentina have moved from military rule to popularly elected civilian governments.

Brazil is far along the same path. The people of Grenada have had restored to them the right to be the arbiters of their own political future. Uruguay has a timetable for a transition to democracy, and its parties have returned to independent activity. Pressure for return to civilian rule is being felt in Chile and Guatemala. This leaves only Cuba, a Marxist-Leninist state; Nicaragua, which has been steadily moving in that direction; and a handful of dictatorships outside this pattern.

This trend toward democracy, which reflects the most profound aspirations of the people of Latin America, has received wholehearted and effective encouragement from the Reagan Administration. Dictatorship in any form, leftists or rightist, is anathema in this hemisphere, and all states within the region have a responsibility to see that dictatorship gives way to genuine pluralist democracy.

Nor is the trend toward democracy confined to Latin America. In the Philippines, for example, the democratic tradition of that republic is evident in the strong popular pressure for free elctions and a revitalized Congress. The government has begun to respond to these aspirations, and we are encouraging it to continue this hopeful process so important to the long-term stability of the Philippines. Likewise in the Republic of Korea, we are encouraged by President Chun's [Doo Hwan] commitment to undertake in the next few years the first peaceful, constitutional transfer of power in Korea's modern history.

US Moral Commitment

A policy dedicated to human rights will always face hard choices. In El Salvador, we are supporting the moderates of the center, who are under pressure from extremists of both right and left; if we withdrew our support, the moderates would be the victims, as would be the cause of human rights in that beleaguered country. The road will be long and hard, but we cannot walk away from our principles.

The cause of human rights is at the core of American foreign policy because it is central to America's conception of itself. These values are hardly an American invention, but America has perhaps been unique in its commitment to base its foreign policy on the pursuit of such ideals. It should be an everlasting source of pride to Americans that we have used our vast power to such noble ends. If we have sometimes fallen short, that is not a reason to flagellate ourselves but to remind ourselves of how much there remains to do.

This is what America has always represented to other nations and other peoples. But if we abandoned the effort, we would not only be letting others down, we would be letting ourselves down.

Our human rights policy is a pragmatic policy which aims not at striking poses but as having a practical effect on the well-being of real people. It is a tough-minded policy, which faces the world as it is, not as we might wish or imagine it to be. At the same time, it is an idealistic policy, which expresses the continuing commitment of the United States to the cause of liberty and the alleviation of suffering. It is precisely this combination of practicality and idealism that has marked American statesmanship at its best. It is the particular genius of the American people.

George Shultz is the secretary of state under the Reagan administration.

"This Administration has tended to use human rights only as a weapon with which to attack its adversaries."

viewpoint **26**

US Human Rights Policies Harm National Interests

Robert F. Drinan

After months of confusion and contradiction the Reagan Administration stated in November 1981 that the promotion of human rights would be central to U.S. foreign policy. The White House, however, has little to point to as human rights victories in its first two years. The record demonstrates that the Administration's prime preoccupation in the field of human rights is with nations deemed to be friendly to the Soviet Union and unfriendly to the United States. As a result, public criticism of our "friends" on human rights grounds is thought by the Administration to weaken their relationship to us.

The Reagan Administration takes no position on the five major human rights treaties that have been signed by previous Presidents but not ratified by the Senate. Indeed, this is the first Administration in history that has not publicly supported U.S. ratification of the Genocide Convention signed by President Truman in 1948.

This approach is a sharp reversal of the law and the practices that made the years 1974 to 1980 the "golden age" of human rights. A law signed by President Ford bans economic and military assistance to countries that engage in a pattern of gross violations of basic human rights. Another law signed by President Carter requires that U.S. representatives to six multilateral development banks channel assistance only to those nations without a consistent pattern of gross violations of human rights. Other laws forbid U.S. aid to any nation for internal law enforcement purposes, while legislation passed in 1981 and signed by President Reagan stipulates that aid to Argentina, Chile, El Salvador and Nicaragua is now contingent on Presidential certification to Congress that specific human rights standards have been fulfilled.

Robert F. Drinan, "Human Rights and the Reagan Administration," *America*, March 5, 1983. Reprinted with permission of America Press, Inc., 106 West 56th St., New York, NY 10019. © 1983 All rights reserved.

The record of compliance with these laws by the Reagan Administration is dismal. Reviewing its position on human rights in several nations, one has to reach the sad conclusion that the adamant anti-Soviet posture of representatives of the Administration has blinded them to the very important value of placing a special emphasis on human rights in U.S. foreign policy.

Central American Human Rights

The repudiation by the Administration of a firm accent on human rights has been particularly visible in Latin America. In 1978 Congress banned all military assistance and arms sales to Argentina. The Reagan Administration successfully sought repeal of this law, but Congress added a requirement that, prior to giving military aid, the President must certify significant improvements in human rights. The certification must consider whether there has been an accounting for the "disappeared" and whether there has been a release of prisoners held without charges.

As of early January 1983 the Reagan Administration had not certified that Argentina qualifies for aid, but the White House says that its failure to certify is not related to the human rights situation. The certification is expected any day, but the recent discovery of more than a thousand corpses of the "disappeared" along with new closings of periodicals and new disappearances may further postpone the date of the certification.

The Reagan Administration also reversed previous U.S. practice on multilateral bank loans. It voted in July 1981 in favor of $310 million in such loans for Argentina, although the law forbids such votes in favor of nations that are gross and consistent abusers of human rights. The willingness of the Reagan Administration to overlook human rights violations in Argentina was demonstrated in other ways. In 1981 the Administration agreed to a compromise arrangement that reduced the effectiveness of a group authorized by the United Nations Human Rights Commission to investigate the status of the "disappeared" in Argentina. The White House received Argentine Presidents Viola and Galtieri on official visits to Washington. United Nations Ambassador Jeane Kirkpatrick traveled to Buenos Aires to proclaim U.S. friendship but declined to meet with human rights groups.

Violations in Chile

In December 1981 Congress enacted a requirement that military assistance and arms sales to Chile could be resumed only if the President certified that there had been a "significant improvement" in human rights in Chile and that progress had been made in bringing to justice those indicted by a Federal grand jury for the 1976 murders in Washington of Orlando Letelier and Ronni Moffitt. The Reagan Administration has not tried to certify that either of these conditions has been met. This is a position for which the Reagan Administration should be praised, but this strong human rights stand is undercut by its reversal of previous policy by voting in favor of $126 million in multi-lateral development bank loans to Chile. There are strong forces within the State Department that want to certify that Chile should receive U.S. aid. If this opinion prevails and the Government of General Pinochet receives aid, it will be hard to discern any minimal standard on human rights compliance being observed by the Reagan Administration.

"This total abandonment of even lip service to human rights in El Salvador inevitably weakens American credibility elsewhere with respect to human rights."

In late January 1983 the Reagan Administration once again certified that improvements in the human rights situation in El Salvador merited continued military aid. In December 1982, following a meeting with President Magana of El Salvador, President Reagan stated that he had already made up his mind and that he intended to certify El Salvador once again. All of the groups that monitor human rights in Latin America have denied sharply that the situation has improved in El Salvador. No real progress has been made in the case of the four murdered U.S. church-women, since the arrest of the five low-ranking national guardsmen does not resolve the question of the culpability of officers involved in the killings or the cover-up.

More perhaps than in any other country, the commitment of the Reagan Administration to maintain the current Government in power in El Salvador and to help it in securing a military victory

over rebel forces brings about the setting aside of any consideration of human rights. This total abandonment of even lip service to human rights in El Salvador inevitably weakens American credibility elsewhere with respect to human rights.

Aid to Guatemala

The Reagan Administration has been intensely interested in restoring military assistance and arms sales to Guatemala. This aid was terminated in 1977 because of Guatemala's horrendous record on human rights. In 1981 the White House evaded this prohibition by selling $3.2 million in trucks and jeeps to Guatemala, alleging that these vehicles did not amount to security assistance.

The Administration claims that there has been an improvement in human rights since the coup of March 23, 1982, that brought General Efrain Rios Montt to power. Even if this is true in Guatemala City, the slaughter of Guatemalans goes on in the countryside. In December 1982 President Reagan met with President Rios Montt and informed the press that Guatemala was getting a "bum rap" on human rights. The White House has announced that it will support an $18 million loan to Guatemala from the Inter-America Development Bank to build a rural telecommunications system.

If the Administration blinks at human rights abuses in El Salvador and Guatemala, it is more outspoken in criticizing the violations of human rights in Nicaragua than in any other nation in the world. Every real or imagined abuse of human rights by the Sandinist Government is proclaimed from the housetops. The rhetoric is grounded more in the Administration's opposition to the ideology of the Government in Managua than to any concern for human rights. Indeed it seems clear that the activities of the U.S. Government in giving support to the anti-Sandinist guerrillas provide a rationale or an excuse for the abuses of human rights engaged in by the Nicaraguan Government.

Paraguay and Human Rights

The pattern in Paraguay is similar to that in Central America. The United States, reversing previous policy, voted in favor of a $7.8 million loan from the Inter-American Development Bank to Paraguay. The State Department claimed an improvement in human rights, a claim that cannot be squared with the findings of Amnesty International. The fact is that the state of siege suspending constitutional guarantees continues in effect in Paraguay, as it has since 1954.

The Reagan White House also voted in favor of a $40 million loan to Uruguay despite the fact that Uruguay has one of the highest ratios of political prisoners to population of any country in the world. The pervasive opposition to Communism that is so ingrained in President Reagan's approach to Latin America results in support for the Duvalier

Government in Haiti. Partly because of the opposition of this regime to Castro, the Reagan Administration is unwilling to grant political asylum to the several thousand Haitians currently seeking asylum in the United States. But the Administration, seeing an apparently Communist regime in Ethiopia, decided in July 1982 to provide temporary refuge to some 15,000 Ethiopians in the United States. Minimizing further the extent of human rights violations in Haiti, the Administration has authorized the granting of direct foreign assistance to that country as well as credits and guarantees under the Arms Export Control Act.

The Administration's policies on Latin America have isolated the United States from collective action with other countries in the United Nations. On Dec. 3, 1982, for example, the United States voted with only 16 other nations on a matter related to Guatemala. The United States acted in a similar way on a vote regarding Chile and stood without a single NATO ally in a vote on El Salvador.

Anti-Communist Foreign Policy

An attitude that gives priority to encouraging anti-Communist regimes over emphasizing human rights is also central to President Reagan's foreign policy outside of Latin America. In South Korea the Administration reversed prior US. policy of abstaining on loans to that country in various multilateral lending institutions. In 1981 and 1982 the United States voted to support over $300 million in loans to Korea. In September 1982 the Commerce Department cleared the sale of 500 electric shock batons to Korea for "crowd control." The State Department protested and the Administration postponed the sale indefinitely.

The Administration is claiming that the release of Kim Dae Jung to come to the United States for medical treatment is a triumph for its policy of "quiet diplomacy." There may be some truth in this claim, but the fact remains, as the South Korean opposition leader Mr. Kim noted in Washington on Dec. 24, 1982, that his political followers in Korea do not enjoy freedom to form trade unions or participate in the political process.

Military considerations have also brought about an easing in human rights standards in America's relationship with the Philippines. In 1982 the United States, reversing previous policy, voted in favor of 15 loans totaling over $107 million from the multilateral development banks to the Philippines. The warm reception given by the White House to President Marcos in September 1982 apparently did not result in any agreement by the Marcos Government to be more observant of human rights.

A combination of anti-Communist and promilitary sentiment has brought about an alteration of America's traditional policies toward South Africa. While condemning apartheid, the Reagan Administration has extended financial assistance to the all-white Government in Pretoria. The Commerce Department has issued at least 12 licenses for the sale of high technology, and the Reagan Administration, on Nov. 3, 1982, supported a loan of over $1 billion from the International Monetary Fund to South Africa. The annual State Department report on the status of human rights required by the Congress last year claimed without supporting evidence that South Africa is moving towards a "modification" of apartheid and that "political change as an organic process is underway in South Africa."

"Military considerations have also brought about an easing in human rights standards."

The perception of Zaire as a bulwark against Soviet influence in Africa has led the Administration to increase aid to that nation even though the regime of President Mobutu has not been known since it began in 1965 as a regime that respects human rights.

Poland and Reagan

The muting of criticism concerning violations of human rights in nations that are friendly to the United States changes radically in the Reagan Administration's approach to Communist countries. The imposition of martial law in Poland brought an avalanche of rhetoric and the imposition of economic sanctions against the Soviet Union. After Western Europe defied the prohibition of the transfer of U.S. technology to aid in the construction of the Soviet Union's natural gas pipeline, the Reagan Administration was required, in effect, to withdraw the proposal even though the human rights situation in Poland had not improved.

The Reagan Administration was also tough on Rumania because of its new heavy education tax on those who desire to emigrate. The Administration is similarly aggressive and articulate on abuses of human rights within the Soviet Union. The imprisonment of Helsinki monitors, the continued exile of Andrei Sakharov and the abuse of psychiatry have all been eloquently denounced.

It is uncertain, however, whether this policy is working to help Soviet Jews who desire to emigrate. In 1982 the number permitted to leave the Soviet Union sank to 2,680, the lowest number since 1970 when emigration began. The total for 1982 contrasts sharply with the 9,447 permitted to leave in 1981 and the total of 51,320 granted exit visas in 1979.

Totalitarian & Authoritarian Regimes

The termination of the grain embargo and the offering of a long-term grain deal to the Soviet Union appeared to be contrary to the most fundamental premises of the Reagan Administration, especially since not even an attempt was made to obtain human rights concessions in exchange for the sale of grain. One can presumably expect the continuation of the sharp contrast in the different approach to totalitarian and authoritarian nations, even though that vocabulary has now been de-emphasized within Administration circles. It is an approach at variance with fundamentals of human rights law as enacted by the Congress starting in 1974. As a result, it has united all of the human rights groups. They were brought together by their successful fight against the proposed appointment of Ernest Lefever as the Assistant Secretary of State for Human Rights.

Since that time human-rights activists have been trying to limit the damage to human rights by the negative policies of the Reagan Administration. The task of these groups in the next two years is overwhelming. It is their job to try to blunt the devastating impact on dissidents and insurgents around the world of a policy perceived by them to be one that minimizes, if not eliminates, human rights as a factor in U.S. foreign policy. These people felt that the United States made a significant, even a monumental, contribution to the growth of human freedom by the adoption and the enforcement of a policy which disassociated the United States from violations of those human rights that are internationally recognized as the minimum safeguards for a civilized society. What these people are asking, along with human rights activists everywhere, is that the Reagan Administration set aside its double standard and be even-handed in its attention to human rights. This Administration has tended to use human rights only as a weapon with which to attack its adversaries.

> "The human rights dimension to U.S. foreign policy has been too institutionalized by Congress. . .for any one Administration to be able to eliminate it."

The legislation enacted by the Congress in the 1970's requiring compliance with human rights in non-Communist countries is designed not to contradict but to complement the policy of containment of Communism adhered to by the United States for some three decades. The policy of containment is based on respect by the United States for the human rights of persons who live under totalitarian governments. The human rights dimension of U.S. foreign policy that developed in the six years before the Reagan Administration was designed to broaden the mandate and the mission of the United States in advancing human rights everywhere in the world. Ultimately that mandate came, of course, from international law and the Charter of the United Nations which in Articles 55 and 56 makes the ''promotion'' of human rights an essential function of the United Nations and an important and inescapable duty of each of its members.

One likes to think that the human rights dimension to U.S. foreign policy has been too institutionalized by Congress and has become too attractive to the entire world for any one Administration to be able to eliminate it as an integral and important part of America's foreign policy. But what may remain of that policy. . .is not certain.

Robert F. Drinan, a Roman Catholic priest and former member of the House of Representatives for Massachusetts, is a professor of law at the Georgetown University Law Center, Washington, D.C., and president of Americans for Democratic Action.

"There is only one human rights political tradition in the world today, and this is embodied in the political system known as democracy."

viewpoint **27**

Anti-Communism Must Govern US Human Rights Policy

Elliott Abrams

I begin with the Declaration of Independence, since the principles contained therein are what Abraham Lincoln called, "the definitions and axioms of free society." As everyone here knows, the Declaration holds four truths to be self-evident: that all men are created equal; that they are endowed by their Creator with certain inalienable rights, among which are life, liberty and the pursuit of happiness; that governments, whose proper role is to ensure these rights, may only be instituted by the consent of the governed; and that, when government becomes destructive of those rights, the people have the further right to alter or abolish it, and reinstitute another in its place.

As Americans, we have been brought up on these words. Having heard them so many times already, perhaps we are tempted to turn off what the late Martin diamond called "a kind of psychic hearing aid" upon hearing them yet again. Nevertheless, these old words merit our deepest attention. Consider, for example, the idea of "inalienable rights" in the Declaration of Independence. By calling human rights inalienable, our Founding Fathers sought to underscore the fact that these rights do not derive from the state, but in here in the human condition itself. Since the state did not grant us our human rights, it cannot therefore deprive us of these rights. It cannot tell us that our enjoyment of human rights is conditional on our performance of certain duties. By stressing the "inalienable" character of our human rights, our Founding Fathers wished to make it absolutely clear that there is an irreducible area of human activity that is beyond state control.

The importance of these philosophical propositions emerges most clearly when we contrast our own constitution with the Soviet Union's. The Soviet constitution contains long lists of so-called rights. Yet, as Dr. Robert Goldwin has observed, "The rights enumerated in the Soviet constitution are clearly seen as gifts bestowed on the citizens by the Soviet state." In return for the enjoyment of these gifts, the citizens must pay a price. Thus, for example, for the theoretical right to "freedom of speech and press," the Soviet citizen has the "duty to use them 'in accordance with the people's interests and for the purpose of strengthening and developing the socialists system.'"

Punishment for the Soviet Citizen

But what happens if a Soviet citizen refuses to do his duty as defined by the Soviet constitution? Suppose he complains about his inability to say and write what he pleases, to come and go as he pleases? For the crime of engaging in "anti-Soviet agitation and propaganda" he clearly forfeits the gifts bestowed upon him by the state. Perhaps Soviet authorities, as punishment for his ingratitude, will sentence him to three years imprisonment followed by ten years in a labor camp. This was Anatoly Scharansky's sentence.

Perhaps the authorities will strip him of his position and his honors and send him into internal exile. This was Andrei Sakharov's punishment. Perhaps the authorities will simply decide that a man who says terrible things about the Soviet Union must be suffering from "creeping schizophrenia," and belongs in a psychiatric ward. This has happened to many lesser known dissidents over the years. An article in the *Washington Post* on November 21, 1983 told of a turn by the KGB back to straight physical torture in dealing with its victims. Whatever the Soviet authorities decide, however, the individual is defenseless. He had no "inalienable rights" to fall back on, since the Soviet State refuses to recognize *any* sphere of activity that is beyond its control.

Elliott Abrams, speech before the National Council for Social Studies, San Francisco, November 23, 1983.

The argument that we in the United States enjoy civil and political rights, while Soviet citizens enjoy economic "rights," is founded on a lie. For Soviet citizens enjoy *no* rights. Theirs is a world of privileges granted—or revoked—by the state, at its whim.

But enough of the Soviet constitution. Let us look at another assertion contained in the Declaration of Independence—the proposition that governments are instituted to secure human rights. This proposition, of course, has to do with the ends of government, the purposes for which governments are established. These days, political scientists rarely address themselves to the ends or purposes of government. Rather, they seem to have developed a "managerial" perspective, according to which the most important question to ask about any government is "How does it work?" and not "What ends was it designed to achieve?" But let us remember that the Founding Fathers recognized that human beings form political communities to achieve certain purposes, and they believed that the ends people choose to pursue, and the means by which they choose to pursue them, define the nature of their political community.

Founding Fathers and Human Rights

The ends which our Founding Fathers chose to pursue, of course, were human rights. The purpose of government, they declared, was to secure these rights. *Not,* it should be stressed, to promote virtue or piety, privilege or wealth, empire or dominion: only rights. So often have we heard the old words of the Declaration of Independence that we are apt to forget the novelty of its underlying argument. We forget that neither the Hebrew prophets nor the Greek philosophers nor the Roman lawyers nor the medieval schoolmen ever said that the protection of individual liberty was the purpose of government. Thus, Lord Acton, the great British historian, was correct to say that, "in the strictest sense the history of liberty dated from 1776, 'for never till then had men sought liberty knowing what they sought.'"

"US policy is to back the democratic center. If it is not clear, you ought to ask those in the death squads and those in the guerrilla bands why it is that they have not yet captured power."

The notion that the end of government is to secure liberty hardly commands universal assent today. If you held a candid conversation with a diplomat from almost any member state of the United Nations, for example, he would probably tell you that his leaders believe that other national goals—wealth, say, or virtue, or even glory—are much more important than individual liberty. To be sure, this diplomat would add, his government finds it expedient to couch its goals in the language of human rights—and even to propose new human rights, such as the so-called "right to development"—but words are one thing, and reality is something else again. And if this diplomat were being exceptionally honest, he might even confess that efforts to speak of "alternative" human rights tradition only to serve to promote intellectual confusion. Strictly speaking, there is only one human rights political tradition in the world today, and this is embodied in the political system known as democracy.

In drawing up our constitution, the Founding Fathers recognized that they had to design political institutions that were strong enough to undertake the great tasks of nation building, yet not so strong as to endanger human rights. As James Madison put it in *Federalist Paper* number 51, "in framing a government which is to be administered by men over men, the great difficulty lies in this: You must first enable the government to control the governed; and in the next place oblige it to control itself."

The political theory which informed the efforts to create such institutions is spelled out most beautifully in *The Federalist Papers*. "To read and understand them," wrote Carl Van Doren in *The Great Rehearsal*, "[is] the next thing to having had a hand in making the Constitution." The complicated, yet intellectually compelling, train of reasoning that went into the creation of such institutions as federalism, separation of powers, bicameralism, judicial review, indirect representation, the extended public, democracy, constitutionalism and limited government are all contained in this single document. The Founders believed that these institutions were the product of what they called a "new political science." It should be added that the institutions of our government are works of art no less than of science, are as much of the fruits of the creative imagination as a sculpture or a symphony.

Communism and Fear

In the opening stanzas of Dante's epic poem, *The Inferno,* the poet describes how he found himself alone in a dark wood whose very memory "gives a shape to fear." For millions of men and women in our century, fear has taken the shape of two political symbols: the swastika and the hammer and sickle. And for millions of Europeans in 1941, for displaced persons in European camps in 1945, for Hungarians in 1956, for boat people in Indochina, for Afghan freedom fighters, for millions upon millions of immigrants seeking a new life, hope has also taken the shape of a political symbol: the Stars and Stripes. Does acknowledging this fact really reinforce "nationalistic stereotypes?" Might it not be better to reject the fashionable sophistries of our time and to tell students the simple truth: that the United States is the party of liberty in the world today because we are the heirs of a great political tradition—a tradition which not only cherishes human rights, but which understands how to embody these rights in the concrete institutions of government? And in telling students these things, would we not be defending these very institutions against a rampart nihilism which threatens to drain them of their vitality and their vigor?

As I noted, governments must be strong enough to control themselves but not so strong as to resist democratic control by the people. Our goal in Central America is to help the people there build those kinds of democratic governments.

There is a myth about Central America that tells us the key battle there is between right and left. This is just not true; the key battle is between those on the violent right and left who oppose democracy, and the vast majority of the people, who seek democracy.

I hope it is clear to you that US policy is to back the democratic center. If it is not clear, you ought to ask those in the guerrilla bands why it is that they have not yet captured power. If you could ask this question and get an honest answer, the answer would be "the United States."

Aid to Central America

Three-quarters of our aid to Central America is economic. Even for El Salvador, two-thirds of our aid is economic. It is our policy to seek political and economic and social development in the area. Thus, we have been a mainstay of support for land reform in El Salvador, and for the return to civilian democratic rule in Honduras (which finally took place in 1982), and we have sought to maintain the closest alliance to the model in the area, Costa Rica. But let us not have our heads in the sand. There is a security threat in the area, and that one-quarter of our aid which is military is essential. Anyone who doubts this needs only to look at the documents captured in Grenada. These documents reveal the workings of a Leninist party, cooperating with Cuba, and even getting aid from North Korea in its plans to establish a communist dictatorship. Cuba and Nicaragua, and for that matter, the Soviet Union, are busily at work in Central America. What are they doing there? Whatever they are doing, one thing we know for sure: they are not advancing the cause of human rights. When Nicaragua sends guns to the guerrillas in El Salvador, or infiltrates agents into Honduras, or threatens democracy in Costa Rica, its goal is not to improve the human rights situation in those countries. If Cuba or Nicaragua, or the Soviet Union were interested in advancing respect for human rights, they could start at home.

What role should the US be playing now? The road to political, social and economic reform is a long and difficult one. On it, campesinos and labor and church leaders, and democratic politicians are caught quite literally in a crossfire between the violent right and the violent left. Our role should be to support them and protect them as they fight for democracy and social change. We owe them this, which means we owe them more than simply acts of abstention or withdrawal as a human rights policy. It is not enough to withhold this or to refuse that; we should be actively engaged in supporting those who share our values. And this is what they want. If you talk to Christian democratic leaders in Guatemala or El Salvador, or the Archbishop of San Salvador or Managua, or labor leaders in those countries, and listen to them, they do not ask us to get out. Archbishop Rivera y Damas has carefully said that he opposes all military aid in El Salvador, but recognizes that if some countries are aiding the guerrillas it is logical for the government to secure assistance as well. The democratic forces in Central America deserve our help. The worst thing we could all do with respect to human rights in Central America would be to abandon those in the center who are fighting for human rights.

> *"Democracies are our best allies and our goal in Central America is to promote the cause of democracy there."*

American influence in a number of countries is often exaggerated. We do not control any of these countries in Central America. When we have controlled countries rather completely, what has been the result? In Germany and Japan where we were an occupying power we did everything we could to establish democracies, and we succeeded. Surely it is already obvious that we will leave behind us in Grenada another nascent democracy. Democracies are our best allies and our goal in Central America is to promote the cause of democracy there. It is a goal of which we can all be proud.

Elliott Abrams is the assistant secretary of state for human rights and humanitarian affairs under the Reagan administration.

*"What is dishonest—and is a betrayal of
genuine rights—is to try to use rights
merely as a means of other goals."*

viewpoint **28**

Anti-Communism Should Not
Govern Human Rights Policy

Henry Shue

We hold these truths to be self-evident, that all men
are created equal, that they are endowed by their
Creator with certain unalienable Rights, that among
these are Life, Liberty, and the pursuit of Happiness.
That to secure these rights, Governments are instituted
among Men, deriving their just powers from the
consent of the governed. That whenever any Form of
Government becomes destructive of these ends, it is
the Right of the People to alter or to abolish it, and to
institute new Government. . . .

Much nonsense has been written in recent years
about what a radical and moralistic aberration it was
for the U.S. Congress to have been so attentive to
universal human rights during the nineteen-seventies.
The least well-informed have attributed the origin of
the concern with universal rights to President Jimmy
Carter and speculated about its sources in his
personal religious convictions, ignoring the fact that
the fundamental recent legislation about human
rights in U.S. foreign policy—Sections 116 and 502B
of the Foreign Assistance Act—were the law of the
land before the Democrats held their nominating
convention in 1976. Others have looked as far back
as President Woodrow Wilson, and dismiss the
current commitment to human rights as a resurgence
of Wilsonian moralism. Besides confusing decency
and basic morality with moralism, the allegations of
Wilsonian origins are only slightly less superficial
than the imputations of Carterian origins. "A
consistent pattern of gross violations" may be the
unmistakably dreary prose of the twentieth-century
lawyer, but it does not take much insight to perceive
the continuity with "a long train of abuses and
usurpations, pursuing invariably the same object."
Nor is this the most fundamental continuity between
the universal rights by which the founders judged
governments and the universal rights by which the
Foreign Assistance Act, as amended in the nineteen-

Henry Shue, "In the American Tradition, Rights Remain Unalienable," *The
Center Magazine*, January/February 1984. Reprinted with permission from
The Center Magazine, a publication of the Center for the Study of Democratic
Institutions, Santa Barbara, CA.

seventies, now judges governments. . . .

It is not for governments to select, as suits their
own goals, which rights they will respect or promote.
On the contrary, rights constitute the standard by
which governments are to be judged. It is for the
purpose of securing rights that governments are
instituted; and although "governments long
established should not be changed for light and
transient causes," any form of government that is
destructive rather than protective of universal rights
may be altered or abolished. Indeed, it is not merely
"their right, it is their duty, to throw off such
governments." Any third party who assists such an
oppressive government in crushing a people's revolt
aimed at restoring fundamental rights has complicity
in preventing that people from doing its duty, much
less securing its rights.

If, faring badly in its attempt to crush the rebellious
American colonists, the British government had
sought an arms purchase (with long-term credit) from
the Spanish government, a Madrid Office on North
America (MONA) might well have protested that,
given its own bad record of rights violations, the least
Madrid could do would be to avoid complicity in
London's violations.

"Naive moralism," might have been the reply,
"and in any case, if we don't sell arms to the British,
the cynical French probably will." But MONA would
have been right in principle and, in the event, the
French did deal with the other side.

Perhaps things are different now? Some are, and
some are not. The most fundamental principle
embraced by the founders—limited sovereignty—not
only remains but is more firmly grounded than
before. Even sovereign national governments are
limited in what they may do, even—indeed,
especially—limited in what they may do to the people
who are dependent upon them for the protection of
their rights, i.e., their own citizens. The doctrine that
municipal *law* is definitive—that citizens have no

rights except the rights their current municipal laws grant them—is false. National legal systems themselves may be judged by moral principles, especially theories of universal rights. Further yet from the truth is the doctrine that pronouncements of the current regime are definitive—that citizens have no rights except the rights their government grants them. "We do not recognize that right here" is not a dispositive judgment, for there are rights that legal systems and established regimes ought to recognize and protect, irrespective of whether they choose to. That a group of unarmed noncombatants is in Soviet airspace, for example, changes nothing about their human rights to immunity from armed attack. If Soviet law does not recognize this right, Soviet law is morally defective.

The Concept of Limited Sovereignty

Limited sovereignty has recently been reaffirmed in a multilateral treaty—the Charter of the United Nations, ratified by the U.S. Senate. Article 55 of that treaty says, in part:

> The United Nations shall promote....universal respect for, and observance of, human rights and fundamental freedoms for all without distinction as to race, sex, language, or religion.

And Article 56 says:

> All Members pledge themselves to take joint and separate action in cooperation with the Organization for the achievement of the purposes set forth in Article 55.

That every member nation is pledged to take separate as well as joint action to promote universal observance of human rights means that it is no part of the sovereignty of the government of a member nation that it is at liberty to violate the rights of its own citizens. It is the legitimate business of every nation and of the United Nations Organization how every government treats every person, including its own citizens, who otherwise would have nowhere to turn.

"It is not for governments to judge rights and omit the rights that they do not find useful."

The UN Charter articulates a doctrine of even more limited sovereignty than the Declaration of Independence did. The Declaration said:

> Any government may be judged by whether it fulfills its purpose for being, which is to secure the rights of its citizens.

The Charter adds:

> ...and judgment may appropriately be rendered by the community of nations jointly and by other nations separately.

The condemnation by the U.S. government of rights violations by other governments, far from

being a meddling in "internal" affairs, is a responsibility pledged by the U.S. Senate in the ratification of the UN Charter. It is no part of a nation's legitimate business to abuse its citizens. That the people in question are the citizens of a particular state does not mean that they are the property of that state, to be used as its government sees fit. The charge that assessing other sovereign governments by the standard of whether they protect the rights of their people is "intervention into their affairs" is without basis. Even if, for example, the United States had not signaled its approval of the imposition of martial law upon the Philippines in 1972 by doubling its security assistance to the dictatorship, the United States would have the right and the duty to criticize, and to refuse to subsidize, the abuses under "Marcos law."

Picking and Choosing Rights

Equally baseless is the bizarre notion promulgated on its own behalf by the Reagan Administration that each government should be allowed to pick and choose among established human rights its own favorites and attend exclusively to those favored rights. Besides being a formula for the destruction of the fragile international consensus on a core of basic rights—because the Reagan list of favorites omits two out of the three general categories of rights that are internationally recognized as fundamental—this suggestion would be the most radical conceivable departure from the doctrine about the nature of rights implicit in the Declaration of Independence.

Perhaps the Reagan Administration does not accept the proposition that which rights belong to all humankind is either "self-evident" or settled by "nature's God"—if not, the Administration has plenty of company. But there are other, rational grounds on which to arbitrate the authenticity of disputed rights, and the last place that could plausibly be proposed as the arbiter of which rights are authentic, and which are basic, would be some portion of the bureaucracy of some one national government, such as the U.S. State Department.

When in the nineteen-seventies the U.S. Congress decided to add explicit reference to human rights to the laws governing foreign assistance, Congress did not arrogate to itself the authority to decide what the appropriate list of human rights would be, much less did it tailor a list to serve current political purposes....

Machiavellianism and Rights

The notion—articulated in the Department of State's classified policy memo of October, 1981, and embodied in Administration practice before and since—that human rights are primarily to be used as a means toward other ends of foreign policy, specifically, that rights can be treated as a weapon against the U.S.S.R., rationalizes the Administration's attempts at selective enforcement: narrow concentration exclusively upon the category of rights that is supposed most sharply to divide the United States and the Soviet Union. This manipulative attitude does not, unfortunately, lead merely to a bias in the choice of which rights are discussed. The attitude reveals an even deeper incomprehension of the nature of human rights and corrodes any appreciation of how human rights actually function.

Human rights are inconveniences—grit in the gears. Due process is a pain in the neck, torture gets quicker answers. Dissidents disrupt the war effort, the "disappeared" cause no further problems. Human rights are supposed to be nuisances and obstacles, especially for governments. They are not designed to allow the smooth execution of policy but to force policy to take twists and turns around individuals—often troublesome individuals, like stubborn Guatemalan Indians—whose insistence upon their own claims is a most unwelcome complication for people with bigger fish to fry.

"To decide. . . to keep talking about the absence of elections. . . in the adversary nation, but to say as little as possible in public about disappearances. . . in an allied nation, is to fail to respect the integrity of authentic rights."

Rights have a different logic from almost all the other considerations that go into policy. To fail to see this is to fail to understand how rights work. Most of the time reasoning about policy appropriately takes a means/end form. We decide which consequences we want to produce—we choose our ends—and then we select our means accordingly. Or, we look at the means at our command—we examine our resources—and then select our goals accordingly. Sometimes we let our ends dictate our means. Sometimes we let our means dictate our ends. And of course, unless we are hopelessly rigid, we usually do quite a bit of both, through a long series of mutual adjustments. We shave a little off the goal in light of the available resources; and we get busy and find some more resources because we do not want to reduce our goals any further, and so on.

Human Rights Are Constraints

There is nothing wrong with this mutual adjustment of means and ends—it is, in fact, the embodiment of one understanding of rationality—and there is nothing in general wrong with means/end reasoning. But rights do not fit. Rights cannot be accommodated within this pattern. Rights have a logic of their own, because rights are neither means

nor ends. Rights are constraints upon both means and ends. Rights set limits upon our normal—and, within these limits, perfectly legitimate—process of the mutual adjustment of means and ends.

This is not an original thought. It is not even controversial. It is the conventional wisdom about rights. But it has implications about what kind of foreign policy can correctly be claimed to be respecting human rights.

First, rights are not means, and therefore it is unacceptable to pick and choose among them as best serves your ends. This is a point that I have already made, and I list it here only to show how it fits into the over-all argument. It is perfectly legitimate to argue about which rights there are and which ones are basic. Substantive disagreements abound, and no one could be expected to pretend to believe in rights that one thinks are groundless.

What is dishonest—and is a betrayal of genuine rights—is to try to use rights merely as a means to other goals, which appears to be the policy of the Reagan Administration. To notice that within the nation that is one's chief adversary there are no free elections but that relatively few people are "disappeared" (they tend to be sent to mental hospitals and other forms of internal exile instead), while within one's allied states many people are "disappeared" but that partly free elections are held, and then to decide for this reason to keep talking about the absence of elections and of the consent of the governed which do violate basic rights in the adversary nation, but to say as little as possible in public about disappearances, which also violate a basic right, in an allied nation, is to fail to respect the integrity of authentic rights. It is an attempt to subordinate rights to ends of one's own. It is to respect only those limits that do not impede the pursuit of one's goals and to ignore those limits that are in the way. Yet the purpose of rights is to get into the way of politics-as-usual.

Stopping Communism

I take it that the current Administration's reply might be that if they use relatively quiet diplomacy about the execution of Guatemalan Indians and relatively loud diplomacy about the despotism of the Cuban government, they do not do so in pursuit of just any old goal. The goal of such policies is to stop the spread of Communism, especially its spread into Central America and the rest of "our" hemisphere. And this is to say that the goal is really human rights, after all. Since Communist regimes to a unique extent irretrievably, systematically, and severely violate human rights, any manipulation of rights along the way by the United States is for the sake of the ultimate defeat of Communism, which is to say the ultimate triumph of human rights. In this view, some rights may be temporarily sacrificed—or, at least, shortchanged—but these rights are being traded off now for a lot more rights later. Because we are at war against the most diabolical violators of rights in history, it is our duty to do whatever it takes to be sure we win.

I take it that I am spared here the task of assessing all the dubious factual assumptions, especially all the implicit comparative judgments, that would have to be correct if the above were to begin to be a compelling argument. As a description of the world, it is simplistic dichotomies compounded into bad theology—a Manichaean fantasy. Most of the relevant factual arguments and counter-arguments are already well-worn, in any case. I will mostly stick to the logic of that position.

This Administration's policy seems to be Machiavellianism in the pursuit of human rights—ruthlessness now for the sake of rights later—hardball so that rights will triumph in the end. But that does not wash, even in theory.

> "To trade the long-term good will of a whole society for the short-term cooperation of an individual dictator seems a poor trade."

Rights are not ends either. Rights are neither means nor ends. Rights are constraints upon both means and ends. To defend against the charge that rights are being treated as means by replying that they are instead being pursued as ends, would still fail to respect rights for what they actually are. (If the Administration has some more plausible argument for its apparently arbitrary manipulation of categories of rights, I would be relieved to learn about it.) Ends or goals may be deferred, especially if the deferred fulfillment will be greater than the immediate fulfillment would. It is simple prudence to wait, if by waiting you get more. But rights are not goals to be pursued in this fashion.

Building Responsive Institutions

This is not to deny that only the progressive realization of rights, civil or economic, is possible. It cannot simply be declared that infant mortality or police brutality will decline. The necessity of progressive implementation is more widely recognized in the case of economic and social rights, but it is no less true of rights to physical security and civil and political rights. Implementing rights means, . . . building responsive and responsible social institutions that do in fact protect people against the threats to which they are most vulnerable. This takes time—indeed, the task is never really finished. But unavoidable gradualism is not the same as optional deferral of rights until after other projects are

completed. Gradual progress and indefinite postponement are not the same thing.

Lenin is supposed to have said, "A revolution is not a dinner party." The current Administration seems to want to say, "Neither is the defense of democracy." But this spirit is precisely what human rights are intended to thwart. Even in the war there are things civilized people do not do in order to win.

I am criticizing the Administration for inconsistency, if it wants to maintain that human rights is a serious goal of U.S. foreign policy. One could consistently take the position that our adversary is so evil that triumph simply requires ruthlessness, that rights must be ignored completely. That would be a different position and would demand a different assessment. What cannot consistently be done, however, is to claim to be committed to human rights but committed to them as a long-range goal that can be reached only through regular and systematic complicity in severe violations of those rights over the medium term.

In sum, it seems to me that the Administration is attempting to use carefully selected rights as means to embarrass our adversaries. And if the justification of this policy is supposed to be that respect for rights is a long-range goal of U.S. foreign policy, this is merely another way to fail to treat rights as what they are: constraints upon both means and ends.

Moralism and Rights

Surely, it will be suggested, the preceding is a bit harsh toward the Administration, especially if it assumes that human rights may never be violated or that it is never necessary to violate one right in order to fulfill another. Actually the above criticisms do not depend on any such extreme and puristic assumptions; but it is incumbent upon me to spell out a plausible position that lies between Machiavellianism and moralism in the realm of rights. To discuss when rights may be violated is to discuss the ethics of second-best: i.e., "dirty hands," messy compromises, tragic choices. These are supremely difficult issues, and my suggestions will be primitive at best. They will also, I suspect, upset both some advocates of "realism" and some advocates of rights.

First, a wet blanket. It is dramatic to believe that one faces tragic choices. It is thrilling to think that one must do evil in order to achieve good. It is flattering to see oneself as the hero who must soil his very soul so that others need not. Would it be all right to torture a child to death in order to save the world from Soviet-style Communism? Wow! I bet it would. Shades of Dostoevsky! Exciting stuff! If we are going to have to break eggs to make this omelet, let's not be prissy.

All this may reflect inordinate faith in the power of dirty fighting. Ruthlessness is not always so wonderfully effective—the Nazis, for example, did lose in the end. Cautionary note: since necessary evils can be so bracing to perform, we should be quite certain they are actually necessary. Fighting fire with fire can be satisfying, especially if you really hate your enemies. But we should always first be sure that water would not work equally well—or, sad thought, even better.

Guidelines for Hardball

Still, sometimes rights must be violated—or, at the very best, violations of rights must be overlooked. Can we formulate any *Guidelines for Hardball?* I think so.

First, if you are playing dirty because you are determined to win, be sure the dirty playing is actually helping you win. This is obvious in theory but much ignored in practice, in part perhaps because playing dirty can be exhilarating once you really get into it. I am, of course, not suggesting the principle: do it if it helps you win. The principle is: do it only if it helps you win. If the justification for indulging—or, as often happens in the U.S. cases, subsidizing with aid or supplying with weapons, technology, advice, and political endorsement—violations of fundamental rights is that the violations are contributing over the long run to U.S. national security, at least be sure that the U.S. position is in fact being strengthened.

"The practical difficulty about playing hardball with human rights is that people do not appreciate being subjected to malnutrition, torture . . . and other violations of their basic rights."

Ignorance compels me to leave detailed case studies to others, but to my eyes much of our allegedly realistic swashbuckling seems not merely ineffectual but extremely counterproductive. After Ferdinand Marcos eliminated traditional democracy from the Philippines in 1972, we doubled security assistance in the name of making Clark Field and Subic Bay more secure. Already in 1979 when I visited Manila and Cebu for discussions about human rights, it was clear that our main accomplishment had been to attract the Filipino people's hatred of the corrupt opulence and brutal repression of the dictator to ourselves as his foreign sponsor, just as we were then also doing in Iran. Twenty years ago, it would have been difficult to have found two more passionately pro-American societies than the Iranian and the Filipino. U.S. diplomacy has succeeded in alienating the one and is well on the way to alienating the other. To trade the long-term good will of a whole society for the short-term cooperation of an individual dictator seems a poor trade.

The second of the guidelines for hardball is proportionality. The marginal contribution to, for example, U.S. national security of our indulgence of rights violations must be significantly greater than the harm done by the violations. Try to imagine that it was somehow to the advantage of U.S. interests in Guatemala to have a murderous fanatic like Rios Montt on our team. Did it contribute enough to U.S. interests to have been worth the slaughter of so many Indians?

Criteria Simplistic

We appear to operate with the simplistic dichotomy: Is he the enemy of our enemy or not? If he is our enemy's enemy, then he gets a blank check. Think of Turkey and South Africa: Is there any extent of human rights violations that would lead this Administration to do any more than slap wrists? If not, their anti-Communism gives them a blank check (and they know it). This means that as long as these regimes occasionally do a little to support U.S. foreign policy, they can commit a lot of violations within the societies they rule. This means, in turn, that proportionality goes by the board.

The South African government is one of the most totalitarian dictatorships in the world today. Its entire legal system has been designed to prevent majority rule. The family has been invaded by laws controlling the physical movements of individuals in such a way that a breadwinner often cannot live in the same house with his or her spouse, but must live in barracks hundreds of miles away in order to hold a job. Freedom of expression is controlled even for the minority that is permitted to vote. Christian theology has been twisted into a perverse racist ideology, and children are taught that the maintenance of luxury and privilege is the preservation of civilization.

The justification for the gentleness of U.S. criticisms of the refusal ever to consider self-government in South Africa, compared to the perfectly appropriate vehemence of U.S. criticisms of such dictatorships as those in Albania and Bulgaria, is South Africa's supposed contribution to U.S. national security in the form of ready access to strategic minerals.

Benefits to US Security Ambiguous

Part of the difficulty of sensing any approximation of proportionality in such cases is that the supposed benefits to U.S. security tend to be speculative and hypothetical, while the violations of rights are concrete and actual. If the U.S. Air Force quickly needed a large number of planes of a certain sort, and if those planes could only be built using certain strategic minerals, and if we had forgotten to stockpile the minerals even though the U.S.S.R. remembered to, and if Zimbabwe did not also have the minerals in question (or would not sell them because of the U.S. alliance with South Africa), and if

South Africa was still under the control of the current rulers, and if they would not sell the minerals simply for the money involved but only out of good will, then we might need their good will. Would you invest in the stock of a company whose success depended upon the conjunction of so many different factors? Meanwhile, millions of South Africans are being herded into the poorest regions of their country, where it is very difficult to earn enough money to feed their children, and deprived of self-government. Are these stunted (and shortened) lives worth less than the increment in U.S. national security that might depend upon the good will of the South African regime?

The third guideline for hardball is closely related: the violations of rights must be the least evil alternative. Once again, this is obvious in theory but much neglected in practice. To continue with the example of South Africa, suppose that without the planes built with South Africa's strategic minerals, the United States would lose a war that would lead to the imposition of a dictatorship wider and more cruel than the current South African regime. In that case, the test of proportionality would be satisfied.

But why couldn't we have gone ahead and stockpiled the strategic minerals and then aggressively supported democracy for South Africa? Well, it would be expensive; it would add to the nation's deficit. But now we are talking about indulging *apartheid* in order to save money, not in order to defend our national security. We can obtain the strategic minerals either way—it is simply cheaper to do it by deferring our purchases of strategic minerals until we actually need them and meanwhile staying on the good side of the South African regime.

Three Justified Reasons

In sum, I am willing, unlike some of my friends in the human rights movement, to concede that in foreign policy the tolerance of rights violations by allied governments can be morally justified—but only if certain conditions are met. Undoubtedly other conditions must also be met. But at least the following is already clear. It is acceptable to tolerate violations of basic rights that could effectively have been opposed

(1) only if the toleration of the violations contributes in fact to the important goal for the sake of which it is advocated;

(2) only if the contribution to the other important goal is significantly greater than the harm done by the toleration of the violations; and

(3) only if the toleration of the violations is the least evil compromise that will contribute to the other important goal.

I suspect that the facts hold comfort for the purists who find this whole discussion of compromising rights to be objectionable. How many cases satisfy even these three conditions, leaving aside others that

I have failed to specify?

For example, I have used U.S. indulgence of South Africa's systematic racism to illustrate the difficulty of satisfying condition 2. In fact, I do not think U.S. indulgence of *apartheid* even satisfies condition 1. I think we are creating conditions in which we will be hated and despised by the regime that overthrows the regime we are now supporting.

The practical difficulty about playing hardball with human rights is that people do not appreciate being subjected to malnutrition, torture, arbitrary imprisonment, and other violations of their basic rights. It is not easy to cultivate the favor of the violators without incurring the hatred of the violated, who in many cases are likely to form the next government whenever it comes. This is not a moral argument—it is an appeal to national interest—but it is highly relevant for those self-styled realists who want us to deal with the world as it really is. Most of the students now demonstrating against the Marcos dictatorship will live to dance on Marcos' grave. Not even General Alfredo Stroessner, our old pal in Paraguay, can live forever.

Henry Shue is the Director of the Center for Philosophy and Public Policy at the University of Maryland and the author of Basic Rights: Subsistence, Affluence, and U.S. Foreign Policy.

The Monroe Doctrine Compels Intervention

Albert L. Weeks

"The Monroe Doctrine, proclaimed on Dec. 2, 1823, is used by the ruling circles of the United States of America for carrying out systematic interference into the affairs of Latin American states and forcing upon them enslaving treaties.... V.I. Lenin has written, 'Rise up, Latin Americans! Oppose the interpretation of the Monroe Doctrine that America only means North America. Latin Americans dread the U.S.A. and demand independence!'"

From the
Soviet Military Encyclopedia,
Vol. 5, p. 379.

In 1815, there were only two independent nation-states in the New World: the United States and Haiti. In just eight more years, this number had soared: La Plata (the modern nation of Bolivia), Chile, Peru, Colombia and Mexico all fought for and won their independence from Spain, just as we had won our independence from Great Britain.

America strongly supported these Latin-American and Caribbean independent movements, in which such heroes as Simon Bolivar went down in history as liberators.

The year 1823—160 years ago—was the time when the British sent a note to us proposing that we and they "bar France from South America." This event started some thinking in Washington, and President Monroe and his Cabinet put their minds to drafting some sort of statement that would keep the New World free of colonizers—but not only French ones....

Against Russia

Actually, when the final document was released—Dec. 2, 1823—the "Monroe Doctrine" was not

directed primarily at West European states (such as Spain, France, etc.), but against *Russia*.

It was Tsarist Russia that was on Monroe's mind when his doctrine was issued to the American public in the form of a message to both houses of Congress. The Russians had penetrated the continental United States as far south as San Francisco at this time early in the 19th century. The Louisiana Purchase, during Jefferson's administration, had "moved" our country far westward, as we began to feel the nationalist yearning to "flesh out" the country from the Atlantic to the Pacific. With Russians in California, this westward expansion was partially blocked by a foreign presence.

John Quincy Adams, a member of Monroe's Cabinet, thought the leading edge of the planned Monroe Doctrine should be directed at Russia, not France, et al. On July 17, 1823, he frankly informed the Russian ambassador to Washington that Imperial Russia's claim to American territory extending northward roughly from the southern Oregon border, called "Oregon Country" in those days, or 51 degrees North Latitude, was invalid. To Adam's mind, colonial establishments far removed from the colonizing country's shores were "immoral" and "destined to fall." The New World, he warned the ambassador from St. Petersburg, must now be considered closed to further colonization by both West or East European colonizers.

In October, St. Petersburg got around to replying to the Adams brief to the ambassador. The Russian message: Adams represented "expiring republicanism,"—an early form of Khrushchev's "We will bury you!"

Reason for Doctrine

So, the Monroe Cabinet's successive discussions of the impending tenor of the new doctrine revolved about the following:

- Russian extension of her colonial establishments

Albert L. Weeks, "Russia and the Monroe Doctrine," *The Washington Times*, August 16, 1983. cc The Washington Times, 1983. Reprinted with permission.

in the Far West; the tsar's denunciation of democratic principles.

• Rumored European intervention in Latin America to turn back the independence movements there.

• The British proposal for joint U.S.-British cooperation in blocking colonization in the Western Hemisphere (a ruse, in part, since Britain herself wished to enjoy colonialist prerogatives).

As the discussions proceeded throughout the summer and fall of 1823, Adams again commented on that main target of the emergent Monroe Doctrine: Russia. "I remarked," he wrote in his memoirs, "that the communications lately received from the Russian Minister (ambassador) afforded, as I thought, a very suitable and convenient opportunity for us to take our stand against the Holy Alliance (a reactionary, anti-democratic coalition headed by the tsar), and at the same time to decline the overture from Britain."

"The principles are, or should be, more firmly planted in our national consciousness today than ever before."

After some vacillation on the president's part—he did not wish to inflame Russian-American relations or prod Russia into war with Turkey, against whom Greece struggled for independence—Monroe consented to making his historic statement about a New World free of any further foreign expansionism and intervention.

Positive and Negative Principles

The Monroe Doctrine mostly reflected Secretary of State Adam's republicanism, while deleting some of the more vehement appeals for Greek independence or criticism of other countries. Essentially, the doctrine was composed of two parts: positive and negative principles.

Positive principles: (a) "The American continents, by the free and independent condition which they have assumed and maintain, are henceforth not to be considered as subjects for future colonization by any European powers." (b) "The political system of the allied powers (in Europe) is essentially different. . .from that of America. . .We should consider any attempt on their part to extend their system to any portion of this Hemisphere as dangerous to our peace and safety."

Negative principles: (a) "With the existing colonies or dependencies of any European power (in other parts of the world) we have not interfered and shall not interfere." (b) "In the wars of the European powers in matters relating to themselves we have never taken any part, nor does it comport with our policy to do so."

Commenting on the provisions of the Monroe Doctrine, Professor Samuel Eliot Morison, the well-known historian, wrote:

"Critics of Monroe have pointed out that his message was a mere declaration, which in itself could not prevent an intervention which had already been given up; that in view of the exclusive power of congress to declare war, a mere presidential announcement could not guarantee Latin American independence. That may be true, but is irrelevant.

Firmly Implanted Principles

"What Adams was trying to do, and what he and Monroe accomplished, was to raise a standard of American foreign policy for all the world to see; and to plant it so firmly in the national consciousness that no later president would dare to pull it down."

Morison wrote these words in 1964. Little did he know then that a foreign power would intervene—in great force with huge shipments of arms to foreign-supported "mercenary" and subversive guerrillas—in the New World two decades later, precisely on the old Holy Alliance formula of killing liberal-democracy as an "expiring" and/or "capitalist" creed.

Far from its being a matter of presidential "daring" to support the Monroe Doctrine, the present incumbent in the White House is compelled, by circumstances, and his own principles, to honor the 160-year old declaration.

The principles are, or should be, more firmly planted in our national consciousness today than ever before.

Albert L. Weeks is a journalist for The Washington Times.

"What [the US] should not be doing is. . .launching invasions and war games in the service of blind doctrine."

The Monroe Doctrine Is No Excuse for Intervention

New York Times

If you want war, nourish a doctrine. Doctrines are the most frightful tyrants to which men ever are subject, because doctrines get inside of a man's own reason and betray him against himself.... Doctrines are always vague; it would ruin a doctrine to define it, because then it could be analyzed, tested, criticized, and verified.... Somebody asks you with astonishment and horror whether you do not believe in the Monroe Doctrine.... You do not know what it is; but you do not dare to say that you do not, because you understand that it is one of the things which every good American is bound to believe in. Now when any doctrine arrives at that degree of authority, the name of it is a club which any demagogue may swing over you at any time and apropos of anything.

—From "War," by William Graham Sumner, 1903.

The ideologues and idealists who inspired that warning, from a noted conservative, are swinging their club again. They have stampeded the country into Caribbean military ventures in virtually every decade of this century. Their alarms—anti-Spanish or anti-British or anti-Soviet—have rarely proved justified, and their interventions have done vastly more harm than good. But here they go again.

You don't believe in the Monroe Doctrine? You accept the Brezhnev Doctrine of Irreversible Revolution? You want Another Cuba? Never heard of the Domino Theory?

For such slogans, the Treasury is opened, the Navy sets sail, C.I.A. armies cross borders and American commitments are drawn in quicksand. When the people balk, the flags are raised still higher and the President merges all slogans into one unreasoned cry:

> There can be no question: The national security of all the Americas is at stake in Central America. If we cannot defend ourselves there, we cannot expect to prevail elsewhere. Our credibility would collapse, our

alliances would crumble, and the safety of our homeland would be put at jeopardy.

Soviets Not Problem

The problem, it's easy to forget, is not a Soviet attack or missile base but El Salvador, a small, long-misgoverned country whose feeble rulers are unable to put down either a Marxist-led revolt or the counterterror of the right. Though his ambassador said this civil war will take a decade to resolve, Mr. Reagan has made it America's war.

Why? Probably because of Nicaragua, whose welcome revolution produced an unwelcome Cuban-style regime. The Sandinista rebels now running Nicaragua have been rooting for and helping the rebels in El Salvador and, anticipating Yankee hostility, taking arms from Cuba and other Soviet friends.

Mr. Reagan says he'll go to any lengths to stop Nicaragua's interference. But the evidence grows that this is a pretext for efforts to overthrow the Sandinista regime. Honduras has been made a base for American-led campaigns into both El Salvador and Nicaragua, and people in Washington now expect—intend?—that provocations will permit the Honduran Army, supported by American forces, to crush the leftists in both countries.

The Administration insists it will thus provide for the "safety of our homeland" with a few billion dollars and without many American troops. Its private documents, however, already stress the value of at least threatening direct American action.

Managing Central America

With the public unmoved, and Congress torn between doubt and loyalty, Mr. Reagan has now summoned Henry Kissinger and a chorus to justify his course or suggest a better one. But what kind of approach is that to a problem the President puts at the top of his list? This commission is a chorus of amateurs. . . . And Choirmaster Kissinger, though a most agile diplomat, brings no open mind. He long ago raised his own voice in the Administration's sloganeering:

> If we cannot manage Central America, it will be impossible to convince threatened nations in the Persian Gulf and in other places that we know how to manage the global equilibrium. We will face a series of upheavals. . . It escapes me why we have to apply the Brezhnev Doctrine in Central America and assert that any Communist government that has established itself can never be changed.

There they are: Monroe Doctrine, Global Equilibrium, Domino Theory, Brezhnev Doctrine, Irreversible Revolution. He might as well yell "Remember the Maine"—as Mr. Reagan did last month in refusing to rule out combat troops.

"The idea that the whole world is tilting from right to left and threatening to bury the Americas. . . is a dangerous delusion."

The mystery sinking of the U.S.S. Maine in Havana harbor became the bloody shirt of the jingos who pushed for war with Spain in 1898 to stretch America's empire to Puerto Rico and the Philippines. They at least had a naval imperative, as did the Presidents who for the next 50 years colonized the Caribbean for its sea lanes and Panama Canal. If Mr. Reagan would but remember the Canal treaties, which he meanly opposed, he might update his knowledge of Latin reality and diplomatic possibility.

America's Survival

Presidents Eisenhower and Kennedy "lost" Cuba on their watch, but the United States survived. So well, in fact, that for the next 20 years, it mostly ignored Latin America. Mr. Reagan may "win" back Nicaragua, as Guatemala was won back in 1954, but that would only prolong the misery and resentment on which radicals prey and build anti-Yankee plots. We may have forgotten who saddled Nicaragua with the Somoza dictatorship; Nicaraguans have not.

Forget the Monroe Doctrine. It was a young America's prayer for isolation from Europe's conflicts and later a pretext for aggrandizement. It is resented by Latins and, like the Maine, irrelevant to the nuclear age. Keeping Soviet bases out of the Americas is a matter for the superpowers to resolve, as they did in Cuba after a confrontation that neither should want to repeat.

Forget the Global Equilibrium. That is nothing more than a pitch for spheres of influence, and those have to be earned, as in Europe. Nicaragua is no more surely "ours" than Pakistan, or Afghanistan, is

the Russians'. Mr. Kissinger is right to say that mismanaging power anywhere can dissipate power everywhere, but wisdom does not flow only from the barrel of a gun. Nicaragua's deplorable passage from a right- to left-wing dictatorship is an object lesson, not a threat to world peace.

Beware the dominoes, by all means. Nicaragua, like Cuba, should be prevented from exporting weapons, by joint action of hemisphere nations. But blockades won't keep radical ideas from reaching frail societies.

Does that mean acquiescing in the triumph of communism in one Cuba after another, in the doctrine of the Irreversible Revolution? Of course not. Even Cuba will not forever be a Soviet ally. Much depends on what the United States has to offer Latin Americans, including its revolutionaries. Fidel Castro's renown owes as much to our hysterical opposition as it does to his own accomplishments.

Revolutions are unsettling, but not inevitably Communist. If Communist, they are not inevitably pro-Soviet. If pro-Soviet, they are not irreversible. Only the Red Army keeps Eastern Europe Communist; Chinese and Yugoslav Communists have become America's friends. The idea that the whole world is tilting from right to left and threatening to bury the Americas in a Marxist avalanche is a dangerous delusion—just one more doctrine.

Provoking Incidents

There are many things the United States should be doing for hemisphere stability, democracy and prosperity, to defend its genuine interests, diminish Soviet influence and dispel the impression that it is threatened by social justice in Latin America. What it should not be doing is overthrowing containable leftist regimes or fighting for lost reactionary causes, launching invasions and war games in the service of blind doctrine.

The President who remembers the Maine in the Caribbean forgets the Maddox and Turner Joy in Tonkin Gulf. He is inviting, perhaps provoking, incidents, practicing neither vigilance nor diplomacy but adventurism. He is drifting into war and turning minor problems into colossal defeats.

This viewpoint appeared as an editorial in The New York Times *on September 24, 1983.*

"Just as America helps people around the world who are hungry for food, we should help people who hunger for freedom and self-determination."

Intervention Protects Democracy

Jim Courter

As I stand among you today, I have no doubt that I am addressing a class of well-educated young men. I know that today's graduates, as well as those who came before you and those that will follow, are the type of men who make good citizens. Your parents and educators are proud of this fact, and I share in that pride.

So my talk today is not going to be centered around your role as American citizens. Instead, I would like to give you some thoughts about your role—our role, our country's role—as citizens of the world.

Minding Our Own Business

We have all heard people say that our country should mind its own business in the world—they say, "Let other countries solve their own problems, we'll take care of our own." According to this attitude, which I call the "new isolationism", we should not look beyond our own shores, we shouldn't think of ourselves or our country as members of a larger community.

Well, considering the fact that we have plenty of problems to solve here at home, it would be nice if we were able to ignore the rest of the world.

However, the simple fact of the matter is that we *can't* ignore the rest of the world. We're too involved in it to turn away.

Trade is but one example: The imports we buy and the exports we sell link us to every other country on the globe.

Defense is another example of our global involvement. We share the burden of defending the free world with friendly nations who are our allies. I happen to believe that it's time for the Europeans and Japanese to start picking up the tab for more of the defense bills that you and I are paying—in order to

Jim Courter, address at Admiral Farragut Academy in New Jersey, June 4, 1983.

get them to pay more, we need a foreign policy.

In addition, we should remember that our country enjoys, or would like to enjoy, a position of respect and leadership in the world. Even our isolationist friends want to be able to tell the Japanese to open their markets to our exports. And they certainly must have had some strong things to say to Ayatolla Khomeini when he seized our diplomats and made them prisoners a few years ago in Iran.

In other words, even the strongest isolationists find times when they want the world to stand up and listen when American interests are at stake.... A leader can't be effective, he can't be respected, if he chooses to lead where and when it suits him, and to stick his head in the sand when he doesn't want to get involved.

Vietnam Syndrome

Because of our experience in the Vietnam War, the strongest pillar of the new isolationist philosophy is the belief that it is never justified for the United States to take sides in any conflict, especially one involving the use of military force. This may even be the prevailing philosophy in America today....

Since the Vietnam War, several events have occurred which should cause us to re-evaluate the isolationist strains in our thinking.

First, regardless of what your opinion is or was about the Vietnam War, we all have to make the grim observation that everyone's worst fears about that part of the world have come true. After the war, bloodbaths occurred. Cambodia fell like a domino and a holocaust occurred there. Countless Vietnamese risked their lives in small boats to flee communism, and many died on the high seas. There is no hope for democracy in the country they left behind. These are the sad facts.

Let's also recall the seizure of our diplomats in Iran a few years ago. After these defenseless people were seized by force and held by a barbaric regime for no reason whatsoever, few could argue that it wasn't right for President Carter to try to use force to save them. I'm referring, of course, to the military rescue attempt that had to be aborted before our men reached Tehran. We may be disappointed that we failed, but not that we tried.

The third event I want to mention is the Falklands war of 1982. This is a case where a defenseless people, a peaceful people, was told by the Argentine government that they were to have new citizenship and a new form of government. They are British subjects and want to remain that way, but the Argentine dictators had a different idea, and they delivered their message through the barrel of a gun. I believe, and I know many of you agree, that Prime Minister Thatcher was right to send the royal Navy to retake the islands. In doing so, she did the world a service. She told the petty dictators of the world that they can't freely abuse or conquer defenseless people in remote parts of the globe, and that if they do so, there is a price to pay.

Freedom—The Highest Value

What I'm trying to suggest, ladies and gentlemen, is that freedom should be the highest value of our foreign policy, and that while we seek no conflicts, America will defend freedom when necessary.

"Freedom should be the highest value of our foreign policy, and. . .America will defend freedom when necessary."

If you really want to measure the change in our country's attitudes over the last twenty years, please join me in thinking back to the cold January day in 1961 when we inaugurated a new President, John F. Kennedy. In his inaugural address, he inspired us all with a vision of America as an active citizen of the world, helping poor countries, strengthening the United Nations, seeking cooperation with our adversaries, and above all, defending freedom. He said:

> Let every nation know, whether it wishes us well or ill, that we shall pay any price, bear any burden, meet any hardship, support any friend, oppose any foe, in order to assure the survival and success of liberty.

President Kennedy went on to say:

> Let all our neighbors know that we shall join with them to oppose aggression or subversion anywhere in the Americas.

I don't think it's an exaggeration to say that if President Kennedy were alive today to deliver this speech, over a hundred members of the House of Representatives would have a screaming fit and say that he was trying to start a war.

But just as we should heed General Sherman's advice to avoid war at all costs, we would also heed President Kennedy's advice to defend freedom, at any price.

Threat in Central America

President Kennedy's words are very apt today, because as I speak to you today, freedom is being threatened in Central America.

And we are being asked to help defend it by the people of El Salvador, who are the victims of a campaign of destruction and terror by a band of guerrillas who have almost no popular support, and seek to upset the young, struggling democracy there.

As you may have guessed, I am a supporter of President Reagan's policy to defend democracy in El Salvador. Actually, we're not being asked to defend anything, we're being asked to provide training and material help so that the Salvadorans can defend themselves.

Ladies and gentlemen, I could give you lots of technical arguments to support my position. I could talk about the presence of Soviets, Cubans, East Germans and the PLO—yes, the PLO—in Nicaragua. I could talk abut the arms the Soviets are sending to the region. I could talk until I'm blue in the face about the potential threats to our own mainland's security that could come about if things go the wrong way in Central America.

But instead, I'd like to tell you a little story about something that occurred last March 28 in El Salvador, concerning a common person like any one of us here today.

It was election day in El Salvador. People were standing in long lines to get to the polling places. One strong woman, a mother of two, had been standing in line since 5 a.m. Her name is Anna Maria de Martinez. At 9 a.m., Mrs. de Martinez was still waiting patiently in the hot sun, and she was two blocks away from the polling place. She was approached by an American newspaper reporter, who asked her a few questions. As she fanned her face in the heat, Mrs. de Martinez told the reporter:

> I'll wait here all day if I have to. The rest of the world seems to have made decisions about El Salvador. Now it's my turn.

As far as I'm concerned all the beauty and purpose of democracy can be found in this simple, eloquent statement of one Salvadoran voter. We should take note of her determination to have a say in her own government. We should also take note of the fact that Mrs. de Martinez was joined that day by 80% of her country's eligible voters, who overcame tremendous obstacles to vote that day.

What kind of obstacles? First of all, there were long lines and general disorganization at the polls. The greatest obstacles, however, were posed by the guerrillas.

Unsupported Guerillas

Even though these guerrillas claim to represent the best interests of El Salvador, they have almost no support, and they know it. For this reason, elections scare them. They tried to get the people to stay home in an election day boycott, but they failed. So, they turned to what they know best, which is violence. They tried to take polling places by force on election day and hoped that the battles they started would keep people away in fear. They blew up over two hundred vehicles that could have helped bring people to the polls. They even attacked some voters. But the people feared the violence less than the guerrillas feared the will of the people, and the election was a great victory for the cause of democracy.

"Why should we turn away when the Soviets are actively promoting war and bloodshed in our hemisphere?"

I can't resist pointing out that under perfect conditions, we Americans can't even get sixty percent of our voters to the polls. When it rains, we automatically expect about ten percent less turnout. It was raining *bullets* in El Salvador that day, and eighty percent voted.

Over a year has passed since that election, and a new election is being planned. The guerrillas have gained no support in the meantime, and their violence continues. They destroy bridges, trucks, and roads, and are generally waging war on the economy, which is struggling with 40% unemployment. They have made it almost impossible for their country to conduct trade with Honduras, their neighbor to the north. Still, they claim to represent the best interests of the people.

And still, there are people in this country who believe that the legitimate, elected government of El Salvador should negotiate with these terrorists.

I agree with the Salvadoran government—negotiations should begin if the guerrillas agree to stand for election. Short of that, there's nothing else to negotiate about. To offer them a share of power would be to take the ballots of Mrs. de Martinez and her countrymen, and throw them in the trash can.

And further, I agree with President Reagan, who wants to help this young, struggling democracy in its battle against a cowardly band of guerrillas.

Just as America helps people around the world who are hungry for food, we should help people who hunger for freedom and self-determination.

"Imposing" Democracy

Now, the isolationists will tell us that it isn't right to offer our help. We should mind our own business—we shouldn't impose our system on other people, they tell us.

But think about that for a minute. Isn't it a little odd to talk about "imposing" democracy on another country? We're not trying to impose a system of government on El Salvador. We're merely trying to guard the right of people like Mrs. de Martinez and others to choose the system they want, and impose it on themselves.

Furthermore, why should we turn away when the Soviets are actively promoting war and bloodshed in our hemisphere? I ask the isolationists, why?

There's only one reason for us to turn away from our neighbors, and it has to do with perception. You see, isolationists see the world as they would like it to be, not as it really is. Isolationists don't know that there are enemies of freedom in the world—violent enemies, at that. It's a well-known fact in many parts of the world, but it sinks in slowly here in America. The people of Poland know it. The people of Afghanistan know it. They know it in Vietnam and Cambodia, and in Angola, and now in Central America, they know it too. My question is, when will our country re-awaken to this simple fact?

Ladies and gentlemen, I have just spent some time outlining the moral reasons for helping stop Communism and promoting democracy in Central America.

There are countless strategic reasons as well, and they will all come to you if you stop to think how much we depend on the commerce that goes through the Caribbean and the Panama Canal.

And there is also the practical reason that can be summed up in one word: refugees. If you think we have problems now with immigration from Mexico and Latin America, how do you think we will do if Central America goes Communist?. . .

Take your own look at Central America. Ask yourself all the hard questions and look at all the facts. Ask yourself this question: as a citizen of the world, what should America do? Make no decision in haste, and hear all sides of the argument. This is what I have done.

And in doing so, I have looked and looked for some ambiguity, some unseen factor that would prove me wrong in my conviction that we should help these people. I have found none.

I think that we should help Central America resist Communism as a matter of moral duty to the Central American people, and as part of our own duty to defend our security. To shy away from this obligation because of a philosophy that tells us to hide our head in the sand when the going gets tough, would be a tragedy. We can't afford to be isolationists, especially in our own hemisphere.

Jim Courter is a Republican Congressman from New Jersey.

Intervention Provokes Hostility

Frank Church

America's inability to come to terms with revolutionary change in the Third World has been a leitmotif of U.S. diplomacy for nearly 40 years. This failure has created our biggest international problems in the post-war era.

But the root of our problem is not, as many Americans persist in believing, the relentless spread of communism. Rather, it is our own difficulty in understanding that Third World revolutions are primarily nationalist, not communist. Nationalism, not capitalism or communism, is the dominant political force in the modern world.

You might think that revolutionary nationalism and the desire for self-determination would be relatively easy for Americans—the first successful revolutionaries to win their independence—to understand. But instead we have been dumbfounded when other peoples have tried to pursue the goals of our own revolution two centuries ago.

Yes, the United States generally has supported political independence movements, as in India or later in Africa, against the traditional colonial powers of Europe. Those situations were easy for us—we've never been colonialists. But where a nationalist uprising was combined with a Marxist element of some kind or with violent revolutionary behavior, Americans have come unhinged.

This happened most dramatically in the biggest tragedy of American diplomacy since World War II, Vietnam. But it has happened repeatedly in other countries as well, most recently in Nicaragua and El Salvador.

Repeating Old Patterns

Given the size and the seriousness of our failures to deal successfully with nationalistic revolutions, you might think we'd be busy trying to figure out why

Frank Church, "It's Time We Learned to Live with Third World Revolutions," *The Washington Post National Weekly Edition*, March 26, 1984. Reprinted by permission.

we've done so badly, and how we could do better in the future. But on the contrary, we simply stick to discredited patterns of behavior, repeating the old errors as though they had never happened before.

The latest example is the report of the Kissinger Commission on Latin America, which painted events in Central America in ominously stark colors. The commission said that in principle America can accept revolutionary situations, but in Nicaragua and El Salvador we cannot. Why? Because of Soviet and Cuban involvement.

But the sad fact is that the Soviets will always try to take advantage of revolutionary situations, as will the Cubans, particularly in this hemisphere. To solve our problem we have to learn to adapt to revolutions even when communists are involved in them, or we will continue to repeat the errors of the last four decades.

Revolutionary regimes are not easy to live with—particularly for a country as conservative as the United States has become. As Hannah Arendt—no Marxist herself—noted in her classic work, "On Revolution," the U.S. had made a series of desperate attempts to block revolutions in other countries, "with the result that American power and prestige were used and misused to support obsolete and corrupt political regimes that long since had become objects of hatred and contempt among their own citizens."

Coming to Terms with Revolutions

Why does America, the first nation born of revolution in the modern age, find it so difficult to come to terms with revolutionary change in the late 20th century?

One answer involves the nature of our own revolution. It was essentially a revolt against political stupidity and insensitivity. With sparsely populated, easily accessible and abundant lands, the restless and dissatisfied in early America had an outlet for their discontent. The young United States never had to deal with the limitless misery of an impoverished majority.

In the first half of this century, when the country faced the prospect of sharpened class conflict as a result of the excesses of an unbridled capitalism, we were blessed with patrician leaders, Theodore and Franklin Roosevelt, who had the foresight to introduce needed reforms. An intelligent, conservative property-owning class had the sense to accept them.

But our experience is alien to other countries which do not share our natural wealth. In poor countries a desperate majority often lives on the margin of subsistence. A selfish property-owning minority and, often, an indifferent middle class intransigently protect their privileges. Dissidence is considered subversive. It isn't surprising that those who wish to change these conditions resort to insurrection.

They take their lead not from the American, but from the French revolutionary tradition where, in Arendt's phrase, the "passion of compassion" led the Robespierres of the time to terrible excesses in the name of justice for the impoverished masses.

The spectacle of violent, sometimes anarchic revolutionary activity combined with an obsessive fear that revolutions will inevitably fall prey to communism has led us to oppose radical change all over the Third World, even where it is abundantly clear that the existing order offers no real hope of improving the lives of the great majority. As a result, those who ought to be our allies—those who are ready to fight for justice for the impoverished majority—find themselves, as revolutionaries, opposed not only to the ruling forces in their own societies, but to the United States as well.

I am not arguing that revolutions are romantic or pleasant. History is full of examples, from France to Iran, of revolutions born in brutality and often accompanied by extended bloodbaths of vengeance and reprisal, and which ultimately produce just another form of authoritarianism to replace the old. But the fact that we may not like the revolutionary process or its results is, alas, not going to prevent revolutions from happening. On the other hand, the fact that revolutions are going to happen need not mean disaster for the United States. Our past failures do suggest a way we can adapt to revolutions without fighting them or sacrificing vital national interests.

Vietnam Lessons

Consider the case of Vietnam. Our overriding concern with "monolithic" communism led us grossly to misread the revolution in that country. Ignoring centures of enmity between the Vietnamese and the Chinese, our leaders interpreted a possible victory for Ho Chi Minh's forces as a victory for international communism. The war against the

French and then the war among the Vietnamese in our eyes became a proxy war by China and the Soviet Union even after those two powers had split, destroying the myth of "monolithic" communism. Indochina, in the new American demonology, was seen as the first in a series of falling dominoes.

Vietnam did fall to the communists, but only two dominoes followed—Laos and Cambodia, both of which we had roped into the war. Thailand, Malaysia and Indonesia continue to exist on their own terms. The People's Republic of China, for whom Hanoi was supposed to be a proxy, is now engaged in armed skirmishes against Vietnam.

"We have to learn to adapt to revolutions even when communists are involved in them."

Meanwhile, the United States, having been compelled to abandon the delusion of containing the giant of Asia behind a flimsy network of pygmy governments stretched thinly around her vast frontiers, has at last shown the good sense to make friends with China. American influence, far from collapsing, has drawn strength from this sensible new policy, and has been rising ever since. As for communism taking over, it is already a waning force. The thriving economies are capitalist: Japan, South Korea, Taiwan, Hong Kong, Singapore. You don't hear Asians describing communism as the wave of the future.

If any lessons were learned from our ordeal in Southeast Asia, they have yet to show up in the Western Hemisphere, where our objective is not simply to contain, but to eradicate communism, regardless of the circumstances in each case. In pursuit of this goal, we took heed of one restraint. The legacy of resentment against us still harbored by our Latin neighbors, stemming from the days of "gunboat diplomacy," made it advisable, wherever feasible, to substitute "cloak and dagger" methods.

Hence the American-sponsored coup to oust a democratically elected government in Guatemala in 1954. The ousted president, Jacobo Arbenz Guzman, was by American standards a New Deal liberal. But our cold warriors of that era decided he was a red threat. As U.S. Ambassador John Peurifoy, arriving in Guatemala on his special mission, put it: "If Arbenz is not a communist, he"ll do until the real thing comes along."

Unspared Efforts

In Cuba, the United States spared no efforts to get rid of Fidel Castro. We financed and armed an exile expeditionary force in an attempted repeat of the Guatemalan coup, only to see it routed at the Bay of

Pigs. Then the CIA tried repeatedly to assassinate Castro, even enlisting the Mafia in the endeavor; and the U.S. imposed against Cuba the most severe trade embargo inflicted on any country since the end of World War II.

Even where the left gained power in fair and open elections, the United States has been unwilling to accept the results. Hence the Nixon administration's secret intervention in Chile aimed first at preventing the election of and then at ousting President Salvador Allende.

Despite these and other efforts by the United States, another Marxist regime did arise in the hemisphere: Nicaragua. And, true to form, the United States has again financed, armed and promoted an exile army whose objective is the overthrow of the Marxist government.

After spending billions of dollars, and emptying the CIA's bag of dirty tricks, what do we have to show for our efforts? Obviously, the hemisphere has not been swept clean of communism. Cuba and Nicaragua have avowedly Marxist regimes; in El Salvador, an insurrection gains momentum against an American-trained and equipped army, despite an American-sponsored agrarian reform program and our hopes for the election of a reformist president and legislature. The result defies our grand design: The army fights indifferently; the agrarian reform is stymied, and the Salvadoran middle class and traditional landed interests remain determined to elect extreme rightists to the important legislative and executive positions. In other words, the beneficiaries of the existing order refuse to yield their privileges to please the United States.

By our unrelenting hostility to Castro, we have invested him with heroic dimensions far greater than would be warranted by Cuba's intrinsic importance in the world. We are in the process of performing a similar service for the commandantes of Nicaragua and, at the same time, discrediting the legitimate domestic opponents of their political excesses. We left Cuba no alternative to increased reliance upon Russia; we now seem determined to duplicate the blunder with Nicaragua.

Failed Objectives

So by any standard, American policy has failed to achieve its objective, to inoculate the Hemisphere against Marxist regimes. But are we fated to cling to the disproved policy of opposing each new revolution because of Marxist involvement, even though the insurgents fight to overthrow an intolerable social and economic order?

By making the outcome of this internal struggle a national security issue for the United States, as the Kissinger Commission does, we virtually guarantee an American military intervention wherever the tide turns in favor of the insurgents. If this happened in El Salvador, it would be difficult to imagine that the present administration would stop before it had gone "to the source," Nicaragua or even Cuba. In the process, of course, we would fulfill Che Guevara's prophecy of two, three, many Vietnams in Latin America.

We should stop exaggerating the threat to us of Marxist revolution in Third World countries. We know that there are many variants of Marxist governments and that we can live comfortably with some of them. The falling domino theory is no more valid in Central America than it was in Southeast Asia. And it is an insult to our neighbor, Mexico, for it assumes that Mexico is too weak and unsophisticated to look out for its own interests.

We repeatedly ignore the explicit signals from Marxists in Central America that they will respect our concerns. For example, we worry that the commandantes in Nicaragua will invite the Soviets or the Cubans to establish bases in their countries. Yet, the Sandinista government in Nicaragua has explicitly committed itself not to offer such bases to the Russians or Cubans. Instead, they have offered to enter into a treaty with the United States and other regional counries not do do so. And the political arm of the insurgents in El Salvador has also committed itself to no foreign bases on its soil.

"We will marvel at the progress in our own neighborhood, measured from the day we stopped trying to repress the irrepressible."

Why not take them up on these commitments? The United States, with the help of other regional powers who share our interest, including Venezuela, Mexico, Colombia and Panama, has the means to ensure that the revolutionaries keep their word. Mexico and Venezuela are the primary supplies of oil to Central America, including Nicaragua and El Salvador. If Nicaragua violated its treaty obligation to all of those states, the U.S. would have legal grounds and regional sanction for taking action.

Negotiating to Victory

If the threat of communist bases is real, then a negotiated agreement precluding them would surely be perceived as a "victory" for the United States and a "defeat" for the Russians. And with a Nicaraguan treaty agreement with the United States and the countries of the region, the Salvadoran insurgents, should they prevail, could do no less than sign a similar agreement.

What is significant about the Nicaraguan revolution is that although it has followed the classic lines, in comparative terms it has been relatively moderate.

There has been no widespread terror, and the regime has shown itself to be sensitive to international pressure. If we cannot come to terms with the Nicaraguan revolution, then we probably are fated to oppose all revolutions in the hemisphere.

The problem is illustrated in human terms by a vignette of the Kissinger Commission in Nicaragua. According to press accounts, the members of the commission were angered by the confrontational tone of the meetings with the Nicaraguans and their obvious reliance on Soviet and Cuban intelligence.

Imagine the setting: The commission arrives in Nicaragua one week after the Contras, supported by the U.S., blow up a major oil facility. On the one side, a largely conservative commission led by Henry Kissinger, Robert Strauss, William Clements and Lane Kirkland, men in their late 50s or 60s, expecting to be acclaimed for their willingness to listen to the upstart revolutionaries. On the other side, peacock-proud Nicaraguan commandantes in their 30s or early 40s, men and women who had spent years fighting in the mountains, who had seen their friends and comrades die at their side in opposition to the U.S.-supported Somoza dictatorship, and naturally resentful of U.S. support of the counterrevolution. To them, a commission led by Kissinger, the architect of the campaign to destabilize Allende, had to be seen as a facade for the American plan to bring them down. Is it really any wonder that there was no sweet meeting of minds?

Whoever gains power in Central America must govern. And governing means solving mundane problems: the balance between imports and exports, mobilization of capital, access to technology and know-how. The United States, the Western European countries and the nearby regional powers, Colombia, Mexico and Venezuela, are the primary markets and sources of petroleum, capital and technology. The social democratic movements in Western Europe are important sources of political sustenance for revolutionary movements in Central America.

If we had the wit to work with our friends and allies rather than against them, the potential abuses and exuberance of revolution in Central America can be contained within boundaries acceptable to this country. There is no reason to transform a revolution in any Central American country, regardless of whence it draws its external support into a security crisis for the United States.

Logical Objective

The objective of U.S. policy should be to create the conditions in which the logic of geographic proximity, access to American capital and technology and cultural opportunity can begin to exert their inexorable long-term pull. Russia is distant, despotic and economically primitive. It cannot compete with the West in terms of the tools of modernization and the concept of freedom.

But if we insist on painting the Cubas and Nicaraguas of this world—and there will be others— into a corner, we save the Russians from their own disabilities. If, on the other hand, we were to abandon our failed policy and adopt the alternative I suggest, pessimism might soon give way to optimism. After a while, democracy may begin to take root again. The wicked little oligarchies, no longer assured American protection against the grievances of their own people, may even be forced to make the essential concessions. The United States and Cuba might be trading again, joined in several regional pacts to advance the interests of both. And Marxist governments, far from overtaking the hemisphere, will be lagging behind as successful free enterprise countries set the standard and the pattern for the future.

We will marvel at the progress in our own neighborhood, measured from the day we stopped trying to repress the irrepressible and exchanged our unreasonable fear of communism for a rekindled faith in freedom.

Frank Church was a Democratic senator from Idaho. He was chairman of the Senate Foreign Relations Committee from 1979-1980. He died of cancer in 1984.

viewpoint **33**

The Grenada Intervention Was Justified

George Shultz and Kenneth Dam

The following viewpoint consists of statements by two of the United States' official representatives, Secretary of State George Shultz and Deputy Secretary of State Kenneth Dam. Part I is the transcript of a press conference held by Shultz on October 25, 1983. Part II is from a speech delivered to the Associated Press Managing Editors' Conference in Louisville on November 4, 1983.

I

I'd like first, to cover four points:

First, the reasons for the President's decision to commit U.S. forces in Grenada;

Second, our objectives as we undertake this effort;

Third, the chain of events as they led up to the President's decision in the immediate days preceding it; and

Fourth, the situation on the ground, very generally, as it was as of about half an hour ago.

There are two basic reasons that determined the President's decision.

Welfare of American Citizens

First was his concern for the welfare of American citizens living on Grenada. There are roughly 1,000 of them. And what we saw was an atmosphere of violent uncertainty: of the Prime Minister of the country first put under house arrest, freed from house arrest by a large number of demonstrators estimated in the thousands, with that demonstration in one way or another becoming attacked, and with the Prime Minister and some of his Cabinet members being executed. We see no responsible government in the country. We see arrests of leading figures. We see a shoot-on-sight curfew in effect. Reports—their validity uncertain—but reports are rife about arrests, deaths, and so forth and certainly random sporadic

George Shultz, press conference on October 25, 1983. Kenneth Dam, speech before the Associated Press Managing Editors' Conference, Louisville, KY, November 4, 1983.

firing that one could hear.

All of these things are part of an atmosphere of violent uncertainty that certainly caused anxiety among U.S. citizens and caused the President to be very concerned about their safety and welfare. He felt that it is better under the circumstances to act before they might be hurt or be hostage than to take any chance, given the great uncertainty clearly present in the situation. So that is the first reason why the President acted as he did.

Second, the President received an urgent request from the countries closest to the area—the Organization of Eastern Caribbean States—which of course, followed these developments very closely over a long period of time, and intensively in recent days, and which determined for themselves that there were developments of grave concern to their safety and peace taking place. They brought in Jamaica and Barbados and, along with those two countries, made a request to the United States to help them in their desire to ensure peace and stability in their area. So their analysis of the situation, in terms of the atmosphere of violent uncertainty, paralleled our own.

And so in response to the request of this organization and in line with a request that they made pursuant to Article 8 of their treaty, bringing the states together, the President decided to respond to the request and to look after the welfare of American citizens in this atmosphere of uncertainty and violence.

Insofar as our objectives are concerned, there are basically two, and very simple:

• To secure the safety of American citizens—and, for that matter, the citizens of other countries—and to assure that any who wish to leave may do so and

• To help the OECS states establish law and order in the country and establish again governmental institutions responsive to the will of the people of Grenada.

Review of Events

Third, let me just review very briefly the chain of events here.

I think you undoubtedly know that on October 13, Prime Minister Bishop was placed under arrest and subsequently on October 19 the demonstration and the freeing of him from house arrest took place, and then his death—our information is by execution—taking place on that date.

On Thursday, October 20, as information about these developments was coming in to us here in the United States, of course, the President was receiving them, and he had the Vice President chair a meeting in the Situation Room reviewing these events. That meeting took place in the late afternoon. I was not present at the beginning of the meeting since I was testifying before a Senate committee in closed-door session, but I came in with Ambassador Motley [Assistant Secretary for Inter-American Affairs Langhorne A. Motley] about halfway through the meeting. Essentially it was a meeting to review the grave turn of events and to consider their implications for the American citizens on the island.

"The developments on Grenada pose definite security and peace risks to [the Organization of Eastern Caribbean States]."

Subsequent to that meeting and on the recommendation of that group, the President decided to divert some naval ships in the area, among them the task force that was carrying the group that would be the normal routine replacement of the Marines who are in Lebanon, and diverted them in the direction of Grenada. Other ships were also included. That was essentially precautionary so that if the situation became worse, we would have a capability nearby.

There were various discussions during the course of Friday, but on Saturday, October 22, a message came in from Bridgetown in Barbados. It reached me at 2:45 a.m. in Augusta, and I discussed it with Bud McFarlane [Robert C. McFarlane, Assistant to the President for National Security Affairs]. About a half or three-quarters of an hour later, the Vice President convened the key national security advisers in Washington. In their discussion, we joined with him through a secure conference call to again evaluate the situation and the information in the cable.

OECS Request

The information in the cable basically gave the OECS states' analysis of the situation and stated their very strong feeling that they must do something

about it on Grenada and their feeling that they were not able to do it on their own, and so they asked if we would help them. I think you should note that by this time they had not only gathered themselves together, but they had brought Barbados and Jamaica in their counsels.

We shortly got the President up and we went through this material with him and went over the views of various people who were taking part in the Vice President's meeting. The President talked to the Vice President, talked to the Secretary of Defense, heard their views, gave his own reactions.

The meeting chaired by the Vice President reconvened at 9:00 on Saturday morning. The President spoke to them by telephone. I might say we considered whether or not to return, and we felt that if we were going to respond to this request, then the element of secrecy should be maintained; and if there was a sudden change in the President's plans, it would obviously call great attention to that possibility, so we stayed there.

On Sunday, October 23, of course, that night we received the tragic news from Lebanon of the attack on the Marines, and that stunning news caused the President to decide in the early morning hours that we should return right away to Washington, and we did so. During the day on Sunday, we met first from 9:00 to 11:00, and then again later in the afternoon from 4:00 to 7:00.

However, tracking back to the decision on October 22, it was felt that we should explore carefully with the leaders of the OECS and Jamaica and Barbados their information, their analysis, and their intentions. So, Ambassador McNeil and Major General Crist were sent to Bridgetown. They left early Sunday. They met in the afternoon and evening in Barbados with leaders there, and they were on the telephone to us through this period, giving us more information about the evaluation being made in the area and the options that were before us.

Tentative Decision

It was in the meeting on Sunday—that last meeting on Sunday—that the President made what I think one would call a tentative decision that we should respond to this urgent request and that particularly so since their analysis and ours were of a very uncertain and violent situation threatening to our citizens.

On Monday, October 24, of course, the plans were being made, the forces organized, and so forth. The President met in the afternoon from roughly 2:15 to 3:30—something like that—with the Secretary of Defense and the Joint Chiefs and at the conclusion of that meeting made a sort of semifinal military decision, he having had the advice of all his advisers the previous day that on general grounds we should proceed. I think the directive of the President to proceed was signed at about 6 p.m. yesterday. That's kind of the chronology.

Finally, where do we stand on the ground? Both airports at Pearls and Port Salines have been secured. The elements of the Caribbean task force, that is, of the countries from the Caribbean, are at Port Salines. They landed approximately 10:45 this morning. I think there are about 150 there now. The southern campus at the medical college near Port Salines Airport has been secured. There are no reports of injuries to any American civilians.

There are pockets of resistance in the St. George's area. I don't want to identify further precisely where, because this is an ongoing operation, and the military people need to be able to conduct their operation secure from any such disclosure. So that is the situation on the ground very generally at this point.

Questions from the Press

Q. The Charter of the Organization of American States, of which the United States is a member, provides that, "No state or group of states has the right to intervene, directly or indirectly, for any reason whatever, in the internal or external affairs of any other state...[This] prohibits not only armed force but also any other form of interference.... Aren't we in violation of that charter? And if not, why not?

"For all intents and purposes, there is no semblance of a genuine government there."

A. The Organization of Eastern Caribbean States provides for their collective security. Those states are not members of the Rio treaty, under which the clause that you've mentioned would operate. So they have asserted themselves under their treaty and asked us to help them.

As they view it, and perhaps you heard Prime Minister Charles [of Dominica] today express her views, most eloquently, the developments on Grenada pose definite security and peace risks to them, and that is the basis for their desire to act. Some are members of the OAS, but they are not members of the Rio treaty. Their equivalent of the Rio treaty is their own treaty.

Right of Sovereignty

Q. Yesterday, in testifying to the Senate, you said, "At stake is the right of a small country...to decide for itself how to achieve its sovereign objectives free of outside pressure, threat, or blackmail." You were talking about Lebanon there. But why should not that same standard apply to Grenada?

A. It does, and in Grenada what you have at the present time is a set of events like this. In 1979, a constitutional government being in power; it was displaced by a bloodless coup, and Prime Minister Bishop has been in charge since that time.

In the events that I described to you, Prime Minister Bishop was placed under house arrest and then executed. For all intents and purposes, there is no semblance of a genuine government present. There is a vacuum of governmental responsibility— the only genuine evidence of governmental authority being a shoot-on-sight curfew. So in the light of that and in the light of the affinity that the other states feel together, they felt that they had to protect their peace and their security by taking this action and that doing so would help reconstitute legitimate government in Grenada.

Cubans and Soviets

Q. Do you believe that the Cubans and the Soviets were in any way responsible for the execution of Prime Minister Bishop? And to what extent was the action taken, at least in general terms, as a signal to Havana and Moscow that the United States was prepared to act to protect its own security?

A. I've tried to give very carefully what the considerations of the President were, and those are the reasons and the considerations for this action. This was not taken as a signal about anything else. It was taken in the light of the threat to the lives and welfare of American citizens and in the light of a request from the local states which are close to the situation and whose analysis of the situation was parallel to, and in fact went a lot further than, our own.

Q. About the first part of the question, sir, do you have any reason to believe that the Soviets or the Cubans were in any way responsible for the overthrow of the Bishop government?

A. We don't have any direct information on that point. However, the OECS states feel that such is the case. But that is not the basis of this action on our part.

Length of Stay

Q. You have said that one of our two objectives there was to help the OECS states establish law and order and governmental institutions. Does that mean that our troops will remain in Grenada until that is done? And what is your time estimate for how long that will take?

A. Our troops will leave as soon as they possibly can. The forces of the other countries in the Caribbean which have initiated this action will be in the lead and working with Grenadians in trying to establish law and order and some form of provisional government. It will be their decision to make in seeing how this situation unfolds, and we will leave as soon as we possibly can, leaving the island to those who are closest to it.

Q. Does that mean that our troops will stay there until they are satisfied that law and order has been established—they, the other countries?

A. I think they will be leaving very, very promptly, and we will have to decide for ourselves what the proper conditions are. We will work with the people from the other governments involved, and they will have a leading role in making these decisions.

I might say that the situation is one in which, in many of these countries, there really is no armed force at all. Prime Minister Charles expressed herself—I might say to the amusement, I guess, of Secretary Weinberger—she said, "When I took office, I decided the worst thing in the world you could have is an army, so I abolished it. I saved myself a lot of money, and I saved conflict between the military and the police force on the island."

So that's what they have. And their belief is that the way to have law and order is not to have military establishment but just a police force. And I imagine that they will work somewhat along those lines, although Grenada has a population of 100,000, so you have to take measures.

Shift of Balance

Q. The United States has now invaded this island with help from some other area democracies in the Caribbean to save and protect the lives of a thousand people, none of whom so far as we know, I guess, have been injured or killed. Why did it take the deaths of 200 Marines in Beirut to send Commander Kelley [General Paul X. Kelley, Commandant of the U.S. Marine Corps] there to start thinking about additional preventive, precautionary measures to save those lives?

A. Of course, we have been concerned about the safety of our Marines all along as they have been there. It didn't take this terrible tragedy to create that concern. I think it is certainly the right thing to do, to have the Commandant of the Marine Corps go promptly to the area and evaluate the security situation in a fresh way. And I think, also, that when you are establishing a presence in an operating, commercial, international airport, naturally, you make decisions that involve some sort of balance between security risks on the one hand and what it takes for an airport to operate on the other.

I think that, certainly, in the light of the terrible tragedy, that balance needs to be shifted, and the emphasis on security will have to be heightened very significantly. But, of course, we look for Gen. Kelley's report.

I think there is a certain pertinence to your question, because, it seems to me, and the President had to weigh this, with the violent and uncertain atmosphere that certainly was present on Grenada, the question is: Should he act to prevent Americans from being hurt or taken hostage? I think that if he waited and they were taken hostage, or many were killed, then you would be asking me that same question: "Why didn't you, in the light of this clear

violent situation, take some action to protect American citizens there?"

I don't want to get in the position of second-guessing myself, or the President, but rather to say, one has to weigh these considerations and be willing to make a decision in the light of all of the circumstances. And that is what the President did.

British Colony

Q. As you know, Grenada is a former British colony, and the Governor General there was appointed by the British, the person you spoke of a while ago. Mrs. Thatcher has said in Parliament over there that their government advised against this and that the British did not wish to go along with it. I would like to ask you two things flowing from that. First of all, does the fact that the British do not go along with it cause some cloud over the Governor General, the British-appointed person now being the one we look to? And, secondly, in view of their experience on the island, why did the United States disregard their recommendation?

A. We responded to the urgent request of the states in the area, which are now independent states. They're no longer British colonies. Although obviously the British have had great experience there, so have we. The Caribbean is in our neighborhood, too, so we have a very legitimate affinity for those people.

"We have no intention of staying there, and the government that will be produced by the people of Grenada is entirely up to them."

We responded to their request, just as Barbados and Jamaica did. British or other states that may or may not have been asked—I don't have the list of who the OECS asked to help them. But each state has to take its own decision, and the President took ours.

As far as the establishment of authority on the island is concerned, we believe that the Governor General is the logical person, given the fact that there is a vacuum of government there, and we expect that it will occur that way. We are, of course, always impressed with the views of the British Government and Mrs. Thatcher, but that doesn't mean that we always have to agree with them. Of course, we also have to make decisions in the light of the security situation of our citizens as we see it.

Casualties

Q. Can you give us a report on casualties, including whether there have been Cuban casualties in combat with Americans, and the status of the Cubans and the Soviets on the island?

A. I can't give you an account of casualties. I don't have that information at hand, but it will be made available as soon as we have it. I think probably the appropriate place, since they have it, is at the Pentagon.

As far as the Soviet Union and Cuba are concerned, as the operation got underway, we notified both the Soviet Union and Cuba of the fact of the operation, of our intentions, and of our readiness to look to the safety of their people in the island. It's my understanding that the Soviets that are there have been identified; they are safe, and their safety is being looked to. On the other hand, in the case of the Cubans, there are many more there. I think there are some 600 Cubans there—presumably, construction workers. But it is the case that some number—I don't know how many, and perhaps the military doesn't know at this point how many—are resisting and firing at our forces, and, of course, that would cause us to fire back.

Q. Who is in charge of Grenada tonight? I mean, at this minute? Where is Mr. Austin? Are we running the country, or are they still running the country? And, secondly, even though your intention may not have been to send a message, do you think anybody in the Caribbean or anywhere else in the world gets a message from this action?

A. I don't know. I can't identify the whereabouts of Mr. Austin who was not genuinely in charge insofar as we could see, in any case.

As far as who is running the country is concerned, the country has been in a state since the house arrest of Prime Minister Bishop, essentially, of a kind of vacuum of governmental authority. And that still exists although as the forces of the Caribbean task force are able to develop their contacts there, presumably a governmental structure will emerge.

As far as your philosophic question is concerned, of course, those who want to receive a message will have to receive it. That was not the purpose of this operation. The purpose was as I have stated it.

Yankee Imperialism

Q. Traditionally, in this part of the world, there's been a great concern about Yankee force, Yankee imperialism, Yankee aggression, et cetera. How do you intend to counter the impression that the United States is once again using its overwhelming military superiority in this part of the world to achieve a specific, political objective?

A. I think the principal point here is that the concerns and the requests for help came from the states in the region, and they have put their own forces into this picture. The fact that their forces are small in comparison with ours is only a reflection of the fact that they don't invest very much in the way of resources into military capability; and, of course, they don't have much to invest in the first place. It's in the nature of these countries that they're

essentially peaceful. But they have put what they can of their own forces forward, and they have taken the lead in suggesting this, and they are there now in the early stages of this effort. And as law and order returns, they will basically be in charge, not us. So it is no effort on our part to gain control of any other country.

Q. The British, who have been critical of this action, took an independent action against the Falklands last year when they thought it was necessary. If they cannot accept the American justification, how do you think, or how many countries in Latin America do you feel will accept the American explanation now?

A. Certainly, Jamaica, Barbados, and the Caribbean states involved. They have asked us very explicitly, not only in the first instances I brought out but on further probing from Ambassador McNeil, to really be sure that they had analyzed the situation carefully and they were making a thoughtful and thoroughly thought-through request, which they were and are.

"What we found in Grenada may be summed up as the military underpinnings for [a Cuban/Soviet military outpost]."

I think that's the thing you have to rest on, and it seems to me people ought to recognize where this request came from; and, also, the fact that we will leave promptly. We have no intention of staying there, and the government that will be produced by the people of Grenada is entirely up to them as far as we're concerned.

Q. You said that there were contacts with the Cubans and with the Soviet Union to inform them of what we were about to do, or had just done. Have there been any contacts at any level since then, and what have you heard from the Soviet Union about this?

A. I don't want to go into detail about diplomatic exchanges. But, of course, in general, their response has been that they expect us to look to the safety of their citizens. And certainly, as one might expect, they object strenuously to this action.

II

This is the 11th day since the combined U.S.-Caribbean peace force landed in Grenada to protect lives and restore order. That may not be enough time to make definitive historical judgments, but it is not too early to begin to reflect on the meaning of what happened. So I would like today to talk both about the collective action itself and about its larger significance for U.S. foreign policy....

Legal Authority for Action

U.S. actions have been based on three legal grounds.

First, as these events were taking place, we were informed, on October 24, by Prime Minister Adams of Barbados that Grenada's Governor General, Sir Paul Scoon, had used a confidential channel to transmit an appeal to the OECS and other regional states to restore order on the island. The Governor General has since confirmed this appeal. We were unable to make this request public until the Governor General's safety had been assured, but it was an important element—legally as well as politically—in our respective decisions to help Grenada. The legal authorities of the Governor General were the sole remaining source of governmental legitimacy on the island in the wake of the tragic events I have described. We and the OECS countries accorded his appeal exceptional moral and legal weight. The invitation of lawful governmental authority constitutes a recognized basis under international law for foreign states to provide requested assistance.

"Perhaps the first and most basic lesson of events on Grenada is that Cuban activities are not as benign as Fidel Castro would have us believe."

Second, the OECS determined to take action under the 1981 treaty establishing that organization. That treaty contains a number of provisions—in articles 3, 4, and 8—which deal with local as well as external threats to peace and security. Both the OAS [Organization of American States] Charter, in articles 22 and 28, and the UN Charter, in article 52, recognize the competence of regional peace and stability. Article 22 of the OAS Charter, in particular, makes clear that action pursuant to a special security treaty in force does not constitute intervention or use of force otherwise prohibited by articles 18 or 20 of that charter. In taking lawful collective action, the OECS countries were entitled to call upon friendly states for appropriate assistance, and it was lawful for the United States, Jamaica, and Barbados to respond to this request.

Third, U.S. action to secure and evacuate endangered U.S. citizens on the island was undertaken in accordance with well-established principles of international law regarding the protection of one's nationals. That the circumstances warranted this action has been amply documented by the returning students themselves. There is absolutely no requirement of international law that compelled the United States to await further deterioration of the situation that would have

jeopardized a successful operation. Nor was the United States required to await actual violence against U.S. citizens before rescuing them from the anarchic and threatening conditions the students themselves have described.

Clear Distinctions

Some are asking how this U.S. action can be distinguished from acts of intervention by the Soviet Union. Let me say that the distinctions are clear. The United States participated in a genuine collective effort—the record makes clear the initiative of the Caribbean countries in proposing and defending this action. This action was based on an existing regional treaty and at the express invitation of the Governor General of Grenada. Our concern for the safety of our citizens was genuine. The factual circumstances on Grenada were exceptional and unprecedented in the Caribbean region—a collapse of law, order, and governmental institutions. Our objectives are precise and limited—to evacuate foreign nationals and to cooperate in the restoration of order. Our objectives do not involve the imposition on the Grenadians of any particular form of government. Grenadians are free to determine their institutions for themselves. Finally, our troops have already begun to leave; we will complete our withdrawal as soon as other forces are ready to take over from us.

Those who do not see—or do not choose to see—these clear-cut distinctions have failed to analyze the facts. We have not made, and do not seek to make, any broad new precedent for international action. Our actions themselves are well within accepted concepts of international law.

The Rescue Operation

To minimize the potential loss of lives and maximize the chances of success, both the preparations for the multinational peace force and our final decision to participate had to be protected by keeping them secret.

When our forces arrived in Grenada, they immediately came under fire. And the main resistance came from Cubans, not Grenadians. The Cubans were very well armed. They were deployed at the airport, at the medical school where a large number of U.S. citizens were studying, at the Governor General's house, at a Cuban military encampment at Calivigny, and at several other forts and strategic points.

Despite the Cuban-led resistance, hostilities have now ended. U.S. forces are withdrawing. The Rangers left Sunday; the Marines yesterday.

The Governor General has thanked us for our assistance as a "positive and decisive step forward in the restoration not only of peace and order but also of full sovereignty."

The OECS is assisting the Governor General and prominent Grenadians to establish a provisional government capable of restoring functioning institutions and permitting early elections.

Seventeen flights have safely evacuated, at their request, 599 Americans and 121 foreigners. Their accounts of conditions in Grenada and praise for their rescuers speak for themselves. The respected Grenadian journalist Alister Hughes evidently spoke for the vast majority of people in Grenada, Grenadians and foreigners alike, when he said of the Caribbean peace force: "Thank God they came. If someone had not come in and done something, I hesitate to say what the situation in Grenada would be now."

Cuban and Soviet Involvement

While we were still assembling and evaluating the evidence, what we have found suggests that Grenada would have become a fortified Cuban/Soviet military outpost. I mentioned earlier that we had been concerned—well before the events which brought about our collective action—that Grenada could be used as a staging area for subversion of nearby countries, for interdiction of shipping lanes, and for transit of troops and supplies from Cuba to Africa and from Eastern Europe and Libya to Central America.

"A third lesson. . . is that in the absence of democratic institutions and legal safeguards, policy differences tend to degenerate into violence."

What we found in Grenada may be summed up as the military underpinnings for just such uses. We found five secret treaties—three with the Soviet Union, one with North Korea, and one with Cuba—under which these communist countries were to donate military equipment in amounts without precedent for a population of 110,000. We found artillery, antiaircraft weapons, armored personnel carriers, and rocket launchers. We found thousands of rifles, thousands of fuses, tons of TNT, and millions of rounds of ammunition. We found communications gear and cryptographic devices. We found agreements authorizing the secret presence of Cuban military advisers, some of them on a "permanent" basis.

All of the agreements stipulated that arms would be delivered to Grenada only by Cuban ships through Cuban ports. And although the Soviet Union was providing the arms and training free of charge, the Soviet Union required the Grenadians to keep all military arrangements secret and delayed the opening of a Soviet Embassy in Grenada until 18 months after entering into such arrangements.

Broader Lessons

Perhaps the first and most basic lesson of events on Grenada is that Cuban activities are not as benign as Fidel Castro would have us believe.

We have been regularly accused of exaggerating the dangers of Cuban/Soviet activities in countries like Grenada. However, what we found in Grenada suggests that, if anything, we were guilty of *understating* the dangers. We now know that we had underestimated Soviet use of Cuba as a surrogate for the projection of military power in the Caribbean. Examine again what we found—well-armed Cubans called construction workers; fortifications; stock-piled weapons; secret military treaties; personnel from Eastern Europe, Africa, and East Asia, all innocently enjoying a tourist paradise no doubt.

Think again about the facilities that all this would have secured—the Point Salines Airport, which would have enabled a MiG-23 carrying four 1,000-pound bombs to strike and return from Puerto Rico in the north to Venezuela in the south; the Calivigny military training area; a 75,000-watt radio transmitter capable of blanketing the entire Caribbean Basin; the potential for a deep-water harbor.

In light of this evidence, many Americans—and not a few Europeans—might productively reassess their estimate of the security concerns of the American Government and of the noncommunist countries of the Caribbean Basin.

Threat from "Friends"

A second, related point worth thinking about is what happened to Maurice Bishop. His experience graphically shows what could happen to those who put their faith in military assistance and advisers from Cuba and the Soviet Union, but then try to remain nonaligned. The threat to their freedom and survival may well come from the very system their friends have helped them put in place.

In the wake of Bishop's murder, Suriname expelled the Cuban Ambassador and 100 Cuban "technicians." The nine *commandantes* of Nicaragua might also wish to ponder their relationship with their Soviet and Cuban mentors.

A third lesson, and again one of particular importance for the Sandinistas, is that in the absence of democratic institutions and legal safeguards, policy differences tend to degenerate into violence. The way to end such violence is to fulfill their original promises of democracy and free elections.

A final lesson of the events in Grenada is that neighbors have a clear, ongoing responsibility to act in ways consistent with each other's legitimate security concerns. In Nicaragua, for example, Sandinista willingness to negotiate seriously, to reduce reliance on military power, and, most importantly, to stop belligerent behavior toward their neighbors would represent the high road to peace in

Central America.

US Policy in Central America

Taken as a whole, what these lessons imply for Central America is that we must focus our resources on finding more creative ways to foster democratic development and regional cohesion. It is for this reason that we are firmly committed to a comprehensive approach to that region's conflicts.

As President Reagan told a special joint session of Congress on April 27, our policy in Central America is based on four interlocking elements—democracy, development, dialogue, and defense.

• Our policy is to actively support democracy, reform, and human freedom in Central America—as much for El Salvador and Guatemala as for Nicaragua.

• The United States supports economic development and is devoting three times the funds to such development than to military assistance. The Caribbean Basin Initiative, I should note, is as open to Nicaragua as to Costa Rica and Honduras.

"The United States is pursuing a responsive and responsible role in this entire region."

• We support dialogue and negotiations—the internal dialogue of democracy in each country and the multilateral negotiations of nations honestly trying to live peacefully with each other.

• And we have and will continue to provide what the President has called a security shield against those who oppose democratization, economic development, and diplomacy.

Responsive, Responsible Role

In the interests of settling the conflicts in Central America before they reach a crisis stage, the United States is quietly but firmly supporting the regional Contadora process. It is no coincidence that the consensus of the nine countries involved about what is required for peace in Central America is parallel to our own. We support—as do Nicaragua's neighbors, especially the "Core Four" countries of Costa Rica, El Salvador, Guatemala, and Honduras—an end to terrorism, destabilization, and guerrilla warfare; a reduction of military forces and armaments; political reconciliation through free elections and respect for human rights; the removal of foreign troops and military advisers; and the commitment of resources more for economic development and reform than for military buildup and destruction.

What this all adds up to is that the United States is pursuing a responsive and responsible role in this entire region. I believe that we have the confidence to do so, even in the face of violence and uncertainty, because we had already learned what may be the underlying lesson of the collective response to the Grenada crisis: the best source of knowledge about an area is the people of that area—those most directly concerned with what is happening in their own neighborhood.

What Prime Minister Charles and the others told us while the Grenada crisis was building proved to be accurate. The Caribbean leaders faithfully reflected the feelings, the concerns, and hopes of the Grenadian people—and, may I add, of the U.S. citizens there as well. We listened to Grenada's neighbors, and we are doing the same thing in Central America. Our policy is responsive to Central American opinion polls, the statements of respected democratic leaders, and the Contadora "document of objectives." And we are responding in the Caribbean Basin Initiative: we listened when Latin and Caribbean economists told us that they wanted "trade not aid."

Leadership means listening and acting intelligently on what is heard. That is what we did in Grenada. That is what we are doing in Central America. And I believe the American people are coming to understand what their government is doing and why.

George Shultz is the secretary of state under the Reagan administration. Kenneth Dam is the deputy secretary of state under the Reagan administration.

The Grenada Intervention Was Unjustified

Fidel Castro

On October 15, 1976, a little over seven years ago, we gathered here, in this same place, to deliver a funeral address for the 57 Cubans who were vilely murdered in the Barbados plane sabotage, carried out by men who had been trained by the U.S. Central Intelligence Agency. Today we have come once again to bid farewell—this time to 24 Cubans who died in Grenada, another island not very far from Barbados, and a result of U.S. military actions.

Grenada was one of the smallest independent states in the world, both in territory and population. Even though Cuba is a small, underdeveloped country, it was able to help Grenada considerably, because our efforts—which were modest in quantity though high in quality—meant a lot for a country less than 400 square kilometers in size, with a population of just over 100,000.

For instance, the value of our contribution to Grenada in the form of materials, designs, and labor in building the new airport came to $60 million at international prices—over $500 per inhabitant. It is as if Cuba—with a population of almost 10 million—received a project worth $5 billion as a donation.

In addition, there was the cooperation of our doctors, teachers, and technicians in diverse specialties, plus an annual contribution of Cuban products worth about $3 million. This meant an additional annual contribution of $40 per inhabitant.

It is impossible for Cuba to render considerable material assistance to countries with significantly larger populations and territories, but we were able to offer great assistance to a country like tiny Grenada.

Many other small Caribbean nations, accustomed to the gross economic and strategic interests of colonialism and imperialism, were amazed by Cuba's generous assistance to that fraternal people. They may have thought that Cuba's selfless action was extraordinary. In the midst of the U.S. government's dirty propaganda, some may even have found it difficult to understand.

Feelings of Friendship

Our people felt such deep friendship for [Maurice] Bishop and Grenada, and our respect for that country and its sovereignty was so irreproachable, that we never dared to express any opinions about what was being done or how it was being done.

In Grenada, we followed the same principle we apply to all revolutionary nations and movements, full respect for their policies, criteria, and decisions, expressing our views on any matter only when asked to do so. Imperialism is incapable of understanding that the secret of our excellent relations with revolutionary countries and movements in the world lies precisely in this respect.

The U.S. government looked down on Grenada and hated Bishop. It wanted to destroy Grenada's process and obliterate its example. It had even prepared military plans for invading the island—as Bishop had charged nearly two years ago—but it lacked a pretext.

Socioeconomically, Grenada was actually advancing satisfactorily. The people had received many benefits, in spite of the hostile policy of the United States, and Grenada's Gross National Product was growing at a good rate in the midst of the world crisis.

A True Revolutionary

Bishop was not an extremist; rather, he was a true revolutionary—conscientious and honest. Far from disagreeing with his intelligent and realistic policy, we fully sympathized with it, since it was rigorously adapted to his country's specific conditions and possibilities.

Grenada had become a true symbol of independence and progress in the Caribbean. No one

Fidel Castro, speech in Havana, Cuba, November 14, 1983.

could have foreseen the tragedy that was drawing near. Attention was focused on other parts of the world.

Unfortunately, the Grenadian revolutionaries themselves unleashed the events that opened the door to imperialist aggression. Hyenas emerged from the revolutionary ranks. Today no one can yet say whether those who used the dagger of divisionism and internal confrontation did so for their own ends or were inspired and egged on by imperialism.

It is something that could have been done by the CIA—and, if somebody else was responsible, the CIA could not have done it any better. The fact is that allegedly revolutionary arguments were used, invoking the purest principles of Marxism-Leninism and charging Bishop with practicing a cult of personality and with drawing away from the Leninist norms and methods of leadership.

In our view, nothing could be more absurd than to attribute such tendencies to Bishop. It was impossible to imagine anyone more noble, modest, and unselfish. He could never have been guilty of being authoritarian. If he had any defect, it was his excessive tolerance and trust.

Conspirators

Were those who conspired against him within the Grenadian party, army, and security forces by any chance a group of extremists drunk on political theory? Were they simply a group of ambitious, opportunistic individuals, or were they enemy agents who wanted to destroy the Grenadian revolution?

History alone will have the last word, but it would not be the first time that such things occurred in a revolutionary process. In our view, [Bernard] Coard's group objectively destroyed the revolution and opened the door to imperialist aggression.

Whatever their intentions, the brutal assassination of Bishop and his most loyal, closest comrades is a fact that can never be justified in that or any other revolution. As the October 20 statement by the Cuban party and government put it, "No crime can be committed in the name of the revolution and liberty."

Internal Dissension

In spite of his very close and affectionate links with our party's leadership, Bishop never said anything about the internal dissensions that were developing. On the contrary, in his last conversations with us he was self-critical about his work regarding attention to the armed forces and the mass organizations. Nearly all of our party and state leaders spent many friendly, fraternal hours with him on the evening of October 7, before his return trip to Grenada.

Coard's group never had such relations nor such intimacy and trust with us. Actually, we did not even know that this group existed.

It is to our revolution's credit that, in spite of our profound indignation over Bishop's removal from office and arrest, we fully refrained from interfering in Grenada's internal affairs. We refrained even though our construction workers and all our other cooperation personnel in Grenada—who did not hesitate to confront the Yankee soldiers with the weapons Bishop himself had given them for their defense in case of an attack from abroad—could have been a decisive factor in those internal events.

Those weapons were never meant to be used in an internal conflict in Grenada, and we would never have allowed them to be so used. We would never have been willing to use them to shed a single drop of Grenadian blood.

"In Grenada, we followed the same principle we apply to all revolutionary nations and movements, full respect for their policies, criteria, and decisions, expressing our views on any matter only when asked to do so."

On October 12, Bishop was removed from office by the central committee, on which the conspirators had attained a majority. On the 13th, he was placed under house arrest. On the 19th, the people took to the streets and freed Bishop. On the same day, Coard's group ordered the army to fire on the people and Bishop, [Unison] Whiteman, Jacqueline Creft, and other excellent revolutionary leaders were murdered.

Cuba's Restraint

As soon as the internal dissensions, which came to light on October 12, became known, the Yankee imperialists decided to invade.

The message sent by the leadership of the Cuban party to Coard's group on October 15 has been made public. In it, we expressed our deep concern over both the internal and external consequences of the split and appealed to common sense, serenity, wisdom, and generosity of revolutionaries. This reference to generosity was an appeal not to use violence against Bishop and his followers.

This group of Coard's that seized power in Grenada expressed serious reservations toward Cuba from the very beginning because of our well-known and unquestionable friendship with Bishop.

The national and international press have published our strong denunciation of the events of October 19, the day Bishop was murdered.

Our relations with [Gen. Hudson] Austin's short-lived government, in which Coard was really in charge, were actually cold and tense, so that, at the time of the criminal Yankee aggression, there was no coordination whatsoever between the Grenadian army and the Cuban construction workers and other cooperation personnel.

The basic points of the messages sent to our embassy in Grenada on October 12 through 25, the day in which the invasion took place, have been made public. Those documents stand in history as irrefutable proof of our unblemished, principled position regarding Grenada.

Leftist Imperialists

Imperialism, however, presented the events as the coming to power of a group of hard-line communists, loyal allies of Cuba. Were they really communists? Were they really hard-liners? Could they really be loyal allies of Cuba? Or were they rather conscious or unconscious tools of Yankee imperialism?

Look at the history of the revolutionary movement, and you will find more than one connection between imperialism and those who take positions that appear to be on the extreme left. Aren't Pol Pot and Ieng Sary—the ones responsible for the genocide in Kampuchea—the most loyal allies Yankee imperialism has in Southeast Asia at present?

In Cuba, ever since the Grenadian crisis began, we have called Coard's group—to give it a name—the "Pol Potist group."

Our relations with the new leaders of Grenada were to be subjected to profound analysis, as was set forth in the October 20 statement by the party and government of Cuba. In it, we also stated that, due to our basic regard for the Grenadian people, we would not rush to "take any steps regarding technical and economic cooperation which might jeopardize the basic services and vital economic interest of the people of Grenada."

We could not accept the idea of leaving the Grenadians without doctors or leaving the airport, which was vital to the nation's economy, unfinished. Most certainly, our construction workers were to leave Grenada when that project was completed, and the weapons that Bishop had given them were to be returned to the government. It was even possible that our very bad relations with the new government would make it necessary for us to leave much earlier.

Cuban Duty

The thing that placed Cuba in a morally complex, difficult situation was the announcement that Yankee naval forces were en route to Grenada. Under those circumstances, we couldn't possibly leave the country. If the imperialists really intended to attack Grenada, it was our duty to stay there.

To withdraw at that time would have been dishonorable and could even have triggered aggression in that country then and in Cuba later on. In addition, events unfolded with such incredible speed that if the evacuation had been planned for,

there would not have been time to carry it out.

In Grenada, however, the government was morally indefensible. And, since the party, the government, and the army had divorced themselves from the people, it was also impossible to defend the nation militarily, because a revolutionary war is only feasible and justifiable when united with the people. We could only fight, therefore, if we were directly attacked. There was no alternative.

It should nevertheless be noted that, despite these adverse circumstances, a number of Grenadian soldiers died in heroic combat against the invaders.

Unjustified Yankee Intervention

The internal events, however, in no way justified Yankee intervention.

Since when has the government of the United States become the arbiter of internal conflicts between revolutionaries in any given country? What right did Reagan have to be so aggrieved over the death of Bishop, whom he so hated and opposed? What reasons could there be for this brutal violation of the sovereignty of Grenada—a small independent nation that was a respected and acknowledged member of the international community?

It would be the same as if another country believed it had the right to intervene in the United States because of the repulsive assassination of Martin Luther King or so many other outrages, such as those that have been committed against the Black and Hispanic minorities in the United States, or to intervene because John Kennedy was murdered.

The same may be said of the argument that the lives of 1,000 Americans were in danger. There are many times more U.S. citizens in dozens of other countries in the world. Does this, perchance, imply the right to intervene when internal conflicts arise in those countries?

"Imperialists, however, presented the events as the coming to power of a group of hard-line communists."

There are tens of thousands of Grenadians in the United States, England, and Trinidad. Could tiny Grenada intervene if domestic policy problems arose that pose some threat to its compatriots in any of those countries?

Putting aside the fallacy and falseness of such pretexts for invading Grenada, is this really an international norm that can be sustained? A thousand lessons in Marxism could not teach us any better about the dirty, perfidious, and aggressive nature of imperialism than the attack unleashed against Grenada at dawn on October 25 and its subsequent development.

Unproven Assertions

In order to justify its invasion of Grenada and its subsequent actions, the U.S. government and its spokesmen told 19 lies. Reagan personally told the first 13:

1. Cuba was responsible for the coup d'etat and the death of Bishop.
2. The American students were in danger of being taken hostage.
3. The main purpose of the invasion was to protect the lives of American citizens.
4. The invasion was a multinational operation undertaken at the request of Mr. [Paul] Scoon and the eastern Caribbean nations.
5. Cuba was planning to invade and occupy Grenada.
6. Grenada was being turned into an important Soviety-Cuban military base.
7. The airport under construction was not civilian but military.
8. The weapons in Grenada would be used to export subversion and terrorism.
9. The Cubans fired first.
10. There were over 1,000 Cubans in Grenada.
11. Most of the Cubans were not construction workers but professional soldiers.
12. The invading forces took care not to destroy civilian property or inflict civilian casualties.
13. The U.S. troops would remain in Grenada for a week.
14. Missile silos were being built in Grenada.
15. The vessel *Vietnam Heroico* was transporting special weapons.
16. Cuba was warned of the invasion.
17. Five hundred Cubans are fighting in the mountains of Grenada.
18. Cuba has issued instructions for reprisals to be taken against U.S. citizens.
19. The journalists were excluded for their own protection.

None of these assertions were proved, none are true, and all have been refuted by the facts. This cynical way of lying in order to justify invading a tiny country reminds us of the methods Adolph Hitler used during the years leading up to World War II.

Offer of Cooperation

The U.S. students and officials of the medical school located there acknowledge that they were given full guarantees for U.S. citizens and the necessary facilities for those who wanted to leave the country.

Moreover, Cuba had informed the U.S. government on October 22 that no foreign citizens, including Cubans, had been disturbed, and it offered to cooperate in solving any difficulty that might arise, so that problems could be settled without violence or intervention in that country.

No U.S. citizen had been disturbed at all prior to the invasion, and if anything endangered them, it was the war unleashed by the United States.

Cuba's instructions to its personnel not to interfere with any actions to evacuate U.S. citizens in the area of the runway under construction near the university contributed to protecting the U.S. citizens residing in that country.

Reagan's reference to the possibility that Grenada might turn into another Iran—a reference calculated to appeal to the U.S. feelings wounded in that episode—is a demagogic, politicking, dishonest argument.

The assertion that the new airport was a military one—an old lie that Reagan administration had dwelt on a lot—was categorically refuted by the English capitalist firm that supplied and installed the electrical and technical equipment for that airport.

"In order to justify its invasion. . ., the US government and its spokesmen told 19 lies."

The British technicians of the Plessey Company, which has made a name for itself internationally as a specialist in this field, worked alongside the Cuban construction workers, to whose civilian worker status they attest. Several countries of the European community that are members of the Atlantic alliance cooperated in one way or another with the airport. How can anyone imagine them helping Cuba to build a military airport in Grenada?

However, the idea that Grenada was being turned into a Soviet-Cuban base is refuted by the proven fact that there wasn't even one Soviet military adviser on the island.

Spurious "Secret" Documents

The supposedly secret documents that fell into the hands of the United States and were published by the Yankee administration a few days after the invasion refer to the agreement between the governments of Cuba and Grenada by virtue of which our country was to send Grenada 27 military advisers, which could later be increased to 40—figures that coincide with the ones Cuba published on the number of advisers, which was 22 on the day of the attack, to which were added a similar number of translators and service personnel from the mission.

Nowhere in those documents that they have been crowing over is there anything that has anything to do with the idea of military bases in Grenada.

What they do show is that the weapons that the Soviet Union supplied to the government of Grenada for the army and the militia were subject to a clause that prohibited their export to third countries. This refutes the idea that Grenada had been turned into an arsenal for supplying weapons to subversive, terrorist organizations, as the present U.S. administration likes to call the revolutionary and national liberation movement. No weapons ever left Grenada for any other country, and, therefore, Reagan can never prove that any did.

The assertion that Cuba was about to invade and occupy Grenada is so unrealistic, absurd, crazy, and alien to our principles and international policy that it cannot even be taken seriously. What has been proven is the absolutely scrupulous way in which we refrained from meddling in the internal affairs of that country, in spite of our deep affection for Bishop and our total rejection of Coard and his group's conspiracy and coup, which could serve only the interests of imperialism and its plans for destroying the Grenada revolution.

The messages containing precise, categorical instructions to our embassy in Grenada, which have been widely publicized by the government of Cuba, constitute irrefutable proof of the clear position of principles maintained by the leadership of our party and state with regard to the internal events in Grenada.

Cuban Personnel

The civilian status of the vast majority of the Cuban cooperation personnel in Grenada has been shown to the whole world by the hundreds of foreign journalists who saw them arriving in our country and who were able to interview each and every one of them.

Nearly 50 percent of them were over 40 years old. Who could question their status as civilian cooperation personnel and workers with long years of experience on their jobs?

When the U.S. government spokesmen asserted that there were from 1,000 to 1,500 Cubans in Grenada at the time of the invasion and that hundreds of them were still fighting in the mountains, Cuba published the exact number of Cuban citizens who were in Grenada on the day of the invasion—784, including diplomatic personnel with their children and other relatives.

The agencies that sent them and the kind of work they did were also reported, as well as the instructions given them to fight in their work areas and camps if attacked, and the fact that it was impossible—according to the information we had—that hundreds might still remain in the mountains.

Later, the names and jobs of all cooperation workers were published, as well as the known or probable situation of each one.

The facts have shown that the information provided by Cuba was absolutely true. There isn't a single fact in all that information that could be proven false.

Treacherous Attack

The assertion that the Cubans initiated the acts of hostility is equally false and cynical.

The irrefutable truth is that the Cubans were sleeping and their weapons were stored at the time of the air drop on the runway and around the camps. They had not been distributed. There weren't enough to go around, and they weren't distributed until the landing was already underway. And that is when the Cuban personnel went to the places assigned to them for that emergency.

Even so, our personnel, now organized and armed, had time to see the U.S. paratroopers regrouping on the runway and the first planes landing. That was the invader's weakest moment. If the Cubans had fired first, they would have killed or wounded dozens—perhaps hundreds—of U.S. soldiers in those early hours.

What is strictly historical and strictly true is that the fighting began when the U.S. troops advanced toward the Cubans in a belligerent way.

It is also true that when a group of unarmed cooperation personnel was captured, they were used as hostages and forced to lead the way in front of the U.S. soldiers.

"The assertion that Cuba was about to invade and occupy Grenada is so unrealistic, absurd, crazy, and alien to our principles and international policy that it cannot even be taken seriously."

The invasion of Grenada was a treacherous surprise attack, with no previous warning at all—just like Pearl Harbor, just like the Nazis. The note from the government of the United States to the government of Cuba on Tuesday, October 25, in an attempted response to our note of Saturday, October 22, was delivered at 8:30 in the morning, three hours after the landing had taken place and an hour and a half after the U.S. troops began attacking our compatriots in Grenada.

Deceitful Communication

Actually, on the afternoon of the 25th, the U.S. government sent the government of Cuba a deceitful note that led us to believe the fighting would cease in a reasonable and honorable manner, thus avoiding greater bloodshed. Although we immediately responded to that note, accepting that possibility, what the U.S. government did was to land the 82nd Airborne Division at dawn on the 26th and attack with all its forces the Cuban position that was still resisting.

Is this the way a serious government behaves? Is this the way to warn of an attack? Was this the way to avoid greater bloodshed?

Mr. Scoon blatantly declared that he approved of the invasion but that he had not previously asked anyone to invade Grenada. A few days after the landing, Mr. Scoon—lodged in the *Guam* helicopter carrier—signed a letter officially requesting the intervention. Reagan could not prove any of his false assertions.

Slanderous Charge

As a pretext for keeping the *Vietnam Heroico*—which was in the port of St. George's on the day of the invasion—from being used as a means of transportation for evacuating the Cuban hostages from Grenada, it was alleged that it carried special weapons. Its captain was immediately asked if by any chance he carried weapons onboard, and the only thing that was determined was that it had just one fearful weapon—its name: Vietnam.

The slanderous charge that Cuba had given instructions to carry out actions against U.S. citizens in other countries was given a worthy, official, and public reply based on the reality, proven by the history of the revolution, that Cuba has always been opposed to acts of reprisal against innocent people.

The government of the United States has not even condescended to make known the number of people arrested nor the figure of Grenadian losses, including civilian losses. A hospital for the mentally ill was bombed, killing dozens of patients.

"The invasion of Grenada was a treacherous surprise attack."

And where is Mr. Reagan's promise that U.S. troops would withdraw in a week? President Reagan himself in his first address to the U.S. people, at 8:30 a.m. on the day of the invasion, in a speech prepared before the landing, stated that the situation was under control.

That same day, his own spokesman described the resistance the invading forces were facing. The military parade the Pentagon had planned to hold in four hours did not take into account the tenacious and heroic resistance of the Cuban cooperation personnel and of the Grenadian soldiers.

US Control of Information

Who, then, has told the truth, and who has cynically lied about the events in Grenada? No foreign journalists—not even those from the United States—were allowed to see and report on the events on the spot.

The pretext that this prohibition was a security measure for the journalists is both superficial and ridiculous.

What they obviously wanted was to monopolize and manipulate the information so they could lie without hindrance to world public opinion, including the people of the United States. This was the only way they could spread deliberate lies and falsehoods of all kinds—which would be difficult to clear up and refute after their initial impact and effect on the people of the United States.

Even in this, the method used by the U.S. administration was fascist.

What is left now, objectively, of those 19 assertions?

Where are the silos for strategic missiles that were being built in Grenada?

But all those lies that the world did not believe, told by the U.S. president and his spokesmen, made a tremendous impact on U.S. public opinion.

Public Support Manipulated

Moreover, the invasion of Grenada was presented to the U.S. people as a great victory for Reagan's foreign policy against the socialist camp and the revolutionary movement. It was linked to the tragic death of 240 U.S. soldiers in Beirut, to the memory of the hostages in Iran, to the humiliating defeat in Vietnam and the resurgence of the United States as an influential power on the world scene. A dirty, dishonest appeal was made to U.S. patriotism, to national pride, to the grandeur and glory of the nation.

This was how they got a majority of the U.S. people—it is said that it was 65 percent at first and then 71 percent—to support the monstrous crime of invading a sovereign country without any justification, the reprehensible method of launching a surprise attack, the press censorship, and all the other procedures the U.S. government used for invading and justifying its invasion of Grenada.

Hitler acted the same way when he occupied Austria in 1938 and annexed Sudetenland in Czechoslovakia in 1938 in the name of German pride, German grandeur and glory, and the happiness and security of German subjects.

If a poll had been taken in Hitler Germany at that time, in the midst of the chauvinistic wave unleashed by the Nazis, around 80 or 90 percent of the people would have approved of those aggressions.

The deplorable, truly dangerous fact—not only for the peoples of the Caribbean, Central and Latin America, but for all the people of the world—is that, when world opinion unanimously denounced the warmongering, aggressive, unjustifiable action that violated people's sovereignty and all international norms and principles, most of the United States—manipulated, disinformed, and deceived—supported the monstrous crime committed by their government.

Virtue and Heroism?

There is something even more disturbing: when this about-face was effected in U.S. public opinion, many U.S. politicians who initially had opposed these events ended up by condoning Reagan's actions, and the press—censored, humiliated, and kept at a distance from the events—ended up moderating its complaints and criticism.

Are these, perchance, the virtues of a society where the opinion and the political and the informational institutions can be grossly manipulated by its rulers, as they were in German society in the time of fascism?

Where is the glory, the grandeur, and the victory in invading and defeating one of the tiniest countries in the world, of no economic or strategic significance?

"A dirty, dishonest appeal was made to US patriotism."

Where is the heroism in fighting a handful of workers and other civilian cooperation personnel whose heroic resistance—in spite of the surprise element, the shortage of ammunition, and their disadvantages in terms of terrain, arms, and numbers—against the air, sea, and land forces of the most powerful imperialist country in the world forced it to bring in the 82nd Airborne Division when the last stronghold was being defended at dawn on October 26 by barely 50 fighters?

The United States did not achieve any victory at all—not political or military or moral. If anything, it was a pyrrhic military victory and a profound moral defeat.

Revolutionary Spirit Murdered

As we pointed on another occasion, the imperialist government of the United States wanted to kill the symbol of the Grenada revolution, but the symbol was already dead. The Grenadian revolutionaries themselves destroyed it with their split and their colossal errors.

We believe that, after the death of Bishop and his closest comrades, after the army fired on the people, and after the party and the government divorced themselves from the masses and isolated themselves from the world, the Grenadian revolutionary process could not survive.

In its efforts to destroy a symbol, the United States killed a corpse and brought the symbol back to life at the same time. Was it for this that it challenged international law and won the repudiation and condemnation of the world?

Does it feel such contempt for the rest of humanity? Is that contempt really so great that Mr.

Reagan's appetite for breakfast on November 3 was not at all affected, as he declared before the press?

Threats to the World

If unfortunately all this were true—and it seems to be—the invasion of Grenada should lead us to an awareness of the realities and dangers that threaten the world.

Mr. [Thomas] O'Neill, speaker of the House of Representatives, said that it was sinful that a man who was totally uninformed and ignorant about international problems and who doesn't even read the documents was president of the United States. If we consider that the United States has powerful sophisticated means of conventional and nuclear warfare and that the president of that country can declare war without consulting anyone, it is not only sinful but truly dramatic and tragic for all humanity.

An air of triumph reigns in the Reagan administration. The echoes of the last shots in Grenada have barely died away and already there is talk of intervening in El Salvador, Nicaragua, and even Cuba, in the Middle East and southern Africa.

Imperialism's acts of interference and military aggression against progressive countries and national liberation movements continue unabated.

Continued Aggression

In Europe, the first of the 572 Pershing 2 and cruise missiles are already being deployed, surrounding the USSR and other socialist countries with a deadly ring of nuclear weapons that can reach their territories in a matter of minutes.

Not just the small countries, but all humanity is threatened. The bells tolling today for Grenada may toll tomorrow for the whole world.

The most prestigious and experienced scientists and doctors assure us that humanity could not survive a global nuclear war. The destructive power of these stockpiled weapons is a million times greater than that of the unsophisticated bombs that wiped out the cities of Hiroshima and Nagasaki in just a few seconds. This is what the Reagan administration's aggressive, warmongering policy can lead to.

Meanwhile, the arms race is already a reality in the midst of the worst economic crisis the world has witnessed since the '30s. And, with the problems of development of the vast majority of the peoples in the world still to be solved, who can feel confidence in a government that acts as precipitately, rashly, and cynically as the U.S. government did in Grenada?

Reagan did not even bother to listen to the advice of a government as closely linked to him politically, ideologically, and militarily as the British government.

It is not strange that, in a poll taken just a few days ago, more than 90 percent of the British people were categorically opposed to the United States' having the unilateral prerogative of using the cruise missiles that are being deployed there.

In our hemisphere, just a year and a half ago, a NATO power used sophisticated war means to shed Argentine blood in the Malvinas. The Reagan administration supported that action. It did not even consider the Organization of American States or the so-called security pacts and agreements, but scornfully pushed them aside.

Hypocritical Justification

Now, basing itself on the alleged request of a phantasmagoric organization of micro-states in the eastern Caribbean, it has invaded Grenada and shed Caribbean blood and Cuban blood.

Nicaragua paid a price of over 40,000 lives for freedom, and nearly a thousand more sons of that noble people have been killed in attacks made by mercenary bands organized, trained, and equipped by the U.S. government.

"Imperialism's acts of interference and military aggression against progressive countries and national liberation movements continue unabated."

In El Salvador, over 50,000 people have been murdered by a genocidal regime whose army is equipped, trained, and directed by the United States.

In Guatemala, more than 100,000 have died at the hands of the repressive system installed by the CIA in 1954, when it overthrew the progressive Arbenz government.

How many have died in Chile since imperialism staged the overthrow and assassination of Salvador Allende? How many have died in Argentina, Uruguay, Paraguay, Brazil, and Bolivia in the last 15 years?

What a high price our people have paid in blood, sacrifice, poverty, and mourning for imperialist domination and the unjust social systems it has imposed on our nations.

Value of Symbols

Imperialism is bent on destroying symbols, because it knows the value of symbols, of examples, and of ideas. It wanted to destroy them in Grenada, and it wants to destroy them in El Salvador, Nicaragua, and Cuba.

But symbols, examples, and ideas cannot be destroyed. When their enemies think they have destroyed them, what they have actually done is made them multiply. In trying to wipe out the first Christians, the Roman emperors spread Christianity throughout the world. Likewise, all attempts to destroy our ideas will only multiply them.

Grenada has already multiplied the patriotic conviction and fighting spirit of Salvadoran, Nicaraguan, and Cuban revolutionaries. It has been proved that the best U.S. troops can be fought and that they are not feared. The imperialists must not ignore the fact that they will encounter fierce resistance wherever they attack a revolutionary people. Let us hope that their pyrrhic victory in Grenada and their air of triumph don't go to their heads, leading them to commit serious, irreversible errors.

They will not find in El Salvador, Nicaragua, and Cuba the particular circumstances of revolutionaries divided among themselves and divorced from the people that they found in tiny Grenada.

Different Circumstances in Central America

In more than three years of heroic struggle, the Salvadoran revolutionaries have become experienced, fearsome, and invincible fighters. There are thousands of them who know the land inch by inch, veterans of dozens of victorious battles, who are accustomed to fighting and winning—when the odds are 10 to 1 against them—against elite troops, trained, armed, and advised by the United States. Their unity is more solid and indestructible than ever.

In Nicaragua, the imperialists would have to confront a deeply patriotic and revolutionary people that is united, organized, armed, and ready to fight and that can never be subjugated. With regard to Cuba, if in Grenada the imperialists had to bring in an elite division to fight against a handful of isolated men struggling in a small stronghold, lacking fortifications, a thousand miles from their homeland, how many divisions would they need against millions of combatants fighting on their own soil alongside their own people?

Our country—as we have already said on other occasions—might be wiped off the face of the earth, but it will never be conquered and subjugated.

In the present conditions of our continent, a U.S. war against a Latin American people would raise the morale of all the peoples of Latin America and turn their feelings against the aggressors. A bottomless abyss would be opened between peoples who—because they are in the same hemisphere—are called upon to live with one another in peace, friendship, and mutual respect and cooperation.

The experiences of Grenada will be examined in detail to extract the utmost benefit from them for use in case of another attack against a country where there are Cuban cooperation personnel or against our own homeland.

The Cubans who were captured and virtually turned into hostages had an unforgettable experience of what a country occupied by Yankee invading troops is like.

The physical and psychological treatment given the cooperation personnel who were taken prisoner was insulting and a cause for indignation. Promises of all kinds were made to each of them to try to get them to go to the United States. But they were not able to break their steel-like staunchness. Not a single one deserted his homeland.

Cuban Heroism

There was no manipulation of the news, nothing was hidden from the people in our country. All reports concerning the invasion that were received directly from Grenada were transmitted to our population just as they arrived, even though the ones on October 26 turned out to be exaggerated.

As a matter of principle, at no time were efforts made to play down the seriousness of the situation or to minimize the magnitude of the dangers facing our compatriots.

We are deeply grateful to the International Committee of the Red Cross for its interest, dedication, and efficient efforts to identify and evacuate the wounded, sick, and other prisoners and the dead as quickly as possible.

We are also grateful to the governments of Spain and Colombia for the immediate efforts they made in this regard.

In bidding farewell to our beloved brothers who died heroically in combat, fulfilling with honor their patriotic and internationalist duties, and in expressing our deepest solidarity with their loved ones, we do not forget that there are Grenadian mothers and U.S. mothers who are crying for their sons who died in Grenada.

"What a high price our peoples have paid in blood, sacrifice, poverty, and mourning for imperialist domination and the unjust social systems it has imposed on our nations."

We send our condolences to the mothers and other relatives of the Grenadians who were killed and also to the mothers and other relatives of the U.S. soldiers who died—because they, who also suffer from the loss of close relatives, are not to blame for their government's warmongering, aggressive, irresponsible actions. They, too, are its victims.

Every day, every hour, every minute—at work, at our studies and our combat positions—we will remember our comrades who died in Grenada.

The men whom we will bury this afternoon fought for us and for the world. They may seem to be corpses. Reagan wants to make corpses of all our people—men, women, the elderly, and the children!

He wants to make a corpse out of all humanity.

But the peoples shall struggle to preserve their independence and their lives! They will struggle to prevent the world from becoming a huge cemetery! They will struggle and pay the price necessary for humanity to survive.

However, they are not corpses! They are symbols. They did not even die in the land where they were born. There, far away from Cuba, where they were contributing with the noble sweat of their internationalist work in a country poorer and smaller than ours, they were also able to shed their blood and offer their lives. But in that trench, they knew they were also defending their own people and their own homeland.

There can be no purer way to express the generosity of human beings and their willingness to make sacrifices. Their example will be multiplied, and they themselves will be multipled in us. No power, no weapons, no forces can ever prevail over the patriotism, internationalism, feelings of human brotherhood, and communist consciousness which they embody.

We shall be like them, in work and in combat!
Patria o muerte!
Venceremos!

Fidel Castro is the President of Cuba, a position he assumed after the communist revolution in 1959.

"Article 52 of the [UN] charter... clearly permits regional peace-keeping actions consistent with the purposes of the United Nations."

viewpoint 35

International Law Supports the Grenada Intervention

John Norton Moore

Americans rightly expect their nation to act lawfully in international affairs. Because issues of lawfulness are important, we should expect more than the Alice-in-Wonderland legal arguments heard at home and abroad instantly condemning the Grenada mission.

The reality is that the peace-keeping and protection mission requested by the Organization of Eastern Caribbean States is lawful and in full compliance with the charter of the United Nations and that of the Organization of American States. Indeed, by serving human rights, self-determination and international security, the mission serves the core purposes of those great charters.

UN Charter

The U.N. charter provides in Article 2(4) that members shall not use force against the "territorial integrity or political independence" of other states. But Article 52 of the charter equally clearly permits regional peace-keeping actions consistent with the purposes of the United Nations.

Such actions to restore order and self-determination in a setting of breakdown of authority are not enforcement actions requiring Security Council approval and may be undertaken at the initiative of regional arrangements. Article 51 of the charter as clearly permits actions in defense. Such actions, which include humanitarian protection, may be undertaken individually or collectively.

The Grenada mission by the OECS countries and Barbados, Jamaica and the United States is a model regional peace-keeping action under Article 52. It was undertaken in a context of civil strife and breakdown of government following the brutal murder of Maurice Bishop and three members of his Cabinet in

John Norton Moore, "The Legal Basis for Grenada," *The Washington Times*, November 11, 1983. cc 1983 The Washington Times. Reprinted by permission.

an attempted coup. And it was in response to a request for assistance in restoring human rights and orderly processes of self-determination from the only constitutional authority on the island, Governor General Sir Paul Scoon. The legal basis for this peace-keeping mission is at least as strong as for the OAS — not just American — action in the second phase of the 1965 Dominican Republic case.

Humanitarian Protection

The Grenada mission is also a model of humanitarian protection under Article 51 of the charter. The context includes uncertainty as to whether any coherent group was in charge, cessation of government functions, a draconian shoot-on-sight, 24-hour curfew applied to civilians, closure of the airports, a community of threatened non-Grenadans, including 800-1,000 Americans, and at least 18 confirmed deaths.

Although not necessary for the legal case, it is relevant that, under Soviet and Cuban tutelage, Grenada had embarked on a military buildup exceeding the combined military strength of the six other members of the OECS and was assisting in the export of terrorism to other Caribbean nations. From the perspective of these virtually unarmed Caribbean democracies the buildup must have seemed as acute a threat as the 1962 attempted emplacement in Cuba of Soviet missiles was for the United States.

Moreoever, it is still not clear whether the attempted coup was subtly or otherwise encouraged by the Soviets or Cubans in a covert application to Grenada of the Brezhnev doctrine after Bishop showed unease with increasing "socialist bloc" dependence. At the least, the attempted coup occurred in a setting where Cuban armed strength exceeded Grenadan, as was demonstrated in subsequent fighting, and in a setting that was at minimum neo-colonial.

Monroe Doctrine

Although the Monroe Doctrine is not a principle of international law, it is also relevant to recall that a major underpinning of the doctrine is the importance of protecting self-determination in the Americas against threats to reimpose colonialism forcefully.

The Grenada mission, which was jointly undertaken by almost one-third of the OAS membership, is also consistent with the OAS charter. Reflecting the traditional Latin concern, Articles 18 and 20 of the charter broadly prohibit intervention. Articles 22 and 28, however, make clear that regional peace-keeping or defensive actions in accordance with special regional treaties do not violate these non-intervention provisions. It is clear from the negotiating history of these articles that the later OECS treaty is a special regional treaty within Articles 22 and 28. In fact, as is the Inter-American defense treaty for other areas of Latin America, the OECS treaty is the only applicable regional security arrangement for Grenada and the Eastern Caribbean.

In contrast with the empty canvas of interest as to the legal basis for Cuban forces ordered to fight to the death to oppose a lawful regional peace-keeping and rescue mission, the OECS and the U.S. actions have met with a drumbeat of legal misperceptions.

OAS Charter

Most frequently heard is the charge that the action violates the non-intervention articles of the OAS charter. As we have seen, this simply ignores the legal effect of Articles 22 and 28. It also ignores Article 137 which reserves all rights under the U.N. charter. Also urged are a melange of arguments under the OECS treaty that non-members cannot participate, that the treaty applies only to external threats and that the action is impermissible because Grenada did not join in authorizing it.

"A major underpinning of the [Monroe] doctrine is the importance of protecting self-determination in the Americas against threats to reimpose colonialism forcefully."

Space precludes full response to these points, but they are as specious as the alleged violation of the OAS charter. In fact, even a careful reading of Article 3(2)(q), Articles 4 and 6 in their entirety, and Article 16(1) of the OECS treaty, taken in the context of the breakdown of government of Grenada and a request for military assistance from the governor general, should satisfy the fair-minded.

Moving from strictly legal analysis to assessment by reference to fundamental purposes of the U.N. and OAS systems, we should ask: Would continuation of murder and civil strife in Grenada better serve human rights? Would continuation of brutal repression by an unpopular faction and further tightening of Cuban neo-colonialism better serve self-determination? Would continuation of the huge military buildup in a peaceful region of the Caribbean better serve peace?

And even ardent practitioners of the pseudo "even hand" who are troubled by comparisons with the Brezhnev doctrine, should be able to discern the differences. Among other things, the Brezhnev doctrine is not premised on a request from an organization of independent states acting lawfully under Articles 51 and 52 of the U.N. charter. And as OECS coexistence with the Marxist Bishop regime shows, the OECS action, unlike the Brezhnev doctrine, is not for the purpose of imposing a particular form of government on the people of Grenada.

The world has yet to see free elections or an end to human rights abuses in any country where the Brezhnev doctrine has been applied. The Grenada mission seeks to serve rather than subvert these goals.

John Norton Moore is Walter L. Brown Professor of Law at the University of Virginia and former counselor on international law to the Department of State.

The US Violated International Law in Grenada

Inquiry

Ronald Reagan's reckless invasion of Grenada, ordered on the thinnest of pretexts, not only endangered innocent lives, but also confirmed his administration as one that revels in military action, regardless of treaty obligations or international law. Coming on the heels of his blunder in Lebanon, this latest violation of the just and wise principle of nonintervention is scandalous.

Reagan's justification for sending the marines to Grenada, along with armed personnel from six eastern Caribbean islands, could not have been more transparent. First, he said, the action was taken to protect innocent lives, especially some 1000 Americans. In fact, up to the time of the invasion there was no threat to the Americans and no reason to think that those who wanted to leave could not do so. Charles Modica, chancellor of St. George's Medical College, where more than 500 Americans attend school, refused a U.S. government request that he voice concern for their safety. On the Sunday before the invasion, the parents of the students were assured by their children and the Grenadian government that the students were safe. The parents asked Reagan not to "move too quickly or...take any precipitous or provocative actions at this time." Diplomatic notes to Washington from the new regime and Cuba also assured the Americans' safety.

No Threats

A retired American living in Grenada, Don Atkinson, speaking over ham radio, said, "Quite frankly, there had been no threats whatsoever to any Americans.... [The students] had been offered the opportunity to leave the island, if they wished to do so.... The airport had been opened for that purpose."

Moreover, the national security minister of neighboring Trinidad and Tobago, John Donaldson, said he had received permission to send a British West Indies Airways plane to fly out nationals of his country. Donaldson said that with the invasion "all of that now has been washed under the bridge." Canada and Great Britain had also arranged flights, which were blocked by the governments of the invasion force.

Far from safeguarding American lives, the invasion put them at grave risk. Since the overthrow and murder of Grenadian Prime Minister Maurice Bishop, the new regime had warned of an impending American invasion. As if on cue, Reagan, before the invasion was approved, ordered a naval task force, including an aircraft carrier and 2000 marines, toward the island. This move could hardly have secured the safety of the Americans. Though Reagan reportedly hoped to prevent a new Iranian hostage crisis, this first sign of an invasion could well have precipitated one.

The defense of U.S. citizens abroad has historically been invoked to justify military action. Lyndon Johnson used the same excuse in his 1965 Dominican Republic invasion. But even if Americans are really in danger, that does not justify invasion; they travel at their own risk and should not count on an interventionist foreign policy to protect them. It is interesting, however, that the Reagan-boosters of the *Wall Street Journal's* editorial board wrote that Reagan's statement about rescuing Americans was "not meant to be believed."

Treaty Prohibitions

Reagan also said the invasion was intended to "forestall further chaos" and "to assist in the restoration of conditions of law and order." Secretary of State George Shultz talked about the island's "violent uncertainty" (something that doesn't disturb U.S. officials when it is found in South Korea, the

Inquiry, "War in Grenada," December 1983. Reprinted by permission.

Philippines, Chile, or Haiti). But none of these things justify military intervention. The United States is a party to several treaties, including the United Nations Charter, that specifically prohibit the action Reagan took. For instance, Article 18 of the charter of the Organization of American States says:

> No state or group of states has the right to intervene, directly or indirectly, for any reason whatever, in the internal or external affairs of any other state.

Article 20 says:

> The territory of a state is inviolable; it may not be the object, even temporarily, of military occupation or of other measures of force taken by another state, directly or indirectly on any grounds whatever.

Shultz ignored these prohibitions and instead referred to the two-year-old Organization of Eastern Caribbean States (OECS), to which the invaders, *excepting the United States,* belong. Reagan spokesman Larry Speakes said, "The United States is responding to an urgent appeal [by] the Organization of Eastern Caribbean States for assistance.... That is our legal basis for involvement." Shultz elaborated by noting that the OECS treaty provides for member states to engage in collective defense against "external aggression." The administration has put much stock in this justification, claiming that the United States was "invited" into Grenada by the neighboring states that fear Soviet or Cuban activity so close to their shores. At a news conference with Reagan, Eugenia Charles, the prime minister of Dominica, an island neighbor of Grenada, went so far as to say that the action was not an invasion: "This is a question of our asking for support. We are one region; Grenada is part and parcel of us," she said.

"It is wrong for Ronald Reagan to soil this country's honor with 'big stick' intervention and international outlawry."

With this defense of the invasion, Reagan and his allies have blazed new and hazardous trails. Reagan properly mocks the Soviet Union when it says it was invited into Afghanistan or Czechoslovakia, yet with a straight face he tells the American people that we have been invited into Grenada—by third parties. How can Dominica invite us into Grenada? Second, by his silence, he assented to Charles's view that there was no invasion because "we are one region." The Soviets presumably would not mind having that principle become an accepted part of international law.

OECS Criticisms

It should be pointed out that, on their own terms, Reagan and Charles have a weak case. The leaders of Trinidad and Tobago, a member of the OECS,

criticized the invasion; Prime Minister George Chambers said it contravened the majority decision of the OECS summit meeting. Furthermore, the OECS treaty stipulates that any formal decision to invade requires unanimous agreement.

Reagan clearly did not wish to be bothered by such details. No doubt the *Wall Street Journal* echoed his feelings when it wrote, in a remarkably arrogant editorial, "There is little time for the moral complexities—what is an invasion, what treaties govern, what is the definition of sovereignty—that perplex Georgetown salons." What counts, said the *Journal* and presumably Reagan, is that Grenada was in the grip of Soviet and Cuban sympathizers. Yet Grenada, which first became friendly with Cuba after a coup in 1979, posed no threat to the other eastern Caribbean islands. Castro had in fact condemned October's violent coup. The best excuse Reagan could come up with was phrased in metaphors drawn from epidemiology: The virus of communism had to be stopped before it spread to Barbados and Antigua.

The fact is that communism isn't a virus. It is an ideology. The mere presence of a Grenadian government sympathetic to the Kremlin cannot be grounds for preemptive war and the flouting of international law.

We do sympathize with the Grenadian victims of this particularly odious form of statism. But they must rely on their own revolutionary ambitions and voluntary, private help. As American citizens, we cannot countenance the immense accumulation of power the U.S. government would need to be the protector of the world. Nor can we accept the dangers that would come with "the perpetual war for perpetual peace."

We cannot help thinking that what really counted in this matter was Ronald Reagan's desire to get his floundering foreign policy out of the doldrums. He has surely bucked up the militarists on the right. To return to the *Journal* editorial: "this will be immensely liberating [!] in future crises around the world.... If no one will say that what happened in Grenada is wrong, why should a different morality apply in the rest of Latin America?"

We say that what happened in Grenada is wrong. We say it is wrong for the U.S. government to throw its power around—insensible of "moral complexities"—when it doesn't like developments in other countries. We say it is wrong for the president to endanger the American people by deliberately seeking conflict with Cuba and the Soviet Union. And we say it is wrong for Ronald Reagan to soil this country's honor with "big stick" intervention and international outlawry.

This viewpoint was written by the editors of Inquiry, *a Libertarian political monthly publication of the Libertarian Review Foundation in Washington, D.C.*

The US Aided a Tyrannized Grenada

Jeane J. Kirkpatrick

Some of the speakers before this Council in the past few days have attempted to present the events of the past days as a classical invasion of a small country by an imperial power—a simple case of intervention in the internal affairs of others whose moral and legal character is easily discernible. After all, the UN Charter forbids the use of force to settle a dispute, and force has been used by the task force. The charter forbids intervention in the internal affairs of states, and the task force is intervening in the affairs of Grenada. The charter requires respect for the independence, sovereignty, and territorial integrity of states, and when foreign forces land on an island state, it might not at first glance appear unreasonable to contend that the independence, sovereignty, and territorial integrity of the state are not being fully respected....

The events of the past days pose no such morally or legally simple questions as has been suggested by that interesting array of speakers. The prohibitions against the use of force in the UN Charter are contextual, not absolute. They provide ample justification for the use of force against force in pursuit of other values also inscribed in the charter— freedom, democracy, peace. The charter does not require that peoples submit supinely to terror, nor that their neighbors be indifferent to their terrorization.

The events in the Caribbean do not comprise a classical example of a large power invading a small, helpless nation. The impression that there is involved here a violation of the charter which should be straightforwardly condemned by an outraged "world opinion" is not only a delusion, it is, as well, a snare and will leave those caught within it a bit weaker, a bit more confused, a bit less able to defend

Jeane J. Kirkpatrick, statement before the UN Security Council, October 27, 1983.

themselves—a bit more of what Jean-Francois Revel called in his most recent book, *Comment les Democraties Finissent,* "an obliging victim."

Vital Issues

This is another way of saying that although the islands that we are meeting to discuss are small, the issues are as large as any ever discussed here. The use of force is, indeed, central to our deliberations, as are respect for the right of peoples to self-determination and nonintervention in the internal affairs of others. The most fundamental questions of legitimacy, human rights, and self-defense are also present.

The intrusion of force into the public life of Grenada did not begin with the landing of a task force. From 1979 Grenada had been ruled by a government which came to power by coup, overthrowing a corrupt, though elected, predecessor. That government declined to submit to free elections. It succumbed to superior force more than 2 weeks ago when, with the complicity of certain powers, which have in the past 3 days nearly drowned us in crocodile tears over the death of Maurice Bishop and foreign intervention in Grenada's affairs, it first arrested, then murdered Bishop and his ministers. Thus began what can only be called an authentic reign of terror in Grenada. Tragically for them, the people of Grenada had already had large experience with political violence before the arrival of the task force.

The people of Grenada were also sadly accustomed to foreign intervention in their internal affairs. Let us speak frankly about this situation. Maurice Bishop was a man of strong ideological commitments. Those commitments identified him and allied him with Cuba, the Soviet Union, and the member states of that empire which invokes Marxist principles to justify tyranny. Bishop freely offered his island as a base for the projection of Soviet military power in this hemisphere. The familiar pattern of militarization and Cubanization was already far advanced in Grenada. More than three dozen Soviet officials have been detained in just the past 3 days. Truly enormous arsenals of Soviet weapons have been discovered in the last 3 days. The total number of Cuban military personnel in Grenada is still unknown, but it is clear that there were more than 1,000—more than one Cuban for every 100 Grenadians. Even this did not satisfy Prime Minister Bishop's friends. Maurice Bishop was not the victim of an ordinary power struggle. As Jamaica's Prime Minister Seaga put it:

> It became clear as events unfolded that this was...a well-planned and orchestrated coup which was carried out with a savagery and brutality without precedent in the English-speaking Caribbean.
>
> On Wedneday, October 19, after having been released by a large crowd of his supporters, Mr. Bishop, his Minister of Education, Miss Jacqueline Creft, his Foreign Minister, Mr. Unison Whiteman, Mr. Norris Bain, Minister of Housing, Mr. Vincent Noel, leader of the Bank and General Workers Union, Mr. Fitzroy Bain, another trade union leader, had been brutally executed by Cuban-trained military officers who had seized power. We also learned subsequently that the People's Revolutionary Army had fired on a crowd of demonstrators which included many women and children and that several of these have not been accounted for and are presumed to have been killed. An eyewitness reports having seen the child attempting to jump to safety having his legs blown off.

Remote Tyranny

Let us be clear in this chamber tonight. Grenada's internal affairs had fallen under the permanent intervention of one neighboring and one remote tyranny. Its people were helpless in the grip of terror.

Imagine, if you will, that here in New York tonight, just after we return home, some gunmen who had already proved that they would kill on a whim announced that anyone leaving his home, anyone appearing on the streets would be shot on sight. Imagine, if you will, that that condition lasted for 4 days and 4 nights, punctuated by the sounds of gunshots. Ask youself whether friendly forces arriving from some nearby, democratic country to free us would be engaged in a violation of the UN Charter, in an unjustifiable intervention in the U.S. internal affairs, in an unjustified use of force....

Liberating Force

It should not be difficult for any people, especially any democratic people, which has ever suffered a reign of terror from either foreign or domestic tyrants to discern the difference between the force that liberates captive people from terror and the force that imposes terror on captive peoples. Neither the intellectual nor the moral nor the legal problems here involved are really very difficult.

It was indeed, a unique combination of circumstances prevailing in Grenada that led the United States to respond positively to the OECS

request that we assist them in their decision to undertake collective action to secure peace and stability in the Caribbean region. Those circumstances included danger to innocent U.S. nationals, the absence of a minimally responsible government in Grenada, and the danger posed to the OECS by the relatively awesome military might which those responsible for the murder of the Bishop government now had at their disposal. The U.S. response, we believe, was fully compatible with relevant international law and practice.

I turn briefly to each of these points. First, the defense of innocent nationals: The U.S. concern for the safety of its nationals was real and compelling and had absolutely nothing to do with any inclination to "gunboat diplomacy." As pointed out by Prime Minister Seaga in his address to Jamaica's Parliament on October 25, "madmen" wiped out the whole government of Grenada, murdered its leading citizens, imposed a 24-hour shoot-on-sight curfew against its own citizenry.

Murderous Madmen

The madmen responsible for the coup in Grenada did not put their captured adversaries on trial; they simply murdered them in cold-blood. In these circumstances, it was fully reasonable for the United States to conclude that these madmen might decide, at any moment, to hold hostage the 1,000 American citizens on that island. American nationals, scattered throughout the island, were denied the right of free exit, as students returning last night testified to repeatedly. The airport was closed, and entry by humanitarian organizations and others concerned with their welfare was prevented.

"Although the islands that we are meeting to discuss are small, the issues are as large as any ever discussed here."

The United States—having recently been the victim of, as well as the witness to, revolutionary violence in Iran, where, in contravention of all international conventions and the express ruling of the International Court of Justice, U.S. diplomatic personnel were held hostage—could not be expected to sit idly by while the lives of our citizens were again threatened.

Of course, it goes without saying that the United States does not advocate that in normal circumstances concern for the safety of a state's nationals in a foreign country may justify military measures against that country. But normal circumstances presuppose the existence of a government which, regardless of the democratic, nondemocratic, or antidemocratic nature of the system which it pursues, is nevertheless recognized as minimally responsible for not wantonly endangering the lives of its citizens, foreign nationals, and the security of neighboring states in the region. Where, however, terrorists murder the leading citizenry and leadership of their own country, a situation may well arise whereby no new government replaces the former order but anarchy prevails. In these circumstances, the general rule of international law permits military action for protecting endangered nationals. Such was the situation in Grenada.

Vacuum of Responsible Government

The second point I would like to address briefly is that this was, indeed, a unique situation in which there existed a vacuum of responsible governmental authority. The revulsion shared by the international community over the cold-blooded murder of Mr. Bishop's government was nearly universal in scope. The consequences of the coup, however, were not restricted in Grenada. Though a small island, Grenada, because of its massive build-up of arms and material, had become capable of gravely affecting the security of the entire Caribbean region. Those most immediately affected by the situation prevailing in Grenada were, of course, Grenada's neighboring countries, all of which were members of the OECS, the Caribbean regional organization.

"In the hands of sane men, the airstrip would have offered no threat."

Aware that the terrorists were in control of Grenada, it became incumbent upon the states of the OECS to assess the military capability at their disposal and the dangers presented to the security of all the states in the Caribbean region. In assessing this danger, the states of the OECS—most of which have no army at all or armies of less than 200 men— concluded that the hands of the madmen who engineered the coup had reached threatening proportions. For example, although Jamaica's population exceeds by twenty-fold that of Grenada, Grenada's army—its indigenous forces alone— exceeded by one and one-half times the size of Jamaica's Armed Forces. Moreover, a new airstrip was in the final stages of completion by over 600 armed Cubans. In the words of Jamaica's Prime Minister Seaga:

> In the hands of sane men, the airstrip would have offered no threat, but against the background of the insanity of the past 2 weeks, it would be a logical staging area for countries whose interests are similar, which have ambitions for using Grenada as a center for subversion, sabotage, and infiltration within the area and against member states of the Organization of Eastern Caribbean States.

It was in this context that the OECS, viewing with the greatest alarm this combination of brutal men with awesome might, decided to undertake collective action pursuant to its charter. Such action fully comported with relevant provisions of the UN Charter, which accord regional organizations the authority to undertake collective action. When asked to assist this effort, the United States, whose own nationals and vital interests were independently affected, joined the effort to restore minimal conditions of law and order in Grenada and eliminate the threat posed to the security of the entire region.

Collective Regional Action

The third legal point I should like to address briefly concerns collective regional action. Dominica, Barbados, Jamaica, and other Caribbean states have already made it clear the factors which impelled them to invoke their regional treaty arrangements for collective action. As pointed out by their representatives here, the issue was not revolution. This hemisphere has seen many revolutions, and many members of the OECS, like the United States itself, were born of revolution. Each of us in this hemisphere celebrates an independence day.

Nor was it an issue of the type of government Grenada possessed. While the government of Maurice Bishop, which had never secured a mandate from its electorate, was an anomaly and an unwelcome anomaly in the democratic Caribbean Sea, no thought was ever given by the OECS to influencing a change of that government. No effort, may I add, was ever undertaken by the United States to in any way affect the composition or character of that government.

Rather the OECS was spurred to action because, as a result of the murder of Mr. Bishop and almost his entire Cabinet, the military power which Grenada has amassed with Cuban and Soviet backing had fallen into the hands of individuals who could reasonably be expected to wield that awesome power against its neighbors. That the coup leaders had no arguable claim to being the responsible government was, indeed, made clear by their own declarations, the failure of other states to recognize them as a legitimate government, and by the fact that the Governor General of Grenada, the sole remaining symbol of governmental authority on the island, invited OECS action.

In the context of these very particular, very unusual, perhaps unique, circumstances, the United States decided to accede to the request of the OECS for aiding its collective efforts aimed at securing peace and stability in the Caribbean region.

Jeane J. Kirkpatrick is the United States chief representative to the United Nations. This viewpoint is taken from a statement made before the UN Security Council, October 27, 1983.

"In Grenada, American G.I.'s hunted people out of the cellars where they hid and drove them into the streets."

The US Tyrannized Grenada

Lev Makarevich

It was a long time since he'd enjoyed himself so much, Sergeant Hunter told newsmen afterwards, reminiscing about the American invasion of Grenada. They had blazed their way with machine guns and automatic rifles, storming every house, suppressing every seat of resistance, and killing everyone who came their way.

Yes, we're killers, Lieutenant Colonel Taylor, commander of the 1st Battalion of the 75th Division of the U.S. task force, admitted with a faraway look in his eyes.

Who would have ventured not to be a hero among these brave fellows who knew no fear of unarmed people? Occasionally the Rangers displayed the magnanimity of a Jack the Ripper who did not kill everyone who fell into his hands. In Grenada, American G.I.s hunted people out of the cellars where they hid and drove them into the streets to stage the "Grateful Islanders Welcome Their Liberators" show.

American Invasion

This invasion by the West's biggest and strongest power against well-nigh the tiniest of the world's countries has put on the order of the day Mark Twain's suggestion that the U.S. flag should be altered somewhat: the white stripes should be painted over black and the stars replaced with the skull and crossbones.

Today, as in Mark Twain's time, many U.S. politicians think of the future in terms of the past.

At the end of last century U.S. Secretary of State Richard Olney said: "The United States is practically sovereign on this continent, and its fiat is law upon the subjects to which it confines its interposition."

At about the same time Senator Beveridge dilated

on the same subject thus: "Cuba not contiguous? Puerto Rico not contiguous? The Philippines not contiguous? Our navy will make them contiguous!... and American speed, American guns, American heart and brain and nerve will keep them contiguous forever."

No Moral Cost

Here are some samples of present-day rhetoric.

"The deed [the Grenada invasion—L.M.] is political...it demonstrates to radicals in Central America that only logistics, not laws or treaties, will determine the means the United States is ready to employ against them." (*The New York Times*.)

"I don't think there's any moral cost to that action," U.S. Ambassador at the U.N. Jeane Kirkpatrick says.

The Christian Science Monitor dotted the i's when it wrote: "Those justifying the invasion stress, among other things...the island's proximity to the Panama Canal and the oil fields of Venezuela." It demonstrated support to pro-U.S. regimes of El Salvador and Guatemala and served "as a message to Nicaragua."

An "unpatriotic" comment from the liberal *Washington Post* introduced a jarring note: The occupation of Grenada, it said, revived memories of the past. "Updating our image as gunboat diplomats is a tragic mistake."

Tradition of Subterfuge

This is indeed not the first time the U.S. has acted in such a manner.

On February 15, 1898, a powerful explosion shook the battleship Maine lying at anchor in the Havana port. The ship broke in two and foundered. Over 250 people perished.

Many years later it transpired that the explosion was caused by a mine planted by secret agents of the United States which was looking for a pretext to

Lev Makarevich, "Uncle Sam Is True to Type," *New Times*, December 1983. Reprinted by permission.

declare war on Spain and sever Cuba from it. The maneuvre worked. The explosion was played up by the yellow press which thirsted after Spanish blood.

"Everything is now ready," the World screamed, "the Army is ready; the Navy is ready; the Treasury is ready; the Naval Court of Inquiry is ready; the case against Spain is ready; the people are ready."

It was in those days of general elation, when "true" patriots were ready to unsheathe their swords and fight for their country, that the press tycoon Hearst sent the telegram to his correspondent in Havana that reserved for him a place in history: "Please remain. You furnish the pictures and I'll furnish the war. W.R. Hearst."

"Threat" to America

Eighty-five years later the role of the Maine was played by the three-kilometre-long landing strip of an international airport in Grenada that was being built by Cuban workers, the British Plessy firm and the Common Market. In Washington's feverish mind it took the form of a Cuban-Soviet base from which America's vital centres could be threatened.

Washington's worst fears proved "justified." After its armada of land, naval and air forces rolled over the tiny island on October 25, among other trophies a depot of rifles dating back to the Franco-Prussian war of 1870-71 was found, a truly deadly weapon compared with the nuclear missiles, aircraft carriers and supersonic aircraft that now protect the peace of the United States of America.

"American speed, American guns, American heart and brain and nerve will keep them contiguous forever."

The New York Post also managed to see there Soviet "green berets," who allegedly helped to co-ordinate the defensive and the withdrawal operations. It is because of them, the paper hinted darkly, that it took the Marines and Rangers so much time to take possession of the island.

The Italians say that a large dose of big lies can prove lethal. Yet many readers did fall for them.

When taking the decision to invade Grenada—during a game of golf—President Reagan did not stop to think how the average American would take it.

Disregard for Public Opinion

This disregard to public opinion is traditional for the American ruling class. Theodore Roosevelt, who was to become U.S. President, wrote with remarkable frankness in July 1898:

"If I had money enough to keep in national politics it would not be difficult, because the average New York boss is quite willing to allow you to do what you wish in such trivial matters as war and the acquisition of Puerto Rico and Hawaii, provided you don't interfere with the really vital questions, such as giving out contracts for cartage in the Customs House and interfering with the appointment of street sweepers."

"The reaction in Europe is not a source of overwhelming anxiety," a Reagan spokesman told a *Christian Science Monitor* interviewer, suppressing a yawn. As to the Americans, the mass media, now wielding influence such as Theodore Roosevelt could not even dream of, saw to it that they should show the right reaction.

Terror from Yellow Press

"Yankees in Danger!"

By issuing this call, U.S. propaganda has found a very simple but highly effective way to justify the use of the mailed fist. It has been its favourite device for the past one hundred and fifty years.

"No man's life, no man's property is safe. American citizens are imprisoned or slain without cause. American property is destroyed on all sides. There is no pretense in protecting it.... Blood on the roadsides, blood in the fields, blood on the doorsteps, blood, blood, blood! The old, the young, the weak, the crippled—all are butchered without mercy...."

"The bodies had almost lost semblance of human form. The arms and legs of one had been dismembered and laced into a rude attempt at a Cuban five-pointed star, and were satirically placed on the breast of a limbless form. The tongue of one had been cut out, split open at the base and placed on the mangled forehead in a ghostly likeness of a horn. Fingers and toes were missing.... And the ears were all missing.... Our Indians were more cleanly than this."

Thus, the newspaper World in 1896, on the eve of the Spanish-American war as a result of which the United States established its protectorate on Cuba. Over the decades the yellow press has developed to a fine art the knack of striking terror into the hearts of its readers.

Diabolica Designs

There was hair-raising evidence of mass violation of human rights and bloodshed (in Grenada), Jeane Kirkpatrick declared. In these circumstances there could be no guarantee of safety and this was the cause of grave concern to her government, considering that almost 1,000 U.S. citizens were studying and living in Grenada.

"Seizing Americans as hostages and holding them...to embarrass the United States and, more immediately, to forestall American military action in Grenada," such is the diabolical design of the "Grenadian ruffians in power," *The New York Times* added its awe-inspiring word.

It is not hard to imagine what the average American felt after he had been fed such a dose of lies coupled with a photograph frontpaged by most newspapers showing a student who "survived" in Grenada kissing the American soil. It did not take long to convince the American philistine that the invasion of Grenada was a rescue mission and occupation, deliverance from chaos, that the punitive squads were the liberators and acts of terrorism, feats of valour.

Patriotic Pride

"A week after the invasion of Grenada," *The New York Times* wrote, "most members of Congress have either sided with President Reagan or muted their criticism.... But many lawmakers seem to sense a public wave of patriotic pride over the Grenada operation.... This is a success and people don't want to hear about mistakes that were made."

Nicely put, isn't it? Reagan the actor played his part well too, appearing now docile, now wrathful, now lachrymose, now stern and unbending.

"US propaganda has found a very simple but highly effective way to justify the use of the mailed fist."

In his statement of October 25, 1983, Ronald Reagan declared that contingents of U.S. troops have launched a landing operation in Grenada that morning, and that there was no other way left for the United States than to display vigour and firmness.

In his TV appearance on October 27, 1983, Reagan cited the words of General Paul Kelley, Commandant of the Marine Corps, who, while visting a military hospital, saw "a young Marine with more tubes going in and out of his body than I have ever seen in one body.... He could not see very well. He reached up and grabbed my four stars, just to make sure I was who I said I was. He held my hand in a firm grip. He was making signals and we realized he wanted to tell me something. We put a pad of paper in his hand and he wrote: 'semper fi...'" Those who had ever been with the Marines or were Marine fans like him, Reagan went on, must know that "semper fi" was a battle cry, greeting and motto of the Marines being an abbreviation of "semper fidelis"—"always faithful."

Lev Makarevich is a journalist for New Times, *a Soviet weekly magazine of world affairs.*

intelligence positions of importance. In late March, 1980, a Sandinista delegation to Moscow met with Soviet leaders A.P. Kirilenko and Boris N. Ponomarev. This led to signing of the Soviet-Nicaraguan Non-Aggression Pact that required, among other things, stationing of 300 Soviet agents in the Soviet Embassy in Managua.

But something went wrong.

The people of Nicaragua are not satisfied with the way things are going. One of Jack Anderson's reporters recently traveled with a guerrilla band into northern Nicaragua. In Anderson's column on 8 May he wrote, "It quickly became obvious that the guerrillas had the support of the populace. They were fed and protected by local peasants at every step. Traveling on foot, and only at night, to avoid detection by government troops, the guerrillas spent the days hiding out in safe houses, often within shouting distance of government-held towns. If the peasants had wanted to betray them, it would have been a simple matter to tip off the Sandinista militia to their hiding places."

US Involvement

The story of our own involvement began with a National Security Council meeting in November, 1981, where it was decided to train a group of 500 guerrillas in an attempt to stop the arms flow from Nicaragua into El Salvador. This incidentally included US M-16 rifles last seen in Vietnam. Has this effort been successful?

Yes, both in stopping the arms flow and recruits for the program. When we were willing to train 500, over 7,000 men took up arms and were ready to conduct a guerrilla campaign against the Sandinistas. This is important because Nicaragua is the main support base for the entire subversive effort in El Salvador. Monitored radio traffic between guerrillas in El Salvador and a radio in Nicaragua reveal that all supply requests are sent by radio to Nicaragua. Nicaraguan exile sources estimated that if men and arms going into El Salvador from Nicaragua could be cut off, fighting would not be possible after a month without supplies. Those Libyan planes stopped in Brazil were carrying such supplies.

Does it seem strange that the key to military action in El Salvador rests with guerrilla support activity in Nicaragua? Does it seem odd that once contra-guerrilla activity began in Nicaragua, Cuban advisors were withdrawn from El Salvador? The true nature of the guerrilla war in Nicaragua is best expressed by people interviewed and quoted in the Anderson column: "We don't want to fight our Nicaraguan brothers," they said. The ones they're after are the Sandinista leaders and their Cuban, East German, Bulgarian and other foreign advisors.

Cuban Connections

Let's focus now on the Cubans.

By 1978, Cuba zeroed in on Central America and the Caribbean Basin—as part of an overall Soviet strategy of revolution. Soviet arms deliveries to Cuba in 1981 were 66,000 tons and have continued at the same pace each year since. In monetary figures the aid is about $4 billion per year, or over half the USSR's global economic assistance program.

No state in the hemisphere is immune from subversion and attempted revolution. Castro follows a "high-low" track. He is talking to governments and to revolutionaries in the same country.

More ominous is the growing alliance between Cuba and Latin American drug growers and processors. To help support the next revolution in Bolivia and Columbia, arms may be purchased by drug dealers in exchange for assistance in getting drugs to markets in the states. Vice-President Bush, in the May 10 issue of the *Washington Post*, covered the involvement of Cuba more specifically.

"No state in the hemisphere is immune from subversion and attempted revolution."

The Soviet strategy of revolution, conducted in this hemisphere by the Cubans, is a realistic one and should be taken seriously by this country. Their goal? Western access to vitally necessary natural resources will be denied by the victory or operations of terrorist movements, insurgencies, and their political supporters. We are faced with a choice. We can do nothing and be blackmailed into submission or we can take counter-measures against this strategy of revolution and keep our country strong.

Covert Counter-Measures

One necessary ingredient of these counter-measures is our capability to conduct covert action. Much of what we've said today revolves around covert action as a means to stop a hostile country's direction and supply of a guerrilla war in El Salvador. Cuba can be stopped. Nicaragua can be stopped. El Salvador can be saved and other countries now under communist control can be reversed. But what can be said about this type of action in the future? We can have such a valuable tool to use if three conditions are met.

First, covert action must be part of an overall policy set by the President. It has always been a quick fix or something to be thrown into the breach in an emergency.

Second, covert action must involve all relevant parts of the government. This requires overall direction and government wide coordination. The alternative is bureaucratic haggling, as was seen in the aftermath of the Angolan and Chilean situations in the early 1970s.

Third, the President has responsibility for building support for his foreign policy goals. Consensus on goals would obviate many of the Congressional battles we see today.

No Choice

We have no choice in today's world. We ignore covert action and suddenly discover we have to send in the Marines. If we hesitate to send in the Marines we will see the Caribbean a Cuban lake and the US in mortal danger. Covert action however, when used as part of an over-all orchestrated effort, can help this country fight that Soviet strategy of revolution without great expense, with little or no chance of escalation, and help protect the waterways and natural resources that give you and all free people their way of life.

If we fail to take action, I feel we can be isolated or choked off in 1 to 5 years. Only you can make something happen to change this, only you can demand we do something before it's too late.

Let us remember the consequences of Neville Chamberlain's appeasement of Adolf Hitler. 50 million people died because the worlds' democracies lacked the will to stop him early on. Santayana has said that those who do not learn from the mistakes of the past are doomed to repeat them. Keep that in mind.

Max Hugel is a former CIA deputy director.

"Not only have the goals not been met, . . . in most instances, things have worsened because of the covert action."

Covert Operations Are a Menace

Lee Hamilton

Mr. Chairman, there are two basic arguments against the covert action in Nicaragua.

First it has not worked.

The administration has given progressively more ambitious rationales for supporting the covert action.

The initial justification was confined to the interdiction of Soviet and Cuban arms traveling from Nicaragua to the insurgents in El Salvador.

This was subsequently expanded to include the objectives of forcing Nicaragua to turn inward, and forcing the Sandinistas to reassess their revolution and their efforts to export it into neighboring states.

Then, we were told that the purpose of the covert action was to bring the Sandinistas to the negotiating table, to bring them to a more reasonable and less antagonistic attitude toward the whole area.

Most recently the rationale has been expanded still further, to include bringing pluralism and free elections to Nicaragua.

Changing Objectives

Thus the objectives of the CIA have grown from interdiction to changing the internal political structure of Nicaragua.

Over the last 2 years, the covert action has achieved none of these purposes even though the military groups being supported by the action have increased dramatically.

It has not stopped the flow of arms. The Salvadoran guerrillas continue to be resupplied.

It has not forced changes in Nicaraguan policies.

It has strengthened the Sandinistas' resolve, strengthened their support within the country, rallied people to the Nicaraguan Government, and given them justification for increased repressive internal policies.

Lee Hamilton, statement before the House of Representatives, July 27, 1983.

It has not lessened Nicaragua's support for Salvadoran insurgents. Rather that support has continued unabated.

Not only have the goals not been met, they do not seem likely to be met. In most instances, things have worsened because of the covert action.

What has the covert action achieved?

Increased Dangers

It has brought about greater Cuban and Soviet involvement in Nicaragua, more Cuban troops, increased Cuban control.

It has increased the risks of active Cuban military intervention.

It has driven the Nicaraguans ever more deeply into the arms of the Cubans and Soviets. The risk we face in Central America is not a Socialist government in Nicaragua (as distasteful as that may be) but that that government may become subservient to Soviet-Cuban influence. This covert action has greatly increased that risk.

It has also increased the risk of a full-scale war by Nicaragua against Honduras and Costa Rica.

It is perceived throughout the world as an effort to overthrow the Government of Nicaragua. Most of our Latin American neighbors and our European allies have urged us to stop.

If the covert action continues, the prospect is for further escalation. That has been the pattern, and there is no reason to believe that pattern will change.

Future Actions

The administration acknowledges its purposes have not been achieved. How then will they achieve them? The answer is: Through increased pressure. That means more and more U.S. resources to support the war. If this covert war continues, one wonders what the total number of U.S. armed guerrillas will be 6 months from now? What will the objectives be then?

It is not just the history of this covert action that

concerns the majority committee members. It is also the future of this action.

I am not able to discern any limits to this covert action. How many contras are we willing to support? Is there any limit? How far will we expand our purposes? What do we do in the event Cuban troops enter the war?

This Member concludes that the United States is engaged in covert actions without limits, and that the major policy makers have not thought through what to do in the event of major—and by no means improbable—contingencies.

The second basic argument against the covert action is that it is not in the U.S. national interest to be conducting this kind of operation.

Covert Action

First, covert action against Nicaragua is against our laws. The first law in question is the Boland amendment, passed last year, which states:

> No funds may be used by the Central Intelligence Agency or the Department of Defense to furnish military equipment, military training or advice or other support for military activities, to any group or individual not part of the country's armed forces, for the purpose of overthrowing the Government of Nicaragua or provoking a military exchange between Nicaragua and Honduras.

This administration denies any intention to overthrow the Sandinista government. But the validity of the U.S. Government's approach assumes U.S. control of the operation—so that the U.S. intent can be carried out. But the fact is that that control is inadequate. The FDN is an independent force.

"If the covert action continues, the prospect is for further escalation."

This question of command and control is important. It is important because those guerrillas that we have armed are supposed to be an instrument of our—United States—foreign policy. But it is clear that they have their own agenda, their own objectives—and it is that objective, clearly stated by their commander to overthrow the Sandinistas—that they are following.

The administration cannot wash its hands of this affair and deny responsibility for what those it has armed want to do with those arms.

It is also clear that military exchanges are occurring between Honduras and Nicaragua as a result of U.S. support of this covert war. That, too, is contrary to the Boland amendment.

Clear Intentions

The administration's intention cannot be separated from the intent and activities of the military groups we support. The Contras have openly declared their intention to "Liberate Nicaragua," and their activities, the size of their forces, the level of the conflict, the targets they are choosing, all fit with this intention. We may admire Commander Bermudez' goal, but his goals are clearly beyond the bounds set by the Boland amendment. The Contras aim to bring down the Sandinistas. We are now supporting a large army inside Nicaragua. We can no longer deny that we are fighting a mercenary war in Nicaragua to overthrow the government of that country—and that is against our domestic law.

The second law is Article 18 of the charter of the Organization of American States, of which the United States is a signatory. The article says that:

> No state or group of States has the right to intervene directly or indirectly for any reason whatever in the internal or external affairs of any other State.

If the United States were to bring Nicaragua before the OAS, and produce compelling evidence of a Sandinista effort to destabilize the region; then under the Rio Treaty and the OAS Charter, the United States and other affected parties are entitled to demand that collective action be taken. Under present policy, the United States, rather than using this law, has chosen to defy it. We cannot go before the OAS with clean hands.

Violation of Obligations

Furthermore, the Paramilitary war certainly appears to be a violation of U.S. obligations under the OAS Charter and the U.N. Charter.

We in the Congress ought to agree that policy should not supersede law. If the United States signs an agreement, we ought to abide by it.

To assert that the Russians break treaties is no excuse for the United States opening itself to similar charges.

The administration argues that it is acting in legitimate self-defense. This view distorts the legal doctrine of self-defense. In the first place, any action in support of the right of self-defense should be overt, not covert.

Moreover, self-defense comes into play when the national sovereignty is threatened. A general threat of communism to the hemisphere does not automatically constitute a threat to U.S. territory. How is the security of the U.S. threatened by Nicaragua sending arms and supplies to insurgents in El Salvador? Self-defense does not license the United States to undertake a covert activity against Nicaragua for its actions against a third country when neither U.S. security nor U.S. troops are directly threatened.

The doctrine of self-defense under the U.N. Charter of the OAS Charter does not allow any signatory, in an act of self-defense, to send mercenary troops inside another signatory country. Self-defense does not allow the United States to conduct a war inside

Nicaragua because Nicaragua sends arms to El Salvador.

In addition, self-defense involves proportionality. There is no proportionality between the damage inflicted on the United States by the Sandinistas and the damage the United States is inflicting on Nicaragua. Civilian casualties in the war zone in Nicargua are rising, as are reports of tortue and maiming by the Contras. And internationally recognized borders are being violated on a daily basis by armed incursions.

Risks of Wider War

Second. There are sound policy arguments against the covert action as well as legal arguments. The more fighting escalates in Nicaragua, the greater the danger of regionalization of the war. Skirmishes along the Honduran and Costa Rican borders will intensify, more Cuban troops and advisors will be brought in, and a full-scale invasion could be launched, provoking a vigorous U.S. response. A major war on Central American soil, would be a calamity for victor and vanquished alike.

Third. Some promising proposals for resolution of this conflict have now been put forward. They have been put forward by friends, the Contadora group, as well as foe Nicaragua. They call for a response that will test the sincerity of Nicaragua's proposal. It is not sufficient to say, as the President did, that negotiations will be extremely difficult as long as the Sandinistas are in power because they are being subverted or directed by outside forces.

My own judgement is that there exists a real opportunity for negotiation at this time. There is a new resolve to talk. But the region, and much of the world is confused by a U.S. policy which repeats rhetoric of support for the peacemaking efforts of the Contadora groups and decides to increase military involvement in the region, including plans for a sharp increase to the Contras seeking to overthrow the Sandinistas. The position of the Contadora group is that the territory of one state should not be used to conduct acts of aggression against the territory of another state. The United States cannot consistently support the Contadora and also support the Contras.

Damage to Credibility

Fourth. The covert action does long-term damage to our standing in the world. The United States is seen as interventionist, even imperialistic. The Soviets have been handed an underserved propaganda advantage which they are using effectively against U.S. interests. Our allies in Europe have condemned forthrightly the U.S. intervention. The countries of the hemisphere are united in opposition to intervention from any external sources. Secretary Schultz concluded that we were able to conclude a Lebanon withdrawal agreement because the Lebanese and Israelis are convinced of our fairness,

trustworthiness and decency. This covert action undermines our reputation as a fair, decent, trustworthy power. It is damaging our ability to exercise leadership throughout the world. This covert action is simply not the kind of thing the United States should be encouraging or conducting.

Fifth. The covert action is still officially covert. This holds the American Government up to ridicule and charges of official deception. The United States is doing, and all the world knows we are doing, that which we deny we are doing. It makes the legitimate covert activity of the Central Intelligence Agency more difficult to carry out, and saps public confidence in the Agency.

"I am not able to discern any limits to this covert action. How many contras are we willing to support?"

Finally, let me say that when the United States acts out of character, it is ineffective. I believe that conducting this secret war in this place, at this time, and in this matter, is not in keeping with our character or our ideals. Because it is not, and because it is unpopular with the American people who oppose it by about 2:1 in a recent poll, we are hesitant and ineffectual in our execution of that policy.

In conclusion, I do not propose an end to this covert war as a favor to Nicaragua—or to please Cuba or Western Europe.

The covert action should be stopped because:

It is not working;

It is harmful to U.S. interests;

It is risking a wider conflict; and

It is diminishing the chances for successful negotiations.

Lee Hamilton, Democratic Congressman from Indiana, made this statement at the US House of Representatives during the floor debate of HR2760, an amendment to a bill authorizing intelligence operations for 1983 and prohibiting US support for military or paramilitary operations in Nicaragua.

"The purpose of counterintelligence is...to learn about and to neutralize the activities of the nation's enemies."

US Intelligence Operations Need to Be Increased

Arnold Beichman

What a cushy job it must be today to run the Soviet KGB, the USSR secret police and espionage agency. There is longevity and job security, not as in the old Stalin days when, after a few years as head of the secret police, you were taken out and shot.

Better yet, Yuri Andropov, who runs the KGB, sits on the Politburo secure in the knowledge that his once redoubtable adversaries, the CIA and the FBI, have for the last seven years been so weakened that they are no longer serious competition. Even now, when there is some possibility that Congress may allow the CIA and FBI to function once more, it will still be years before these agencies will be sufficiently secure against KGB penetration and disinformation.

Penetration of the CIA by the KGB is now an established fact. On October 29, David H. Barnett, a former CIA agent, confessed that he had been selling important secrets to the Soviet agency for some years—including a top-priority clandestine CIA operation in Indonesia in the 1960s. Mr. Barnett also confessed that he had revealed to the KGB the identities of thirty covert CIA employees.

CIA Deficiencies

The organizational deficiencies have multiplied since 1975 because of Congressional investigations, Executive orders and, above all, because of the serious decline of U.S. counterintelligence capacity in the CIA and the FBI. This was the conclusion of many specialists who attended the third meeting of the Consortium for the Study of Intelligence (CSI). It is now possible, for example, to assign Soviet agents to the U.S., literally by the shipload. In 1978, there were 1,300 Soviet and 700 Soviet-bloc officials permanently assigned to the U.S. as diplomats, media and trade representatives, and staff to international organizations. The number of Soviet-bloc graduate students has increased from the usual 35-40 to 200. During 1977, there were almost 60,000 Soviet-bloc visitors to the U.S. Of these visitors, 14,000 were commercial, scientific, and cultural delegates, while the remaining 40,000 were crewmen who enjoyed complete liberty while Soviet ships were docked in 40 U.S. deepwater ports.

Now I have it on good authority that before Congress put the FBI on its "most wanted" list, the FBI routinely covered KGB suspect agents on a one-to-one basis, that is, one FBI surveillance expert to one KGB suspect. Today, as Mr. Andropov knows well, the ratio has dropped to 1-to-4. There are just too many KGB targets floating about the U.S. today, while some 300 FBI staffers are busy checking applications from all kinds of dubious sources under the Freedom of Information Act. Let me quote former Assistant Attorney General Antonin Scalia, now a professor at the University of Chicago Law School:

> A story that I often tell is, when I was at the Justice Department, concern was expressed by the National Aeronautics and Space Administration that it was receiving a regular series of requests from AMTORG, the Soviet trading company. And they asked the Justice Department was there anything they could do about it under the Freedom of Information Act and, of course, the answer was no. The Act doesn't make any distinction with respect to citizens or aliens or foreign companies, so it's not an unreal problem, but the Act was quite clearly drawn that way and intentionally so. I don't think that it was an oversight.

Thus foreigners and foreign governments, regardless of whether friend or foe, have the right under American law to information from *all* agencies of the American government.

Intelligence Crisis

If this state of affairs were limited to a few agencies, the damage might be controllable. But the damage goes far beyond that—it threatens the very existence of counterintelligence, without which there

"Can Counterintelligence Come in from the Cold?" by Arnold Beichman is reprinted by permission from *Policy Review*, Issue No. 15 (or Winter 1981). *Policy Review* is a publication of The Heritage Foundation, 214 Massachusetts Ave. NE, Washington, DC 20002.

can be no operative intelligence system. To put it simply, the crisis of U.S. intelligence is a crisis of counterintelligence.

Newton S. Miler, former chief of operations in the counterintelligence staff of the CIA under James Angleton, recently told the CSI that America did not have an effective counterintelligence capability. He told us that neither the CIA nor the FBI neutralizes Soviet and Soviet-bloc intelligence activity in the U.S. There are even people who believe that the CIA has been "turned around" and that revitalizing the agency, instead of starting a new one, would merely strengthen the possible KGB penetrators in the CIA right now, such as any Barnetts who still may remain undiscovered. The importance of counterintelligence has been emphasized by Richard Helms, CIA director from 1966-72, who has said, "Counterintelligence is terribly important, because without an effective counterintelligence program—both in the CIA and the FBI—the problem of double agents and infiltrators is insurmountable."

"The CIA and the FBI have for the last seven years been so weakened that they are no longer serious competition (for the KGB)."

Still worse is the fact that throughout these five years the powerful Congressional intelligence oversight committees have paid little or no attention to the presence of the KGB in the U.S. Nor have such powerful newspapers as the *New York Times* and *Washington Post*—which for years occupied themselves with relentlessly exposing our intelligence agencies—paid any attention to the KGB. I know of no Congressional committee which is presently working on an investigation of the KGB. Unfortunately nothing much can be done on such a matter because there are weightier debates going on in Washington. There is, for example, a dispute over Carter Administration amendments to the National Intelligence Act of 1980 and to the Foreign Intelligence Surveillance Act (FISA) of 1978. In one case, the row is over an amendment to the FISA whether to "extend the emergency surveillance period of 24 to 48 hours"! This situation justifies Senator Frank Church's observation: "I wonder if we are competent to manage an intelligence gathering program on anything." Senator Church should know.

Intelligence Security

The importance of a counterintelligence agency is to ensure that the other parts of the intelligence community can be trusted—that is, those sections which deal with covert operations, clandestine collection and analysis and estimates. If counterintelligence operatives are inefficient or intimidated, the enemy success is inevitable.

Success or failure in counterintelligence depends largely upon the ingenuity of counterintelligence officers as well as on the initiative and courage of sources of information. In other words, successful counterintelligence depends upon the quality of its personnel—the counterintelligence analyst, the counterintelligence case officer, and the agent or informant. But the quality of the personnel is insufficient to guarantee good results. There must be positive incentives to good performance and under the present system, certainly during the last seven black years for U.S. intelligence, there have been disheartening disincentives.

The counterintelligence analyst, farthest removed from danger or betrayal, must perform an unpleasant duty if he is to be loyal to his assignment. He must constantly question the *bona fides* of sources and the validity of information which is usually hard-won, often unique. Such questioning of information, especially from defectors, reflects—or may be interpreted as reflecting—on the judgment of others in the intelligence community and in the government itself. Often the counterintelligence analyst is questioning the judgment of officials of much higher rank than his.

The counterintelligence case officer has an even more difficult road. He is the actual counter-spy. His duty is to investigate, to maintain surveillance, to infiltrate, to carry out "experiments"—e.g., feeding data to certain persons through certain channels and then watching for results to confirm or disconfirm suspicions about individuals within his own service who may have been deceived or used or have actually gone over to the other side. If there had been any successful counterintelligence activity in Britain could the Philbys, Blunts, and Macleans have flourished?

The Agent

The agent (i.e., the source of informant) is in the most difficult, if not the riskiest, position of all. If his identity becomes known, he may be killed. Lester Dominique, a federal informant, was recently found bludgeoned, beaten with chains, disemboweled with a machete. His name has been inadvertently left in open court documents.

The agent, the informer who penetrates an organization, must do the things required of anyone living in the environment he is penetrating. Such work is usually unpleasant, often dangerous and sometimes illegal. Adding to the informant's agonies is the fact that he is no longer regarded as a useful member of the society which is he serving, whatever his motive may be. In the 1950s, an informer's job was glorified in a TV serial, "I Led Three Lives." But by the 1970s, the undercover operative no longer enjoyed much esteem. Thus E. Drexel Godfrey, a former senior CIA official, wrote in *Foreign Affairs* (January 1978) that those in the business of corrupting others actually end up corrupting American society. Such a statement, unprovable by its nature, borders on the metaphysical and tells us little about how to combat in peacetime enemies determined to destroy that same society.

Although formal proof is lacking, it may be that the size of the overall counterintelligence program has increased both in manpower and in money during the last few years. Compared with the early 1970s, some parts of the counterintelligence community—parts of the CIA's counterintelligence staff and the FBI domestic security program—have been cut. Other sectors have been augmented—the FBI's foreign counterintelligence staff and Department of Defense sections.

Despite this apparently good news, it is far from clear that the total resources devoted to counterintelligence are adequate to the needs of the 1980s, especially when the KGB has had such an easy time for several years. However, the most formidable obstacles to U.S. counterintelligence have been specific laws, judicial opinions and regulations enjoying the force of law which together have created a host of disincentives to effective counterintelligence.

Legal Obstacles

Laws whose norms are clear-cut are not the problem. Counterintelligence operatives now know that they are barred from engaging in activities once considered permissible. But other rules are nowhere near as clear; lawyers themselves will argue about the meaning of regulations and judicial decisions. Thus, for instance, it is not always possible to guarantee an informant's anonymity. Finally, as is the custom with Congress when confronting a delicate issue, some rules are made intentionally vague—to satisfy competing pressure groups—on the assumption that the questions will be finally resolved by the courts. What is the counterintelligence operative to do in the meantime? His interest is to stay at a safe distance from a law or regulation until the matter is settled conclusively.

The totality—laws, court cases, presidential orders, guidelines, the interpretations which the CIA and other agencies offer of these norms; the hearings and statements of powerful legislators and their staffs—create a legal and legislative climate which hampers counterintelligence performance. That is the opinion of both retired counterintelligence officials and former informants.

Let me make something clear. I do not argue that counterintelligence should be free of rules, standards and prohibitions. Restrictions are necessary to protect civil liberties. However, the constraints which have been put into effect since the 1970s have been narrowly focused to the detriment of counterintelligence performance. It should be possible to devise rules that can both assist the counterintelligence mission and protect civil liberties from potential abuse by the government.

Function of Counterintelligence

The legal restrictions arise from a misunderstanding of what counterintelligence is and what it is not. Counterintelligence cannot be identified with criminal proceedings, because counterintelligence deals with activities whose primary characteristics is not criminality but hostility to the nation's security. The purpose of counterintelligence is not to prevent crimes and to punish criminals but rather to learn about and to neutralize the activities of the nation's enemies.

"There must be positive incentives to good performance and under the present system. . . there have been disheartening disincentives."

In criminal investigations, it is hard to imagine that the government would have a right to keep tabs on wholly innocent persons. In the field of intelligence and counterintelligence it is sometimes necessary to observe the activities of perfectly loyal citizens in order to learn about the activities of hostile intelligence services.

The counterintelligence officer's relationship with a hostile spy is not comparable to that between a policeman and a criminal. The hostile spy may not even be doing anything criminal because covertly influencing public policy in the U.S. is not a crime. Punishing him is not the task of counterintelligence. Its tasks are fourfold:

(1) to protect our own intelligence operations.

(2) to discover deception and disinformation.

(3) to uncover secret political operations directed against the U.S.

(4) to keep spies and terrorists from being successful.

It is not part of counterintelligence operations to go beyond identification of an enemy agent. Counterintelligence officers generally argue against arresting hostile operatives; once known, they become harmless. The Foreign Intelligence Surveillance Act of 1978 requires special proceedings to obtain warrants for surveillance; the requirements are a parody of criminal law. Even more ludicrous is that in the course of the trials required to convict spies it is often necessary to reveal more information than the spies, during their operations, had actually succeeded in obtaining.

It is not my intention to depict counterintelligence

officers or other CIA officers as nature's noblemen, worthy of exemption from the accepted rules governing the behavior of other appointive officials. Counterintelligence officers have a job to do which, by its nature, may be unpleasant and discomforting to a democratic society. Not all democratic standards can be applied in dealing with the operatives of a government which operates by a totalitarian standard and which judges victory solely on its success in weakening a democratic society.

In confronting this highly successful Soviet espionage organization, American government officials—regardless of party—have simply not understood the counterintelligence mission, either in the CIA, the FBI or the Defense Department. I say "regardless of party" because it was President Ford's Attorney General, Edward Levi, whose guidelines regulating counterintelligence activities are effectively in force today. They have remained substantially unaltered throughout the Carter Administration.

Criminal Standard

The main concept which informs the guidelines is the criminal standard—the notion that an individual should not be subject to investigation unless it can be demonstrated that he is or probably will be involved in a criminal undertaking. One set of guidelines (publicly available) establishes thresholds which cannot be crossed unless it can be demonstrated that a U.S. citizen or resident alien actually has committed or is about to commit a crime. Advocating or discussing the violent overthrow of the government or the commission of terrorist acts is not enough. The FBI has interpreted these rules to mean that it cannot even collect publications of domestic organizations unless there is "probable cause" to believe that a crime is imminent.

"It should be possible to devise rules that can both assist the counterintelligence mission and protect civil liberties from potential abuse by the government."

According to the guidelines, should the FBI come across information that an organization may be planning to violate the law (for example, a report that someone is buying explosives) then the FBI may slightly increase surveillance of the group and establish a "limited investigation." This means no electronic surveillance, no mail cover, no placing of informants in the group.

Such "intrusive" techniques are permissible only when a "full investigation" has been authorized by FBI headquarters on the basis of "specific and articulable facts" describing "(1) the magnitude of the

threatened harm; (2) the likelihood it will occur; (3) the immediacy of the threat; (4) the danger to privacy and free expression posed by a full investigation."

Here is the classic catch-22. How do you obtain the information to justify a full investigation without first using the investigatory techniques which are expressly forbidden in a "limited investigation"? The answer is you cannot do so.

These guidelines impose similar obligations on the field agent; they must write justifications for investigations which they may be reluctant to commit to paper because all they have is a hunch and imperfect data. It must often seem better to drop the case.

Further Obstacles

These are only the unclassified guidelines. The classified guidelines deal with foreign counterintelligence activities, but retired FBI and CIA officials indicate that the principles embodied in the one are not substantially different from the principles in the other.

These "domestic" and foreign guidelines reportedly have limited counterintelligence operations to a criminal standard so strict as to prohibit surveillance of the Puerto Rican terrorists who, released after serving twenty-five years in prison, vowed to strike again.

There are some observers who take an optimistic view of the future for U.S. intelligence and counterintelligence. I do not. Unless we are first made aware of the titanic effort directed by the Soviet Politburo to attenuate American power and will, and finally we realize that this effort is succeeding, no reform, no alignment, no new philosophy, and no new technical expertise are going to help one whit.

Arnold Beichman is a visiting scholar at the Hoover Institution and currently resides in British Columbia. He is co-author of Andropov: New Challenge to the West, *a political biography of Yuri Andropov.*

US Intelligence Operations Need to Be Reduced

John Stockwell

Following several years of shocking revelations about the United States intelligence service, we now have a unique opportunity to rethink our objectives in the Third World, especially in Africa, and to modify our intelligence activities to complement rather than contradict sound, long term policies. The revelations, and their related publicity, have been a healthy exercise, making the American public aware of what enlightened people throughout the world already knew, that CIA operations had plumbed the depths of assassination, meddlesome covert wars, and the compulsive recruitment of foreign officials to commit treason on our behalf; activities which, if they did not border on international terrorism, certainly impressed their victims as harsh and cruel, whatever their bureaucratic authentication and national security justification in Washington.

American citizens may be less aware of the widening credibility gap the United States suffers in the Third World because our leaders have responded to repeated crises by mouthing benign platitudes about peace and humanity while secretly ordering the CIA to attempt violent solutions. Can you believe the American President? The Secretary of State? In 1975 they publicly called for an embargo on the shipment of arms into Angola, while secretly ordering the CIA to deliver 1,500 tons of arms into the civil war. History has exposed numerous similar discrepancies in the Congo, Cuba, Chile, Vietnam. In June 1978 President Carter angrily accused Fidel Castro of encouraging the Katangese invasion of the Shaba. Castro denied the charge. Who was telling the truth?

Even more important for Americans to understand are the implications of the mounting reservation with which we are now viewed in the Third World. No longer are we the Ugly Americans, arrogant in our unsophisticated chauvinism; nowadays virtually every legitimate, well-meaning American who sojourns in the Third World encounters the exasperating obstacle of suspicion of being "CIA," and the connotation even in friendly minds is pejorative.

Inadequate Response

So far our reaction to the scandalous CIA revelations would hardly reassure anyone that we have learned our lesson about secret intelligence organizations, and mended our ways. To begin with, not one CIA miscreant has been reprimanded, much less punished, for the crimes and irresponsible activities they have undertaken in the Third World— without exception they are still drawing CIA salaries or pensions. (Richard Helms was punished—a wrist slap—only for lying to the Congress, not for the operation he supervised in Chile.) And in 1976 President Ford actually expanded the CIA's charter to give it license to conduct covert operations in countries friendly to the United States and in those not threatened by subversion. After taking office, President Carter enhanced the role and influence of the CIA director by making him the "intelligence czar" while reaffirming the CIA's authority to conduct covert action anywhere abroad, to dally covertly with the press, and to recruit on United States college campuses (overt recruitment of American staff employees and covert seduction of young foreign students into CIA roles which are treasonous against their own countries.)

True, the current CIA director, Admiral Turner, announced a massive housecleaning of the CIA and President Carter reworked the boards, panels, and committees which are commissioned to oversee the CIA. It was not lost on the world, however, that the objective of these moves was to strengthen the CIA and to deflect continued criticism. Admiral Turner's announced purpose in cleaning house was to make

John Stockwell, "The Case Against the CIA," *Issue: A Quarterly Journal of Africanist Opinion*, Spring/Summer 1979. Reprinted by permission.

the CIA "lean and efficient," ominous words to people who traditionally have been victims of the CIA's activities. Nor have these adjustments been administered in any credible way. Turner's housecleaning was abortive. After firing the first 200 employees (of an announced plan to dismiss 800) in the "Halloween Massacre" of 1977, he gave it up, claiming weakly, as every CIA Director before him had done, that early retirements were relieving the Agency's "dead wood" problem. To inhibit further exposure of the CIA's misdeeds, the Government (with President Carter's public blessing) has sued one CIA whistleblower, Frank Snepp. And the Senate Intelligence Committee responded to evidence that CIA managers had deliberately given it misleading testimony to subvert its oversight responsibility during the Angolan operation of 1975-1976 by exercising itself with a perfunctory, year-long investigation. Eventually it shelved this formality without recommending disciplinary or corrective action. The lesson is obvious: if the Senate tolerates false testimony about major operations like the Angola program in which thousands of human beings are killed, then it is more a neutered collaborator than an overseer, and President Carter's reassurances of adequate supervision of the CIA are implausible.

Self-Conscious Chauvinism

In fact, the only adjustment President Carter has made which promises to be very effective was the order to the attorney general to police the agency from operating illegally within the United States. If done vigorously this will inhibit the CIA from such things as illegal mail openings and using us as guinea pigs in secret drug/sex experiments. This self-conscious chauvinism is transparent; we have endeavored to protect ourselves from the CIA while increasing its effectiveness against non-Americans.

"Spy vs. spy intrigue—the CIA vs. the KGB—is an anachronism which should be relegated as soon as possible to its appropriate place in mythology."

If we mean what we say to the world about Peace and human rights, and if we value our credibility both as a world leader and as traveling, functioning private citizens, we cannot have our foreign representation permeated with cynical intelligence operatives. More than exercising restraint in fielding CIA case officers to every corner of the world, we must set a courageous example by abstaining from covert activities even when they are marginally justifiable.

The most common final argument one hears to justify the CIA is that as long as the other side has "those people" we must field our own team to keep our guard up. This is adolescent posturing, an unfortunate element of Soviet/American competition in the Third World in which each side has struggled to minimize its effectiveness, much like giveaway checkers. The Soviets blunder away their alliance with Egypt while we besmirch ourselves with the Angolan debacle. Nothing of lasting importance is decided in the alleys and gutters of the world. Spy vs. spy intrigue—the CIA vs. the KGB—is an anachronism which should be relegated as soon as possible to its appropriate place in mythology. If the Soviet Union is determined to discredit itself with KGB skullduggery, let's not retaliate by soiling ourselves with CIA shenanigans.

At present we have over thirty CIA stations on the African continent, a hundred case officers under official cover, and two dozen or so "outside" case officers under non-official cover. It is highly doubtful that any of these operatives are in fact contributing strategic intelligence which would not be provided adequately by overt State Department officers and other collection systems. And yet the lot of them are invariably known as "CIA" in their host communities as they energetically attempt to prove themselves to Washington by recruiting local agents. The CIA has been in business for thirty years. In some posts the local residents have knowingly watched a dozen generations of case officers come and go.

Unnecessary Expansion

No one, not even the CIA, can argue plausibly that our national security is very much at stake in Ouagadougou, Niamey, Ndjamena, Bangui, or Nouakchott. But in recent years the agency has nevertheless succeeded in expanding its presence into such places by arguing that small African posts offer unique access to the "hard targets," the Soviet, Chinese, North Korean and Eastern European officials. The CIA has in fact had little success in recruiting any such officials in Africa who could report strategic information, but each station has justified the maintenance of a stable of covert agents, Africans and resident Europeans, for the hypothetical, indirect access they offer to the hard target individuals. This illegal network probably totals five hundred agents (spies). Their presence is about as popular in the host countries as the recent efforts by the South Korean government to bribe our own legislators were to ourselves.

Even Lusaka, which is the CIA's pivotal station in Southern Africa because of the mounting Zimbabwe crisis, contributes little vital intelligence which could not be had by our State Department officers. It maintains contact with various liberation movements, but each of these movements has indicated its willingness to work directly with legitimate United States representatives. And the presence of CIA case officers in Lusaka, Praetoria, Maputo and Dar Es Salaam perennially tempts the administration to experiment with covert ploys. Does President Kaunda need some special weapons, does Joshua Nkomo want an errand run, would Ian Smith like to have his back scratched? The threat of CIA adventuring in Zimbabwe is far from hypothetical. The CIA is there and, with or without National Security Council approval, it is ready and eager to act. Unfortunately, during the Angolan operation the agency demonstrated that its sympathies were solidly with the white redoubt in southern Africa; it collaborated intimately with the South African troops inside Angola while the Lusaka, Praetoria and Kinshasa stations vigorously promoted even greater involvement with South Africa.

We are still haunted by the legacies of former CIA operations in the Congo, Katanga, Vietnam, Cuba, Chile, and Angola. Can we hope that such costly blunders will not be repeated if we do not substantially modify the CIA?

Something for the World

We are a great nation with a system of government which claims to offer the individual maximum protection, freedom and opportunity. We have something valuable to offer the world, if we believe in ourselves sufficiently to trust in our true strengths. Unfortunately, we also have an ignominious flaw: latent, arrogant insensitivity which, combined with our violent heritage, has blighted our record with incidents like the slaughter of the Moros in the Philippines, the Rattlesnake Buttes massacre, and My Lai. The Phoenix program was more subtly rationalized, but killed more people than the others. The sacrifice of the Kurds in Iraq in 1975 was equally callous. And in 1975 three men in Washington were primarily responsible for ordering the poorly rationalized Angolan operation which led to thousands of Angolan deaths. In May 1978 the CIA director, Admiral Turner, and the Africa Division chief, James Potts, approached Senator Clark, asking him to waive his amendment of 1976 so they could heat up the Angolan civil war to cause problems for the Cubans there. Only clark's refusal to cooperate with this "strategic" nonsense saved numerous Angolan lives.

The ironic truth is that not one of these scarlet incidents worked to the United States long term national interests, and in each case humane and constructive alternatives were available. To say that such conduct is debasing and that it is destructive of the world's chance for peace is only to state the obvious.

Perhaps the most important disclosure of 1976 was that the CIA's spy apparatus is an ineffective tool for gathering strategic intelligence. The Pike Committee analyzed a series of major intelligence failures in situations of enormous importance to the United States national security and to world peace and found that the CIA had lost track of the Soviet army for two weeks before the invasion of Czechoslovakia, that it had failed to monitor and report India's development of the atomic bomb, and that its faulty reporting during the Yom Kippur War had led us to the brink of World War III, military confrontation with the Soviet Union. Congressman Pike concluded that the CIA's intelligence production was lousy. In Africa, the Angola program itself was highlighted with repeated intelligence failures, typical of the CIA's clandestine services. The SHABA crises of 1977 and 1978 further illustrated that, outside of the capitals where they live and compete with State Department officers, the CIA has little intelligence coverage. The stakes are too great for us to continue to indulge ourselves with spy games which our thirty-year CIA experiment has proven ineffective and destructive.

The appropriate role of American intelligence is to accumulate by the most modern methods strategic information to enable our government to cope with real global challenges. Already this is done by our highly effective and enormously expensive technical collection systems....

"We have something valuable to offer the world, if we believe in ourselves sufficiently to trust in our true strengths."

In Africa, as with the rest of the Third World, we should exercise positive leadership and minimize covert activities which are so threatening to the stability of precarious young governments, and ultimately so damaging to our own long term interests. We should drastically reduce our CIA presence in Africa, thereby restoring the credibility of our diplomats, Peace Corps, businessmen, professors and tourists. Had we done so long ago we would have avoided the Congo, the Ugandan, the Angolan debacles, and our name would not have been so closely identified with the white renegades called "mercenaries" whose presence in several African crises has stirred such resentment, or with white South Africa, or with the losing trend in southern Africa. Should we withdraw the CIA from Africa today we would not be a whit less well informed, our national security in no way jeopardized, and we would reduce the tension in an already volatile continent by exactly the measure of our current CIA activities there.

John Stockwell was with the CIA in South Africa and is the author of In Search of Enemies: A CIA Story.

"We are better off in the long run if our ideas get sponged down by outside critical minds."

US Intelligence Needs Congressional Supervision

Les Aspin

Editor's note: Hughes-Ryan, referred to in the following viewpoint, was the 1974 amendment to US Intelligence legislation providing for Congress to oversee CIA operations.

I am introducing legislation entitled the "Intelligence Activities Act of 1980." This legislation will do two things. It will provide for a stronger congressional tether on the intelligence community and, at the same time, address the major problems of which the CIA itself complains. This bill is intended neither to emasculate the intelligence services nor to allow them free run on the globe. It is an honest effort to provide those restraints that will prevent a return to the "good old days" that proved to be an embarrassment to us as a nation while at the same time recognizing that our intelligence services cannot be expected to operate in a fishbowl like some social service agency. I think the Intelligence Activities Act of 1980 is just such a balanced approach....

Twenty-seven congressmen and 19 senators is not an unreasonable number to be briefed about so crucial a matter of public policy as covert actions. The key to avoiding covert action disasters is the assurance that a cross-section of people will consider it. A number of covert actions blew up in our faces in the past because they were terrible ideas to begin with. They were put together by a handful of true believers who prevented anyone who might question their judgment from having a say. The Nixon administration, for example, set up the 40 Committee to oversee intelligence operations. But when the White House had an inspiration it thought some members of the committee might find less than inspiring, it simply bypassed the committee. That's how we got track II in Chile and how we first helped and then cynically shut off help to the Kurds.

Les Aspin, speech before the US House of Representatives, March 18, 1980.

To be sure, the requirement to brief congressional committees is no guarantee that foolish covert actions will be avoided. The committees do not have and are not seeking the power to veto an intelligence operation, nor do they have any unique wisdom. But bringing more people into the process forces those doing the planning to think through what they want to do, to confront arguments against it, and opens them up to opposition or ridicule if they have a patently ridiculous proposal. For example, a reporting requirement could have prevented some of that foolishness against Castro, such as the effort to make his beard fall out.

Where Are the Leaks?

Of course, the more who know of an operation, the greater the opportunity for leaks. But where are all these leaks supposedly caused by *Hughes-Ryan*? We are doing a fair amount of covert operations now and have been for some time; they are not being leaked. I have sat through whole days of briefings on covert actions and never seen anything about them in print. What I do see, however, are articles saying the Nation is paralyzed because of Hughes-Ryan.

What concerns me is the subtle twist being given to logic. Those who wish to rescind Hughes-Ryan are in effect reasoning with the public as follows: (a) You do not see any leaked stories in the newspapers about covert actions; ergo, (b), there are no covert actions going on, and (c) this means our foreign policy is crippled. But this argument is fallacious since covert actions continue daily. In truth, we should be reasoning thus: (a) You do not see any leaked stories in the newspapers about covert actions; ergo, (b), we have clearly demonstrated that Congress can exercise oversight of the intelligence community without any serious problems.

There is, however, one real problem with the reporting requirement in Hughes-Ryan—a perceptual problem: just how cooperative are foreign intelligence services and sources willing to be when they think so many talkative Congressmen are being brought into the informational loop. I hear many expressions of concern relayed by the CIA from foreign intelligence agencies, though I have often wondered if the CIA's publicly expressed fears about foreign cooperation have proved self-fulfilling and made the problem more serious. I would not deny that the gesture of restricting access to covert action information to my colleagues and I on the two intelligence committees could enhance cooperation abroad. My bill encompasses that gesture of restricting notification to the two intelligence committees, augmented by the leadership of the other committees....

Public Disclosure

Turning to the second provision, we hear of a need to amend the Freedom of Information Act so the CIA will not have to release so much information. But let us look at realities. The freedom of information provisions that concern the CIA were enacted in 1974. Can the CIA or anyone else point to a single word that the CIA has been forced to release against its better judgment in the intervening 6 years?

"Twenty-seven congressmen and 19 senators is not an unreasonable number to be briefed about so crucial a matter of public policy as covert actions."

But again, we do have a real perceptual problem emanating from friendly foreign intelligence services and potential sources. The bill I am introducing, therefore, proposes to add to the statutes a very brief and simple statement that would make clear that nothing in the law requires any intelligence links or informational exchanges with foreign governments or sources to be publicly disclosed.

This section does not mean that illegal acts or improprieties could be covered up through this provision. For example, any arrangement with a foreign intelligence service that permitted it free rein to operate against its nationals in this country regardless of American law would be uncovered by the strengthened procedures for congressional oversight.

Perceptual Problems

So we see that the real problems posed for our intelligence community by the Hughes-Ryan amendment and the Freedom of Information Act are perceptual problems. They cry out for a perceptual solution. And that is what the Intelligence Activities Act of 1980 provides—no overkill, just a solution that focuses directly on the real problem.

There are other problems with Hughes-Ryan—problems not for the CIA, but for congressional oversight.

First, Hughes-Ryan says that without notification to Congress, no money may be spent by "the Central Intelligence Agency for operations in foreign countries, other than activities intended solely for obtaining necessary intelligence."

That neatly provides two loopholes. First, covert operations could be assigned to intelligence agencies other than the CIA—and there are lots of them. How many people are aware, for example, that the Drug Enforcement Administration has intelligence agents all over the world. Second, sensitive intelligence collection operations are exempt from such review although one of the biggest intelligence flaps in modern history—the downing of Gary Powers' U-2—involved an intelligence collection operation. Another, the *Glomar Explorer,* involved the expenditure of hundreds of millions of dollars without real congressional review.

Hughes-Ryan erroneously assumes that intelligence collection is neutral and that foreign policy can only be tripped up by covert action—defined in the profession as programs designed to influence the outcome of events abroad through clandestine activity ranging from propaganda to paramilitary.

Hughes-Ryan should be amended so that congressional committees—be they two or eight or something in between—are informed of covert action, intelligence collection, and other high-risk intelligence activities mounted by any agency of the Government.

"In a Timely Fashion"

Second, as we frequently hear, Hughes-Ryan says that Congress should be notified "in a timely fashion." The CIA points to that phrase and interprets it to mean it need tell Congress only after it has launched a covert action, by which time it has become much more difficult to change direction.

Over the years, I have accepted that interpretation of the phrase "in a timely fashion." And I have publicly labeled that a defect of Hughes-Ryan. However, upon closer examination, I fear that we in Congress have allowed ourselves to be buffaloed into accepting an unreasonably narrow interpretation of the law.

We passed legislation that called for prior notification. The bill I am introducing today will make that specific so there need be no further dispute.

But, as with the matters I discussed earlier, there is still a matter of perceptions. For just as critics of the Hughes-Ryan provision calling for notification to eight committees think hundreds of Congressmen and Senators are notified, so critics of the "timely fashion" phrase in Hughes-Ryan tend to think the CIA notifies the committees of nothing in advance. I want to make clear that the CIA has usually, though not always, given the House Intelligence Committee advance word of covert action plans. The problem is that the CIA has insisted from the beginning that it cannot be required to inform Congress in advance. The language of my bill is intended to pin down the intelligence community. The language in my bill, however, really breaks no new ground; it simply fixes with certainty both current practice and the original intentions of the Congress.

A large part of the American public remains ill at ease about the intelligence community and fearful that the rights of individuals can be trampled easily by agencies that have the statutory power to operate behind a cloak. The intelligence community and its supporters can argue that these fears are groundless and that the abuses of the past have been banished forever. In effect, they are saying that the American public has a perception problem about the intelligence community.

Rules for Intelligence Community

I do not accept that. Their abuses were real enough once. They can happen again. We ought to address the problem by writing into the statutes rules the intelligence community must comply with. We need not excessively hamper the intelligence community, and we would be addressing the concerns of a significant segment of the public.

First, an American should not be treated as a second class citizen by the U.S. Government simply because he travels abroad. An American should not be considered a fair target for any kind of surveillance simply because he has left Dubuque for Dunkerque. The bill I am introducing will do that. For example, to institute an electronic surveillance of an American abroad, a warrant would be required, based on a criminal standard, as it is for such surveillance in the United States. If the Government wants to open the mail or search the home or office of an American, at home or abroad, under my bill they will have to obtain a warrant based on strict probable cause of a crime, and will have to serve the warrant on the subject of the search.

Second, the integrity of some of the leading institutions of our society—specifically, the clergy, the press, and academia—can be undermined if their counterparts abroad believe that ministers, newsmen, or teachers are actually sent abroad by the CIA to ferret out intelligence information. The internal regulations of the CIA now prohibit such paid relationships, but the Director of Central Intelligence can waive these provisions, and has said that he has been willing to do so. My bill explicitly prohibits such relations, with no waivers.

In the past covert actions were commonly laid out by a small circle of people often devoted to ends over means. It is those means that got us into trouble in many parts of the world. The processes that have been set up since then were designed not to emasculate intelligence operations, but to block the folly of the unchecked bureaucrat. We have not worked with these procedures for a half decade. They have worked reasonably well, but both the intelligence community and its congressional overseers have grounds for legitimate complaint. The law does need to be fine tuned—fine tuned to relieve the intelligence community of perceptual impediments to its legitimate work, fine tuned to improve the congressional oversight process, and fine tuned to assure the public that it will be protected from molestation by agencies that cannot by definition operate in public.

A Better End Product

Many in the intelligence community would prefer to return to the good old days. The fewer people it has to go to the better, in its eyes. I might note that most school superintendents would prefer not to have to run their ideas past school boards. Most county executives could do without the bother of getting approval from county boards. Most corporate presidents would just as soon skip those meetings with the board of directors. We all like to think that we have great ideas and we would like to carry them to fruition without having other people first toss darts at them.

"Can the CIA or anyone else point to a single word that the CIA has been forced to release against its better judgment?"

But whether we plan covert operations, corporate strategies, or congressional campaigns, we are better off in the long run if our ideas get sponged down by outside critical minds. It might not be great for the ego, but it provides a better end product. . . .

The goal should not be to loosen the ties that bind the CIA to Congress, but rather to strengthen them. We should no more permit the CIA to prowl the realm of public policy unchecked than we would allow the Agriculture Department or the Nuclear Regulatory Agency to do so.

At the same time, the goal should be to assist the CIA in carrying out the duties assigned to it by the law. We cannot ask any agency to perform assigned tasks and then turn around and impose restrictions that prevent that agency from doing its job.

Les Aspin, Democratic Representative from Wisconsin, introduced legislation to control the US intelligence community.

"The CIA officers, knowing that hundreds of Congressmen and staffs can be briefed on any particular covert action, may be reluctant to undertake operations."

viewpoint **44**

US Intelligence Is Hampered by Congressional Supervision

John Ashbrook

Covert action is influencing other countries through clandestine means. It may range from placing articles in local newspapers to subsidizing political movements friendly to the United States. Soviet covert action includes such things as forgeries and support for terrorist movements. We would not want our country to act like the Soviet Union. But, we would want it to have the ability to counteract Soviet operations.

Under the present law, the President of the United States must find that a particular covert action is of importance to the United States, and must personally sign off on each one. In addition, eight separate committees, four in the House and four in the Senate, have a right to be briefed on every covert action. As a result, covert actions that might be beneficial to the United States have been inhibited. The CIA officers, knowing that hundreds of Congressmen and staffs can be briefed on any particular covert action, may be reluctant to undertake operations which, while very beneficial to the United States, could be extremely sensitive. In addition, requiring that the President sign the Finding removes the possibility of "plausible denial." There may be times when a President would like to deny that the United States is engaged in a particular covert action. He could not easily do so if his signature was on the Finding.

Purpose of Prior Reporting?

The present mood of Congress would reduce the Committees to which covert actions have to be reported from eight to two. These would be the two Intelligence Committees. However, there are some who desire that covert actions be reported in advance to Congress rather than after they take place. In practice, in almost every case, covert actions have been reported to Congress in advance. But what is the purpose of prior notification? If there is prior notification, there is the possibility that the covert action could be prevented. But under our Constitution, the conduct of foreign policy is in the hands, not of Congress, but of the President. Congress has no right to prevent the President from carrying out his foreign policy either overtly or covertly. But if Congress is to play a proper role in intelligence oversight, it must be fully informed of all covert actions. A compromise developed by Congressman Zablocki and adopted by the House Foreign Affairs Committee would require prior notice, but would allow exceptions in particularly sensitive cases—for example, if human life were in danger. That seems like a sensible compromise. But in reality there is no real reason for prior reporting as long as there is full reporting after the event. Congress can play no role in determining whether the President should or should not order a particular covert action. That is the President's responsibility. Congress can make its views known through the budget process and through oversight so that the President will not go far beyond what Congress, representing the American people, desires him to do. Prior notice increases the possibility of leaks and particularly in very sensitive operations we need to minimize leaks as much as possible.

A few years ago, many in Congress felt that covert actions should not be carried out at all, and many more felt that they should be carried out only in the most extreme circumstances. Our experience in Iran and then in Afghanistan has changed quite a few minds on this subject. The present mood of Congress is to allow, and even to encourage, covert actions by the CIA to suport American foreign policy. Covert action cannot be a substitute for foreign policy, it can only be an aid. It has been described as the middle ground between doing nothing and sending in the Marines.

John Ashbrook, statement issued in April 1980.

In many situations in the world, American needs can be met and American policy supported only by carefully considered covert action. Covert action programs could be developed in some countries in support of youth organizations or trade unions. There are parts of the world where the only youth organizations or the only trade unions are those controlled by the local communists, supported with funds by the Soviet Union. The opportunity for the United States to help provide an alternative, through covert action, may mean the difference in the future between a country dominated by the communist, an enemy of the United States, or a country part of the free world, friendly to the United States.

Other covert actions could help convince threatened countries that they should defend themselves against Soviet aggression rather than acquiesce. Covert actions could be undertaken in support of peace initiatives in volatile areas of the world. Others could be developed to prevent activities by international terrorist groups.

Soviet Operations

There is a real world out there, and Americans living in an ivory tower will not be able to cope with it. The House Intelligence Committee recently received an unclassified report from the Central Intelligence Agency on Soviet covert operations. This report revealed that the Soviet Union is spending over three billion dollars a year for covert actions and propaganda. This includes two hundred million dollars to terrorist groups, so-called national liberation movements, and over fifty million dollars in subsidies to foreign communist parties.

Intelligence Committee has never asked for the names of sources. It has asked for and has always received all of the information it needs to evaluate the activities of the Central Intelligence Agency.

Congress should look into the possibility of requiring reporting on covert action to the two Intelligence Committees, even when the action is not carried out by the CIA, but by other entities of the executive branch. This is not to suggest that normal diplomatic activities must be reported, but that those activities, carried out in a manner in which the hand of the United States Government is not obvious, should be reported regardless of the agency that carries it out.

Covert action is a useful weapon for the United States Government in carrying out its responsibilities. But for over a decade the CIA's covert action capability has atrophied. There are many reasons for this.

But in the long run, the needs of the American people are best served by having a competent and effective covert action capability. We must make sure that this capability is rebuilt in the CIA, that the funds and assets are available when the needs of the American people require that they be used.

John Ashbrook, Republican Representative from Ohio, issued this statement about Congressional supervision of intelligence operations in April 1980.

"Prior notice increases the possibility of leaks."

There was a view for a period of time in Congress that the United States should not play a part in the world. That view has been overtaken by events. There is a widespread belief among the American people, and this is reflected in Congress, that the United States has a responsibility to protect its own interests and those of its allies in the complex and hostile environment that the world has become. In order to do this, a combination of open diplomacy and covert action is necessary.

The best guarantee against executive branch abuses is Congressional oversight. With a two-party system, and extensive access to executive branch information, the American people can be assured that neither the CIA nor any other portion of the executive branch will abuse its powers. We recognize, however, that the CIA must protect its confidential sources, both individuals and foreign liaison services. The House

"A conscientious citizen committed to democracy and living in a democratic society need not always commit himself or herself to non-violent methods."

45

Terrorism Is Sometimes Justified

Kai Nielsen

Mass-media talk of the role of terrorism and violence generally tends to be emotional with a high level of ideological distortion. I shall try to clear the air and establish that we cannot, unless we can make the case for pacifism, categorically rule out in all circumstances its justifiable use even in what are formally and procedurally speaking democracies. . . .

When and where [terrorism] should be employed is a tactical question that must be decided—though not without some general guidelines—on a case-by-case basis. It should be viewed like the choice of weapons in a war. It cannot reasonably be ruled out as something to which only morally insane beasts or fanatical madmen would resort. In the cruel and oppressive world in which we find ourselves, it, like other forms of violence, can be morally justifiable, though typically, but not always, its use is a sign of weakness and desperation in a revolutionary movement and thus, in most contexts, but not all, is to be rejected, at least on prudential grounds.

A humane person who understands what it is to take the moral point of view will deplore violence, but—unless that person thinks that pacifism can be successfully defended—he or she will recognize that sometimes the use of violence is a *necessary* means to a morally worthwhile end and that moral persons, while hating violence in itself, must, under these circumstances, steel themselves to its employment. Such moral persons will, of course, differ as to when those occasions will occur and will differ over what constitutes a morally worthwhile end. . . .

Justifiable Violence?

"Acts of Violence" are acts that are usually taken by the people who *so label them* as both illegal and morally unjustified; but it does not follow that under

all circumstances "acts of violence" are unjustified. Surely they are *prima facie* unjustified, for to inflict harm or injury to persons or their property always needs a careful, rational justification.

There are two diverse types of circumstances in which questions concerning the justification of violence need discussing. We need to discuss (1) revolutionary violence—the violence necessary to overthrow the state and to bring into being a new and better or at least putatively better social order—and (2) violence within a state when revolution is not an end but violence is only used as a key instrument of social change within a social system that as a whole is accepted as legitimate. It is often argued that, in the latter type of circumstance, a resort to violence is *never* justified when the state in question is a democracy.

Let us first try to ascertain whether this is so. Consider, first, the situation in which a democratic state is engaging in institutionalized violence. Suppose, for example, that there is heightened trouble in the black community. It takes the form of increased rioting in the black ghettos. And suppose further that it is not adequately contained within the ghettos but that sporadic rioting, not involving killing but some destruction of property, breaks out into white middle-class America. Suppose further that there are renewed ever more vigorous cries for "law and order" until finally a jittery, reactionary, but still (in the conventional sense) "democratically elected," government begins systematically to invade the black ghettos and haul off blacks in large numbers to concentration camps (more mildly "detention centers") for long periods of incarceration ("preventive detention") without attempting to distinguish the guilty from the innocent. Would not black people plainly be justified in resorting to violence to resist being so detained in such circumstances if (1) they had good reason to believe that their violent resistance might be effective and (2) they had good reason to believe that their counter-violence would not cause more injury and suffering all round than would simple submission or nonviolent resistance to the violence directed against them by the state?

Even in such vile circumstances, it could be claimed that the blacks should nonviolently resist and fight back only through the courts, through demonstrations, through civil disobedience, and the like. This is perhaps fair enough, but, if the counterviolence continues and the camps begin to fill up without the nonviolent efforts producing any effective countervailing forces, then the employment of violence against these repressive forces is morally justified.

Utilitarian Considerations

In such circumstances there would be nothing unfair or unjust about violently resisting such detention. Violence, and not just force, has been instituted against the blacks—the state having exceeded its legitimate authority—and the blacks are not behaving unfairly or immorally in resisting an abuse of governmental authority—democracy or no democracy. In deliberation about whether or not to counter the institutional violence directed against them, the blacks and their allies should make tough and careful utilitarian calculations, for these considerations are the most evidently relevant considerations here. To utilize such calculations, they must try to ascertain as accurately as they can, both their chances of effectively resisting and the comparative amounts of suffering involved for them and for others from resistance as distinct from submission or passive resistance. If in resisting police seizure some police are likely to be injured or killed, and if this means massive retaliation, with the police gunning down large groups of blacks, and if the concentration camps are not modeled on Auschwitz but on American wartime camps for Japanese-Americans, it would seem to be better to submit and to live to fight another day. But, if instead the likelihood was that even in submitting to extensive brutalization and indeed death for many, if not at all, would be their lot, then violent resistance against such a "final solution" is in order, if that is the most effective way to lessen the chance of seizure. A clear understanding of what in each situation are the empirical facts is of central importance here. But what is evident—to put it minimally—is that there is no principled reason in such circumstances as to why even in a democracy counterviolence in response to institutionalized violence cannot be justified.

Suppose that a democratic superpower is waging a genocidal war of imperialist aggression against a small underdeveloped nation. Suppose that this superpower has invaded it without declaring war, suppose further that it pursues a scorched earth policy, destroying the land with repeated herbicidal doses, destroys the livestock, pollutes the rivers (killing the fish), and then napalms the people of this country, civilian and military alike. Suppose that repeated protests and civil disobedience have no effect on the policies of this superpower, which goes right on with its genocide and imperialist aggression. Suppose, further, that some conscientious and aroused—but still nonrevolutionary—citizens turn to acts of violence aimed in some small measure at disrupting and thus weakening this institutionalized violence. It does not at all seem evident to me (to put it conservatively) that they have done what in such circumstances they ought not to do, provided that the effects of their actions hold some reasonable promise of hampering the war effort. (Even if they were mainly symbolic and in reality did little to slow down the violent juggernaut, I would still find them admirable, provided that such actions did not in effect enhance the power of the juggernaut.)

> "If the use of revolutionary violence . . . were to lessen . . . suffering, degradation, and injustice more than would any other practically viable alternative, then it is justified."

If, on the one hand, only more suffering all round would result from such violence, then resort to violence is wrong; if, on the other hand, such acts of violence would likely lessen the sum total of human suffering and not put an unfair burden on some already cruelly exploited people, then such violence is justified. . . .

Democracy and Violence

Let me now turn to a less extreme situation. Suppose that the members of a small, impoverished, ill-educated ethnic minority in some democratic society are treated as second-class citizens. They are grossly discriminated against in educational opportunities and jobs, segregated in specific and undesirable parts of the country, and not allowed to marry people from other ethnic groups or to mix socially with them. For years they have pleaded and argued their case but to no avail. Moreover, working through the courts has always been a dead end, and their desperate and despairing turn to nonviolent civil disobedience has been tolerated—as the powerful and arrogant can tolerate it—but utterly ignored. Their demonstrations have not been met with violence but, rather, have simply been nonviolently contained and then effectively ignored. And finally suppose that this small, weak, desperately impoverished minority has no effective way of emigrating. In such a circumstance, is it at all evident that they should not act violently in an attempt to attain what are in effect their human rights?

There is no principled reason as to why they should refrain from certain acts of violence. The strongest reasons for their not so acting are the prudential ones that, because they are so weak and their oppressors are so indifferent to their welfare and dignity, their chances of gaining anything by violent action is rather minimal. But again the considerations here are pragmatic and utilitarian. If there were good reason to think that human welfare—a justly distributed human happiness, the satisfaction of needs, and avoidance of suffering—would be enhanced by their acts of violence, then they would be justified in so acting.

We may conclude that, although violence ought *prima facie* to be avoided, a conscientious citizen committed to democracy and living in a democratic society need not always commit himself or herself to nonviolent methods....

Revolution and Violence

I turn now to the justification of the use of violence to attain a revolutionary transformation of society. As Herbert Marcuse put it in "Ethics and Revolution," "Is the revolutionary use of violence justifiable as a means for establishing or promoting human freedom and happiness?" The answer I shall give is that, under certain circumstances, it is.

To discuss this question coherently, we need first to make tolerably clear what we are talking about when we speak of "revolution." Revolution is "the overthrow of a legally established government and constitution by a social class or movement with the aim of altering the social as well as the political structure." Moreover, we are talking of a "left revolution" and not of a "right revolution," in which the revolutionary aim is to enhance the sum total of human freedom and happiness....

Reasonable and humane persons will generally oppose violence, but in some circumstances they may agree that violence is justified. However, to be justifiable the violence must be publicly defensible.

Violence admits of degrees and of kinds. It is, for example, extremely important to distinguish between violence against property and violence against persons. The sacking of a ROTC office is one thing; the shooting of the ROTC officers is another. But it is surely evident that violence of any considerable magnitude—particularly when it is against person—is not justified as a purely symbolic protest against injustice. (This is even more evident when the persons in question are innocent persons.) There must be some grounds for believing that this protest will have an appropriate beneficial effort. It is—concentration camp-type circumstances apart—both immoral and irrational to engage in violence when all

is in vain, for this merely compounds the dreadful burden of suffering....

If we turn, with such considerations in mind, to the great revolutions of the modern period, keeping in mind that it would have been impossible for modern conditions to have come into existence without them, it is evident that "in spite of the terrible sacrifices exacted by them," they greatly enlarged the range of human freedom and happiness....

Terrorism as Tactic

In this context we should view terrorism as a tactical weapon in achieving a socialist revolution. "Terrorism" and "terrorist," we should not forget, are highly emotive terms. Burke referred to terrorists as hell-hounds, and the word "terrorist" is often simply a term of abuse. A terrorist is one who attempts to further his or her political ends by means of coercive intimidations, and terrorism is a systematic policy designed to achieve that end. I shall view terrorism here in the context of socialist revolutionary activity....

> *"There must be some grounds for believing that this protest will have an appropriate beneficial effect."*

Terrorist acts of assassination—as distinct from the massive acts of terroristic repression utilized by brutalitarian governments—rarely make any serious difference to the achievement of a revolutionary class consciousness and the achievement of a socialist society. Rather—as happened after the terrorist assassination of Tsar Alexander II in 1881—fierce reactions usually set in.

Justified Terrorism

Like all acts of violence in a political context, terrorist acts must be jusitifed by their political effects and their moral consequences. They are justifed (1) when they are politically effective weapons in the revolutionary struggle and (2) when, everything considered, there are sound reasons for believing that, by the use of that type of violence rather than no violence at all or violence of some other type, there will be less injustice, suffering, and degradation in the world than would otherwise have been the case.

We must, however, be careful to keep distinct, on the one hand, individual or small-group acts of terror to provoke revolutionary action or to fight back against a vicious oppressor—the paradigm terrorist actions—and, on the other, terrorism as a military tactic in an ongoing war of liberation. For any army, vastly inferior in military hardware but with widespread popular support, terrorism in conjunction with more conventional military tactics might very well be an effective tactic to drive out an oppressor. It is in this context that we should view such acts in South Vietnam and in Algeria. Where we have—as in Rhodesia—a less extensive struggle, it may still very well be justified. But the terrorist tactics of the F.L.Q., the Weathermen, or (probably) the Irish Provisionals are something else again. They seem in the grossest pragmatic terms to have been counterproductive. We have the horror and the evil of the killings without the liberating revolutionary effect—an effect that would be morally speaking justified, in which all human interests are considered and other viable alternatives are considered, if the likelihood would be of preventing on balance far more human suffering and opposition in the future. (In these last cases it is very unlikely.)...

"Like all acts of violence in a political context, terrorist acts must be justified by their political effects and their moral consequences."

There is a sense of moral satisfaction—of justice having been done—when some thoroughly tyrannical brute has been gunned down by revolutionary terrorists or money for the poor has been extracted from the ruling class through political kidnappings; but, again, as Rosa Luxemburg cooly recognized, this sense of moral satisfaction tends to lull people into inaction. People are likely to be deceived into believing that something effective is being done and are thus less likely to come to see the absolute necessity of making a socialist revolution for attaining a mass proletarian base of class-conscious, committed workers....

In an ongoing revolutionary struggle in which workers are already struggling against an overt and brutal oppressor who will not make significant concessions or give them any significant parliamentary rights, terrorism can be a useful and morally justified tactic. We can see this exemplified—as I have already noted—in Algeria and South Vietnam. But, once significant democratic concessions have been wrung from the ruling class, it is not only a useful tactic, it is positively harmful to the cause of a socialist revolution, though it should also be recognized, as my hypothetical examples evidenced, that, where these democratic concessions are being seriously overridden, situations can arise in which a violent response on the part of the exploited and oppressed is justified.

I recognize that arguments of the type I have been giving will with many people cut against the grain. They will feel that somehow such calculative considerations conceptualize the whole problem in a radically mistaken way. They will say that we simply cannot—from a moral point of view—make such calculations when the lives of human beings are at stake.

Choice of Evils

My short answer is that we can and must. Not wishing to play God, we must sometimes choose between evils. In such circumstances, a rational, responsible, and humane person must choose the lesser evil. Sane people capable of making considered judgments in reflective equilibrium will realize that judgments about the appropriateness of the use of revolutionary violence are *universalizable* (generalizable) and that, without being moral fanatics, they will be prepared to reverse roles, though of course, a member (particularly an active member) of the ruling class, placed as he or she is in society and with the interests that he or she has, is in certain important respects one kind of person and a proletarian is another....

The thing to keep vividly and firmly before one's mind is this: that, if anything is evil, suffering, degradation, and injustice are evil and that proletarians and the poor generally are very deeply afflicted with these evils. Some of them at least are avoidable; indeed some that we already know how to avoid flow from the imperialistic and repressive capitalist system and from its country cousin, state capitalism. If the use of revolutionary violence in the service of socialism were to lessen this suffering, degradation, and injustice more than would any other practically viable alternative, then it is justified, and if not, not.

In the past, revolutionary violence has been so justified, and in the future it may very well be justified again, even in what are formally democracies. Terrorism, by contrast, has a much more uncertain justifiable use. There are extreme cases—as with a charismatic leader such as Hitler—in which a terrorist assassination is very likely not only a good political tactic but, from a socialist and humanitarian point of view, morally desirable as well. More significantly and more interestingly, terrorist tactics may very well be justified in the liberation struggles in Chile, Angola, and Mozambique. Morally concerned rational human beings must go case by case. However, in the bourgeois democracies, in which concessions have been made and in which certain vital liberties exist, it is not a justifiable tactic but is rather a tactic that will harm the cause of revolutionary socialism.

Kai Nielsen is professor of philosophy at the University of Calgary. He is an editor of The Canadian Journal of Philosophy *and the author of many books and articles on philosophical subjects.*

"Even if the highest good is achieved and even if it truly is a higher good, that alone does not justify the terrorists' tactics."

viewpoint 46

Terrorism Is Never Justified

Nicholas Fotion

One might suppose, when first coming to think about acts of terrorism, that moralists could simply say that these acts are wrong. One might also be tempted to suppose that moralists who cannot show that such acts are wrong are not much good for anything. It is not as if in being expected to condemn terrorists they were being asked to make close moral calls, as when in baseball the runner and ball arrive at first base within a fraction of a second of one another. Condemning terrorism, it would seem to the ethical novitiate, is like calling a runner out who is only halfway to first base when the ball has already settled into the first baseman's glove.

It is disturbing, therefore, to read an account [by Kai Nielsen] of terrorism and violence that says, "Victimizing people is always at least *prima facie* wrong, indeed it is terribly wrong," that also urges a careful consideration of all moral options including terrorism but that, nonetheless, seems to open wider the door to terrorism and violence than these cautionary thoughts suggest it would. It is also disturbing when this account is both biased in the direction of a particular political ideology and implies that terrorism is acceptable if it is successful.

To be sure, I too will argue that victimizing people is always a *prima facie* wrong and that one ought to look at all the options as he or she should in theory in dealing with any moral issue—even terrorism. Nonetheless, I will go on to argue that the beginner in ethical theory is nearer the mark in condemning terrorism than are some sophisticated moralists who, in the end, permit more terrorism than they should. I will hedge a bit myself by permitting some forms of terrorism. It may be, for example, that certain forms are justified in dealing with an enemy in war who is himself engaged in terrorism. Further, there are

many forms and degrees of terrorism, and it would be foolish in a *carte blanche* fashion to condemn them all for all possible settings. Nonetheless, if there are exceptions so that some forms of terrorism are justifiable, there are nevertheless other forms, especially those in which the terrorist directs his acts against innocent people, that should always be condemned.

I will back my contention by focusing attention initially upon the recipients of the terrorist's activities rather than upon the actor himself. These recipients can be divided into those who are victims and those who are terrorized; and of these two, I will deal with the former first.

Victims Not Essential

Terrorists do not have to have victims to do their work. It is possible for them to terrorize a population, a class of people, or a government simply by displaying their power in a threatening way. One can, for example, imagine a situation in which terrorists threaten to use an atomic weapon that everyone knows they have in their possession. However, in a vast majority of the cases familiar to us, some individuals will be victimized so as to make it clear that the terrorists mean to be taken seriously.

The terrorist's victims may not be, although they are often, terrorized in (and/or following) the process of being victimized. Yet, they must be hurt in some way if they are to have the status of victims. The victims can be robbed, tortured, raped, starved, killed, or abused in any number of other ways. They may also carry some guilt. When they do, we begin to hedge a bit by saying, "Of course terrorism is wrong. However, in cases such as these we can see why terrorism might be acceptable." But these are not the kinds of cases that disturb us the most. They should still disturb us if for no other reason than that the terrorist's victims should have been treated as if they were innocent until proved guilty. Thus, in killing an allegedly guilty person, the terrorist is, in effect, administering the death penalty without offering the victim due process of law.

Although the unilateral actions of the terrorist are bad enough when the victims chosen deserve (in some sense) the treatment they have received, the terrorist's actions cannot help but be seen in a worse light when the victims are innocent. There are, of course, degrees of innocence and guilt; but terrorists who choose their victims in a random or nearly-random fashion cannot help but victimize many people who are innocent of political or other wrongdoing. Think of a child, an uneducated peasant, a housewife, a white-collar worker, and even a person who shares the political views of the terrorist (but is against the tactics of terrorism) who may be randomly killed, maimed, or assaulted. Each is literally treated as an object to be used—we might even say used up—to further the terrorist's ends.

Victim as Object

In fact, in being treated as an object, the innocent victim is worse off than the (alleged) guilty victim. Insofar as the latter is judged to have done a wrong, he is thought of as a human. After all, it is humans, not dogs and cats, who make political errors and commit moral wrongs. For the terrorist the innocent victim is neither a human in this judgmental sense nor a human in the sense of simply having value *as a* human being. Of course the terrorist needs to pick a human being as a victim. But he does this because choosing human victims brings about more terror than does choosing either dogs or cats for victims or inanimate objects for destruction. But this does not involve treating them *as* humans. Rather, they are victimized and thereby treated as objects *because* they are humans.

No doubt terrorists can reply to these accusations by saying that they regret all the death and suffering that they are causing; and, insofar as they do, they show at least some respect for their human victims. Further, we might contend that they do not consider the victims to be anything but objects. Rather, the terrorists find it necessary to sacrifice (valued) humans for some greater good.

But surely more than an expression of regret is required to establish that terrorists are treating their victims as humans and/or that they value them as humans. Minimally what would be required is a careful set of calculations showing us just how much value was placed on their victims and just how they made the calculations that resulted in their victims' losing out to the greater good. But even this is not enough. Without some behavioral consideration, some nonverbal gesture in the direction of showing that their victims actually received some consideration, it is tempting to say that the terrorists' regrets are insincere or simply represent so much

rhetoric. This is especially so if their victims are selected at random without regard to age, gender, biological and social status, past accomplishments, and failures and are chosen only with regard to their racial or ethnic status (i.e., because they are Jews, Chinese, etc.).

Heavy Moral Burden

So the moral burden of terrorists who direct their harmful acts against innocent people is a heavy one. It is heavier still when we realize that their calculations ought to take account not only of the innocent people that they are victimizing as a type, but in terms of their numbers as well. How many will they "regretfully" sacrifice? Philosophers talk about the fallacy of the slippery slope, that is, of assuming that, when a person begins drinking, for example, that person will inevitably become an alcoholic. But surely some slopes are more slippery than others, and terrorists are on one of the most slippery of all. Because terrorists have a higher calling that allows them to victimize an individual, the very logic of their argument dictates that they find more victims to initiate and sustain terror. That their own argument greases the slope and thereby tempts them not to set a limit on the number of people that they will turn into victims on behalf of their higher good is, in fact, another indication of the object status to which they relegate their victims.

"If mere bombings do not terrorize because... people have become inured to them,... why not add rape and torture to the agenda?"

But the moral burden is heavier still. Not only are terrorists greasing the slope with a logic that allows them to create quantitatively an almost unlimited number of victims, but they are greasing it for quality as well. If mere bombings do not terrorize because they simply maim and kill, or because people have become inured by them, terrorist logic dictates a slight tactical change. Why not add rape and torture to the agenda? Why not concentrate on victimizing children? Surely, the terrorists might say to themselves, these "variations" will bring about more terror. Very likely they will, but they must also increase the terrorists' moral burden.

Even if the terrorists admitted that they carry all these moral burdens, they have an effective counterargument available. They can say that in spite of its burdens, their tactics can and often do work. they succeed in terrorizing certain peoples and governments so that the "greater good" is brought about. Thus, insofar as terroristic tactics are successful, they are justified. It is as simple as that.

This argument is deceptively persuasive. However, when fully understood, although it may still persuade a few, I believe that most will not be moved by it. To show why, it is necesssary to focus next upon the second group of people who receive the attentions of the terrorist, namely, the terrorized.

The Terrorized

The first thing to note about those who are terrorized, obvious though it is, is that they are also harmed. To be terrorized is at least to suffer temporary emotional trauma and often permanent damage as well. More than that, terrorized persons may themselves harm others. In a terrorized condition, a person will often act violently while making demands on government officials, searching for food that others have, and seeking other things as well. In his irrational (terrorized) state, the terrorized person may even do things that will further harm himself.

The second thing to note, especially if the terrorism is aimed randomly at a general population, is that it will affect many innocent people. Again this may seem obvious; but, if the burdens of the terrorist are to be weighed, each harm that he does needs to be identified. So, to reach those people or officials who must in some sense capitulate to their demands, terrorists more than likely must harm two separate layers of innocent people (i.e., their victims and those terrorized)—actually three if one counts those harmed by the terrorized persons while they are in a terrorized condition. The terrorists destroy or very nearly destroy their victims and unhinge the terrorized. Along the way of getting what they consider to be the higher good, they are up to no good at all. Their means in fact are about as evil as their imaginations can conceive and their powers carry out. So *successfully* terrorizing people in and of itself counts heavily against an overall assessment of what the terrorists are up to. It is their "highest good" alone, when achieved, that sustains their argument, in theory at least, by counterbalancing the burdens of wrongdoing that they have committed against their victims and the terrorized.

Justification as "the Higher Good"

Looking, then, at the "higher good" portion of the terrorists' argument, notice that even if the highest good is achieved and even if it truly is a higher good, that alone does not justify the terrorists' tactics. To do that, they must show us that no other tactical option is available that has a reasonable chance of bringing it about. After all, because they chose morally the worst, or just about the worst, possible means, they owe us an explanation as to why just these means are chosen over all others. Why, for instance, did they not choose to terrorize the opponent's military establishment? Certainly, if the

campaign against it were pressed, the establishment might be significantly damaged. It is true that military people have an unpleasant habit of shooting back when attacked, and for that reason attacking them may be more dangerous than victimizing unarmed citizens. But this observation could hardly be turned into a morally convincing principle that, when revolutionary work becomes a bit hazardous, it is permissible to attack children, women, and other noncombatants. In fact, when one comes to think of it, the option of attacking the opponent's military establishment is always present. It is easy enough for the terrorist to say that there are not other options available but difficult to convince people that this is so. Indeed, people's feeling about this matter may be one key reason for its being so difficult to sympathize with terrorists. That is, the terrorist case is inconvincing, not just because the moral burden of attacking innocent people is so very heavy, but also because it is very difficult to show convincingly that there is no other way to get the revolutionary job done. Given different situations, different options will open up. Nonviolent resistance will work in some contexts; testing the laws to the limit will work in others. In still others, terrorizing the offending government officials directly may be an option that, for all its dangers, at least keeps innocent people from becoming victimized or terrorized. Still, the option of attacking the opponent's military establishment is always available; and because this is so, the terrorist tactics of attacking innocent people at random will seem intuitively to be morally wrong to most people.

"It will do the terrorists little good to argue that when they talk about 'having no other choice' they do not mean this literally."

It will do the terrorists little good to argue that when they talk about "having no other choice" they do not mean this literally but mean instead "having no other choice *as good as* killing innocent people." To clarify their meaning in this manner weakens their position considerably, for it is now obvious that the terrorists have a real choice. They cannot plead, after all, that the only choice that they have is to kill or be killed. Such an excuse would be sufficient in the case of one person who has killed another in self-defense, having no choice but to kill to save himself—even when the slain victim's threat was not malicious or deliberate. The terrorists' rhetorical claim that they have no choice but to kill their innocent victims is simply false. They are not *forced* to act as they do. Rather, it is their *decision* to adopt those tactics that both victimize and terrorize innocent people.

Public Evaluation

Further, now that it is obvious that their tactics are a matter of conscious and deliberate decision making, it makes sense to ask that public calculations be made to see if the terrorists have chosen well. To be sure, it is difficult to disprove their claim to have chosen well. But this is not so much because their position is so strong as because it is so difficult to imagine how *any* overall calculation can be made either of the position's strengths or of its weaknesses. Indeed, some calculations can be made; but they hardly help the terrorists to defend themselves against charges of gross immorality. It is the nature of the terrorists' tactics that some of their moral debts are calculable. We can count their victims and, in a crude fashion, measure some effects of their terror as these moral debts are so visible and are incurred by them in advance. In contrast, their credits tend to be promissory and/or often identified as credits by them in terms of their own ideological standards rather than in terms of the standards of a wide spectrum of people. The overall calculations (which could show that the moral costs of terrorism are less than the gains) are hard to produce. In addition, the terrorists must demonstrate that their form of behavior creates greater overall moral profit than does (1) terrorizing the opponent's military establishment and (2) any other option available. Such a demonstration would involve putting into a set of calculations not only the value of bringing about the higher good in the first place, but also such things as (1) the value of bringing it about a month (a year) sooner because terrorism was used rather than some other means, (2) the military and economic costs associated with terrorism as against the costs of using other means, and (3) the civilian costs associated with terrorism as against the costs of using other means. These and other difficult-to-come-by calculations leave terrorists in an awkward position, to say the least, as they need them to help justify their tactics.

The argument that put them in such a position can be summarized as follows: Given the high moral costs of their tactics, they can say that they have (literally) no choice if they are to act to bring about their "higher good." But what they say here is empirically false. The terrorists always do have another choice. They can choose, if no other option is available, to engage in a terroristic war against their opponent's military establishment. So they must admit that they are not literally forced to adopt the tactics that they do but, rather, that they choose to do so. But their choice, which victimizes and terrorizes innocent people and thereby carries a visibly heavy moral burden, becomes even more unattractive when we realize how difficult it is to prove that it is significantly better than other choices that could have

been made. Thus, even if successful in bringing about their cherished goals and even if they come to us with claims of victory and success, it would not be inappropriate for us to withhold our moral congratulations. Instead we might ask them in their moment of triumph, "What assurances can you give us that some less bloody way was not better?"

"Terrorists take upon themselves a high initial burden of moral wrongdoing."

Now there are many replies that terrorists can give to get out of these difficulties. I cannot, of course, deal with all of them, although I feel that all can be answered in such a way as to condemn all forms of terrorism of innocent people. I will, however, present three replies that they could give and deal briefly with each one.

Burden of Proof

First, they may argue that the argument against them places an undue burden of proof upon them. If they cannot prove that their tactics are the best of a bad lot, neither, they could argue, can the defenders of the other options prove that theirs are any better. However, in making this reply the terrorists forget that they carry a special burden of proof because they carry a special burden of wrongdoing. We do not ask people to justify their actions when they harm no one in the process of attempting to achieve a good or alleged good. If they fail, we say, "Too bad," and perhaps urge them to try again. But the more their efforts harm others, the more we expect an accounting that makes sense. Thus, even if the terrorists are successful, it is difficult to make sense of tactics that involve such initial high costs and are difficult to assess. A related additional argument that puts the terrorists' tactics in a still worse light is that, if they fail, we are left with a heavy moral deficit with little or nothing on the positive side to counterbalance it.

The terrorists' second response is a desperate one at best. They can deny that the calculations needed to assess the merits of their position are difficult to make by claiming that calculations can be made because their victims and those that they terrorize count for nothing. They are most likely to say this when those who are the objects of their attention belong to a hated ethnic (racial, national, etc.) group, so that it is at least possible for them to get support for their tactics among their own group. But surely it will be difficult for them to get support for their discriminatory policies beyond their group if for no other reason than that they are violating the universalizability principle:

As ethical judgements become more general, specific references to "me," "here" and "now," "them," "there" and "then" are eliminated and as long as any such references remain there is room for an appeal to a more general principle. The point at which the justification of a moral decision must cease is where the action under discussion has been unambiguously related to a current "moral principle," independent (in its wording) of person, place and time: e.g., where "I ought to take this book and give it back to Jones at once" has given way to "anyone ought always to do anything that he promises anyone else that he will do" or "It was a promise." If, in justifying an action, we can carry our reasons back to such universal principles, our justification has some claim to be called "ethical." But, if we cannot do so, our appeal is not to "morality" at all: if, for example, the most general principles to which we can appeal still contain some reference to us, either as individuals or as members of a limited group of people, then our appeal is not to "morality" but to "privilege." [Stephen Toulmin, *The Place of Reason in Ethics*]

Morally, then, it is a bankrupt policy to turn the hated ethnics into worthless objects. It amounts to appealing to privilege rather than to ethics.

Historical Insignificance

Somewhat less desperately the terrorists could claim that their victims and those that they terrorize count for something but that, in the sweep of history, the many good things produced by the revolution reduce its victims to insignificance. Aside from sounding both cavalier about other peoples' lives in saying this and also overly optimistic about the merits of the revolution, this reply is beside the point. The issue is, again, not just whether terrorist tactics have greater utility than doing nothing. Rather, it is whether they can be shown to be more beneficial than other options that have fewer initial moral costs.

"Terrorists, having placed themselves in precisely the same moral position [as the tyrants they seek to replace], have morally disqualified themselves from coming into positions of political authority."

The terrorists' third reply is not to deny the worth of those that they victimize and terrorize but to deny their innocence. Whole ethnic groups or classes of people can be said to share the guilt of some past deed or practice, they might argue. This being so, they claim that they bear virtually no moral burden for their actions.

In response, one may ask whether they are all *equally* guilty. Is the terrorist implying that the hated ethnic leader is no more guilty than a hated ethnic thirteen-year-old? Is the hated ethnic secret agent no more guilty than the hated ethnic athlete? Whatever guilt the athlete and the thirteen-year-old carry must certainly be so diluted as to pale into innocence. To claim that all of "them" are guilty equally, or even guilty enough so as to deserve becoming objects of the terrorists' attentions, is simply to be uttering half- (or quarter-) truths at best, or redefining "guilty" arbitrarily.

Conclusion

My arguments against terrorism are really quite simple. They attempt to make explicit the reasons why people are instinctively repelled, especially by those forms of terrorism in which innocent people are the targets. Three basic arguments were presented.

The first is that terrorists take upon themselves a high initial burden of moral wrongdoing. It is a two-layered burden in that they victimize some and terrorize others. This burden might possibly be overcome if there were no other way to achieve the greater good that the terrorists want so badly. However, and this is the key premise in the second argument, there is always another way. Because there is and because the other way carries with it a lesser moral burden, the terrorists' position is now doubly unattractive morally.

The third argument is that more than any other tactician, terrorists need to show us how they figure that their way is superior to all others. But this showing is difficult to come by. The terrorists are left in limbo—needing to justify themselves but being unable to do so.

Of course, even if they could produce calculations that made sense to others (besides their most ardent followers), the others might show that there was a better way than the terrorists'. Consider whether it really makes a difference if the terror is applied *before* or *after* the terrorists come to power. Keep in mind that officials who use terror are also terrorists, even though they are sometimes called oppressors or tyrants instead. Whatever we may call them, we rightly feel that they do not deserve to stay in power if they resort to terrorism aimed at innocent people. By using such tactics they have morally disqualified themselves to rule, although in fact they do rule. Terrorists, having placed themselves in precisely the same moral position, have morally disqualified themselves from coming into positions of political authority.

Nicholas Fotion is a professor of philosophy at Emory University and the author of Moral Situations. *He has written numerous articles on such topics as paternalism, medical ethics, consciousness, wickedness, and the philosophy of language.*

"We should declare, as foreign policy, that international law allows us to pursue international terrorism to its core."

The US Should Use Force to Combat Terrorism

Stuart S. Malawer

What is it about the Defense Department's Long Commission report that is most troubling? Is it the fact that everyone with any common sene knew that truck bombings had become a way of life and death in the Middle East long before the Marine bombing? Yet the report details how only now the U.S. military belatedly recognizes this deadly truth. Or is is that the report labels the state control of terrorism a new phenomenon, which we will are not capable of guarding against? Yet terrorists previously bombed the U.S. Embassy in Beirut and held American captives in the U.S. Embassy in Tehran.

Why has the most casual observer learned these truisms, but no U.S. policymakers, nor the U.S. military?

In his recent State of the Union message, the president declared unequivocally that "we must not be driven from our objectives of peace in Lebanon by state-sponsored terrorism." President Reagan promised to request legislation to help combat terrorism generally. What should be the legal and policy responses of the administration to this dreaded and deadly form of warfare?

Form of Warfare

The Long Commission report concludes that state-supported terrorism is a form of warfare prevalent throughout the world and has often replaced more traditional forms of warfare. Unfortunately, the U.S. military is not equipped to combat this. Thus U.S. foreign policy should not rely on military force, but on diplomacy. Astonishing!

I strongly believe that diplomacy is futile without the prerequisite force behind it. How can we have an active and forceful foreign policy when our military is not able and, indeed, has not even been told of the

Stuart S. Malawer, "Terrorism: What to Do?" *The Washington Times,* February 20, 1984. cc 1984. The Washington Times. Reprinted by permission.

necessity, to defend itself against bombs carried by trucks, along with those delivered by airplanes, presumably with their combat insignias glistening in the sunlight. Incredible!

The Long Commission report declares that "terrorism is 'warfare on the cheap' and entails few risks." Why is this? We can certainly use conventional and special forces to up the ante and to create dire risks. Bombing raids, preemptive strikes, and cross-border commando raids can help sever the link of state support. Why not counterbombings by Mack trucks (to give such operations a clear American imprint) in the capitals of Syria and Iran and aimed both at military targets and those directly linked to the terrorists?

If terrorism is an act of war, why not respond with overwhelming strength? The Israelis in the Middle East, the British in Northern Ireland, the French in Africa, and South Africans in southern Africa learned these lessons long ago. The United States is only beginning to grasp this idea in Central America, but, obviously, not yet in the Middle East. There is a general need to improve the American military vastly to ensure the better projection of American power and protection of American interests abroad.

International Law

What should the U.S. response be? As a matter of international law, we should declare, as foreign policy, that international law allows us to pursue international terrorism to its core, that is, to the government of the state which sponors and cooperates with it. International terrorism is an act of war violating the rules of the game as provided in Article 2(4) of the U.N. Charter, which prohibits the illegal use of force against states. The mere making of this declaration ought to act as a deterrence to terrorism.

Force should be employed to uphold the core principle of the Charter, the prohibition against the use of force to intervene directly or indirectly in the territorial integrity of states. Such force should be used to uphold principles of the Charter even though a state is not subject to an armed attack under Article 51, which also allows for the use of force in those situations. When the principle of non-intervention is breached, it ought to be our view that the principle gives rise to a legal and legitimate military response, which includes conventional and counterterrorist military action.

Effective military force is an essential instrument of foreign policy and diplomacy. Although military force has very real limitations, especially when not utilized competently—witness Vietnam and Lebanon—it provides defense, deterrence and protection of American interests when used properly. Neither international law nor constitutional law ought to be formulated, interpreted or applied in the 1980s in a manner to preclude the enforcement of the rule of law in international affairs. The fathers of our Republic did not intend to circumscribe the president's ability to use proper and legitimate force in order to uphold the cardinal rules of customary international law and the vital national interests of the United States.

Discredited American Policy

Much of American foreign policy has been discredited, since the international law rules upon which it has been based have been subverted by Third World and communist states. Those states simply do not observe such rules and practices. Thus, American foreign policy based on pious hopes is futile, because we are making policy based upon rules which are not reciprocally observed.

"American foreign policy based on pious hopes is futile, because we are making policy based upon rules which are not reciprocally observed."

We ought to enunciate our views on the rules of international law and the U.N. Charter so as not to obscure our real reasons for using military force, when we perceive such use as legal and legitimate in the context of the world in which we live. A lack of such legal candor only further obfuscates our political and military policies abroad. Greater clarity would certainly aid American foreign policy by contributing to building a domestic and alliance consensus which is so critical to effective diplomacy. Such a consensus might have prevented the fiasco of the failed American policy in Lebanon.

We should not be shackled to an expansive interpretation of international law when unprincipled adversaries run roughshod over it. Idealistic legal and political theories of domestic and international societies must reflect more accurately the brutal facts of international life.

Dangerous Period

The Reagan Republican foreign policy recognizes this truth. The Democratic philosophy of foreign affairs and diplomacy, as epitomized by the Carter-Vance years, denounces this reality and continues to proclaim its folly.

Ambassador Jeane Kirkpatrick's dire warning in *The Reagan Phenomenon* (1983) has great currency for the decade of the 1980s. As she has stated so perceptively, "The new period we have now entered is, I believe, an exceedingly dangerous one—perhaps the most dangerous we have faced—and its outcome is far from clear. It is...conceivable that an affluent and technologically advanced democratic civilization may succumb to one that is distinctly inferior in the wealth and well-being of its people."

Stuart S. Malawer is a professor of law and teaches foreign policy and international trade at the George Mason University Law School.

viewpoint **48**

The US Should Use Legal Means to Combat Terrorism

Daniel Patrick Moynihan

I offer as my thesis today the threefold proposition that much of the current disorientation in American foreign policy derives from our having abandoned, for all practical purposes, the concept that international relations can and should be governed by a regime of public international law. Further, that this ideal has not yet been succeeded by any other reasonably comprehensive and coherent notion as to the kind of world we *do* seek. And finally, that among the consequences of the disappearance of law as a guiding principle in American foreign policy has been the steady elevation of the role of terrorism, to the point where it is now a common instrument of the foreign policies of a number of nondemocratic governments.

At a recent gathering at the Center for National Policy in Washington, one speaker cited international law as a standard by which to judge the desirability of a policy. Zbigniew Brzezinski replied that among the shortcomings of international law as a useful framework for thinking about foreign policy is the fact that it does not provide us with an answer to international lawlessness, such as terrorism. What Dr. Brzezinski seemed to be saying was that, in a world where terrorism is a growing problem, international law is increasingly irrelevant.

Irrelevant International Law?

What I would ask you to consider is whether the reverse might, in fact, be true: whether, in a world where international law is increasingly thought to be irrelevant—or at least is so treated by those who conduct U.S. foreign policy—terrorism will flourish.

Could it be that the inattentiveness of the West, and of the United States in particular, to considerations of law has contributed to an international political climate that allows other states to believe that we will not hold them accountable to standards of civilized and peaceable behavior, such as might be embodied in a tradition of international law? Consider the consequences of this for the United States.

The idea that a world ruled by law would be an ideal one—certainly a peaceful one—is almost as old as the idea of law itself. But it was only in the last part of the nineteenth century that it came to be seen as a practical vision and a reasonable choice that governments might make in determining their behavior. It was part of the prevailing optimism of the time.

There was terrorism then, to be sure. In many ways the series of assassinations of public figures and bombings of citizens in cafes that spread through Europe and North America in the years before World War I—the first modern wave of terrorism—was more alarming than anything we face today. But governments of that time had no reason to consider the problem to be anything other than a matter of law enforcement: find the murderers and prosecute them. (I promptly grant that the question is much complicated by state-sponsored terrorism. The government of North Korea recently undertook to blow up the government of South Korea. The international community has developed almost no effective means of coping with such acts. Yet this does not mean we cannot; still less that we should not.)

Early Optimism

The optimism that prevailed early in this century was part of that era's broad confidence in the continuing expansion of freedom through democracy and law, a confidence epitomized by Woodrow Wilson. No man, before or since, so engaged the passions and the hopes of all mankind as Wilson did in the months after the end of World War I. Wilson's

Daniel Patrick Moynihan, address before a terrorism conference in New York City on December 13, 1983.

ideals of normative world order were embodied in the League of Nations. And though the United States did not join it, we did not abandon the proposition that law ought to be central to the conduct of states.

It fell to Franklin D. Roosevelt to achieve Wilson's objective, by establishing the United Nations. The U.N. represented a more experienced and perhaps more practical Wilsonianism, its ideals somehow vindicated by the devastation of World War II, which was seen as the consequence of the unwillingness of the democracies to insist upon and defend those ideals.

How very long ago that all seems. We no longer believe that democracy is the way of the future; nor do we believe that international law provides a guide to policy making.

Aimless US Policy

Yet though we no longer believe in what we once did, we have not replaced it with anything. It is the resulting aimlessness and normlessness in U.S. foreign policy that seems to me to be a source of so many of our immediate problems.

For example, in response to the Soviet invasion of Afghanistan, President Carter spoke of his personal disillusionment with Leonid Brezhnev. In fairness, Mr. Carter did try to do something; he proposed a grain embargo. But his reaction was based on his shock at having been lied to by a man he had embraced when last they had met. That the Soviets had violated international law was not the ground on which we acted. Our response was, at an important level, a normless one.

President Reagan seems to have followed a similar pattern last September when the Soviets shot down Korean Air Lines flight 007. Ronald Reagan said this was "a terrorist act" about which the Soviet government had "flagrantly" lied. His language grew harsher still—yet the President *did* nothing. William Safire noted at the time that Reagan had "sounded off more fiercely than Theodore Roosevelt and has acted more pusillanimously than Jimmy Carter." Why? Because the President did not know how to respond. Indeed, on September 9 the President replied to critics such as Safire by asking plaintively, "Short of going to war, what would they have us do?"

Reagan's question points to the disappearance of the idea of law as an alternative; that in between doing nothing and going to war there are no intermediate sanctions. So, we did nothing.

"Right to Covert Activity"

Not long afterward, as if to confirm that considerations of *realpolitik* are as paramount in Washington as in Moscow, the President turned his attention to Central America. Commenting on the activities of the Central Intelligence Agency there, he said: "I do believe in the right of a country, when it believes that its interests are best served, to practice covert activity . . ."

Now this is a wholly normless statement. It could as easily be said that the Soviet Union has a right to shoot down civilian airliners if "it believes that its interests are best served." The President said precisely what the Soviets believe.

I don't think the President recognizes the trap we have fallen into. A country has the right to do what it has the right to do—not what it thinks serves its interests. That is the difference between the Hobbesian state of the war of all against all and a state of law.

"If we permit ourselves to view terrorism simply as being politically undersirable in certain contexts, and overlook it in certain other contexts, then we have told the world that we do not find it fundamentally unacceptable."

We are committing ourselves to the world described in those wonderful lines from Wordsworth, in "Rob Roy's Grave":

The good old rule
The Simple plan
That they should take who have the power
And they should keep who can.

Having no sense of norms, or of law, we do not object to lawlessness as such. So we find ourselves disoriented, apparently unable or unwilling to confront the lawlessness of terrorism *as lawlessness*. If we permit ourselves to view terrorism simply as being politically undesirable in certain contexts, and overlook it in certain other contexts, then we have told the world that we do not find it fundamentally unacceptable.

The costs to Americans shall in the end be measured not in the size of explosions, such as that detonated in the Capitol building on November 7. Had the timing been different, two dozen senators could have been killed; but senators can be replaced. No, the costs are to be measured in the concrete barricades that have been constructed around government buildings throughout Washington, and in the diminished access Americans will thereafter have to their own government. A government, I suggest, that has not paid adequate attention to the role of law in world affairs.

Daniel Patrick Moynihan is a senator from New York. This viewpoint is from his keynote address at a conference on terrorism sponsored by the State University of New York's Institute for Studies in International Terrorism, in cooperation with the American Jewish Congress.

"The European allies of the US are regarded as hostages."

European Missiles Hold Europe Hostage

New Times

Europe stands before a kind of Rubicon. Will it or will it not be possible to spare it the presence of new American missiles? The future of the continent depends in large measure on how this question is decided. Either the process begun in Helsinki and continued in Madrid will develop, maintaining equilibrium and peace on European soil, or the situation will sharply deteriorate and the storm clouds that have gathered over Europe will spread to other continents, increasing the danger of nuclear war.

The meeting of the Warsaw Treaty Foreign Ministers' Committee in Sofia, therefore, particularly stressed the need for further efforts to prevent the deployment of new American missiles in Europe and gradually free it from both medium-range and tactical nuclear weapons. This is no easy task. Washington is clearly bent on forcing its way into Europe with its new missiles at all costs. It is deliberately dragging its feet at the talks in Geneva and is secretly, without waiting for December, shipping parts of the missile systems across the ocean. The socialist countries are well aware of all these subterfuges, but they are displaying restraint and patience. Statesmen, in our opinion, should not build policies on emotions and act contrary to common sense, as it is done in the White House.

The participants in the Sofia meeting expressed the conviction that the possibility for reaching agreement at the Geneva talks that would meet the interests of the peoples still exists. They pointed out that if agreement is not reached at the talks by the end of the year, the talks should be continued, given the renunciation by the United States and its NATO allies of their schedule for deploying new medium-range nuclear missiles. In these conditions, the Soviet

Union is ready to continue maintaining its unilateral freeze on the medium-range missile systems deployed in the European part of its territory and to proceed with the unilateral reduction of such systems which was started simultaneously with the introduction of the freeze.

Christmas Gifts

But apart from the Geneva talks, the leaders of the countries for which the United States is preparing "Christmas gifts" should surely have something to say. After all, it is not a question of Christmas tree crackers. It is no secret that the Pershing and cruise missiles are offensive weapons. In other words, the doctrines of "containment" and "flexible response" with which the United States has long been lulling people's vigilance in the West has actually turned out to be a "first-strike" doctrine. It is not for nothing that the U.S. Administration avoids replying to the Warsaw Treaty countries' appeal to follow the example of the Soviet Union which has assumed the commitment not to be the first to use nuclear weapons.

The U.S. Administration's plans were spelled out in President Yuri Andropov's recent statement: "The operation of stationing these American nuclear missiles in Europe is seen from the Washington control tower as perfectly simple and maximally advantageous for the United States—advantageous at the expense of Europe. The European allies of the U.S. are regarded as hostages. This is a frank, but cynical policy. But what is really unclear is this: do those European political leaders who—disregarding the interests of their peoples, the interests of peace—are helping to implement the ambitious militaristic plans of the U.S. Administration give thought to this?"

The participants in the Sofia meeting again drew attention to the fact that the states which would allow the stationing of new medium-range nuclear

New Times, "The Possibility Is Still There," October 1983. Reprinted by permission.

missiles in their territories would assume a grave responsibility before all the peoples for the consequences this would entail for peace in Europe.

A Washington Trap

Their guilt would be all the greater because many political parties, primarily the Communist, as well as public organizations and the working masses in Western Europe itself have been warning the ruling circles against reckless moves. British Labourites and most of the Land organizations of the Social Democratic Party in the Federal Republic of Germany have come out against the deployment of American missiles on their soil. Hundreds of thousands are taking part in anti-war demonstrations, because they do not want to be caught in the trap Washington is setting. And the mighty protest wave is growing.

"Storm clouds that have gathered over Europe will spread to other continents."

European public sentiment shows that the socialist countries' peace proposals fully accord with the aspirations of the continent's peoples. No one should entertain any doubts about the ability of the socialist countries to ensure their security in any conditions. But we do not distinguish the well-being of our peoples and their security from the well-being and security of socialist foreign policy, the secret of its influence in the world.

This viewpoint appeared as an editorial in New Times, *a Soviet weekly magazine of world affairs.*

European Missiles Hold the US Hostage

Gary L. Guertner

The nation's first general and President warned his countrymen against entangling alliances that might tie their security to the "vicissitudes" of European politics. The Reagan administration's decision to deploy intermediate-range nuclear missiles in Europe ties the United States into a complex web of deterrence and war-fighting strategies that neither George Washington nor the contemporary American public could have imagined or desired. These weapons substantially increase the risk that nuclear war in Europe will escalate in intensity and trigger Soviet attacks on the continental US.

The modern SS-20 missile represents a qualitative change in the Soviet threat to Europe, but by no means is it a new threat. That threat is as old as the Soviets' earliest nuclear deployments in the 1950s.

Political Crisis

Why then the political crisis, the arms control deadlock, and the US administration's insistence on proceeding with its own theater force modernization?

The threat to Europe is not Soviet intermediate-range missiles, but the credibility of the US nuclear deterrent in an age of nuclear parity. Europeans, most notably West Germans, fear that the Soviet Union no longer believes the US will retaliate in the event of a nuclear attack on Germany. The Soviet threat of escalation against the US weakens the American nuclear umbrella over West Germany. US missiles based in Germany that can reach the Soviet Union will, it is argued by German officials, reinforce deterrence by guaranteeing that nuclear war will not be isolated to Europe's central front. Through "strategic coupling," the US nuclear umbrella will create a hostage relationship that links US and German security by making both countries prompt

Gary L. Guertner, "The US as Europe's Nuclear Hostage," *The Christian Science Monitor*, August 12, 1983. Reprinted by permission of the author.

nuclear targets.

The Russians have tumbled beautifully to the German strategy. In a speech before an East German military audience, Soviet Minister of Defense Dmitri Ustinov threatened, "If Washington thinks that we will reply to the use of Pershing and cruise missiles by hitting targets in Western Europe alone, it is deeply mistaken. Retribution will follow inevitably, and against the US itself."

Strengthening Deterrence

The strategy of coupling US and German security through intermediate-range missiles in the Federal Republic serves the greater German interest of strengthening deterrence, but does it serve US interests if deterrence fails?

It has been the US objective since the early 1960s to raise the nuclear threshold through a strategy of flexible response. Flexible response places emphasis on the initial conventional defense of Europe. It has never been popular with West German strategists because defending with conventional weapons increases the likelihood of trading space for time and reinforcements. The use of nuclear weapons is foreseen only if defeat is threatened. By that time the battle will have penetrated deep into the heavily populated West German heartland where collateral damage from nuclear weapons would be highest and credible threats to employ them lowest.

West Germans prefer to think in terms of "forward defense," early use of nuclear weapons, and striking Warsaw Pact forces in their own territory. In short, West Germans understandably emphasize deterrence over warfighting and see deterrence maintained over the long run only if there is a shared US-European community of risk.

American interests are by no means the same. With political unrest in Eastern Europe combined with an American administration that seriously questions the legitimacy of Soviet security interests there, the risk of unintended war cannot be ignored. If deterrence fails, US interests and objectives are served by the lowest possible level of violence in the narrowest possible theater of operation. With additional nuclear weapons deployed in Europe that are capable of reaching Soviet territory, Moscow will be more inclined to strike out at the nearest nuclear threats. If European-based American nuclear weapons respond, the Soviet threat to expand the theater of conflict to the continental US is real.

Soviet Perspective

It is also important to understand that from the Soviet military perspective the deployment of intermediate-range missiles in Europe is a significantly new strategic threat. These weapons will not be isolated to a theater of war outside Soviet territory. The extremely short flight time and accuracy of the Pershing II threatens Soviet nuclear command and control structures. A preemptive threat against these systems is one of the few conceivable paths to "victory" in nuclear war. The Soviets are therefore not likely to concede on any agreement that balances Soviet theater forces against American weapons with prompt strategic reach—especially if they are not counted by SALT II or START.

"Through strategic coupling, the US nuclear umbrella will create a hostage relationship."

Few Americans would be willing to play the role of nuclear hostage to European security if they understood the issue in these terms. If intermediate-range nuclear weapons negotiations become deadlocked, and the administration proceeds with the full deployment of new missiles, the role of a US hostage to European security will become increasingly apparent. This may result in an anti-NATO backlash precipitating public and congressional opposition not only to US nuclear participation in NATO, but also to the current size of American conventional forces deployed there. This would be particularly true if European governments used US theater nuclear weapons to legitimize conventional force reductions of their own.

Two Options

There are two possible approaches to the problem. One is to accept or negotiate modifications in Soviet proposals to cut back their 250 SS-20s to the level of British and French missiles. These forces combined with US nuclear-capable aircraft in Europe, submarine-based nuclear missiles, some 6,000 short-range, battlefield nuclear weapons, and 300,000 troops pose a substantial deterrent and a highly visible US commitment to the defense of Europe.

A second approach if NATO security requires a response to Soviet theater nuclear modernization programs is offshore basing of sea-launched cruise missiles or additional designation of US submarine-launched missiles to NATO. These forces would pose a far more survivable deterrent than land-based missiles.

For the West Germans such forces offer a military solution to the problem, but not a political solution, since offshore basing weakens the credibility of the West German-American hostage relationship. For American security, however, it is safer to entertain German doubts than Soviet assurances of prompt escalation if deterrence fails.

Gary L. Guertner is a professor of political science at the US Army War College.

The Atlantic Alliance Is Essential

Richard R. Burt

This conference could not be more timely. And the need to view trans-Atlantic developments with care could not be more critical. As a former journalist, I am aware that those outside government have the opportunity to observe the ebb and flow of current affairs with a unique perspective. As a government official, I am also aware that this opportunity is not always seized as often as it might be. It is for this reason that *Time* and the conference organizers deserve our most sincere thanks and appreciation. Indeed, those of us enmeshed in the day-to-day of policymaking are in need of the criticism and vision of people such as yourselves and gatherings such as this. Without the benefit of perspective, we are less likely to shape historical forces than to be shaped by them.

I believe we have arrived at a critical juncture in the annals of the Atlantic alliance. Let me hasten to add that this is not because we are in a deep crisis as some would have us believe. Rather, we are in the midst of what can best be described as a grand debate. It is a debate over the very essence of the Atlantic alliance—its purpose, its shape, its future.

This is hardly the first time the alliance has been in the throes of self-examination and self-criticism. Indeed, the Atlantic alliance was born amidst controversy. The entire notion of peacetime engagement in the affairs of Europe went against the grain of American history. Postwar America was anxious to bring its boys back home and bring about a parochial peace with prosperity.

Formative Years

Nor were the formative years of the alliance easy ones for Europeans. Reconstruction and recovery were foremost in everyone's mind. Arming to prevent

Richard R. Burt, speech before the Time Conference on the Atlantic Alliance, Hamburg, Germany, April 25, 1983.

yet another war demanded all too scarce resources; forging bonds of trust with recent foes demanded the intellectual courage to look ahead rather than back.

But on both sides of the ocean, the uncommon men of the immediate post-war era made difficult, and sometimes unpopular, decisions. In the United States two world wars had shown all too clearly the folly of isolationism. It was understood that Jefferson's famous injunction against "entangling alliances" did not have permanent application. In Europe it was understood that the security of the Continent against the emerging Soviet threat required permanent association with a noncontinental power. Out of these twin recognitions the alliance came to life. The initial debate had been decided.

The alliance of the 1950s was an alliance overwhelmingly dominated by the United States. Deterrence depended on U.S. nuclear superiority to offset a Red Army which never demobilized. Decisions were largely reached in Washington and communicated through NATO in Paris. For the most part, we spoke, Europe listened; we led, Europe followed.

By the 1960s it was increasingly evident that such a formula had grown obsolete. Europe was no longer prostrate. Economic recovery had succeeded. The alliance was no longer based on a simple security guarantee but had evolved into a true military coalition with integrated national forces. And Europeans were less and less willing to accept American leadership without question. The conditions for a second great debate had materialized.

Nuclear Politics

Many of the strains accompanying these developments were manifested in the nuclear realm. Then, as today, nuclear politics went to the heart of the alliance. Two principal issues emerged in the nuclear debate of the 1960s. The problem was in part military. The American guarantee was no longer as convincing, given Soviet strides in developing their nuclear arsenal. How could the U.S. strategic deterrent compensate for conventional weakness and deter Soviet strategic forces simultaneously? Equally, the problem was political. Europeans wanted some say in the life-and-death decisions affecting nuclear weapons.

Washington's proposed approach for dealing with these problems—the NATO multilateral nuclear force—only exacerbated these tensions. Fortunately, the ultimate solution had the opposite effect. The doctrine of flexible response, formally adopted by the alliance in 1967, provided for a continuum of forces—conventional, theater nuclear, and strategic nuclear—by which deterrence could be maintained at all levels. And a new institution, the NATO Nuclear Planning Group, was created. Responsibility for nuclear policymaking would henceforth be shared. The basic Atlantic bond was maintained.

"The balance of power in Europe is central to world stability."

But in the best tradition of Hegelian logic, yesterday's synthesis has given way to today's antithesis. There is no little irony in this. In the 1960s, European concerns reflected a perceived lack of U.S. commitment to maintain the American nuclear guarantee; in the 1980s, the most vocal elements in Europe view with alarm American efforts to ensure the credibility of this same nuclear guarantee.

Thus, in 1983, we are once more hearing from many quarters that the alliance is no longer relevant, or viable, or both; that only radical surgery can prolong the patient's life. If I read the signs correctly, a third grand debate is underway. The reasons for this happening now are several.

First, the passage of time has dulled the initial Atlantic impulse; the alliance no longer seems as relevant to the concerns of young people bearing outlooks formed by experiences far from those of the postwar era.

Second, European states and institutions have advanced in capacity, wealth, and independence. Many on both sides of the Atlantic view the alliance as an anachronism, a product of an era of American strength and European weakness, which no longer exists.

Third, U.S. and European interests are not always identical or even complementary. We are often economic competitors. We often have differing views of Third World or regional crises. We at times have contrasting assessments of the Soviet Union, the threat it poses, and how best to manage East-West relations.

Fourth, a prolonged period of economic recession has increased competition for budgetary allocations. Providing more for defense and deciding how much each member of the alliance ought to provide are increasingly contentious.

Finally, shifts in the military balance and the emergence of U.S.-Soviet strategic parity, in particular, have raised anew the issue of American reliability. The credibility of the U.S. strategic deterrent is sometimes doubted. The emergence of Soviet superiority at the intermediate nuclear level has raised new questions as to the coupling of the defense of Europe and the U.S. strategic deterrent.

That a great debate over the future of the Atlantic alliance should evolve out of such circumstances is hardly odd; indeed, it would be odd, if one were not to take place. Not surprisingly, we are seeing challenges to the basic Atlantic model coming from all parts of the political spectrum. Both sides of the Atlantic are participating. What I should like to do today is make my modest contribution to this debate.

The Atlantic Model

In the United States, it is significant that we are not witnessing a revival of traditional isolationism. Fortress America is not being promoted as a model of American well-being. Perhaps the notion is simply too discredited to hold much attraction; perhaps most have simply come to accept that the United States is too dependent upon, and interdependent with, the rest of the world to pursue this simplistic and dangerous option.

Other challenges to the Atlantic connection exist, however. There is, for example, an American school of thought that has come to be known as "global unilateralism." Adherents of this school begin with an appreciation of the global scope of U.S. interests. They note the broad range of possible threats to the United States. And they would reduce the U.S. commitment to Europe so that we could enhance our flexibility to act everywhere.

This approach is flawed. All interests are not vital; all are not equal. The balance of power in Europe is central to world stability and American involvement in Europe is central to the balance there. Moreover, our range of ties, commercial and cultural, cannot be duplicated or done without. The reality is that there is no cheap way of protecting these interests. Deterrence, to be credible, requires a large U.S. continental commitment; it also requires that we act together as a true coalition.

A second challenge is perhaps better known to you. For want of a better phrase, I call it "Atlantic reconstruction." It manifests itself in several places— the Congress and the media most notably—and in several ways by, for example, threatening troop withdrawals or not funding defense programs critical to the defense of Europe.

The roots of this American movement are to be found in the soil of frustration and resentment. There is a growing belief in the United States that Europeans are not doing their share, be it to defend themselves or to defend common interests around the world. Sometimes tied to this view is the belief that Europe's commitment to detente outweighs its commitment to the alliance, that Europe is more concerned with its economic well-being than with Western defense. The reconstructionists want to end this alleged "free ride." They wish to send a signal to Europe to stimulate a larger European defense effort.

Roots of the Movement

As is often the case, neither analysis nor prescription is accurate. That we all need to do more to strengthen deterrence is obvious. And that there is a requirement for equity on defense efforts in a coalition of democratic states is also clear. More must be done, and the Reagan Administration has worked hard to increase defense spending on both sides of the Atlantic. At the same time, we have sought to deflate misconceptions about allied contributions to the common defense. There is not enough awareness, for example, that should conflict arise in Europe, 90% of NATO's land forces and 75% of its sea and air forces would be European.

There are those who argue that we could improve the situation by cutting U.S. efforts. I do not doubt that by doing less in Europe the United States would, indeed, "send a signal." Unfortunately, it would be the wrong signal with the wrong result. In the name of enhancing deterrence and defense, those who would cut back America's contribution could well achieve precisely the opposite. Reducing U.S. strength and raising questions about the U.S. commitment are hardly self-evident ways of promoting peace and stability.

European Alternatives

An even greater debate is taking place on this side of the Atlantic. This is to be expected, given the immediacy of the issues here. Let me address briefly what I see as the principal alternatives being presented.

Neutralism. Three schools of thought appear to dominate. The first would exchange the alliance for neutralism. Some go as far as to see this neutralism embracing all of Europe, West and East. It is argued that a Europe without allegiance to either bloc and without significant military forces would be a safer haven, less likely to be drawn into a confrontation between the two superpowers. Somewhat differently, it is asserted that Europe (and especially Germany) could make its most important contribution to peace by serving as a bridge between the two superpowers, explaining one to the other.

These are romantic visions. With or without its Eastern neighbors, a weak and neutral Western Europe would be under the sway of the strongest continental power, the Soviet Union. What is needed for peace is less a bridge than a bulwark. Our problems with the U.S.S.R. are not caused by a lack of communication, although communication is important. Our problems with the U.S.S.R. are caused by a lack of Soviet restraint and respect for the interests and well-being of others.

Armed Independence. Some recognize these realities and, instead, argue for a Western Europe that is strong, independent of the United States, and able to provide fully for its own security. An image of a European military entity is held up, the analogue to European political cooperation and economic integration. In this model, Europe would thus be able to mediate between the two powers from a position of strength—able to deter one without being tied to the other. European interests would prosper, we are told.

"A weak and neutral Western Europe would be under the sway of the strongest continental power, the Soviet Union."

I can do no better in describing this school of thought than by quoting Hedly Bull of Oxford University:

> The course that the Western European countries should now be exploring may be called the Europeanist one. It requires the countries of Western Europe to combine more closely together, increase their defense efforts, and take steps toward reducing their military dependence on America.

Professor Bull's vision, too, suffers from a lack of realism. Europe at present lacks the requisite political basis for constituting such collective management of its security. It is not clear that European states would be willing to make the necessary political commitments and economic investment. And it is not at all certain that the emergence of an independent, armed Europe—with conventional and nuclear forces alike—could occur without crisis or even conflict. Indeed, the security and stability we all know and enjoy now could be jeopardized by such development.

Reconstruction. A third approach is embodied by proposals now coming from opposition parties in northern Europe. In many respects, these ideas are the mirror image of the proposals offered by American reconstructionists. The European reconstructionists have several goals: to lessen the influence of the United States; to reduce the likelihood of nuclear war in Europe; to carry out a more independent policy toward Moscow; and to promote European interests around the world as they see fit. They seek not to leave the alliance so much as to change it from within.

Even such "reformist" policies are not without major difficulties; indeed, they draw upon several of the worst features of the two alternatives just discussed. We should not delude ourselves. Conventional defense needs strengthening. But more robust conventional defense efforts will not make nuclear forces irrelevant or redundant. Soviet conventional and nuclear advantages must be offset, whether by deployments, arms reductions, or both. The bond between forces in Europe and U.S. strategic deterrence, or coupling, must be maintained. At the same time, conventional force improvements will prove costly; a consensus for a major increase in the level of defense effort has yet to emerge. And heightened European independence from the United States has its risks; Europeans cannot choose when they wish to enjoy the fruits of alliance and when they do not. There is room for disagreement and difference within the alliance but not for selective commitment.

> *"The bond between forces in Europe and U.S. strategic deterrence, or coupling, must be maintained."*

Neutralism, armed independence, reconstruction—these are the three basic European alternatives to the current Atlanticist framework for Western security. Cutting across these approaches are various themes which would also alter the current Atlantic bridge in a decisive manner.

Antinuclearism

Antinuclearism is one such idea. The aim is to reduce or, if possible, eliminate the presence of nuclear weapons in Europe and with them the risk of nuclear war. The most ardent enthusiasts of this proposition would do so unilaterally in hopes of eliciting parallel Soviet restraint.

But I agree with (former Secretary of Defense) Harold Brown's observation about U.S.-Soviet arms competition: "When we build, the Soviet Union builds; and when we don't build, the Soviet Union still builds." Moreover, unilateral actions by the West would undermine our best chance for meaningful arms control negotiations. More seriously, unilateral nuclear disarmament would threaten deterrence and heighten the vulnerability of the West, too.

Nor can there be a policy of "no first use" of nuclear weapons. The effect would once again be decoupling and thus erode, not enhance, deterrence. It is the prospect of the use of nuclear weapons and the full weight of American might which helps to keep the peace in Europe.

Wishing away the possibility that nuclear weapons will be used is not enough. Declarations are simply words. Meanwhile, Soviet conventional, chemical, and nuclear capabilities are real and increasing. Were the alliance to adopt a policy of no first use of nuclear weapons, the danger of conventional war—which would be incredibly destructive in our age—would be increased and with it the possibility of nuclear tragedy. More than 50 million people perished in World War II; we cannot adopt policies which would heighten the risk of conventional, not to mention nuclear, war in Europe.

Arms Control

Lastly, there are those who remain within the alliance or Atlantic house but who place all their hopes on arms control. Arms control—whether some version of a nuclear freeze or negotiations more broadly—is held up as the panacea for Europe's dilemma. Only arms control, it is alleged, offers the means to limit the threat, reduce the levels of weapons and the spending on them, and promote renewed detente.

But such hopes cannot live in isolation. Arms control will only prosper if the Soviet Union has incentive to negotiate; what is required to bring this about is a sound military foundation on our part. Nor can arms control be expected to persuade the Soviet leadership to eschew the role of force; Soviet policy at home and abroad depends on it too much. Arms control has the potential to buttress our security and deterrence; it cannot take the place of our collective efforts to do the same.

What Is at Stake

In more normal times, debates involving competing conceptions of alliance security would be welcomed. Over years or even decades, we would perhaps create a new consensus. But 1983 is not a normal time. To the contrary, 1983 could well turn out to be the most important year in the history of the Atlantic alliance since its inception.

The reason for so stating is clear. To a degree unlike any other year since 1949, the determination and credibility of the alliance are being tested. How we implement the December 1979 decision on intermediate nuclear forces will have a major impact on our future. Those who would apply their abstract or idealized notions of how best to structure the Atlantic relationship to determine the outcome of the INF (intermediate-range nuclear forces) debate should only do so with a full understanding of what is at stake.

Not surprisingly, this temptation exists. There are those in the United States who wonder why we should go to such lengths to bring about the implementation of the decision. They are unhappy that so many facets of the U.S.-European relationship are held hostage to the INF decision and cite the possibility that deployment of U.S. missiles in Europe could heighten the risk of a direct Soviet nuclear attack on the American homeland.

On this side of the Atlantic, there are those—particularly the new neutralists—who maintain precisely the opposite. They argue that new U.S. weapons based on the Continent would enable us to localize or limit an East-West nuclear exchange to Europe. Others simply argue that the new missiles are not necessary because the Soviet Union has no intention of exploiting its current INF monopoly. Or, in yet another variation, there are those who are prepared to wait indefinitely for arms control to solve the security problem created by SS-20 deployment. In every case, they seek to opt out of implementing the 1979 decision.

Obvious Fallacies

The fallacies in each of these approaches are manifest. The United States cannot be secure for long in a world in which Western Europe is not. Americans who would weaken or remove the U.S. nuclear guarantee would jeopardize the prospects for stability and peace everywhere. In the name of reducing risk to themselves, they will have raised it for everyone.

European opponents of deployment are also mistaken. The effect of new U.S. missiles would not be to limit or localize a nuclear exchange in Europe but rather to prevent one. Indeed, it is in part through the threat of escalation and full American involvement that we help to promote stability and deterrence in Europe. Indeed, no better proof for this proposition exists than Defense Minister Ustinov's recent comment that the Soviet Union would respond to a strike by U.S. systems in Europe by directly attacking the United States. If that's not coupling, I don't know what is.

No New Deployment

Those who maintain no new deployments are needed, whether owing to Soviet good will or the prospects of arms control, are simply deluding themselves. It is probably true that Western Europe could live with a Soviet preponderance of force; but to expect the Soviets not to exploit any advantage for its own paranoic, political purposes is to ignore every lesson of history. Similarly, the U.S.S.R. cannot be expected to negotiate seriously in the absence of any incentive to do so; deployment, either in promise or in fact, remains our best and only way to get the Soviets to come to the negotiating table in good faith.

In short, the implementation of the INF double-track decision has become the touchstone for Western security in the 1980s. The decision continues to have a sound political and a sound military rationale. It was taken in response to an unprovoked Soviet buildup which continues unabated. It represents continued alliance commitment to a concept of deterrence predicated on the notion that American power tied to Europe is the best way of promoting European stability and peace. The commitment of the Reagan Administration and allied governments to pursuing both tracks—arms control and, if need be, deployment—of the 1979 decision is now unshakeable.

"The United States cannot be secure for long in a world in which Western Europe is not."

My support for decisions taken some 3½ years ago and my criticism of various alternative visions of the alliance should not be interpreted as complacency. The flaws of the various alternatives I have described should not be taken as a complete dismissal of their validity. Nor should it be understood as a complete endorsement of the status quo. If I may modify an old American adage for my purposes here tonight, I would simply advise against fixing the alliance more than it is broken. Or, to shift metaphors, I would simply urge you to beware of cures worse than the disease.

Reform Is Needed

This is not a call for standing pat. Reform is needed. So too is close consultation. We must upgrade not only our nuclear deterrent but also our conventional forces. More must be done to safeguard common interests outside the formal treaty area. We must ensure that our commercial relations with the East are consistent with our political and security requirements. And we must continue to be imaginative and flexible in our search for meaningful arms control agreements.

We must be careful, though, in how we proceed. Europe in the 30 years since the Second World War has been spared armed conflict. We have achieved levels of prosperity and freedom without historical precedent. Too much is at stake to go ahead precipitously or recklessly. The alliance and the basic Atlantic model or structure remain relevant and viable. Only within its contours can we harness the resources of the West in a manner which maximizes effectiveness and minimizes the burden on our free societies and strained economies.

There is a wonderful line from the novel, *The Leopard*, by the Italian author Giuseppe di Lampedusa. "If we want things to stay as they are, things will have to change." To a degree this is true. Indeed, the history of the alliance is a series of adaptations to evolving circumstances. The alliance of 1983 is not the alliance of 1949.

Yet, there must also be limits to our departures. The essentials of the Atlantic model that is the alliance have served us well and should be saved.

The alliance can continue to safeguard our interests if we are as wise about what to keep as we are about what to change.

Richard R. Burt is the United States assistant secretary for European affairs.

"The question must arise whether the countries of the cape of the Eurasian land mass are any longer worth that much attention and commitment."

The Atlantic Alliance Is Obsolete

Patrick Cosgrave

There can be little doubt that the Atlantic Alliance is in poor shape. Neither on the question of Afghanistan nor on that of Poland was it possible for the United States and the governments of western Europe to remain firmly in step for long. With the exception of the United Kingdom and, to a lesser extent, Italy, all the European NATO powers have displayed vacillation and trepidation on the issue of the manufacture and eventual deployment of cruise missiles and neutron warheads on their territories. President Reagan's remarks—off the cuff and partially incomprehensible though they were—on the various thresholds of nuclear exchange caused no end of a kerfuffle in Europe.

The impatience and incredulity (covered though it has been with an almost unfailing courtesy) of the Administration towards allies who seem determined neither honestly to accept the implications of American nuclear protection nor stoutly to bear the cost of bringing their own conventional forces to a level of convincing deterrence was expressed by Mr. Weinberger in an interview on August 12, 1981. "I had," said the Secretary of Defense, "a German representative (who) suggested that the real answer was for us to encourage Europe to increase their conventional weapons so that we wouldn't have to have the neutron warhead. This is a fine academic argument, but it's made in the face of a decision made last week by the German government to reduce its defense spending. . ." Finally, the differences between the EEC Council of Foreign Ministers and the U.S. on the Middle East, as exemplified in the Venice Declaration, are notorious.

Mention of this last area of disagreement points up the increasingly institutionalized nature of American-European differences. Contrary to what many

"America versus Europe," by Patrick Cosgrave is reprinted by permission from *Policy Review*, Issue No. 15 (or Winter 1981). *Policy Review* is a publication of The Heritage Foundation, 214 Massachusetts Ave. NE, Washington, DC 20002.

Americans—including many American politicians—believe, the European Economic Community, as established by the Treaty of Rome, and as enlarged by subsequent treaties, has no military or defense dimension. It is, however, the ambition of the EEC governments to formulate a common foreign policy. The attempt to do this on the matter of the Middle East represented partly a conviction that the European powers—notably Britain and France—had something special to contribute because of their historical experience of the area, and partly a desire in principle to take a stand different from, if not directly at variance with, that of the U.S.

NATO and the EEC

Thus, any American government faces two areas of potential friction with its European allies—within the NATO alliance, in strategic and, to a lesser extent in political, matters; and, in relation to the EEC, on foreign policy generally.

The clash of opinion in the United States is no longer—as it was in the 1960s—between interventionists in foreign policy and isolationists, like Senator (now Ambassador) Mike Mansfield. A new—and more subtle and sophisticated—element has entered with the rise of the globalists, who are inclined to feel that the U.S. has interests of potentially equal weight all around the world. They see the major task of defining U.S. interest in the coming decade as to appropriate attention and resources in just measure between them. Since Europe has been given strategic first priority in American thinking since the war, the question must arise whether the countries of the cape of the Eurasian land mass are any longer worth that much attention and commitment, particularly when their interests and policies (the two are not always the same) diverse so increasingly from the perceived interests and articulated policy of the United States. . . .

The relative harmony—as against the EEC—that prevails between the NATO powers (though NATO does have problems) can be explained by the simplicity of its aims and methods, as opposed to those of the EEC. It is vastly easier to make coherent the policies and tactics of an organization which has the simple and overriding aim of mutual defense against a single and perceived enemy. There may, of course, be a number of conflicts over the nature of the menace or—as has been the case to some extent in recent years—over political acceptability. The newly burgeoning European nuclear disarmament movement, for example, has made it less easy for some western European governments readily to continue to accept the leadership of the United States on certain major issues, such as the deployment of cruise and the Alliance's negotiating posture towards the Soviet Union and the Warsaw Pact. These are not problems to be burked or ignored. Nevertheless, the existence of the EEC clearly makes far harder the tasks of those statesmen on both sides of the Atlantic who appreciate the singular importance of keeping up the NATO shield, and keeping sharp the NATO sword.

The Alliance's Banker

First, there is the problem of wealth and expense, a subject on which the Europeans seem consistently and constantly confused. The United States, besides providing the great bulk of NATO's manpower, equipment, and commitments is the Alliance's banker and paymaster. As such she is constantly demanding a greater defense investment for the purposes of the Alliance from the European powers. To such cajolings the Europeans constantly plead, if not poverty directly, then the heavy demands of other commitments. Yet, it is a regularly recurring claim (or boast) of European politicians that, properly organized the Community can be an economic match for—and rival to—any other world power or group of powers, including the United States. It is not easy for an American politician, even with the best will in the world, readily to accept the reasonableness of both of these positions. And the strain is becoming greater all the time.

For a second problem enters here. While the whole development of the EEC since the signing of the Treaty of Rome—with the possible, and in any event marginal, creation of the directly elected European "Parliament"—has been economic, the ultimate aspirations enshrined in the Treaty are political. I have already mentioned that the first pragmatic object of the founders of the Community was to make another Franco-German war impossible. They sought in the first instance to achieve this by the creation of the European Coal and Steel Community, the idea being to bring together the resources needed to support warfare under multi-national authority. Of course, they realized that no federalist, or quasi-

federalist, organization could hope to exist without the underpinning of a mutually satisfactory economic structure. For many of them, however, the ultimate objective was a common foreign policy. And, given that modern foreign policy is increasingly a matter of economic relations, the search for a common policy inevitably involved the lineaments of developing economic policies.

The Atlantic Gulf

Writing at a time before the United Kingdom joined the EEC, Mr. Roy Jenkins, (then Britain's Chancellor of the Exchequer) in his book *Afternoon on the Potomac,* described how he and Secretary for the Treasury William Simon were constrained to wait for days in stuffy ante-rooms while EEC ministers hammered out a common position on the economic issues at stake. From such experiences, Mr. Jenkins, already an ardent proponent of his country's bid to enter the EEC, came to the conclusion that almost any terms were acceptable in order to procure membership of this club.

"European powers. . . have been particularly opposed to the American determination to use her informal alliance with Israel as the lynch-pin of her policy."

Nowadays, of course, Mr. Jenkins's humiliating experience is, for American politicians and diplomats, a very common one. It has cropped up particularly in recent years on Western policy toward eastern Europe and Russia; and on the development of Western policy in the Middle East. European powers—though there are considerable variations of opinion and emphasis among them—have been particularly opposed to the American determination to use her informal alliance with Israel as the lynch-pin of her policy. Since the Americans are so deeply committed in terms of *material* and prestige in the Middle East, and the Europeans are not, American politicians have been angered over what they see as European attempts to fish in troubled waters, by going around and outside the system created by the Camp David Accords.

The Europeans reply the Americans are, quite simply, wrong to imagine that they can use Camp David as the centerpiece of a major effort by diplomacy to produce stability in the region. Second, and more significantly, they insist that, because the issues at stake in the area are of some international importance, it is imperative that Europe have an *independent* view of them. This doctrine—that of being *necessarily* different from everybody else—is, historically, a particularly French one, and was most dominant in General de Gaulle's period of power. It creates, of course and quite simply, a horrendous series of diplomatic delays. If there *must* be a common European position, then it will take a good deal of time to formulate. (For example, the Mitterand government in France is overtly and strongly pro-Israeli. Its position, following President Giscard's long cultivation of the Arabs, necessarily upsets the agreed position of the Europeans.) During its formulation, or its umpteenth re-formulation, diplomatic activity between the EEC governments and the United States comes to a halt. This is understandably irritating to the Americans in any case. When the issue—as on the economic matters I discussed earlier—involves direct American interests, it is far more than merely irritating, and inevitably calls in question the whole post-war trend of United States policy towards western Europe.

Seeking a Common Policy

One must surely question the desirability of so much effort being spent, at such potentially damaging cost, on the procuring of agreement—often itself expressed in an anodyne fashion—on matters which Europe cannot significantly influence. There has always been a strong element of fantasy in EEC aspirations, and it is nowhere more marked than in the seeking of a common foreign policy. Moreover, the fact that is sought to express such policy through the person of the Chairman of the Council of Ministers, and the fact that the job changes every six months, makes consistency, if not *ad hoc* coordination, impossible.

"To formulate common European policies is perhaps to exaggerate, even sometimes to create, a permanent division between Europe and America."

But the attempt may have seriously damaging consequences. To formulate common European policies is perhaps to exaggerate, even sometimes to create, a permanent division between Europe and America. It is a matter of common observation that allies seldom agree. But there is no necessary condition that the line of division should be the Atlantic Ocean. Before this institutionalized common foreign policy, indeed, even the least popular American position could usually depend upon finding some supporters among the NATO allies. Alliance divisions were then both internal to Europe and constantly shifting. Sometimes the West Germans, sometimes the British, even very occasionally the French would take the American side against other

Europeans. This had for Europeans the healthy effect that Americans were intimately involved in the earliest stages of European arguments and were, so to speak, anchored to Europe thereby. But the first effects of attempting to formulate a common foreign policy are to exclude America from the early stages of European policy-making and to compel into line those European countries which, otherwise, might have taken the American position. In matters covered by the common policy-making apparatus, therefore, America can never hope to find allies among its European allies (unless, of course, the happy chance occurs that America and the whole EEC agree). The line of division will invariably be the Atlantic Ocean. It is not difficult to see that, over time, this must promote irritation, suspicion, and discord between the two sides of the Atlantic.

Diplomatic observers, indeed, have not perhaps realized just how far this process has already gone. To take a striking example, the EEC representatives at the United Nations held about 300 meetings to "coordinate" UN votes in a recent ten-week period. And it was apparently the feeling of the U.S. delegation that these meetings usually produced decisions inimical to U.S. interests and wishes. The attempt to create a "different" and "independent" European foreign policy, therefore, is likely to result nine times out of ten in an anti-American foreign policy (just as the attempt to create a common economic and trade policy has harmed and undercut American economic interests). This casts an ironic light on the early U.S. hopes that such unified approaches would be in natural harmony with America's own policies.

A House Divided

The truth is—and the Americans too rarely understand this—that the European powers have, on a great number of issues, singularly different interests and perceptions. For many years until recently the United States—often with the best will in the world—has sought to treat western Europe as a single unit. It was more than a little pleased that, in their apparent developing federalism, these states appeared to be seeking to ape the American experience. But European perceptions are not merely different from American perceptions, they are different from one another.

For example, West Germany is, naturally and reasonably, pre-occupied with the division of Germany into two countries. From time to time each of her governments engages in a burst of *Ostpolitik* activity, which has for its ultimate aim the end of the national division. Quite apart from the fact that the U.S.S.R. would never permit the ending of the division, it is exceptionally doubtful whether any of the other major western European powers would welcome it either. Forty years of peace has by no means ended suspicions of Germany, or rather suspicions of what a united Germany might become, even if only in the economic field. Staunch though the Federal Republic has generally been as an American ally, moreover, there have been times—notably after the invasion of Afghanistan—when she took a conciliatory line toward the Soviet Union that not merely irritated, but angered, the United States. It was to be explained, of course, with reference to the current state of her exchanges with East Germany. While that may not excuse it, it makes it more understandable. It follows from all this that, whereas the United States should seek neither to follow its traditional policy of seeking to negotiate with western Europe as a bloc, nor seek to divide it in such a way as would arouse the resentment of the European allies, it would in the future be better to conceive of them as separate entities, and to seek to conciliate them individually as the opportunity arises.

Britain's Case

There is also, however, the special case of Britain. The special nature of Britain's case has become much more apparent since the Argentinian invasion of the Falkland Islands. Several considerations should be borne in mind when considering the British position, and all form part of the background to the affair of the Falklands. First, as I mentioned earlier, the United Kingdom joined the EEC late. She was able to play (by her own choice) no part in its original construction or in its period of important early development. As a consequence she found, on entry, an organization already set in its ways, and not at all agreeable to an island power which still had, diminished though they were, worldwide trading connections and responsibilities. Second, the advent to power of Mrs. Margaret Thatcher in 1979 brought to the British helm a political leader who, though anxious to stay in the EEC, was by no means committed to its fundamental principles and who was determined to fight for British rights as she saw them, whatever the consequences for Britain's partners. Third, in her Britain had a Prime Minister of singularly pro-American bent. (Her last conservative predecessor, Edward Heath, had been markedly anti-American, partly because he wished to disarm European suspicions that—in General de Gaulle's phrase—Britain would be America's Trojan horse in Europe.) Thus, before the Falklands crisis broke, Britain's relationships within the EEC were, to put it at its lowest, uneasy.

Lesson of the Falklands

Some of the consequences of the Falklands War are already becoming clear. The most important, so far as Britain is concerned, is the psychological revolution it has brought about in the nation. Whatever the United States—or any other concerned power—might wish, there is no conceivable possibility of Britain returning the islands to Argentina or handing them over to some form of international trusteeship. Any such move would destroy a Prime Minister whose reputation has been made by her resonse to the initial invasion. It seems, moreover, that Mrs. Thatcher is prepared now to undertake the development of the islands—for so long neglected by Britain—particularly in regard to fishing and oil. It is, however, the cost in blood, rather than the potential for profit, which will determine future British policy.

"The line of division will invariably be the Atlantic Ocean."

It is a striking thing that no likely alternative Prime Minister in Britain would have launched the Task force at all. In that sense General Galtieri's gamble was not as ill-considered as is generally supposed. In her action Mrs. Thatcher not merely revealed the bent of her own mind—nationalistic in essence—but released an upsurge of nationalist feeling in the country which most of the political establishment had thought long passed out of existence. It is symbolic of the confused swirl of attitudes to which the crisis gave rise that it was not merely the Labour opposition that sought to hold back action, but Edward Heath, the Conservative who brought Britain into the EEC, as well. Mr. Heath argued that our large scale interests in Latin America, and the necessity to devote our energies to Europe, precluded military action over undeveloped islands 8,000 miles away. Now, the fact that a small Western power acted so decisively, and at such considerable cost, in defense of an interest which most other countries regarded as at best marginal may have all sorts of consequences for international relations. But both the fundamental and immediate question is the consequences it will have for Britain's relations with her main allies.

Britain's Latitude

British opinion went through several phases. The first thing to note is that of all her friends—the United States, the Europeans and the Commonwealth—only the Antipodean members of the latter organization have won unqualified gratitude. This gratitude was stimulated by the act of the New Zealand government in placing a frigate at the disposal of the Royal Navy. In the early stages even those opposed to British membership of the EEC reacted with gratitude to the organization's speedy imposition of sanctions on Argentina, and with suspicion to the even-handedness of the United States. As of the end of May that attitude has been completely reversed. EEC sanctions were imposed initially for a limited period and to procure their renewal—even then with Ireland and Italy standing out—Britain had to pay a heavy price in terms of its contribution to the Community budget. At the same time, Secretary Haig's mediation efforts having failed, the prompt and generous American provision of supplies to the Task Force—widely publicized in Britain—created a flood of feeling towards America of a kind not seen since the war.

Thus, in terms of traditional British policy, which was supposed to rest on three legs, American, Commonwealth, and European, the balance of national sentiment and opinion has shifted decisively towards the first two legs and, in practical terms for the future, towards the American. What should the United States make of all this?

"The potential cost to the United States of maintaining the status quo *in the Alliance may be considerable."*

Before setting off on his European trip, President Reagan reiterated the traditional post-war American position on Europe—that the defense of the sub-continent was an integral American interest and that to make that defense strong, political and economic cooperation with Europe must be fostered. However that policy works out, the United States will also have to face, post Falklands, the fact that one of her allies will, for the foreseeable future, be an Atlantic power with a base in the South Atlantic. This is bound to affect, in one way or another, the relationship of both countries to Latin America.

Cost of the Alliance

At the same time, given the economic stresses described in the early part of this essay, which lie beneath all the diplomatic and defense consideration which any American administration must consider, the potential cost to the United States of maintaining the *status quo* in the Alliance may be considerable. It is likely to become more considerable as American global interests—particularly in the Far East—develop. There are more and more Americans prepared to argue that, at the very least, the United States should give equal weight to its interests in the Pacific, and perhaps even in the Middle East, as she does to those in Europe. This is a development fraught with consequences for the Europeans. It is likely, too, that President Reagan's successors will, increasingly, be men who do not have the automatic European orientation that we in Europe have come to expect from American presidents. My own view is that the likely development is a gradual loosening of the ties that bind the United States to Europe. But I see also a distinct possibility that one western European power—Britain—will find herself once more growing closer to the United States. This will be all the more so because the defense plans of even the Thatcher government—which foresaw considerable cutbacks in naval expenditure before the Falklands erupted—are now bound to be scotched. National opinion will not accept a policy which would mean that a Task Force like Admiral Woodward's could not be launched. Now, there is a respectable school of thought—to which I myself belong—which has for some time believed that Britain's major contribution to NATO in Europe should in fact be naval. America and Britain would in these circumstances find themselves moving in the same direction: away from a strategic attitude that places overwhelming emphasis on the land defense of Europe, with a consequent neglect of the West's other interests around the world; and toward a greater priority for naval and highly mobile forces designed to protect these wider interests. But there is equally no doubt that such a policy, if adopted, is bound to cause problems with our land-fixated continental allies.

In terms of European defense the fundamental decision must, of course, be American. If the United States retains the traditional idea of the centrality of Europe in her strategy—an attitude of mind which ensured that she eventually and practically supported Britain in the South Atlantic—then matters will go on much as before. But so many factors are acting against the continuance of that presumption, not least the developing nature of the EEC, its drift to a position of organized economic rivalry with the U.S., its gropings toward a distinctive world role, and the difficulties that Americans and Europeans (notably the West Germans) have in agreeing upon a common nuclear policy. It is becoming apparent that, since 1945, America has been pursuing two policies that are, in the final analysis, logically incompatible: a close alliance with Europe, and the encouragement of European unity. We are all entering a new, dangerous, and unfamiliar world. In that world, the traditional U.S. policy of encouraging European unity may no longer serve American interests.

Patrick Cosgrave is a journalist, historian, and former political correspondent of the London Spectator. *He is the author of* Churchill at War: Alone.

The US Should Remain in Southeast Asia

Richard D. Fisher Jr.

Southeast Asia faces a growing Soviet military threat. Just last November, about ten nuclear capable Tupolev Tu-16 "Badger" medium-range bombers were deployed at what is for all purposes the Soviet "base" in Cam Ranh Bay, Vietnam. The Badger's 1,500 mile combat radius enables it to strike the capitals of Brunei, Indonesia, Malaysia, the Philippines, Singapore, and Thailand—the members of the Association of Southeast Asian Nations (ASEAN). This unprovoked Soviet military escalation radically alters the region's strategic balance.

The deployment of the Badgers follows nearly a decade of Soviet military-political expansion after U.S. forces left Indochina. As such, Soviet power in Southeast Asia now threatens vital Western economic and strategic interests. Soviet naval and air forces in Vietnam can interdict merchant and military naval traffic in the South China Sea and disrupt the vital Indonesian and Malaysian straits. Secure air and shipping lanes are crucial to the economies of ASEAN, Northeast Asia, and Taiwan, and for the United States to meet its political commitments in Asia and the Persian Gulf. Soviet strategic objectives, military-economic activity in Indochina, espionage, and subversion are directed toward increasing Soviet power in Southeast Asia.

Continued U.S. economic and military aid to ASEAN members, and continued maintenance of a regional military presence through bases in the Philippines are important contributions to regional security. However, even closer cooperation between ASEAN members and increased U.S. activity in the region are needed to meet the growing Soviet threat. The current U.S. presence is not enough to play an active regional role even though ASEAN leaders look to the United States as the only power able to counter

Richard D. Fisher Jr., "Moscow's Growing Muscle in Southeast Asia," *Asian Studies Center Backgrounder*, April 4, 1984. Reprinted by permission of the Heritage Foundation, 214 Massachusetts Ave. NE, Washington, DC 20002.

Soviet advances in the region. Many Americans ignore Southeast Asia because of the all too recent memory of Vietnam. Despite the "Vietnam syndrome," the United States must continue to be a force for peace in Southeast Asia....

Soviet Bases

Moscow was able to translate its military support for Vietnam into access to Vietnamese military facilities. Moscow's massive shipment of arms in late 1978 enabled Hanoi to conquer Kampuchea in December 1978. When China reacted with a limited invasion of Vietnam in February 1979, Moscow increased its military aid and sent a naval show of force.

This assured access gives Moscow a long desired strategic link between Northeast Asia and the Middle East and a warm water port from which to threaten Southeast Asia's sealanes. Moscow regards its basing rights as a major form of compensation for its economic and military assistance to Hanoi, which is estimated currently at $4 to $6 million a day. Hanoi continues to insist that it has not granted bases to the USSR. But particularly in Cam Ranh Bay, local Soviet control is nearly complete. Only senior Vietnamese officials are allowed on the base. Indeed, Soviet patrol boats are believed to have fired on Vietnamese fishing boats washed near shore during storms.

Soviet naval units are the most visible Soviet military presence in Southeast Asia. They began operating out of DaNang in mid-1979, but moved to American built facilities at Cam Ranh Bay by late 1979. In Cam Ranh, the Soviets have installed additional piers, bomb proof submarine shelters, a floating drydock, underground fuel storage tanks, and electronic navigation aids. Electronic intelligence gathering equipment in Cam Ranh monitors U.S. and Chinese military movements and communications traffic. Satellite communications equipment allows close contact with the Soviet General Staff in

Moscow. Tupolev Tu-142 "Bear" long-range reconnaissance and targeting aircraft operate from DaNang and Cam Ranh Bay.

Cam Ranh Bay

Soviet use of Cam Ranh Bay has grown from about 8 ships in 1979 to about 22 ships by late 1983. Combat vessels include up to 4 submarines, nuclear and conventional powered, and up to 6 surface ships. The aircraft-carrying anti-submarine cruiser MINSK has made several port calls in Cam Ranh Bay. This Kiev-class ship carries the 250-mile range SS-N-12 cruise missile, which is able to deliver either a nuclear or conventional warhead. The recent transfer to the Pacific Fleet of another Kiev-class ship, the NOVOROSSIYSK, increases Soviet capability to deploy significant naval force to Southeast Asia. With the deployment of Tu-16 bombers to Cam Ranh, the Soviets now have in Vietnam all the elements of their tactical naval surface warfare strategy: preemptive cruise missile and torpedo strikes from aircraft, submarines, and surface ships, coordinated by a land-based command staff. This translates into a present and direct threat to U.S. naval forces and Asian merchant ships passing through the South China Sea.

The transfer of Tu-16s to Cam Ranh alters the region's strategic balance. They place increased pressure on U.S. forces in Southeast Asia and are a weapon the ASEAN nations cannot match. The 1,500 mile unrefueled radius of the Tu-16 enables it to strike every ASEAN capital, cities and military installations in Northern Australia, and U.S. bases in the Philippines. Its ability to carry free fall bombs and cruise missiles armed with nuclear warheads adds an intermediate range complement to Moscow's Siberian-based intercontinental ballistic missiles and submarine launched ballistic missiles.

"Soviet expansion in Southeast Asia threatens US strategic interests."

Referring to the DaNang and Cam Ranh based Tu-142 "Bears," Singapore Foreign Minister Suppiah Dhanabalan recently stated, "They are not just flying around...they are on missions." The military forces of ASEAN would be hard pressed to defend against Soviet forces now in Vietnam.

Other Soviet Military Activities

Hanoi is dependent upon Soviet military aid to defend itself against China and continue its occupation of Laos and Kampuchea. From 1955 to 1975 Moscow gave Hanoi about $300-$500 million annually in military aid. Today, this figure has nearly doubled. Except for aging American weapons captured in 1975, the Vietnamese, Laotian, and Kampuchean armed forces rely on Soviet supplied weapons. Soviet military aid to Laos and Kampuchea from 1979 to 1982 was over $100 million, with much more indirect aid being provided by "paying" for Vietnamese troops stationed in each country....

Moscow is now supporting guerrillas directed at Thailand. In early 1983, Soviet Deputy Foreign Minister Mikhail Kapitsa threatened that Vietnam would assist insurgents in countries that were supporting Kampuchean groups opposed to the Vietnamese installed Heng Samrin regime. Following this, Vietnam, along with Soviet, Polish, Cuban, and Czech advisors, set up about 20 training camps inside Laos to train Thai guerrillas.

Economic Dependence

The communist regimes of Indochina—Vietnam, Laos, and Kampuchea—all depend on Soviet economic support. The U.S. imposed a trade embargo on Hanoi after its conquest of South Vietnam in 1975. Other Western nations followed suit after Hanoi's 1978 invasion of Kampuchea and remain adamant that Hanoi will not benefit from Western aid and trade as long as it occupies Kampuchea.

Thus, Hanoi has had to rely on economic support from the Soviet Union and Soviet-bloc countries. Hanoi received over $3 billion in economic aid during its 1976-1980 Five Year Plan period. Current annual economic aid is about $600-$700 million. In 1982, direct Soviet aid to Phnom Penh was $82 million. Moscow pledged $600 million to Laos for its 1981-1985 Five Year Plan. There are about 4,000 Soviet economic advisors in Vietnam, 3,000 in Laos and 600 in Kampuchea. By comparison, total U.S. FY 1984 economic aid to all ASEAN nations is $170.7 million.

Moscow and Hanoi have devised a diabolical scheme by which Vietnam repays the USSR—exploiting the Vietnamese labor force. An estimated 100,000 Vietnamese are working in the Soviet Union and Eastern Europe; up to 70 percent of their wages are kept as repayment.

Hanoi admits near total dependence on the Soviet Union for petroleum products and about 90 percent dependence for fertilizer, iron and steel, cotton and machine tools. Despite all of this aid, Vietnamese per capita annual income in 1982 was only $160....

US Policy

Current U.S. policy toward Southeast Asia has two major facets: deference on major issues to ASEAN (and China), and the growing Soviet threat through defense commitments and military-economic aid. In conjunction with this policy, the U.S. also supports ASEAN's policies vis-à-vis Kampuchea and a continued aid and trade embargo of Vietnam.

Economically, ASEAN today is collectively the fastest growing region in the world. However, its continued growth is dependent upon unobstructed participation in the international economic system. The United States is a major partner in ASEAN's economic growth. The U.S. is the first or second major trading partner of each ASEAN country. But besides being an important market for U.S. products, Southeast Asia is an important source of strategic materials such as oil, rubber, and tin.

But growing economic interaction with the U.S. does not satisfy ASEAN leaders. They want Washington to play a greater political and military role in Southeast Asia. Increased military aid is part of the answer. A direct military commitment would be difficult for the U.S. in view of the American public's fear of becoming involved in another Vietnam. Military aid has the additional advantages of enabling the ASEAN states to enhance their own defense capabilities, increasing the cooperation between the respective U.S. and recipient armed forces, and signalling continued American commitment to resist Soviet expansion in the region.

The Philippines currently is the largest Southeast Asian recipient of U.S. military aid. The Administration's current military assistance proposal to the Philippines is part of President Reagan's 1983 pledge to obtain $900 million in security assistance over five years. Compared to military assistance packages given to other U.S. allies, this is a small price for the strategic benefits that Philippine bases provide the U.S.—particularly considering the proximity of Soviet bases in Vietnam. Thailand, as a "front line" state, is ASEAN's second major recipient of U.S. aid, which totalled $135 million in 1983.

U.S. aid is vital for Thailand to repel Vietnamese incursions. The Administration and Congress should approve a recent Thai request to purchase F-16 jet fighters with the advanced 100 series engine. Current U.S. policy permits the sale of F-16s with the less powerful J-79 engine to this region. The presence of Tu-16 bombers in Cam Ranh Bay and the possibility that Moscow could give Hanoi advanced MiG-23 fighters heightens the Thai need for advanced fighter aircraft. The sale will also send a political signal to ASEAN that the United States continues to be a willing partner in helping the member states to meet their defense needs.

Regional Defense Cooperation

The growing Soviet threat in Vietnam and the U.S. commitments to defend Northeast Asia and the Persian Gulf against Soviet threats makes inter-ASEAN defense cooperation an essential part of Southeast Asian security. Already, the U.S. conducts naval and marine exercises with Thailand. The 1971 Five Power Defense Agreement brings together Australia, New Zealand, Britain, Malaysia, and Singapore for consultation on regional security and periodic exercises. On an inter-ASEAN level, Indonesia has conducted naval exercises with Singapore, Malaysia, Thailand, and the Philippines.

Singapore has conducted air defense exercises with Thailand and Malaysia. Because these exercises have been sporadic, greater multi-service cooperation is needed.

Singapore's recent purchase of E-2C "AWACS" type surveillance aircraft, for example, presents an opportunity to build an integrated air defense of the Malaccan Straits region with Malaysia and Indonesia.

"Increased military aid is part of the answer."

Ideally, as the defense capabilities of the states of Northeast and Southeast Asia are enhanced, a cooperative interregional response to meet the common Soviet threat should emerge. The United States can and should be prepared to play a positive role in encouraging such cooperation.

Relations with Hanoi

America's withdrawal from Indochina drastically cut U.S. influence in Southeast Asia. Many urge the U.S. to normalize relations with Hanoi as a means to seek a settlement in Kampuchea, lessen Soviet regional influence, and solve the emotionally charged issue of Americans missing in action from the Vietnam War. If the U.S. normalized relations with Hanoi before significant positive movement by Hanoi on any of these issues—which are of concern to ASEAN as well as the United States—the only significant U.S. leverage over Hanoi would be lost. Quiet U.S. diplomatic contact with Hanoi to explore outstanding issues is useful. But Hanoi must demonstrate its willingness to act responsively before it is readmitted to the world community.

Noncommunist Resistance in Kampuchea

Another more direct way the United States can increase its regional role is to actively support the noncommunist resistance groups in Kampuchea. These groups are currently fighting a guerrilla war against the Vietnamese operating in the mountains along the Thai-Kampuchean border, and drawing much support from refugee camps inside Thailand. The groups include the 30,000-man Khmer Rouge, the 12,000-man Khmer People's Liberation Front (KPNLF) led by former Prime Minister Son Sann, and the 5,000-man Moulinaka led by former head of state Norodom Sihanouk. The latter two groups are noncommunist.

The groups formed a coalition in June 1982 on the advice and pressure of ASEAN, China, and the United States. The coalition seeks to present itself as a legitimate opposition to the Vietnamese-installed Heng Samrin regime in Phnom Penh, protected and kept in power by Hanoi's 150,000-170,000 troops. ASEAN is supporting the coalition with the eventual hope of freeing Kampuchea from Hanoi's control.

It is in the U.S. interest to join ASEAN's efforts in backing the Kampuchean resistance. Yet, the U.S. must also help prevent the genocidal Khmer Rouge from returning to power.

Conclusion

Soviet expansion in Southeast Asia threatens U.S. strategic interests, as well as the economic security of America's Asian allies. Soviet military bases in Vietnam are a threat to the maritime lifelines of ASEAN, Taiwan, and Northeast Asia. Soviet support for Hanoi's occupation of Kampuchea and support for insurgents directed against Thailand demonstrate Moscow's continued goal of expanding the circle of communist states.

Commercial trends point to greater U.S.-Asian trade and industrial cooperation. Consequently, the U.S. must increase the level of its military-political activity in Southeast Asia to counter Moscow's growing military presence—which now threatens the security of the greater Pacific Basin.

Increased military aid to ASEAN states, such as the sale of F-16A fighter aircraft, is needed to enhance their defense capabilities to meet the growing Soviet military presence in Vietnam. Continued U.S. access to Philippine bases is vital for U.S. and free-Asian defense. Thus, the U.S. should not stint in providing economic-military aid to the Philippine government.

The U.S. should quietly encourage greater inter-ASEAN defense cooperation. This can be accomplished through more frequent military exercises and the purchase of common weapons to increase interoperability.

Military aid should be provided to noncommunist groups in Kampuchea fighting the Vietnamese occupation forces. This will raise the cost of Hanoi's Soviet-sponsored aggression and bolster ASEAN's political will to resist the spread of communist totalitarianism.

The Reagan Administration has demonstrated its willingness to join with allies in other parts of the world to resist Soviet expansion. Similar resolve must be shown in Southeast Asia.

Richard D. Fisher Jr. is a research assistant in the Asian Studies Center of The Heritage Foundation.

"Southeast Asian issues are best dealt with outside the framework of superpower competition."

The US Should Withdraw from Southeast Asia

Stephen D. Goose

Ten years after the Vietnam War ended, Southeast Asia is once again viewed by most Americans as a remote place of little value to the United States. Despite the hundreds of billions of dollars spent and the 58,000 lives lost in more than a decade of war, most people do not know or care what is happening militarily in that part of the world.

American citizens almost never hear the common refrain of the 1960s: "Vital national interests are at stake in Southeast Asia." The spotlight is now on the wars and the Marxist threat in Central America, on the wars and the Soviet threat in the Middle East and "Southwest Asia," on missile talks, missile deployments, and supposed Soviet nuclear superiority in Europe. When attention is focused on Asia, it is usually turned to the north, to Japan's response to U.S. pressures to expand Japanese military forces and responsibilities, to the alternating currents of Sino-Soviet recriminations and rapprochement, to the ever-escalating arms race and tensions between North and South Korea.

But it is a widespread misconception that U.S. foreign and military policy underwent a radical change in Southeast Asia following the defeat in Vietnam. Those who think that the United States has withdrawn militarily from the region had better look again. While American force levels have, of course, declined significantly from wartime peaks, military strategy and structure remain much the same. The United States maintains an extensive network of naval, air, and ground bases in Asia as part of the forward-deployment strategy, born of the Cold War, to which the United States still clings. It relies on the stationing of large numbers of soldiers, planes, ships, and weapons, even nuclear weapons, in foreign countries and areas to "contain" the Soviet Union

and to further other U.S. objectives.

Containment remains, as it has for nearly four decades, the guiding light of American foreign policy, although the term has gone out of favor. "Deterrence," whether in reference to nuclear or conventional warfare, is the popular word today. The Reagan administration has resurrected the most severe and rigid Cold War thinking, rhetoric, and actions. This can be seen in its record military budgets, its unprecedented nuclear weapons buildup, its record military assistance levels, its expanded plans for the Rapid Deployment Force and Special Operations Command, and other actions. In Southeast Asia, as elsewhere, the administration has been laboring hard to build a "strategic consensus," politically and militarily, against the Soviet Union.

Though Congress and the administration have talked about the need for other countries to assume more of the military burden, the notion of America as the world's policeman and protector is once again driving U.S. military planning. Secretary of State George Shultz recently said, "It is necessary and proper that we encourage these countries that share the benefits of a peaceful and proper world order to assume greater responsibility for maintaining it.... Our goal in asking others to increase their efforts is to gain added strength together, not to decrease our own efforts...our overall responsibilities will not be diminished in importance nor shifted to others."

Trade and Oil

The United States has been both encouraging the nations of Southeast Asia to build up their military forces and, with very little fanfare, beefing up its own military forces and increasing its military involvement in the region. Despite the lack of headlines, Southeast Asia, and Asia in general, remain of great importance to the United States. Trade with nations in the Asia/Pacific region exceeded that with any other region in 1982, totaling

Stephen D. Goose, "No Retreat: America in Southeast Asia," *Inquiry*, August 1983. Reprinted with permission of the author and the Center for Defense Information, Washington, DC.

$136 billion, or roughly 30 percent of all U.S. foreign trade. In addition, $106 billion of oil traversed the Indian and Pacific Oceans, much of it through the Southeast Asian straits, en route to world markets.

In regard to Southeast Asia, government and public attention in the United States has focused on two issues: one, the Soviet military buildup in the region, and, two, the Vietnamese occupation of Kampuchea (Cambodia) and the possibility of an attack on Thailand. But these are only two aspects of the increased militarization of the region.

US Military Involvement

For decades, through Republican and Democratic administrations, the United States has tried to play the role of guarantor of peace and stability in Asia. Nine presidents, from Roosevelt to Reagan, have made clear military commitments to Southeast Asian nations. Both President Reagan and Secretary of Defense Weinberger, for example, have stressed that the Manila Pact, signed in 1954 and committing the United States to the defense of Thailand, is a "living document." In late 1982 Weinberger went on what was billed as a five-nation "tour of reassurance" to Thailand, Singapore, Indonesia, Australia, and New Zealand, touting closer military cooperation and stronger opposition to the Soviet naval buildup in the region.

"Those who think that the United States has withdrawn militarily from the region had better look again."

Early in the Carter years, it seemed that the United States intended to cut back its military forces in Asia. Then-Secretary of Defense Harold Brown noted that major developments in the region—especially the Sino-Soviet split and the fact that the United States no longer plans force levels on the basis of a U.S.-China conflict—were leading the United States to alter its "Asian deployments, base structure, and...defense posture." The highlight was to be the withdrawal of most ground combat troops from Korea. Reductions in the U.S. 7th Fleet in the Western Pacific and in the 13th Air Force in the Philippines were also contemplated.

Boosting US Strength

The changes never came about, despite the lack of significant new military developments in the region, and Carter instead began boosting U.S. military strength in Asia, giving the region a higher military priority and increasing U.S. military assistance to Asian nations. The Reagan administration has greatly accelerated those trends.

The United States has nineteen major air bases, seven major naval bases, and six major ground-force bases in East Asia and the Pacific, plus important intelligence and communications facilities in Australia. In Northeast Asia, the United States has large facilities in South Korea and Japan. In Southeast Asia, the major facilities are in the Philippines and Guam. The United States has about 124,000 military personnel stationed throughout East Asia and the Pacific, along with the some sixty ships of the 7th Fleet and roughly 600 Air Force, Navy, and Marine combat aircraft. These would be the "front-line" defense units for any Asian conflict in which the United States got involved. This country also has about twice as many men and twice as much equipment based outside the region that are earmarked as reinforcements in Asia.

If every item of the military budget is allocated to some particular mission—be it defense of the United States, or war in Europe, Asia, Latin America, or elsewhere—the cost of U.S. forces committed to Asia would total about $45 billion.

Adding New Ships

There have been many additions to and improvements in U.S. forces in Asia over the past few years, and many more are planned. The United States has added new ships, new aircraft, more spare parts and expendables, more construction money for facilities and housing, and a host of other items. The first Trident nuclear ballistic missile submarine, the U.S.S. *Ohio*, was added to the Pacific Fleet in the fall of 1982. The newly refurbished battleship, the U.S.S. *New Jersey*, armed with Tomahawk cruise missiles and new electronics gear, has just joined the Pacific Fleet. The only B-52 nuclear strategic bombers based outside of the continental United States are in Guam. Over the last half of 1983, the Strategic Air Command will replace the B-52D bombers there with improved B-52G models.

The largest U.S. military presence and military facilities in Southeast Asia are in the Philippines. The United States has 14,400 military personnel stationed mainly at three bases: Subic Bay Naval Base, Clark Air Base, and Cubi Point Naval Air Station. Subic Bay is the largest U.S. naval base in the Western Pacific or Indian Oceans. The United States has just renewed its base rights agreement with the Marcos government for the fiscal years 1985-1989 at a cost of $475 million in economic aid and $425 million in military aid. (Of the $425 million, $125 million will be grants and the remainder will be concessional loans paid over a twenty-year period.)

The Philippine bases are essential only if the United States persists in its forward-deployment, containment strategy. Their primary purposes are logistics, supplies, refitting, and overhaul, not protection of the sea lanes, anti-submarine or other combat operations. Yet recent improvements in American airlift and sealift capabilities make the bases less important. Moreover, the base arrangements with the repressive and unpopular Marcos regime make a mockery of U.S. human-rights policy.

Expanding Military Bases

The United States is looking to expand its military bases in Asia, and Southeast Asia in particular. For several years, talks have been underway with Australia about building a new naval base. Cockburn Sound and a location on the Gulf of Carpentaria have been mentioned. American officials have said that the U.S. Navy may build a base in Singapore "in the foreseeable future."

The United States has also increased its joint military projects and training programs in Southeast Asia, signifying that it is ready to fight again in that area and that the enemy is the Soviet Union. A special section on the Pacific in a recent edition of *Air Force Magazine* noted that "maritime scenarios designed to counter a growing Soviet naval and air threat are now incorporated into many PACAF [Pacific Air Forces] exercises."

The large number of U.S. forces in Asia are there mainly to demonstrate American will, resolve, and intent to honor commitments, not to protect sea and air lanes. Yet, reliance on military power has proven to be a most dangerous and ineffective means of achieving political objectives.

US Military Assistance

Under President Reagan, military aid and sales of increasingly sophisticated arms have come to dominate U.S. foreign policy to an unprecedented degrees. Weapons exports are seen as one of the best ways, if not the best way, to win friends and achieve foreign-policy objectives around the globe. Arms agreements with foreign nations totaled a record $24 billion in fiscal 1982, far surpassing the $18 billion level in 1975. The nations of Southeast Asia accounted for $3.4 billion of the 1982 total, with Australia being the largest single customer worldwide after Saudi Arabia.

On several occasions over the past few years, the United States has responded to increased tensions on the Thai-Kampuchean border by rushing new military equipment to Thailand. These shipments, which make no significant difference in the ability of Thailand to defend itself against Vietnam, have fulfilled primarily a political function, assuring Thailand (and Vietnam) of the American defense commitment. It is not at all clear that the American public shares a commitment of that depth.

During the four years of the Reagan administration (counting the actual levels for 1981 and 1982, the estimated level for 1983, and the proposed level for 1984), the United States will have signed about $6.2 billion in arms agreements with Southeast Asian nations. Australia ($4.3 billion) is far and away the

biggest customer, followed by Thailand ($743 million).

This makes the United States the largest weapons supplier to the noncommunist nations of the region. According to the U.S. Arms Control and Disarmament Agency, during the five-year period from 1976 to 1980, the United States and the Soviet Union each delivered roughly $2 billion in arms to Southeast Asian nations. For the USSR, $1.9 billion went to Vietnam, the remainder to Kampuchea and Laos.

"Reliance on military power has proven to be a most dangerous and ineffective means of achieving political objectives."

Since the American withdrawal from Vietnam in 1975, the members of ASEAN (the Association of Southeast Asian Nations—Thailand, Malaysia, Singapore, the Philippines, and Indonesia), as well as Australia and New Zealand, have undertaken an unprecedented arms buildup with the encouragement of the Reagan administration. The buildup has been prompted by the belief that U.S. combat forces will no longer fight their battles; apprehension about Vietnamese military aggression, especially in Thailand; and fear of increased Soviet activity in the region.

From 1975 to 1981 (the last year for which figures are available), the five ASEAN nations nearly tripled their combined military spending from $2.79 billion to $7.62 billion. From 1980 to 1981 alone, this spending rose 24 percent, or $1.5 billion. Another traditional measure of military strength, manpower, has also increased significantly for ASEAN nations since 1975, growing by 140,000 (or 22 percent) to a combined total of 768,000 men under arms.

ASEAN's charter does not provide for a military alliance, but the organization is becoming just that, to an unprecedented extent. Moves have been made to share intelligence, exchange personnel, exercise together regularly, and standardize command systems and weapons.

The Soviet Military Buildup

Roughly one third of all Soviet conventional forces are in the Far East. The Soviet Pacific Fleet, based at Vladivostok, is the largest of the four Soviet fleets. In recent years several developments have caused concern in the United States and among Southeast Asian nations: About one-third, or 108, of all Soviet SS-20 nuclear missiles are based in the Far East; the Soviets are stationing Backfire bombers in the Far East; over 600 fighters have been replaced with more capable aircraft; the Soviets are operating more frequently in the South Pacific and Indian Oceans;

and their operations have been greatly facilitated by access to the Vietnamese naval base at Cam Ranh Bay and airfield in Danang.

None of these developments is reason for alarmist overreaction, however. Major improvements in Soviet Far East forces have been anticipated for some time, since they have in the past been the last to receive upgraded equipment. They do no more than parallel the major improvements in U.S. Pacific forces. Similarly, the United States should not be surprised at increased Soviet use of Vietnamese facilities, because of their usefulness for the increased operations in the Indian Ocean both superpowers have been conducting since 1979.

Greater Manpower

The Soviet Union has more than twice the manpower and combat aircraft in its Pacific Forces than the United States, but its requirements are also far greater. The Soviet Union must take into account the more than 4 million men in the Chinese armed forces, and the 6000 (admittedly outdated) Chinese fighter aircraft, plus the formidable forces of Australia and the ASEAN nations.

Soviet air power remains too far away from its land bases in Northeast Asia to be effective in Southeast Asia. Even with access to Danang, Soviet air power is relatively weak in Southeast Asia. There are few Soviet aircraft in Vietnam, and the Soviet Union still has no fixed-wing aircraft carriers, which are crucial to substantial power projection. Soviet military forces have little capability for sustained offensive action against any nation in the region. They lack the replenishment and resupply ships necessary for long-range sustained operations.

"The cost of U.S. forces committed to Asia would total about $45 billion."

The U.S. Navy today, as in the past, is superior to the Soviet navy in the Pacific, particularly in the South Pacific. When asked earlier in 1983 if the balance of naval power in Asia has shifted away from the United States in favor of the USSR, Vice Admiral M. Staser Holcomb, commander of the 7th Fleet, replied, "No question, we have an edge in the Indian Ocean. We have a marked edge in the South China Sea.... I maintain that the strengths of the 7th Fleet, properly applied, would prevail over the Soviet Pacific Fleet."

Soviet air and naval forces in Southeast Asia give the Soviets a military and political presence, and perhaps allow them to apply psychological pressures, but no direct military threat is expected. The USSR would not find it militarily profitable to invade any Southeast Asian nation or to attack merchant shipping in peacetime. Soviet military forces in Southeast Asia and the Pacific simply do not warrant or justify increases in U.S. forces.

Despite the economic successes of some nations, about eight wars are being fought in Southeast Asia; some have been going on for decades. Wars in Kampuchea, Laos, East Timor (Indonesia), and the Philippines have flared again in recent years, while the ones in Burma and Malaysia have remained fairly constant. Thailand's internal guerrilla wars have cooled down, but the confrontations with Vietnam have heated up. China seems ready to try teaching Vietnam another lesson.

Burma, Thailand, the Philippines, and Indonesia are each fighting at least two or more distinct internal guerrilla conflicts, while Vietnam fights in both Kampuchea and Laos, worrying also about China and about maintaining control in its own south. The main driving force behind these diverse conflicts is nationalism, not communism.

The United States seems to be unnecessarily worried and bellicose about whether Vietnam will take its war in Kampuchea into Thailand. An invasion by Vietnam is extremely unlikely. Its resources are already stretched dangerously thin.

Most attention has been focused on the war in Kampuchea and whether the United States should continue to back China and ASEAN by refusing to recognize the Vietnamese-backed government of Heng Samrin or to deal directly with Vietnam. After several years, it seems clear that a policy change is needed. Isolating and attempting to "bleed" Vietnam has obviously not worked. It has only forced Hanoi deeper into debt to the Soviet Union and has not produced results on the battlefield.

The United States seems never to have learned the major lesson of its involvement in Southeast Asia: The policy of containment, where the United States assumes overriding responsiblity for halting the spread of Soviet influence and power and for preserving world peace, has not been effective. The United States cannot and should not play the role of policeman, protector, and intervener in Southeast Asia. Its abilities are too limited and the costs too high.

Primary responsibility for the resolution of intraregional conflicts, whether military, political, or economic, should be borne by the nations of the region. Southeast Asian issues are best dealt with outside the framework of superpower competition. The nations of the region do not want to be run by the United States, the Soviet Union, or China, but rather to be left in peace by all foreign powers.

Stephen D. Goose is a senior research analyst at the Center for Defense Information.

"Japanese manufacturing strength is overwhelming many important industrial sectors in the United States."

Japan's Success Is at US Expense

Thomas Ferguson and Joel Rogers

For a generation, unresolved trade, defense and foreign policy conflicts have been storing dynamite beneath the surface of U.S.-Japanese relations. In the late 1950s, the first flood of Japanese steel and other exports pouring into the West Coast provoked outraged cries from American producers and labor unions, and military agreements between the two governments triggered widespread rioting in Japan. Tensions mounted steadily during the boom years of the 1960s, as the U.S. market absorbed an ever-widening array of Japanese manufacturing and consumer goods. They became dramatically visible in the early 1970s after the Nixon Administration's surprise opening to mainland China and its famously protectionist New Economic Program. Nixon's actions stunned the Japanese, precipitating a crisis in U.S.-Japanese relations whose containment required an unprecedented mobilization of multinational elites in both countries. Since the two great Nixon *shokku*, however, most of the forces driving a wedge between the United States and Japan have grown stronger. Now, as planeloads of increasingly grim-faced businessmen, journalists and government officials from both countries crisscross the Pacific, warning about the consequences of rapidly worsening relations, it is clear that an explosive day of reckoning for the United States and Japan may finally be at hand.

In the United States, these accumulating pressures have set off a torrent of discussion. While no simple summary of the emerging "Japan debate" can exhaust its complexity, most analysts agree on the major issues. Virtually everyone, for example, acknowledges that Japanese manufacturing strength is overwhelming many important industrial sectors in the United States; the only disagreements are over the extent of the carnage and the seriousness of the threat to particular industries. And almost everyone agrees that Japan's nontariff barriers to trade with the United States are high, although there is dispute over which plays a greater role—cumbersome customs and inspection procedures or the more formal restrictive practices. There is also virtually unanimous agreement that Japan spends a disproportionately small percentage of its gross national product on defense, in effect enjoying a free national-security ride at American expense. And many think that Japanese expenditures on nonmilitary foreign assistance are inadequate.

But while most American observers are of one mind about the major sources of friction between the two powers, there is much less agreement on what to do about them.

Pressuring Japan

Some policy initiatives are relatively uncontroversial. While they may not have thought through the long-term consequences of encouraging the Japanese to rearm, all significant segments of elite American opinion, from Senator Jesse Helms to Secretary of Defense Caspar Weinberger, agree that the Japanese should be pressured to spend more on defense, thus taking some of the international security burden off the United States and weakening Japan's economy. And while this sentiment is often accompanied by the fear (only rarely expressed) that Japan's enhanced regional role might complicate our relations with the People's Republic of China, the Soviet Union and the rest of Asia, a consensus is forming that Japan should be pressed to contribute more nonmilitary assistance to South Korea, Thailand and other nations in the area. It is clear, too, that scarcely any American interest objects to the Administration's unheralded attempt to mobilize the Organization for Economic Cooperation and Development (O.E.C.D.) to limit Japanese subsidies to

Thomas Ferguson and Joel Rogers, "The Great Japan Debate," *The Nation*, February 13, 1982. *The Nation Magazine*, Nation Associates Incorporated © 1982.

its growing high-technology industries. Nor will objections be raised to future attempts to shoehorn more American exports into Japan.

But on the crucial issue of American imports from Japan, U.S. opinion is sharply divided. Both the shape of ultimately desirable policy and amount of pressure to be applied to the Japanese are in dispute. Once again, the business community's response to a major policy issue is split between those firms and industrial sectors that can compete in a global economy and those that cannot.

The Protection Controversy

As has been the case for more than a generation, the top priority of American commercial bankers, multinational firms, grain companies and most (though perhaps no longer all) investment bankers, along with the elite media, the big foundations and parts of the Reagan Administration, is the protection and expansion of a liberally structured world economic system. Although the mounting trade imbalances between the United States and Japan are thinning their ranks and driving many to endorse "temporary" trade restrictions (in the hope of heading off deeper and permanent constraints), these groups still hew as closely as possible to the path of international cooperation and free trade. They are perfectly willing to pressure the Japanese to open their product and capital markets, to facilitate the selling of American services (like banking services) to Japan and to sell that nation more coal and Alaskan oil (which, if the relevant restrictions in the Export Administration Act of 1979 were rescinded, would immediately reduce the U.S. trade deficit by several billion dollars, as well as provide huge profits for Exxon, Sohio and Arco).

"Almost everyone agrees that Japan's nontariff barriers to trade with the United States are high."

At home, they are happy to join calls to build up America's export capacity and international competitiveness through enhanced productivity, increased savings and greater investment in research and development. But they are strongly opposed to slamming the trade door shut. (Representative of this business faction were the so-called "Wise Men" of the recent Japan-United States Economic Relations Group, an association that brought together American businessmen and academics with close ties to Japan and their Japanese counterparts. Members included such luminaries of the multinational community as Edson Spencer, the chief executive of Honeywell, a firm with several Japanese subsidiaries, Akio Morita, the chairman of Sony, and, until his elevation to the presidency of the World Bank, Bank of America president A.W. Clausen.)

By contrast, businessmen and workers in weak sectors of the economy like the automobile industry find the theoretical benefits of free trade outweighed by the urgent need to block the foreign competition that is displacing them. For them, in the end neither increased exports nor the union give-backs and other labor concessions now being generated by the pressure to compete with the Japanese will be enough. They want protection, and they want it now.

Japanese Promises

Following a Cabinet shuffle, the Japanese government has recently promised to raise defense spending, encourage imports from the United States and investigate more "orderly marketing agreements" to govern trade with America. If implemented, such proposals would alleviate some of the pressures on U.S.-Japanese relations, but there are reasons to doubt that they will ever be fully executed. Domestic pressures may force the Liberal Democratic Party government to drag its heels on increasing defense spending. Promises to boost imports may be worth little more than the year-old agreement on Nippon Telephone & Telegraph's closed-bidding practices, which after all the hubbub yielded only minuscule contracts for American supplies. The orderly marketing agreements may end up like the recent automobile agreement, which posed limits on the number of Japanese cars to be sold in the United States, but not on the prices of those cars. Since the agreement, Japanese manufacturers have upgraded the automobiles sold here, thus avoiding much of their prospective loss by merchandizing higher-priced models, while the collapsing U.S. car market permitted an increase in Japanese market share over that envisioned at the time of the agreement.

If future agreements turn out as badly, the Reagan Administration will be forced to act, and the Japan debate will reach fever pitch. It will be urgent at that time to understand how that debate, while not entirely irrelevant, has systematically failed to identify those issues in U.S.-Japanese relations most critical to public welfare here. It will be important to recognize that rather than posing a threat in itself, the Rising Sun mercilessly illuminates major problems in American social structure and political process. Only then will it become clear that at the crux of the "Japan problem" lies the controlling paradox of U.S. domestic politics in the 1980s: growing misery for the working population amid considerable overall economic strength. Understanding this paradox, however, requires a more nuanced view of America's position in the world economy than that popularized by the Japan debate.

Many participants in the Japan debate have correctly highlighted the importance of the diminished American position in the global economy. Often, however, these critics convey the impression that the entire competitive position of the United States is in immediate jeopardy. Nothing could be further from the truth. American positions in agriculture, many raw materials (coal, for example, exports of which will certainly grow), some manufactures (notably aircraft, although that industry is becoming increasingly competitive) and service industries like banking remain tremendously strong. While the huge amount of oil that the United States will probably import throughout the rest of the century will severely strain the balance of payments, there is no chance that America will be left with nothing to sell to the rest of the world.

Equally misleading are related assessments of declining industrial sectors and lowered productivity and manufacturing growth in the domestic economy. Especially in the context of relations with Japan, it is vital to recognize that important new industries continue to emerge in the United States. In the fields of telecommunications, information processing and biotechnology, revolutions are under way—high-technology revolutions in which America is almost certain to lead, rather than lag behind, Japan. As a consequence, while U.S. aggregate growth figures may not be spectacular in the coming years, only a financial collapse could prevent some measure of real economic growth in the 1980s.

But if the overall economic position of the United States will survive any likely challenge from Japan Inc., the same cannot be said for the American standard of living. For Japan, together with several Third World countries, which are themselves challenging Japan in some important sectors, has definitely surpassed the United States in most of the basic industries that have until now made up the core of its industrial power. It will be Japan, supplemented sometimes (as in textiles and steel) by other countries, which will henceforth produce the radios, appliances, cars and other goods that were once made in Buffalo, Detroit, Gary and other U.S. industrial centers.

Surplus Workers

By itself, this historic shift would make for a first-class disaster in the United States, for it is apparent that most of the workers in these older industries cannot hope to find employment in the expanding high-technology sectors. Telecommunications, biotechnology and other such fields simply do not need that much labor. Indeed, a good deal of the information-processing revolution is about doing far more work with far less labor, as the growing interest in industrial robots (a Japanese specialty) shows. Nor will displaced production workers find much consolation in the mostly low-wage service and other auxiliary jobs that even a completely Japanese-dominated auto or appliance industry would require,

or in the other generally low-paying service employment that might be opened up by the press of vast ranks of the unemployed on existing wage structures. In addition, the pressure on these workers will be greatly increased by the reduction of white-collar and secretarial employment attending the spread of the "office of the future," the slowdown in government employment and last, if scarcely least, the arrival of vast numbers of Mexican immigrants.

Disastrous as they are, these trends in the domestic economy will be exacerbated by the Reagan Administration's bundle of tax, fiscal, monetary, defense and regulatory policies. As Japanese imports eliminate more and more manufacturing jobs in this country, Reagan's cuts in spending for Federal programs will leave workers with no place to turn for long-term assistance. The high interest rates that are the inevitable accompaniment to the Federal Reserve System's tight-money policies will accelerate the decline of America's industrial base by making expenditures for modernizing plants prohibitive. The shift to more defense spending will bid away labor and other resources from firms trying to compete with the Japanese and generally bleed the civilian economy, opening production gaps that will be filled by yet more imports.

"Japan spends a disproportionately small percentage of its gross national product on defense, in effect enjoying a free national-security ride at America's expense."

Nor will the celebrated supply-side tax cuts help. Coupled with the choking effect that high interest rates have on investment, accelerated depreciation schedules and other tax write-offs will probably hasten the abandonment of the old industrial base without providing compensating rises in employment from new investment. And the expected deregulation of natural gas will send producer costs soaring throughout the Middle West and the Northeast.

Possible Countermeasures

Were the Japan debate addressed to meeting the needs of the whole population, any number of useful measures might be contemplated to alleviate or even to surmount the Japanese threat to the American industrial and employment base. The tax system, for example, could be redesigned to encourage exports, even within the limits of the international agreements to which the United States is already party. The government could begin applying some of the same standards to multinational enterprises that many Third World countries do, driving harder bargains and retaining a bigger share of such benefits as exist for the United States. Formalizing through legislation what it is already doing informally with Japanese car companies, the government could insist that sellers in the American market set up factories here or otherwise act to preserve the value added to the goods they make by American production processes. Similarly, the United States could manage its public oil and mineral holdings with the same concern with which OPEC nations superintend the exploitation of their oil reserves.

"Business and workers in weak sectors of the economy like the automobile industry find the theoretical benefits of free trade outweighed by the urgent need to block the foreign competition."

Even more important, the Japan problem could be attacked at its source. The demand-restriction policies pursued by most postwar American administrations could be replaced by policies that explicitly sought full employment and economic growth as part of a coordinated national economic strategy. Under such an approach, imports would simply mean lower prices, not the ruin of entire regions of the country.

Public policy debate does not proceed in a vacuum, however. Given the current structure of American politics and power, we need no Metternich or Machiavelli to discern the improbability of such responses or discussion. A high-salience debate over employment and national economic policy, for example, is the last thing desired by multinationalists in either the United States or Japan. Whatever effect higher employment would have in reducing pressure against imports, such a debate would inevitably linger over the critical role that the unrestricted mobility of capital across regional and national boundaries plays in the U.S. economy. Public examination of this first principle of multinationalism would be anathema to the business and other elites that interlock on the boards of organizations like the Trilateral Commission, the Japan Society, the U.S.-Japan Foundation, the Japan-U.S. Friendship Commission and Washington, D.C.'s Japan-U.S. Culture Center, as well as to the American consultants and lobbyists for the Japanese, a list of whose names takes up forty pages in the attorney general's 1980 report on administration of the Foreign Agents Registration Act.

Preferred Solution

For these successful multinationalists, who profit from the lower inflation rates produced by American demand restriction and who enjoy the increased purchasing power afforded by Japanese imports, the preferred solution to the Japan problem will remain the same: the familiar calls for cooperation on defense and energy policy, a continued lowering of barriers to the free flow of capital and goods, increased productivity at home and steady pressure on those wage earners in the United States who are employed in industries competing with the Japanese to expect less and less. (The artistic and cultural exchanges between the two countries lavishly promoted in recent years will presumably continue.)

But if those who would benefit from a continuation of present policies toward Japan can hardly be expected to bite the hand that so generously feeds them, what can be expected of the losers, the workers and businessmen who will be squeezed out?

For workers, the situation is truly grim. The increasingly desperate state of organized labor is obvious, as is the fact that labor is best organized in those industries that are most threatened by Japanese competition. Indeed, as the trend toward Japanese manufacturing superiority plays itself out, if labor fails, as it has thus far, to make compensating gains among service and other workers, organized labor will virtually disappear as a force in American public life. Equally obvious, however, are all the limits on the willingness and the ability of unions to act effectively on the Japan issue. A few important labor leaders, like International Ladies Garment Workers president Sol (Chick) Chaiken, are themselves part of the multinationally-dominated U.S.-Japan network. (Chaiken, who reportedly harbored hopes of being named U.S. ambassador to Japan upon the re-election of Jimmy Carter, serves on both the Trilateral Commission and on the advisory board of the U.S.-Japan Foundation.) Little help can be expected from labor leaders. Another obstacle is the incremental nature of the Japanese threat. New imports do not flow into the United States in one giant, undifferentiated flood; they come in separate streams that imperil one or a few industries at a time. Such "salami tactics" make it easy to pick off unions one by one, especially when they are coupled with carefully nourished illusions that the problems of severely decayed U.S. industrial sectors are only temporary—that, for example, the auto industry will "come back" in full force in a few years' time.

Ineffective Shield

More critically, unions are not structured like broad-based political parties but are concentrated in specific parts of the American industrial machine. Accordingly, the natural response of powerful unions (weak ones simply disappear) is to seek piecemeal protection for themselves, a strategy whose consequences are almost invariably disastrous both for the public welfare and, eventually, for the labor movement itself. The "protection" thus afforded shields only a small percentage of the work force (mainly those with seniority), along with the union leadership, since such unions rapidly become the objects of deep resentment as the protected industry inevitably shrinks and the underlying sources of its weakness remain untouched. Everyone else is thrown to the wolves, or urged to move to Texas. Such unions rapidly become the objects of deep resentment, as the costs of "protection" are shifted haphazardly onto consumer (that is, other workers), who end up paying higher prices for inferior products, and onto successful businesses that lose resources inefficiently deployed in the failing industry. (The conjunction of the piecemeal character of this effort and its haphazardness should be emphasized. Were protection embraced as part of an explicit national economic policy to promote employment and growth, the government could compensate those whose jobs or businesses were eliminated and prevent enterprises past all hope of revitalization from forever wasting resources. In the absence of such a concerted effort, piecemeal protection is probably the worst of all possible trade policies.)

Demand restriction's depressing effect on employment also undermines the identification of organized labor and the poor. In his recent *Witness to Power*, John Ehrlichman provides illuminating details on the way George Shultz (then Secretary of Labor, now a high official of Bechtel, a director of the Council on Foreign Relations and prominent adviser to Reagan) played off black groups against construction unions during the Nixon Administration. High unemployment insures that blacks, women and other notoriously underpaid portions of the work force spend their time fighting for shares of a limited job pool, rather than mobilizing to secure work for all. Mounting unemployment will also probably inspire fiercer labor resistance to automation. Where successful, such efforts will affect the general welfare in much the same way that piecemeal protection does.

Politics of Protectionism

But if most American workers are unlikely to mount effective resistance to current trends in U.S.-Japanese relations, the same cannot be said of the other big losers under those policies: the American businessmen whose markets are melting in the heat of the Rising Sun. Ever since the early 1960s, when Republicans wrote an import-restriction clause into the G.O.P. national platform, foreign economic policy has figured importantly in American politics. Its pivotal role is particularly evident during Republican Presidential primaries, which regularly feature nationalist protectionist candidates slugging it out with more reserved figures from the free-trading "liberal wing" of the party.

Ronald Reagan, of course, emerged from just such a fight, and as we have observed in these pages and

elsewhere, his Administration is sorely divided over trade policy. Since coming to power, it has often preached free trade and has taken several measures to facilitate imports, but it has also sought to protect select industries. In the always troublesome case of the steel industry, for example, the Administration first raised the trigger prices on imported steel and then, after failing to dissuade domestic producers from filing antidumping suits against their European competitors with the International Trade Commission, supported their right to sue in that venue, rather than litigating within the machinery of the General Agreement on Tariffs and Trade, the Europeans' preferred forum. In the automobile industry, the Reagan Administration negotiated an import-restriction agreement with Japanese car manufacturers (albeit a modest one), something that Jimmy Carter had refused to do for Detroit even in the face of an oncoming election. The Reagan Administration also supported a new restrictive multifiber agreement, and reportedly decided in December to toughen its stance against the Japanese.

"The increasingly desperate state of organized labor is obvious, as is the fact that labor is best organized in those industries that are most threatened by Japanese competition."

While recent moves such as U.S. Steel's purchase of Marathon Oil may slacken some firms' interest in trade limitation, business leaders in the declining industrial sectors remain highly mobilized to fight for it. Consider, for example, the elevation of John Connally, the American political figure most prominently identified with a hard line on Japanese imports, to the board of directors of Ford.

More ominously, protectionist opposition to Japan Inc. is also likely soon to find common voice with military and national-security elites. Historically, national protectionism and expansionist militarism have often come as parts of one terrible package, but elective affinities aside, it is clear that the decay of the U.S. industrial base will eventually affect American security. In a country already overly fascinated with the god Mars, the protectionists' appeal to such concerns is likely to have wide resonance, however vital the importation of electronic components from the Far East will remain for the weaponry itself.

Atrophy of Democracy

It is in this general context of protectionist versus free-trading business elites that the current Japan debate is joined. And, as pressures mount in the coming months for some solution to the Japan problem, these will be the major forces doing battle, as they have so often during the last several decades, to decide the future course of U.S. public policy. Notably absent from the debate are the poor and the working class, whose fate will also be decided. For them, the drastic decay of mass participation in American politics, the atrophy of democratic institutions amid pervasive antistatist rhetoric and the failure to forge themselves an adequate political instrument all virtually insure a denial of their interests. Despite widespread hopes to the contrary, they will not be saved by Jesus, or Ronald Reagan, or supply-side economics, or the opening of refugee camps in Houston.

"Japanese sectoral supremacy will destructively interact with American domestic politics to send a tidal wave of misery to these shores."

Indeed, the interaction of domestic elite struggle and democratic decline with the changing shape of the global economy is what the Japan problem is really about. What the puzzle denotes is the process by which, in the context of the world economy, limited Japanese sectoral supremacy will destructively interact with American domestic politics to send a tidal wave of misery to these shores. That this process has not been highlighted by the current Japan debate is wholly unsurprising, for that discussion has thus far been typical of other American ventures into Pacific mythology. As many of the finest writings on the American experience in the Far East remind us, U.S. policies toward that region, while always advertised as regional expressions of "national interest" in the face of encroaching foreign powers, commonly have more to do with satisfying powerful demands within the domestic system. Now, once again, such dynamics are at work in the shaping of Far Eastern economic policy. And once again, the search for an Asian villain only distracts from the pile-up of victims at home.

Thomas Ferguson and Joel Rogers are members of the political science departments at the Massachusetts Institute of Technology and Rutgers University, respectively. They are the authors of a column that appears regularly in The Nation.

Japan's Success Is Not at US Expense

Norman Gall

Japan's recent conquest of new markets has provoked fear and rage among Western businessmen, union leaders, and politicians concerned with maintaining employment and productive capacity, and threatens to disrupt the postwar system of international trade. Yet according to the latest World Bank figures, Japan exports a smaller share (15 percent) of its national product than most industrial countries, coming closer to the low export profile of the U.S. economy (10 percent) than those of most European nations, which exceed 30 percent. Moreover, Japan's manufactured exports are less than its share of population among the industrial countries, and less in absolute terms than the manufactured exports of the U.S. and Germany. Indeed, with half the population of Japan, Germany exports considerably more manufactured goods.

No doubt Japan still is and will remain one of the world's leading industrial economies. Yet unperceived by most Westerners, Japan's economy is entering a phase of "maturity" akin to that of the older industrial nations. Thus since the 1973 oil crisis, despite Japan's extraordinary achievements in energy conservation and in maintaining the competitiveness of its manufactured exports, real economic growth has declined to 3 percent yearly—according to Japan's Ministry of International Trade and Industry (MITI), the minimum needed "just to insure the stability of Japanese society"—and to about one-third to one-fourth the levels of the previous "boom decades." Annual gains in labor productivity have declined in the same proportion. While these rates are higher than those of the Western economies, that is because Japan still is younger industrially. On the other hand, Japan soon will have the oldest workforce of all industrial

countries because (thanks to a bulge in its birth rate during the early postwar period) its population is aging faster than any other nation on earth.

An Aging Industry

At the same time, we are witnessing the erosion of the economic viability of some of Japan's key "strategic" industries—shipbuilding, aluminum, oil refining, petrochemicals, nonferrous metals—that were favored with priorities and subsidies over the past half-century in Japan's drive toward heavy and chemical industrialization. In these and other industries, the domestic Japanese market is increasingly being penetrated by imports. "Despite a widely-held view that the Japanese economy is 'closed,'" says a new Hudson Institute report, "the cases of declining industries on record to date show that at some point Japanese companies, like those in other countries, are unable to sustain price/cost differentials with the rest of the world." In the official view of MITI: "Just as Japan is being admired for the strength of its economic power, major changes are taking place within its industrial structure. The very foundation of that industrial activity which must support Japan's future economic performance is in danger." Thus, while Japan was the world's leading steel producer two years ago, a sudden rise in cheap imports in 1982-83 has taken away one-fourth of the home market from Japanese companies which are now pressing the government for protection.

In addition to all this, Japan since 1973 has been running the largest government deficits of any major industrial country, eating steadily into the huge pool of personal savings—highest in the world—that once could finance both government deficits and industrial investment. Thus savings has been following investment on a downward path, while Japan's international competitiveness is being undermined gradually by rising consumption at home, the closing of overseas markets, and the challenge in its home

Norman Gall, "The Rise and Fall of Industrial Japan," reprinted from *Commentary*, October 1983 by permission; all rights reserved.

market of imports from abroad.

The Black Ships

According to Braudel, "industrial functions are called into existence by commercial activity, which creates the demand for them; they therefore presuppose a certain level of economic maturity." Yes, trade breeds manufacturing, and Japan was forced to trade again with the West after the visit in 1853 of Commodore Perry's "black ships," ending more than two centuries of seclusion imposed by the Tokugawa shoguns. But how was Japan able to overwhelm its Western trading partners with a flood of cheap manufactured goods, of ever-increasing sophistication and quality, so soon after the reopening of trade?

"Japan's precapitalist development singularly paralleled that of Western Europe."

Scholars of many different stripes have been chewing on that question for a long time. In his new book, *MITI and the Japanese Miracle: The Growth of Industrial Policy, 1925-1975*, Chalmers Johnson of the University of California tells how the elite bureaucracy of MITI rode piggy-back on the militarization of Japanese politics and society in the 1930's to carry out a transition from low-class industry (silk, cotton textiles, toys) to high-class industry (steel, chemicals, motor vehicles, airplanes). Building on this foundation, Japan in the postwar decades became a "plan-rational state." Johnson explains:

> The United States government has many regulations concerning the antitrust implications of the size of firms, but it does not concern itself with what industries ought to exist and what industries are no longer needed. In the plan-rational state [Japan], the government will give the greatest precedence to industrial policy....The real equivalent of the Japanese Ministry of International Trade and Development in the United States is not the Department of Commerce but the Department of Defense, which by its very nature and functions shares MITI's strategic, goal-oriented outlook.

Japan's First Priority

Other scholars—including Takafusa Nakamura of the University of Tokyo—have taken Johnson to task for exaggerating the importance of MITI, for underrating the role of the private sector, and for stating that Japan's first priority since 1925 has been economic development. Nakamura has just published two major works in English on the prewar and postwar Japanese economy that provide a much more far-reaching view. Nevertheless, he shares Johnson's

fascination with the embarrassing and often unpalatable linkages between warfare and economic development, and he elsewhere actually reinforces Johnson's analogy between MITI and the Pentagon. In his *The postwar Japanese Economy*, Nakamura argues that present systems of lifetime employment, industrial investment, forced mergers, industrial subcontracting, and sweeping bureaucratic powers over industry all developed in the wartime emergency that began with the 1937 invasion of China and ended with the surrender to the United States in 1945. "To a great extent, the system which was created during the war was inherited as the postwar economic system," he writes. "The industries which were expanded during the war became the major postwar industries; wartime technology was reborn in the postwar export industries; and the postwar national lifestyle, too, originated in changes that began during the period of conflict."

The trouble with interpretations like this is that they concentrate too much on recent events and not enough on the underlying strengths that bred the great flowering of Japanese economic development in the half-century before 1929. Perhaps Japan's success, both in the prewar and postwar decades, would have been easier for Westerners to understand if Japan were not so far, culturally and geographically, from the "white men's club" of nations along the two great industrial belts that, until 1929, produced four-fifths of the world's industrial goods. The first was the European belt that spread over the centuries along the irregular series of iron and coal deposits that stretch from the British Midlands to the Ruhr, Silesia, and Russia's Don basin. The second was the North American belt that followed both shores of the Great Lakes from western New York, Pennsylvania, and Ontario into the huge but now depleted Mesabi iron range of Minnesota. While these two industrial belts developed as men learned better use of their coal and iron, Japan groped along the path of a resource-poor seafaring nation, Holland, in nurturing trade and industry.

Genius of the Dutch

Indeed, the Dutch were the Japanese of the 17th century. Like the Japanese three centuries later, the Dutch built upon an early trade in bulk commodites to introduce new methods of making ships and textiles—the advanced products of the time—in the service of a trading network that spanned the world. "The Dutch had a genius, if not an obsession, for reducing costs," writes the Italian historian Carlo Cipolla:

> The Dutch succeeded in selling anything to anybody anywhere in the world because they sold at very low prices, and their prices were competitively low because their costs of production were more

compressed than elsewhere. The Dutch decidedly moved toward mass production. In an increasing number of activities they endeavored to maximize their profit by maximizing the volume of sales. Even Dutch painters produced their masterpieces at low prices and in prolific quantities.

Like the Japanese centuries later, Dutch entrepreneurs thrived on low domestic interest rates—3 percent in Amsterdam against 6 percent in London—which made it easier to invest in trade and industry. And like the Dutch before them, the Japanese thrived as interlopers on other peoples' trade. Just as the Dutch aggressively cut themselves into the established business of the city-states of Italy and the North German Hanseatic League, the Japanese became suppliers of cotton fabrics to Europe's Asian and African colonies during World War I, while the colonial powers were otherwise distracted. The momentum thus gathered enabled Japan to overtake the British as the world's leading textile exporter by 1933.

Selling Beer to Germany

By then, too, Japan was further irritating and embarrassing the industrial powers by selling beer to Germany, silk to silk-making Italy, and American flags to the American Legion. Meanwhile, as the Dutch did centuries before, the Japanese were creating new markets by selling a bewildering variety of manufactured products so cheaply that they were within the reach of people who never could afford them before. In Chile, for example, they were marketing handsome English-style bicycles in 1934 for $8 each, half the price of the competing German model. American microscopes wholesaled at $7.50, while Japanese copies wholesaled for 61 cents in Japan in 1935 and were landed in Boston, duty-paid, for $1.95. By the 1930's U.S.-Japanese "trade frictions" were beginning to take the shape of the disputes of the 1970's.

"The main source of economic growth was not exports but investment."

In 1935 the U.S. got Japan to agree to "voluntary" restraints on textile imports and then imposed "here and there" controls on imports of wool-knit gloves, zippers, rubber shoes, electric bulbs, toys, matches, brushes, carpets, pottery and porcelain, imitation pearls, canned fish, and pencils.

Today, the mix has changed. However, even as Japan in 1980 became the world's leading producer of steel and automobiles, overtaking depressed U.S. industries and throwing overpaid U.S. workers out of work, the Japanese economy was beginning to yield to the same forces that governed the rise and decline of earlier powers.

Thus the Dutch encountered protectionist legislation in Russia, Prussia, Denmark, Norway, and Spain in the early 18th century; the Japanese today are facing the same kind of closing of their export markets. So, too, high wages and taxes began to undermine the competitiveness of Dutch products just as foreigners were beginning to make the same things and close their home markets, after many Dutch industries had expanded to meet export demand; the same thing is happening to Japan today. Again, just as cheap Dutch textiles previously invaded the home markets of Genoa, Venice, and Milan, wiping out their industries, cheaper English cloth later invaded the Dutch market—wiping out the workshops of Leyden and Utrecht in the 18th century almost as fast as they had mushroomed a century earlier; today, the same way, the Japanese home market is being invaded by cheap Korean steel, textiles, machine tools, and electrical appliances.

Japanese Imports

The point is illustrated in Ronald P. Dore's jewel-like book, *Shinohata: A Portrait of a Japanese Village*. "I'm afraid the [printed gift] towels are more expensive this year," apologizes an old cloth merchant quoted by Dore. "Luckily the dyers still had the plates from last year or the expense would have been terrible. They can't get people to do this kind of thing nowadays. They've even started sending work to Korea to be done. It's terrible the cost of labor these days."

The complaint of the cloth merchant in Shinohata bears witness to a sweeping change in the traditional economic system upon which Japan built in order to burst onto the world economy with so much force. Only recently have we come to appreciate the strength and character of that traditional system and the degree to which Japan's precapitalist development singularly paralleled that of Western Europe. In his newest book, *The Wheels of Commerce*, Braudel summarizes the recent work of many scholars by observing that Japan grew institutionally

> in a kind of anarchy not unlike that of the European Middle Ages. Everything developed simultaneously in the diversified arena of Japan as the country gradually formed itself over the centuries: a central government, feudal lords, towns, peasantry, an artisan class, the merchants. Japanese society bristled with "liberties" like the liberties of medieval Europe, which were privileges behind which one could barricade oneself for protection and survival.

The strength and adaptability of the traditional system are richly described in Nakamura's new book, *Economic Growth in Prewar Japan*. One-fourth of all farmers managed second businesses by the end of the Tokugawa shogunate (1803-64). They ran small bars and eating houses, made bean curds and candies, sold tobacco, vegetable oils, and lumber, and hired themselves out as craftsmen and laborers, while their wives and daughters raised silkworms and wove cloth and straw matting when not working in the fields. Landlords were pawnbrokers and moneylenders, fertilizer and dry-goods merchants, and owned small *sake* and soy-sauce factories, whose number doubled between 1892 and 1899 alone.

Adapting Western Machines

Accoridng to Nakamura, Japanese industry adapted imported Western machines to make them cheaper and simpler to copy and to make factory oeprations more labor-intensive. For silk-reeling machines from France and Italy, capital costs were reduced by making parts from wood instead of copper, iron, and brass; wire replaced glass and earth replaced brick. Big cotton-spinning factories could not become profitable until they added night shifts, increasing the ratio of cheap labor to expensive capital. Power-weaving made little progress until a big hydroelectric construction effort began after 1910, enabling capital per worker to double during the 1920's in the textile industry.

Preindustrial Japan was not a poor country. Fisheries in its surrounding waters were so abundant that they provided not only a ready protein supply for the islanders, but also a supply (in the form of dried fish) of fertilizer, contributing to the large increases in farm productivity during the Tokugawa era. Japan's mineral wealth was such that it was a leading supplier of silver and copper to Europe in the 16th and 17th centuries. These exports continued through the Dutch trading station on an island in Nagasaki harbor even after trade with other Western countries was banned in 1637. By the 18th century Japan was one of the most urbanized societies outside Europe. In an earlier book, *Education in Tokugawa Japan* (1965), Dore estimated that 54 percent of males and 19 percent of females had been though primary school in 1875 (as compared with England at the height of the Industrial Revolution, when only one child in four or five was ever getting to school).

So much, then, for the traditional view of Japan making a sudden transition from feudalism to capitalism as it burst upon the world scene after the visit of Commodore Perry's "black ships."...

Between 1954 and 1960 private investment quadrupled, while exports doubled, accelerating the parade of booms. In 1956-57 came the "Jimmu boom," so named by Japanese journalists because no such prosperity was remembered since the Emperor Jimmu ascended the throne in 660. Next came the 1959-61 "Iwato boom," bringing good times not seen since the even more remote period when the Sun Goddess Amatarasu Omikami was lured from her sullen seclusion in the Iwato cave.

Income Doubling Plan

By then, the historic Income-Doubling Plan had been launched by Prime Minister Hayato Ikeda (1960-64), one of Japan's legendary super-

bureaucrats. In his book, *The Postwar Japanese Economy,* Nakamura tells how the Income-Doubling Plan—which outpaced all expectations, doubling personal income in seven instead of the planned ten years—was fueled by a "strikingly large budget expansion," with public-spending increases averaging 25 percent yearly in the early 1960's and plant and equipment investment averaging 40 percent. The "accompanying rising prosperity" led into the "Izanami boom" (1967-69), when the economy grew by 13 percent yearly, harking back to the still more misty past when the goddess Izanami coupled with her brother and gave birth to the islands of Japan.

Through all these booms, the main source of economic growth was not exports but investment. From 1952 to 1970 annual private investment increased more than tenfold, financed by an enormous growth in household savings, which peaked at 24 percent of disposable income in 1974 (as compared with only 6 percent in the U.S. today)....

US Exports

Now as then, Japan is the largest overseas customer for U.S. exports, but the U.S. economy is much more dependent on exports today than it was a half-century ago. At the same time, Japan's two main markets and competitors in industrial exports, Germany and the United States, fearful of reviving the nightmare of the 1930's, are determined to maintain both free trade and their own home markets open to the degree permitted by domestic political constraints. Meanwhile, Japan itself has become a major exporter of capital as well as goods, with the Tokyo money market becoming the world's second-largest after Wall Street. Many foreign companies and governments raise funds there. Japan thus is following the historical path of the Dutch in the 18th century, Britain in the 19th, and the U.S. in the 20th, all of whom became capital exporters at the peak of their industrial ascendancy.

"The Japanese can still get along without more things than any other industrial people."

In this new role, Japan is cooperating intimately with banks and governments in other creditor-nations in attempts to manage today's international currency and debt difficulties. In addition, a fast-growing number of small and medium-sized Japanese companies have joined giants like Nissan and Matsushita (Panasonic-National) in investing in factories overseas. In some months of last year, investment income from abroad accounted for most of Japan's current international earnings. In this way the structure of Japan's balance of payments is changing from that of a developing country to something akin to Britain a century ago or the United States today. . . .

"Our" Kinds of Problems

In the process of becoming more like us, the Japanese are finding themselves faced with the challenge of managing the same kinds of problems that also plague us. How they meet this challenge will be a fascinating and fateful story in the years immediately ahead. For the incorporation of Japan over the past century into which might be called the world system of capitalism and democracy has been the latest example of the recurrent mutual stimulation between distant cultural and industrial centuries that is one of the most positive and painfully-sculpted features of human development.

We do not know whether it is still true, as *Fortune* observed a half-century ago, that "The Japanese can still get along without more things than any other industrial people." On the one hand, there is the huge increase in consumption of recent decades and the cost and welfare burdens imposed by tiny farms, tiny shops, and other inefficient economic units that have become net takers from the system. On the other hand, Japan over the centuries has shown a remarkable capacity to cut back consumption in different ways, from the practice of infanticide and abortion to maintain living standards in the 17th and 18th centuries, to its radical simplification of imported industrial machinery and processes early in this century, to its pathbreaking achievements in oil conservation in the 1970's. In its new role at the center of a much larger system, Japan now may either be trapped by its excesses or generate new ideas and patterns that could be very useful in insuring the continued vitality of capitalism and democracy not only in Japan itself but in the United States and the other Western countries as well.

Norman Gall is a contributing editor for Forbes *and resides in Brazil. His articles on Latin America have been published in* Commentary *over the years.*

"The goal is to enhance the ability of the US and China to take cooperative and complementary military actions in wartime."

China Is a Good US Ally

Banning Garrett and Bonnie S. Glaser

For more than a decade, American policy toward the U.S.-Soviet Union-China triangle has been premised on the assumption that Soviet fears of Sino-American collusion provide useful peacetime pressure on Moscow and complicate Russian military planning. However, in the past two years, the Reagan Administration has assigned less importance to China in U.S. global strategy than previous administrations. Some officials, noting the slow pace of China's economic and defense modernization and the likelihood of a continued imbalance of forces between China and the Soviet Union, have concluded that Chinese weaknesses reduce Beijing's strategic usefulness to the U.S. as a deterrent to the Soviet Union. They also have pointed to China's efforts to distance itself from the U.S. and its positive responses to overtures from Moscow as calling into question Beijing's reliability as a strategic partner.

The Soviets are not as sanguine as some American officials. Moscow is not reassured by the favorable Sino-Soviet military balance, the slow progress in China's economic and military modernization, or the vascillations in China's peacetime relations with the U.S. and the U.S.S.R. Soviet public and private statements indicate that Moscow is not confident of its wartime ability to manage a two-front conflict with NATO in the west and China in the east. The Soviets fear U.S. wartime aid to China in a Sino-Soviet war, and Chinese participation in a U.S.-Soviet conflict. In some limited conflict scenarios with China, the Soviets may be confident of their ability to intimidate China through the controlled use of conventional or even nuclear forces. In the Soviets' "worst case," however, China poses a far more formidable threat than its outdated tanks and first-generation nuclear missiles would suggest.

Banning Garrett and Bonnie S. Glaser, "The Strategic Importance of Sino-American Relations," *USA Today*, July 1983. Copyright 1983 by Society for the Advancement of Education.

Struggle for Eurasia

Soviet military writings emphasize the possibility of protracted global war that may continue beyond massive nuclear exchanges and leave the U.S.S.R. vulnerable to political coercion or attack by its previously weaker neighbors. Such a conflict could begin as a U.S.-Soviet confrontation without Chinese involvement. Even if a global war does not initially involve the Chinese, the U.S.S.R. must plan to defeat a Chinese enemy that may seek to take advantage of a war-ravaged Soviet Union by seizing Soviet territory or attacking the Russian heartland in a prolonged struggle for Eurasia.

The Soviets fear China may have a superior post-nuclear survival and revival capability and that it could pose a serious threat to the Soviet Union in a protracted post-nuclear struggle in which the technological level of the two powers is roughly equalized. From this perspective, the problem for the Soviet planners is to determine the potential surviving conventional as well as nuclear forces that could threaten Moscow's control of Soviet territory, and to prepare to defeat those forces and insure slower recovery of the enemy relative to the U.S.S.R. The Soviets thus must plan to destroy Chinese conventional as well as nuclear forces and to retard China's post-nuclear recovery by attacking its economic and infrastructure facilities.

Chinese Advantages

The Chinese are aware that they have advantages over the Soviet Union in the size of their population and the decentralization of their economy, despite the relative backwardness of their conventional and nuclear forces. China's "people's war" strategy emphasizes these advantages in conventional, nuclear, and post-nuclear phases of war. In a conventional conflict, China threatens to "engulf" an invading Soviet army and "attack the enemy's rear areas, destroying its communications and transportation facilities (including oil pipelines), cut off its supplies, harass its forces, tie them down and wear the enemy out," according to a recent Chinese commentary.

The Chinese are also preparing for possible escalation in use of tactical nuclear weapons against invading forces and for retaliation against a Soviet nuclear strike with their own strategic weapons. The Chinese Communist Party journal *Red Flag* recently noted: "We have devised and produced our own atomic and hydrogen bombs, long-range guided missiles and other sophisticated strategic weapons for self-defense." The Chinese perceive and plan for the possibility of protracted nuclear war and recognize the deterrent value of the post-nuclear threat they pose to their otherwise more powerful northern neighbor. They emphasize the survivability of their strategic nuclear systems to insure their ability not only to immediately retaliate, but also to counter-attack the Soviets "at any uncertain time"—even days, weeks, or months later.

The Soviet Military Buildup

Since the mid-1960's, the Soviets have been expanding and improving their forces deployed against China, which now total some 50 divisions backed by advanced tactical aircraft. They also have increased deployment in the Far East of theater nuclear weapons, including MIRVed SS-20 intermediate-range nuclear missiles and Backfire nuclear bombers. Since the mid-1970's, the Soviets have been increasingly concerned that the U.S. and China might cooperate militarily in wartime, thus further complicating their already demanding strategic environment. Soviet diplomacy and the buildup of Soviet military power have aimed at reducing the likelihood of such a coordinated two-front war against the Soviet Union on the one hand, and at acquiring sufficient military power to defeat all of Moscow's enemies simultaneously on the other.

"Chinese leaders have encouraged the US to expand its military presence in Asia."

During a period of increased Soviet-American tensions and a new buildup of U.S. nuclear forces, Soviet leaders have sought to capitalize on growing differences between the U.S. and its allies and friends. This has included exploiting Western European fears generated by the Reagan Administration's rhetoric about nuclear war and the planned U.S. deployment in Europe of Pershing II's and Ground-Launched Cruise Missiles (GLCM's). The Soviets have also sought to exploit Sino-American differences over Taiwan and other issues and to ease tensions in Sino-Soviet relations, thus reducing the likelihood of wartime cooperation between Washington and Beijing.

Chinese Response to Moscow

China's cautious, but positive, response to Moscow's recent overtures and its aloofness from Washington have been prompted by Beijing's perception of a changed peacetime international situation. Since early in the Reagan Administration, the Chinese have been denouncing the U.S. for being "hegemonist"—a term which for several years Beijing had reserved for the Soviet Union. Chinese leaders have charged the U.S. with returning to hegemonist policies that threaten the sovereignty of other nations and increase the risk of global conflict. At the same time, the Soviet Union has not taken new steps to threaten Chinese security since the invasion of Afghanistan—"good behavior" which Beijing has rewarded by reopening normalization talks.

However, China's tactical maneuvering does not indicate Beijing has adopted a strategic posture that is equidistant between the superpowers. China's criticism is aimed at peacetime differences with Washington over issues such as Taiwan and trade and U.S. policies toward the Middle East and southern Africa. Meanwhile, Beijing's continued denunciations of Soviet occupation of Afghanistan and its support for Vietnam's occupation of Kampuchea, along with the U.S.S.R.'s military presence on China's border, are expressions of Chinese concern about the wartime threat posed by the Soviet Union. At the same time, Chinese leaders have encouraged the U.S. to expand its military presence in Asia and the Pacific as a counter to the Soviet Union, and Beijing's deterrent strategy continues to rely in part on Moscow's fear of a two-front war and of American assistance to China in the event of a Sino-Soviet conflict.

Peacetime Bickering

Despite peacetime bickering between Beijing and Washington, the *realpolitik* basis for Sino-American strategic and military cooperation has not changed. The U.S. and China do not have identical global aims, but they each play a vital role in the other's security strategy and share a desire to deter the Soviet Union from the use of force against other nations. The aim of the U.S. in cooperating militarily with Beijing is not to build China into a powerful, unilateral military force capable of projecting its power against other states. Rather, the goal is to enhance the ability of the U.S. and China to take cooperative and complementary military actions in wartime, Sino-American relations form an important link in Washington's global coalition strategy—which includes the NATO alliance and U.S.-Japanese security ties—to counterbalance Soviet power. A properly managed U.S.-Chinese strategic partnership will contribute to this global deterrence of the Soviet Union by increasing the likelihood of a coordinated two-front war should Moscow escalate a conflict.

The Soviets will object to such coordination, but they are not apt to reject initiatives from Washington or Beijing aimed at stabilizing and improving peacetime relations. While the Soviets have repeatedly threatened—privately as well as publicly—that Moscow would take unspecified countermeasures if the U.S. were to provide China with arms, they have not taken direct action against China or the U.S. since the first American moves toward military ties with China in the late 1970's.

"The US and Red China differ on policy, but they both benefit from a mutual military alliance opposed to the USSR."

The common security interests of the U.S. and China have persisted, but the strategic dialogue between Washington and Beijing has lapsed in the last two years as each side has become suspicious of the other's intentions. The U.S. is wary that China aims to achieve a bilateral improvement in relations with Moscow at the expense of shared strategic interests with Washington. China questions the sincerity of Pres. Reagan's commitment to U.S. government pledges on Taiwan, and doubts the reliability of a U.S. Administration that has downgraded the strategic importance of its friends and allies. Beijing and Washington must stabilize their bilateral relations and hold regular high-level consultations to better understand each other's strategy—and each other's role in that strategy. The U.S. should demonstrate to Chinese leaders that it will adhere to the August Communique on arms sales to Taiwan, and Chinese leaders should take concrete steps to show Washington they are willing to advance strategic cooperation.

Banning Garrett and Bonnie S. Glaser are Washington-based defense consultants. The authors have completed a study for the Defense Department entitled "Soviet and Chinese Strategic Perceptions in Peacetime and Wartime."

"The US and the rest of the world haven't gained very much from their friendlier relations with China."

viewpoint**58**

China Is Not a Good US Ally

William P. Hoar

The Republic of China is both strategically and economically important to us, as was noted last year in *American Legion* magazine by Dr. Ray S. Cline, former Deputy Director of the Central Intelligence Agency:

"Trade between the United States and the Republic of China in 1982 amounted to about $14 billion, according to statistics compiled by the U.S. Department of Commerce. This volume places the ROC as the seventh largest trading partner of the United States, below Canada, Japan, Mexico, the United Kingdom, West Germany and Saudi Arabia. In Asia the ROC stands second, topped only by Japan, in trade with the United States. . . . Its people live comfortably: about 80 percent of the homes have color TV sets, 95 percent have refrigerators, and 86 percent have motorcycles."

"Control of Taiwan by the PRC would mean loss of American access to the central island in the offshore chain of Asian insular and peninsular states. In this West Pacific rampart, Taiwan is the bridge, guardian of the sea lanes linking Japan and South Korea with Southeast Asia, the Indian Ocean and the Persian Gulf. Keeping the island free from either PRC or Soviet encroachment is absolutely essential to the security of the West Pacific. The island has often been said, because of its harbors and airbases, to be the equivalent of a whole fleet of unsinkable aircraft carriers. In peacetime we can depend on Subic Bay and Clark Field in the Philippines. In the event of hostilities, the Philippine bases would not be tenable, if Taiwan ends up in hostile hands. Both Japan and South Korea would be isolated and in danger of blockade or attack.

This material is an excerpt from "Courting Red China" by William P. Hoar, which first appeared in the March, 1984 issue of *American Opinion*, (Belmont, MA 02178) and is reprinted by permission of the publisher. All rights reserved.

Income Diversity

Whereas the Red China regime and the ROC on Taiwan both started with per-capita income of about fifty dollars a year in 1949, the Free Chinese on Taiwan today have an income one thousand percent as great as on the Mainland. *U.S. News & World Report* notes that the Red Chinese want "the American technology needed to modernize China's economy and quadruple China's per capita income to $1,000 annually by the year 2000." Meanwhile the Republic of China is *already* producing at two-and-a-half times that figure.

Comrade Zhao, of course, wants to "reunify" the Chinese. And Yeh Chien-ying, chairman of the Standing Committee of the Communist National People's Congress, has made the same pitch to those not under Red rule. Free China's James Shen puts the matter in perspective: "What completely gave Yeh away was his offer of financial help if Taiwan's local finances should be in difficulty. . . ." This ludicrous pretense, of course, was cited when Jimmy Carter broke diplomatic relations with Taipei in late 1978 and exchanged Ambassadors with the Red Chinese— the "sole legal government of China." The Free Chinese, told but a few hours before of the *fait accompli,* were not even given the advance warning of derecognition that had been afforded by France, Japan, and Canada.

Broken Treaty

Taipei's reaction: "In the last few years, the United States Government has repeatedly reaffirmed its assurances to maintain diplomatic relations with the Republic of China and to honor its treaty commitments. Now that it has broken its assurances and abrogated the treaty, the U.S. Government cannot expect to have the confidence of any free nations in the future." Indeed, if Taipei had not sent its diplomatic files home, or destroyed them, they would have been turned over to the Reds with China's pre-1949 properties in the U.S.

Never mind that even the *New York Times* marvels at the Republic of China, reporting on January 22, 1984: "...if the island has suffered in its isolation, it has not done so materially. Taiwan is thriving economically, with a gross national product that hit $49.7 billion last year. Its per capita income of $2,444 is one of the highest in Asia. It even ran an embarrassingly large surplus of $6.6 billion in its trade with the United States in 1983. Taiwan's resilience is rooted in a propensity for hard work and thrift among its 18.7 million people.

"Taiwan has promoted trade with the rest of the world to the point that exports now account for more than half of the island's gross national product. Last year, its economy grew by 7.1 percent, well above the Government's 5 percent target. American business investment alone has reached $1 billion. The luxury goods displayed in the stores, and the motorcycles, attest to Taiwan's rising affluence. Yet its citizens saved nearly a third of their income last year, one of the highest thrift ratios in the world."

Betrayal of Friends

We have betrayed a friend; has it bought us an ally in Red China? Hardly. Writing in the *Asian Wall Street Journal,* Professor Robert Downen of the Georgetown Center for Strategic and International Studies predicts that terminating our defense commitment to the ROC could have grave economic and political repercussions throughout Asia and the rest of the world. And, the "disturbing denial of [*Red*] Chinese support for U.N. condemnation of the KAL incident last September only hints at the wider lack of political concord with Washington over Third World policy (in the Middle East, El Salvador and Grenada, to cite a few examples), bilateral trade disputes and differences of ideology and national interest. It is misleading and simplistic, to say the least, to suggest that major advances in U.S.-Chinese relations hinge primarily on a settlement of differences over Taiwan."

The tyranny in Red China is so complete that even so private a matter as owning a dog has been banned, and hundreds of thousands of animals have been drowned, strangled, electrocuted, or bludgeoned to death "voluntarily" by their owners. Had they not done so, the authorities were ready with a fine of twenty-five dollars (about ten percent of annual per-capita income, remember) and the dogs would have been killed anyway by the party's canine death squads. So far cats have been spared, presumably because they eat mice. Human beings are just as expendable. The United Nations actually honored Peiping for a population-control program involving widespread female infanticide and the kidnapping on Party orders of pregnant women who are forced to

have abortions even in the third trimester. This does seem to bother Western "Liberals" a trifle. Jonathan Mirsky, China correspondent for the London *Observer*, commented last year in *The Nation:*

Permission to Conceive

"Under the draconian birth control law, couples must ask the party's permission to conceive. Party cadres maintain tight surveillance so that unauthorized pregnancies can be detected. Women must display their sanitary napkins on demand, for example, to show they aren't pregnant. Thousands of women have been forced to have abortions. When an unauthorized baby is born, the parents' wages may be cut, and the family denied social services. Those who adhere to the one-child limit receive bonuses."

"The tyranny in Red China is so complete that even so private a matter as owning a dog has been banned."

The Chinese dictatorship revolves around the *danwei,* or unit, in which one labors. Under the population-control program, reports Sinologist Fox Butterfield, "each province and city has been awarded quotas for the number of babies they can sire per year, and the unit then determines which families may use the quota. Local clinics often publicly post charts showing what method of birth control each family is using—with a red star for those people who have been sterilized." The unit, reports Butterfield in *Free China Review* for January 1984, "is no joking matter. For in addition to providing people their jobs and their housing, I came to learn, it also gives families their ration coupons, for everything from rice and cooking oil to soap and bicycles; it arranges their medical care, school for their children, and after they retire, jobs for their offspring too, under China's unique system of inherited jobs."

Nor is there any of the vaunted social equality under the Chinese Reds. The Party is of course on top of all, but even there one finds twenty-four grades of Communists. And pay is graduated from eleven dollars a month for an apprentice worker in a factory to two hundred twenty-five dollars for a general.

Omnipresent Tyranny

The tyranny is omnipresent. As President Reagan was entertaining Comrade Zhao at the White House, word reached the West of Catholic clergymen receiving ten-year sentences for "anti-Socialist activities." And 76-year-old Bishop Joseph Fan, one of the last bishops ordained by the Pope before the split with the Communist-backed "church" in 1957, was given another ten years to go with his previously ordered twenty-one years of imprisonment. His latest crime, according to a spokeswoman for the State Religious Bureau, is ''colluding with anti-Chinese foreign forces [*the Vatican*] to jeopardize the security of the motherland.''

No freedom of religion, speech, travel, or education is permitted by our new ''friends.'' President Reagan says: ''For our part, we recognize the differences between our two countries, but we stand ready to nurture, develop and build upon the many areas of accord to strengthen the ties between us.'' *What* areas of accord? One can hardly argue with columnist Patrick Buchanan, who makes the case that ''the victory of Mao's armies in 1949 appears, in retrospect, the most unmitigated disaster suffered by a great nation in the 20th century. With this crude peasant, tenth-rate poet and crazed megalomaniac in absolute power, China, for 25 years, lurched from one national lunacy to another. The great purges, butchering millions, were followed by the forced collectivization of the farms. The disastrous Great Leap Forward was succeeded by the even more calamitous Cultural Revolution.''

Modernization Nightmare

Today's nightmare is Red China's ''Four Modernizations'': agriculture, industry, science and technology, and the military. For a while the U.S. Department of Agriculture thought about canceling several ''cooperative'' projects because the Communists had not lived up to their end of the bargain, carrying on loudly about the defection of tennis player Hu Na. But the deals are now back on line. There are ten thousand Red Chinese ''students'' in the U.S., and a plethora of arrangements are in place to provide the Peiping dictatorship with access to U.S. science, technology, and industry. Prime examples are the nuclear deals.

In return for Peiping's word that it will not advocate the use of nuclear weapons or provide them to other countries we are culminating an agreement to ''share'' our nuclear-power technology. The ''Liberal'' *Boston Globe* calls this a ''favorable outcome of the Zhao visit,'' despite that paper's opposition to America using this same technology. Tufts professor of Asian politics Donald Klein comments benignly: ''. . .there is no 'antinuke' lobby in China, and China clearly intends to use nuclear technology for a massive electric-power program to fulfill the 'Four Modernizations.' Some problems remain, but Washington hopes that President Reagan will sign a nuclear accord during his April visit in Peking.''

Reform Through Labor

Of course if there is an ''antinuker'' in Red China he is busy in some gulag learning the error of his ways under a program called *lao gai* or ''reform through labor.'' Besides, Zhao has promised the West

''reasonable profits at minimal risk.'' So one reads in the *Washington Post*, another nest of Luddites when it comes to U.S. nuclear power: ''The Reagan administration has been negotiating with Peking since 1981 on an agreement that would free U.S. companies to participate in China's plans to build eight nuclear reactor plants by the year 2000. Potential U.S. sales have been estimated as high as $25 billion.''

While our guidelines are being revised to provide upwards of one billion dollars in military-related sales to Red China this year, the Red shopping cart is still making the rounds. ''Before long,'' we are told, Red China's Defense Minister Zhang Aiping will be in Washington with fresh demands. Prime Minister Zhao has said the only real problem will be how to pay for U.S. weaponry.

''No freedom of religion, speech, travel, or education is permitted by our new 'friends.'''

The World Bank will no doubt be of help. In early January, that body announced it will triple its Red China ''loans'' to two billion dollars a year. Since becoming eligible in 1980, Peiping has been provided by the World Bank and the affiliated International Development Agency with more than a billion dollars in free loans (0.75 percent service fee) payable in fifty years. Another $450 million has come from the International Monetary Fund. The U.S. Government backs such lending practices with our taxes.

World Bank Money

John Cooper, head of the Heritage Foundation's Asian Studies Center, reports: ''Within two or three years, China may be the largest recipient of World Bank money.'' Edward R. Lim, a senior economist and representative of the Red Chinese Government, says Peiping would like to get ''as much concessionary'' (International Development Agency) funding as it can; then as much World Bank capital; and, then commercial loans. Lim says he is ''quite encouraged by what is going on in China'' and that he believes the country's leadership is ''committed to present policies.''

''Such talk,'' comments Steven Beckner of the *Washington Times*, ''which has the full, self-deluded encouragement of the Reagan administration, must have been equally common and fervently believed in the 1920s, when many Westerners convinced themselves [*V.I.*] Lenin's 'New Economic Policy' represented a flowering of liberalism in the Soviet Union.''

One hardly knows where to start in making a list of those companies anxious to make a profit from building up the Red Chinese dictatorship. American Motors Corporation, for example, has just begun a joint venture with Peiping. (Cymbals clanged, drums were beaten, and firecrackers were set off to frighten away evil spirits.) The American company will make Jeeps to be used by the Red Chinese Army, with others for export. While U.S. autoworkers are paid twenty-two dollars per hour, workers in the Red plant are expected to be paid sixty cents an hour. Then there is the latest in a series of McDonnell-Douglas pacts that was recently announced—no surprise from a firm that makes U.N. Day a company holiday—providing "coproduction" of transport aircraft.

Slave-Labor Exports

Two-way U.S. trade with the Red Chinese reached a peak of $5.5 billion in 1981, then fell, but is expected to grow in 1984 by as much as thirty-five percent. Leaders in the pack include Exxon Corporation and Occidental Petroleum (headed by Lenin's old friend Armand Hammer), which have accelerated exports to start work drilling for petroleum in the South China Sea. On the other hand, despite complaints from the American textile industry, cheap slave-labor products being shipped here are also expected to increase according to the National Council for U.S.-China Trade.

That Council proudly lists all its member firms and the deals made in *China Business Review* (Suite 350, 1050 17th Street, North West, Washington, D.C. 20036). Other traders operate through the National Committee on United States-China Relations. Their propaganda comes out of 777 United Nations Plaza, New York City 10164.

Remember that part of the ploy in our making the Communist Chinese stronger is that this is supposed to worry the Soviet Communists. But the Establishment *Insider* journal *Foreign Affairs* (see Spring 1983, for example) insists that Sino-Soviet relations will likely improve and that "the PRC can hope to extract the largest number of concessions from Washington by moving deliberately but slowly toward a new relationship with Moscow." Despite this, say these seers, we should remain very close to the Red Chinese.

Little to Gain

The *Wall Street Journal* buys part of that line: "...a friendly China can be useful in keeping the Soviets guessing." But the *Journal* remains suspicious, saying: "...we don't want to seem ungracious, and we like his [Zhao's] suits too. But something about this mutual admiration didn't sit very well. It occurred to us that, for all the pleasant chatter, the U.S. and the rest of the world haven't gained very much from their friendlier relations with China." Just so.

And President Ronald Reagan might do well to pay attention to who is cheering in his corner. For example, "Liberal" columnist Philip Geyelin has gushed in the *Washington Post* that "Reagan has probably done more than any American president to tighten U.S. ties to the People's Republic, with agreements or progress on industrial cooperation, high-tech exports, textile trade, nuclear energy and arms sales [*limitations*] to Taiwan....Five years ago, Reagan was calling 'normalization' a 'chancy game' and accusing Jimmy Carter of 'political expendiency.' Reagan now sees 'normalization' as a game worth chancing—geopolitically. And unless you think the timing of his trip to Peking in the middle of the Presidential primaries is sheer coincidence, you would have to conclude that he is no more above 'political expediency' than was Carter."

On the other side of the ring is James Shen of Free China, who exclaims: "My name will go down in history as the last Ambassador of the Republic of China to the United States. What a dubious distinction indeed!" One notes with terrible sadness Ambassador Shen's remark that America's leaders have for years been selling our "loyal friend and long-time ally, the Republic of China, down the river, a bit at a time, but down the river just the same."

William P. Hoar is a feature columnist and associate editor for The Review of the News, *an authoritative national conservative newsmagazine as well as a frequent contributor to* American Opinion..

"A strong China inhibits the Russians."

The US Should Sell Arms to China

Richard Pipes

Question: Professor Pipes, why do you favor the sale of American weapons to China at this time?

Answer: We and China have a common interest in stopping Soviet expansion. A strong China inhibits the Russians because it confronts Moscow with resistance in the East as well as in the West. For that reason, a militarily strong China is very much in our interest.

Furthermore, every time the Russians become threatening, we can draw a little bit closer to the Chinese. That's wonderful leverage in our common interest. That kind of action registers in Moscow; don't think it doesn't.

Question: In arming Peking, would we run the risk of provoking a dangerous Soviet response—perhaps even an attack on China?

Answer: I don't normally worry much about Soviet anxieties, but in the case of China the Russians are indeed extremely sensitive—almost irrationally so. An all-out campaign by the United States to arm China could trigger a violent response from them. Therefore, an American policy of selling arms to China must be carefully calibrated.

In this instance, we should put ourselves in the Soviets' shoes and ask: Will a specific weapon worry Moscow only to the point where it says the situation may get out of hand, so let us stop? Or will the Soviets say the situation has already gotten out of hand, and so we had better strike while we may? There's a fine line there. A broad spectrum exists between doing nothing and doing too much.

Question: Just how far should the U.S. go in providing the Chinese with weapons?

Answer: Broadly speaking, we would do well to limit arms supplies at this time to defensive weapons—those that would enable the Chinese to give the Russians a very rough time in case of a Soviet attack or some greater worldwide conflagration. Of course, it's very hard to say when defensive arms become offensive. Clearly, however, we must not sell them offensive strategic nuclear systems. As for conventional weapons, I would not worry too much about upsetting the balance of power in that region.

Actually, the Chinese seem more interested in technology than in hardware. We might share with them data on ballistic-missile defenses—helping them to devise systems against possible nuclear attack. I favor that. I do not favor an all-out effort—the kind that we would make on behalf of our allies in the North Atlantic Treaty Organization.

Desperately Weak

Question: Are the Chinese really so desperately weak that they need U.S. weapons and technology at this time?

Answer: They are extremely primitive. Peking's military establishment is prepared for a World War I type of conflict, but they confront a possible World War III scenario. They have to make enormous leaps. Our know-how might go a long way toward modernizing China's forces.

Question: Isn't there a danger that this technology or weaponry could also menace U.S. allies such as South Korea or Taiwan?

Answer: Of course, if you look into the 21st century, that may well happen. But China is not an aggressive power. If you look at Russian history, you find a legacy of expansion going back 600 years. China does not have that tradition.

There is no question that someday we may not see eye to eye with China. But that is why we ought to exercise great moderation and keep our options open on the arms question. Still, for the foreseeable future, our common enemy is the Soviet Union. You have to take care of dangers as they present themselves.

Richard Pipes, "Sell U.S. Arms to China? Yes." *U.S. News & World Report*, July 21, 1980. Reprinted from *U.S. News & World Report*; Copyright, 1980, U.S. News & World Report, Inc.

Question: Aren't we running the risk of being drawn into Asian conflicts by this Chinese military connection?

Answer: Quite the contrary. We may inhibit the Chinese from plunging ahead into wars. We can acquire an influence that we didn't have before. For example, if the Chinese 10 years from now were more heavily dependent on the U.S. for weapons and actually contemplated aggressive action, we would be in a position to decide whether to supply essential spare parts and ammunition. The moment you give or sell weapons you have a certain amount of leverage over the recipient.

Jeopardizing Our Relationship

Question: In your view, would we jeopardize our future relationship with China if we failed to supply arms?

Answer: You mean that we must draw much closer to the Chinese, or else drift apart? I don't think that is necessary, and I am not making this argument. I see America's relations with China this way: We have no outstanding quarrels. There are no territorial disputes. The Chinese are not penetrating into areas where we feel we have vital interests. On the other hand, our political systems are so far apart that there's no natural propensity to draw much closer together.

"China is not an aggressive power."

So the relationship comes down to this: We have a common interest in blunting the thrust of Soviet expansion. China sees the Soviet threat in a very somber light; so do we. I do not believe China is presently menaced by the Soviet Union. If China were menaced, the situation would be different. Then the question of supplying arms would assume much greater importance in the relationship between China and the U.S.

Question: If China and Russia should be reconciled, wouldn't the Chinese be more dangerous for the U.S. if they were armed with American weapons?

Answer: Actually, military links between China and the United States are likely to reduce the possibility of rapprochement between China and Russia. I don't see much prospect of a reconciliation anyway. The mutual antagonisms are extremely strong in both countries.

It could happen, I believe, only in an extreme scenario in which the Chinese perceived the United States and NATO to be so weak as to be perfectly helpless. The Chinese then might decide that they could not stand on their own and might feel compelled to seek rapprochement with the Soviet Union.

Moscow, of course, would love a rapprochement with China. It is the Chinese who don't want it. They have had their fingers burned. They find the Soviet government so treacherous that they want nothing to do with it.

Richard Pipes is a Baird professor of history at Harvard University.

viewpoint **60**

The US Should Not Sell Arms to China

O. Edmund Clubb

The geopolitical factor occupies a prominent place in the developing Sino-American relationship. The significance of Sino-American relations for the Sino-Soviet and American-Soviet conflicts is clear. The United States hopes to "play the China card" against its prime adversary, the Soviet Union. The Chinese leadership plans, along parallel lines, to "play the American card" and, to that end, would like to weld the United States with other nations into what the Maoist strategists have termed "the broadest possible united front" against China's prime enemy.

The Reagan administration has continued along the road taken by its Democratic predecessor, with some new emphases as regards both the mainland and Taiwan. Secretary of Defense Caspar W. Weinberger stated in London on April 4 that, if the Soviet Union were to intervene in Poland, the United States could impose trade sanctions on the Soviet Union and sell weapons to China. It was in that atmosphere that Secretary of State Haig made his official visit to Beijing in mid-June, 1981, to discuss, among other things, "security ties" between the two countries and the matter of American arms sales to Taiwan.

On June 13, while Haig was enroute to Beijing, it was reported that he proposed to tell the Chinese that there existed a "strategic imperative" for the two nations to have closer political, economic and security ties, because of a growing Soviet threat to both the United States and China. The day before, in Beijing, the official press carries a *New China News Agency* commentary stating that

> China has made it explicitly clear that it would rather refuse United States arms than consent to United States arms sales to Taiwan, an interference in China's internal affairs. . . .

The Chinese had staked out their bargaining position.

O. Edmund Clubb, "America's China Policy," *Current History*, Summer 1981. Reprinted by permission of Current History, Inc.

Friends, Not Allies

In a news conference at the end of his three-day visit, Secretary Haig said that his talks with key Chinese leaders foreshadowed the fact that the Reagan administration "will be marked by a major expansion of Sino-American friendship and cooperation." Noting that the two countries were only friends, not allies, he announced that the United States had decided in principle to sell arms to China, but that details of arms sales would be worked out in the course of a visit by a high-level Chinese military mission to Washington, D.C., in August, with Chinese requests for specific arms to be handled on a case-by-case basis. With regard to Taiwan, Haig reported that he had informed the Chinese side that the unofficial relationship between the American and Taiwanese peoples would continue. Significantly, no joint communique was issued. There had apparently been some areas of difference in the American and Chinese views. Nonetheless, on the day of Haig's departure from Beijing, Washington disclosed that in 1980 an electronic station, jointly operated by the United States and China, had been established in China's remote Xinjiang-Uighur Autonomous Region for the purpose of monitoring Soviet missile tests— with the intelligence shared by the two countries. The collaboration between the two was more intimate than had previously been made public.

The Sino-American policy course has been roughly charted, but it does not promise to be always smooth. As for the sale of weapons to China, the United States Central Intelligence Agency's National Foreign Assessment Center made public an analysis in early August, 1980, in which it was concluded that the modernization of China's armed forces would probably be a process spread over decades; Chinese leaders "now more than ever recognize that they must correct fundamental weaknesses in the economy before they can undertake an extensive upgrading of defense capabilities.'' And in September, subsequent to that estimate, the National People's Congress decided to cut the military budget by $2 billion, reducing it to $13.1 billion. How can China modernize its armed forces in the forseeable future, unless the United States supplies both capital and training?

Border Problems

The Reagan administration has said that before negotiating arms sales for China the United States will consult with Japan and other friendly nations. How many will be found in agreement? China has border and power problems not only with the Soviet Union but with other neighbors. The Japanese Institute of Foreign Affairs recently urged measures to prevent China from becoming a military and economic threat to the free world. In February, 1981, a writer connected with the North Atlantic Treaty Organization's Economic Directorate referred to this statement and to China's many unsettled border claims and noted that

> It is therefore highly questionable if a militarily strong China—which implies Western assistance in enhancing its military capabilities—can contribute to peace and stability in South-East Asia.

And he remarked that a basic principle of Chinese strategy ''has always been to encourage rival states to wear each other down, to use the 'barbarian to fight the barbarian.'''

"China has border and power problems not only with the Soviet Union but with other neighbors."

And this is what makes it difficult for the United States to move from détente to full entente with China. The stated American objective of welding China into the world community in a way designed to promote world peace and order is politically wise and commendable. But the Communist rulers of the People's Republic have what is for the most part a radically different world outlook from that of the United States. The evolution of current American policy vis-a-vis China and Taiwan is a potentially explosive issue to be addressed with circumspection and with regard for a multitude of related factors in the complex Asian sector of today's world.

O. Edmund Clubb, a retired US Foreign Service Officer, is a contributing editor to Current History, *a world affairs journal.*

The Philippine People Do Not Support US Military Bases

A. Petrov

For over a month now, the Philippine capital has been living, as it were, under martial law. Checkpoints and patrols everywhere in the Manila district and the adjoining areas. Riot police in full combat gear. Troops, personnel carriers and tanks standing by. Helicopters circling in the air.

At the end of September, Manila was the scene of violent demonstrations involving hundreds of thousands. The biggest ones were held in front of the Presidential palace, in Makati, the capital's business centre, and outside the U.S. Embassy. On September 21, there were fierce clashes on the approaches to the Presidential residence. Palace guards and Marines opened fire on the raging crowds, killing eleven and injuring hundreds.

Participants in a protest rally in front of the U.S. Embassy burnt an effigy of President Reagan and chanted slogans demanding the dismantling of the American war bases in the Philippines and an end to U.S. intervention in the country's internal affairs. Despite the additional "security measures" taken by the authorities, the demonstrations and unrest continue.

The Aquino Assassination

Most observers agree that the mass riots were sparked off by the assassination of Benigno Aquino, leader of the bourgeois opposition and, in the past, the principal rival of President Ferdinand Marcos. Aquino was murdered on August 21 at Manila airport when, surrounded by bodyguards and security officers, he was coming off the plane on his return from the U.S., where he had lived for three years after spending eight years in a military prison in the Philippines on charges of subversion and plotting against the government.

A. Petrov, "The Roots of the Crisis," *New Times*, October 1983. Reprinted by permission.

On the very day of the assassination, various bourgeois opposition groups blamed it on the Marcos administration, and later called for a nationwide civil disobedience campaign, including strikes and anti-government demonstrations. The campaign aimed at forcing President Marcos, who has ruled the country for 18 years, to resign. By decision of the opposition leaders, it was to start on September 21, a month after Aquino's assassination. At the same time, the opposition blocked the government enquiry into the assassination by accusing the investigating commission of bias, so that at the beginning of October every one of its members resigned. A spokesman for President Marcos declared that the opposition had no stake in the circumstances of the assassination being cleared up at an early date, intent as it was on deriving maximum political capital from it. The authorities deny having had anything to do with the murder and blame it on "communist elements."

Wave of Unrest

The present wave of unrest, observers say, is the highest since the introduction, in September 1972, of a state of emergency, which was lifted in January 1981. Following the demonstrations in Manila and other big cities, a series of attacks was launched by the armed detachments of the Maoist-type underground "New People's Army," and by Moslem separatists in the south of the country.

At the height of the unrest, President Marcos appealed to the population to maintain peace and ignore the calls for violence. He promised a thorough and objective enquiry into the Aquino assassination and punishment of the culprits. He rejected the opposition's demand for his resignation and warned that the state of emergency would be reintroduced if the anti-government demonstrations and riots continued.

The present aggravation of tension in the

Philippines, many observers believe, is not merely the result of a power struggle, but of much deeper causes: the grave state of the economy, the increase in unemployment and poverty, and the widespread discontent at the corruption and abuse of power in the administration, and the government's endless concessions to Western creditors and foreign monopolies which are detrimental to the national interests.

The present demonstrations, like the actions of the democratic forces that preceded them, also have a clearly pronounced anti-U.S. orientation. One of the principal demands is for the dismantling of the American war bases in the Philippines, these being a key element in the shackling "special relations" binding the republic to the former metropolitan country.

Pentagon Outposts

The two biggest ones, Subic Bay and Clark Field, both in Luzon Island in the north of the Philippine archipelago, are strong points of the U.S. Navy and strategic aviation in this part of the Pacific. They also serve as outposts for the interventionist Rapid Deployment Force. The two bases are manned by 18,000 American servicemen. Ships of the U.S. Seventh Fleet enter Subic Bay for repairs, to take on fuel and equipment and afford rest to the crews. Of late, American nuclear-powered aircraft carriers and nuclear-missile cruisers have called there with increasing frequency.

"The Philippine government ignored the growing movement for the dismantling of the American bases and the removal of the nuclear weapons."

The United States' "interests" in the Philippines are not confined to the military installations. The investments of American and U.S.-based transnational corporations total more than $2,000 million. American banks account for nearly half of the Philippines' external debt of $18,000 million.

President Marcos has repeatedly deplored Washington's using the "special relations" to secure unilateral advantages and interfere in the Philippines' internal affairs. In particular, there was talk of revising the status of the U.S. military bases. However, the latest round of U.S.-Philippine negotiations which ended in May produced only a few minor amendments to the existing agreement. The Pentagon retains the right to the unrestricted use of the bases. In 1984-89, the Philippine government is to get $900 million in "compensation," as against $500 million in the preceding five years. Half of the

$900 million will go for the purchase of arms.

In agreeing to the prolongation of the U.S. military presence, the Philippine government ignored the growing movement for the dismantling of the American bases and the removal of the nuclear weapons stored in the archipelago. Spokesmen of the movement stress that the presence of these weapons holds the threat of destruction to the country's 50 million population in the event of the Washington hawks unleashing a nuclear conflict.

The negative effects of the U.S. military presence are also making themselves felt in the social and economic spheres. Democratic public opinion is angered by the U.S. bases having become breeding grounds of crime, narcomania and prostitution, major transshipment points in the drug, arms and contraband traffic. The 40,000 Filipinos employed at the bases are the object of ruthless exploitation and discrimination. They are fighting for a better deal. At the beginning of October they held a general strike, the biggest ever in the history of the bases, to press their wage claims. The American command was forced to agree to the workers' demands.

Washington is worried by the rise of anti-imperialist and, in particular, anti-American sentiment in the Philippines, seeing it as a threat to its "interests" there. President Ronald Reagan's visit to the Philippines, initially planned for early November as part of his tour of a number of Asian countries, was to reaffirm these "interests."

Double Game

Generally speaking, the U.S. is playing a double game in the Philippines. While in no way curtailing its relations with the Marcos government, it is also looking for support among the opposition.

"Washington is prepared to jettison the favoured status it has extended to Marcos for 18 years...." says the *Washington Post*, "and take whatever steps it considers necessary to preserve American interests in the Philippines." The *New York Times* quotes a high-ranking State Department official as saying that the Marcos regime is approaching its decline and the U.S. would not wish to find itself in a position similar to the one it found itself in after the overthrow of the shah in Iran.

Writing in the same paper, William Sullivan, who has served as U.S. Ambassador both in Manila and in Teheran, puts forward a whole complex of "urgent and resolute" measures that Washington should take in the Philippines. In expressions befitting a viceroy, he expatiates on what kind of government the Philippines needs, and declares that the United States alone is capable of devising "a formula for political transition." "Only we," he asserts, "can lead such a transition." If this is not a case of blatant interference in the affairs of a sovereign state, of Washington's striving to shape Philippine policy and control the country's political life, what is?

Aggravating Stability

It is symptomatic that even before Aquino's assassination the American press indulged in speculation about President Marcos' "poor health," about a "plot brewing in the army" and the like. After the assassination, Washington's "concern" over the "instability" in the Philippines (an instability which the U.S. is aggravating by its actions) became especially clamorous. The Pentagon is reported to have increased the number of U.S. servicemen in the Philippines, while American banks indicated that they would not "hurry" to extend fresh loans to Manila. The Manila stock exchange panicked, black-market currency speculation assumed unprecedented proportions, the flight of capital reached the record level of $200 million in September. At the beginning of October the Philippine peso was devalued by over 20 per cent, the second devaluation within six months.

"The Philippine people desire an end to US intervention in their country, both economically and militarily."

At about the same time, Washington announced the "postponement" of President Reagan's visit to Manila. Some Western observers hold that in the present conditions, Washington would like to "dissociate" itself somewhat from the Marcos government. But there is another, more obvious reason: the U.S. President clearly fears that his visit might further aggravate anti-American sentiment in the Philippines.

U.S. imperialism's manoeuvres, both before and after the Aquino assassination which sparked off the fresh wave of unrest in the Philippines, are evidence of its unceasing attempts to influence developments in that country. As before, its aim is to consolidate its military, political and economic positions in the Philippines and secure the continued presence of the U.S. strategic bases there.

A. Petrov is a journalist for New Times, *a Soviet weekly magazine of world affairs.*

The Philippine People Support US Military Bases

John C. Monjo

No discussion of the Philippines and U.S.-Philippine relations can begin without reference to the unique, long-term bilateral relationship of our two countries. It is vital that we underline the need for a policy that looks to the long term in our relationship. Close ties between the United States and the Philippines go back to the turn of the century, and those ties include the shared suffering of World War II as well as that exhilarating moment of Philippine independence on July 4, 1946. Strong bilateral economic relations that still exist are a key element—the United States is still both the primary source of foreign investment in the Philippines and the largest market for Philippine goods. Both the U.S. Government and the private sector have played an important role in the economic development of the Philippines.

Perhaps because of our shared history, the United States and the Philippines have tended to view international security and political problems and issues in much the same way. In good times and bad, the Philippines has often stood by our side. A key element in our bilateral friendship has been our common interest in security and regional stability, as manifested in our 1947 Military Bases Agreement, our 1952 Mutual Defense Treaty, and continuing close cooperation in defense and security matters. Just recently we rapidly and amicably concluded a review of our Military Base Agreement. The two military facilities in the Philippines fulfill a vital function in maintaining regional security and stability—a role that has been noted positively by virtually all of the countries of East Asia—and that stability in turn contributes to the remarkable economic growth of the entire area.

Another essential element of the relationship, of course, is people—those American teachers and government officials who introduced English and new institutions in the early days, the comrades in arms in World War II, those members of Philippine Governments from President Roxas to President Marcos with whom a series of U.S. Administrations—both Republican and Democrat—have dealt amicably and productively over the years, the 1 million or so Filipino-Americans and Filipinos who live in the United States today and enrich our culture and society. Until last August, that number included Senator Benigno Aquino, who 3 years earlier was released from a Philippine military prison for a heart operation in the United States, and his family.

The Assassination

The Aquino assassination has rocked the Philippines. It was a tragic event that has beclouded the reputation of the Philippine Government. Many Filipinos, and not all of them opposed to the current government, suspect the complicity of elements of the government in the crime. It raises very disturbing questions that demand answers. It puts into grave doubt the competence of the airport security forces, who themselves are suspect of at best gross negligence in their duties. We do not have the answers to those questions yet. As we have stated, we look to the Government of the Philippines to provide them.

This is a matter, first and foremost, that concerns the Philippine Government and the Philippine people. But the U.S. Government has made clear to the Government of the Philippines, both publicly and privately, that, in view of our close relationship, the United States also has and continues to have the deepest concern over the assassination of Senator Aquino. We fully expect the Philippine Government to act swiftly and vigorously to track down the perpetrators of this crime, as President Marcos promised in his statement on the day of the murder.

John C. Monjo, address before the Subcommittee on Asian and Pacific Affairs, the House Foreign Affairs Committee, September 13, 1983.

At this point, we still know very little about the assassination that is not already a matter of public record. Not enough evidence has yet been found to substantiate or to rule out any of the several possible explanations which have been mentioned so far. The circumstances of the murder and the identity of the alleged assassin, whom the Philippine Government describes as "a notorious killer, a gun for hire," make us doubt that one man alone could have been responsible for this clearly political assassination.

The Investigation

The United States welcomed the idea of naming a high-level panel to investigate the assassination. The members of the commission as it is presently constituted, headed by the current Chief Justice, are former members of the Philippine Supreme Court. Opposition leaders and others have expressed concern that certain of the members are too closely identified with the government.

"The United States is still both the primary source of foreign investment in the Philippines and the largest market for Philippine goods."

Despite the international interest in the investigation, it will necessarily be a domestic Philippine matter which the Philippine authorities must carry out to its conclusion. The commission, of course, must be judged ultimately by its work. It is clearly too early now to make any judgments when the investigation has barely begun.

U.S. participation in the investigation has been limited to the FBI providing, in response to a Philippine request, technical assistance in tracing the alleged murder weapon and in a fingerprint check. For our part, we have not offered any other assistance.

The Assassination and U.S. Policy

In the public statement issued on the day of the assassination, the U.S. Government went on record in denouncing the assassination as a "cowardly and despicable act which the United States Government condemns in the strongest terms." We stated that "the United States Government trusts that the Government of the Philippines will swiftly and vigorously track down the perpetrators of this political assassination, bring them to justice, and punish them to the fullest extent of the law." We also expressed our condolences to Senator Aquino's wife and children and to his family, friends, and supporters in the Philippines. Ambassador Armacost represented the United States at the funeral.

The United States is following the investigation of the Philippine authorities closely. We have asked the Philippine Government to keep us informed as the investigation, which has just begun, develops. The Government of the Philippines is fully aware of our interest. To supplement our public statement, we have privately told senior officials of the Philippine Government of our strong concern that the investigation be thorough and impartial. The Philippine Government has reacted positively to this expression of U.S. interest.

Military Bases

Other aspects of our bilateral relationship are continuing. There are several economic and trade problems that need attention. We are also moving ahead with the Philippine Government to implement provisions of our recently concluded review of the Military Bases Agreement.

The Aquino assassination does not appear to have changed pre-existing Philippine attitudes about the U.S. military presence in the Philippines or about our economic and security assistance programs. There were no anti-American manifestations during the funeral or when hundreds of thousands of mourners accompanied the Aquino cortege right past the U.S. Embassy. Our embassy in Manila is also in touch with broad elements of the Philippine body politic in an effort to keep abreast of developments and to make our views known.

Following the assassination, much media attention has been directed to the President's planned visit to the Philippines, a stop on his trip to East Asia, this November. The White House responds to all questions about the President's travel. What I can say to you at this time is that there are no current plans to change the President's announced itinerary. Naturally any new developments would be carefully weighed.

Stability and Elections

With the assassination of Senator Aquino, the opposition has lost its most charismatic leader. Senator Aquino had hoped to return home to persuade the Marcos government and his fellow members of the opposition to find electoral solutions to the Philippines' political problems. Now that Senator Aquino is gone, the leaders of the moderate opposition must decide what they will do. The Marcos government, for its part, will also have to deal with the new political situation as it prepares for the 1984 parliamentary election.

We cannot foretell how the political events will play out. For our part, we hope that both the government and the moderate opposition will deal with this new political reality in a way that contributes to political stability, the strengthening of democratic institutions, and respect for human rights. In this regard it is more important than ever that the

May 1984 parliamentary election be one in which the legitimate opposition will have a free and fair opportunity to participate. If the ground rules for the election permit the legitimate opposition to participate, then it could be the most significant electoral exercise in the Philippines since the declaration of martial law in 1972.

Elections widely seen as fair and equitable can contribute significantly to stability and the avoidance of political polarization. It is no accident that the communists, and their armed force, the New People's Army, do not want such elections, just as they are the ones who gain the most from the political turmoil caused by the Aquino assassination. Some moderate members of the opposition, frustrated by the murder, could become more willing to throw in their political lot with the extreme left in their desire to bring about political change. The manner in which the Philippine Government and the moderate opposition leaders ultimately respond to the new political reality and, in particular, how they will deal with the 1984 election will go a long way toward determining whether political polarization will, in fact, take place.

Philippine Politics

Over the years, the presence of U.S. military facilities and how best to deal with the United States on bases issues have been an integral part of Philippine political life. Some Philippine nationalists have traditionally viewed the bases as remnants of the colonial past. Others have taken ambivalent stands on the bases, which, with the Mutual Defense Treaty, have constituted the country's guarantee against foreign attack since independence in 1946. All administrations in the Philippines have favored the presence of the bases, while their political opponents have tended to be critical of the incumbent's handling of the bases issue.

We fully understand that our vital military facilities in the Philippines—as such facilities in other countries—cannot be effectively operated without at least the tacit support of the host government and the host peoples. Fortunately, we believe that the U.S. facilities continue to enjoy substantial support in the Philippines and, indeed, throughout the East Asia region.

The Administration intends to continue with its plans to ask the Congress for the security assistance it pledged to seek in connection with this year's Military Bases Agreement review. We believe the agreement reflects U.S. and Philippine interests.

The Philippine Economy

My statement would not be complete without some comments on the Philippine economy, which has also received considerable attention lately. In the decade of the 1970s, the Philippine economy, under the guidance of an able team of technocrats backed by President Marcos, made solid, if not spectacular,

strides, with growth rates averaging 6%. Then in this decade, growth dropped off sharply, largely as a result of the worldwide recession which reduced the demand for the country's traditional exports. Most recently, with the upturn in the world economy, there have been some favorable developments, including higher prices for Philippine products, which should help in efforts to overcome the Philippines' balance-of-payments problems. The Philippine Government has been willing to take some tough measures. Moreover, the 1984 parliamentary elections, provided they have the hoped for political stabilizing effect, should significantly support investor confidence in the Philippines.

"The United States and the Philippines have tended to view international security and political problems and issues in much the same way."

The Aquino assassination had initially led to concerns about possible adverse effects on the economy. However, we have not seen indications that this event has seriously affected lending and investing attitudes. In any event, the medium- and long-term outlook is favorable because the underlying factors such as the availability of trained and capable manpower, resources, and geographic location remain conducive to growth and development.

Benigno Aquino's murder is a tragedy for the Philippines. Filipino political leaders in both the government and the opposition recognize the gravity of their political problems. How they work out their differences is, of course, their responsibility. We continue to believe that a free and fair electoral process in which Filipinos can place their confidence is the key to the resolution of the political problems left in the wake of the Aquino assassination. We trust that all the responsible political leaders of the Philippines share this view.

John C. Monjo is deputy assistant secretary for East Asian and Pacific affairs. This viewpoint is a statement given before the Subcommittee on Asian and Pacific Affairs of the House Foreign Affairs Committee on September 13, 1983.

"Aggression feeds on itself, and...it frequently visits itself upon people who thought they could avoid it by ignoring it."

Containment Is the Best Third World Policy

Noel C. Koch

Each year the Executive Branch goes to the Congress with a foreign assistance budget request. That request is one of the battlegrounds upon which the nation's priorities are thrashed out.

Part of that budget goes to foreign aid, and some of that aid is just that. Out of the pockets of the taxpayer, it goes to nations which need and want our help, and it is given freely in the sense that the recipient doesn't have to pay it back.

That part of the total budget comes to about 2 percent of federal expenditures in any given year and reflects the singular political fact that "There is no constituency for foreign aid." Providing money, food, or technical assistance to a developing country doesn't produce the votes that a clover-leaf or a dam or a defense contract back home produce. I don't say that cynically; it's a simple fact of our democratic process.

There are other mechanisms that provide assistance in one form or other—the International Monetary Fund, the World Bank, and others are instrumentalities in which we also play a role, though that role is much more convoluted than it is in the assistance we provide directly.

One major component of foreign aid is security assistance. I think it is fair to say that the most benign perception of security assistance is that it goes to help others defend themselves. A less generous and more suspicious view is that it enables its recipients to make war on others—both outside and within their own borders.

Security Umbrella

Part of this notion has it that beneath this umbrella of security assistance "America, the munitions merchant" goes about arming the world—seeking, by

Noel C. Koch, "Thirld World Problems and International Security," *Defense*, February 1984.

its own lights, to make the world safe for democracy and succeeding only in making it unsafe for humanity. And all this is done with the taxpayers' dollars—which, by the way, could be far better spent on clover-leafs and dams and housing projects.

There is a programmatic misunderstanding here, to begin with. The next time you hear a senator or congressman inveighing against security assistance and how much money it costs, you should know that most of the money involved is off-budget. It goes to recipients not in the form of grant aid, but largely as loans. More than half of the administration's security assistance request currently before the Congress is on a loan basis. These loans are made at the prevailing interest rate, with a few notable exceptions, and they must be repaid. And, with a few notable exceptions, they are repaid.

Security Assistance

In other words, the term "security assistance" is in large part a misnomer It is no more assistance than a mortgage from a bank. The bank benefits. So do we. Security assistance, far from being a drain on the taxpayer, is a revenue-producer. We charge a 3 percent surcharge to defray our management costs, and virtually without exception all goods and services are procured in the United States. This creates jobs throughout the country. This is also true of foreign military cash sales, which are a straight buy, without credit.

There are various kinds of security assistance. The largest is foreign military sales credits, which reflect most of the features I have been discussing.

Military Grants

There are also three forms of security assistance that are provided largely or totally as a grant. The first of these is the Economic Support Fund. In Fiscal Year 1984, we requested almost $3 billion for the Economic Support Fund, about 85 percent of which would be grants. The Economic Support Fund, which is administered by the Agency for International Development, provides balance of payments assistance, project aid or commodity import assistance, and other improvements to a country's civilian infrastructure. Although the Economic Support Fund is an important element of the overall security assistance program, I should like to emphasize that the Economic Support Fund may not be used to buy military goods and services.

The second of these is international military eduction and training. All international military eduction and training is grant aid. This is just what the name implies. We teach military personnel from other countries various skills. Some of this is done abroad, but most of it is done here. Along with the training, it allows us to inculcate certain values of democratic consequence—such as the subordination of the military to the common good of the nation. It also allows us to form friendly personal relationships, which often pay off as the student goes home and ascends through the ranks of his own military structure.

"If we can curb the appetite of aggression by providing others the means to defend themselves. . . then we think that's a pretty good investment."

And there is the Military Assistance Program, which this administration revived in Fiscal Year 1982 to assist economically hard-pressed countries meet their debt burdens. Until recently, these new funds were used, with few exceptions, for spare parts and supplies for major equipment provided in the past, but funds to cover new purchases are once more being appropriated by Congress.

Weapon Silencers

There are constraints on our assistance. There are types of assistance that we do not provide at all. For example, I was approached recently to provide silencers for weapons. We don't do that; we are not allowed to do it. Nor do we provide aid under security assistance for civilian law enforcement entities.

Recipients of material under security assistance are not permitted to transfer that material to third parties without the express permission of the United States Government, or to use it for aggressive purposes.

The administration does not unilaterally decide the level and content of country programs. Congress must authorize all program resources and must be notified in advance of proposed major weapons systems sales (over $14 million). Congress exerts a strong hand and makes its views known in detail. For example, Congress generally votes more money for Israel and Egypt than the administration requests, while slashing other programs. Indeed, about half of all our security assistance goes to just those two countries. The remainder is spread in various forms over almost 100 countries.

There are larger questions that deserve our consideration. Should we have a security assistance program at all; does it work, or might it be counterproductive and, if so, what do we do about it?. . .

Women and War

I know it is considered gauche to call attention to differences of gender, but I think a difference needs to be recognized. Long ago I read *Lysistrata*, and more recently I have read enough private campaign polls to know that a constant in the difference between men and women is that women don't like war. Or, at least they're the ones least afraid to acknowledge that they don't like it. Sharing this attribute with them are men who have actually engaged in it.

The point is: All this talk about the Soviets being an expansionist power is often met by women with a resounding "So what!" I'm never sure of a proper response for that. "What" usually seems to me self-evident, and so if it doesn't seem evident to others, the exchange seems to break down.

We do, however, have some fairly contemporary evidence, and some not so contemporary, to suggest that aggression feeds on itself, and that when it's been fed sufficiently it frequently visits itself upon people who thought they could avoid it by ignoring it.

Curbing Aggression

In a nutshell, and expressing the proposition purely in terms of self-interest, if we can curb the appetite of aggression by providing others the means to defend themselves, rather than by going to war ourselves, then we think that's a pretty good investment.

It seems to me that argument makes sense when we single out countries such as Thailand; this country faces a threat from Vietnam, which occupies Laos and Kampuchea. Or when we single out El Salvador or Honduras, which face a country like Nicaragua, with far and away the largest military force in all of Latin America. . . .

One always approaches different cultures and different political constraints with a sense of trepidation. Having traveled to every continent except Antarctica, I have a sense of being part of a minority—and a small minority, at that—which cherishes values that, having evolved over centuries, and having been fought and died for, and having produced wealth and choice and liberty, seem preferred almost by nature in a kind of natural political selection. And yet, we are a minority for all that, which lead one to ponder this question of preference.

If we're right, why don't others acknowledge it by adopting our conventions? I don't know; I only know they mostly do not.

So we see nations which apparently choose to maintain themselves outside the communist orbit, yet not within our own. And we fall into a cultural, political, and economic crack between communism and the Free World. Here we have a dilemma.

Helping Friendly Governments

The primary purpose of security assistance is to help friendly governments challenged by external threats. Frequently, however, internal pressures stemming from domestic tensions—ethnic, religious, regional, racial—also threaten these governments. And these internal problems are not helped by purchasing expensive weapons or otherwise burdening fragile economies with defense expenditures.

"The primary purpose of security assistance is to help friendly governments challenged by external threats."

Such situations are further aggravated when the ruling group feels it necessary to reward or appease the military with excessive salaries or extravagant military purchases not truly required by the threat to national security, which drain off scarce resources that could be used for development. Thus, we need to avoid a process of circular causation in which the effort to provide security ironically produces economic problems which contribute to greater instability.

Tailoring Arms Sales

Our challenge is to tailor our security assistance so that it is sufficient to the requirements of any real external threat and yet conducive to a peaceful and productive amelioration of internal instabilities. We are looking at a number of ways to meet this challenge.

By the end of the Carter administration, there were no grant Military Assistance Program funds for Africa. Our Fiscal Year 1984 request was for more than four-fifths Military Assistance Program money. We have sharply reduced, and plan to eliminate entirely, foreign military sales credit for countries, such as those in Africa, which cannot afford it. We seek to meet legitimate needs through the Military Assistance Program.

There are proposals being readied to move security assistance on-budget and thus inflict the discipline of the budget on ourselves, rather than creating credit card armies for those who cannot afford the payments.

In the Pentagon, we are looking very closely at how we can direct security assistance toward civic action: nation-building by the military elements of our assistance recipients. This would mean less emphasis on lethal systems and more on the hardware and the skills that can build roads, dig wells, clear land for planting, rebuild ports and harbors, and generally contribute to the economic infrastructure of the nation, all within the service of its real security. Out of this should come skills transferable to civilian employment. Out of it should come a new sense of the relationship between the military and the people—so they are seen truly as protectors and contributors rather than as privileged parasites.

Former Soviet Clients

We are looking for ways to help our friends who used to be Soviet clients take the equipment they have and restore it, rather than buying new equipment. This increasingly finds us in the seemingly fantastic situation of saying, "Why don't we see if we can fix those East German trucks you bought when you were cozy with the Soviets, rather than buying nice, shiny new, expensive American trucks." They don't believe what they are hearing. Some of our defense contractors probably wouldn't believe it, either.

But the point is we do not fit the stereotyped image of the arms merchant, and we are trying to help our friends defend themselves and not help them destroy themselves.

We must, all of the above notwithstanding, acknowledge that many nations are threatened and, being threatened, deserve and ought to have the means to defend themselves.

So the real issue is how to provide those means. We believe, in spite of the criticism—much of which is well-founded, and all of which is well-intentioned—that on balance, America's record in this arena is a good one.

Non-Alignment

To put that record in perspective, we must see that we are dealing with nations that most frequently want genuinely to remain non-aligned, nations which are understandably touchy about matters of sovereignty, and nations which are not always well equipped to manage all those elements of a security assistance relationship which they would like to have.

Many see a modern, heavily-equipped military not merely as a defense requirement, but as a symbol of nationhood—like a national airline, for example, and just as costly. To argue against acquiring such a symbol is often seen as an argument against the country's very right to nationhood, and in the Third World, this is a delicate thing.

One of the standard arguments we hear in favor of providing security assistance, where objective considerations seem to mitigate against it, is that if we don't provide it, the nation will go to the Soviets for help. I'm frequently skeptical of this argument and its implicit threat, but taking it at face value, and looking at the matter outside the parameters of East-West competition—looking at it in terms of the interests of the aid recipient—we can ask why is it better for us to provide assistance than to abandon the ground to the Soviets.

US vs. USSR Objectives

There are distinct differences in the objectives of the two powers and the ways they run their assistance programs. Those differences go to the heart of the question of non-alignment, or neutrality.

The Soviet objective is to create through security assistance a profound degree of dependence on the part of the aid recipient. This is accomplished in several ways. One is by not teaching the recipients how to maintain the equipment provided to them. Thus, maintenance can only be carried out by Soviet technicians, and this in turn requires that a large number of technicians be permitted into the country. They come with the hidden mission of exerting their influence throughout the recipients' military, political, and social affairs. By sheer force of numbers, they frequently succeed.

Another method of maintaining dependence is to stock in-country only the most limited supplies of spare parts and repair items. Major maintenance requires requisitioning on a case-by-case, as-needed basis or returning the equipment to the Soviet Union or Eastern bloc nations. The result of this approach is that should the relationship be broken, the departing Soviets leave behind a military force whose equipment is almost immediately useless. Africa is a virtual junkyard of Soviet equipment resulting from this doctrine. So while the host government may become disenchanted with their relationship with the Soviets, it takes a considerable measure of courage to get them to leave. It means going back and beginning again the effort to build their forces.

Insidious Loans

Finally, I noted earlier that the United States usually requires payment for its hardware and other assistance. So do the Soviets...but their approach is insidious. They often offer long grace periods with seemingly low rates of interest. But in, say, eight or ten years when the bills come due for equipment that often is obsolete or obsolescent by then (and may have been when it was initially transferred), the Soviets demand cash on the barrelhead. Unlike Western nations which will roll over debts or provide bridging loans, the Soviets demand hard currency or quid pro quos such as recasting the debtor's governmental system along the Soviet model, access

to natural resources, fishing rights, disadvantageous trade arrangements, or allowing the establishment or expansion of Soviet military bases. The relationship rapidly becomes analogous to that between migrant workers and the company store. The end result is de facto slavery.

Let me briefly describe the plight of Ethiopia and Angola, two of the major beneficiaries of Soviet assistance. Both nations are plagued by civil wars that scream out for diplomatic resolution. Were the United States the benefactor of these nations, I can assure you we would be limiting military aid while pushing hard for meaningful negotiations. We do this routinely; indeed, it is what we did in the 1960s and 1970s when Haile Selassie ruled Ethiopia.

The Soviets, on the other hand, have turned the military aid spigot wide open, leading their clients in Luanda and Addis Ababa to seek spectral military victories. In point of fact, the military situation is steadily worsening in both countries.

A Debt to the Soviets

The Angolans pay for this equipment and the well-fed Cubans who accompany it with much of their oil revenues while normal municipal services are becoming a thing of the past and people literally fight for scraps of food in the street. Ethiopia is not blessed with oil; it is saddled with an ever growing debt to the Soviets that will take generations to pay off. However, this is a burden that many Ethiopian children will never have to bear since dozens of them starve to death every day.

"Out of it should come a new sense of the relationship between the military and the people—so they are seen truly as protectors and contributors."

Meanwhile the Soviets are ensconced along the Red Sea and in the South Atlantic, the two main routes for Persian Gulf oil to flow to Western Europe and the United States. What will happen if Angolan or Ethiopian leaders decide the price isn't worth the candle and try to oust the Soviets as Sadat and Nimieri courageously did in the past? They will look around and see thousands upon thousands of Cuban combat troops and remember the fate of Maurice Bishop.

Noel C. Koch served as a special assistant to Presidents Nixon and Ford and is a former assistant to the postmaster general.

"The Third World demonstrates vividly that containment is the wrong policy for the wrong time."

Containment Is Not the Best Third World Policy

Robert Armstrong

In his address to the United Nations in September 1983, President Reagan—echoing John Foster Dulles—urged the world to choose sides between the United States and the Soviet Union: "The members of the United Nations must be aligned on the side of justice rather than injustice, peace rather than aggression, human dignity rather than subjugation."

However well this Manichean view of the world may have served to structure U.S. foreign policy in the 1950s, it is foolish and dangerous in 1983. The Soviet Union is no more the embodiment of evil than the United States is of good: both are societies with great accomplishments and grave flaws. It is precisely these fallacious moral absolutes that make the world so dangerous. If one nation in the nuclear age declares another to be evil, its destruction becomes easier to justify. The relations between great powers are delicate, and the rhetoric of "good and evil," and "us and them" are of little help in managing them.

Worse than just politically reckless, this notion is bankrupt as a framework for international relations. The world will not be divided into two halves again. Bipolarity ignores the political and economic realities of the rest of the world: Africa, Asia, the Middle East, Latin America and the Caribbean—the so-called Third World—and the other industrialized powers of Europe and Japan.

At this moment in history, many of those nations refuse to take up battle positions on one side or another of what they regard as an artificial divide. For over 20 years Third World nations have worked together to build a framework for international relations which avoids the trap of U.S./Soviet conflict. Their vision has given precedence to their common problems of hunger and poverty and their common desire to give the concept of human rights concrete

"Containment and the Third World," Robert Armstrong, *NACLA: Report on the Americas*, November/December 1983. Reprinted by permission of The North American Congress on Latin America, 151 W. 19 St., New York, NY 10011.

meaning for their inhabitants. In Europe and Japan, political leaders demand a world in which the economic and political realities of their nations are not reduced to weapons in a terminal confrontation between the superpowers. No amount of rosy joint communiques from the summit meetings of Western leaders can disguise this tension.

The Rise of the Third World

Future historians will probably regard as the most important event of the turbulent 20th century the emergence as new nations of the former colonies and neo-colonies of Europe and the United States. Before World War II, the countries of Africa, Asia and much of the Near East were European colonies. The Caribbean islands belonged to Britain, France, the Netherlands or the United States. Latin American nations, though formally independent, functioned as neo-colonies of the United States.

With the end of the war, the colonial empires of Europe collapsed. During the next thirty years new nations emerged from the old colonies in a wave of nationalism which rivalled in significance the birth of the European nations in the 16th and 17th centuries. But this new nationalism confronted a world in which the U.S. and the Soviets faced each other in a deadly game—one in which, at least according to the players in Washington, there was no room for spectators.

With considerable diplomatic adroitness and political courage, the new nations found ways to stay on the sidelines. Unlike the European nation states of three hundred years earlier, they put aside many of their own differences, sought common counsel and forged a new internationalism. Today, those principles find expression in the Non-Aligned Movement, the Group of 77 and—above all—the United Nations.

After World War II, the United States was well-positioned to take advantage of the demise of the

European empires. On one hand, it enjoyed vast economic and industrial resources; on the other, it was not burdened by a long colonial heritage. Hard as it may be to believe today, in 1945 the United States was widely perceived as an anti-colonial, anti-imperialist power. Ho Chi Minh, the founding father of Vietnam, modeled his country's declaration of independence from French colonialism on the American Declaration of Independence. With its own historical memory of British colonialism, the United States was leery of keeping colonies in the European manner. When it acquired Cuba, the Philippines and Puerto Rico in the wake of the 1898 Spanish-Cuban-American War, there was debate within elite circles over the legality of possessing colonies under the U.S. Constitution. In 1904, the United States granted Cuba independence, while retaining the right—in what would become the classic style of indirect colonialism—to veto any laws it did not care for. In 1946, it granted political independence to the Philippines and in the same period encouraged a limited exercise of local autonomy for Puerto Rico.

Obsession with Communism

But the obsession of the United States with international communism and the concomitant expansion of U.S. global influence robbed the American image of its lustre. CIA adventures in Iran and Guatemala, U.S. support for the French in Vietnam, the anti-colonial uprising in Puerto Rico in 1950 and Dulles' rigid demand that the world's nations should define themselves for or against "Godless communism" chilled the enthusiasm of the emerging nations for U.S. tutelage. Instead, they looked to each other for solutions outside the constraints of the U.S./Soviet confrontation.

"The Reagan Administration... approach to the Third World is in the classic tradition of 'divide-and-conquer.'"

The seeds of this new initiative were planted in Bandung, Indonesia in 1955 when 29 former colonies met for the first time in the absence of the European powers and the United States. Most historians credit three men with leading the process of giving a voice to the decolonized world; they were Yogoslavian president Josip Broz—better known as Tito—Jawaharlal Nehru, prime minister of India and Gamal Abdel Nasser, the president of Egypt. From their joint discussions and continuing talks with leaders of the new nations came a new doctrine called nonalignment.

What the three leaders desired was the diplomatic means to avoid Cold War alignment without per se creating a Third World bloc, a nationalist agenda of

radical social content with major international influence. Each of the three premiers had different reasons for carving out an international position beyond the U.S. and Soviet umbrella.

Reducing Superpower Tension

In Yugoslavia, Tito had broken with Stalin and maintained a pro-Western foreign policy. After Stalin's death, under Khrushchev's doctrine of peaceful coexistence, Tito reasoned that Yugoslavia's security would be best served by reducing superpower tensions.

India's leaders, meanwhile, regarded their country as a major world power, less by virtue of any economic or military strength than from its moral force—in great part the legacy of Gandhi. Major power status and the obligations of morality obliged India, said Nehru, to an "independent policy."

Nasser had come to power in 1954 after a military coup two years earlier had ovethrown a corrupt monarchy. Wishing to escape from traditional patterns of Western domination without being absorbed into the Soviet camp, Egypt was searching for political and economic changes to benefit its impoverished population. It desired no role in the superpower face-off and had no pretensions to global power itself—a pragmatic attitude more typical of other post-colonial nations.

By the end of the decade, tensions between the Soviets and the United States had worsened with the "U-2 Incident" in which a CIA spy plane was shot down. The election debate between Richard Nixon and John F. Kennedy centered on missile gaps and getting tough with Castro. Events in Africa in 1960 gave early warning of the importance of the New Third World nations. Sixteen nations became independent and joined the U.N. In South Africa, police had killed 67 blacks and wounded nearly 200 at Sharpeville. In the Congo, the post-independence government had collapsed and the U.N. had been required to intervene. In Algeria, a fierce guerrilla war continued against the French.

Tito visited Africa early in 1961 and found support for a meeting of like-minded radical nationalist states. Invitations went to leaders of 17 nations to attend a preliminary meeting in Cairo; from that emerged a conference in Belgrade, Yugoslavia, attended by the leaders of 25 countries, from September 16, 1961—the first meeting of the Movement of Non-Aligned Nations.

Non-Alignment

Since then the Movement has held six full summit meetings, and since the mid-1970s there have been annual meetings at the ministerial level. A permanent executive, the Coordinating Bureau, was established in 1970 and later mandated to coordinate an informal caucus at the United Nations. An official spokesperson (currently Indira Gandhi) holds the position for the three years between summits. As originally formulated, non-alignment meant the "assertion of state sovereignty in Afro-Asia," but over the years the term has come to cover nations in the Middle East and Latin America. Its foreign policy is "peaceful coexistence, equal state relations, cooperation for development and an end to colonialism."

Conservative critics of the movement accuse it of being no more than a repeat of the 19th century notion of diplomatic neutrality. Sympathizers counter that more than a diplomatic position, non-alignment is an ideology. For some nations, it may be better described as a "counter-ideology to the pressures from the 'Free World' and the 'Socialist system.'" For others, it is a way of managing internal political stress.

Unlike classic neutrality, argues Peter Willets in his book *The Non-Aligned Movement: The Origins of Third World Alliance,* the term does not suggest a passive, isolationist policy of non-involvement. It opposes the Cold War, supports anti-colonial struggles and has taken sides in disputes between the developed and developing worlds. To accept the Cold War as inevitable, say the non-aligned, is "[a] view [which] reflects a sense of hopelessness and helplessness." Yet even in the Cold War, the non-aligned may side with one superpower or another, provided each issue is decided "on the merits" and not as a matter of bloc support. In short, non-alignment is an active position.

The Group of 77

While the Non-Aligned Movement has concerned itself with a new international political order, its economic counterpart has been the Group of 77. The Group derives its name from the 77 Third World countries which lobbied at the U.N. General Assembly in 1962 to win the convocation of what came to be known as UNCTAD—the U.N. Conference on Trade and Development. Over 100 countries now consider themselves to be part of the Group of 77.

UNCTAD's first meeting in 1964 set the tone for the strained, sometimes angry, North-South dialogue which has persisted ever since. With the prolonged global recession of recent years, the troubled and inconclusive search for a more equitable distribution of the world's wealth has grown even more urgent. From it has emerged the plea from the countries of the South for a New International Economic Order (NIEO).

In the view of the Group of 77, the prevailing economic order is obsolete and unjust. They argue that internal reforms are essential in the developing countries, that the international division of labor must be reorganized to give the Third World greater control over its resources, and that the activities of transnational corporations must be regulated. Under the NIEO any nation will have the right to choose its own economic system without interference or external threat—including the right to regulate, expropriate or nationalize foreign investment.

The U.N. and the Third World

The United Nations has become the most important and prestigious forum for the views of the Third World. As conceived by Roosevelt and Churchill during World War II, the U.N. was to be a forum in which all nations would participate through a body called the General Assembly. World security, however, would be guaranteed by five nations—the United States, Great Britain, France, China and the Soviet Union—acting through a smaller body, the Security Council, in accordance with traditional spheres of influence. Post-war reality failed to support that conception, however: Britain lost its status as a world power; Western influence in China ended with Mao Zedong's communist triumph. Antagonism between Moscow and Washington essentially created two spheres of influence.

"From the perspective of containment, countries were little more than arenas for East-West confrontation, chess pieces in that larger game."

In the relative stalemate that ensued, the new nations came to see the U.N. as the best vehicle for placing a new agenda before the world. In 1960, the U.N. General Assembly passed a crucial resolution calling for worldwide decolonization; later resolutions fixed a timetable for decolonization and established the machinery for holding the colonial powers accountable. The number of U.N. members swelled and so did the influence of the Third World nations.

They expressed that influence primarily in the General Assembly, where the principle of 'one state, one vote' operates. Real power still resides in the Security Council: though its numbers have grown, the five original members still have veto power. Nonetheless, in diplomatic circles appearances count for much. General Assembly resolutions cannot simply be ignored, and behind recent U.S. attacks on the U.N. lies the realization that this country has lost the ability to control the institution it created.

Through the United Nations, the Non-Aligned Movement and the Group of 77 have been able to act as distinct groups with a high degree of cohesion, especially on broad North-South issues. It is their resolutions which have kept the questions of the Cold War, disarmament and anti-colonialism at the forefront of the U.N.'s concerns. Tensions among Third World nations, including East-West tensions, have caused the influence of the Non-Aligned Movement to ebb and flow, especially now when there is sharp internal debate over its tilt to the Soviet Union. Yet its role as an autonomous pole in international relations is of greater importance than ever.

> ## "Divide-and-conquer is indeed a staple US response to the Third World challenge."

For the Third World, U.S. foreign policy since World War II has been a consistently depressing affair. When not trying to subvert them, U.S. foreign policy has tended to ignore Third World efforts to find a common stance on political and economic issues. The easiest course has been to deny the existence of the Third World as a category, a political force or an expression of human needs. From the perspective of containment, countries were little more than arenas for East-West confrontation, chess pieces in that larger game where a country could be 'lost' even if it professed non-alignment.

Soviet foreign policy, meanwhile, understood early on the significance and power of this new force and sought its support and friendship—undoubtedly with one eye on its conflict with the United States. Khrushchev himself proposed the decolonization resolution in the 15th session of the General Assembly in 1960. And in its approaches to the Third World, the Soviet Union was not burdened by the legacy of colonialism and neo-colonialism. Its example of rapid industrial development out of conditions of poverty which any African or Latin American would have recognized fascinated Third World leaders.

To be sure, there is diversity within the Third World, just as repeated U.S. administrations have asserted: it contains large, wealthy countries and small, destitute ones; some are blessed with natural resources, others have none; in some, tiny elites control the wealth, in others there is more equitable distribution. Speaking at the Non-Aligned Summit in Havana in 1979, Tanzanian president Julius Nyerere admitted that within the Group of 77, "We are not all friends. Some countries represented here are at war with one another. Our per capita income varies from $100 to $2,000 per year. Some of us have minerals; others, none. Some lack access to the sea; others are isolated by enormous oceans." But, Nyerere warned, "Divide-and-conquer is an old technique of domination. The industrialized countries are aware of its utility."

Divide and Conquer

Divide-and-conquer is indeed a staple U.S. response to the Third World challenge. After the oil embargo in 1973, the United States set about dividing OPEC while offering selective concessions to member countries. But the oil crisis, coupled with the decline of the U.S. economy relative to its principal Western competitors, showed up the fact that the West was no longer a political or economic monolith. The 1970s brought new tests for both the Atlantic Alliance and U.S.-Japanese relations. The European countries increased their trade with the Soviet Union, while Japanese products penetrated deep into the U.S. economy. The United States and its Western allies had divergent strategies for dealing with the South. One initiative came from the United States itself— from within the elite but outside the prevailing administration consensus. That was the Trilateral Commission, whose fate has already been discussed.

Increasing Arms Flows

How has the Reagan Administration responded to these shifting realities? Its approach to the Third World is in the classic tradition of "divide-and-conquer." It has stressed bilateral negotiations; it increases arms flows and training to local armies; it invokes the "magic of the marketplace" when asked what is to be done. It ferociously asserts the old order and is prepared to defend it with military force. Its answer to the Third World is, "Do it our way or else!"

It is still not clear how this intransigence and the new Cold War will affect the North-South dialogue, but U.S. policy shows every sign of wanting to destroy it. The position of the Third World, meanwhile, is scarcely at its brightest. Its internal unity is strained for a variety of reasons. The effectiveness of oil as a weapon has declined; wars between Third World nations create unpredictable problems; the gap between the resource-rich and resource-poor countries of the Third World has widened, and there is serious discord over the role of the Soviet Union in Third World affairs.

But the questions of world peace and social justice which gave birth to Third World cooperation are still the most pressing questions on the world's agenda, and they will remain so until the end of the century. The Third World demonstrates vividly that containment is the wrong policy for the wrong time. International relations will never again be reduced to the simplicities of 1946; today, the interdependence of the world is not a question of polemics: it is a question of reality.

Robert Armstrong is a member of the research staff of The North American Congress On Latin America (NACLA). Founded in 1966, NACLA is an independent non-profit organization focusing on the political economy of the Americas.

"Commercial contacts established by the West have improved material conditions out of all recognition over much of the Third World."

viewpoint**65**

US Influence Helps the Third World

Gerald R. Zoffer

One of the most awesomely expensive undertakings of our times, still growing in terms of disbursements with no end in sight, is the program of Western aid to the so-called Third World.

In its early beginnings, the Third World aid program was incorporated in President Truman's Message to Congress in January 1949. Point Four of that Message called for Western aid to underdeveloped countries. A simple enough, practical undertaking hardly intended to jar the sensibilities of economically better-off nations. Nevertheless, there was an implication involved that didn't register at the time.

As Prof. P.T. Bauer points out in his excellent and detailed study of the Third World aid program, *Equality, the Third World and Economic Delusion,* "Point Four was an early instance of lumping together the non-Western world into one aggregate or collectivity."

An egalitarian point of view seized the leaders of the advanced nations, and by the 1970s large-scale and practically unconditional wealth transfers came to be widely regarded as a matter of right of the recipients, with the recently issued Brandt Report a highwater mark in the insistence of large-scale transfers to the Third World.

Two Worlds

The simplistic view is that there are two worlds, the "haves" and the "have-nots." The "have-nots" are said to comprise fully two-thirds of the world's population. The names of Third World countries have been thrown around with enough abandon to make it unnecessary to list them here, but basically they are located in underdeveloped parts of Africa, Asia and Latin America.

Gerald R. Zoffer, "Fables and Truths about Aid to the Third World," *Human Events*, March 6, 1982. Reprinted by permission.

The overall picture Western media have given us of these countries is one of unremitting poverty, wretchedness, hunger and despair, all the result of Western neglect. The subliminal message is that the "poor" have the right to siphon off the wealth of the "rich" in order to smooth out the social injustices that have accumulated between the two worlds.

As part of its fallacious approach, Third World aid takes no note of the difference between people in their ability to earn money. We readily accept differences between people in terms of their artistic, intellectual, musical and athletic abilities, but not on their economic ability. As a result, many are convinced that those with high incomes have come by them via exploitation rather than by effort.

Income Differences

Extend this notion and you have the concept that "rich" nations have become so by exploiting others. This is a common Communist claim, but in an aside, Prof. Bauer points out that "the differences in income and living standards are quite as pronounced [under communism] as in some market-oriented societies—and this after more than half a century of mass coercion."

There are some basic simplistic notions that have been propounded over the years that deserve comment and rebuttal. Former head of the World Bank Robert McNamara has averred that "the greatest single obstacle to the economic and social advancement of the majority of peoples in the underdeveloped world is rampant population growth."

Retorts Bauer: "The recent rapid increase in population in less-developed countries reflects a steep fall in morality. This represents a substantial improvement in conditions, since people value a longer life."

Population and Poverty

McNamara is unable to reconcile the rapid population increase in densely populated Hong Kong and Singapore since the 1950s with the large increases in real income and wages in those areas. Nor does he explain the fact that the population of the Western world has more than quadrupled since the middle of the 18th Century. "Real income per head is estimated to have increased by a factor of five or more," writes Bauer. "Most of the increase in income took place when population increased as fast as, or faster than, in the contemporary less-developed world."

There have been no famines reported from such densely populated regions of the less-developed world as Taiwan, Hong Kong, Singapore, Malaysia and cash-crop-producing areas of West Africa.

Prof. William Townsend of Essex University, who writes extensively on poverty, attributes the poverty of deprived nations "to the existence of a system of international social stratifications, a hierarchy of societies with vastly different resources in which the wealth of some is linked historically and contemporaneously to the poverty of others. This system operated crudely in the era of colonial domination and continues to operate today."

The Poorest Countries

Rebuts Bauer: "This cannot be so. The poorest and most backward countries have until recently had no external economic contacts and often have never been Western colonies. It is therefore obvious that their backwardness cannot be explained by colonial domination or international social stratification."

During the 1950s and 1960s a familiar figure on the Third World scene was Kwame Nkrumah of what is now Ghana. He described Western capitalism as a "world system of financial enslavement and colonial oppression and exploitation of a vast majority of the population of the earth by a handful of the so-called civilized nations." He is discreetly silent on the fact that until his emergence as leader, Ghana (the former Gold Coast) was a prosperous country as a result of cocoa exports to the West.

In 1975 Julius Nyerere, president of Tanzania, declared "If the rich nations go on getting richer and richer at the expense of the poor, the poor of the world must demand a change." He should be reminded that when the West established substantial contact with Tanganyika (Tanzania) in the 19th Century, it was an empty region thinly populated with tribal people exposed to Arab traders. Its relatively modest progress since then has been the work primarily of Asians and Europeans.

A Long Relationship

Taking a long look at the relationship of the Western world to the Third World, Dr. Bauer makes these points:

• Far from the West having caused the poverty of the Third World, contact with the West has been the principal agent of material progress there. The materially more advanced societies and regions of the Third World are those with which the West established the most numerous diversified and extensive contacts: the cash-crop-producing areas and entrepot ports of Southeast Asia, West Africa and Latin America; the mineral-producing areas of Africa and the Middle East; and cities and ports throughout Asia, Africa, the Caribbean and Latin America. The level of material achievement usually diminishes as one moves away from the foci of Western impact.

"The poorest and most backward countries have until recently had no external economic contacts and often have never been Western colonies."

• Since the middle of the 19th Century, commercial contacts established by the West have improved material conditions out of all recognition over much of the Third World, notably in Southeast Asia, parts of the Middle East, much of Africa (especially West Africa) and parts of east and southern Africa. Also, very large parts of Latin America, including Mexico, Guatemala, Venezuela, Colombia, Peru, Chile, Brazil, Uruguay and Argentina.

• Before 1890, there was no cocoa production in the Gold Coast or Nigeria, only a very small production of cotton and groundnuts, and small exports of palm oil and palm kernels. By the 1950s all these had become staples of world trade, made possible by Westerners who established public security and introduced modern methods of transport and communications.

• As late as the second half of the 19th Century, Black Africa was without even the simplest, most basic ingredients of modern social and economic life. They were brought there by Westerners over the last century or so. They include wheeled traffic, law and order, the application of science and technology to economic activity, clean water and sewage facilities, public health care, hospitals, the control of endemic and epidemic diseases, and formal education.

Gerald R. Zoffer, the author of Economic and Collapse, *has written extensively on economics.*

*"Foreign domination of the economy
was probably the key factor contributing
to the poverty and under-development in
the Philippines."*

US Influence Harms
the Third World

Esther Epp-Tiessen

The twenty or thirty women who had crammed into the tiny living room watched in awed silence as the demonstrator explained the unique features of each piece of Tupperware. One set of canisters, she noted proudly, could be stacked, thereby saving counter space. Another group of canisters could be used to store food in the refrigerator or could serve as lunch boxes for one's children. A serving dish boasted a new kind of snap-top cover, and a collection of tumblers was now available in a variety of colors.

The scene could have been any North American community. But it was not. This particular Tupperware party took place in a small village in the southern Philippines. Like Coke and Pepsi, McDonalds, and Levi jeans, Tupperware had come to the Third World!

I attended that party. My husband, Dan, and I had recently arrived in the country for a three-year term of service with the Mennonite Central Committee. As part of our orientation, we had moved to the port city of Davao to study the Cebuano language. There we lived with a Cebuano-speaking family in the village of Dona Pilar. It was the 32-year-old daughter and breadwinner of this family who had hosted the party and who invited me to attend.

Foreign Domination

My heart sank as Divina put the question to me. Even prior to our arrival, Dan and I had made a strong commitment to try to avoid supporting foreign-owned corporations in the country. Our readings and conversations with people had convinced us that foreign domination of the economy was probably the key factor contributing to poverty and under-development in the Philippines. Our short time in the

Esther Epp-Tiessen, "I'll Take Three Bowls and a Cake Saver," March/April
1984 *Daughters of Sarah*, 2716 W. Cortland, Chicago, IL 60647. A bimonthly Christian feminist magazine available for $8 a year.

country only reinforced those beliefs. The more we could do to support indigenous industries, the better. To attend a Tupperware party therefore seemed a betrayal of some of my deepest convictions.

At first I responded to Divina's invitation by sharing my feelings with her. But my mumblings about American corporate imperialism left her so confused, I knew even then that I would attend the party and—alas—would also buy an article or two. The high value that Filipinos place on maintaining smooth inter-personal relationships meant that I could not refuse Divina. I may have upheld my own scruples, but I would have seriously damaged my relationship with her. Moreover, I would have upset the delicate balance of *utang* (indebtedness). Because I had been invited to the party, I was under obligation to attend and to purchase.

Because of an earlier appointment on the Sunday afternoon of the party, I arrived home after it had begun. The neighborhood women sat attentively listening while the demonstrator picked up each item in turn and described it. At the appropriate pauses, they whispered to each other about how nice it would be to have "that." Children played on the floor with the small Tupperware gadgets each of their mothers had received as a thank-you for attending. Several husbands watched from the windows or open doorway. This was evidently a big event.

Ironic Situation

The irony of the entire situation struck me forcefully as I watched the proceedings from a corner. It seemed so inappropriate. For one thing, none of the women present could really afford to purchase the articles for sale. Though they were by no means among the country's poorest, their ragged dresses, unemployed husbands, and thin children all spoke of a life that was certainly difficult. One set of bowls amounted to two days' wages for many of them. And the colorful sandwich container complete with carrying handle which especially caught their fancy, cost the equivalent of a week's income.

To my great surprise, however, the women signed up for pitchers, mixing bowls, serving dishes, and canister sets. Two of them even ordered the 129-peso ($17) sandwich container. Of course none of them had the money to pay for their items. They would have to borrow from someone and then pay back the debt in monthly installments with sizable amounts of interest. Judging by their oohs and ahs, they were obviously enamoured with the Tupperware items. But my guess is that many of them purchased something for the very Filipino reason that they could not offend the hostess by not buying. The fact that the hostess could win a gift lamp if her guests purchased a certain quota of items only added to the pressure these women faced.

"As a result of 450 years of direct colonial rule, first by the Spanish and then by the Americans. . .Filipinos generally have a low opinion of themselves."

Another upsetting thing about the entire incident was that Tupperware was really the last thing those women needed. As the demonstrators drew attention to a large cake container, I could not help wonder how many of them had ever baked a cake. Even if they had had ovens—which they did not—it is doubtful that they would have used them to bake cake; cake is just not a part of the Filipino diet. The big ice cream container was just as absurd. One woman told me later that her family might eat ice cream once per year, and that would be a single cone purchased at an outdoor ice cream stand.

Colonial Mentality

Perhaps most frustrating was that this party reinforced the colonial mentality that is so prevalent in this country. As a result of 450 years of direct colonial rule, first by the Spanish and then by the Americans, and another forty years of neo-colonial domination, Filipinos generally have a low opinion of themselves. Rather than taking pride in themselves and their accomplishments, they long to be like the white foreigner and do what he or she does. Foreign-made jeans or "origs" are better than domestically-produced ones, English Hollywood movies "have more class" than local Tagalog films, and Pepsi and Coke taste better than home-grown fruit juices. If Filipinos cannot all emigrate to the States—which a great many would like to do—they at least want to acquire those things which they believe all Americans possess. This Tupperware party no doubt

convinced many of the women attending that they had to have Tupperware in order "to be someone."

Much has been written on how foreign-owned corporations exploit the peoples of the Third World. The arguments usually focus on how such firms grab land from peasant farmers, how they repatriate profits, how they mistreat their workers, how they prop up ruling elites. I have no idea where the Tupperware corporation comes out in any of these areas.

But it nevertheless seems painfully clear that Tupperware is engaged in exploiting the Filipino people. By trying to persuade poor women to buy items which they cannot afford, which they do not need, and which only enhance their sense of dependence on foreigners, Tupperware is using them in ways which demean them both economically and spiritually. Filipinos are becoming poorer and less self-reliant so that shareholders in another country can receive higher dividends. What makes this especially saddening is the fact that it is done with so little effort. Because party participants are indebted to their hostess for inviting them, they buy readily. The traditional Filipino trait of "indebtedness" makes the job of the Tupperware salesperson rather easy. At the same time it makes the exploitativeness of each sale all the more glaring.

Two weeks after the party I received my set of three Tupperware bowls. I debated whether to hide them in the back of our kitchen cupboard or to use them as visual aids when sharing thoughts on foreign economic domination. I eventually gave them away.

Esther Epp-Tiessen and her husband, Dan, are serving in the Philippines as country representatives for the Mennonite Central Committee.

US Corporations Benefit the Third World

Lee A. Tavis

Multinational corporations are the lightning rods which attract much of the world's frustration over the economic and social conditions of poor peoples and countries. The affluence which these firms represent contrasts sharply with the poverty of the countries in which they are located.

Third World peoples know that they are poor and we are not. They see us on television, read about our "good life" in newspapers and magazines, and watch our workers in their countries. For most of these people, their best is not as good as our worst. The vast majority of them live in squalor, as have their parents and grandparents, and have no hope of getting out. Sometimes their frustrations boil over, and the local multinational corporation is a convenient target. The same holds for the Third World host governments: those concerned with improving the living conditions of their peoples, those who see global development as a zero-sum game with the developed countries gaining at the expense of the less fortunate, or for the political opportunist.

In fact, people in the less-developed part of our world don't live very well. Although they make up three-fourths of the world's population, they consume less than one-fourth of its resources. More than 700 million people are classified as destitute; it is estimated that 70 percent of the children suffer from malnutrition; as many as 300 million people are physically or mentally retarded as a result of inadequate diets.

Alleviate Poverty

Multinationals help to alleviate these conditions. As the economic link between the disparate segments of our world, multinationals transfer productive

Lee A. Tavis, "Multinationals as Foreign Agents of Change in the Third World," *Business Horizons*, September/October, 1983. Reprinted with permission.

capability from the industrialized economies to those not so far along in their development process. These firms bring an ability to develop and apply technology, and to infuse managerial skills. They excel in training laborers. Multinationals work with local suppliers, helping them to meet quality specifications. They provide access to capital markets and the important capability to analyze economic potential. The global resources and diversification of these firms enable them to weather bad times in individual operating locations. In these ways, multinationals contribute to productivity and are an important component of the economic growth in the less-developed world.

Multinationals occupy a unique position and have a unique responsibility to the people and country in which they are operating. The responsibilities are sometimes unexpected and often great, but so is the potential for benefiting both the company and the local people and economy. In order to reap the benefits and meet the responsibilities, however, managers need the expertise to respond to challenges as difficult as any faced by corporate management. Consider, for example, the problems inherent in manufacturing in a Third World country.

By working for a multinational firm, local employees may be improving their material standard of living, but their lifestyles are undergoing dramatic dislocations. Multinationals rely on production technology drawn from the industrialized countries for their contribution to local productivity. In their fields or shop floors, work procedures are regimented, hours are specified, women are employed, promotion is based on accomplishment rather than family connections. Although these managerial techniques enhance local worker productivity, they are frequently new, strange, and foreign to the workers. Imagine the impact on a small farmer who has spent his life, as did his parents and grandparents, tilling his two acres beside his wife and children with their work hours tied to the season and the sun. Now he leaves his family every day at a specific time to work with others on routinized tasks, perhaps in a factory on the same land that he farmed just the previous year. You can imagine the effect this might have on his own and his family's sense of identity.

Worker Migration

The physical environment suffers dislocations too. As workers and their families migrate to places where work might be found, communities and cities swell beyond the capacities of sewer, water, roads, schools, and medical facilities. The improved material standard of living for these workers and families is achieved at the cost of congestion and the external pressures on the family unit associated with urban life.

Think of the issues all of this raises for the multinational manager. The involvement of the corporation in the lives of the employees at the job site, and in their families and surrounding communities, is far more broad than it is in our modern industrialized world.

The extent of this involvement means that a multinational manager must consider dimensions of his or her firm's activity that are not part of the decision process in the United States. What does a manager do when accident rates are high because workers are malnourished and come to work hungry; when disease among the workers, families, and communities is endemic and health care is woefully inadequate; when water supplies are nonexistent or polluted; where property taxes disappear into local government coffers with no apparent improvement in the community; when governments at the municipal or national level are more concerned with controlling their populace than enhancing their welfare. For many multinationals, these local conditions are the rule rather than the exception. In these circumstances, the firm must get much more involved with local peoples than it would in Western industrialized countries.

Necessary Involvement

This involvement is necessary because there is no one else to do it. When the local institution doesn't handle the job, the multinational is called upon to fill the void. For example, when there is no effective labor legislation or when unions don't represent their membership, the multinational manager has to set wage rates and decide on the tradeoff between wages and fringe benefits. Confronted with severe poverty, the multinational becomes involved with health, food, and housing for its employees. With no institution in society to protect traditional cultures, it often falls to the multinational manager to somehow judge the rate of modernization, or development, that

employees can handle. When other institutions don't meet the need, this added social role is imposed on the multinational. Because the multinationals must go it alone in many of these endeavors, some view them as exercising excessive power. To the manager, there is simply a lack of signals from the environment concerning the proper limits on the activities of the corporation.

In spite of all these difficulties, multinationals can make an important and beneficial difference to the people and communities in their foreign location. For example, a company called Castle & Cooke brings modern agricultural technology to rural areas. At its Dolefil subsidiary on the island of Mindanao at the southern tip of the Philippines, Castle & Cooke grows pineapples on a rocky, sandy mountainside plantation of 35,000 acres and has increased significantly the productivity of that land. A bustling local community has grown up around the plant where wages have a multiplier effect, and local industries such as transportation and construction have appeared as a result of the Dolefil policy to buy locally.

"Third World peoples know that they are poor and we are not. . . .the local multinational corporation is a convenient target."

Another example is the Caterpillar Tractor Co. in Brazil. It has production facilities in the sprawling metropolitan area of Sao Paulo and the smaller city of Piracicaba about 100 miles to the northwest. Engines and transmissions produced in these factories are combined with components manufactured by Brazilian firms to make equipment for local construction and agriculture. Caterpillar enhances productivity through the application of manufacturing technology gradually developed through production experience over the years, and through an extensive training program for Brazilian managers and skilled laborers in the United States and England (one- to two-year assignments) as well as at the local production sites. Caterpillar also works closely with its Brazilian suppliers, transferring technology in areas such as heat-treated steel.

Foreign Agent of Change

As multinationals enhance productivity, they become an agent of development in these countries— a foreign agent of change. Companies like Castle & Cooke or Caterpillar Tractor introduce new products into the Third World and new ways of making them. They contribute to economic development and, in the process, change people's lives. Castle & Cooke has drawn 9,000 workers to its pineapple raising and canning operation in the Philippines, with many families migrating from areas more than 300 miles away. In one generation, many of these families have adjusted from remote rural and, in some cases, tribal, lifestyles to urban communities. Caterpillar employs about 2,800 workers in its Brazilian operations. In Sao Paulo, many workers are drawn from the very poor favelas of the city while in Piracicaba most of the work force were formerly cane cutters on the surrounding sugar plantations.

> *"When the local institution doesn't handle the job, the multinational is called upon to fill the void."*

Dolefil was the central factor in providing or helping to organize the availability of water, food, transportation, sewage, medical care, and education. As the community established an identity, new problems of congestion, dust, and soil erosion had to be solved. In metropolitan centers, multinationals find a different set of developmental priorities. With workers spread throughout a larger community, the company's focus is more directly on the worker and his family. In Brazil, Caterpillar serves rolls and coffee to arriving employees since so many of them come to work hungry. Lunches are heavily subsidized, often providing the workers' only full meal of the day. Medical facilities are provided at the plant site where physical examinations are stressed and the widespread endemic diseases treated. The company heavily subsidizes family medical care in plans similar to our Health Maintenance Organizations, paying up to 80 percent of the cost. The uniqueness of the developmental needs at each location set off against the capabilities of each multinational subsidiary to serve those needs means that a firm's developmental response must be initiated at the local operating location.

Tradeoffs Are Tough

A multinational, of course, cannot meet all of the development needs at each location. Resources flowing to one use must be diverted from somewhere else in the firm. In our Castle & Cooke example, an expansion of the Dolefil hospital or the provision of water-seal toilets for the surrounding community uses resources that then would not be available elsewhere in the system. These resources might be drawn from a Honduran banana farmer who sells his product to the Castle & Cooke Standard Fruit Subsidiary in the form of a lower price for his bananas. These tradeoffs are tough. The Honduran farmer and his family may well be only marginally surviving while, at the Dolefil site, open toilets lead to epidemics of dysentery and adequate medical care is available only

at the Dolefil hospital.

Another alternative would be to take these resources from the shareholders in the form of reduced dividends, but investors in efficient financial markets will elicit a return to compensate for the risk they perceive based on the dividends anticipated. To get the needed resources from the consumers through higher prices is equally difficult since both pineapples and bananas are sold in competitive international markets where we as consumers control the price. Workers in the United States often exert the same kind of control.

A balance must thus be found among constituents in the developed world (such as providers of capital, consumers, workers) and those in the Third World. The efficiency of the product and capital markets in the industrialized countries coupled with the power and sophistication of governmental authorities and other institutions, places constraints on the resources that can be channeled to development needs within the less efficient markets and less effective and powerful institutions of the Third World. The other dimension of the tradeoff—the allocation of scarce benefits across so many constituents in the Third World in such desperate need—is no less difficult. The existence of a multinational corporate developmental responsibility surely places managers squarely in the middle of the disparate conditions among the people and countries of our world.

Roar of Discontent

Making these tradeoffs between developmental needs and the demands of competitive markets stretches the capabilities of even the best manager. Contributions to development do not have the solid ring of assets on the books, sales, or earnings; they take a long time to achieve their final impact; their loudest shout is usually "cost." Too often these developmental considerations are swept aside by the requirements of financial markets in industrialized countries, international competition, or a roar of discontent at the site of some Third World operation.

Thus, in Third World settings, managing the expanded social-economic multinational organization calls for important extensions of management planning and information networks. The developmental component of decisions must be identified locally, the impact measured, and information communicated to decision centers if the Third World developmental charge is to be responsibly met. For the long-term, however, the root problem must be addressed—the disparity in our world. Multinationals serve this need through their contribution to local productivity based on an understanding of overall developmental needs. There is still another, often unrecognized, area in which multinationals can be of service. This is in assisting with the information-processing capabilities of governments and other local institutions. If multinationals are to serve the true needs of the developing world in a less contentious environment, the sophistication of local institutions must be enhanced. These organizations must be managed better and represent their constituents more effectively.

"Contributions to development do not have the solid ring of assets on the books, sales or earnings."

Multinationals can help local institutions and governments by collecting and processing information relating to their industry; counseling with unions in setting up effective grievance procedures; providing technological and financial assistance to local supplier or buyer cooperatives; encouraging the involvement of local church groups as intermediaries between the multinational and local constituents. All of these activities will contribute to the development of local institutions. And, the more effective the local groups, the less contentious the local environment, the more opportunities for cooperation as opposed to politicized conflict, and the better for both the multinational and the local community. There are examples of multinational contribution in each of these cases that attest to the importance of more effective local institutions for the long-run benefit of the firm as well as constituencies in the less-developed countries.

What Multinationals Do Best

As local suppliers, buyers, governments, and labor organizations grow in their ability to represent their own constituents, the multinational can retrench from its extended role to focus on the traditional enhancement of productivity within clearly established boundaries set by representative host governments, efficient markets, or in negotiation with responsible institutions. This is to focus on what multinational corporations do best in a socially developed, more balanced, less contentious world.

Until this happy state of circumstances arrives, the manager finds that he must get at that developmental response right now—decisions can't wait. Better than other members of our society, managers understand that they must act today while working toward a better world for tomorrow. To them, the thunder over multinational presence in the Third World comes as no surprise, but neither does the possibility of and responsibility for improving the lives of people in that other, less-developed, part of our globe.

Lee A. Tavis is a C.R. Smith Professor of Business Administration at the University of Notre Dame.

viewpoint **68**

US Corporations Exploit the Third World

Amata Miller

Our systems—socio-economic, political, educational, religious—are in crisis today. Crisis always presents both dangers and opportunities. One danger is that those who gain from the systems the way they are will dig in, consolidate their power, use more and more repressive means to retain their positions. I believe that is happening in Latin America and, to some extent, in our own country at present.

However, a second aspect of systems in crisis is a very crucial one for us as Christians. Crisis also provides an opening for change, an opportunity for new values. At a time when there is a call, and a need, for change, Christians have a responsibility to enter in with constructive action.

Thirdly, remember the comments of democratic socialist Michael Harrington after he traveled to India and other Asian countries in the mid-1970's. He argued that the worst thing that could happen for the poor of the world today would be the collapse of Western capitalism, because we have nothing with which to replace it. The result would be more repression and more violence and the poor would suffer most from the chaos.

However, Harrington does believe in the vision of a socialist society where there is more equality, more humane social structures. The United States, he said, is at the center of an oppressive system, and most of us are not even aware of it. He called that lack of awareness our "cruel innocence." If we could become aware of the part we play in this complex system, that could be the beginning of change.

Lastly, not only religious people but also secular humanists, industrialists, cyberneticists, diplomats, and people from the grassroots are calling for a new structure based on new kinds of values—respect for

persons, solidarity and cooperation rather than competition, stewardship rather than consumption and wasteful use of resources, and non-violent ways of dealing with conflict in a thermo-nuclear world.

The Economic Dilemma

The basic economic dilemma comes because we are persons whose needs and wants are virtually unlimited, while we always face limited resources with which to meet those wants. Think of the world, the limited planet, on which we all live together and where one out of every four people does not have his or her most basic needs met. Then consider that even we are seldom satisfied, that we always want more. The economic dilemma arises because scarcity in relation to wants always presents us with the necessity of choice.

The economic choices that face us are always of three types: (1) Out of all the things that we could make and do with our resources, what *will* we make and do? (2) What is appropriate technology, given the available resources? (3) Whose wants will we satisfy and to what degree?

Thinking of those choices, consider a world population approaching 6,000,000,000 by the year 2000. Most futurists argue that it will not be the physical limits of the earth that will pose the serious problems. It will be the failure of human beings to organize the procedures for using those resources to meet human needs.

Economic Development

Economic development is the process by which a society organizes itself to provide progressively for the wants of its people. Basically, economic development has two elements: (1) generating goods and services to meet human wants and needs, and (2) distributing those among people to meet their needs. The process of development is not only a process of increasing the GNP, although the measuring rod of

Amata Miller, "Multinational Corporations in Developing Countries." Reprinted with permission from *engage/social action* magazine, May 1982. Copyright 1982 by the General Board of Church and Society of the United Methodist Church.

capita income and changes in it.

As a nation, we believe in the magic of democracy. We have also believed that the market will do the same thing for the Third and Fourth World countries that it has done within our own country. It has been our belief that over a period of time the market will raise the level of living of all people. It will narrow the gap between the rich and the poor; it will diminish the number of absolutely poor. That belief has been the basis of US foreign economic policy in the post WW II period.

However, in the late 1960's the World Bank undertook a study of the effect of all their loans and grants over the period of the past twenty years. The study found that, although growth had indeed, been very rapid and per capita growth had been abnormally rapid in the poor countries of the world, distribution had worsened, the gap between the rich and poor within poor countries had widened, and the gap between rich and poor countries had widened. So, they came to the conclusion that the magic of the market was not working in the world context as it had within the developed countries.

"The magic of the market was not working in the world context as it had within the developed countries."

The process of economic development has many components, including a number of socio-political preconditions. Countries have to have some degree of political stability, some degree of recognition of the need for change. There also has to be some economic leadership to bring things together. There have to be raw materials within the country or imported. Human resources—people with skills to be employed—are necessary. The people have to be located in relation to resources in ways that they can be brought together to satisfy human wants. In addition, there have to be some woman-and-man-made resources—some capital goods such as machines, tools, and buildings. Obviously to get capital goods, there has to be some technical expertise and some investment capital.

The Dilemma of Multinationals

Furthermore, countries have to have some kind of an entrepreneurial group, either public or private, to bring all these other elements together. This is where some of the dilemma of the multinational corporations begins. They can provide this group in countries that do not have a highly developed middle class and business orientation. In other countries the public sector provides the entrepreneurial element.

In the early stages of modernization, multinationals often help countries discover their raw materials and to ascertain what the areas for growth may be. However, the rest of the life of the people tends to be carried out in traditional economic sectors. So food self-sufficiency is generated by peasants in the way it had been done for centuries.

Multinationals, at this stage of a country's development, are often seen as agents of development. They provide a table base for the government. They develop physical growth assets such as mines, roads, and so forth. Their influence tends to be isolated. They have limited political influence and few close ties with the lives of the people. At this point, they are fairly easy to control from the perspective of the host country.

Likely to Dominate

As a country continues to develop a begins a demographic transition of moving people out of rural sectors into urban areas, multinational corporations are likely to dominate certain sectors of the economy. They may be very present in the factory, financial or transportation sectors. They now begin to become a disfunctional force because they help to stimulate flows of people from their traditional rural areas into the cities, which are usually ill-prepared to employ and take care of them.

At this point the multinationals become identified as the instrument causing the problem. Getting control of, or regulating multinationals becomes more difficult for the host country at this stage, particularly since only one part (or perhaps division) of the multinational enterprise may be housed in the country.

The third stage of development is what we have in our own country and other advanced countries. Here the multinationals have become so integrated into the entire fabric of life that the people take them for granted. We are not much surprised or concerned that we have huge corporations dominating all aspects of manufacturing in our country. We hardly think of them as exploiting or influencing us.

However, at this stage countries are maximally vulnerable to the operation of multinationals. The middle class of the country tends to be dependent upon the employment opportunities provided at middle management levels in the corporations. So political linkages and vested interests become tied up with the political process.

At this point the multinationals also exert their influence widely throughout the society, not only through their own power, but also through the kinds of dependency relationships they have widely built up. They tend to be preoccupied with stability and security, so the military-industrial complex begins to develop. At this stage the question becomes: How do you develop a means of drawing corporations to public accountability in an arena of political democracy?

When we look, therefore, at multinationals to see

what impact they have on economic development of a country, we have to be aware of the stage of development of the host country. To evaluate the impact of multinationals on developing countries, we have to ask a series of questions:

- What are they producing?
- For whom is it produced?
- What resources does it use up?
- Is it better than previous means of production?
- What kind of human resource development does it foster?
- From where is the capital coming?
- Is it diverting capital from other, more important, needs?
- What are alternatives to the multinational company?
- What kind of linkages are being created by this company?
- What kind of spin-offs are there, both positive and negative?
- What is the political power being exerted by the company?

Looking at the whole system within which nations develop, we must ask the question: Why are poor nations poor? The answer lies in a very complex structural reality with many pieces.

We live in a world in which the dominant economic system is ours. The dominant rules of the game that dictate what happens in world markets where the poor, as well as the rich, nations must go to trade, and where multinational corporations are major actors, are our rules. Under these rules, everyone is expected to take care of himself or herself; poor nations in the marketplace are also expected to take care of themselves. The rules say that the best way to make sure that the world's resources are allocated most effectively, or are used to create the greatest good, is to leave the international markets free to function in relation to supply and demand. Competition among parties with equal bargaining power will prevent any one person or group from exploiting any other.

A System of Dependency

However, the Third and Fourth World countries are saying to us—in their call for a New International Economic Order—that we have got to find a way to address the fact that there is *not* free competition in the international market, which is dominated by rich nations and large, rich corporations. The system of dependency in the international market has a number of elements:

- *The system of world trade* has "a stacked deck." In varying and complex ways, multinationals play a major role in this system. The deck is stacked against poor nations in three ways:

(1) They are restricted to producing products mainly in their primary state. (About two-thirds of all the trade income of the poor countries comes from

selling agricultural products or minerals in their raw state.) Profits go to the middle-person (often a multinational corporation) and the primary producer receives very little.

(2) Because of the way the markets are structured and because of poverty, poor nations compete in limited markets. We, and other rich nations, have various tariffs and non-tariff barriers against products from poor countries. These barriers are set up, often as a result of the multinational lobby, to protect our markets.

When we have a recession in the United States, it sets off shock waves in international markets, causing serious depressions in poor countries, which depend on selling their goods and services to us. When a country has a good crop year, many other countries also probably have good crop years, so prices drop. Neighbor countries, who would be their best customers, are also poor.

"There is not free competition in the international market, which is dominated by rich nations and large, rich corporations."

(3) Even under best of market conditions, prices of industrial products, which poor nations must buy, tend to increase steadily, while the price of the raw products they sell fluctuate with supply and demand.

- *Aid flows,* which are necessary to supplement the earnings of poor nations' trade, are shrinking and are increasingly given in the form of loans rather than grants. This means increasing debt burdens for poor countries.

- *The debt burden* has become increasingly high as interest rates have risen and poor countries are pressed even harder, making them prey to the harsh conditions of consortiums, including multinational banks.

- *Investment by private parties*—multinationals and others—follows the market where the profit capabilities are best. Therefore, it does not go to the poorest countries.

- *The net "brain drain"* from Third and Fourth World Countries is greater than the flow of aid, so poor structures lose their scarce resource of educated scientific and technical personnel.

- *The arms race,* in which the United States is clearly the primary force, diverts scarce resources. It generates inflation because it uses limited resources for military goods rather than for the production of food, clothing and shelter. It generates unemployment because it is capital intensive rather than labor intensive. The arms trade is the most buoyant sector of world trade today, and the United

States is the primary arms merchant.

The time has come for change. While the situation may seem overwhelming, unless we Christian people, together with others who want to bring about a more humane world order, seek to bring about transformation, change will not begin.

Economist James Robertson, in his small book titled *The Sane Alternative,* looks to the future and says we have three alternatives: (1) We can have a business-as-usual future. (2) We can have a technical-fix future. Or (3) we can have a SHE future—a future that is *sane, humane,* and *ecologically sound.* He says that we need to hold the vision that we *can* bring about a more humane world, a world in which structures and systems serve people.

"About two-thirds of all the trade income of the poor countries comes from selling agricultural products or minerals in their raw state."

A long time ago St. Augustine wrote that hope has two daughters: (1) anger and (2) courage. Anger so that what ought not to be cannot be. Courage so that what must be will be. Christians need to have that kind of hope—infused with a touch of anger and a great burst of courage carrying us forward into action for a just world order.

Sister Amata Miller, I.H.M. is an economist and adjunct professor at Marygrove College in Detroit, Michigan.

"The conditions imposed on US companies by the seabed regime were no worse than those encountered in many Third World countries."

viewpoint**69**

Proposed Sea Treaty Promotes US Interests

John T. Swing

Nine years ago, representatives of 147 countries sat down to the task, as ambitious and important as it would be difficult, of drafting a comprehensive Law of the Sea Treaty covering every aspect of ocean activity. What was envisioned was nothing less than a constitution for the oceans, which would set the pattern of governing them, for decades or longer.

To the surprise of many skeptics, on December 10, 1982, 117 countries signed the Treaty, which had been painstakingly and sometimes painfully negotiated, on the very day it opened for signature at Montego Bay, Jamaica. Not only did the number of countries signing so soon represent a record of considerable importance for the international system, but the countries came from all sectors of the international community, geographic and economic.

Among the very few countries announcing that they will not sign is the United States. Yet the United States had played an active role in shaping the document that finally emerged, following a line consistent with and approved by the three previous U.S. Administrations. Thus, the decision of the Reagan government to chart a different course during the final stages of the negotiations in 1981 and 1982, and ultimately to reject the Treaty altogether, came as a shock to countries around the globe. The U.S. action was distressing to America's allies and its friends in the Third World and clouded the prospect which the Treaty promised: a single universally respected "rule of law" for the oceans.

Treaty Objectives

To understand what happened and why, it is necessary to look back and ask what U.S. objectives were and to what extent the Treaty fails to meet them, at least in the mind of the current Administration. In this context, it is well to

remember that there were in fact two separate, if related, negotiations being conducted under the single umbrella of a comprehensive conference.

• There were what might be called the jurisdictional negotiations. Their purpose was to pick up where the First and Second Law of the Sea Conferences of 1958 and 1960 had failed in establishing outer limits of coastal state jurisdictions. Beginning with the Truman Proclamation in 1945, claiming the oil in the U.S. continental shelf in the Gulf of Mexico, these claims attempted to extend sovereignty well beyond the traditional three-mile limits of coastal state jurisdiction.

In those negotiations the principal U.S. objective was to maintain freedom of navigation for both merchant and military ships and the freedom of overflight for aircraft in and over the waters beyond the traditional three-mile territorial seas. Among the United States' subsidiary objectives were the establishment of international safeguards to protect the marine environment, especially from the growing threat of vessel source pollution and to preserve the freedom of scientific research.

• There were organic negotiations which dealt with a different although related problem: the establishment of an international regime to manage the exploitation of the deep seabed mineral resources, principally manganese nodules rich in nickel, copper and cobalt, "beyond national jurisdiction," whatever the outward limit of national jurisdictions might be. The United States had agreed in 1970 that such seabed resources were "the common heritage of mankind" to be exploited internationally "for the benefit of all mankind." In these negotiations, it sought to attain reasonable access for its private companies to the deep seabed minerals, under terms and conditions that would justify the large capital investments involved and make it possible for them to make a fair profit.

John T. Swing, "Law of the Sea," *The Bulletin of the Atomic Scientists*, May 1983. Reprinted by permission of the author.

Achieves US Objectives

How well does the Treaty signed in Jamaica meet this set of objectives? On the jurisdictional side, with the exception of scientific research, the United States by any standard largely achieved all of its important objectives. Thus, while the Treaty reflects a growing trend by providing for a universal 12-mile territorial sea, it developed a new "transit passage" regime for 116 straits around the world. These straits, being less than 24 miles wide, would otherwise have lost their high-seas status and become territorial waters subject to the control of coastal states. In the territorial sea, the only international right is that of "innocent passage," which forbids the underwater transit of submarines and overflight without the prior consent of the coastal state. Imagine what that might have meant during such a situation as the 1973 Arab-Israeli war. Since land overflight was denied by the United States' European allies, it could resupply Israel only by relying on the right to fly over the straight of Gibraltar, then an international waterway.

High-seas freedoms of navigation are also protected in the newly created "exclusive economic zones" extending 200 miles off the shoreline of a coastal state and in what otherwise would have become internal waters of the world's archipelagoes.The Philippine and Indonesian, or Malay, archipelago are but two examples.

Freedom of Navigation

Preservation of navigational freedoms was also important to the United States in the environmental area, where the United States had two important yet conflicting objectives: It wanted a regime that would protect shipping around the world from arbitrary rules and regulations proposed by coastal states in the name of protecting the marine environment but actually imposing undue burdens on freedom of navigation. At the same time, it wanted international recognition of rules under which it could protect its own shoreline from the kind of damage that resulted from the *Argo Merchant* disaster off the coast of Nantucket or the *Amoco Cadiz* off the coast of France.

The final draft could hardly have better served both of these U.S. objectives. . . .

Control Over Exploitation

If the Law of the Sea Treaty results in a net gain for the United States, why did President Reagan on July 9, 1982 announce that the United States would not sign it? The answer is to be found on the organic side of the negotiations, centered on building a new institution for the management of seabed resources, the manganese nodules, that lie "beyond national jurisdiction." It is here, for better or worse, that ideology both from the left and right played an important part. The more radical countries of the Third World (Algeria and Libya are good examples) saw the negotiations in "North-South" terms. They

wanted a regime over which, by reason of "one nation, one vote," they would outnumber the developed countries and have total control over the exploitation of the resources and could grant access to the industrial countries only when it suited their discretion.

"Free enterprisers" in the United States and the other industrial countries started from an opposite pole. They viewed their debt to the "common heritage" as requiring no more than a basic and presumably minimal license fee to be paid to the international authority, in return for which they would be free to take what they wished from the deep seabed. . . .

"The final draft could hardly have better served both of the U.S. objectives."

This was approximately the situation when the Reagan Administration took office. Its first act, on the eve of the Tenth Session of the Conference in March 1981, was to announce that the United States would not negotiate further until the Treaty was completely reviewed. This effectively stalled negotiations for the rest of 1981.

Hardliners vs. Pragmatists

In the meantime, it became apparent that there was a battle within the Reagan Administration between the hardliners and the pragmatists over the position that the United States should take concerning a Treaty that was approximately 95 percent complete at the time Reagan took office. The hardliners, particularly the domestic economic advisors in the White House, had a profound distaste for almost all aspects of the deep seabed regime as it had emerged. They rejected such deviations from the free-market theory as production ceilings or the mandatory transfer of technology, no matter how they might be circumscribed in the actual text. And they disapproved of the whole concept of the "common heritage" itself, which implies the sharing of ownership and management responsibility with other countries. They wished to assure direct access to strategic minerals on the seabed, which they considered a necessary part of the Administration's rearmament against the East. They preferred, in fact, to be entirely free of the Treaty.

The pragmatists for their part argued that, given the major gains for the United States in other provisions of the Treaty, one final effort should be made to make the seabed regime marginally acceptable. And they won the first battle when, on January 29, 1982, President Reagan announced that the United States would return to the negotiations that spring to seek to accomplish six objectives. In the Administration's view, the Treaty should:

- not deter development of resources;
- assure national access;
- provide decision-making that fairly protects the "economic interests and financial contributions of participating states";
- not allow amendments to enter into force without approval of the U.S. Senate;
- not set "other undesirable precedents for international organizations";
- be likely to be ratified by the U.S. Senate, which would at the minimum require eliminating the mandatory aspect of technology transfer, and would avoid participation by and funding of national liberation movements, including the Palestine Liberation Organization....

Many pragmatists argued that, with these changes, the conditions imposed on U.S. companies by the seabed regime were no worse than those encountered in many Third World countries, and that the Treaty, while by no means perfect, should be accepted. On the other hand, the texts did not make the extensive fundamental changes that the actual instructions to the U.S. delegation, largely written by the hardliners, required. Financial arrangements, the production ceiling and the governance provisions were carried forward virtually unchanged. More flexible instructions, however, might have made it possible for the United States to achieve two small but important changes suggested by a neutral group of 11 Western countries friendly to the United States: eliminating the mandatory aspect of technology transfer; and changing the amendment procedure so that an amendment, even when ratified by the necessary majority of other states, would not be binding on a state that had not or would not ratify it. While these changes might not have tipped the balance in favor of the Treaty in the minds of the hardliners, they would have made the overall result far more palatable to more moderate Treaty critics; and they certainly would have helped in the U.S. Senate....

Outright Rejection

Perhaps fearing that such a result would undercut their own opposition, the hardliners within the Administration pushed for and achieved, on July 9, 1982, the early presidential announcement of outright rejection of the Treaty. This virtually eliminated any hope of further changes or concessions. They had lost a battle when the United States returned to the negotiations, but they won the campaign.

Where do we go from here? During the weeks before the meeting at Montego Bay the United States had lobbied actively against signature among its advanced industrial allies. This effort met with only partial success. The United Kingdom and West Germany, both of which had already signed an agreement with the United States to avoid overlapping claims, withheld their signatures, at least for the time being, citing the unattractive aspects of the regime for the deep seabed. Japan, which along with France had voted in favor of the Treaty on April 30, also curtsied to pressure from Washington by announcing that, with the advent of the new U.S. Administration, the matter was still under consideration. Informally, however, the Japanese assured delegates that Japan *would* sign, following the projected meeting between President Reagan and Premier Nakasone to be held early in 1983....

"The United States had agreed in 1970 that such seabed resources were the common heritage of mankind."

One important distinction must be made. All of the countries named, including the United States, signed the "final act," a procedural certification that they had participated in the negotiations that led to the Treaty. Countries that sign the "final act" are empowered to participate in the Preparatory Commission, which is empowered to draft the detailed rules and regulations that will govern deep seabed mining under the Treaty. Countries that sign the Treaty will be voting members of the Commission; those that sign only the "final act" can participate as observers but have no vote. All of the countries important to deep seabed mining, with the exception of the United States, have indicated that they will participate in the work of the Commission. Even if it should continue to maintain its position against signature or ratification the United States has nothing to lose by participating in the work of the Commission. A valuable insurance policy, apparent to all of the other advanced industrial countries, will have been lost.

The Right to Mine

Whether or not others ultimately join the United States in rejecting the treaty outright, the battle lines now seem to be drawn between a handful of countries and the rest of the world. The U.S. position is that its nationals have the right to mine manganese nodules in the areas "beyond national jurisdiction" as a traditional freedom of the high seas, regardless of the fact that the vast majority of other nations around the world do not recognize such a right. Conversely, it argues that the balance of the Treaty, the many provisions emerging from the jurisdictional negotiations to which the United States has no objection, will become "customary international law," exactly because they will be so widely accepted. As "customary law" the United States will be able to take advantage of them, the argument goes, even though it refused to sign the Law of the Sea Treaty itself.

This line of argument is not without real problems. Even before 1970 and the unanimous adoption of the "common heritage" resolution by the U.N. General Assembly, there was doubt that a high-seas freedom to mine nodules went far enough to encompass international recognition of the right that U.S. companies claimed they needed to keep others out of an area to be defined by geographic coordinates on the seabed "beyond national jurisdiction." Today, the argument is likely to be even more tenuous if only because, 12 years after the "common heritage" resolution and the international negotiations that followed, most countries will deny that such a freedom exists now, if it ever did. A resolution to the dispute is likely to depend on the outcome of protracted litigation in courts around the world, beginning with the International Court of Justice, which may soon be asked to deliver a declaratory opinion on the matter.

"The decision of the Reagan government to. . .reject the Treaty altogether came as a shock to countries around the globe."

In any case, uncertainty in and of itself is likely to have a chilling effect on unilateral mining by U.S. companies. The reason is simply that the title to the nodules is in doubt and outside financing for the huge investments that would be necessary is unlikely to flow without some form of government subsidy or guarantee which, at least under the Reagan Administration, can hardly be counted on. Having staked its entire position on the need for direct access by U.S. flag vessels to the strategic minerals on the seabed, there is no small irony in the realization that American companies may ultimately choose to mine under the flag of one of their consortia partners whose state is a signatory to the Treaty, thereby achieving exactly the opposite result to that intended by the Administration. Either way, the economics of deep seabed mining are so doubtful that it is unlikely that there will be any mining before the end of the century.

Automatic Benefits

There are also problems with the contention that, because Treaty provisions have or certainly will receive wide adherence, the United States can automatically benefit from them without signing the Treaty. For example, it is true that a large number of coastal states have already claimed 200-mile economic zones, supporting the argument that such a limit is already recognized as customary law; but the rights and obligations that each country has decreed for its particular zone differ widely. Will Mexico, for one, extend the benefits of its partial relaxation of claims within its 200-mile zone, required by the Treaty, to countries like the United States that haven't signed? The result is by no means sure, since Mexico is just as likely to continue to enforce stricter regulations against non-signatories, lacking a bilateral agreement to the contrary.

The United States can, of course, strike dozens of bilateral agreements with other states as the only way of knowing where it stands in myriad situations in myriad places of importance around the world, provided it is willing to pay whatever price other countries care to exact. Or, at the other extreme, it can live with the resulting uncertainty and ultimately rely on force or the threat of it: to protect its mining ships against other countries' attempts to stop U.S. "plunder" of "the common heritage," and to secure rights of passage or other "rights" that conflict with the positions of other states.

Avoiding Conflict

While force may be the only true fallback, the wisdom and efficacy of such a course is doubtful in situations less than war. After all, the main impetus for a comprehensive Law of the Sea Treaty was the need to establish widely accepted rules with the central purpose of avoiding conflict which had steadily grown more likely when the consensus on what the laws were began collapsing in the years following the Truman Proclamation of 1945. (The Treaty itself is replete with devices for conflict resolution including compulsory conciliation, arbitration and its own special tribunal.)

Western democracies depend on stability that can in turn be assured only by reliance on the rule of law. Whatever ideological satisfaction the Reagan Administration feels it gained by turning its back on the Treaty, the long-term interests of the United States and indeed the Western world as a whole are likely not to have been well served.

John T. Swing is vice-president and secretary of the Council in Foreign Relations. He served on the US delegation to the third UN Conference on the Law of the Sea from 1974 to 1981.

*"The Treaty would give control of the
vast ocean riches to the Third World."*

The Sea Treaty Sells Out US Interests

Phyllis Schlafly

The United States (along with only three other
countries) voted against the Law of the Sea Treaty on
April 30, 1982, while 130 countries (mostly Third
World) voted Yes, and 17 countries (including most
of Western Europe) abstained.

The United States made the correct decision, and
the Reagan Administration is to be commended for
standing firm against the United Nations and Third
World pressure and propaganda. If the Treaty, or any
facsimile thereof, rears its head again, it should be
rejected by the Administration and by the U.S.
Senate.

The Law of the Sea Treaty is the culmination of
eight years of effort by Third World nations to gain
control over the development and use of our deep
seabed mineral resources. If ever signed and ratified,
the Law of the Sea Treaty would be a sellout of
American interests even greater than the giveaway of
the U.S. Canal at Panama by the Panama Treaty
(which was rammed through the Senate by President
Jimmy Carter in 1978).

We have nothing to gain and everything to lose by
signing the Treaty. It would jeopardize vital American
interests. The Treaty is a trap in which the United
States would be compelled to pay billions of private-
enterprise dollars to an international authority while
socialist, anti-American nations harvest the profit. Its
international controls and regulations would deny to
U.S. ocean-mining companies the assured,
continuing, and non-discriminatory access to strategic
ocean minerals which we need for our industrial and
military defense.

The Treaty would give control of the vast ocean
riches to the Third World, which has contributed
nothing to the tremendous technology and financial
investment necessary to bring those riches to the
surface. The Treaty would cheat the American
companies which have done and will do most of
what is necessary to make those minerals usable.

The Law of the Sea Treaty text excludes the
essential principles of free-market economics which
provide the basic incentives for private investment in
mineral resource development. It is clear from the
proposed treaty that deep-ocean minerals
management would be patterned after socialist
governments rather than free economies.

The proposed Law of the Sea Treaty has been
incubating since 1973. It ripened almost to the
plucking state in the last months of the Carter
Administration. When Ronald Reagan discovered that
it was due for signing within weeks after his
inauguration in early 1981, he fired the U.S.
Ambassador who negotiated it, plus six of his top
aides. This precipitated two more conferences before
the signing by other countries on April 30, 1982.

What's Wrong with the Treaty

The Law of the Sea Treaty would surrender major
political and strategic advantages to the Soviet Union
to the direct disadvantage of the United States.
Putting it bluntly, the Soviet Union is self-sufficient
in the minerals found in seabed nodules, but the
United States is not. The Treaty would take the
ownership of the ocean minerals away from us, and
force American private-enterprise companies to use
their technology and capital to mine the minerals for
the benefit and under the control of unfriendly, anti-
American countries.

The Sea Treaty would create an International
Seabed Authority (ISA) with sovereignty over three-
fourths of the earth's surface. It would have more
power than the United Nations, and the United States
would have even less decision-making power than we
have in the UN.

The International Seabed Authority would set both
general production controls and specific production

Phyllis Schlafly, "U.S. Should Sink the Law of the Sea Treaty," *The Phyllis
Schlafly Report*, August 1982. Reprinted by permission.

limits for ocean mining sites. The one-nation-one-vote procedure would assure that the ISA Assembly would always be dominated by the Third World.

In the International Seabed Authority Assembly, we would have only one vote and no veto. Since 80 percent of the nations signing the Treaty are from the Third World, they would have effective control of the Assembly, plus a clear numerical superiority in the Executive Council, plus control of the important subsidiary committees. The United States is not assured of a seat on the Executive Council. We would not have enough votes, even in combination with our allies, to propose even procedural changes.

In the Council of 36 countries, 25 seats would be guaranteed to Third World countries and three seats would be guaranteed to the Soviet Union. How many seats would be guaranteed to the United States? You guessed it—none. We would have to compete with all our allies for the remaining eight seats.

If an American corporation wants to make the tremendous investment involved in mining the ocean floor, it must first give all its geological data to the Council and then seek approval from the Council to explore. The Council has full discretion to approve or deny the request. If the request is approved, one-half of the area requested would be awarded to "Enterprise," an international entity operating in competition with the American company but using the American company's geological data, technology, and money.

"The Treaty would cheat the American companies which have done and will do most of what is necessary to make those minerals usable."

"Enterprise" would enjoy discriminatory advantages. It would receive the mandatory transfer of our highly sophisticated, defense-related ocean mining technology. This very setup would make it impossible for private companies to compete without governmental subsidies or other incentives.

In order to finance the start-up of the Enterprise, the United States would be required to contribute at least $125 million in long-term, interest-free loans, and another $125 million in loan guarantees. That would only be the start of the annual assessments on the U.S. Treasury.

The Treaty provisions for settling commercial and other disputes under the ISA are arbitrary, subject to political pressures, and provide no assurance of consistent, even-handed decisions under predictable rules. The arbitration of important disputes would be controlled by judges from Third World countries, many of whom are openly hostile to U.S. interests.

The International Sea Authority has all sorts of extra rip-off powers. It can impose rigid production ceilings so the United States could never become independent in strategic materials. It could even hand out benefits to "liberation groups" such as the PLO and SWAPO.

The Treaty also provides for 12-mile territorial seas and 200-mile exclusive economic zones rather than the historical 3-mile limit. This would erode freedom of navigation and overflight over the high seas.

How Did We Get in This Noose?

The United Nations is now based on the absurd rationale that the world is a homogenous democracy that can be governed by a procedure called "one nation one vote." It can't, because most of the nations in the UN don't understand or respect American freedom, yet are bitterly envious of its political, social, and economic benefits.

"Nations" all have the same vote in the UN General Assembly even though they may have fewer people than some of our cities. Some of those alien nations look upon the UN as a device by which the economic have-not or socially-criminal nations can gang up on the wealthy, successful, free nations, and extort as much as they can.

They do this by fostering a guilt complex among the wealthy nations, by diplomatic intimidation, and by hoisting the banner of "international cooperation" as a cover for bankrolling illegitimate regimes by American handouts. As Americans grow wary of the many conduits that have funnelled U.S. cash through international "loan" and "development" organizations, the Third-World confidence men keep concocting new methods.

The Law of the Sea Treaty is one of their more sophisticated schemes to steal from the United States. We are fortunate that Ronald Reagan stayed the hand of our diplomats just as they were reaching for the pen to sign on the dotted line early in 1981. In plain words, the Law of the Sea Treaty is a scheme to force American business interests to sink billions of investment dollars down on the ocean floor, and then let the Third World and Socialist/Communist blocs rake in the sea-bed's riches.

It all started back in 1958 when Malta (a nation with half the population of Washington, D.C.) proclaimed that the ocean's floor is the "Common Heritage of Mankind" and should be governed by an international treaty. By 1970, the UN voted to convene an official Law of the Sea Conference; its broad mandate enabled the "disadvantaged" countries to polarize the issues and hurl their demands on the wealthy nations.

By 1974, Algeria used the UN platform to launch an "official" call from the Third World for a "New International Economic Order." The purpose? To use the Law of the Sea Treaty as the primary vehicle to bring about a global redistribution of the wealth from developed nations to the less-developed nations.

There are two fundamental political issues in these negotiations. The poor nations want to con us into using our financial and technological resources to bring up the mineral wealth off the ocean floor and give it to them. The Socialist/Communist nations want to deny the United States access to the strategic minerals which are on the ocean floor (such as cobalt, nickel and manganese) because the Soviets know that our traditional land-based sources are in politically unstable countries far from our shores.

So those two blocs of nations are trying to force us into an International Seabed Authority which would have sole control of all sea-mining rights.

What Is the Problem?

The United States is a giant island of freedom, achievement, wealth and prosperity in an unfriendly and envious world. We have almost everything we need to maintain our safety and economy, but the items we lack are absolutely essential.

One of these essential items is manganese. It is essential to harden steel, and steel is essential to 20th century life. We import most of our manganese from Russia, southern Africa, and other faraway places, so our lifeline of supplies can be easily cut off by unfriendly governments.

A marvelous solution to this problem is available. The ocean floor from our West Coast to Hawaii is rich in nodules of manganese, and American private-enterprise companies have the capital and the technology to mine them.

The oceans are generally recognized as the earth's largest area of untapped resources, including oil, gas, minerals, and seafood. Scientists today believe that the ocean floor has layers of potato-sized nodules which can provide a virtually perpetual supply of certain minerals.

The sea-bed is believed to have enough copper nodules to supply the world for 1,000 years, enough nickel for 23,000 years, enough manganese for 34,000 years, and enough cobalt for 260,000 years. Most of these minerals lie beyond the continental shelves. The question of who will reap the harvest is unresolved.

The importance of America's access to strategic minerals can no longer be ignored. We import about half of our domestic petroleum needs, and we depend on foreign sources for 22 of the 74 non-fuel raw materials essential to a modern industrial economy.

In the years ahead, U.S. security interests may depend on our access to the vital minerals on the bottom of the ocean. The financial investment required to bring them to the surface is tremendous because the minerals are scattered on the ocean floor at depths of up to 20,000 feet.

The sea mining companies, whose investment, ingenuity, and technology are essential to surface the minerals, believe that the proposed UN Law of the Sea Treaty unreasonably limits the amount of minerals to be mined and puts an excessive financial burden on the United States by forcing U.S. firms to transfer precious technology to potential competitors.

The Law of the Sea Treaty is also a clear violation of the 1980 Republican Platform which promised that "a Republican Administration will conduct multilateral negotiations in a manner that reflects America's abilities and long-term interest in access to raw material and energy resources." The Platform specifically criticized the Law of the Sea Conference, "where negotiations have served to inhibit U.S. exploration of the sea-bed for its abundant mineral resources.

"The United States is a giant island of freedom, achievement, wealth and prosperity in an unfriendly and envious world."

American dependence on imported oil is only a part—and only the obvious part—of American dependence on imported materials which are not only strategic, but absolutely essential to our standard of living. Americans may not be as consumer-oriented toward cobalt, bauxite, chromium, manganese, and platinum as they are to gasoline, but those minerals are just as important to our economy and their availability is just as tenuous.

The United States has imported more than 90% of our needs for each of those non-fuel minerals during the past several years. Unless we develop North American resources, or engage in major stockpiling, we will remain dependent on the good will of the source nations to sell to us and the good will of the Number One Navy in the world, the Soviet fleet, to leave the sea lanes open to our ships.

Those five non-fuel minerals are vital both in war and in peacetime to our transportation, electronics, manufacturing, mining, chemical processing, and construction. Whether we are talking about automobiles or tanks, jet airliners or fighter planes, housing or shipyards, we must have those minerals.

Cobalt is essential for jet engines, magnetic materials for electronics, metal cutting, and mineral tools. Zaire and Zambia account for about half of the known resources; other sources are Belgium and Finland. In 1979 we imported 97% of our needs.

Bauxite is essential to aluminum, and is also important to refractories, chemicals, packaging, mechanical equipment, and abrasives. It comes from Jamaica, Australia, Surinam, and Guinea. In 1979 we imported 93% of our needs.

Chromium is essential to metallurgical, refractory, and chemical industries. We import it from South

Africa and the Soviet Union; Zimbabwe (Rhodesia) also has superior sources. In 1979 we imported more than 90% of our needs.

Manganese is essential to steel, pig iron, dry cell batteries, and various chemical processes. South Africa and the Soviet Union have 80% of the known sources; it also comes from Gabon, Brazil and France. In 1979 we imported 98% of our needs.

Platinum-group metals are essential to automobiles, chemical processing, the electrical industry, and petroleum refining as catalysts. South Africa and the Soviet Union have 90% of the known resources; some also come from the United Kingdom. In 1979 we imported 90% of our needs.

The strategic minerals list goes on and on. In 1979 we imported 100% of our columbium, mica, strontium, and rutile titanium. We imported more than 50% of 30 other essential minerals.

More than 98% of our imports of strategic minerals must come by water. Are we sure we can keep the sea lanes open? We used to have—35 years ago—the strongest merchant marine force in the world. Today we rank a lowly tenth, and the Soviets have taken a commanding lead in both naval and merchant marine strength.

"The Reagan Administration is to be commended for standing firm against the United Nations and Third World pressure and propaganda."

The Soviet Union is not dependent on freedom of the seas or on importing strategic minerals. The Soviet Union imports only nine critical minerals, and in no case does it import more than 50% of any mineral. Furthermore, the Soviets can get most of their imports by land rather than by sea.

One historical comparison shows our vulnerability today. During the World War II year of 1943, 25% of our ships bringing us bauxite were sunk by German submarines in the Caribbean. The Germans started World War II with 59 diesel submarines, and the U.S.S.R. has about 270 today, most of them nuclear.

American ingenuity must be permitted to mine the rich nodules of scarce materials which lie on the ocean floor between California and Hawaii. Our continued existence as a progressive industrial power depends on both the development of North American sources and the adequate stockpiling of essential minerals.

The Resource War

"He who runs alone will win the race" is reputed to have been said by Benjamin Franklin. Whether he said it or not, this truism is certainly applicable to the race that the Soviet Union is running to win the contest for strategic materials.

Russia has all but ceased mineral exports and has begun to import such important minerals as cobalt, platinum, chromium, and manganese. Control of strategic raw material sources appears to be the objective of current Soviet activities.

Although a land-lock nation, Russia has built the greatest blue-water navy in the world and a state-owned merchant fleet which is the third largest in the world.

Like every other aspect of the Soviet economy, the resource war is the result of a political plan laid down by the top bosses. In 1973, Leonid Brezhnev told a meeting of Warsaw Pact leaders in Prague: "Our aim is to gain control of the two great treasure houses on which the West depends: the energy treasure house of the Persian Gulf and the mineral treasure house of central and southern Africa."

The implementation of that national plan is the most logical explanation for the Soviet presence and influence in southern Africa, which is the source of much of the Free World's strategic minerals. Soviet Major General A.N. Lagovskiy was correct when he called America's dependency on foreign countries for certain essential minerals the "weak link" in American military capability.

The nonfuel minerals which our country imports from Africa and other faraway points are just as essential to our modern industrialized economy and to our military defense as our petroleum imports. General Alton D. Slay, Commander of the Air Force Systems Command, told the House Armed Services Committee last November 13: "With growing Soviet strength, we see ourselves in a position of heavy dependence on foreign sources for defense materials, little capability to increase defense production quickly, an alarming slow-down in national productivity growth rate, and a questionable record in the quality of what we do produce."

General Slay bluntly called the United States a "have not" nation in essential nonfuel minerals. He added, "It is a gross contradiction to think that we can maintain our position as a first-rate military power with a second-rate industrial base. It has never been done in the history of the modern world."

Phyllis Schlafly was a member of President Reagan's 1980 Defense Advisory Group. She is a leading conservative activist and the author of five books on defense and foreign policy. This viewpoint was taken from her newsletter The Phyllis Schlafly Report.

"South Africa is critically important to the survival of the West."

The US Should Support South Africa

Robert Slimp

Undoubtedly the most controversial country on the continent of Africa is the Republic of South Africa. This beautiful land, whose cities are as modern as our own, is a country of contrasts, contradictions and abundance.

South Africa is gifted with a myriad of assets which include immense mineral riches, enormous agricultural wealth, and an extraordinary and varied population.

Big booming bawdy Johannesburg, a city of nearly two million has been called the "New York" of Africa. Actually this ultra modern metropolis with its skyscrapers surrounded by huge mounds of dirt from its gold mines, more resembles Dallas or Denver than the Big Apple. Surprisingly it will celebrate only its 100th birthday next year. Cape Town with one million people looks a lot like San Francisco, and Pretoria, an extremely clean city filled with modern high rises, has a charm and distinction all its own.

OPEC of Minerals

South Africa is the OPEC of the mineral world. It supplies 65 percent of the world's gold, nearly 90 percent of its platinum and diamonds (the United States receives 98 percent of her industrial diamonds from South Africa). In addition South Africa supplies about half of the world's uranium, 42 percent of the world's vanadium and 81 percent of the world's chrome. She also has substantial deposits of copper, lead, plus 61 percent of the world's manganese. Certainly the West cannot afford to ignore this vast storehouse of mineral wealth. The strategic sea lanes around the Cape of Good Hope are so vital that Lenin once remarked that "the road to Berlin, Paris, London, and the United States runs through Cape Town." Indeed we Americans receive 70 percent of

Robert Slimp, "The Bright Side of Dark Africa," *The Union Leader*, March 22, 1984. Reprinted with permission.

our imported oil around the Cape. Hence South Africa is critically important to the survival of the West.

Small wonder that this fabulously wealthy country, though containing only 6 percent of Africa's population, generated 50 percent of the continent's electricity, manufactures 74 percent of its railway cars, 42 percent of its motor vehicles, and a whopping 94 percent of its books, magazines and newspapers.

And yet in spite of all her assets, South Africa is pictured by much of the Western news media, the United Nations, the World Council of Churches, the Communist bloc and even by the Democratic Party Presidential hopefuls as a dictatorial police state where the white minority exercises cruel control of the black population. So widespread is this feeling, that it is difficult to put in a good word for South Africa without being called controversial or even "racist."

Getting Recognition

What are the facts: This country of 472,359 square miles has a history very similar to our own. Today, those countries as told to me by George Matanzima, president of the Transkei, "We may not yet be recognized by the United States and Britain, but we are recognized by ITT, IBM, Coca Cola, Ford and even Kentucky Fried Chicken, and that's where the big bucks come from. That's the kind of recognition that counts."

In many ways the white man has been good to the black man. Remember the whites were there first. It must be admitted in all candor, that everything that runs on two wheels, grows in two rows and stands more than two stories tall was brought to South Africa by the European. The black population has exploded because of the white man's medicine and because the white man stopped their tribal fighting. That is certainly a better record than we Americans enjoy. Our forefathers killed off most of our American Indians while winning the West. The Boer was more humanitarian.

But, in spite of this record, the rest of the world will not leave South Africa alone to solve her own affairs. The whites thus far are the only ones who have the vote and although they represent only five million people out of 25 million, they hold the power and they govern. However, many South Africans feel that they are doing an extremely good job of taking care of their 17 million blacks, two million colored and 800,000 Indians and 200,000 other Asians, including 50,000 Malays.

Housing for Blacks

There are beautiful housing areas for blacks, Indians, and coloreds. The government spends 20 million annually on housing for blacks alone. Today, blacks have all the freedoms but one, and that is the right to vote, the right to govern himself outside of his homelands. And this right to vote is what is causing all of the problems. The outside world simply does not want to understand. Hence because of the bad press given to South Africa world wide, this country remains a pariah nation, or as Prime Minister Pieter Botha puts it: "We are the pole cat of the world."

"There is a grim joke in most of the black states north of the Limpopo, 'one man one vote one time.'"

Of course the Communists are exploiting this explosive situation. They are stirring up unrest among the non whites and they are succeeding. "Our servants are sometimes a bit rebellious these days," says Shirley Bell, a Pinetown housewife. "Sometimes my maid goes to political meetings and then she is very sullen and hard to get along with for the next few days." Sometimes this rebellion breaks out in the open as was the case of the Soweto riots in 1976.

Rhodesia vs. Zimbabwe

Is there a solution to this problem? The answer is no. What black nation to the north should a Black South Africa pattern herself after? Mozambique, Angola, Zimbabwe are all one party Marxist dictatorships. There is a grim joke in most of the black states north of the Limpopo, "one man one vote one time." What Rhodesians were promised at Lanchester House in London in 1979 was that they would have a future in a black ruled Zimbabwe. Dictator Mugabe has ignored this promise made for him by the British. The whites have not been allowed to have their own schools. They have been taxed out of their businesses, terrorized out of their farms.

More whites have been killed since Mugabe took over in April, 1980 than lost their lives in the long bush war of 1974 to 1979. The slogan on Zimbabwean T shirts: "Kill a white a night" is no joke. Beautiful Rhodesia has been replaced by a ruin: Zimbabwe.

The future of South Africa seems to be unfolding like a three act play in which Act I was the destruction of Rhodesia, Act II is to be the destruction of South West Africa dubbed "Namibia" by the United Nations, and Act III, the grand finale will be the destruction of the Republic of South Africa. This is the plan, not only of Moscow, but also the World Council of Churches and the liberal Democratic candidates for President of the United States. Even our own State Department in the person of African Affairs "expert" Chester Crocker is putting severe pressure on the South African government to capitulate and to give the blacks the vote now. Should this happen, the vast mineral wealth of this troubled land and the vital Sea Lanes around the Cape of Good Hope will fall into Marxist hands. If this happens, it will mean the end of the aircraft industry and will make it almost impossible to continue a viable defense system against our Soviet enemies.

Already the South Africans are fighting our battle against communism in Angola where the South Africans confront 30,000 Cubans and 3,000 East Germans. If the Reagan administration would put as much pressure on Moscow and Havana as it puts on Pretoria for a settlement, our future would be much brighter.

Reverend Robert Slimp returned from a South Africa tour and wrote this report of what he saw in that nation.

"It is time for Congress and other American institutions to tell South Africa: Enough is enough."

The US Should Denounce South Africa

Anthony Lewis

The South African Government had a beautiful advertisement in a number of American publications recently. "South Africa," it said, "is involved in a remarkable process of providing fair opportunities for all its population groups."

The ad told about how the Government is making houses available to black families at low prices—"an integrated part of its drive towards home ownership for everyone." At the bottom an attractive picture showed three black children playing outside a nice row house.

Growing up Black

In the interest of completeness, South Africa might take another advertisement giving further details on those happy black children: on the realities they face as they grow up. Here are a few.

• They and other blacks, 70 percent of the population, may not vote for members of Parliament or take any other part in the country's government.

• They are barred from living in "white areas"—87 percent of South Africa—unless they are among the minority who qualify for permits under intricate laws.

• The police may stop them at any time and demand their passbooks showing where they may live. If they have the wrong stamp in the book, they will be fined or imprisoned after a trial lasting a few minutes—and then shipped to a desolate "homeland" where there are no jobs.

Remote Resettlements

• They may be farmers in a black community that has owned the land for generations. But if that area is declared "white," they may suddenly be moved to a remote resettlement area where the only structures are rows of metal privies.

• If they join any serious movement to demand political rights for the majority of South Africans, they are likely to find themselves arrested, detained in solitary confinement without trial, tortured.

• Far from being "integrated" in the American sense of that word, their lives will be totally segregated. They will be confined to separate and grossly unequal schools, housing, trains, hospitals.

A "Free World"

Advertisements notwithstanding, Americans are increasingly aware of the realities of life in South Africa. More and more want to do something about the practice of massive institutionalized racism by a country that calls itself part of the "free world."

Those American feelings are taking concrete form in a spreading legislative phenomenon. Three states—Massachusetts, Connecticut and Michigan—have passed laws forbidding the investment of public funds in companies that operate in South Africa. More than 20 cities, the largest Philadelphia, have similar laws. Many universities are under student pressure to take such action in regard to their funds.

Congress has taken a step of a more direct kind. Last fall, in passing legislation to increase the U.S. contribution to the International Monetary Fund, it provided that the U.S. delegate must "actively oppose" any I.M.F. loan to South Africa unless the Secretary of the Treasury certifies in writing that a loan would benefit "the majority of the people," and meet other nonracial tests.

Prohibit Loans

Then the House added significant amendments to the Export Administration Act. They would prohibit U.S. commercial bank loans to the South African Government except for nondiscriminatory housing, schools or hospitals; prohibit any further American private investment there; forbid the importation of Krugerrands, and make all U.S. companies in South

Africa comply with the so-called Sullivan Code against discrimination. (Half the U.S. firms there now ignore the voluntary code.)

The Senate is to take up the export legislation shortly, and is expected to pass it without considering South African issues. There will then be a fight in conference, with House members trying to keep some of the South African restrictions in the final version. If they succeed, it will be hard for President Reagan to veto a bill that includes essential trade provisions.

"If there is anything that recent history teaches, it is the evil, the corrupting, dangerous evil, of racism."

Legislative steps of that kind are not going to lead to a change of heart by the South African Government: of course not. But they do keep Americans from participating in evil. And if there is anything that recent history teaches, it is the evil, the corrupting, dangerous evil, of racism.

Namibian Independence

The United States must continue diplomatic efforts in relation to South Africa's external policy: the effort to bring Namibia to independence, for example. But it is also necessary for Americans to make clear our opinion of internal South African policy. Those who rule the country will hear the message, and they do care what Americans think of them.

The ranking members of the House African subcommittee—Howard Wolpe, a liberal Democrat, and Gerald Solomon, a conservative Republican— were right when they wrote South Africa's Prime Minister that "there can never be a normal relationship between our two countries as long as the inhuman and destabilizing doctrine" of racial separation continues. It is time for Congress and other American institutions to tell South Africa: Enough is enough.

Anthony Lewis is a columnist for The New York Times.

The US Should Withdraw Its Corporations from Africa

Gail Hovey

Since 1978, the Western media have been announcing an imminent settlement of the Namibian question. This journalistic optimism, initially created by the Carter administration's call for a negotiated settlement and kept alive under Reagan, is not based on a realistic assessment of the situation in Namibia or the actions of the Pretoria regime. South Africa, in defiance of both the United Nations and international law, remains very much in control of the territory, and in fact has recently tightened its grip. Meantime —a little-reported factor—South African and Western interests continue a relentless exploitation of Namibian resources, in some cases to the point of near-depletion.

The United Nations, through the Council for Namibia, is the lawful authority in the territory. South Africa challenged this authority by holding elections in 1978 without U.N. involvement, then establishing an administrative structure based on ethnic divisions. The vast majority of the Namibian people never accepted this South African move. Not surprisingly, the government created under this scheme collapsed in January 1983, and South Africa resumed direct control, appointing a new administrator general to run the country.

Destabilizing Force

Efforts to achieve an internationally negotiated settlement have always foundered on various South African objections. The latest one, advanced with the encouragement of the Reagan administration, insists that there can be no settlement in Namibia until Angola expels the Cuban troops dispatched to the Luanda government. South Africa cites their presence as the reason for unrest in the entire region, and charges SWAPO (the South West Africa Peoples

Organization), whose troops maintain bases in Angola, with bloodshed and terrorism in Namibia. Never mind that Angola is an independent nation, or that the Angolan government invited Cuba to send troops to help repulse repeated South African incursions into Angola, or that SWAPO is fighting for the independence of Namibia. Never mind the facts or history, for in shifting attention to the presence of Cuba in Angola, South Africa has drawn world attention away from its own illegal occupation of Namibia and from the role it is playing in destabilizing the entire southern African region. War has been going on in northern Namibia since the late 1960s. Now, the South Africans have concentrated their attacks on southern Angola, occupying territory and villages. They have taken aggressive military action against Lesotho and Mozambique, and aided antigovernment forces in Zimbabwe, Mozambique and Angola. They, not the Cubans, are the source of unrest and instability in the entire region.

The struggle for Namibian independence has a special urgency since every day that it remains under the control of South Africa is one more day in which the profits from its vast but finite natural resources are appropriated by foreign corporations.

Fishing, agriculture and mining produce nearly 50 percent of Namibia's Gross Domestic Product (GDP) and 90 percent of its exports. Most of this production is controlled by South African and Western companies and over the years the amount of GDP remitted abroad has steadily increased. From 1950 to 1956, some 17.2 percent of GDP was appropriated by the foreign corporations. By 1977, a United Nations study estimated that 36 percent of Namibia's GDP was remitted abroad. This has created a profoundly distorted economy in which foreigners become wealthy, Namibia is not developed, and its black population remains, in the midst of impressive wealth, one of the poorest in the world.

Three Mines

The pattern is demonstrated most dramatically in the mining industry. In 1978 minerals made up 60 percent of Namibia's exports and the mining industry produced 32 to 37 percent of the GDP. The industry is dominated by three major corporations: South Africa's Consolidated Diamond Mines, the British-controlled Rossing Uranium Ltd., and the U.S.-owned Tsumeb Corporation which runs the largest and most profitable base-mineral mine in the country. These three operations control about 95 percent of mineral production and exports.

In a classic case of greed and exploitation, the vast profits from these mines have not been invested to develop Namibia but have been repatriated to enrich foreign investors. For example, in the ten-year period ending in 1975, Tsumeb's net earnings averaged $16.8 million a year. During that decade an average of $15.9 million per year was paid in dividends. Over 90 percent of the net income from Tsumeb was sent out of the country. The specter that hangs over the country is that by the time Namibia is finally controlled by the Namibian people, much of the mineral wealth will have been depleted.

"Tsumeb Corporation, the largest US-owned firm in Namibia, illustrates the depletion of Namibia's resources."

Fears of likely depletion of resources have already come true in the fishing industry. In 1975 Namibia was the largest producer of canned pilchards (a herring-like fish) in the world and in the mid-1970s the industry contributed as much as 13 percent to the GDP and 15 percent of exports. The industry is entirely owned by South African companies with Namibian blacks supplying the labor.

Ruined Industry

Today the industry is in ruins. Massive overfishing promoted by a desire for quick profit took precedence over the need to protect a vital natural resource. Warnings were ignored, and a record 1968 catch of 1.5 million tons of pilchards was reduced to a mere 12,000 tons by 1980. In 1976, 5,000 blacks had jobs in the fishing industry; by 1980, fewer than 500 jobs remained. Finally, in 1981 pilchard fishing was banned altogether. The future of the industry depends on whether or not the fish shoals will be allowed sufficient time to build up after their devastating exploitation.

The third main sector of the economy, agriculture, produces about 14 percent of the GDP and 20 to 24 percent of exports. The bulk of this agricultural income is generated by sheep and cattle ranching.

The sheep are raised to produce karakul pelts or Persian lamb which is made into expensive coats for an external market. Most of the cattle are exported on the hoof to South Africa. Namibia sells its agricultural products to South Africa, or through South Africa to Europe and North America. Namibia buys from South Africa the food it needs to feed its people. The bulk of the staple food of the black population, maize, has to be imported.

The creation of this agricultural situation is an important part of the historical oppression of the Namibian people. By destroying the Africans' herds and appropriating their land, the colonizers robbed the population of their ability to feed themselves and forced them to seek wage labor. Namibia's foreign-owned economy is totally dependent on cheap black labor. Ninety percent of traditional African land has fallen into the hands of white farmers, and the 1970 census reported that on average whites had 65 times as much useful land per person as did blacks. Even this staggering figure is misleading. In Ovamboland, the most densely populated area of the country, an average white farmer has 170 times as much land as the average black farmer.

Some 240,000 blacks are still involved in subsistence agriculture, but this produces no more than 2.5 percent of total marketed agricultural output. These peasant farmers cannot support themselves and are dependent on the wages earned by the remaining 241,000 workers, employed in the white-owned sectors of the economy. Most of these 241,000 workers are men and 40 percent of them are migrants, forced to leave the poverty-stricken rural reserves for jobs in mining, manufacturing, commercial agriculture and other white-owned enterprises.

Who Profits?

An examination of the Tsumeb Corporation, the largest U.S.-owned firm in Namibia, illustrates the depletion of Namibia's resources, the profits reaped by foreign corporations and the exploitation of Namibia's migrant labor force. Tsumeb is jointly owned by Newmont Mining Corporation and AMAX Inc. It operates the main mine at Tsumeb, about 200 miles north of the Namibian capital of Windhoek, as well as three smaller mines: Kombat/Asi West, Matchless, and Otjihase. Namibia's largest base metal producer, Tsumeb's main products are copper, lead, and zinc. In addition, it mines silver, gold, cadmium, arsenic, and pyrite, as well as operating the only copper and lead smelters in the country. The major customers for its products are Japan, South Africa, Belgium, Italy, and West Germany.

The deposits have been mined since the turn of the century. Tsumeb took over in 1947 and until the mid-1970s production amounted to about 80 percent of the country's total base metal output. Since the mid-1970s there has been a substantial cutback, primarily because of declining metal prices on world markets. In addition, the ore deposits at the main mine have been seriously depleted after so many years of extraction. In 1947, one ton of ore at Tsumeb contained 9.5 percent copper and 29.3 percent lead. By 1981, comparable figures were 3.61 percent copper and 7.32 percent lead. Mine managers were predicting that reserves would be exhausted by the early 1990s.

Although Tsumeb's richest days are over, the mine has been incredibly profitable for its owners. The average annual return on the original investment from 1950 to 1970 was 348 percent. Even in the last six years when net annual income had fallen to $8.8 million, dividend payments have averaged $8.7 million.

90 Percent 'Migrants'

This extravagant profit-taking has been at the expense of Namibia's workers. Working conditions at Tsumeb have the reputation of being among the worst of any major mining company in the country. Tsumeb operates a company town next to its major mine where all aspects of the miners' lives are dependent on the corporation. In 1979, there were 5,695 workers, 1,313 of whom were white and 4,382 of whom were black. Ninety percent of the black miners are migrants, forced to live in bachelor dormitories, separated from home and family for months at a time.

According to an Investor Responsibility Research Center study, since 1977, Tsumeb has claimed a single uniform wage scale based on job category, not on race. However, since whites remain entrenched in the top jobs, there is still profound discrimination based on race. Average wages for whites in 1977 were $774 per month, and $97.80 for blacks. By 1979, wages had increased to an average of $1,222 for whites, and $130 a month for blacks. The level of exploitation represented by this wage scale is demonstrated by comparing Tsumeb wages, which include non-cash payments, to the subsistence level for a family of six in Windhoek, which in 1978 was put at $190 per month.

Workers' Complaints

Following a major strike in 1971, Tsumeb management promised to address workers' complaints that focused on the migrant labor system and the lack of promotion opportunity due to race discrimination. But as of 1980 only 185 black men out of a work force of over 4,000 had new homes for themselves and their families. By the end of 1981, only 23 workers were receiving training in apprentice school and only 65 black workers had jobs traditionally held by whites.

Tsumeb's most important owner is the Newmont Mining Corporation, which is incorporated in

Delaware with its principal office in New York City. It owns, directly and indirectly, 35.9 percent of Tsumeb stock and appoints six members to Tsumeb's Board of Directors. Newmont has used its impressive profits, not to improve conditions for black workers or to facilitate economic development in Namibia, but to project itself into the front rank of the world's mining industry. In 1982 Newmont was the fourth largest copper producer in the U.S. and the seventh in the world. Because of timely diversification into such fields as energy, precious metals and cement, Newmont has weathered the depressed state of the copper market, and continued to declare profits.

Three-Cornered Tangle

Newmont illustrates the complex connections which bind together corporate interests in Namibia, South Africa, and the United States. In 1981, Consolidated Gold Fields—an associate of the Anglo-American Corporation of South Africa—acquired 22.4 percent of Newmont equity to become the largest single owner of Newmont. Anglo itself is now the single largest foreign investor in the United States.

"Working conditions at Tsumeb have the reputation of being among the worst of any major mining company in the country."

Newmont's principal partner in Tsumeb is AMAX Inc., which is incorporated in New York and has its principal office in Greenwich, Connecticut. AMAX is the largest mining company in the United States. Directly and indirectly, it owns 31.2 percent of Tsumeb stock and appoints six of the 15 directors.

Besides AMAX and Newmont, there are 15 other U.S. corporations with investments in Namibia and about 40 more that have marketing outlets or franchise agreements. Both Caltex Oil (owned by Texaco and Standard Oil of California) and Mobil Oil operate service stations throughout Namibia. Both are also involved in South Africa where together they account for about one third of all U.S. corporate investment.

U.S. Oil Companies

Because South Africa is occupying the territory and waging war on Namibia and because there is an OPEC embargo against South Africa, these U.S. oil companies are directly involved in helping South Africa's war machine run, directly involved in maintaining the illegal occupation of Namibia. Yet Mobil has publicly defended its role of supplying oil to the South African military. In its 1981 proxy statement Mobil management made the following statement:

Mobil's management in New York believes that its South African subsidiaries sales to the police and military are but a small part of its total sales.... Total denial of supplies to the police and military forces of a host country is hardly consistent with an image of good citizenship in that country. The great bulk of the work of both police and military forces in every country, including South Africa, is for the benefit of all its inhabitants.

Mobil's statement is, of course, directed to an American public remote from and largely indifferent to the "benefits" conferred on black people in South Africa and Namibia. In South Africa the police and military forces exist to protect an openly discriminatory minority white regime. In Namibia, South Africa maintains an estimated 90,000 troops and police to control a population estimated to be about 1.5 million—approximately one soldier for every 17 Namibians. The mission of this force, one of the largest occupation commands in the world, is to maintain flagrantly illegal South African control over Namibia's land, people and resources. Mobil and other foreign companies working in collusion with the "host country" are partners in oppression.

Decree Number One

The theft of Namibia's resources has long been a concern to SWAPO and the international community. After the United Nations revoked the South African mandate in 1966, it set up the Council for Namibia to administer the territory until independence. South Africa has prevented the Council from entering the territory. Nonetheless, the Council has played a critical role in keeping the question of Namibia before the U.N. One of its most important acts was to pass Decree Number One in 1974. The decree was explicitly designed to prevent the exhaustion of Namibia's resources before independence by making it illegal to extract or export Namibia's wealth without the consent of the Council.

Although the U.N., acting through the Council for Namibia, is the only lawful authority in Namibia, Namibia's major economic partners have ignored U.N. efforts to protect the country's wealth. The United States has an official policy of discouraging new investment in Namibia and has made it clear that investments made by U.S. nationals after 1966 will not receive U.S. government assistance in protection of such investments against claims by a future lawful government of Namibia.

Yet this policy has not prevented U.S. corporations from continuing and expanding their operations in Namibia. The Department of Commerce makes it clear that the policy is not a prohibition on investment. It is not illegal to invest and individual corporations are free to make their own decisions. In effect, the U.S. government and private American firms ignore Decree Number One and continue to rob the Namibian people of their country's wealth.

"Constructive Engagement"

The United States bears a special responsibility for the progressive impoverishment of Namibia because it is the U.S. that has taken the lead in the negotiating process. When the Carter administration came to power in 1977, a new situation existed in southern Africa. Mozambique and Angola were recently independent and the African states at the U.N. were pushing for effective international action in support of Namibian independence. They wanted economic sanctions against South Africa.

"Namibia's foreign-owned economy is totally dependent on cheap black labor."

Carter argued instead for negotiations with South Africa. When the Security Council, with U.S. support, imposed a mandatory arms embargo against South Africa in November 1977, African states were led to believe that the U.S. was finally putting real pressure on Pretoria.

But a settlement did not materialize, and under the Reagan administration U.S. policy shifted from supporting such measures as an arms embargo to a strategy of "constructive engagement." According to this policy, South Africa will only be persuaded to abandon its illegal control of Namibia if closer economic, political and military ties to the West are established. Thus, under Reagan, the arms embargo has been relaxed, economic ties have been strengthened, and official criticism of South Africa's aggression against its own people and against its neighbors has been muted.

Until the South Africans leave not only Angola but also Namibia, until there is an end to apartheid in South Africa, there can be no peace in southern Africa. Bishop Dumeni went on to explain why this is a matter that should be of grave concern to the American people. "Our people believe that the U.S. government has the power to persuade the South African government to come to ceasefire and U.N.-supervised elections. But we see that the U.S.-South African government relationship is very important to them, rather than the suffering of the people of Namibia.... We know who holds the keys to this matter. It is Botha [Prime Minister of South Africa] and President Reagan. They have the power. The bloodshed of my people is now their responsibility."

Gail Hovey is research director of the American Committee on Africa. The information in this viewpoint is based on the Committee's report: "Namibia's Stolen Wealth."

The US Should Not Withdraw Its Corporations from Africa

Tom Wicker

He was one of the most prosperous merchants in Soweto. "Prosperous" is a relative term in that sprawling, shapeless "township" on the outskirts of Johannesburg (the name "Soweto" is actually an acronym for "southwest townships"). There, those in authority, who are white, allow the residents, who are black, to operate only small "mom and pop" businesses that cannot compete with the white merchants in Johannesburg.

Still, among blacks, he made a better-than-average living from his small grocery store, and he played an active leadership role in Soweto, perhaps the world's largest black ghetto. I had come to ask him about the use of American economic power in South Africa, although in late 1978, after three weeks of conversations with South African blacks and whites, I no longer expected a definitive answer.

My host, a big, cordial, well-dressed man, had the charm and humor that mark so many South African blacks and that perhaps enable them to survive the indignities of apartheid. He was one of the few of Soweto's million or more inhabitants who owned his own house. He did not, however, own the land on which his house stood, because the Government forbids blacks to own land in the townships. Like other black homeowners, he risks the loss of his home if for some reason the Government withdraws his permit and reclaims the land. But the risk seems well worth taking since the alternative is a four-room, two-family Government rental house that has no indoor plumbing.

Life and Business

The low brick house into which I was welcomed was cool and dim within, and neatly furnished. Over a British-style afternoon tea, my host and another

South African black businessman talked about life and business in Soweto and their frustrations at Government restrictions on their entrepreneurial instincts.

They believed they could make a killing with a soft-drink bottling plant in Soweto, but the Government would not permit the enterprise. And so, in a hot and dusty city without running water in most of its houses, the oceans of soda pop that are consumed would continue to be obtainable only from white bottlers and wholesalers in Johannesburg.

"We are made to keep small all the time," the friend complained, and my host added: "Shall we die never having accomplished a thing in life?"

A grandiloquent sentiment? Perhaps. But these men *have* to live in Soweto and accept its restrictions, unless they want to move to one of the so-called "homelands" for blacks—rural areas where jobs are few and business prospects dismal. Under South Africa's complex system of "influx control," the nation's 19 million blacks must live where they're told to, by a Government elected by five million whites. Blacks must also carry passes at all times; if they should be on the streets of Johannesburg after 6 P.M., for example, they are supposed to have written justification from their employers for being there.

What Should the US Do?

So I asked my question—one that must trouble any reasonably compassionate American who moves beyond South Africa's glittering cities into the black townships and sees at close range the harsh restraints of apartheid, the faces of its victims and the clear exploitation of black labor on which the South African economic system is built.

What should Americans do, I wanted to know, with the economic power generated by 320 American firms with subsidiary operations in South Africa, 21 of them employing more than 1,000 persons each?

Such investments have a book value of $1.6 billion; in 1976, U.S. trade amounted to $1.35 billion in exports to South Africa and $925 million in imports from that country. Should we continue these investments and trade exchanges with the aim of influencing the South African Government toward the abolition of apartheid? Or, as many American liberals and generations of college students have demanded, should we "pull out" of investments already made, refuse new ones, sacrifice trade relationships, in unequivocal condemnation of the great moral and historical wrong being perpetrated in South Africa?

An hour earlier, an impassioned black high-school student—spiritual heir to the hundreds who died in the Soweto riots of 1976—had blurted to me that "Americans are the worst!" So-called American companies in South Africa, he charged bitterly, were really run by South African whites who wanted only "to keep blacks down." The student believed the Americans let these South African managers do as they wished in order to increase American profits. But since nothing, he declared, could "stop the revolution," Americans would do well to "clear out" of South Africa. And "the sooner they go," he said, "the sooner the crunch comes."

Doing Themselves a Favor

The Soweto businessmen were predictably more temperate and less certain. They agreed that South African whites, aided by American investment, were "doing themselves a favor and enriching themselves out of us." And, in the event of an American economic pullout, they did not feel that South African blacks would suffer too much.

"Despite lapses. . . American officials in South Africa nevertheless believe American companies are now seriously trying to follow nondiscriminatory employment practices."

"We can always live our simple life," my host said, in a variation of the old African faith that "the bush will provide." Besides, he said, blacks in South Africa "are used to starving. . .starving is just part of us." On the other hand, as businessmen, they believed that American investment, properly directed, *could* help blacks economically, and in that way perhaps increase their strength and political power.

Why couldn't an American company offer to put, say, a light manufacturing plant squarely in the middle of Soweto, where it could immediately provide jobs for the unemployed, estimated at perhaps a third of Soweto's working-age population?

And why couldn't the American company see to it that perhaps half the board of directors was black? Confronted with such a proposition, my host insisted, white South Africa either would have to accept it or concede to the world that apartheid was not the "separate development" the whites claimed but a system of blatant exploitation.

A Heated Topic

The two black businessmen felt that on the whole American investment, despite obvious problems, was probably a good thing—always providing it actually helped blacks economically and subscribed to the "Sullivan Principles," under which American firms pledge to follow nondiscriminatory employment practices. (The principles are named for their author, the Rev. Leon H. Sullivan, a Philadelphia black leader and member of the boards of some corporations—including General Motors—active in South Africa.). . .

In the United States, economic association with South Africa is one of the few subjects that can still set off heated arguments—and one of the still fewer that can cause tired liberal blood to boil.

Under pressures from students, faculty, big donors and important alumni, numerous universities have moved to rid their investment portfolios of the South African taint. Earlier this year, Columbia University sold $2.7 million worth of stock in three banks— about 1 percent of the university's investments. Two of the banks had refused to disclose whether they made loans in South Africa; the other was extending credit to the Government in Pretoria.

Stanley Sheinbaum, a regent of the University of California, who favors disinvestment for the effect it might have on attitudes here and in South Africa, pointed out in a memo to Gov. Edmund G. Brown Jr. that "pulling out" of South Africa was more difficult than many people realized and would have less economic impact than they hoped. The university, he said, would have to sell 60 percent of its holdings in American firms; but after having done so, it would have withheld from South Africa only 0.4 of 1 percent of its investment dollars, the percentage of its holdings in American firms actually devoted to their South African business operations.

The South African question troubles American businessmen, too—if for no other reason than that it troubles so many of their stockholders. Under their pressure, or out of a sense of social responsibility or business prudence, more than 100 American companies have adopted the Sullivan Principles; numerous banks are now prohibiting or curtailing credit to South Africa, and at least seven major corporations (including General Motors, Ford, Eastman Kodak and Gulf and Western) have announced that they will not expand their South African investments. Control Data Corporation has limited the types of equipment and services it will sell the South African Government in an effort—as the Control Data announcement put it—not to help that Government in "abridging human rights and dignity." Polaroid has severed its connection with a company that had served as its distributor in South Africa.

6,000 American Firms

There are more than 6,000 American firms doing business in South Africa, at least on an agency basis, and almost every American businessman who has an interest there justifies it by claiming that his company is either helping blacks, influencing Pretoria toward reform, or both. Unfortunately, businessmen and student radicals alike tend to see the South African question in simplistic terms. One side sees "staying in" as essential to South African reform, and regards "pulling out" as abandoning the struggle. The other side believes "pulling out" would put effective moral and economic pressure on white South Africa, and charges that "staying in" is equivalent to "financing apartheid."

Economic facts and my own observations suggest that American investment in South Africa—about 17 percent of total foreign investments there, and only 1.2 percent of all U.S. investments abroad—is not that crucial. Neither, in my judgment, is U.S.-South African trade, which was just over 8 percent of South Africa's total trade in 1976.

"Critics of 'pulling out' make much of the fact that the new managers might not have much sympathy for the Sullivan Principles."

It is true that American bank loans outstanding to South Africa in 1976 totaled about the amount needed for that country's oil and defense imports that year. It is also true that South Africa's greatest economic weakness is its lack of oil. But what basically enables that country to import oil while building up its defense forces is its enormous gold exports, boistered by high gold prices. Every $10 per ounce on the world price of gold means about $230 million in foreign exchange for South Africa, which has more gold resources than any other nation.

And even if Ford or General Motors were to pull out, they could not literally dismantle their plants and remove them physically. Someone—most probably a European auto maker—would move in, or the Government would find some means to operate the plants. Critics of "pulling out" make much of the fact that the new managers might not have much sympathy for the Sullivan Principles.

Difficult to Divest

An American company divesting itself of a South African property would run afoul, too, of numerous Government regulations that could make it difficult to return to stockholders the true value of the assets sold. These regulations also would limit the adverse impact on South Africa's balance of payments.

On the other hand, a recent Government ruling allows all earnings after Jan. 1, 1975, to be freely repatriated to the parent company. American officials told me that in 1976 American companies brought home nearly two-thirds of the profits earned in South Africa, rather than reinvesting these earnings in operations in that country—an important form of "disinvestment," if followed over the years.

One measure of the actual economic power of the United States in South Africa is that wholly or partially owned American businesses employ only 11 percent of the national work force. That includes about 70,000 blacks out of millions in the working-age population. Even multiplied by family dependents, that's not much economic leverage.

A recent study by Arndt Spandau, professor of business economics at the University of the Witwatersrand in Johannesburg, demonstrated that a 40 percent drop in foreign—not just American—investment would decrease total disposable income in South Africa by only $281 million, or about 1.3 percent. Unemployment would rise by only 90,000, but include more than 60,000 blacks.

So total American economic withdrawal—even if it were possible—would hardly be so severe a blow as to cause South Africa to overturn its whole political structure. The opposite might even result. A total oil embargo, for example, might produce a South African military lunge from Namibia (South-West Africa) through Angola to the oil fields of Cabinda; numerous South Africans seem to believe their Government militarily and politically capable of such an act, if it were pushed to the wall.

A Trade Boycott

A trade boycott, in the unlikely event it could be made effective, would have greater consequences. Dr. Spandau calculated that a 50 percent boycott in 1976 would have cut South African exports by nearly $5 billion and thrown 1.1 million people out of work. But that was an economic study. What would be the political effect? Proponents say it would demoralize the Government, increase business pressures and speed reform. My belief is that it would be more likely to stiffen Afrikaner intransigence, making peaceful change less likely.

By increasing black unemployment and restiveness, a boycott might hasten violent change, or efforts to bring about such change. But should the United States, or any country, pursue violent change in another country as a matter of policy? Against the well-armed and determined South African Government, blacks might well shed rivers of their own blood without necessarily achieving ultimate power.

Pretoria has made it clear, moreoever, that if the West acts economically against South Africa, the adverse effects will immediately be passed on to dependent countries—Botswana, Lesotho, Swaziland, all poor black nations with whom the West has no quarrel—possibly even to an independent Namibia and Mozambique. The last, though black and Marxist, is noticeably not an advocate of economic sanctions against South Africa, which virtually runs Mozambican ports and railways, is its best customer, and in other ways vitally supports Mozambique's economy.

I believe Americans who argue that the way to achieve reform is to pull out entirely are overestimating their country's power to influence events elsewhere in the world—a common American failing. Pullout advocates also overestimate the changes of concerted action with other nations. William Whitelaw, deputy prime minister in the newly elected British Conservative Government, said in 1978 that halting Britain's considerable trade with South Africa would add 250,000 persons to the already severe British unemployment total and cost Britain more than $4 billion a year in "gross income." Together with the low level of interest in human-rights activism in South Africa's other major trading partners—France, West Germany and Japan—this suggests how unlikely concerted Western economic action really is.

"Total American economic withdrawal. . . would hardly be so severe a blow as to cause South Africa to overturn its whole political structure."

But merely "staying in" is not much more promising. In interviews with people in all strata of South African society and government, I was impressed with the stubborn complexity of South Africa's racial dilemma: five million whites living at Western levels of economic and political development, who believe themselves intolerably threatened by the idea of majority rule by 19 million blacks.

Working out a system in which the rights of all races and groups will be equally protected will be a lengthy and difficult task—not a matter of a little pressure or a few quick reforms. And although foreign investments are undoubtedly important (they account for about 20 percent of total private investments), what finally happens between South Africa's huge mass of subjugated blacks and its dominant minority of whites will depend far less on the outside world than on South Africans themselves.

A Dictating Rule

The Government of South Africa is Afrikaner and Afrikaner history dictates to this unique people their right and obligation to rule, and an almost fanatical will to maintain their independence, language and culture; any system much less coercive than apartheid, many feel, would threaten all of these. And that same history has inculcated in them an abiding suspicion of the English whites, who twice subjugated "Afrikanerdom" (as Afrikaners refer to their culture) to colonial domination. While the English still dominate South African business, they have little political power, and most of them seemed to me not much more liberal on race matters than the Afrikaners. Few whites in South Africa favor majority rule.

Pretoria has repeatedly risked Western economic boycott on the question of independence for Namibia. Obviously, it doubts the West would impose economic sanctions. And in neighboring Rhodesia, there is a graphic example of the general ineffectiveness of such sanctions, which the West may now be about to end. South Africa, moreover, is a far more lucrative Western trade partner than Rhodesia.

South Africa already is undergoing one international embargo—on arms sales—without visible effect on its racial policies. In the aftermath of the Soweto riots, which raised questions about its internal stability, Pretoria can no longer get long-term foreign loans except at staggering interest rates. But that hasn't produced significant reform either.

South Africa is noticeably failing to attract new capital and in the first half of 1977 even suffered a net capital outflow of $700 million; in the first nine months of 1978, this loss rose to $1.5 billion. Unemployment has doubled in recent years and inflation hovers at 11 percent, with growth rates far below what is needed to provide the new jobs required every year for an expanding work force, particularly the black work force. Even though these economic debilities have been partially caused by foreign concern about South Africa's political stability, there still has been no move by Pretoria toward substantial reforms to meet foreign criticism. How much worse would foreign powers have to make things—or could they?—before South Africa felt itself forced to do away with apartheid?

Agents of Social Reform

And if South Africa's Government is not an easy one to influence, since when have multinational corporations and big American banks been eager agents of social reform anyway? They invested in South Africa if not overtly in support of apartheid, at least in spite of it, and because the climate for making money was good—it usually is where there is a plentiful supply of unorganized cheap labor. And there's obviously a limit to corporate interest in raising wages and encouraging unions.

The Sullivan Principles—which are less stringent than a similar code promulgated by the European Economic Community—do not, for example, require black unions in plants that have agreed to the principles. The parent corporation has only to agree to "support the elimination of discrimation" against black union rights, which barely exist. This is one reason why some critics charge that American companies adopt the Sullivan Principles more to impress American stockholders than to effect real reform.

Limited reforms strengthening black union rights were announced this year. But neither black nor white unions have effective strike powers, because strikers can be fired and easily replaced with black strike-breakers from the ranks of the unemployed. White unions continue to dominate most skilled-labor industries.

Black Unionism

To be fair, some American companies have made efforts to encourage black unionism. Ford, for one, has entered into a subterfuge at one of its plants that has had that effect. Companies are not allowed by law to agree to a "checkoff"—the deduction of union dues from paychecks; but Ford deducts "funeral benefits" from its unionized black workers' wages.

Blacks within white-dominated unions are not much better off. P.J. (Arrie) Paulus, the white leader of the important Mineworkers Union, told me last year that "Bantu" (a disparaging term for blacks) mineworkers were "migrants" and therefore had no union rights of their own. As members of his union, he said, they were paid about $1,460 yearly, while whites earned about $10,800. Blacks do not rise higher than the rank of "black boy," or No. 2 man to a crew leader.

"You have to know a black," Mr. Paulus carefully explained, to realize that "he wants someone to be his boss. They can't think quickly. . . . You can take a baboon and learn him to play a tune on a piano . . . but it's impossible for himself to use his own mind to go on to the next step. Here it's exactly the same."

But Mr. Paulus's reason for opposing equal pay for equal work, one of the Sullivan Principles, is not based on his opinion of black capabilities. Rather, he said, the bosses would surely take advantage of such a scheme to raise black wages only slightly while bringing white wages down substantially to the common level. This statement not only exposes the rank exploitation that "separate development" really is, but also raises the question whether even strict

adherence to the Sullivan Principles would be as socially fruitful as might appear.

Despite lapses (in an "integrated" Holiday Inn, a white desk clerk makes 400 rand—about $480 a month while a black clerk makes only $90 for the same work). American officials in South Africa nevertheless believe American companies there are now seriously trying to comply with the Sullivan Principles.

Housing Efforts

Companies such as Ford and General Motors have made substantial efforts to provide decent housing for black workers. Ford is planning to build a "middle-class community" for white-collar blacks, and not just for its own workers, in the industrial city of Port Elizabeth. General Motors is spending a reported $4 million to build integrated cafeterias and washrooms at its plants, although one plant unsuccessfully tried to avoid integrating the toilets by taking down "white" and "black" signs and replacing them with white doll symbols on some doors, and black doll symbols on others.

When Borg-Warner integrated its cafeteria, a white union walked out. But the company stuck to its position, and eventually the South African Government "winked" at what is, after all, a violation of South African law. In fact, the Government tends to wink at Sullivan-code actions that violate relatively minor apartheid laws. How it would react to major challenges is uncertain.

In view of all this, I believe Americans should neither "pull out" entirely nor "stay in" with exaggerated hopes for racial reform in South Africa. I see no reason whatever, for example, for either the American Government or American banks to provide loans or credits to the South African Government; in fact, such loans are now infrequent and several American banks—among them Maryland National, Wells Fargo and First Pennsylvania—have said they will make no more.

Loans with Strings Attached

Exceptions, however, might be useful. If South Africa's Electricity Supply Commission (ESCOM), a state agency, wanted to sell bonds in this country, American banks might buy some—but only on condition that a stated share of the proceeds be used to electrify Soweto. My businessman-host was one of the few Sowetans who had household electricity. More than 80 percent do not, despite the dominating presence in the middle of their city of the huge coal-fired Orlando generating plant. It feeds power only to Johannesburg's white residents, not to Soweto, and it is run by ESCOM.

As for commercial loans, the Evans Amendment to Export-Import Bank regulations, adopted by Congress last year, requires that recipient firms demonstrate that they are following a code of practices similar to the Sullivan Principles. This kind of "directed" investment could prove more positive than cutting off bank loans altogether.

American firms with direct investments in South Africa could—if they would—challenge apartheid laws seriously. It is all very well for such companies to build decent housing for blacks and coloreds (people of mixed black and white descent). But by insisting on racially mixed housing as an alternative to substantial disinvestment, American companies could challenge the Group Areas Act that now enforces separate townships for the races. If South Africa permitted the mixed housing, that much of a hole would be torn in the fabric of apartheid. If not, the company making the effort might recover its losses in worldwide—particularly third world—good will.

In trade matters, exports or sales that specifically help maintain apartheid—sales of almost anything to the South African police, for example—have no justification. And American firms undoubtedly could do more to make Sullivanlike principles profitable and necessary not just for foreign companies but for South African buyers and suppliers as well. Targeted boycotting of the most exploitative South African firms—those with the worst records of wage discrimination, for example, or with the most blatant hostility to black unions—might ultimately have powerful political effect.

Symbolic Importance

Such efforts, however limited in their practical impact in South Africa, would have symbolic importance in a country that wants to be regarded as part of the West. They would be even more important in the eyes of third-world countries, where Americans are often seen, in the words of that Soweto student, as money grubbers and closet racists mouthing hypocritical human-rights slogans.

And even if nothing much happened as a result of efforts like those suggested, Americans could feel better about themselves if they made clear their disapproval of what former Senator Dick Clark described as "the only country in the world in which men and women are systematically denied fundamental freedoms in virtually every sphere of human endeavor on the sole basis of the color of their skin."

South African blacks warn against merely "polishing our shackles"—a phrase sometimes attributed to Nelson Mandela, 16 years a prisoner on Robben Island but still the best-known living black leader. It is a warning—essentially the same voiced by my Soweto host—against actions that make black life in South Africa merely somewhat more bearable, or better for the few, without really changing conditions fundamentally, perhaps making change even less likely.

This is a standard against which American economic and political actions ought always to be measured. But if Americans cannot reasonably hope, by their own actions or even by concerted Western action, to force a solution to South Africa's profound race dilemma, they still are entitled—obligated, some of us would say—to act toward South Africa in consonance with the ideals of their own democracy and the words of the Declaration of Independence and the Bill of Rights.

Can supporting the power of an idea—and none has more power than the idea of freedom—ever merely "polish the shackles" of the oppressed? Isn't it much more likely to corrode those shackles, however slowly? That may be the best that Americans can hope to achieve in South Africa. The rest will be up to the South Africans, the 19 million as well as the five.

Tom Wicker is an associate editor for The New York Times.

"It isn't nutmeg that's at stake in the Caribbean and Central America; it is the U.S. national security."

The US Must Defend Its Security in Central America

Ronald Reagan

Late last year, I visited Central America. Just a few weeks ago, our Ambassador (to the United Nations), Jeane Kirkpatrick, also toured the area. And in the last few days I have met with leaders of the Congress to discuss recent events in Central America and our policies in that troubled part of the world. Today I'd like to report to you on these consultations and why they're important to all of us. . . .

Let me just show you how important Central America is. Here at the base of Central America is the Panama Canal. Half of all the foreign trade of the United States passes through either the canal or the other Caribbean sealanes on its way to or from our ports. And, of course, to the north, as you can see, is Mexico, a country of enormous human and material importance with which we share 1,800 miles of peaceful frontier.

And between Mexico and the canal lies Central America. As I speak to you today, its countries are in the midst of the gravest crisis in their history. Accumulated grievances and social and economic change are challenging traditional ways. New leaders with new aspirations have emerged who want a new and better deal for their peoples. And that is good.

The Threat to US Security

The problem is that an aggressive minority has thrown in its lot with the communists, looking to the Soviets and their own Cuban henchmen to help them pursue political change through violence. Nicaragua has become their base. And these extremists make no secret of their goal. They preach the doctrine of a "revolution without frontiers." Their first target is El Salvador.

Important? To begin with, there's the sheer human tragedy. Thousands of people have already died and,

Ronald Reagan, speech before the National Association of Manufacturers in Washington DC, March 10, 1983.

unless the conflict is ended democratically, millions more could be affected throughout the hemisphere. The people of El Salvador have proved they want democracy. But if guerrilla violence succeeds, they won't get it. El Salvador will join Cuba and Nicaragua as a base for spreading fresh violence to Guatemala, Honduras, Costa Rica—probably the most democratic country in the world today. The killing will increase and so will the threat to Panama, the canal, and, ultimately, Mexico. In the process, vast numbers of men, women, and children will lose their homes, their countries, and their lives.

End the Killing

Make no mistake. We want the same thing the people of Central America want—an end to the killing. We want to see freedom preserved where it now exists and its rebirth where it does not. The communist agenda, on the other hand, is to exploit human suffering in Central America to strike at the heart of the Western Hemisphere. By preventing reform and instilling their own brand of totalitarianism, they can threaten freedom and peace and weaken our national security.

I know a good many people wonder why we should care about whether communist governments come into power in Nicaragua, El Salvador, or other such countries as Costa Rica and Honduras, Guatemala, and the islands of the Caribbean. One columnist argued last week that we shouldn't care, because their products are not that vital to our economy. That's like the argument of another so-called expert that we shouldn't worry about Castro's control over the island of Grenada—their only important product is nutmeg. . . .

People who make these arguments haven't taken a good look at a map lately or followed the extraordinary buildup of Soviet and Cuban military power in the region or read the Soviets' discussions about why the region is important to them and how they intend to use it.

It isn't nutmeg that's at stake in the Caribbean and Central America; it is the U.S. national security.

Soviet military theorists want to destroy our capacity to resupply Western Europe in case of an emergency. They want to tie down our attention and forces on our own southern border and so limit our capacity to act in more distant places, such as Europe, the Persian Gulf, the Indian Ocean, the Sea of Japan.

Soviet Theorists

Those Soviet theorists noticed what we failed to notice: that the Caribbean Sea and Central America constitute this nation's fourth border. If we must defend ourselves against a large, hostile military presence on our border, our freedom to act elsewhere to help others and to protect strategically vital sealanes and resources has been drastically diminished. They know this; they've written about this.

"No significant sector of the public anywhere in this hemisphere wants to see the guerrillas seize power in El Salvador."

We've been slow to understand that the defense of the Caribbean and Central America against Marxist-Leninist takeover is vital to our national security in ways we're not accustomed to thinking about.

For the past 3 years, under two Presidents, the United States has been engaged in an effort to stop the advance of communism in Central America by doing what we do best—by supporting democracy. For 3 years, our goal has been to support fundamental change in this region, to replace poverty with development and dictatorship with democracy.

These objectives are not easy to obtain. We're on the right track. Costa Rica continues to set a democratic example, even in the midst of economic crisis and Nicaraguan intimidation. Honduras has gone from military rule to a freely elected civilian government. Despite incredible obstacles, the democratic center is holding in El Salvador, implementing land reform and working to replace the politics of death with a life of democracy.

The good news is that our new policies have begun to work. Democracy, with free elections, free labor unions, freedom of religion and respect for the integrity of the individual, is the clear choice of the overwhelming majority of Central Americans. In fact, except for Cuba and its followers, no government and no significant sector of the public anywhere in this hemisphere wants to see the guerrillas seize power in El Salvador.

The bad news is that the struggle for democracy is still far from over. Despite their success in largely eliminating guerrilla political influence in populated areas, and despite some improvements in military armaments and mobility, El Salvador's people remain under strong pressure from armed guerrillas controlled by extremists with Cuban-Soviet support.

Struggle Is Not Over

The military capability of these guerrillas—and I would like to stress *military* capability, for these are not peasant irregulars; they are trained, military forces. This has kept political and economic progress from being turned into the peace the Salvadoran people so obviously want.

Part of the trouble is internal to El Salvador, but an important part is external—the availability of training, tactical guidance, and military supplies coming into El Salvador from Marxist Nicaragua. I'm sure you've read about the guerrillas capturing rifles from government national guard units. And recently, this has happened. But much more critical to guerrilla operations are the supplies and munitions that are infiltrated into El Salvador by land, sea, and air—by pack mules, by small boats, and by small aircraft.

These pipelines fuel the guerrilla offensives and keep alive the conviction of their extremist leaders that power will ultimately come from the barrels of their guns. All this is happening in El Salvador just as a constitution is being written, as open presidential elections are being prepared, and as a peace commission—named last week—has begun to work on amnesty and national reconciliation to bring all social and political groups into the democratic process.

It is the guerrilla militants who have so far refused to use democratic means, have ignored the voice of the people of El Salvador, and have resorted to terror, sabotage, and bullets, instead of the ballot box.

During the past week, we've discussed all of these issues and more with leaders and Members of the Congress. Their views have helped shape our own thinking. And I believe that we've developed a common course to follow.

Now, here are some of the questions that are raised most often.

Five Pertinent Questions

First, how bad is the military situation? It is not good. Salvadoran soliders have proved that when they're well trained, led, and supplied, they can protect the people from guerrilla attacks. But so far, U.S. trainers have been able to train only one soldier in ten. There's a shortage of experienced officers. Supplies are unsure. The guerrillas have taken advantage of these shortcomings. For the moment, at least, they have taken the tactical initiative just when the sharply limited funding Congress has so far approved is running out.

A second vital question is: Are we going to send American soldiers into combat? And the answer to that is a flat no.

A third question: Are we going to Americanize the war with a lot of U.S. combat advisors? And again, the answer is no.

Only Salvadorans can fight this war, just as only Salvadorans can decide El Salvador's future. What we can do is help to give them the skills and supplies they need to do the job for themselves. That, mostly, means training. Without playing a combat role themselves and without accompanying Salvadoran units into combat, American specialists can help the Salvadoran Army improve its operations.

Over the last year, despite manifest needs for more training, we have scrupulously kept our training activities well below our self-imposed numerical limit on numbers of trainers. We're currently reviewing what we can do to provide the most effective training possible, to determine the minimum level of trainers needed, and where the training should best take place. We think the best way is to provide training outside of El Salvador, in the United States, or elsewhere, but that costs a lot more. So the number of U.S. trainers in El Salvador will depend upon the resources available.

Question four: Are we seeking a political or a military solution? Despite all I and others have said, some people still seem to think that our concern for security assistance means that all we care about is a military solution. That's nonsense. Bullets are no answer to economic inequities, social tensions, or political disagreements. Democracy is what we want, and what we want is to enable Salvadorans to stop the killing and sabotage so that economic and political reforms can take root. The real solution can only be a political one.

This reality leads directly to a fifth question: Why not stop the killings and start talking? Why not negotiate? Negotiations are already a key part of our policy. We support negotiations among all the nations of the region to strengthen democracy, to halt subversion, to stop the flow of arms, to respect borders, and to remove all the foreign military advisers—the Soviets, the Cubans, the East Germans, the PLO (Palestine Liberation Organization), as well as our own from the region.

A regional peace initiative is now emerging. We've been in close touch with its sponsors and wish it well. And we support negotiations within nations aimed at expanding participation in democratic institutions, at getting all parties to participate in free and nonviolent elections.

What we oppose are negotiations that would be used as a cynical device for dividing up power behind the people's back. We cannot support negotiations which, instead of expanding democracy, try to destroy it; negotiations which would simply distribute

power among armed groups without the consent of the people of El Salvador.

We made that mistake some years ago—in Laos—when we pressed and pressured the Laotian Government to form a government, a co-op, with the Pathet Lao, the armed guerrillas who'd been doing what the guerrillas are doing in El Salvador. And once they had that tripartite government, they didn't rest until those guerrillas—the Pathet Lao—had seized total control of the Government of Laos.

"We cannot support negotiations which, instead of expanding democracy, try to destroy it; negotiations which would . . . distribute power among armed groups."

The thousands of Salvadorans who risked their lives to vote last year should not have their ballots thrown into the trash heap this year by letting a tiny minority on the fringe of a wide and diverse political spectrum shoot its way into power. No, the only legitimate road to power, the only road we can support, is through the voting booth so that the people can choose for themselves; choose, as His Holiness the Pope said Sunday, "far from terror and in a climate of democratic conviviality." This is fundamental, and it is a moral as well as a practical belief that all free people of the Americas share.

U.S. Position in Central America

Having consulted with the Congress, let me tell you where we are now and what we'll be doing in the days ahead. We welcome all the help we can get. We will be submitting a comprehensive, integrated economic and military assistance plan for Central America.

First, we will bridge the existing gap in military assistance. Our projections of the amount of military assistance needed for El Salvador have remained relatively stable over the past 2 years. However, the continuing resolution budget procedure in the Congress last December led to a level of U.S. security assistance for El Salvador in 1983 below what we'd requested, below that provided in 1982, and below that requested for 1984. I'm proposing that $60 million of the moneys already appropriated for our worldwide military assistance programs be immediately reallocated to El Salvador.

Further, to build the kind of disciplined, skilled army that can take and hold the initiative while respecting the rights of its people, I will be amending my supplemental that is currently before the Congress to reallocate $50 million to El Salvador. And these funds will be sought without increasing the overall amount of the supplemental that we have already presented to the Congress. And, as I've said, the focus of this assistance will remain the same—to train Salvadorans so that they can defend themselves.

Because El Salvador's problems are not unique in this region, I will also be asking for an additional $20 million for regional security assistance. These funds will be used to help neighboring states to maintain their national security and will, of course, be subject to full congressional review.

Secondly, we will work hard to support reform, human rights, and democracy in El Salvador. Last Thursday, the Salvadoran Government extended the land reform program which has already distributed 20% of all the arable land in the country and transformed more than 65,000 farm workers into farm owners. What they ask is our continued economic support while the reform is completed. And we will provide it. With our support, we expect that the steady progress toward more equitable distribution of wealth and power in El Salvador will continue.

And third, we will, I repeat, continue to work for human rights. Progress in this area has been slow, sometimes disappointing. But human rights means working at problems, not walking away from them. To make more progress, we must continue our support, advice, and help to El Salvador's people and democratic leaders. Lawbreakers must be brought to justice, and the rule of law must supplant violence in settling disputes. The key to ending violations to human rights is to build a stable, working democracy. Democracies are accountable to their citizens, and when abuses occur in a democracy, they cannot be covered up. With our support, we expect the Government of El Salvador to be able to move ahead in prosecuting the accused and in building a criminal justice system applicable to all and, ultimately, accountable to the elected representatives of the people.

"We were told. . . that the government was the oppressor of the people. Came the elections, . . . it was the guerrilla force threatening death to any who would attempt to vote."

And I hope you've noticed that I was speaking in millions, not billions. And that, after 2 years in Federal office, is hard to do. (Laughter) In fact, there are some areas of government where I think they spill as much as I've talked about here over a weekend.

Fourth, the El Salvador Government proposes to solve its problems the only way they can be solved

fairly—by having the people decide. President Magana had just announced nationwide elections moved up to this year, calling on all to participate, adversaries as well as friends. To help political adversaries participate in the elections, he has appointed a peace commission, including a Roman Catholic bishop and two independents. And he has called on the Organization of American States and the international community to help. We were proud to participate, along with representatives of other democratic nations, as observers in last March's Constituent Assembly elections. We would be equally pleased to contribute again to an international effort, perhaps in conjunction with the Organization of American States, to help the government ensure the broadest possible participation in the upcoming elections, with guarantees that all, including critics and adversaries, can be protected as they participate.

Let me just say a word about those elections last March. A great worldwide propaganda campaign had, for more than a year, portrayed the guerrillas as somehow representative of the peoples of El Salvador. We were told over and over again that the government was the oppressor of the people. Came the elections, and suddenly it was the guerrilla force threatening death to any who would attempt to vote. More than 200 buses and trucks were attacked and burned and bombed in an effort to keep the people from going to the polls. But they went to the polls; they walked miles to do so. They stood in long lines for hours and hours. Our own congressional observers came back and reported of one incident that they saw themselves—of a woman who had been shot by the guerrillas for trying to get to the polls, standing in the line, refusing medical attention until she had had her opportunity to go in and vote.

More than 80% of the electorate voted. I don't believe here in our land where voting is so easy, that we've had a turnout that great in the last half century. They elected the present government, and they voted for order, peace, and democratic rule.

Finally, we must continue to help the people of El Salvador and the rest of Central America and the Caribbean to make economic progress. More than three-quarters of our assistance to this region has been economic. Because of the importance of economic development to that region, I will ask the Congress for $65 million in new moneys and the reprogramming of $103 million from already appropriated worldwide funds, for a total of $168 million in increased economic assistance for Central America. And to make sure that this assistance is as productive as possible, I'll continue to work with the Congress for the urgent enactment of the long-term opportunities for trade and free initiative that are contained in the Caribbean Basin Initiative.

In El Salvador and in the rest of Central America, there are today thousands of small businessmen, farmers, and workers who have kept up their productivity as well as their spirits in the face of personal danger, guerrilla sabotage, and adverse economic conditions. With them stand countless national and local officials, military and civic leaders, and priests who have refused to give up on democracy. Their struggle for a better future deserves our help. We should be proud to offer it. For in the last analysis, they're fighting for us, too.

US Assistance Needed

By acting responsibly and avoiding illusory shortcuts, we can be both loyal to our friends and true to our peaceful democratic principles. A nation's character is measured by the relations it has with its neighbors. We need strong, stable neighbors with which we can cooperate. And we will not let them down. Our neighbors are risking life and limb to better their lives, to improve their lands, and to build democracy. All they ask is our help and understanding as they face dangerous armed enemies of liberty and that our help be as sustained as their own commitment.

"Our neighbors struggle for a better future, and that struggle deserves our help, and we should be proud to offer it."

None of this will work if we tire or falter in our support. I don't think that's what the American people want or what our traditions and faith require. Our neighbors struggle for a better future, and that struggle deserves our help, and we should be proud to offer it.

We would, in truth, be opening a two-way street. We have never, I believe, fully realized the great potential of this Western Hemisphere. Oh, yes, I know in the past we've talked of plans. We've gone down there every once in a while with a great plan, somehow, for our neighbors to the south. But it was always a plan in which we, the big colossus of the north, would impose on them. It was our idea.

On my trip to Central and South America, I asked for their ideas. I pointed out that we had a common heritage. We'd all come as pioneers to these two great continents. We worship the same God. And we'd lived at peace with each other longer than most people in other parts of the world. There are more than 600 million of us calling ourselves Americans— North, Central, and South. We haven't really begun to tap the vast resources of these two great continents.

Without sacrificing our national sovereignties, our own individual cultures, or national pride, we could,

as neighbors, make this Western Hemisphere, our hemisphere, a force for good such as the Old World has never seen. But it starts with the word "neighbor." And that is what I talked about down there and sought their partnership, their equal partnership in we of the Western Hemisphere coming together to truly develop, fully, the potential this hemisphere has.

Last Sunday, His Holiness Pope John Paul II prayed that the measures announced by President Magana would "contribute to orderly and peaceful progress" in El Salvador, progress "founded on the respect," he said, "for the rights of all, and that all have the possibility to cooperate in a climate of true democracy for the promotion of the common good."

My fellow Americans, we in the United States join in that prayer for democracy and peace in El Salvador, and we pledge our moral and material support to help the Salvadoran people achieve a more just and peaceful future. And in doing so, we stand true to both the highest values of our free society and our own vital interests.

Ronald Reagan was elected president of the United States in 1980.

"When we argue that aligning ourselves with the right wing military dictators of Latin America is not truly in the interests of the United States, the people of this country will agree with us."

US Security Is Not at Stake in Central America

Michael D. Barnes

One of the reasons that the upcoming election is so important is that it is going to determine whether the United States continues its slide toward direct involvement in a Central American war, or whether we will elect a President who is capable of recognizing that our interests are best served not by war but by negotiated political settlements and economic progress and development.

As Chairman of the Subcommittee on Western Hemisphere Affairs, I have worked hard, along with several of my colleagues in the Congress, to get this choice across to the American people. We have not yet succeeded. People still don't realize that, unless he changes his policies, a vote for Reagan is a vote for war in Central America. People still don't realize that the Democratic Party offers a better alternative, one that responds both to their desire for peace *and* to their desire for security in our region. . . .

During his campaign, Ronald Reagan told us to ask ourselves whether we were better off or worse off than we were four years before, and to vote accordingly. It's a fair proposition. And in that spirit, I propose that we ask ourselves whether Reagan's policies have left us better or worse off today in Central America than we were when he took office three years ago. The answer is obvious to any serious observer.

We are losing the war in El Salvador. Democracy and human rights are vanishing dreams. Even the Secretary of State admits that the situation has deteriorated so markedly that he would not have been able to make the required certification of human rights in El Salvador if the President had not vetoed the certification bill which I introduced and which passed both houses of Congress without serious opposition. We are rapidly approaching the

point in El Salvador when the only options remaining to us will be to let the guerrillas take over, or to send American troops in to fight them. The President hopes he will not have to make this decision until after next November 6, but I'm not so sure.

Counterproductive Policies

In Nicaragua, Sandinista control and repression have increased. *Everyone* we said our policies were supposed to protect—the Miskito Indians, the political parties, the private sector, the press, the church—is worse off now than they were three years ago. We and Nicaragua's neighbors are at the brink of war with that country, a war that everyone involved is certain to lose.

In Honduras, hopes for democracy are withering in the face of a ten-fold increase in American military aid under Reagan (from $4 million in 1980 to $40 million in 1984). Poor Honduras has been turned into what one cynic has called "the USS Honduras"—an American battleship in Central America devoted not to its own development, but to American strategic objectives. The supreme authority in Honduras is not the elected President, but the Commander of the Armed Forces—if it is not the United States Ambassador. And while Honduras devotes its scarce resources to preparing for the war that we and its Generals want it to fight with Nicaragua, the economy worsens and the people's misery increases.

Guatemala continues to be governed by a military regime that violates human rights with impunity. Just within the past few weeks we have learned once again of the murder in Guatemala of employees of our own Agency for International Development, with apparent complicity by the Guatemalan military. Reagan's only policy for dealing with the situation in Guatemala has been to try every few months to get Congress to approve military aid for Guatemala. I admit that it is hard to know what to do of a positive nature in Guatemala, but it is easy to know what

Michael D. Barnes, address before the Women's National Democratic Club in Washington, DC, December 12, 1983.

would have a negative effect, and military aid is it. Fortunately, Congress has so far refused to go along.

Only in Costa Rica, which was on the verge of bankruptcy when Reagan took office, can it be said that the situation has improved—but only because Democrats in Congress literally forced the Administration to give Costa Rica desperately needed economic assistance.

Threat of War

Overarching all this is the dire threat of regional war. When Ronald Reagan took office three years ago, except for brief border skirmishes the Central American countries had not fought with each other in 100 years. Ronald Reagan appears to be about to change that. A Republican member of the Kissinger Commission said to me when we were in Central America recently that Central America in 1983 reminded him of Europe in 1938—there is an inevitability of war in the air.

"Everyone we said our policies were supposed to protect is worse off now than they were three years ago."

Americans are entitled to ask their government, "How did you get us into this mess? How did you manage to take a situation where we had some options, some hope for the future, and destroy all those options in three short years? How did you manage to bring us to the brink of war in a region where international war has been virtually unknown? How can it be that, in the one area of the world where we ought to be able to exercise the most effective influence in defense of our interests, we face the imminent collapse of our policies?"

We are where we are in Central America because Reagan and his advisers have made fundamental miscalculations about the nature of the situation and the appropriate American response. The first was to believe that they could draw a line in the dust in El Salvador and win a quick, easy victory. They thought that if we were tough enough, and stood up to the bad guys, the bad guys would give up. It didn't happen, and isn't happening, because the analysis is wrong. El Salvador is fundamentally a political problem with a modest military dimension, so you have to deal with it politically. Being tough is not enough.

The conflict in El Salvador is happening because of generations of violence, repression, and inequality, and because political avenues for redressing grievances have been closed. Under the Administration's policy, they are still closed. That is why many of the guerrillas continue to fight.

Our side is losing the war because its army won't fight. It won't fight with the quarter-of-a-billion dollars that Reagan has given it in military aid, and it won't fight if Reagan gives it double that amount.

Bay of Pigs Fallacy

The second miscalculation that Reagan made was to think we could send a few thousand contras into Nicaragua and the people would rise up and throw off their oppressors. This is the classic Bay-of-Pigs fallacy—and only an Administration committed to not learning from history would fall victim to it.

That expected result isn't happening, either, and for the same reason that it isn't happening in El Salvador: the analysis is wrong. The contras we are supporting are viewed as foreign invaders, not liberators. The McCarthyites in the Administration would have us believe that anyone who says that is pro-Sandinista, but that has nothing to do with it. It's just a fact.

Unfortunately, there is no evidence that the Reagan Administration has given up its goal of overthrowing the Sandinista government. The demands that we make of the regime go far beyond security arrangements for ourselves or Nicaragua's neighbors. They include basic changes in the nature of the regime itself. It is hard to imagine what proposals the Sandinistas could make that they haven't already made. But we just keep demanding more, refusing to settle for anything less than the dismantling of the regime.

It isn't going to happen. Sandinista response is very clear. They are prepared to negotiate security arrangements, because they respect our power and they know that they can't expect to be left alone if they threaten our interests in the region. And they are prepared to make some concessions domestically. But they are not prepared to negotiate away their power. If they are going to go down, they are going to go down fighting.

Dangerous Military Escalation

And so I am very fearful that the Reagan Administration is about to make its third and most costly miscalculation: that if the Sandinistas refuse to surrender, we can take care of them militarily at an acceptable cost. Unless we abandon our policy of refusing to talk and increasing the pressure until the Sandinistas give up, we are going to have war, because they aren't going to give up.

So that is where we are headed: toward sending American boys to defeat the guerrillas that El Salvador's own army won't fight, and to overthrow a Sandinista government that the people of Nicaragua don't want to overthrow themselves.

Sure, we're strong enough to do it, if we want to. The reason we shouldn't do it is not because we're not strong, but because we're not stupid. Because what happens after we kill all the guerrillas in El

Salvador, which we undoubtedly have the power to do? What happens after we drive the Sandinistas back into the hills, which we also have the power to do? What happens after we inflict—and take—all those casualties? What happens is that we are stuck—trapped in a situation we can't get out of, because if we leave, the people who we held at bay with our guns will just come back. And they will come back stronger, riding the anti-American wave that we created with our occupation.

Is that what the American people want? I suggest that they do not—especially considering that there are alternatives that can promote and protect our interests better at less cost.

As Niccolo Machiavelli—someone Ronald Reagan would like to think he emulates—once wrote, "Everyone may begin a war at his pleasure, but cannot so finish it."

How can we avoid beginning this Central American war that we will find ourselves unable to finish on acceptable terms? How can we stop our slide down the slippery slope?

We Democrats in the Congress have been saying that we ought to be seeking political and economic solutions to political and economic problems.

Need for Negotiated Settlement

In El Salvador, it is in our interest to take the left up on its increasingly urgent requests for talks leading to a negotiated settlement. Our power has helped create a strong incentive for the guerrillas to seek a negotiated settlement. They deeply fear direct United States intervention. They know that if they won a military victory they would face a United States-supported counterrevolution, just as the Sandinistas do, and that the United States would seek to deny them access to the resources they would need for the reconstruction and development of their country. And the democrats among them know perfectly well that they would not survive a military victory by the armed left. They would quickly be pushed aside by the people with the guns, the hard-core Marxist/Leninists.

For all these reasons, many on the left want to move the struggle to a political plane. Since that is what we purport to want, why don't we declare victory and do it? Why do we continue to hide behind the obvious absurdity that the only thing to be negotiated is the left's surrender?

We should encourage our allies in El Salvador to enter into negotiations with the left. The left has a well developed agenda for negotiations; the government has yet to make a serious proposal. But while the parties themselves will have to agree on their agenda, the basic outlines of a settlement seem fairly clear.

First, a cease-fire must be negotiated. Then, the government has a right to seek a commitment by the left that power will be decided by means of free elections, and agreement by the left on practical steps to bring those elections about within a reasonable time frame. The left has a right to seek participation in the arrangements leading to those elections, and a restructuring of the security apparatus which will permit them to participate safely. Both sides have a right to seek the creation of conditions not only for free elections on election day, but also for free political participation and expression prior to the elections and freedom from political retaliation after the elections. Democracy is a process, not an event, and unless you have a democratic process, the event of an election is meaningless, as has been demonstrated all too often in Latin America. Both sides will have to deal with the problem of what to do with their respective armies and the flow of arms from outside. And finally, they will have to agree on verification procedures, presumably international ones, for all those arrangements.

"So that is where we are headed: toward sending American boys to defeat the guerrillas that El Salvador's own army won't fight."

What must we do to get the negotiations started? The answer to that question partly answers the question of why we don't do it. Because the obstacle to negotiations is not the left; it's the right. To bring about negotiations, we would have to go to the mat with the right wing. We would have to make it plain to them that we support a political settlement of the conflict, and that we will cut them off if they try to sabotage such a settlement. And then we would have to have the courage to stick to that stand. It is because this Administration, as tough as it thinks it is, doesn't have the courage to do that, that we don't have negotiations in El Salvador.

A negotiated settlement is a tall order, but it is not impossible. Defeating the guerrillas militarily without United States troops *is* proving to be impossible. We should recognize reality and seek the possible. It is the only rational way out.

Respecting the Sandinista Government

With respect to Nicaragua, instead of avoiding talks, we and our allies should be seeking to engage the Sandinistas in the talks that they have themselves proposed leading to a settlement of the issues that make Nicaragua a threat in our eyes and those of its neighbors. We have nothing to lose and everything to gain by such talks, *unless* our objective is to do away with the Sandinistas, which is the only thing we cannot accomplish through talks.

Once again, although only the other side has made

serious proposals for talks, it is fairly clear what a settlement would look like. We have a right to seek enforceable agreements on those factors which we and Nicaragua's neighbors perceive to be threatening, including the size of Nicaragua's armed forces, their supply of foreign arms, their support for subversion in neighboring countries, the level of foreign military advisers, and other such factors that are traditionally the subject of treaties and executive agreements. In return, the other countries involved would have to agree to reciprocal reductions in their own war-making capabilities, and to accept the existence of the Sandinista revolution. Finally, there would have to be agreement to maintain a sufficient degree of openness and respect for human rights within Nicaragua to satisfy the conscience of the region—not that many countries in the region have much of a conscience in this regard, but it just has to be part of a workable bargain. This would require an end to the persecution of the Miskito Indians, guarantees of freedom of religion, press and expression, some opportunity for political participation by non-Sandinista political parties, and some kind of amnesty for the guerrillas. We must accept the fact, though, that the Sandinistas are going to remain the dominant force in their political system for the foreseeable future. Unless we are prepared to accept that, there's no deal, and we're back to the war option.

"In El Salvador, it is in our interest to take the left up on its increasingly urgent requests for talks leading to a negotiated settlement."

So it is not difficult in principle to outline the elements of negotiated settlements and to identify obstacles to them. It is not so easy to develop the actual formulas that will work, but on that I believe that we should defer to the Contadora Group—the four countries of Mexico, Venezuela, Colombia, and Panama that have been trying to bring about talks. The Contadora Group consists of friends of all sides in these conflicts. We are ourselves a protagonist. They are in a better position than we are to find the right formulas and sponsor the talks.

Our role is to encourage our own clients to negotiate, rather than discouraging them as we are doing now, and then to support the settlement that emerges. Equally important, as part of and subsequent to a settlement, we have to be willing to put our money where our rhetoric is. If this region is as important to us as Reagan is always saying it is, and I believe it is, then we should be prepared to devote major resources to the economic reconstruction of the region and to helping the people of the region satisfy their basic human needs in a context of freedom and democracy.

A One Percent Solution

Many of you have heard me propose what I call "the one-percent solution," where we would take one percent of our defense budget and devote it to economic development in the region. I hope the Kissinger Commission, which I serve as a congressional adviser, will recommend something like that.

These are some of the alternatives that Democrats have been advocating as ways that we should be protecting and promoting our interests in Central America without going to war there. We should be pursuing political settlements. Why won't the Reagan Administration do that? The reason, clearly, is that the policy of the Reagan Administration is to try to turn back the clock and re-impose traditional United States hegemony by strengthening traditional nondemocratic elites, particularly the military. The Administration's approach is based on the assumption that the center is incapable of resisting the left, so we have to put our money on the right.

There are two things wrong with that approach, and we Democrats have a responsibility to say what they are. First, the costs of reimposing the old order, even if it were possible, would be staggering, and have not yet even begun to be paid. Second, the approach is antidemocratic to the core; it assumes that it is against the interests of the United States for our neighbors in Central America to be able to organize themselves politically so as to achieve a better life for themselves and their children—that their aspirations are outweighed by our security interests. The Reagan approach is not worthy of the American people, and we can confidently go before them in 1984 and say no. When we argue that aligning ourselves with the right wing military dictators of Latin America is not truly in the interests of the United States, the people of this country will agree with us.

We Democrats have a better idea. It is better in terms of promoting our national security, and it is a better reflection of who we are as a people. It is a policy based on the confidence that we are strong, not the fear that we are weak. It is a policy that aligns us with, rather than against, the aspirations of the people of Central America for peace, free political expression, and an opportunity to participate in the development of their countries. And because of that, it is the only policy that can bring to this region the stability that constitutes the only real protection for our national security.

Michael D. Barnes, Democratic Representative from Maryland, is the chairman of the Subcommittee on Western Hemisphere Affairs of the US House of Representatives.

"The crucial issue in Latin America is: will we allow the Communists to take over another country and let the dominoes fall all the way to the Rio Grande?"

viewpoint **77**

America Must Discourage Communism in Central America

Phyllis Schlafly

Hardly anybody wants to come right out and say what the real issue is in Central America. Contrary to the thrust of the questions at President Reagan's press conferences, the real issue is not human rights, democracy or elections; it's not a phony comparison with Vietnam; it's not what the public opinion polls say; it's not even the personality of Henry Kissinger.

The crucial issue in Latin America is: will we allow the Communists to take over another country and let the dominoes fall all the way to the Rio Grande? Is the Monroe Doctrine really as dead as Khrushchev once boasted?

Why do we care if a few more "people's republics" like Castro's Cuba emerge in Latin America? Is the defense of Central America from Communism in the self-interest of the United States?

If there were no other reason to care, the refugee problems would be enough. Every country where a Communist regime has taken over has witnessed a mass exodus of refugees. Thousands of them have reached the United States from faraway countries.

If the Communists take over Central America, their refugees would not have to show the uncommon courage of the "boat people"; they would be able literally to walk across our borders. Our problems and our costs would be massive.

Central America is clearly the most important to American security of the more than a dozen wars of "national liberation" which the Soviets are waging around the world. If the Soviet-Cuban backed forces take El Salvador, then Honduras and Costa Rica will fall soon after. Mexico would become a problem we could not escape, and it would be a real problem with its corrupt, openly pro-Communist government, its 100% inflation, and its impoverished peasantry so eager to come to the United States.

The Communist arms build-up is going on all the

time. The Soviet Union has poured at least $2 billion into Cuba and Central America in the past two years and built Cuba into a world-class military power. In April, Brazil even intercepted four Libyan transport planes loaded with arms bound for El Salvador.

Soviet Military Assistance

Yet, when the press got a chance to question President Reagan at a news conference, they asked him to explain AMERICAN naval vessels in the Caribbean; they didn't ask him about arms-carrying Russian ships!

The press asked President Reagan to justify giving American servicemen the right to defend themselves if they were attacked, but failed to ask him about the presence of Russian troops and advisers in the Western Hemisphere, or the fact that Soviet military advisers in Cuba outnumber U.S. military advisers in all Latin America by a ratio of 25 to 1. Reagan properly responded by saying "what's new?" about allowing American GIs to defend themselves against attack.

The liberals complain incessantly about the miniscule amount of aid President Reagan has requested to prevent the Communists from capturing another country. Incidentally, it's only one one-hundredth (1/100th) the sum we are giving to the International Monetary Fund to bail the big banks out of their bad loans to Communist and Third World countries. The liberals just don't talk about the immense Soviet military aid.

Falsifying the Human Rights Issue

Few things show the liberals' bias so much as their phony demand for "human rights" in El Salvador. That beleaguered nation did have an election in March 1982; more than 80 percent of the eligible voters participated and voted anti-Communist even though they were under the terrorist threat of "vote in the morning and die at night."

Phyllis Schlafly, "The Stakes in Central America," *The Phyllis Schlafly Report*, September 1983. Reprinted by permission.

The liberals crying about "human rights" in El Salvador are the same people who told us that Chiang Kai-shek was corrupt and reactionary while Mao-Tse-tung was an agrarian reformer; and now we have Communist China. The liberals told us that Batista was corrupt and reactionary while Castro was an agrarian reformer; and now we have Communist Cuba.

The liberals told us the Shah of Iran was corrupt and reactionary while Khomeini was merely a religious leader; so now Iran has the most reactionary regime of the 20th century. The liberals told us Somoza was corrupt and reactionary and the Sandinistas were idealistic reformers; so now we have Communist Nicaragua, and it is also a base for exporting Communism to its neighbors.

This year is the 160th anniversary of the Monroe Doctrine—our pledge not to allow any new European colonies in the Western Hemisphere. Our credibility is at stake in El Salvador and Nicaragua. If we can't defend our interests there, no one will believe we can or will defend ourselves anywhere.

Covert Activity in Central America

The anti-Reagan media and the Congressional liberals would have us believe that there is something evil, new and un-American about covert activity in Nicaragua. On the contrary, if you have read Solzhenitsyn, you would know that it is always a social good to save a nation from Communism. Furthermore, there is a successful precedent for U.S. covert activity to overthrow a Communist government in Central America. It happened in Guatemala in 1954; and thereby hangs a little known piece of history.

President Dwight Eisenhower determined that a Communist government in Central America was intolerable to U.S. security and a violation of the Monroe Doctrine. He appointed a distinguished U.S. career diplomat, Whiting Willauer, to head the operation.

Willauer was a brilliant man, a lawyer and a linguist, who had served as U.S. Ambassador to several countries. He had been special representative to the Philippines to reconstitute the civilian economy after World War II. He had held an important position with General Claire Chennault's Flying Tigers during World War II, he was the legal coordinator of Admiral Richard Byrd's second Antarctic expedition, he held a pilot's license, and he was an expert diver, having received an award for dangerous rescue work.

In 1954, Willauer was appointed Ambassador to Honduras for the specific purpose of helping to overthrow the Communist regime in neighboring Guatemala. Willauer headed the U.S. team consisting of Ambassador Robert Hill, John Puerifoy, and several CIA men.

The Willauer team accomplished a unique

objective: the successful overthrow of a Communist regime; and Guatemala has been free from Communist control ever since. Allen Dulles later gave Willauer a commendation which stated that the Guatemalan revolution could not have succeeded without his guiding hand.

On December 10, 1960, Secretary of State Christian Herter called Willauer into his office and said that President Eisenhower had "a very special job" for Willauer. He was asked to be the senior partner of a two-man partnership with a top CIA man in directing an operation that had started in March that year, run by Cubans but backed by the CIA.

"If you have read Solzhenitsyn, you know that it is always a social good to save a nation from Communism."

Five days later, Willauer started work as the top representative of the U.S. Government on the Bay of Pigs invasion to overthrow Castro in Cuba. After the Eisenhower Administration was replaced by the Kennedy Administration in January 1961, Secretary of State Dean Rusk personally telephoned Willauer and asked him to continue on the same job.

Kennedy and Cuba

Within weeks, however, the tide turned in the Kennedy Administration. At a meeting in Rusk's office on February 8, Willauer reviewed the invasion plans for top State Department officials. It became apparent that, while Willauer's main objective was to make the Bay of Pigs invasion a success, the others were more interested in what other countries would *think* of the invasion.

On February 14, Willauer's CIA partner phoned Willauer and said, "We can't talk to you any more. We can only talk to other people." Not only the CIA, but everyone in the State Department clammed up and refused to talk to Willauer about anything. They simply froze him out of further plans without a word, even without getting the benefit of Willauer's expertise for whomever replaced him as project director.

We all know now that the Bay of Pigs invasion was one of America's most humiliating defeats. Castro's air force was not knocked out; the Swan Island radio station "somehow" failed to broadcast the signal alerting the Cuban underground to revolt; the Lignum Vitae Island radio station was forbidden to tell the Escambray guerrillas to cut the only rail line from Havana to the Bay of Pigs; some invaders armed with 30-caliber machine guns received 50-caliber ammunition; others armed with Garand rifles received cartridges made for Springfields; paratroopers had no sleep for two nights and no food or water for seven hours before jumping into Cuba; and American warships steamed away without even offering the out-gunned invaders a Dunkirk-type evacuation.

A few months later, Whiting Willauer died of a broken heart, knowing if he had been kept on the job, people now dead would be alive, and seven million people would have been liberated from Communism. Five years later, in a frank interview with journalist Stewart Alsop, Kennedy's Secretary of Defense Robert McNamara said about the Bay of Pigs: "You know damn well where I was at the time of decision—I recommended it."

President Reagan's options in Nicaragua are not easy, but they are clear. He can liberate a Central American country from Communism as Eisenhower did in Guatemala; or he can acquiesce in a planned defeat and leave a nation enslaved by Communism as Kennedy did.

Kissinger and Latin America

A recent *New York Times*/CBS public opinion poll (printed on the front page as though it were important news) is a good example of how phony news is manufactured. The poll claimed that "despite months of controversy over U.S. policies on Central America, most of the American public does not know which side the Reagan Administration supports in either El Salvador or Nicaragua."

" 'Which side does the Reagan Administration back in El Salvador and Nicaragua—the Communist or the anti-Communist?' The big majority of American people would have had no trouble giving the accurate answer."

The *Times* pompously advised its readers that this survey of 1,365 adults nationwide has only a 3 percent margin of error. However, that's only the margin of error on the question that was asked. The big error was in the wording of the question.

Instead of asking if the Reagan Administration backs the government or the anti-government forces, the survey question should have been, "Which side does the Reagan Administration back in El Salvador and Nicaragua—the Communist or the anti-Communist?" The big majority of American people would have had no trouble giving the accurate answer.

The issue in Latin America is not whether one faction or another is in control in various little countries, but whether the Kremlin-Castro axis will get another base in the Western Hemisphere. Ronald Reagan and the American people understand that

issue rather well, even if the *New York Times* pollsters don't.

Henry Kissinger has bounced back from the damaged inflicted on his reputation by Seymour Hersh's book *The Price of Power* into the chairmanship of a commission to advise the President about Latin America. Unfortunately, Kissinger seems to have an inferiority complex when he deals with the Communists, and they usually get the better of him.

Phony "Missile Gap"

In 1960, Kissinger fell hook, line and sinker for the phony "missile gap," John F. Kennedy's presidential campaign slogan. Kissinger wrote in his 1961 book: "It is generally admitted that from 1961 to at least the end of 1964, the Soviet Union will possess more missiles than the United States. . . . The missile gap in the period of 1961-1965 is now unavoidable. . . It may mean that we could lose if the Soviet Union struck first. In that case, we would be fortunate if we escaped a surprise attack."

By 1970, Kissinger had discovered the truth about that time period. He wrote: "In as late as 1962, during the Cuban missile crisis, the Soviet Union had around 40 ICBMs. We had over 1,000 bombers and over 200 missiles that could reach the Soviet Union. . . .In short, our strategic superiority was overwhelming." Richard Nixon put the ratio of our 1962 strategic superiority over the Soviets as 8-to-1.

A comparison of these two Kissinger writings reveals how he imagined the threat of a Soviet strategic force substantially more powerful than ours, how he thought this nonexistent Soviet missile force had such a margin of superiority over us that they had a first-strike capability against us, and how he believed the Kremlin dictators had the will to use this missile force so that we would be "fortunate" if they did not surprise-attack us.

Kissinger's 1961 vision of the United States "losing" to the Soviets was a kind of sick defeatism. There never was any factual basis for this fear; there was every possible reason for absolute confidence that, in a confrontation, the Soviets would lose; and that is exactly what did happen in the Cuban Missile Crisis of 1962.

Kissinger's tour de force was the SALT I agreements which he negotiated and got Nixon to sign in 1972. Under SALT I, the United States accepted inferiority at the ratio of 3-to-2 in Soviet-U.S. missiles and submarines.

Kissinger's rationalization for this inferiority was this: "As a result of decisions made in the 1960s, and not reversible within the timeframe of the projected agreement, there would be a numerical gap against us in the two categories of land-based and sea-based missile systems whether or not there was an agreement. . . .Therefore, any time over the next five years (1972-77) we were confronting a numerical margin that was growing, and a margin, moreover, that we could do nothing to reverse in that five-year period."

Kissinger lives in a make-believe world in which the Soviet Union (which can't even feed itself) is ten-feet tall. He thinks that the United States (which has a Gross National Product twice that of the U.S.S.R.'s) is a pitiful helpless giant who can't catch up.

If Kissinger carries his surrender syndrome to his Latin America task, the Communists will soon take El Salvador and start the falling dominos in the Western Hemisphere. One can only hope that Kissinger has learned something in recent years from the rejection of SALT II and from Ronald Reagan's defeat of Jimmy Carter.

Low Frontier of Unconventional War

The bombing in Beirut should remind us that we face a third dimension in warfare in addition to strategic (nuclear) and conventional (non-nuclear). Usually called unconventional warfare, General John K. Singlaub also calls it the "low frontier."

Unconventional warfare has many faces. It includes terrorism, sabotage, guerrilla actions, passive resistance, and support of dissident groups. It also includes economic warfare, political warfare, psychological operations, subversion, disinformation activities, and propaganda.

The Soviets have a full-scale operation in all types of unconventional warfare. It is probable that the Soviets have just as much a margin of superiority over us in this third dimension of warfare as they do in ICBMs and in tanks.

The Soviets are quite familiar with the writings of the ancient Chinese military strategist, Sun Tzu (350 B.C.), who said that the best general is he who avoids violence and achieves conquest by surrender of the enemy.

A major part of the Soviet's unconventional warfare against us since the end of World War II has been a "peace offensive." Years ago, Louis Budenz, former managing editor of the Communist *Daily Worker*, titled his book *The Cry is Peace* to describe this Soviet propaganda campaign. Like the thief who cries "Stop, thief!" to distract attention from his crime, the Soviets accuse America of disrupting world peace.

Of course, there are different kinds of peace. We certainly don't want the peace of surrender as they have in North Korea, North Vietnam, Laos, Cambodia, Cuba, Angola, and Eastern Europe. Nor do we want the peace of the 1,500 slave labor camps that form the Gulag Archipelago.

General Singlaub believes that Western strategy must recognize the entire spectrum of conflict and exploit the weaknesses of the enemy. In a recent speech, he made constructive suggestions for an American strategy to cope with the third dimension.

1. Adopt a national strategy which recognizes the entire spectrum of conflict, and has a policy for dealing with all facets, including the low frontier of unconventional conflict (as well as strategic and conventional). Our strategy must have a sound, offensive non-military component.

2. Exploit the weaknesses of the Soviet empire. No football game was ever won by a team which stayed on its own side of the 50-yard line. The Achilles heel of the Russian empire is the disaffection of the peoples behind the Iron Curtain; the captive peoples behind the Iron Curtain are our best allies.

3. Stop the process of our self-surrender through subsidizing the Communist system. We must limit the flow of technology, food, and credits to the U.S.S.R.

"Like the thief who cries 'Stop, thief!' to distract attention from his crime, the Soviets accuse America of disrupting world peace."

4. Face up to the fact that Mainland China will never be a U.S. ally under any scenario that one could reasonably imagine. Such wishful thinking is a real danger to our security.

5. Recognize that the centerpiece of Soviet ideology is the continuing "class struggle." The Soviets are at war all the time, even when not using guns.

6. Use the Voice of America and Radio Free Europe to counteract Soviet and Chinese disinformation. VOA and RFE broadcasts should explain the facts about political and economic freedom.

7. Beef up the Special Operations forces in our Army, Navy, and Air Force; and reestablish the intelligence collection capabilities of the CIA.

8. Loosen legislative restraints which frustrate our ability to defend American diplomatic and military personnel in other countries. For example, current law forbids us to use U.S. funds to train police forces in other countries (even though some small countries cannot afford to train their own police sufficiently to provide local protection to our embassies). The recent bombing in Beirut was the 50th attack on our embassies abroad in recent years.

Phyllis Schlafly was a member of President Reagan's 1980 Defense Advisory Group. She is a leading conservative activist and the author of five books on defense and foreign policy. This viewpoint was taken from her newsletter The Phyllis Schlafly Report.

"If the United States were not controlled by its obsession about communism and even traces of marxism, we might be able to. . .provide alternatives to Soviet or Cuban support."

viewpoint **78**

American Obsession with Communism Is Self-Defeating

John C. Bennett

In the political debate about the administration's policy in Central America few questions are raised about the presupposition of that policy. Politicians facing election are reluctant to challenge them. In general terms, however, the policy's opponents often point out that the indigenous sources of revolution—regional poverty and oppression—are more important than is influence from outside, from the Soviet Union or Cuba. In what follows I shall try to give more substance to that general point.

The clearest sign of how wrong our policy is can be seen in our preference for the government of El Salvador over that of Nicaragua. The administration is doing everything it can to defend the one and to overthrow the other. If the comparison were made in human terms without ideological blinders, this preference would be seen to be a moral absurdity. *CHRISTIANITY AND CRISIS* has prepared its readers for some time to see that this is the case.

The government of El Salvador, which we so strongly support, contains murderous elements that get out of control. Its moderates seem captive of the army and the right wing. Its economic reforms are off and on, grudgingly supported because of American pressure, opposed by the powerful right wing, and wholly inadequate to provide fundamental political and economic change. To say that in defending that regime we are defending democracy, as is so much emphasized by President Reagan, is also an absurdity.

Sandinista Government Unrepressive

The government of Nicaragua is a postrevolutionary government, and as such it is relatively restrained and humane. It is seldom that postrevolutionary governments avoid ruthless counterrepression. In spite of disillusionment among many of their

early admirers, disillusionment that stems in part from the very lofty standards associated with the revolution, the record of the Sandinistas has been free from the most serious repression. Their government does employ censorship, and its early pluralism has been too much reduced. It permits a considerable private sector, though its exact extent is debated. Political parties keep their identity pending an election.

Tom Wicker on a very recent visit reported "a general absence of police terror and brutality, a deeply rooted Catholicism, and a relaxed atmosphere that seems to a visitor more nearly a signal of hope than fear." The spirit of the people is much praised by visitors. One sign of the government's concern for people is the fact that even critics of the regime praise its system of medical care and accomplishments in attaining much greater literacy.

The Catholic hierarchy is now in opposition, and the several priests in government are under pressure from Rome because their political activity is disapproved; but at many levels priests and nuns and missionaries and evangelical leaders who live with the people support the revolution from religious motives. The "basic Christian communities," which are now opposed by the hierarchy, remain a strong religious movement supporting the revolution. The melding of Christian and Marxist influences at work in this revolution may well be unique.

Marxism Cause for US Panic

Marxism is a strong element among the ruling junta, but how hardline it becomes may depend on how much it has to struggle to defend the revolution against opponents supported by the United States. It does not take much evidence of a Marxist presence to convince many people in Washington that a nation is on the way to becoming a full-fledged totalitarian state and an agent of Soviet power.

Our country has wronged the people of Nicaragua

John C. Bennett, "Central America: False Premises," *Christianity and Crisis.* September 19, 1983. Reprinted with permission.

for three generations. For decades our marines intervened and controlled the nation; then we established the regime of the Somoza family, which was an ugly tyranny for decades. Now our administration has chosen to do what it can to plunge Nicaragua into a civil war that has already killed many Nicaraguans, has done much to bleed the economy and may result, if our side gets its way, in years of disorder followed by an ugly tyranny that might be another American puppet. (Fortunately, our side is not likely to have its way.) That is a great wrong for our government. To do all of this out of far-fetched ideological calculations and from a misreading of the long-term interests of our own country is an even greater wrong. It is this fundamental error in American policy, as it affects the people of Nicaragua, that is seldom mentioned in our political debates.

I have mentioned the great difficulty postrevolutionary governments have in avoiding a period of terror against their opponents and have suggested that the Nicaraguan revolution, in spite of all current criticisms of it, may be an exception. Americans may misjudge the difficulty of the problems of a postrevolutionary government because their own revolution was won under most exceptional circumstances; its chief opponents were 3,000 miles away and were much divided. The leaders of the American revolution were fortunate also in having behind them the British political tradition, and they had an experience of self-government in the colonies. Hannah Arendt in her *On Revolution* praised the unusual success of the American revolution and credited that success partly to the fact that it was a political and not a social revolution; it was not a revolution against poverty. Central American revolutions do not have such an advantage.

Two US Misconceptions

Underlying the dominant American thinking about Central America are two misconceptions about the dynamics of the area. One is the assumption that all that is needed are a few reforms that an American government is glad to encourage, including elections regardless of whether minimally fair electoral procedures are possible. Some of those countries need revolutions to change the location of political and economic power. The displacement of oligarchies allied with American economic interests is not on our government's agenda.

The other misconception, to which I have already referred, is that external Marxist influences are the cause of needed revolutions rather than a factor that has helped to organize the forces of revolution, which themselves are indigenous and arise out of the desperate poverty and oppression from which most people have long suffered. In the eyes of most Americans the signs of Marxist influence discredit the revolutions themselves. A nation that is to any degree influenced by Marxism or communism is assumed to be a lost entity that we can no longer influence, lost to the Soviet or Cuban camp.

If we made a distinction between the revolution and the Marxist forces that have helped to organize it and defend it, we might be able to use our imagination, our tactical skill, the admired aspects of our democratic society, and our national energy to help provide alternatives to Soviet or Cuban support. We might have done this 25 years ago in the case of Cuba; instead we tried to strangle the Cuban revolution and caused Castro to become dependent on the Soviet Union. We are in the process of making the same mistake in the case of Nicaragua.

"So long as we continue our arrogant interference to preserve frozen patterns of a corrupt past, we shall remain their enemy."

If the United States were not controlled by its obsession about communism and even traces of Marxism, we might be able to deal with greater empathy and more rationally with neighboring nations in need of revolutionary change. It would be helpful to realize that the Soviet Union has not been generally successful in maintaining control over nations at a great distance from the Red Army. The picture of the Soviet Union as cumulatively gaining power over distant countries, which is important in presidential rhetoric, is false. There are many reasons why a nation in this hemisphere would resist becoming dependent on Soviet power. Why not give more attention to such issues as nationalism, their desire for self-determination, the faded appeal of the Soviet system, the effects of Soviet heavy-handedness, and to alternative paths we might help to make possible? It would be better to think on these things rather than on frozen ideological stereotypes.

US Responsibility for Oppression

It would be well for those who make American policy to listen to a not unfriendly voice from abroad, that of *The Guardian*. That journal asks:

> How can it [the United States] learn to live in peace in its own hemisphere with people who are waking up to the fact that their condition of oppression—for which the United States bears some historic and present responsibility—is not forever immutable? The United States can adapt to change or seek to resist it. It cannot—even with the marines—prevent it.

Much is made of the effect on our national security of events in Central America. More attention should be given to the effect on our security of piling new resentments upon old resentments because of our continuing acts of intervention. George Ball is one of a group of elder statesmen who are not running for office and who thereby speak out more freely on many issues. He gives a picture of the future of Latin America and its possible relations with the United States that is far more fateful than all our present ideological calculations. In the year 2000, he says, there will be 600 million people in Latin America with 60 percent under the age of 25.

> Thus we must coexist in the same hemisphere with a swelling freshet of increasingly disenchanted young people rebelling at their inheritance of poverty, discrimination, and repression. So long as we continue our arrogant interference to preserve frozen patterns of a corrupt past, we shall remain their enemy.

There is more wisdom in that statement than in all the speeches of our political leaders today. Such wisdom was apparent a few years ago in the struggle to get the Panama Canal treaties ratified when those treaties were opposed by Ronald Reagan and his associates. Ultimately, our caring about what happens to those 600 million people for their own sake is more important than even the realization that we are in danger of incurring the enmity of so many Latin Americans.

John C. Bennett is senior contributing editor for Christianity and Crisis, *a Christian journal of opinion.*

"It is recognized internationally that Nicaragua is the victim of an unjustified military aggression."

The US Should Not Oppose the Nicaraguan Government

Tomás Borge Martínez

"A great nation gains in honor and prestige by respecting the sovereignty of small, weak nations, rather than by oppressing those who fight to secure their rights." These are the words of General A. C. Sandino, who led the fight against U.S. Marine intervention in Nicaragua in 1927-33 and served as inspiration for the Sandinista National Liberation Front.

It is recognized internationally that Nicaragua is the victim of an unjustified military aggression. This aggression is in violation of international laws and the very laws of the United States. As many facts concerning this aggression are well known by now, there is no need to enter into details about it.

There is another, less apparent form of aggression, an aggression of constant lies, half-truths, accusations based on false premises, and interpretations motivated by bad faith.

It is obvious that this latter form of aggression was planned months ago in order to justify to an uninformed public a later military aggression. This is an affront to the intelligence and good will of the people of the United States.

What is said of Nicaragua? That the revolution has altered its original program and that the present government has liquidated democratic liberties to establish a totalitarian regime.

Several political parties covering a broad span of the political spectrum are active in Nicaragua today. We distinguish clearly between legitimate opposition and counterrevolutionary opposition: the latter is based on anti-national premises that seek a return to dictatorship and the forfeiting of our people's needs to the interests of other nations.

We asked our people to give us five years to reorganize a country destroyed by war. Part of this

reorganization is setting the institutional bases for elections to be held in 1985. Have the American people, after 200 years, forgotten that the United States required thirteen years of reorganization before the first national elections were held in 1789?

Today the process is moving forward. Our council of state is studying the political systems of other countries, including the United States, in order to see what aspects are pertinent to our reality, and to develop our own democracy.

A law of political parties, which guarantees political parties access to power through the electoral process, has been approved by our legislature.

Economic and Social Progress

Political pluralism is growing side by side with a strong mixed economy. In 1982, the private sector received 60.5 per cent of the credits approved by the banks. That sector also obtained 68.8 per cent of the authorized foreign exchange. More than 70 per cent of the land and 60 per cent of industrial activities are private. The agrarian reform is not based on whether the land is privately held or not; rather, it is founded on the productive use of the land.

Don't these facts disprove the statements made by the government of the United States concerning Nicaragua's political and economic reality?

In Nicaragua today there is a greater percentage of private enterprise than is the case in countries such as Venezuela, Mexico, and Brazil, to state a few examples.

In just four months in 1980 we reduced illiteracy from 51 per cent to 12 per cent, and we have developed programs to prevent relapse into illiteracy. The entire child population is incorporated into the school system. (Some of these schools have been attacked by the CIA-financed counterrevolutionary forces.) The number of children attending primary school has doubled, and there is an increase of 53 per cent at the secondary level. There has been a 92 per

Tomás Borge Martínez, "Washington's Lies and Half-Truths," *The Washington Post*, July 31, 1983. Reprinted by permission.

cent increase in university registration.

The achievements in health care during the last four years have been greater than the accomplishments during the previous 150 years. We have eliminated diseases such as poliomyelitis, reduced tuberculosis, virtually eradicated malaria, reduced infant mortality by about 50 per cent, and increased the number of vaccinations by 190 per cent. The entire population is incorporated into the program of preventive medicine. Nicaragua is recognized by international organizations to be at the forefront in public health care. Both education and health care are available to our people free of charge.

Is this not respect for human, economic, and social rights? Is the Reagan administration fighting against this? What other country in Latin America has accomplished so much in such a short period of time, in spite of sabotage and the opposition of the most powerful country of the planet?

Full Religious Freedom

We have been accused of religious persecution. Many religious organizations have stated the contrary.

Since 1979 full freedom of religious expression exists in Nicaragua for the first time in our history. There are 240 priests in the country, most of whom support the revolution. Sixty per cent are foreigners. They offer more than 300 masses daily in more than 350 churches located in 155 parishes. Catholic orders, including the Dominicans, Calazans, Jesuits, and Maryknolls, as well as dozens of Protestant churches, including the Moravians, are all represented in Nicaragua. The Protestant and evangelical churches have quadrupled their membership since 1979. Several Catholic priests serve as ministers of state, and a Jesuit priest, Father Fernando Cardenal, is one of the leaders of the Sandinista Youth Organization.

"To pose the issue of the Central American crisis as part of the East-West confrontation could be considered ridiculous if it did not have such dramatic consequences."

Is this reality consistent with the accusations leveled against us by the government of the United States? And if there are doubts as to whether we have freedom of religion, why don't they come to Nicaragua and see firsthand, as have so many honest and open-minded U.S. citizens who have changed their opinion after visiting our country?

Recently we have been accused of anti-Semitism. In Nicaragua no one is persecuted because of his religion, race, or political beliefs. Those who

participated directly or indirectly in the genocide carried out against the people of Nicaragua by the Somoza dictatorship were punished. Two individuals of Jewish origin had their properties confiscated because of their involvement in the above-mentioned crimes. We are sending documentation to Rabbi Morton Rosenthal, who initiated these charges against us. Moreover, we have invited him to come to Nicaragua so he can see for himself how mistaken he has been.

If, in the process of reviewing the case of the alleged confiscation of a synagogue, the government finds sufficient grounds to consider that the building—though registered in the name of an individual very much linked to the Somoza regime—is in fact patrimony of the Jewish community, the government will facilitate its return.

No East-West Implications

To pose the issue of the Central American crisis as part of the East-West confrontation could be considered ridiculous if it did not have such dramatic consequences.

When we were fighting against Somoza, the Soviet Union gave neither arms nor advice to us Nicaraguans.

Following the revolutionary victory, Nicaragua has established diplomatic and commercial relations with the Soviet Union and other socialist countries, within the normal parameters that are the rights of all modern states that are fighting to keep from dying.

Our people are fighting to keep from dying of hunger. Our struggle is against hunger and backwardness. Hunger and backwardness create a conflict between the selfishness of bloody dictatorships and the people. What does the East-West conflict have to do with gastroenteritis, illiteracy, and the genocide of repressive military rulers?

I think that this argument is a brutal sophism to deceive the people of the United States, to justify the aggression of a powerful, rich country against a small, impoverished, weak country. This argument is a deliberate lie whose only force lies in its constant repetition.

Central America has been victimized by dictatorships, each of which might have provided chapter and verse for the apocalypse. It has been calculated that the National Guard, Somoza's army, in the course of nearly half a century, assassinated more than 300,000 Nicaraguans. Since 1954, more than 10,000 persons have been assassinated in Guatemala, and the Salvadorans since 1979 have offered more than 50,000 victims to the holocaust.

They accuse us of being dominated by the Cubans and the Soviets. All Nicaraguans remember that, in the evil hour of Somocismo, the maximum authority in our country was the ambassador of the United States. We overthrew Somoza, fundamentally, in order to be the masters of our own decisions. This is a Sandinista principle of elementary national pride.

I can affirm, with full knowledge of the facts, that neither the Cuban ambassador nor Fidel Castro, with whom we have frequently conversed, nor the Soviet Leader, . . . with whom we have also spoken, has ever told us what we must do. To think the contrary would be to accept that we have no criteria of our own, that we are simply puppets. If we were nincompoops, if we were so dishonorable as to sell out to somebody, there can be no doubt whatever that it would be much easier and much more comfortable to sell ourselves to the government of the United States. We Sandinistas never have been, are not, and never will be anybody's satellites. The Manichean concept that a country which has stopped being a satellite of one country has to become a satellite of another country is simply inconceivable to us.

Our concept of nonalignment is not inconsistent with our right to establish relations with other countries based on the principle of mutual respect. What is more, it is our hope that the United States will become one of those countries. We are not to be blamed that there exist those who maliciously confuse the diversification of our relations with alignment.

Another accusation that has been launched against Nicaragua is that we are fomenting an arms race in Central America. Let us see what the real facts are:

Nicaragua was first threatened and then invaded. We have the right and obligation to defend ourselves, as we also have the obligation not to attack other countries. We do not propose to invade Honduras, and neither do we propose—however unnecessary it be to mention this—to invade the United States. Nicaragua has clearly demonstrated over the past four years that it is not a threat to the national security of any country. It is not we who have constructed naval bases in the Gulf of Fonseca, military training bases outside our borders, military air bases from which C130s daily unload munitions. We do not violate the airspace of any country with espionage overflights, nor do we send against the coasts of any country powerful naval task forces, complete with aircraft carriers and missile cruisers.

Faced with the escalation of armaments in Central America, clearly directed against us, we have the elemental right of self-defense. In this regard, we are certain that we will receive aid from all around the world, including the American people.

The problem of Central America is not the supposed expansionism of Cuba or the Soviet Union in the region. It is not the aggressiveness of Nicaragua with respect to its neighbors. The problem is the philosophy of the big stick: the inconceivable concept that the United States believes it has the right to decide who should govern our countries, and to become irritable if other peoples determine styles and forms that fail to please whatever U.S. president happens to be in office.

Negotiations: Blocked by U.S.

We have made numerous proposals for dialogue, for negotiations. The response of the United States has always been either silence or an escalation of threats and aggression. It has responded similarly to proposals launched by such countries as Mexico and France. We always insist that our problems are with Honduras, whose territory is being used as a base of U.S. military operations and attacks against Nicaragua.

"We want peace. We need peace in order to work, to study; in order to sing, to laugh."

Because of that, negotiations must be of a bilateral nature with those two countries. The U.S. response, and consequently that of Honduras as well, is that the so-called regional problem that Nicaragua supposedly represents must be negotiated multilaterally.

Very well. In order to avoid pretexts, on July 19 [1983] we announced that we are disposed to negotiate multilaterally. We proposed a nonaggression pact with Honduras. We proposed the absolute end to all supplies of weapons by any country to the forces in conflict in El Salvador, so that the Salvadoran people may resolve their problems without foreign interference. We proposed an end to the militarization of the area and to the use of any territories to launch aggressions against any other country. We also proposed the noninstallation of military bases and respect for the self-determination of each country. Who can doubt that all of these are measures conducive to peace?

This has been recognized by personalities such as Bernardo Sepulveda, foreign minister of Mexico, who stated publicly that the six-point proposal presented by the government of Nicaragua "is a step forward in the process toward peace in the region."

And what has been the response? In the first instance, the dispatch of powerful naval fleets to "carry out maneuvers" along our Pacific and Atlantic coasts. At the same time, statements that the principal obstacle to peace was "the leftist government of Nicaragua."

But the international reaction remains on the side of reason and common sense. The presidents of Panama, Venezuela, Colombia, and Costa Rica have stated their opposition, as has the president of Mexico, who warned that a generalized war in Central America "would result in victory for neither side" and called on the international community to take steps "to stop the outbreak of an irrational war before it destroys the legitimate yearning for peace and development."

The foreign ministers of France and Japan have also made similar statements. The Social Democratic Party of Germany and the Labor Party of Great Britain have demanded that their respective governments expressly condemn the policy of the United States toward Central America.

It seems that the unanimous statements in favor of peace and against war have somewhat moderated the U.S. government's language a bit. In its most recent declarations it says that the United States "is not preparing a war" against Nicaragua, and it hopes peace can be achieved "without bloodshed."

But the facts contradict these affirmations. The aircraft carriers are there. U.S. troops are carrying out "prolonged maneuvers" in Honduras. The CIA continues financing the counterrevolution. The Green Berets continue training the Honduran army. And we continue contributing the dead.

We want peace. We need peace in order to work, to study; in order to sing, to laugh; in order to simply live.

We want peace. *Why don't they leave us in peace?*

What wrong have we done to the people of the United States? We have offered the hand of friendship. Why does their government respond with a clenched fist?

We want peace, but we are disposed to defend ourselves. Neither our petition for peace nor our determination to defend ourselves is rhetorical.

Our people, like Sandino, prefer "to die as rebels rather than to live as slaves."

George Washington, that apostle of truth, would have applauded this determination of our national hero and this heroic determination of the Nicaraguan people.

Perhaps the gravest error is to believe that the force of arms is superior to the force of truth, or to the force of peoples who have conquered their liberty.

Tomás Borge Martínez is a leader of the Sandinista National Liberation Front (FSLN) and a member of the Directorate of the Nicaraguan Revolutionary Government.

"If the United States refuses to aid the anti-Sandinista forces, . . . it will be morally responsible for selling the Nicaraguan people into slavery."

The US Must Oppose the Nicaraguan Government

Miguel Bolaños Hunter

Before coming to power, the Sandinistas signed accords with the free enterprise sector, the Catholic Church, and the existing political parties, in order to unite the entire country against Somoza. Once that was accomplished, however, all these sectors were betrayed. Private enterprise has been virtually destroyed by state controls and nationalizations. Although freedom of expression was promised, it lasted no longer than three months after the triumph of the revolution. The church is now being attacked and maligned, as a result of disturbances provoked by the Sandinista front to discredit and neutralize its political power. Today, the church recognized by the Sandinistas as legitimate representative of the Catholic followers is the "Church of the Poor," previously known as the "People's Church." The new church is not recognized by Rome, and Archbishop Obando y Bravo of Managua has officially discredited its activities.

When the Sandinistas assumed control of the government in 1979, they had to share power with democratic forces, a situation which they never had any intention of maintaining. They consolidated their position by taking control of all the propaganda media, the army, the internal police, the prisons, and a very large part of what by then appeared to be a democratic political system. Thus, as the revolution developed, opposing political forces did not have any opportunity to argue their case against the changes imposed by the Marxist Sandinistas.

During the campaigns, the Sandinistas subtly discredited those opposition elements that the FSLN (Sandinista National Liberation Front) leadership wished to portray as aligned with the Somocista National Guard. Through the use of disinformation, front organizations, youth organizations, teacher

Miguel Bolaños Hunter, "Inside Communist Nicaragua: The Miguel Bolanos Transcripts," *The Backgrounder*, September 30, 1983. Reprinted by permission of the Heritage Foundation, 214 Massachusetts Ave. NE, Washington, DC 20002.

organizations, and a barrage of Sandinista propaganda, the Marxists successfully prevented the opposition from becoming recognized as a viable alternative to Communism, thus assuring that no force within the opposition became a political threat to them. . . .

The Campaign Against the Church

The project to neutralize the church, the most powerful force opposing the Sandinistas, is directed toward denigrating the church hierarchy, associating it with the Somoza guard, and identifying it with the United States and the Nicaraguan wealthy classes.

The Sandinistas have used different types of operations to accomplish this. One is the use of government-organized mobs, called "divine mobs" by Comandante Tomás Borge. Such mobs are placed in parishes, where they pose as devout Catholics. They gradually gain power by supporting priests who back the revolution. The idea is to divide the church and to make it look as though the church establishment is the enemy and these "progressive" priests are for the people. . . .

In a related incident, Archbishop Obando y Bravo removed a pro-Sandinista priest from a parish in Santa Rosa. In retaliation, the Sandinista mobs played the role of parishioners and created an uprising, taking over the church. The mob took away religious items and turned the building into a warehouse. The government filmed the "spontaneous" incident for propaganda purposes.

The mobs that heckled the Pope during his visit to Nicaragua were also organized by State Security. They prevented large numbers of Catholics who wanted to participate in the papal Mass from getting close to John Paul II.

Harassment of Business Leaders

Harassment of the business community began in 1980 with the assassination of business leader Jórge

Salazar, head of the Nicaraguan Businessmen's Association (COSEP). I am personally aware of this incident; the head of all the F sections, Alejandro Royero, gave me details of all the players and how it was planned to send José Moncada, Cerna's assistant, as a double agent to induce Salazar to join an armed movement against the Sandinistas that Moncada supposedly led. Salazar was killed when they went to a gas station to pick up arms. Moncada was armed and Salazar was not. The security guards shot at Salazar only. Following the incident Moncada was sent to Cuba. He returned from Cuba in 1983 and holds a high position in State Security.

"The more serious censorship of journalists is done upon their exiting the country."

Business leaders have also been subjected to harassment. The jailing of nine businessmen in February 1982 was part of an operation to scare them into leaving the country and to make them aware that they were not immune from Sandinista repression. The idea is to make it so that those who remain will cooperate with the Sandinistas.

Press Manipulation

Since 1979 the Sandinistas have been working with the foreign press through F-2 Unit D. This security unit collects information about all the correspondents who come to Nicaragua, categorizing them as useful, manageable, or hostile. For example, on numerous occasions, whenever a network crew would arrive at their hotel, members of the F-2 D unit were secretly sent to their rooms to review videotapes made by groups such as CBS, NBC, or ABC. Sometimes the tapes were confiscated and replaced with blank tape. The crew's notes were read and cassette tapes listened to—all this while the crew was on assignment for a long period away from the hotel. The minister of tourism has assisted in creating a group for surveillance of the international press, which on a regular basis bugs reporters' rooms. Hotel clerks are in reality security agents, all coordinated by State Security. This process really begins at the airport, where passports of reporters are photographed and files are kept on them.

The more serious censorship of journalists is done upon their exiting the country at the airport. All information is reviewed without their knowledge while they await departure. All passports are checked against the files taken on their arrival. . . .

One correspondent in Managua for a widely respected American press organization has been working as an agent of the F-2 D unit since December 1982. Though he is not being paid, he is receiving direction from State Security. He is sometimes critical of the Sandinistas in his dispatches, but it is only to maintain credibility. For example, he will do interviews with leaders of democratic groups and then give the information to the Sandinistas. His employer does not know that he is working for the Sandinistas. However, he is not a full agent, because State Security believes that the CIA could have planted him and that he could be a double agent. There are many other journalists working like him.

Manipulating Missionaries

Journalists are not the only ones used to promote the image of the Sandinistas abroad. A number of religious representatives have been manipulated; one of the most prominent among them is the Catholic Maryknoll order of missionaries. The Sandinistas' foreign minister, Miguel D'Escoto, is a Maryknoll priest and the former editor of *Maryknoll* magazine, a Catholic publication which has printed stories favorable to the Sandinistas and very critical of the rest of the governments of Latin America. D'Escoto has used his influence in the Catholic Church in the United States to gain support for the Sandinistas.

The Maryknoll order represents a very influential Catholic force both in Latin America and in the United States. The Sandinistas have realized they need the promotion of a religious group to have a credible image in the United States. Maryknoll is only one of several religious organizations in support of the Sandinista regime that promote the FSLN abroad. . . .

Human Rights Abuses

The Sandinista security forces systematically employ methods of interrogation against their opponents that deny their basic human rights. When the Sandinistas bring someone in for interrogation, they usually need only to confirm information or to obtain names they do not yet have. They apply the KGB method of psychological torture. Even the jails are constructed for psychological torture; their layouts have been brought from Cuba and are based on KGB models.

The F-1 interrogators are trained by Cubans, who themselves trained for five years in the Soviet Union. They have the ability to reduce anyone's resistance within two days. Outside Managua the methods are not so sophisticated. In the north, anti-Sandinista rebels are often brutally killed *en masse*. If fifteen are captured, two will be taken to Managua for debriefing, where they are put on TV, and the rest will be killed. Often they are killed by stabbing, but there is also the "vest cut." In this, the prisoner's arms and legs are cut off while he is alive, and he is left to bleed to death. It is an old technique used by Somoza and Sandino.

Stedman Fagoth, the leader of the Miskito Indians, was one of those who were psychologically tortured. He gave F-1 more information than he realized. Because of the interrogation, he negotiated with the Sandinistas. Later, however, we realized it was an intelligent move on his part, because it allowed him to get away. The Argentine Victor Frances was interrogated in this manner when he was kidnapped in Costa Rica and brought back to Managua. It was then that he was forced to make statements about U.S. and Argentine involvement in helping the anti-Sandinista rebels.

Involvement by the Communist Bloc

Intervention by Cubans, Soviets, and other elements of the socialist bloc exists on a grand scale in all areas of Nicaraguan society today. There are Soviet and Cuban political advisors, and, as a consequence, there is rapid movement toward a Marxist economy. There is already a plan to establish firm economic ties with the Soviet Union.

Renan Montero (*nom de guerre*), commander of the Nicaraguan intelligence service, is a former colonel in Cuba's intelligence service who became a nationalized Nicaraguan citizen. He was ordered to work with the Sandinistas fifteen years ago, in efforts to help them sieze power and set up Communism in Nicaragua. Sandinista leader Tomas Borge was so pleased with his work that he asked Fidel Castro to allow Montero to remain permanently in Nicaragua.

Today, Nicaragua has 3,000 Cuban soldiers (not counting high-level advisors) and a covert team of 2,000 soldiers working as technical advisors, building roads and handling heavy machinery. Their purpose is to help Nicaragua in case of an attack or emergency. There are 400 Cuban advisors to the army alone, and forty high-level officials on the staff of the regular army. There are 200 Soviet military advisors in Nicaragua, of whom fifty are high-level officials working with the army. There are also high-level Cuban and Soviet advisors working with intelligence and counterintelligence. The Cubans' role with the regular army involves military training of low-ranking Nicaraguan soldiers, as well as developing all aspects of army security and defense....

Soviet Arms in Nicaragua

Arms from the Communist bloc have flowed freely into Nicaragua. Today the army, the militia, and the police, including the security police, special troops, and commandos, are outfitted with Soviet arms. Armaments that have been sent by the Soviet Union to Nicaragua include bazookas, machine guns, mines, and hand guns, as well as "Katuska" rocket-launchers and .45 cal. recoil-less rifles.

There are 100 Soviet tanks in Nicaragua and, according to the head of the Nicaraguan air force, eighty Soviet MiGs are waiting in Cuba until

Nicaraguan pilots return from training in Bulgaria. There are armored transport vehicles of Soviet manufacture and Soviet-made artillery. Nicaragua has also received radar-guided surface-to-air missiles (SAMS) and the heat-seeking SAM-7 missile. Two subterranean missile bases have been established. One is located in the Sandino International Airport; the other is in a restricted area near Managua, in a project called *Granja*.

The Soviets have rented the port of South San Juan. They are expected to repair and recondition it for receiving their large fishing vessels. But, while they need the port for economic reasons, international Communism also needs this port for arms delivery directly to Central America. Afterwards, of course, there is the possibility of submarine use.

"Intervention by Cubans, Soviets, and other elements of the socialist bloc exists on a grand scale in all areas of Nicaraguan society today."

Furthermore, the Soviets are building a channel through Nicaragua so they will not have to depend on the Panama Canal. If Panama breaks ties with Nicaragua, the Soviets will have to build much faster. Aside from the port they are building in San Juan del Sur, on the Pacific, they are also going to build two more ports—one on the Lake of Managua, close to the capital city, and another on the Lake of Nicaragua. It is the same route that Americans thought of using before deciding on the Panama route.

Exporting Revolution

Nicaragua has become the base of operations for the spread of international Communism in the Western Hemisphere. Cuba is an island and easily watched. However, Nicaragua has a commercial airport, and ships can leave Nicaragua more easily than Cuba.

Nicaragua has become the psychological center of support for revolutionary reawakening. The M-19 of Colombia, Montoneros of Argentina, FMLN of El Salvador, EGP of Guatemala, and the armed groups of Costa Rica and Argentina all have their centers of operations in Nicaragua. These are preparing for a new invasion of Argentina and Colombia.

Aid to Guerrillas in El Salvador

In El Salvador, the Sandinistas are offering total help, advice, and direction on how to manage both the war and international politics. Salvadoran guerrillas have been and continue to be trained in Nicaragua. The Sandinistas have helped the

Salvadorans with their air force, army, and navy, in transporting arms into El Salvador. Some of the arms come from Cuba via Nicaragua....

The Salvadorans have two command centers in Nicaragua: one for communications and the other to meet with the Nicaraguan High Command. The Salvadoran High Command stay in Managua all the time, unless they go back to rally the troops. They are then flown in for a day and flown back. The political people have homes in Nicaragua.

The New Privileged Class

The slogan of the Sandinistas is, "Only workers and peasants will obtain power and last until the end." Why? Because workers and peasants are used to feeling inferior and are without high expectations. In transferring to a Marxist system, they cannot see the difference between the privileged classes under Somoza and the new privileged class under the Marxists.

In a few sectors, the poor do live better, but it is a limited standard preventing them from any achievements. The poor cannot become professionals and work for themselves; they will be controlled as they are in Cuba. And, as in Cuba, the people who belong to the ruling party will remain the privileged class, having good salaries and living in the best places.

"Communism has come to this hemisphere because the area is of vital economic and strategic importance to the United States."

Despite talk about the "new society in Nicaragua," the leaders who were going to construct this new society spend money on themselves. The *commandantes* feed themselves with the best food while the people are reduced to rationing.

People want to join the party because that is where the good life is. The Sandinistas recently bought seventy new cars for their nine *commandantes.* All the *commandantes* have foreign bank accounts. It is called "money of the people."

When Cerna and Borge returned from a trip to the Soviet Union, they gathered 600 top government and party officials together to see all the things they had bought with the money that belonged to the ministry. Among their purchases were many cases of Bulgarian wine and caviar.

For party members, there were no waiting lines but a commissary well stocked with items which in the open market are heavily rationed and in great shortage. The Nicaraguan people have realized that the Sandinista directorate has become like the

members of the Somoza family they fought so hard against.

Recommendations for US policy

The Sandinista leaders were trained in Cuba from the early 1960s. Their training was ideologically, politically, and militarily supervised by Fidel Castro. To think that the model of the Nicaraguan revolution is unique, and to think that there exists the possibility that this revolution is different from others, is naive. A revolution is never spontaneous, and in recent history, all revolutions have been motivated and created by one of two forces, capitalism or Communism.

International support was given to the revolution, not as a Communist revolution, but as a spontaneous revolution. The Sandinistas fabricated propaganda for domestic and international consumption portraying the Nicaraguan revolution and the FSLN as one and the same. Thus, little by little, world public opinion was led to believe that the radicalization of the revolution was actually a normal response to domestic conspiracy against the revolution.

The window which international Communism has opened in Nicaragua must be closed. This involves not only aiding the rebels but also playing "hard ball" with the international forces supporting the Sandinistas. They include the Socialist International and groups in Mexico, Venezuela, and France. The United States must persuade these international forces to cut the support they give the Sandinistas. This will pressure the Sandinistas into defining themselves and their revolution.

The United States has a moral responsibility to educate the Western world about the reality of the Sandinistas. Through a well organized propaganda campaign, the Sandinistas are viewed as democrats who will permit elections in 1985. The United States must warn the world about the Sandinistas as it warned about the Nazis in World War II. The Nazi strategy is the same as the Communist today, the ambition to conquer the world.

U.S. policy should give far more attention to Latin America. The United States must open up Latin export economies and increase its economic assistance to the region. The United States will reap the benefits of these actions.

The most direct assistance to the Salvadoran guerrillas is coming from the Sandinista Front, not the Cubans, in the same way in which the Cubans gave assistance to the Nicaraguan revolution. The practical experience needed to conquer El Salvador is based in Managua. The Salvadoran government must be helped, militarily and economically. Pressure must continue against Marxist rebels. The United States should not force the Salvadoran government to give the rebels the legitimacy they should earn only through the democratic process.

The United States should provide Honduras and

Guatemala with military training and assistance. In the case of Honduras, it is a necessity to prepare the Honduran military to defend themselves from an attack by Nicaragua. Honduras has been a prime target of Nicaraguan military strategy. Costa Rica too is threatened by Nicaragua, but not militarily as much as politically. The democratic forces of the United States must realize that the Costa Rican democracy is now threatened by Nicaraguan triumph.

The Sandinistas have been fighting for twenty years to implant Communism. It is totally illogical to think that they would have friendly relations with the United States when they believe that it is their historic mission to export Communism to the rest of Latin America. Those Americans who naively think that negotiations will solve the problems don't know the Sandinistas. Negotiations serve only to buy time for the Sandinistas. This is something they tell you quite openly within the Sandinista organization: negotiation is used only to buy time to consolidate power.

Communism has come to this hemisphere because the area is of vital economic and strategic importance to the United States. The only option for the United States is to support those who are trying to defeat the Sandinista regime. If the United States refuses to aid the anti-Sandinista forces, which are growing stronger in internal support, it will be morally responsible for selling the Nicaraguan people into slavery. And in a few years, the United States will have to respond to Communist gains throughout the rest of the American hemisphere.

Miguel Bolaños Hunter was a counterintelligence officer in the Nicaraguan Revolutionary Government until he defected and fled to Costa Rica in 1983.

"Honduras is an infant democracy which deserves to be nurtured and encouraged by the US."

The US Is Protecting Democracy in Honduras

Richard Araujo

Honduras is the poorest country in Central America, and may be facing the most difficult period in its modern history. Its fragile democracy and its stability are threatened by economic crisis as unemployment and underemployment each approach 45 percent. Having achieved civilian rule through an electoral process at a time when violent disputes ranged along its borders, the 3.6 million Hondurans now are threatened by possible armed conflict with Nicaragua and with attempts at destabilization by outside guerrilla forces.

To bolster faltering Honduras, the Reagan Administration has been providing it with economic and military assistance. Assistant Secretary of State Thomas Enders has described the Reagan Administration's policy in Latin America and the Caribbean as a "policy to use our limited resources to support democracies and encourage those nations in transition to democracy." Efforts by the Administration to carry out such a policy in Central America have been attacked by Congress. The lawmakers, in fact, are threatening to cut back military aid to Honduras. This is very puzzling, for Honduras is an infant democracy which deserves to be nurtured and encouraged by the U.S.

Honduras is one of four Latin American nations to make the transition from military to civilian rule during the Reagan Administration. In April 1980, concern about violence in El Salvador and Nicaragua, and for the stability of Honduras, prompted the Honduran military to allow elections for a constituent assembly. Presidential elections followed in November 1981, and civilian rule resumed on January 27, 1982.

Honduras has become a key element in the struggle for El Salvador. Leftist forces in El Salvador are using Honduran territory to channel weapons and supplies from Nicaragua and to stage attacks on the Salvadoran army. Honduran air space is violated repeatedly by planes from Cuba and Nicaragua transporting aid to the Salvadoran guerrillas. The violence raging within its neighbors has driven some 46,000 refugees into Honduras, creating an enormous economic burden. How long the fragile Honduran democracy can survive such pressures is uncertain. Without U.S. help, however, it will not survive for long....

Honduras and its Neighbors

The most critical problem facing Honduras is the Marxist-Leninist regime in neighboring Nicaragua. Until the 1979 Sandinista revolution, Honduran relations with Nicaragua were cordial; since then, they have deteriorated substantially due to violations of its territories by Sandinista forces aiding Salvadoran guerrillas. Among the most recent violations have been Radio Sandino jamming of domestic Honduran newscasts. Recent months have seen the forging of a quasi-alliance between the democratically oriented nations of the region. On January 19, 1982, Honduras, El Salvador and Costa Rica signed a document proclaiming the "Central American Democratic Community."

Nicaragua has denounced this community. A front page article in the Sandinista newspaper *Barricada* described the union as a "regrettable error." It noted that, "Nicaragua cannot recognize this decision as just. Neither can Nicaragua consider the decision a political solution that will lead to the establishment of peace in the region."

Nowhere in the Democratic Community treaty is there mention of excluding a neighboring country, such as Nicaragua, although it does mention that the "arms race in Central America, in increasing tensions in an irresponsible manner, places the stability of the region in danger." It also "condemns terrorism and

Richard Araujo, "Backing Honduras: Taking a Stand for Democracy," *The Backgrounder,* May 3, 1984. Reprinted by permission of the Heritage Foundation, 214 Massachusetts Ave. NE, Washington, DC 20002.

subversion'' in the region.

Since this treaty was signed, administrations in all three countries have changed. Yet in view of the perceived continuing threat of destabilization, relations among these three nations continue to be close. This agreement has been viewed by the U.S. as an encouraging sign of commitment to the development of democracy. The Reagan Administration has become increasingly aware of the importance of efforts by Central American nations to foster the development of democracy in the region.

Nicaraguan-Honduran Disputes

The danger mounts of full-scale armed conflict between Honduras and Nicaragua. Honduras finds it difficult to patrol its 700 kilometer border with Nicaragua because it lacks sufficient military personnel and roads to this uninhabited area. Nicaragua, on the other hand, enjoys a more developed road system to its border with Honduras and has a huge military force. Indeed, the present Sandinista forces are four times larger than the pre-Sandinista National Guard Army of Dictator Anastasio Somoza. Today's forces, moreover, are calculated to be eight times more powerful than Somoza's. The present 138,000-man combined Army and Militia, in fact, is larger than all the military forces of the rest of Central America combined.

"The most critical problem facing Honduras is the Marxist-Leninist regime in neighboring Nicaragua."

While Nicaragua continues to charge Honduras with border violations, Nicaraguan violations against Honduras receive little media coverage. Since early this year, Nicaragua has been interfering with the broadcasts of Honduras' main radio station. This interference has been traced to a powerful transmitter of between 10 and 15 thousand kilowatts, placed near the Gulf of Fonseca (bordering El Salvador, Honduras and Nicaragua) inside Nicaraguan territory. The Honduran army recently sighted a convoy of Sandinistas transporting weapons to Salvadoran guerrillas some 70 miles inside Honduran territory....

Policy Recommendations

Honduras is entering a second year of negative economic growth, high unemployment and economic barriers. This is due not only to world economic conditions, but also to the violence at its border. The U.S. should recognize Honduras' fragile situation and the particular problems that it confronts. As such, U.S. policy should include aid for the Honduran private sector. Hondurans fear violence from guerrilla

activity less than hunger, poverty and unemployment. International institutions should be encouraged to grant loans to help offset Honduras' deficit. Productivity must be boosted by increased imports of agricultural and industrial products. This in turn will generate greater employment and reduce the threat of social violence. Moreover, the Administration should encourage private lending institutions to extend short-term loans for the continued industrial development of Honduras.

Development assistance under the Caribbean Basin Initiative (CBI) should be increased from $29 million in FY 1983 to $35 million for FY 1984. The overall CBI economic assistance program for FY 1983 of $63.1 million should be increased in line with Honduras' immediate needs. The present U.S. sugar quota for Honduras should be raised to at least 3.0 from the present low 1.0 percent to give its sugar surplus a chance in a competitive world market.

The Administration should request additional funds to increase AID projects already in progress as well as develop educational and health programs. This includes the completion of a hydro-electric plant in El Cajon, which will enable Honduras to cut petroleum imports and to export electricity. Development of the Olancho Pulp and Paper project would allow Honduras to make greater use of its forest resources.

Military Assistance Increased

Military assistance should not only be continued but increased to a level meeting the immediate needs of the present crisis and for Honduras to safeguard its national security. The present buildup of military forces and anti-air systems in Nicaragua poses a grave threat not only to Honduras but to all of Central America. Recent shipments of arms to Nicaragua demonstrate that the escalation will continue. Congress should approve a $17 million supplemental to the $21 million already requested by the Administration for military education and training in FY 1983. This amount should be increased in FY 1984 from the Administration's request of $41 million in MAP and IMET to $50 million combined. This would enable the Honduran government to purchase surveillance equipment similar to the current U.S. radar in the area.

The Honduran Armed Forces, however, must not be allowed to interpret such military support as encouragement for a military takeover. This would be viewed by Congress as anti-democratic and could result in a cut-off of all aid to the country. This must be made clear to the military in view of its past corruption and abuse of government. It should also be made clear that the United States will not allow terrorism and subversion to destabilize a democratic ally.

The Suazo government has made two significant moves to demonstrate its commitment for democratic development. It has joined with Costa Rica and El

Salvador in a Democratic Community and it has presented a peace proposal before the Organization of American States and U.N. This proposal calls for general disarmament in Central America; termination of arms traffic in the area; reduction in the number of foreign advisors (El Salvador has 50 U.S. military advisors to Nicaragua's 2,000 Cubans); an agreement for a multilateral agreement that will strengthen the democratic pluralistic system, including rights of free expression of political will. The U.S. should encourage the other democratic nations of Latin America and Europe to support the government of Honduras and to acknowledge its efforts to develop a democratic union in the region.

"Should Congress restrict assistance for Honduras as it has for El Salvador, it will be clear to friendly and democratic countries in Latin America that they cannot rely on the United States for support."

U.S. policy should aid Nicaraguan democratic forces in exile to gain recognition before the OAS Permanent Commission and the U.N. Security Council. This would not only give them a public forum from which to voice their grievances, but also would alleviate political pressures on the Honduran government.

In the event of crisis in Central America, the U.S. should encourage a more active role by the Organization of American States. To date, it has backed the elections in both Honduras and El Salvador and opposed terrorism in any and all of Latin America. The OAS' Human Rights Commission should be encouraged to take a more prominent role in investigating human rights abuses against the Miskito population from Nicaragua, Salvadoran refugees and Guatemalan refugees. Congress should review the findings of such a commission before even considering curtailing U.S. assistance to Honduras.

Supporting Honduran Democracy

An unprecedented 80 percent of the Honduran people went to the polls in November 1981 to elect the current civilian government. Since then, Honduran democracy has survived some of the most difficult challenges faced by any Honduran administration.

Honduras suffers from grave economic and political pressures caused by the world recession and attempts by Nicaragua to destabilize its democratic government. Honduras is being victimized by Nicaraguan aggression against Honduras' border

region. When the Sandinistas were only a guerrilla movement four years ago, they were able to launch their attack on the Somoza regime from this same, hard to control, region inside Honduras.

Should Congress restrict assistance for Honduras as it has for El Salvador, it will be clear to friendly and democratic countries in Latin America that they cannot rely on the United States for support.

U.S. legislators must take a stand for democracy and freedom. It is time to send a clear message to Latin America that the U.S. remains part of the Americas, and that stability and democratic evolution in all of the Americas is of major concern to the U.S. government and its people. If the U.S. no longer wishes to be viewed as supporting only authoritarian regimes in the area, it must promote its image as an advocate of democracy among the affected countries. There is no better place to start than Honduras.

Richard Araujo is a policy analyst on Latin American affairs for The Heritage Foundation.

"Democracy in Honduras is more fiction than reality."

The US Is Undermining Democracy in Honduras

Jack Nelson-Pallmeyer

As our plane began its final descent into Honduras, three Americans could be seen jogging on the runway. They were the first of many visible signs of the growing U.S. military presence here. Honduras is the key to U.S. foreign policy in Central America.

Along with several Protestant pastors, some Catholic nuns and priests, a few students, a printer, and a veterinarian, I recently visited Honduras and Nicaragua. We were there to assess the impact of U.S. policies on the people of Central America.

Honduras is the poorest country in Central America, the second poorest in the hemisphere. (Only Haiti is poorer.) Even to the most casual observer, the poverty is stark and the inequality between social groups is striking. Despite its poverty and inequality, Honduras has avoided the violent social upheaval of its neighbors—El Salvador, Guatemala, and Nicaragua. The contrast is more a condemnation of its neighbors than a compliment to Honduras. Recent Honduran governments have done little more than keep a lid on social tensions through modest land reform and tolerance of open criticism. This is changing rapidly. Today an atmosphere of intimidation and fear permeates Honduras.

My friends who were concerned that I was visiting "totalitarian" Nicaragua will be surprised to learn that I felt perfectly safe there. But I was frightened in "democratic" Honduras. I felt this way, as did many others in my group, not because I have an affinity for totalitarian regimes but because I experienced Nicaragua as more open than Honduras.

Delays in Honduras

Our problems began immediately on arrival. Although each of us had thirty-day visas issued by the Honduran consulate, we were delayed at the airport for two hours while immigration authorities discussed whether to admit us. The only explanation was that we were a group and they didn't know we were coming. I was surprised by the treatment we received not only because of the democratic label attached to Honduras but also because I expected that a government closely linked to U.S. policy would be eager to please Americans. The opposite seemed to be true. Even as we waited at the airport, we were under close surveillance by plainclothed Honduran police.

We were eventually given permission to enter the country, but our visas were ignored and we were told we could stay only three days. Only after a twenty-four hour wait and the intervention of the head of Honduran immigration was our permit extended to fit our schedule. Apparently the real issue was a profound uneasiness about independent Americans moving through the country trying to understand tensions within Honduran society.

In this light, the deaths of two American journalists (killed two days after we left Honduras) can be understood. Both journalists were sympathetic to the Nicaraguan revolution, and they were killed in an area where just days before two Swedish journalists had been sprayed with machine-gun fire. This area was completely controlled by Nicaraguan counterrevolutionaries supported by the United States and Honduras. The Swedish journalists believed they had been fired on by counterrevolutionaries or members of the Honduran army.

Honduran authorities were apparently concerned that many people in our group had religious connections. The church in Honduras, at least in some areas, has been critical of the present human-rights situation in the country. Also we entered the country in an area dominated by American fruit companies. The area had recently been the site of significant labor strife, including the disappearances

Jack Nelson-Pallmeyer, "Who Is Totalitarian?" *theOtherSide*, February 1984. Reprinted with permission from theOtherSide magazine, 300 W. Apsley St., Philadelphia, PA 19144. Copyright © 1984.

of key labor leaders. Indeed, we spoke to many labor leaders who indicated that they were putting themselves in great danger simply by meeting with us. At the end of one meeting, a labor leader told us, "Welcome to Honduras, but don't stay long because people disappear here." If this sounds a bit dramatic, his words became more believable as we traveled through the country.

"When the president of the Honduran Assembly says that matters of human rights, military security and the role of the military in politics don't concern him, clearly democracy is moving from fragile to nonexistent."

Between San Pedro Sula and Tegucigalpa, all trucks and public vehicles must stop at three checkpoints. Honduran citizens are often required to sign their names at these checkpoints—an interesting way to monitor the movement of citizens in a "democratic" country. At the first checkpoint, our private bus was stopped. Two armed members of FUSEP (the Honduran national police) boarded our bus and checked our passports carefully. They were followed by a plainclothesman who identified himself as a DIN agent. (DIN is widely acknowledged to be a Honduran death squad closely associated with the military.) After rechecking all our passports and asking questions about our group, we were allowed to proceed. It was clear from the questions that they had prior knowledge of us. As our Honduran bus driver said, "They knew we were coming."

Totalitarian Honduras

At the second checkpoint, two members of FUSEP boarded our bus, checked our passports, and searched our luggage. I remember thinking at the time that the treatment we were receiving in Honduras was precisely the kind of treatment that the average American would expect in "totalitarian" Nicaragua: harassment, monitoring of our actions, the powerful presence of the military, restrictions on movement and speech. Yet my experience in Nicaragua less than a year earlier and again immediately after our stay in Honduras involved absolutely no restrictions. I wonder what kind of campaign is under way to convince the American people that Nicaragua is totalitarian and Honduras democratic?

At the second checkpoint, FUSEP members confiscated a variety of written materials. They confiscated papers listing our itinerary and describing several of the groups with which we had met. It seemed possible that this material would be used in

reprisals against Hondurans. So immediately on leaving the checkpoint, we destroyed all the notes and information we had received from people in Honduras. In addition, we removed all film from our cameras and put them on our person, again fearing confiscation and later reprisals against the people with whom we met. As it turned out, we made it through the third checkpoint without incident.

That evening we met with the president of the Honduran Human Rights Commission, Ramon Custodio. His stature in Honduras is often compared to that of Oscar Romero, the former archbishop of El Salvador. Romero was murdered because he defended the rights of the poor and because he urged the United States to stop military support of the repression in his country. Custodio spoke to us about the growing repression within Honduras, including increasing instances of arrests without charge, long detention without trial, disappearances, torture, and political murders. He spoke about the hope which existed in his country a year and a half ago when a civilian government replaced military rule. And he grieved over a betrayed democracy and about the growing political power of the Honduran military financed by the United States.

Unfortunately, the comparison between Ramon Custodio and Oscar Romero may eventually include their deaths. Many believe that Custodio will soon be killed. While he never said he was in danger, each of his words carried great weight. You could sense that you were in the presence of a person who had already passed through death. It was the truth and not the fear of death which ruled his life. If Custodio is murdered, it will be a great loss for Honduras. Tragically, few Americans even know the name of this man resisting U.S. policies.

Honduran Democracy Fictional

We began to conclude that democracy in Honduras is more fiction than reality. This observation was confirmed by meetings at the U.S. embassy in Honduras and with the president of the Honduran Assembly. At the embassy we met with Shepard Lowman, deputy chief of mission. He indicated that the military plays a stronger role in Honduras, a much stronger role than U.S. citizens would find acceptable at home. He insisted, however, that General Gustavo Alvarez Martinez respects the constitutional government headed by President Suazo. General Alvarez is the head of the armed forces, and he is often portrayed as the real political leader in the country. Lowman told us that the military had supported the transition to civilian rule because the Honduran economy was collapsing and the military did not want to be held responsible. He also indicated that President Suazo and General Alvarez shared many common goals and that they needed each other. When asked why they needed each other, Lowman responded, "They know it would be more difficult to get as much U.S. assistance with a military government in Honduras." In other words, the facade of civilian rule makes a huge Honduran military buildup possible. It allows the Reagan administration to use Honduras as a base for its foreign policy in the region, including the destabilization of Nicaragua and the intensification of the war in El Salvador.

When we told Lowman about delays, searches, and confiscation of our materials by Honduran security forces, he told us not to be concerned. Honduran security forces "would know [whom we met and our itinerary] as part of the normal course of events," he said. Democracy clearly has a different meaning in Honduras.

When we asked about numerous reports of disappearances, he became visibly flustered. "There are disappearances and there are disappearances," he said. "I mean, have these people disappeared, or have they disappeared?" If this doesn't make any sense to you, it didn't to us either. One had the impression that Shepard Lowman was hoping to convince us that disappeared people in Honduras are simply on vacation.

Our meeting with J. Efrain Bu Giron, the president of the Honduran Assembly, was even more disconcerting. I asked Giron whether United States support for the Honduran military and the increasing role of the military in Honduran politics was undermining a fragile democracy. I also asked whether Honduran support for the counter-revolutionaries seeking to overthrow the Nicaraguan government was aggravating tensions that could lead to war. Giron responded, "These are political matters; therefore they do not concern me." We asked about the violation of human rights, including frequent disappearances and the detention of people for long periods without formal charges (a clear violation of the Honduran constitution). "These are matters for the police," Giron said. "I don't know anything about this. Nonetheless, there are no human rights violations in Honduras." He went on to say that "communists have no rights." The problem, of course, is that throughout Central and Latin America the label "communist" is applied to anyone who is critical of the government or its economic priorities.

No Concern for Human Rights

When the president of the Honduran Assembly says that matters of human rights, military security, and the role of the military in politics don't concern him, clearly democracy is moving from fragile to nonexistent. Not surprisingly, when the United States decided to train Salvadoran and Honduran troops at a new base at Puerto Castilla, the Honduran Assembly debated the issue after the fact. All my experiences in Honduras confirm what others have suggested: the United States and the Honduran military run the country while the Honduran Assembly is a shadowboxer outside the main arena.

One stated goal of U.S. policy in Central America is to promote stable democracies. The willingness of the United States to sacrifice the Honduran democracy to broader regional objectives exposes its stated goal as a lie. It also suggests an unstated goal: the overthrow of the Sandinista government in Nicaragua. The United States justifies a hard-line policy toward Nicaragua by charging that Nicaragua is running guns to the rebels in El Salvador and poses a military threat to Honduras. . . .

The Nicaraguan people are asking the people of the United States to break the chains of submissiveness to a foreign policy which is undermining the people of Honduras, Nicaragua, and the rest of Central America. We must work to end U.S. military support for Honduras and for the counterrevolutionaries, and we must work for immediate bilateral negotiations between the United States and Nicaragua. In a deeper sense than we know, our sovereignty is tied to the sovereignty of the Nicaraguan people.

Jack Nelson-Pallmeyer is the coordinator of the American Lutheran Church and the Lutheran Church in America Hunger and Justice Project in Minnesota.

"All [the Salvadoran armed forces] require from us is a supporting budget of about $100 million a year, which would be used for training programs and basic equipment."

viewpoint **83**

The US Should Aid the Salvadoran Army

Alvin H. Bernstein and John D. Waghelstein

No American combat presence is required in El Salvador to defeat the Marxist-Leninist insurgency there. The United States does not have to risk confrontation with any power beyond the Caribbean. It need not choose between the domestic dangers of a protracted war and the humiliation of cutting losses and deserting allies. The Salvadoran armed forces can handle the Farabundo Marti Liberation Front (FMLN) themselves. All they require from us is a supporting budget of about $100 million a year, which would be used for training programs and basic equipment—no fancy high-tech items required. They also need an understanding of their adversaries' vulnerabilities and a knowledge of the strategic principles of counterinsurgency warfare.

There are now between 6,000 and 8,000 guerrillas in El Salvador facing government security forces of some 40,000. Yet the outnumbered guerrilla force can create great problems by using the tried and proven tactics of revolutionary war. The guerrillas' strategy avoids confronting the larger armed forces of the host government and attacks the national economy instead. It assumes, correctly, that a poor country like El Salvador cannot sustain a long, debilitating internal war. By concentrating their limited forces and by using the intelligence system they established before the outbreak of hostilities, the guerrillas can initiate surprise attacks on public utilities and on supply and communications centers. They thereby manage to keep the bulk of the Salvadoran military tied down guarding those vulnerable targets that cannot go undefended. At the moment, 60 percent to 80 percent of all Salvadoran troops are occupied in defending such installations as power stations and dams against guerrilla demolition attacks. These attacks against the economy can be extremely effective and are

devilishly difficult to prevent—as the events in Lebanon have made clear to Americans in particular. In El Salvador they are designed to make the current regime appear unstable and ineffectual so that the government loses the foreign aid and the private investments it so desperately needs. Should the army attempt to disperse its limited forces to meet the sporadic guerrilla sorties, it will risk becoming more vulnerable at all points.

Helping the Salvadoran Army

The Salvadoran armed forces are only now just being prepared to deal effectively with the guerrilla tactics of counterinsurgency. They find themselves in a position similar to the one we occupied in the midsixties in Vietnam, where we were able to force a Clausewitzian main battle against an enemy who, when confronted, would either melt into the jungle or retreat across a border. We must now help the Salvadorans learn from our mistakes so that they do not repeat them.

First, the Salvadoran soldier must learn the subtle art of locating his enemy's base camps. We can help him by monitoring with our satellites the arms shipments from the socialist bloc countries that make their way to Cuba and Nicaragua via ports in Indochina or Algeria. We can even reveal to them, to some extent, the land supply routes in Central America and their supply concentrations in El Salvador itself. To be successful in this enterprise, there must be on-the-spot human surveillance, and to this end, U.S. advisers have been training long-range reconnaissance patrols, whose success to date has been encouraging. These are squads of about six men who are trackers trained especially to operate at night, when the guerrillas travel and are most easily located.

In the army's attempt to discover the enemy's base camps, it is also essential for the Salvadoran soldier to enlist the support of the man-in-the-street and the

"How to Win in El Salvador," by Alvin H. Bernstein and Colonel John D. Waghelstein, is reprinted by permission from *Policy Review*, issue #27 (or Winter 1984). *Policy Review* is a publication of the Heritage Foundation, 214 Massachusetts Ave. NE, Washington, DC 20002.

peasant-in-the-field. Contemporary left-wing rhetoric notwithstanding, the FMLN does not enjoy much popular support, except possibly in the sparsely populated, strategically unimportant areas of Chalatenango and Morazan along the Honduran border. The overall support of the people is, therefore, within the reach of the army. Should it be achieved, it will help limit recruitment opportunities for the guerrillas and also provide an invaluable source of information because the peasants are in an excellent position to know the movements and the locations of the guerrilla forces. Obtaining the cooperation of these *campesinos* against the Salvadoran guerrillas requires courage, tact, even diplomacy. It is crucial and takes time to teach.

Damaging the Guerrillas

Once the guerrilla is located, he must be damaged. In each of the country's 14 provinces, the Salvadoran army requires at least one well-equipped, 350-man hunter battalion, which will be broken down operationally into smaller teams capable of scouting guerrilla movements, destroying his base camps, and disrupting his supplies. With this kind of trained, mobile force, the Salvadoran army can both defend vital public services and mount a tactical offensive to keep the guerrilla on the run, foraging and scrimping for his food, no longer a determined terrorist but a dislocated nomad.

"Victory in El Salvador requires patience: It may take several years to build up an officer corps and counterinsurgency force sufficient to wear the guerrillas down."

The army needs skilled, well-trained officers to command these hunter battalions. Historically, the Salvadoran military academy has produced only some 25 to 35 officers each year. Moreover, the Salvadoran army has suffered from a long-standing, outmoded, and socially exclusive officer corps. American training programs are in the process of changing that. In 1982, 470 Salvadoran cadets completed a 12-week officers' training program at Fort Benning, Georgia. In 1983 more than 600 Salvadoran cadets enrolled. Thus, a far higher percentage of the applicants to the Salvadoran military academy received officer training, and a far less socially exclusive corps has infused the military command hierarchy.

Well-drilled troops and well-trained officers need proper equipment. Currently, much of the Salvadoran soldier's armory is obsolete. His standard infantry rifle should be replaced by M-16s so that he can have at least as much firepower as the guerrilla he faces,

who is equipped with excellent Soviet small arms as well as with some American models that were captured in Indochina. The Salvadoran army also needs boots that do not rot in the damp, ponchos and fiber helmets, state-of-the-art communications equipment (which the guerrillas already possess, purchased on the open market), lightweight body armor, and freeze-dried campaign rations.

Medical Improvement Necessary

Improvement in the army's medical care and medical supplies is also essential. Too few combat medics are available, and those who are, are often inadequately trained. Woefully short on medical supplies, the medics need helicopters to evacuate their wounded. The arrival in 1983 of a U.S. 26-man army medical team has helped with these problems, but much more remains to be done. In Vietnam one of every nine or ten wounded American or South Vietnamese soldiers died. For Salvadorans, the death toll has been one of three wounded.

In the final analysis, however, the effort to keep a Marxist-Leninist guerrilla force from shooting its way into power in El Salvador will depend upon interdicting the guerrillas' remaining supply routes. Substantial successes recorded so far give cause for considerable optimism. The Salvadoran navy has already closed the old sea passage from Nicaragua to the Bay of Jiquilisco. In May 1983 it converted three 100-foot cutters to patrol boats and began employing them as "mother ships" or buses from which to launch 25-foot Boston whalers equipped with 250-horsepower Johnson engines for hot pursuit of the smugglers. Air surveillance has drastically curtailed the number of plane drops from Nicaragua: The number of unidentified aircraft sighted in El Salvador fell from 100 in the last six months of 1982 to fewer than 10 in the first half of 1983. Moreover, in 1982, Honduran troops began patrolling their territory between Nicaragua and El Salvador for the first time, sharply cutting the flow of overland supplies. Still, the guerrillas continue to receive sophisticated radio equipment, medical supplies, and demolition gear, mostly via land routes through Honduras and Guatemala. This diminishing operation must be squeezed more tightly, above all for psychological reasons: A cutoff in foreign supplies would demoralize the guerrillas in addition to hampering their effectiveness.

Providing No-Risk Aid

True to their form, some members of Congress are dragging their heels in supporting limited, no risk aid. More than that, Congress has actually placed some impediments to progress in El Salvador. Among the many positive reforms initiated by the junta after the October 1979 coup was a much-publicized and much-needed land reform. History has shown repeatedly that although land reform is almost always terrible economics, it is often a political necessity. So it is in El Salvador, where generations of inequity have resulted in one of the most skewed land tenure systems in the Western hemisphere. The Salvadoran land reforms went a long way toward lessening the guerrillas' appeal to the *campesinos*. Since land reform has become something of a *sin qua non* for continued U.S. support, it is ironic that Congress has passed a law impeding that support. The Helms amendment to the Foreign Assistance Act prohibits "assistance to El Salvador for the purpose of planning for compensation, or for the purpose of compensation, for the confiscation, nationalization, acquisition, or expropriation of any agricultural or banking enterprise, or of the properties or stock shares which may be pertaining thereto."

This legislation has a catch-22 appearance about it. We know that land reform must continue in El Salvador if we are to continue to support their military efforts, and we know that the Salvadoran government must be seen as part of the solution to the host of economic and social ills from which the country suffers. But until the previous owners of the lands are compensated, there will remain a belief among all concerned that the new land law will be repealed. The prohibition on using U.S. funds for the essential act of compensation remains a major bone of contention in the issue of land reform itself and serves no useful purpose. What is needed from Congress is a quitclaim that acknowledges the legitimacy of the land reform and the fact that compensation has duly been paid. This would discourage the old landowners from persisting in their anti-reform activities and would encourage much-needed reinvestment in the economy.

Stopping Human Rights Violations

Another legal impediment to sound policy, an inappropriate holdover from our unhappy experience in Vietnam, is the restriction that prevents our advisers from working with any police force or agency that has an internal security mission. Section 660 of the Foreign Assistance Act of 1961, as amended in the Foreign Assistance Act of 1974, prohibits the use of U.S. funds "to provide training or advice, or provide any financial support, for police, prisons, or other law enforcement forces for any foreign government." The philosophical and moral reasons for such a restriction appear reasonable enough, to be sure. But in El Salvador this legislation is working against human rights. The legislation prohibits U.S. training of the approximately 10,000 men in the national guard, the treasury police, and the national police, who occasionally fight as infantry. In Guazapa treasury police and national guard units fight the guerrillas alongside the army. These forces—accounting for one quarter of El Salvador's troops—are beyond our influence, and partly because of this they have the worst record for

human rights violations. In fact, there have been marked improvements in the treatment of civilians by the army, and more prisoners have been taken, precisely because those units have come under our influence and observation. But we have not been able to respond positively to the request from the commander of the treasury police (and from his predecessor as well), who has asked us to train and supervise his men, knowing full well that along with our instruction in counterinsurgency tactics comes increased respect for human rights.

To contain Communist insurgency in Central America, it is not enough for Congress to provide funds. The funding must be regular and predictable. Too often the Salvadoran military has lost an advantage or wasted precious time waiting on the vagaries of the congressional budget process. In the critical months following the March 1982 election, momentum so painfully won was lost. As a result of holdups in funding from Congress, only a few newly trained, company-sized units were added to the Salvadoran armed forces between May 1982 and September 1983. The guerrillas used this lull to launch a successful military offensive that partially offset their political defeat in the elections. This past May the government inaugurated its new national campaign plan. It includes far-reaching social and economic programs as well as continued efforts of counterinsurgency by the military. The plan will require a gradual but steady expansion of the armed forces to achieve a favorable force ratio against the FMLN. The new offensive will require a commitment to training and equipment on a firm, reliable timetable.

Victory in El Salvador requires patience: It may take several years to build up an officer corps and counterinsurgency force sufficient to wear the guerrillas down. But Marxist-Leninist guerrillas have been defeated in countries ranging from Venezuela to Greece to Thailand. They can also be defeated at little American cost in El Salvador.

Alvin H. Bernstein is professor of strategy at the US Naval War College. Colonel John D. Waghelstein, former commander of American military trainers in El Salvador, is now assigned to the US Army War College.

"Nothing United States military advisers can do can instill morale and elan into an army whose leaders routinely torture and murder."

The US Should Not Aid the Salvadoran Army

Robert E. White and Ricardo Alejandro Fiallos

The following viewpoint is in two parts. Part I is by Robert E. White and Part II is by Ricardo Alejandro Fiallos.

I

As the military stalemate in El Salvador drags on, many in the United States have begun to wonder what if anything we can do to break the impasse. In fact, there may be very little we can do. We may have pushed the Salvadoran military as far as it is able or willing to go—and, indeed, it may be time to cut our losses and accept the revolutionaries' repeated offers to negotiate.

In spite of hundreds of millions of dollars in military assistance and training, the Salvadoran military has proved unwilling to carry the war to the insurgents. With the rainy season now at an end, the revolutionaries will again strike when and where they wish—will again dominate much of the countryside and again demonstrate their superiority over Government forces.

How does the Reagan Administration explain why the revolutionaries fight so much better than Government troops? The Administration talks about the insurgents' foreign supplies of arms—but does not explain why guns from the United States do not work similar miracles for Government forces.

Multilated Bodies

Guns are to a revolution what clay is to brick masonry—useless without kiln, mortar and willing hands. With songs to fire the spirit and poems to commemorate the fallen, the revolution is fed with a constant supply of recruits. They prefer to die in battle rather than wait their turn to have the security forces march them off to ignominious death. Each dawn, mutilated bodies of civilians appear in ditches

to remind the poor of the barbaric system under which they live—under the jackboot of the Salvadoran military. No wonder the revolutionaries move among the people like fish through the sea.

It would be foolish to romanticize the insurgents, but it is stupid and shortsighted not to recognize their strength. Unlike the Reagan Administration, the revolutionaries have demonstrated a remarkable capacity to move from extremism and harsh rhetoric to apparent moderation.

In 1980, several of the guerrilla groups deserved to be compared with Pol Pot. They kidnapped innocent people and murdered them when their ransom demands were not met. They contemptuously brushed aside offers to negotiate a political solution.

All that has changed. Abuses still occur, but the insurgents have learned that observance of civilized norms pays dividends, nationally and internationally. For example, the guerrillas treat captured soldiers with such consideration that returned prisoners are considered security risks by the military. Revolutionary leaders regularly call for a negotiated peace and a political solution.

Widespread Corruption

But what of the foot soldier in the Salvadoran military? For him there are no songs, no poems—above all, no leadership. The young officers who led the October 1979 revolution in favor of land reform and human rights have been either sidelined or exiled. As a result, the officer corps is again infected to the bone with the cancers of brutality and corruption.

Nothing United States military advisers can do can instill morale and elan into an army whose leaders routinely torture and murder. Nothing United States Army trainers can say can put heart and spirit into soldiers led by officers who battle one another for access to the public purse instead of fighting guerrillas. Nothing the Pentagon can supply to the

Robert E. White, "Salvadoran Impasse," *The New York Times*, November 30, 1983. Copyright 1983 by The New York Times Company. Reprinted with permission. Ricardo Alejandro Fiallos, testimony before the Subcommittee on Foreign Operations, April 29, 1981.

army can overcome the contempt the common soldiers feel for officers who spend nights and weekends in the capital city and funnel official funds into foreign bank accounts.

What can the United States do to end the stalemate? Very little, short of sending in our own troops. In June, the then Army Chief of Staff, Gen. Edward C. Meyer, warned the Administration not to send combat forces to El Salvador because "unless you have the commitment of the people, of the indigenous forces, you're not going to solve a guerrilla war."

This common sense advice has not impressed the Administration. In September, the Under Secretary of Defense for Policy, Fred C. Ikle, called for the military defeat of the Salvadoran revolutionaries and the "unconsolidation" of the Nicaraguan Government. In phrases that bridled like sabers, he suggested that we "place forward deployed forces in these countries as in Korea and West Germany."

The security of the United States and the free world depends in great measure on the confidence and self esteem of the American military. Our troops' morale depends in turn on the American people's perception that our armed forces carry out their missions abroad in a manner that does not bring shame on the ideals and traditions of the United States. What kind of madness is it that would identify the good name of the American military with one of the most brutal, corrupt and inefficient armies ever to have disfigured a Western nation?

II

I speak to you this morning as an officer in exile of the Salvadoran Army. Despite the risks which this type of public testimony holds for members of my family who still remain in El Salvador, I feel that it is critical that members of the Congress as well as the people of the United States understand the role played by the high military command as well as the directors of the security forces in El Salvador and the nature of their involvement in the violence which continues to afflict my country.

It is important to understand that the base of power in El Salvador does not lie in the hands of the President of the Junta, José Napoleón Duarte, nor with the other civilian members of the Junta. Rather, it is the high command of the armed forces and, more specifically, Colonels José Guillermo García and Jaíme Abdul Gutierrez, along with the directors of the security forces, who wield the real power in El Salvador. An example of this is evidenced by the fact that despite two official requests from President Duarte to the Minister of Defense, Colonel García, to remove Colonel Francisco Moran as the head of the Treasury Police, due to the involvement of this branch of the security forces in the brutal assassination of various mayors, most of whom were Christian Democrats, Moran still retains his position.

The Army and Death Squads Are One

It is a grievous error to believe that the forces of the extreme right, or the so-called "death squads," operate independent of the security forces. The simple truth of the matter is that "Los Escuadrones de la Muerte" are made up of members of the security forces and acts of terrorism credited to these squads such as political assassinations, kidnappings, and indiscriminate murder are, in fact, planned by high-ranking military officers and carried out by members of the security forces. I do not make this statement lightly, but with full knowledge of the role which the high military command and the directors of the security forces have played in the murder of countless numbers of innocent people in my country.

During the period in which I worked as a doctor in the military hospital, I treated numerous members of the security forces. In inquiring as to the cause of their injuries, which is a normal medical procedure in the hospital, various individuals told me as well as other doctors that they had been injured in the act of "eliminating" civilians.

Let me make it clear that not all of the armed forces in El Salvador are implicated in the types of crimes which I have mentioned. The principal problem lies in the high military command and in the directors of the security forces, not in the ranks of the army, and it is these individuals who, without a doubt, constitute the gravest threat to the future of El Salvador. Until the officials of the high military command are replaced and the security forces completely restructured and brought under strict control, there will be no end to the violence which is destroying my country, and no possibility of establishing a democratic government.

Supporting Repression

Finally, due to the fact that the center of power in El Salvador lies in the high military command and the directors of the security forces, any military assistance or training which the United States provides to the current government is perceived by the people of El Salvador as support for the forces of repression which are destroying the country.

Unless the United States government ceases its support for the current regime and attempts to encourage an end to the state of siege and a political settlement which, by definition, must include the opposition forces, there will be no peace in my country.

Robert E. White is the former US ambassador to El Salvador and is considered a specialist on Latin America. Ricardo Alejandro Fiallos, a doctor by training, is a captain in the Salvadoran Army.

"A sanctuary symbolizes peace and dignity amid threatening violence and barbarity—a symbol pointing to the need for peace with justice in Central America."

viewpoint **85**

The US Sanctuary Movement Protects Salvadoran Refugees

Eric Jorstad

More than one-half million people have arrived in the United States from Central America since 1979. According to the U.S. government, they are here illegally. A few have been given political asylum, but the vast majority are subject to deportation. Their home countries are torn apart by brutal violence; in El Salvador a civil war is raging.

Some local churches in the U.S.—Lutheran, Roman Catholic, Presbyterian, United Methodist, United Church of Christ and others—have declared themselves to be a "public sanctuary" for these persons. They take in families and individuals and provide them with shelter, food, companionship and a place to tell their story. The U.S. attorney general regards this action as a felony, "harboring an illegal alien," punishable by up to two years in prison and a $5,000 fine. The churches regard it as a duty of Christian conscience to help these people, to protest U.S. policy toward Central America and its refugees, and to mark a limit to the power of the U.S. government by providing sanctuary.

After the October 1979 coup in El Salvador and the consequent escalation in violence there, refugees started making their way into the southwestern United States. Initially they had fled across their border into Honduras or Guatemala, but after continued raids on refugee camps by the Salvadoran military, many of them continued on to Mexico, heading for the U.S. At the border they were usually led by a "coyote," a person who collects high fees for providing expert guidance in an undercover crossing.

The Salvadorans' destination was a city with a large Spanish-speaking population, such as Los Angeles, Tucson, El Paso, San Antonio or Chicago, where a "community-in-exile" was formed. By 1983 the Los Angeles community had grown to about 250,000, and

each of the other four cities had about 60,000 refugees. The communities-in-exile have shown a remarkable capacity to bring in and care for new families of refugees, but they have limited resources. Consequently, literally thousands of fugitives landed on the doorsteps of churches in the Southwest.

Churches and Services

From the beginning, churches have sought ways to help. These have included:

• **Legal services.** A fugitive who is apprehended is held in a detention center, usually on $5,000 bond (a higher figure is set for Salvadorans than for other aliens detained by the Immigration and Naturalization Service). Some churches have provided bond money to release these detainees and have supported legal clinics to help them apply for political asylum.

• **Social services.** After having traveled so far, often spending all of their meager resources to pay a "coyote," the refugee families arrive with great need for food, shelter and medical assistance. Some churches have helped provide such social services, and have also raised money for emergency assistance to refugee camps in Honduras and Mexico.

• **Evasion services.** Jim Corbett, a well-known "coyote" who works from religious convictions, not for profit, helps fugitive Central Americans evade INS detection and settle in a community-in-exile. His service, of course, is not a public form of assistance, nor is it publicly provided by any church.

The churches of the Southwest found that these services were helpful, but increasingly limited and frustrating. Legal services are very expensive, especially in cost per person helped, and are not very promising, in light of the INS's poor asylum record for Salvadorans. Social services are also expensive, and quickly begin to seem like a "Band-Aid" approach. How long can one pull drowning people out of a river before trying to go upstream to stop

Eric Jorstad, "Sanctuary for Refugees: A Statement on Public Policy." Copyright 1984 Christian Century Foundation. Reprinted by permission from the March 14, 1984 issue of The Christian Century.

whoever is pushing them in? The same is true for evasion services which, being covert, are unable to address the broader public policy questions.

Many churches providing legal and social services, sometimes with national denominational support, also engaged the INS and government leaders in dialogue to seek a change in policy, specifically that Central Americans be granted refugee or extended voluntary departure status. But the services became increasingly inadequate with the large influx of people in need, and the dialogue proved fruitless.

Then, on March 24, 1982, Southside Presbyterian Church in Tucson, Arizona, and four other churches offered public sanctuary for refugees from Central America. The date was chosen in remembrance of the assassination of El Salvador's Archbishop Oscar Romero, a hero and martyr of radical and peaceful change in El Salvador. Southside Presbyterian soon had more refugees than it could handle, and initiated the idea of a national network of sanctuaries.

"Sanctuary is a powerful way of raising the consciousness of American church people about conditions in Central America and the situation of its refugees."

The movement grew rapidly; today there are some 75 churches across the country providing sanctuary, with hundreds of other congregations and organizations officially endorsing their action. The Chicago Religious Task Force on Central America has assumed national leadership to coordinate and promote the network. *Time* and CBS Evening News have carried the story, and there has been extensive local media coverage in areas where sanctuary has been given. The movement continues to gain strength, with more and more congregations supporting sanctuary or making a study to decide whether they want to offer sanctuary themselves.

The Elements of Sanctuary

The sanctuary movement has succeeded in reaching the media and the public because people seem fascinated by the risks that U.S. citizens are taking to help the refugees evade capture and deportation. The movement's basic goal is to put public pressure on the U.S. government to change its policy toward these refugees and toward their home countries. Action toward that goal is taken in four areas: compassion, resistance to injustice, education and empowerment.

• **Compassion.** Sanctuary is, first, an act of compassion, an expression of the fundamental Christian concern to love one's neighbor. In the story of the Good Samaritan, the consequences of his compassion are acts of care for the injured ''neighbor.'' Similarly, sanctuary is a way of expressing compassion in caring for our suffering neighbors from Central America. It is a way of providing for people in need, not only with social services, but also by giving them haven from the potentially disastrous consequences of deportation.

• **Resistance to injustice.** But sanctuary is much more than an act of relief, and all of its advocates are very clear in emphasizing that this is not the only goal. As an act of resisting what is believed to be the unjust policy and practice of the INS and the unjust foreign policy of the Reagan administration, sanctuary makes a clear statement of protest. The refugees in effect receive extended voluntary departure status (as long as the INS chooses not to violate sanctuary). The force of public conscience and opinion protects them and calls into question the INS policy.

Further, the sanctuary movement claims that the real illegal action is not by the churches involved, but by the INS itself. For the INS policy violates the nation's legal commitment (Refugee Act of 1980) to adhere to the Convention and Protocol on Refugees of the United Nations, and the United Nations High Commissioner for Refugees has determined that Salvadorans fleeing their country are as a group bona fide political refugees. So the INS, the argument continues, will not violate sanctuary because it cannot risk having its policy tested in court.

But whether or not INS policy is ruled illegal, sanctuary is a public symbol that the policy is *immoral* in its threat to the life and safety of the Central American ''illegal aliens'' who are sent back into countries filled with fear and violence.

Sanctuary As Resistance

Sanctuary is also an act of resistance against what its supporters believe to be the unjust foreign policy of the United States toward Central America. There is a close connection between U.S. foreign policy and U.S. immigration and refugee policy. Movement advocates are not trying to house all of the one-half-million refugees in U.S. churches, or to stop with gaining extended voluntary departure status for them. A further aim is to seek a just resolution of the violent conflicts and the oppression which led the exiles to flee in the first place, so that they can return home with hope.

A sanctuary symbolizes peace and dignity amid threatening violence and barbarity—a symbol pointing to the need for peace with justice in Central America and for an end to all foreign military intervention, including that of the United States. In contrast to the usual tactics used to seek change in U.S. foreign policy (e.g., in South Africa, in the Middle East, toward the Soviet Union, or in Vietnam in the 1960s), sanctuary offers unique opportunities to educate North Americans and to empower the Central Americans in solidarity with their northern neighbors.

• **Education.** Sanctuary is a powerful way of raising the consciousness of American church people about conditions in Central America and the situation of its refugees. This can be done best by the refugees themselves. Close interaction and personal fellowship are established between the refugees and the host congregation. The church people have the opportunity to know a human being—always a more powerful experience than simply hearing statistics or general descriptions. The refugees also have a platform from which to tell their stories and describe the particular conditions which drove them to flee. A relationship is built which gives politics a human dimension, for the congregation can understand how U.S. foreign policy has affected the lives of people they know.

The educational impact of sanctuary extends beyond the host congregation into the community. "Rene Hurtado," the Salvadoran refugee at St. Luke's Presbyterian Church, Wayzata, Minnesota, has spoken at dozens of churches around the Minneapolis-St. Paul area, as well as at public forums and demonstrations, and for meetings of college groups, labor unions and other civic organizations. He is always accompanied by someone from the host church as a representative of a sanctuary. An entire area gains new, firsthand information about life and death in Central America.

"Sanctuary also creates an empowering solidarity between Central and North Americans."

The interest of government officials is also alerted—and not all are negative. One U.S. congressman has visited with "Rene," and expressed his support for sanctuary at St. Luke's. One Minnesota senator has spoken in favor of extended voluntary departure, in sympathy with the church's concern. Given the role of the United States in Central America, sanctuary as a personal encounter and public witness offers an important means of education for the American people.

Sanctuary As Power

• **Empowerment.** Not so obvious to North Americans, perhaps, but crucial for long-term change is the empowerment of Central Americans, in solidarity with their neighbors here. When evasion of the authorities is required to guarantee safety, it is very difficult if not impossible for refugees to speak out publicly, and thus they are "depoliticized." But in sanctuary they can contribute to the process of

resistance and change; they can actively participate in the future of their home country.

Bernard Survil, a Catholic priest who has experienced persecution in El Salvador and Guatemala, explains that the refugee in sanctuary has an environment that is "nonpartisan and without the threat of repression or surveillance with its inevitable chilling effect." This situation, he goes on, "involves the refugee in the liberation process." Anonymity might be easier and less risky; underground life can become comfortable. By no means do all refugees want to enter sanctuary. But those who do can experience empowerment by taking an active role in their own future and that of their compatriots back home. They become "diplomats," opening a new hope. Sanctuary thus gives refugees an experience of self-determination otherwise unavailable to them publicly in the United States.

Sanctuary and Solidarity

Finally, sanctuary also creates an empowering solidarity between Central and North Americans. The provision of both protection and a platform sets up a partnership in the work for change. Jim Corbett, the "coyote" who is active in the sanctuary movement, summarizes this aspect:

> Most of our refugee services to date have been paternalistically organized, denying the refugees a voice, weakening their community development, and preparing them to serve Anglo America as a highly exploitable underclass. By fusing humanitarian and political concerns and by providing an opportunity for the refugees to be seen and heard, the sanctuary movement opens a way out of the bog of condescension that is created when well-meaning sympathizers develop programs modeled on establishment charities.

Sanctuary is thus distinguished from legal and social services as it helps refugees move out of dependency into partnership, being not a one-way service but a two-way relationship. Obviously the refugee needs protection from the sanctuary, but both refugee and host—as both Central America and the United States—stand in need of liberation.

The situation of the Central American refugees challenges the self-understanding of the North American church, by asking that our practice conform to our principles. The question is not whether the church can or will take a stand, but with whom the church *is* standing. The final goal of the sanctuary movement is to make this challenge.

Eric Jorstad is the former consultant to the American Lutheran Church's Office of Church and Society of Minneapolis and is currently a pastor at St. James Lutheran Church in Detroit.

The US Sanctuary Movement Is Illegal and Unnecessary

The Cardinal Mindszenty Foundation

Are our churches above the law? Is political confrontation the good news proclaimed by the Gospel? Has an eleventh commandment been discovered which declares: thou shalt turn houses of worship into press clubs issuing propaganda releases favorable to leftist guerrilla movements in Central America?

The answer to all these questions is a resounding "yes" if you or your church are playing the hottest new game sweeping the country. It is called "Sanctuary" and it uses real people as pawns, real churches as a playing board for the action, and a strategy for winning that requires cunning, deceit and disarming one's opposition before he makes a move.

"Sanctuary" is being played in all earnest in scores of churches from coast-to-coast and its popularity is increasing among those religious activists who can be counted on to jump on any bandwagon plastered with the latest leftist ideological bumpersticker slogans condemning U.S. imperialism, Yankee interventionism, or alleged American exploitation of the poor.

Players of the "Sanctuary" game piously claim that it is not a game at all. They are simply helping political refugees from such countries as El Salvador and Guatemala find haven in the United States. What they are doing, actually, is smuggling a select number of highly vocal illegal aliens into the country; housing them in their churches where the press is invited to interview and publicize their presence; and then daring U.S. Immigration and other authorities to challenge their illegal actions.

The "Sanctuary" Angle

The first U.S. church to come up with the "Sanctuary" angle was the Wellington Avenue

"'The Sanctuary' Game," *The Mindszenty Report*, May 1984. Reprinted by permission of The Cardinal Mindszenty Foundation, St. Louis, MO 63105.

United Church of Christ in Chicago. Nearly two years ago its officers informed U.S. Immigration and Naturalization Service that they were going to bring illegal aliens into the country in defiance of the law. It was not long thereafter that the American Civil Liberties Union (ACLU) was involving itself on the question of such illegal aliens, issuing a report on the dangers facing these political refugees if deported back to their own countries.

Other groups based in Washington, D.C., with names like El Salvador Asylum Project and Refugee Policy Group began appearing in the press with regularity. Their concern, too, was that illegal aliens deported from the U.S. would be returning to certain death at the hands of governments of Central America who are fighting guerrilla insurgents.

Meanwhile, the "Sanctuary" game was being coordinated by a group called Chicago Religious Task Force. It was helping smuggle illegal aliens to so-called "Sanctuary churches" across the country and providing information and other assistance to church groups deciding to play the game. Most of the Chicago group's activities were shrouded in secrecy at first, but plans were being made for a big propaganda event that would gain nationwide media attention.

The So-Called "Freedom Train"

Felipe and Elena Excot and their five children—refugees from "repressive," pro-U.S. Guatemala—were selected by the Chicago Task Force to ride in a weeklong, 1,400-mile motorcade from the Windy City to Weston, Vermont, where they would be offered sanctuary in a Benedictine monastery with great fanfare and media attention. Here is how *Newsweek* magazine of April 2, 1984 described the media event under the headline "This is a Freedom Train":

"A few motorists honked. Some flashed peace signs. Most simply stared at the caravan of cars studded with signs proclaiming, 'U.S. Out of Central

America' and 'This Is a Freedom Train.' Leading the procession as it made its way from Chicago to a Benedictine monastery in Weston, Vt...., Felipe and Elena Excot and their five children—illegal aliens from Guatemala—rode in a brown Ford van, marimba music playing on a portable tape recorder. At each stop the Excots stayed in churches, slept on floors, ate food donated by parishioners—and dared the U.S. Immigration and Naturalization Service to arrest them.

"The Excots' journey was part of the 'sanctuary movement' of religious groups that has helped an estimated 350 Central American illegal aliens settle in the United States last year...the Excots' sponsors, the Chicago Religious Task Force on Central America, made this trip openly to protest what they say is a sudden attempt by the Reagan administration to break up their underground network...U.S. citizens convicted of assisting illegal aliens can be subject to up to five years in prison. But until now the INS has followed a tacit hands-off policy toward the sanctuary movement, largely out of unwillingness to force its jurisdiction over houses of worship. Religious leaders also suspect U.S. officials want to avoid the bad publicity of arrests in churches."

Generating Publicity

Publicity generated by the Excots' trek from Chicago to the Benedictine Weston Priory, as the *Newsweek* article proves, was one of the reasons for staging this made-for-the-media event. The Excots were painted by other press accounts as simple, hard-working peasants fleeing for their lives from Guatemala: "He will help the monks till their vegetable gardens and help cut wood for the stoves used for heating," said a March 25 Associated Press story; "His wife whose small hand loom was the only personal belonging she brought from Guatemala will teach the brothers to weave."

The "simple peasants," however, had more than planting beans and cucumbers or looming colorful serapes for the Benedictine monks in mind when facing the press "as church bells rang" upon their arrival in Vermont. Felipe told the Associated Press that he "has a duty to tell Americans how governments supported by their tax dollars force Christians in Central America to bury their Bibles and hide their communion wafers." He had been branded a subversive, Felipe added, "for teaching villagers to read and for getting farmers to buy fertilizer and rent trucks together at harvest time. He said the army calls that communism." Poor peasant farmer Felipe Excot, as *Newsweek* points out, is also a "Catholic theologian" who hopes "to raise the consciousness of the American people to what is happening in Central America."

Julio and Maria (no last name) are political refugees from El Salvador living in sanctuary at the Immanuel Lutheran Church in St. Louis. Their message is similar to that of Felipe Excot. "We need to tell the people of North America what's happening in El Salvador," Maria is quoted in *The RiverFront Times,* a small "alternate" newspaper which affords the "Sanctuary" game players—as do other such publications around the country—a forum to reach wider, sympathetic audiences already predisposed to leftist politics.

Forget About Communism

"Forget about the ominous warnings about Communist takeovers" in Central America, Julio adds. The left are the good guys with "proposed agendas" to end the various conflicts in Central America while the "ultra-right, believed responsible for the vast majority of political murders, hasn't budged." The solution say "Sanctuary" refugees Julio and Maria: "One way to force them to relinquish power is to cut off American aid."

Like the Excots, Julio and Maria and other "Sanctuary" aliens are not interested in seeking legal political asylum in the U.S. because that is not the object of the "Sanctuary" game. Julio and Maria along with many other illegal refugees tell *The RiverFront Times* they will soon depart from St. Louis on a "lobbying campaign" to Washington, D.C., where they hope to testify about their experiences and opinions and meet with key Congressmen on Central American issues.

"Players of the "Sanctuary" game piously claim that it is not a game at all."

No one knows, of course, how many illegal aliens from Central America are presently in the U.S. "Some estimates," says *City Newspaper* of Rochester, New York, put the number of Salvadorans alone at between 300,000 and 500,000. That number may be too high, but the "Sanctuary" players have some definite ideas in mind about what they want the government to do about the problem. "Sanctuary supporters," says the Rochester paper, are pushing for legislation granting "extended voluntary departure" status for all illegal Central American aliens now in the U.S.

Extended Voluntary Departure

What EVD or "extended voluntary departure" status means is those illegals would be granted the right to remain in the U.S. and obtain permission to work until "hostilities" in their respective countries are ended. Such status is now being granted to citizens of Lebanon, Ethiopia, Uganda, Afghanistan, and Poland presently in the U.S., and "Sanctuary" spokesmen want illegals like Julio and Maria and Felipe and Elena Excot extended the same rights.

"This bill really shouldn't be controversial," says Carol Wolchok, a full-time ACLU lawyer who is lobbying Congress for legislation submitted by Massachusetts Congressman Joe Moakley granting EVD status to illegal Central American refugees. While admitting the Moakley bill is "trying to force the administration's hand" on the illegal alien question, the "Sanctuary" players quickly point out that EVD will not entitle these illegals to such government assistance programs as welfare, Food Stamps and Medicaid. Anyone familiar with ACLU tactics knows, however, that once EVD status is granted to illegals, ACLU lawyers will be in the nation's courtrooms arguing such denial of welfare benefits is unconstitutional, probably criminal, and a national disgrace.

A Christian Tradition?

Sanctuary, say the game players, is a Christian tradition dating back to Biblical times when sanctuaries were established as places of refuge for persons fleeing from violence or from the penalties of law. To injure a person in sanctuary or to remove him forcibly was considered a sacrilege. Question: Is it not also a sacrilege to use our churches as havens for Marxist propaganda agents representing the guerrilla and terrorist elements in their countries responsible for violence, acts of sabotage, criminal extortion, robbery and blackmail?

"Runaway slaves in the Civil War days were seeking freedom while today's "Sanctuary" illegals speak for forces that would enslave their countries under Communism."

In more recent times, the "Sanctuary" players point out, many churches in the United States often took a role in the Underground Railroad movement of the 1850's, helping transport and harbor runaway slaves. The new sanctuary movement claims to revive and reconstitute the Underground Railroad with churches playing a key role in helping illegal Central American political refugees make their way to sanctuary churches all across the country. Question: Is there not a great deal of deceit in this comparison? Runaway slaves in the Civil War days were seeking freedom while today's "Sanctuary" illegals speak for forces that would enslave their countries under Communism.

It is true that Christian churches were given the right to sanctuary as far back as the time of Roman Emperor Constantine, who also issued the Edict of Milan which freed Christianity from 300 years of persecution. Over the years the abuse of sanctuary, which tended to encourage crime, led to its curtailment and abolition. Today modern penal codes no longer recognize the right of sanctuary. The "Sanctuary" game players are breaking the law and hiding behind their church doors, taunting authorities to arrest them or admit they've lost the game.

"A spokesman for the Immigration and Naturalization Service in Washington," an Associated Press dispatch appearing in the March 25, 1984 *Louisville Courier-Journal* newspaper tells us, "said U.S. law does not recognize sanctuary...however, it is the Service's policy not to take special enforcement actions against the sanctuary movement." But, why not?

If a church were running a prostitution ring out of its basement surely the law would not be hesitant in acting to shut it down. The same with a gambling operation or a distribution center for drugs. When churches become headquarters for political intrigue, they are no longer above the law.

The "Sanctuary" game players are religious Pharisees, sanctimoniously beating their breasts over the plight of illegal, pro-Marxist aliens. The game they play is another example of how the Left uses religious channels for propaganda and promotion of political objectives. It needs to be thoroughly exposed for the fake it is.

Population and Marxism

The illegal alien problem is growing more serious. A Marxist takeover of Central America, some estimate, would generate up to 20 million refugees seeking asylum in the United States. Add that to the millions of poor Mexican peasants who cross the U.S. borders illegally and the problem will become staggering.

There is already a massive Hispanic migration from Mexico flowing into Texas and other western states. There are some known Marxist agitators organizing and propagandizing among Mexican-American farm workers and other aliens. The U.S. Catholic Bishops' Campaign for Human Development, for example, funds a San Antonio-based organization called the Mexican American Cultural Center where Peruvian Fr. Gustavo Gutierrez, the most prominent of the world's "liberation" theologians, teaches his brand of revolutionary Christianity. The Center also has ties to the Chicago-based Industrial Areas Foundation where the late radical Saul Alinsky operated and where he trained religious agitators and propagandists.

It was Alinsky, a self-described professional radical espousing class warfare, who told his students to "seek out controversies and issues...people must be made to feel frustrated, defeated, lost and fruitless...The job of the organizer is to maneuver and bait the establishment so that it will publicly attack him as a dangerous enemy. A revolutionary organizer must shake up the prevailing patterns of people's lives...agitate...create disenchantment and discontent with the current values to produce a passion for change.''

The involvement of the Catholic church with Alinsky-type revolutionaries seeking to agitate and create class conflicts between Hispanics and other Americans is a disgrace. Few Americans, outside of those living on states bordering Mexico, know of this serious problem.

The Cardinal Mindszenty Foundation conducts educational and research activities concerning communist objectives, tactics and propaganda. The Foundation sponsors study groups, speakers clubs, conferences, and films.

"Our task now...is to help our neighbors...set in place the policies...that will make them both prosperous and free."

The Kissinger Report on Central America

National Bipartisan Commission on Central America

In this report, we propose significant attention and help to a previously neglected area of the hemisphere. Some, who have not studied the area as we have, may think this disproportionate, dismissing it as the natural reaction of a commission created to deal with a single subject. We think any such judgment would be a grave mistake.

It is true that other parts of the world are troubled. Some of these, such as the Middle East, are genuinely in crisis. But the crisis in Central America makes a particularly urgent claim on the United States for several reasons.

First, Central America is our near neighbor. Because of this, it critically involves our own security interests. But more than that, what happens on our doorstep calls to our conscience. History, contiguity, consanguinity—all these tie us to the rest of the Western Hemisphere; they also tie us very particularly to the nations of Central America. When Franklin Roosevelt proclaimed what he called his "Good Neighbor Policy," that was more than a phrase. It was a concept that goes to the heart of civilized relationships not only among people but also among nations. When our neighbors are in trouble, we cannot close our eyes and still be true to ourselves.

Second, the crisis calls out to us because we *can* make a difference. Because the nations are small, because they are near, efforts that would be minor by the standards of other crises can have a large impact on this one.

Third, whatever the short-term costs of acting now, they are far less than the long-term costs of not acting now.

Fourth, a great power can choose what challenges to respond to, but it cannot choose where those

Report of the National Bipartisan Commission on Central America, January 1984.

challenges come—or when. Nor can it avoid the necessity of deliberate choice. Once challenged, a decision not to respond is fully as consequential as a decision to respond. We are challenged now in Central America. No agony of indecision will make that challenge go away. No wishing it were easier will make it easier.

Perhaps the United States should have paid more attention to Central America sooner. Perhaps, over the years, we should have intervened less, or intervened more, or intervened differently. But all these are questions of what might have been. What confronts us now is a question of what might become. Whatever its roots in the past, the crisis in Central America exists urgently in the present, and its successful resolution is vital to the future....

Seven Common Threads

Certain common threads run through all the chapters.

• First, the tortured history of Central America is such that neither the military nor the political nor the economic nor the social aspects of the crisis can be considered independently of the others. Unless rapid progress can be made on the political, economic and social fronts, peace on the military front will be elusive and would be fragile. But unless the externally-supported insurgencies are checked and the violence curbed, progress on those other fronts will be elusive and would be fragile.

• Second, the roots of the crisis are both indigenous and foreign. Discontents are real, and for much of the population conditions of life are miserable; just as Nicaragua was ripe for revolution, so the conditions that invite revolution are present elsewhere in the region as well. But these conditions have been exploited by hostile outside forces—specifically by Cuba, backed by the Soviet Union and now operating through Nicaragua—which will turn any revolution they capture into a totalitarian state, threatening the region and robbing the people of their hopes for liberty.

• Third, indigenous reform, even indigenous revolution, is not a security threat to the United States. But the intrusion of aggressive outside powers exploiting local grievances to expand their own political influence and military control is a serious threat to the United States, and to the entire hemisphere.

• Fourth, we have a humanitarian interest in alleviating misery and helping the people of Central America meet their social and economic needs, and together with other nations of the hemisphere we have a national interest in strengthening democratic institutions wherever in the hemisphere they are weak.

• Fifth, Central America needs help, both material and moral, governmental and nongovernmental. Both the commands of conscience and calculations of our own national interest require that we give that help.

• Sixth, ultimately, a solution of Central America's problems will depend on the Central Americans themselves. They need our help, but our help alone will not be enough. Internal reforms, outside assistance, bootstrap efforts, changed economic policies—all are necessary, and all must be coordinated. And other nations with the capacity to do so not only in this hemisphere, but in Europe and Asia, should join in the effort.

• Seventh, the crisis will not wait. There is no time to lose. . . .

No Room for Partisanship

We have approached our deliberations in a nonpartisan spirit and in a bipartisan way, and we believe that the nation can and must do the same. . . .

The international purposes of the United States in the late twentieth century are cooperation, not hegemony or domination; partnership, not confrontation; a decent life for all, not exploitation. Those objectives must be achievable in this hemisphere if they can be realized anywhere. . . .

Challenges in Central America

The hemisphere is challenged both economically and politically. While that double challenge is common to all of Latin America, it now takes its most acute form in Central America.

First, the commanding economic issue in all of Latin America is the impoverishment of its people. The nations of the hemisphere—not least those of Central America—advanced remarkably throughout the 1960's and 1970's. Growth was strong, though not nearly enough was done to close the gap between the rich and the poor, the product of longstanding economic, social and political structures. . . .

Second, the political challenge in the hemisphere centers on the legitimacy of government. Once again, this takes a particularly acute form in Central America.

Powerful forces are on the march in nearly every country of the hemisphere, testing how nations shall be organized and by what processes authority shall be established and legitimized. Who shall govern and under what forms are the central issues in the process of change now under way in country after country throughout Latin America and the Caribbean. . . .

Democracy is becoming the rule rather than the exception. The nations of Central America are also, each in its own fashion, engaged in a struggle over how a nation shall be governed. . . .

Democracy Encourages Stability

Experience has destroyed the argument of the old dictators that a strong hand is essential to avoid anarchy and communism, and that order and progress can be achieved only through authoritarianism. Those nations in Latin America which have been moving to open their political, social and economic structures and which have employed honest and open elections have been marked by a stability astonishing in the light of the misery which still afflicts the hemisphere. The modern experience of Latin America suggests that order is more often threatened when people have no voice in their own destinies. Social peace is more likely in societies where political justice is founded on self-determination and protected by formal guarantees.

"The United States must be concerned by the intrusion into Central America of aggressive external powers."

The issue is not what particular system a nation might choose when it votes. The issue is rather that nations should choose for themselves, free of outside pressure, force or threat. There is room in the hemisphere for differing forms of governance and different political economies. Authentically indigenous changes, and even indigenous revolutions, are not incompatible with international harmony in the Americas. They are not incompatible even with the mutual security of the members of the inter-American system—if they are truly indigenous. The United States can have no quarrel with democratic decisions, as long as they are not the result of foreign pressure and external machinations. The Soviet-Cuban thrust to make Central America part of their geostrategic challenge is what has turned the struggle in Central America into a security and political problem for the United States and for the hemisphere.

There is no self-determination when there is foreign compulsion or when nations make themselves tools of a strategy designed in other continents....

Responding Positively

A contemporary doctrine of U.S.-Latin American relations cannot rest on insulating the hemisphere from foreign influence. It must also respond in an affirmative way to the economic and political challenges in the hemisphere; U.S. policy must respect the diversities among the nations of America even while advancing their common interests. Three principles should, in the Commission's view, guide hemispheric relations; we have sought to apply them to our considerations of Central America.

• The first principle is democratic self-determination....

• The second principle is encouragement of economic and social development that fairly benefits all....

"In Central America today, our strategic and moral interests coincide."

• The third principle is cooperation in meeting threats to the security of the region....

The remainder of this report sets forth the ways in which this Commission believes a consistent economic, political and security effort, one which coordinates the best efforts of the people in Central America, its neighbors, and the United States, can be maintained. The way in which that combination of crises is addressed—or any failure to address it with both the urgency and the comprehensiveness it requires—will profoundly affect not only our national interest but the larger interests of the hemisphere as well.

The Crisis in Central America

Central America is gripped today by a profound crisis. That crisis has roots deep in the region's history, but it also contains elements of very recent origin. An understanding of it requires some familiarity with both....

There has been considerable controversy, sometimes vigorous, as to whether the basic causes of the crisis are indigenous or foreign. In fact, the crisis is the product of *both* indigenous and foreign factors. It has sources deep in the tortured history and life of the region, but it has also been powerfully shaped by external forces. Poverty, repression, inequity, all were there, breeding fear and hate; stirring in a world recession created a potent witch's brew, while outside forces have intervened to exacerbate the area's troubles and to exploit its anguish.

Those outside forces have given the crisis more than a Central American dimension. The United

States is not threatened by indigenous change, even revolutionary change, in Central America. But the United States must be concerned by the intrusion into Central America of aggressive external powers....

The period of the 1930's was terribly disruptive in Central America. As the bottom dropped out of the market for Central America's products, a wave of instability swept the region; for the first time traditional oligarchic rule came under serious challenge....

By this point, two main political traditions were operating in Central America—and an emerging third one.

First, there was the old authoritarian tradition. This historically dominant force still drew considerable strength from the difficulty of establishing democratic forms in the fragmented, violent, disintegrative context of Central America.

Second, there was a democratic tradition enshrined in political constitutions but of only marginal importance in practice....

The third strain—socialism—also appeared in a variety of forms in Central America amid the turmoil of the 1930's and has remained present ever since, frequently mixed into both democratic (as in Costa Rica) and Marxist or even communist elements....

Only in Costa Rica was the final formula democratic. After a brief but decisive civil war in 1948, regular elections have since led to periodic rotation in power by the two dominant groups.

Elsewhere, efforts were made to combine or reconcile the traditional and the liberal orientations, and at times even to hint at the socialist one.

In Nicaragua, for example, after the death of Anastasio Somoza Garcia (1896-1956), his elder son Luis made various attempts to relax the harsher aspects of the old authoritarianism—to allow a greater sense of pluralism and freedom. In Honduras, military and civilian parties rotated in office or else ruled jointly in an arrangement whereby military officers controlled security matters and acted as political arbiters, while the civilian elites managed the economy, held key cabinet positions, and staffed the bureaucracy. In Guatemala, after the United States helped bring about the fall of the Arbenz government in 1954, politics became more divisive, violent and polarized than in the neighboring states. But even there, there were efforts to combine civilian and military rule, or to alternate between them, in various shaky and uneasy blends....

None of these regimes was truly democratic, but the trend seemed to favor the growth of centrist political forces and to be leading toward greater pluralism and more representative political orders. This trend gave hope for peaceful accommodations and realistic responses to the profound social changes occurring in the countries of Central America....

In Nicaragua, the political opening that had seemed to be promised in the 1960's was now closed off by Somoza's second son, Anastasio, Jr., who took power in 1966. His rule was characterized by greed and corruption so far beyond even the levels of the past that it might well be called a kleptocracy; it included a brazen reaping of immense private profits from international relief efforts following the devastating earthquake of 1972. And as opposition to his regime increased, repression became systematic and increasingly pervasive.

In Guatemala, the more or less centrist civilian and military governments of the 1960's gave way in the 1970's to a succession of extremely repressive regimes....

In El Salvador, the pattern was similar. Military-based regimes that had been moderately progressive in the early 1960's had become corrupt and repressive by the 1970's. The annulment of the victory by civilian Christian Democratic candidate Jose Napoleon Duarte in the 1972 election ushered in a period of severely repressive rule. It was in this context, with its striking parallels to the developments in Nicaragua and Guatemala, that the present crisis in El Salvador began.

It is no accident that these three countries—El Salvador, Guatemala, and Nicaragua—are precisely where the crisis for U.S. policy is centered. While there were of course significant national variations, all three went through a roughly parallel process in which a trend toward more open, pluralistic, and democratic societies gave way to oppression and polarization, precipitating the crisis which has now spread throughout Central America....

Modernization and Poverty

While measures of absolute poverty are inevitably arbitrary and subject to considerable margins of error, studies show that in El Salvador, Guatemala, Honduras, and Nicaragua during the 1970's about half of the urban population and three-quarters of the rural population could not satisfy their basic needs in terms of nutrition, housing, health, and education. The population explosion magnified the problem of inequitable distribution of national income. As we have seen, the number of Central Americans almost tripled in 30 years. The World Bank projects a further increase in the region's population to 38 million by the end of the century. Except in Costa Rica, rapid urbanization and population growth overwhelmed the limited resources that governments were prepared to devote to social services—or that private organizations could provide. This was true in all fields—education, health, housing, and nutrition.

In short, the economic growth of the 60's and 70's did not resolve the region's underlying social problems. About 60 percent of the populations of El Salvador, Guatemala, Honduras, and Nicaragua (before the revolution) remained illiterate. Ten of

every one hundred babies born died before the age of five, and, according to reliable nutritionists, 52 percent of the children were malnourished. Somewhere between four and five million people in the region were unemployed or underemployed. They and their families were often living on the edge of starvation....

The economic collapse of the late 1970's, coming as it did after a period of relatively sustained growth, shattered the rising hopes of Central Americans for a better life. Though the period of modernization by no means lifted most Central Americans out of poverty, it did arouse expectations that the quality of life would improve. The frustration of these expectations, along with the disappointment of efforts to bring about political change in the region, thus offered fertile opportunities for those both in the region and outside of it who wished to exploit the crisis for their own advantage.

Growth of Communist Insurgency

By 1979, in terms of modern military capabilities Cuba had become perhaps the strongest power in the Western Hemisphere south of the United States. It was also the country best prepared and most eager to exploit the intensifying crisis in Central America....

"Curbing the insurgent's violence in El Salvador requires...cutting them off from their sources of foreign support."

In the early years, the major Cuban effort to export revolution to Central America occurred in Guatemala. There, Castro gave support to an armed insurgency that began in 1960. Though the Soviet Union was relatively inactive after the Cuban Missile Crisis, Castro provided arms, financing and training to the MR-13 guerrilla movement and later to the rival Armed Forces of Revolution (FAR). This was not an isolated tactic. Cuba was following the same practice in this period with similar movements in Venezuela, Columbia and Peru....

In 1978 Castro disappointed those who thought he had abandoned the export of revolution in this hemisphere. He saw new opportunities. Guerrillas were once again in the field in Guatemala; the elements of a promising insurgency were present in El Salvador; and, above all, a particularly inviting situation presented itself in Nicaragua where the Samoza dictatorship was beginning to crumble. The United States was still suffering the after-effects of Vietnam and Watergate. At the same time, Castro's Soviet patrons, who had not actively supported the armed struggle during the 1960's, were coming around to his view that the time for guerrilla war in Central America had arrived.

Their conversion to the doctrine of armed violence became complete with the collapse of Somoza in Nicaragua. Although Venezuela, Costa Rica, Panama, and other Latin American countries assisted the revolutionaries in Nicaragua, and although the refusal of the U.S. to supply arms helped precipitate Somoza's fall, Cuban support was a particularly important factor in the Sandinista triumph. It was Castro who unified the three Nicaraguan guerrilla factions and provided the weapons, supplies, and advisers that enabled the Cuban-oriented *comandantes* to establish themselves as the dominant group in the revolution. . . .

The Present Crisis

As we have seen, Central America's contemporary crisis has been a long time in the making. By the late 1970's, the increasingly dangerous configuration of historic poverty, social injustice, frustrated expectations, and closed political systems was suddenly exacerbated by world economic recession and by intensified foreign-promoted communist insurgency. And just as the economic collapse and political impasse offered an opportunity for the insurgents, the insurgency aggravated the economic and political crisis by spreading violence and fear. To varying degrees, but with many common elements, this crisis is reflected in the situation of each of the five Central American nations.

"Military aid should. . . be made contingent upon demonstrated progress toward free elections. . . and the termination of the activities of the so-called death squads."

Nowhere is the link between economic decline and insecurity more apparent than in El Salvador, once perhaps the leading beneficiary of the Central American Common Market. El Salvador today faces violence and destruction that threaten economic collapse. Planting and harvesting have been disrupted, buses and trucks burned, bridges and electric pylons dynamited. The cumulative direct cost of the war to the economy has been estimated at more than $600 million, with indirect costs far higher. El Salvador's economy is now less than three-quarters the size it was in 1978, and national income on a per capita basis is roughly at the level of the early 1960's.

The insurgents themselves acknowledge that destruction of the country's basic infrastructure is a key ingredient in their strategy to bring down the government. They seek victory through both economic and military attrition. Although their

absolute numbers have not increased over the last three years, and although they have not attracted the broad popular support they hoped for, the guerrillas after four years of experience in the field demonstrate an increasing capacity to manuever, concentrate their forces and attack selected targets. They maintain sporadic control over areas in the eastern provinces and pose a hit-and-run threat virtually everywhere outside the major urban areas. Guerrilla forces regularly attempt to intimidate and coerce local populations with shootings, abductions and other strong-arm tactics. And the human costs of the war have been immense. Displaced Salvadorans driven from their homes and leading a precarious existence within the country number in the hundreds of thousands. Many thousands more have left El Salvador as refugees. . . .

The Need for Revolution

There was little dispute among the witnesses appearing before the Commission that, in the words of one of them, "El Salvador needed a revolution"—a democratic revolution. The unemployment, steadily deteriorating social conditions and a very young population is potentially explosive. . . .

Although the current situation differs substantially from country to country, there are many common elements.

The region as a whole has suffered severe economic setbacks. All five nations are markedly poorer than they were just a few years ago. Intra-regional trade has fallen drastically. The Common Market is threatened with extinction as the resources necessary to sustain it dry up. Political violence and the menace of the radical left have caused huge flights of capital. Investment, even in the leading agricultural export sectors, has come virtually to an end. . . .

The configuration of economic recession, political turbulence and foreign intervention makes the crisis in Central America both exceptionally difficult and exceptionally ominous. Although turmoil has often accompanied economic difficulty in Central America, it has never before been so calculated to create chaos and want. This both intensifies the conflict and accelerates the economic and political decay of the region.

The prospect of even greater calamaties should not be underestimated. None of the five Central American states is free of war or the threat of war. As the conflicts intensify, and as Nicaragua builds an armed force with firepower vastly greater than anything ever seen before in Central America, the threat of militarization hangs over the region. Were this to happen, it could further warp Central America's societies and shut off the possibilities for internal and external accommodations. . . .

The importance of the United States to the region's economies has been a powerful element in shaping

Central American attitudes toward us. Beginning in Costa Rica almost a century ago, U.S. capital developed the banana industry and monopolized it throughout the isthmus. For decades, the United Fruit Company was known in the area as "the octopus." It controlled much of the region's transportation and communications. Bananas were vital to the economies of several countries, and United Fruit dominated the international markets for the fruit. Since the 1950's patterns of both land ownership and distribution in the banana industry have diversified. United Fruit itself no longer exists; its successor, United Brands, is widely regarded as both a model citizen and a model employer. But the questionable practices followed by the fruit companies in those early years, together with the power they wielded over weak governments, did a lot to create the fear of "economic imperialism" that to some degree still persists among Central Americans.

"The consolidation of a Marxist-Leninist regime in Managua would be seen by its neighbors as constituting a permanent security threat."

This is only one side of the history of U.S. relations with Central America. The U.S. government has also made extensive positive efforts to advance Central American development, beginning at the turn of the century with a public health campaign against yellow fever. During the Second World War the Institute of Inter-American Affairs, headed by Nelson Rockefeller, was established. The Institute developed a system of "Servicios"—bilateral organizations to finance and manage projects in health, education and housing. Through the decade of the 1950's the Servicios provided training and experience to a new generation of Central American technicians and professionals.

With the launching of the Alliance for Progress in 1961, the role of the United States in Central American development underwent a major transformation. This was a bold and unprecedented effort to encourage comprehensive national planning and to promote a wide array of social, political, tax and land reforms, supported by significantly increased resources from the United States, the newly created Inter-American Development Bank, the World Bank and other aid donors. The assistance from the United States, and perhaps equally as significant, the personal identification of President Kennedy with the program, was a critical factor in the surge of Central American development which began in the 1960's.

U.S. assistance was instrumental in the creation of effective central banks and private intermediate

credit institutions, and in the establishment of agricultural cooperatives, housing projects, roads, health centers, population assistance, and technical training. The Alliance for Progress also provided major funding and cooperative planning to the Central American Common Market, which was perhaps its most important single contribution to Central American growth during this period.

In essence, the Alliance was a compact between our government and the governments of Latin America. The goals of the Alliance were three: economic growth, structural change in societies, and political democratization. But as we have seen, it was only in the first area that significant progress was made. Central America's growth rate of over 5 percent per capita during the 1960's far surpassed the 2.5 percent target for all of Latin America laid down in the charter of the Alliance. An impressive inventory of physical infrastructure was constructed in the five Central American countries during this period, including schools, hospitals, low-cost housing, and sewage systems.

But the other two goals of the Alliance, structural change and political democratization, proved much more difficult to achieve.

Direct private investment in Central America by U.S. firms also continued to grow during these years. While that investment might seem small in relation to total U.S. investment abroad (currently about 2.4 percent, including Panama), it was large in Central American terms. It has contributed substantially to the region's growth, as many Central Americans are quick to acknowledge. At the same time, it has been a constant target of the propaganda of the radical left, which has played upon the theme of economic hegemony and "imperialism."

Central America's dependence on trade with the United States has, of course, always been high. Though the portion of the region's exports that came to the United States declined from 61 percent in 1955 to 36 percent in 1975, the U.S. still led all other countries as a market for Central American products and commodities. While such dependence remains a sensitive issue, investment from the U.S. and trade relations with the U.S. are critically important to the economies of Central America....

US Interests

When strategic interests conflict with moral interests, the clash presents one of the classic challenges to confront societies and statesmen. But in Central America today, our strategic and moral interests coincide....

• To preserve the moral authority of the United States....

• To improve the living conditions of the people of Central America. They are neighbors. Their human need is tinder waiting to be ignited. And if it is, the conflagration could threaten the entire hemisphere.

- To advance the cause of democracy, broadly defined, within the hemisphere.
- To strengthen the hemispheric system by strengthening what is now, in both economic and social terms, one of its weakest links.
- To promote peaceful change in Central America while resisting the violation of democracy by force and terrorism.
- To prevent hostile forces from seizing and expanding control in a strategically vital area of the Western Hemisphere.
- To bar the Soviet Union from consolidating either directly or through Cuba a hostile foothold on the American continents in order to advance its strategic purposes.

In short, the crisis in Central America is of large and acute concern to the United States because Central America is our near neighbor and a strategic crossroads of global significance; because Cuba and the Soviet Union are investing heavily in efforts to expand their footholds there, so as to carry out designs for the hemisphere distinctly hostile to U.S. interests; and because the people of Central America are sorely beset and urgently need our help....

The Future

The people of Central America have lived too long with poverty, deprivation and violence. The current turmoil must not be allowed to shatter their hopes for a brighter future.

They have endured too many generations of misrule to let their aspirations for democratic political development be dashed in this generation on the rocks of fear, division and violence. Not least, their own security—and ours—must no longer be threatened by hostile powers which seek expansion of influence through exploitation of misery....

Security Issues

We ardently wish that there were no need for a security chapter in a report on Central America. But there is.

The region is torn by war and the threat of war. It needs peace in order to have progress. It needs security in order to have peace.

The conflicts that ravage the nations of Central America have both indigenous and foreign roots. Restoring peace and stability will require a combination of social and political reforms, economic advances, diplomatic pursuit and military effort....

We have stressed before, and we repeat here: indigenous reform movements, even indigenous revolutions, are not themselves a security concern of the United States. History holds examples of genuinely popular revolutions, springing wholly from native roots. In this hemisphere Mexico is a clear example. But during the past two decades we have faced a new phenomenon. The concerting of the power of the Soviet Union and Cuba to extend their presence and influence into vulnerable areas of the Western Hemisphere is a direct threat to U.S. security interests. This type of insurgency is present in Central America today....

"We can reduce Soviet opportunities and increase the incentives for others to abstain from forging ties with Moscow that damage U.S. and regional interests."

In El Salvador two separate conflicts have raged since 1979. One conflict pits persons seeking democratic government and its associated rights and freedoms against those trying to maintain oligarchical rule and its associated privileges. A second conflict pits guerrillas seeking to establish a Marxist-Leninist state as part of a broader Central American revolution against those who oppose a Marxist-Leninist victory.

In each of these conflicts one of the parties has pursued its goals by violence. Both traditionalist death squads and murderous guerrillas have attacked political party, labor and peasant leaders working to establish and consolidate democratic institutions, killing them and dismantling their efforts to build democracy....

Both violent groups are morally and politically repugnant to this Commission, which strongly supports the consolidation and defense of democratic institutions in El Salvador....

It is not only for the sake of democratic reform and human rights that we oppose the death squads. Their violent attacks upon Salvadoran democrats handicap the struggle to resist the armed insurgency of the guerrillas. This Marxist insurgency not only opposes democracy and is committed to the violent seizure of power, but also threatens U.S. security interests because of its ties to Nicaragua, Cuba, and the Soviet Union. The policy challenge facing the United States is to untangle these two conflicts—to support the forces of democratic reform against the death squads while at the same time helping El Salvador resist subjugation by Marxist-Leninist guerrillas....

Marxist-Leninist Influences

Because this chapter addresses the question of security, it will focus initially on the threat posed by Marxist-Leninist insurgencies in Central America. It will then put forward proposals to end human rights abuses by the death squads.

The externally-supported guerrilla insurgency that confronts us in El Salvador and elsewhere in Central America is really a new kind of war. It differs as much from indigenous revolts as it does from conventional wars. It is more complex, both in concept and in execution. By now the world has had enough experience with it so that its nature is known and its patterns are predictable.

An examination of any particular externally-supported insurgency requires an understanding of a) the internal conditions that invited it, and b) the external forces that support it. Both are essential elements, and the interaction between them is one of the key factors that make these wars so difficult for governments to win and so devastating for the people who become their victims....

Whatever the social and economic conditions that invited insurgency in the region, outside intervention is what gives the conflict its present character. Of course, uprisings occur without outside support, but protracted guerrilla insurgencies require external assistance. Indeed, if wretched conditions were themselves enough to create such insurgencies, we would see them in many more countries of the world.

Propaganda support, money, sanctuary, arms, supplies, training, communications, intelligence, logistics, all are important in both morale and operational terms. Without such support from Cuba, Nicaragua and the Soviet Union, neither in El Salvador nor elsewhere in Central America would such an insurgency pose so severe a threat to the government. With such support, guerrilla forces could develop insurgencies in many other countries. The struggle in El Salvador is particularly severe because it is there that external support is at present most heavily concentrated.

"Whatever the social and economic conditions that invited insurgency in the region, outside intervention is what gives the conflict its present character."

Therefore, curbing the insurgents' violence in El Salvador requires, in part, cutting them off from their sources of foreign support.

If reforms had been undertaken earlier, there would almost surely have been no fertile ground for revolution, and thus no effectively developed insurgency. But once an insurgency is fully under way, and once the lines of external support are in place, it has a momentum which reforms alone cannot stop. Unchecked, the insurgents can destroy faster than the reformers can build.

One reason for this is that an explicit purpose of guerrilla violence is to make matters worse: to paralyze the economy, to heighten social discords, to spread fear and despair, to weaken institutions and to undermine government authority—all so as to radicalize the people, and to persuade them that any alternative is better than what they have. By disrupting order, the strategy of terror strikes at the foundation of authority. By helping to provoke the use of counter-terror, as Carlos Marighella wrote in his classic terrorist tract, *Minimanual of the Urban Guerrilla*, guerrillas can transform "the political situation in the country...into a military situation in which the militarists appear more and more to be the ones responsible for terror and violence, while the problems in the lives of the people become truly catastrophic."...

Because the Marxist-Leninist insurgents appeal to often legitimate grievances, a popular school of thought holds that guerrilla leaders are the engines of reform. They characteristically reinforce this by inviting well-meaning democratic leaders to participate in a Popular Front, taking care, however, to retain in their own hands a monopoly of the instruments of force. If the insurgents were in fact the vehicles for democratic and social progress, the entire security issue would be moot; they would no longer be the problem, but rather the solution.

Unfortunately, history offers no basis for such optimism. No Marxist-Leninist "popular front" insurgency has ever turned democratic *after* its victory. Cuba and Nicaragua are striking examples. Regimes created by the victory of Marxist-Leninist guerrillas become totalitarian. That is their purpose, their nature, their doctrine, and their record....

The Cuban-Soviet Connection

Soviet policy in this hemisphere has followed the pattern of Soviet policy elsewhere in the world: Moscow has exploited opportunities for the expansion of Soviet influence. In the aftermath of the Cuban Missile Crisis, the Soviets concentrated on expanding their diplomatic, economic and cultural ties in Latin America and on strengthening the influence of local communist parties in broad electoral fronts, trade unions and the universities. In this respect they differed from Castro, who continued to support a course of armed struggle in Venezuela, Colombia, Guatemala, and several other countries. But later the fall of Allende in Chile and the subsequent right-wing takeovers in Uruguay, Argentina, and Bolivia discredited the Soviet expectation of the "peaceful path" to communism in Latin America....

As a mainland platform, therefore, Nicaragua is a crucial steppingstone for Cuban and Soviet efforts to promote armed insurgency in Central America. Its location explains why the Nicaraguan revolution of 1979, like the Cuban revolution 20 years earlier, was a decisive turning point in the affairs of the region. With the victory of the Sandinistas in Nicaragua, the levels of violence and counter-violence in Central America rapidly increased, engulfing the entire region.

Through most of its history, the United States has

been able to take for granted our security in our own hemisphere. We have come to think, as Walter Lippmann wrote four decades ago, "that our privileged position was a natural right." In fact, it was the rivalries in Europe and the supremacy of British seapower that allowed us to uphold the Monroe Doctrine with minimal effort for more than a century—until the intrusion of communism into Cuba.

The ability of the United States to sustain a tolerable balance of power on the global scene at a manageable cost depends on the inherent security of its land borders. This advantage is of crucial importance. It offsets an otherwise serious liability: our distance from Europe, the Middle East, and East Asia, which are also of strategic concern to the United States. Security commitments in those areas require the United States to supply its forces overseas at the far end of trans-oceanic lines of communication whose protection can be almost as costly as the forces themselves.

At the level of global strategy, therefore, the advance of Soviet and Cuban power on the American mainland affects the global balance. To the extent that a further Marxist-Leninist advance in Central America leading to progressive deterioration and a further projection of Soviet and Cuban power in the region required us to defend against security threats near our borders, we would face a difficult choice between unpalatable alternatives. We would either have to assume a permanently increased defense burden, or see our capacity to defend distant trouble-spots reduced, and as a result have to reduce important commitments elsewhere in the world. From the standpoint of the Soviet Union, it would be a major strategic coup to impose on the United States the burden of defending our southern approaches, thereby stripping us of the compensating advantage that offsets the burden of our transoceanic lines of communication.

Protecting Communication

Such a deterioration in Central America would also greatly increase both the difficulty and the cost of protecting these lines of communications themselves. Under present plans, some 50 percent of the shipping tonnage that would be needed to reinforce the European front, and about 40 percent of that required by a major East Asian conflict, would have to pass from the Gulf of Mexico through the Caribbean-Central American zone. These same sea routes also carry nearly half of all other foreign cargo, including crude oil, shipped to this country.

The Soviets have already achieved a greater capability to interdict shipping than the Nazis had during World War II, when 50 percent of U.S. supplies to Europe and Africa were shipped from Gulf ports. German U-boats then sank 260 merchant ships in just six months, despite the fact that Allied

forces enjoyed many advantages, including a two-to-one edge in submarines and the use of Cuba for resupply and basing operations. Today this is reversed. The Soviets now have a two-to-one edge overall in submarines and can operate and receive aircover from Cuba, a point from which all 13 Caribbean sea lanes passing through four chokepoints are vulnerable to interdiction. . . .

"The Soviets have already achieved a greater capability to interdict shipping than the Nazis had during World War II."

As Nicaragua is already doing, additional Marxist-Leninist regimes in Central America could be expected to expand their armed forces, bring in large numbers of Cuban and other Soviet bloc advisers, develop sophisticated agencies of internal repression and external subversion, and sharpen polarizations, both within individual countries and regionally. This would almost surely produce refugees, perhaps millions of them, many of whom would seek entry into the United States. Even setting aside the broader strategic considerations, the United States cannot isolate itself from the regional turmoil. The crisis is on our doorstep.

Beyond the issue of U.S. security interests in the Central American-Caribbean region, our credibility worldwide is engaged. The triumph of hostile forces in what the Soviets call the "strategic rear" of the United States would be read as a sign of U.S. impotence. . . .

Problems of Guerrilla War

Despite these high stakes, the debate over Central America has been polarized in the United States. One reason may be the seeming paradox in which important security questions are raised by small conflicts in an area which we have customarily neglected. . . .

The fundamental dilemma is as follows: both the national interests of the United States and a genuine concern for the long-term welfare of Central America create powerful incentives to provide all necessary assistance to defeat totalitarian guerrillas. At the same time one of the principal objectives of the guerrilla forces is to destroy the morale and efficiency of the government's administration and programs.

We thus labor under an immediate handicap. Unlike the Soviet Union in Afghanistan, the U.S. cannot—and should not—impose its own administration, even for such laudable objectives as implementing political, social and economic reforms; it cannot place its own experts in each village and town to gather political intelligence; and it cannot supervise the conduct of each soldier and policeman in all dealings with the population. For these goals, the U.S. Government must rely on the abilities and good faith of the government under attack.

But that government—already fragile because of history and structure and conflicting attitudes—is being systematically weakened further by the conditions of guerrilla warfare in which it must function....

The Darker Side

There is, of course, a darker side as well in El Salvador. The United States obviously cannot accept, let alone support, the brutal methods practiced by certain reactionary forces in Central America. Some of these actions are related to counter-insurgency.... It is designed to terrorize opponents, fight democracy, protect entrenched interests, and restore reactionary regimes.

Whatever their aims, these methods are totally repugnant to the values of the United States....

The Need for Military Assistance

The present level of U.S. military assistance to El Salvador is far too low to enable the armed forces of El Salvador to use these modern methods of counter-insurgency effectively. At the same time, the tendency in some quarters of the Salvadoran military towards brutality magnifies Congressional and Executive pressures for further cuts in aid. A vicious cycle results in which violence and denial of human rights spawn reductions in aid, and reductions in aid make more difficult the pursuit of an enlightened counter-insurgency effort.

"Military aid should, through legislation requiring periodic reports, be made contingent upon demonstrated progress toward free elections."

The combination of the tactical guidance given by U.S. advisers and levels of aid inadequate to support that advice creates a potentially disastrous disparity between U.S. military tactics and Salvadoran military resources. U.S. tactical doctrine abjures static defense and teaches constant patrolling. But this requires the provision of expensive equipment such as helicopters. In their absence, the Salvadoran military abandon their static defenses for intensive foot patrolling, only to find the strategic objective they had been guarding destroyed in their absence....

Democratic Competition

A final problem is philosophical. Our historic tendency as a nation is to think about diplomacy and military operations as antithetical. The fact is that the principles outlined here will enhance the prospects of a political solution.... Experience suggests that a lasting political solution will become possible only when the insurgents are convinced that they cannot win through force, and are therefore willing to settle for the next best option: taking advantage of opportunities for democratic competition and participation....

Human Rights

The question of the relationship between military aid and human rights abuses is both extremely difficult and extremely important. It involves the potential clash of two basic U.S. objectives. On the one hand, we seek to promote justice and find it repugnant to support forces that violate—or tolerate violation of—fundamental U.S. values. On the other hand, we are engaged in El Salvador and Central America because we are serving fundamental U.S. interests that transcend any particular government.

Our approach must therefore embrace, and pursue, both objectives simultaneously. Clearly, sustained public and international support rests heavily on our success in harmonizing our dual goals. Against this background, we have stressed the need to make American development assistance strictly conditional on rapid progress towards democratic pluralism and respect for human rights, as well as economic performance. Respect for human rights is also of great importance to improved security in Central America, as well as to the self-respect of the United States. We recognize, however, that how the problem is addressed in this regard is vital because Central America is crucial to our national security....

With respect to El Salvador, military aid should, through legislation requiring periodic reports, be made contingent upon demonstrated progress toward free elections; freedom of association; the establishment of the rule of law and an effective judicial system; and the termination of the activities of the so-called death squads, as well as vigorous action against those guilty of crimes and the prosecution to the extent possible of past offenders. These conditions should be seriously enforced....

As an additional measure, the United States should impose sanctions, including the denial of visas, deportation, and the investigation of financial dealings, against foreign nationals in the United States who are connected with death-squad activities in El Salvador or anywhere else....

Conclusion

The Commission has concluded that the security interests of the United States are importantly engaged in Central America; that these interests require a significantly larger program of military assistance, as well as greatly expanded support for economic growth and social reform; that there must be an end to the massive violation of human rights if security is to be achieved in Central America; and that external support for the insurgency must be neutralized for the same purpose—a problem we treat in the next chapter.

The deterioration in Central America has been such that we cannot afford paralysis in defending our national interests and in achieving our national purposes. The fact that such paralysis resulted from the lack of a national consensus on foreign policy in the United States would not mitigate the consequences of failure. We believe that a consensus is possible, and must be achieved, on an issue of such importance to the national security of the United States.

We would hope, moreover, that a clear U.S. commitment to such a course would itself improve the prospects for successful negotiations—so that arms would support diplomacy rather than supplant it. . . .

The Search for Peace

Americans yearn for an end to the bloodshed in Central America. On no issue in the region is there a stronger consensus than on the hope for a diplomatic solution that will stop the killing and nourish freedom and progress. The Commission shares this deeply felt goal. . . .

The general strategic objective that should animate U.S. diplomacy in dealing with the present threats in Central America can be simply stated: to reduce the civil wars, national conflicts and military preparations there at least to the dimensions of the Central American region.

As a nation we are certainly not opposed to indigenous reform in Central America. Nor are we threatened by indigenous revolutions that use local resources and appeal to local circumstances.

What gives the current situation its special urgency is the external threat posed by the Sandinista regime in Nicaragua which is supported by massive Cuban military strength, backed by Soviet and other East bloc weapons, guidance and diplomacy, and integrated into the Cuban network of intelligence and subversion. . . .

Agreement Verifiable

Any agreement in Central America must be verifiable. Equally important, it should also avoid any possible loophole that would permit the Soviet Union and Cuba to argue that whatever is not specifically prohibited is allowed. We should make sure that any agreement we reach is unambiguous. We should also remember that language and legalisms alone, however well crafted, will not provide airtight assurances in future cases not foreseen in the drafting. It will be important to give clear expression to the spirit of whatever obligations are undertaken, and to monitor continually how that spirit is

respected. We must guard carefully against a gradual erosion of our position in any agreement worked out in Central America. . . .

In sum, we believe that there is a chance for a political solution in Central America if the diplomacy of the United States is strategic in conception, purposeful in approach, and steadfast in execution. Our broad objectives should be:

• To stop the war and the killing in El Salvador.

• To create conditions under which Nicaragua can take its place as a peaceful and democratic member of the Central American community.

• To open the way to democratic development throughout the isthmus.

El Salvador

Obviously, the future of Central America will depend in large part on what happens in El Salvador. That nation most immediately faces critical choices about the course of its internal politics; it is wracked more severely by internal strife and conflict than any of its neighbors; it most requires intelligence and subtlety in the day-to-day conduct of U.S. diplomacy. . . .

"The Commission believes that the Sandinista regime will pose a continuing threat to the stability in the region."

In the political field two broad options have been presented: either elections, or what is commonly referred to as power-sharing. . . .

The Commission has concluded that power-sharing as proposed by the insurgents is not a sensible or fair political solution for El Salvador. There is no historical precedent suggesting that such a procedure would reconcile contending parties which entertain such deeply held beliefs and political goals, and which have been killing each other for years. Indeed, precedent argues that it would be only a prelude to a take-over by the insurgent forces. . . .

Free Elections Pursued

We believe that a true political solution in El Salvador can be reached only through free elections in which all significant groups have a right to participate. To be sure, elections do not solve a nation's problems. They can be the beginning, but cannot be the end, of political development. This is particularly true in El Salvador, which is threatened by a fragmentation of political life affecting most, if not all, of its institutions.

How elections are conducted will be crucial. Given prevailing conditions in El Salvador, all factions have legitimate concerns about their security. Neither supporters nor opponents of the regime can be expected to participate in elections so long as terrorists of the right or the left run free. No political efforts at reconciliation can succeed if the Government of El Salvador itself aids and abets violence against its own people. Unless it effectively curbs the actions of the death squads—unless it provides basic security for teachers, editors and writers, labor and religious leaders, and generally for the free and secure expression of opinion, the political process recommended here will break down. A secure environment must be established for all who wish to take part, whether leftists, centrists or rightists. The U.S. Government—to be credible—must insist that these conditions be met....

"Coexistence would have to involve an end to Cuban support for insurgency in Central America and promotion of revolutions elsewhere in Central America."

What happens in El Salvador will have important consequences in the other nations of Central America. If the shaky center collapses and the country eventually is dominated by undemocratic extremes, this will lead to increased pressures on El Salvador's neighbors. For Guatemala and Nicaragua, the experience of El Salvador could carry a clear message: the best means of earning the support of the United States, and of promoting political, social, and economic development, lies in adopting both the form and the substance of democracy.

In addition, events in El Salvador will have a major impact on developments in Nicaragua and on Nicaragua's relations with its neighbors. It is to these factors that we now turn....

Nicaragua

Nicaragua is tied into the Cuban, and thereby the Soviet, intelligence network. The Commission encountered no leader in Central America, including democratic and unarmed Costa Rica, who did not express deep foreboding about the impact of a militarized, totalitarian Nicaragua on the peace and security of the region....

The consolidation of a Marxist-Leninist regime in Managua would be seen by its neighbors as constituting a permanent security threat. Because of its secretive nature, the existence of a political order on the Cuban model in Nicaragua would pose major difficulties in negotiating, implementing, and verifying any Sandinista commitment to refrain from supporting insurgency and subversion in other countries. In this sense, the development of an open political system in Nicaragua, with a free press and an active opposition, would provide an important

security guarantee for the other countries of the region and would be a key element in any negotiated settlement.

Marxist-Leninism Intolerable

The notion that the United States should cope with a Marxist-Leninist Nicaragua, militarily allied to the Soviet Union and Cuba, through long-term containment assumes an analogy between conditions in post-war Europe and the present circumstances of Central America. The experience of the post-war period, however, shows that containment is effective as a long-term strategy only where U.S. military power serves to back up local forces of stable allies fully capable of coping with internal conflict and subversion from without. In such circumstances, the United States can help to assure the deterrence of overt military threats by contributing forces in place, or merely by strategic guarantees....

Though the Commission believes that the Sandinista regime will pose a continuing threat to stability in the region, we do not advocate a policy of static containment....

Framework for Regional Security

The Commission believes that a comprehensive regional settlement could be based on the principles enumerated below. Such a settlement would not imply the liquidation of the Sandinista Government or the formal abandonment of its revolutionary ideals, but only that it submit itself to the legitimating test of free elections. It is therefore not beyond the realm of possibility that Nicaragua, and the other nations of the region, would in the end embrace it. The basic framework would be an agreement on Central American security negotiated among the Central American "five" (Costa Rica, El Salvador, Guatemala, Honduras and Nicaragua), containing these key elements:

• Respect for the sovereignty, independence, and integrity of all Central American countries.

• A broad and concrete commitment to democracy and human rights.

• A verifiable commitment by each nation not to attack its neighbors; nor to transfer arms overtly or covertly to any insurgents; nor to train the military personnel of a Central American country; nor to practice subversion, directly or indirectly, against its neighbors.

• A verifiable commitment by each country not to possess arms that exceeded certain sizes, types, and capabilities. The total permissible scale of military forces in each nation could be stipulated as not to exceed an agreed level substantially lower than now. No military forces, bases, or advisers of non-Central American countries would be permitted.

• United States respect for and cooperation with the agreement. This would include a readiness to support the Central American military and security arrangements, and a commitment to respect whatever domestic arrangements emerge from legitimating elections, as long as there is continuing adherence to the basic principles of pluralism at home and restraint abroad.

• Commitments by all countries to pluralism, to peaceful political activity, and to free elections in which all political parties would have a right to participate free of threat or violence. Particularly, the pledges by Nicaragua of July 1979 to the OAS, and reaffirmed by the Contadora group, would be fulfilled. All insurgent groups would stop military activity.

• Permanent verification. The United States would be prepared to offer technical assistance to ensure effective verification. The Contadora countries could play a major role.

• The Central American nations that are parties to the agreement could invite other countries to be associated with it. They could also request that others in the hemisphere undertake mutual pledges of non-interference.

• Adherence to the agreement would be a condition for participating in the development program outlined in Chapters 4 and 5. The Central American Development Organization would, as suggested there, maintain a continuing audit and review of compliance with the commitments to nonintervention abroad and democratization at home.

• Foreign and other ministers of the Central American members, together with the United States, Mexico, Panama, Colombia, and Venezuela as observers, would meet regularly to review the arrangement and compliance with it. The council would develop procedures for conflict-resolution among member states....

Bringing Peace and Stability

A settlement of this nature would bring peace and stability to Central America. It would insulate the region from great power rivalry. Dilution of its terms would carry risks. A failure of negotiations because not every term was fulfilled would carry other risks....

This diplomacy must carry with it penalties for failure to comply with any agreement reached....

Cuba and the Soviet Union

Both the role played by the Sandinista regime in Central America and the threats in neighboring countries gain added importance for the region and for the United States because of Cuba's active engagement. As we have seen, Cuba has long been committed to revolutionary violence as an essential part of its ideology; indeed, that commitment is reflected in its national constitution. In turn, Cuba is closely allied with the Soviet Union and other communist bloc states, gaining support from them and promoting their interests in the Caribbean Basin region....

In 1962 the United States hoped that, by the exercise of American will and the projection of American strength, Cuba would be neutralized as a threat to Central and South America. More than twenty years later the threat is still there—and in guises that are arguably more dangerous to the stability of the region than the IRBMs of the 1960's.

The United States has a clear interest in reducing Cuba's role as a surrogate for the Soviet Union in the hemisphere. Yet because of their mutual dependence—Cuba in gaining arms, economic aid, and diplomatic support; the Soviet Union in gaining greater access to the region—it is not likely that the United States will be able to separate Moscow from Havana under present circumstances. As in the past, Moscow may at times seek to limit particular acts of Cuban adventurism within the region when such acts impose excessive risks, conflict with other Soviet objectives, or offer little opportunity. But Moscow is unlikely to be either able or willing to require Cuba to abandon its revolutionary principles and activity.

Should Havana, for whatever reason, change its basic attitude and be prepared for genuine coexistence with the United States, we, in turn, should be prepared to negotiate seriously. Such coexistence would have to involve an end to Cuban support for insurgency in Central America and promotion of revolutions elsewhere in Central America and promotion of revolutions elsewhere in the world. We, in turn, should then be prepared to live with Cuba and lift existing restrictions.

"In El Salvador itself, those seeking to establish democratic institutions are beset by violence from extremists on both sides."

In the meantime, the United States has a dual task: to create those economic conditions in Central America that thwart the export of revolutions and to make clear the risks of expanded violence. Social reform, economic advance and political stability in Central America will discourage Cuban adventurism in the region. But we must also bring home to Havana a due appreciation of the consequences of its actions....

Negotiations with Soviet Union

The Commission sees little promise in negotiating with the Soviet Union over Central America. The Soviets would almost certainly use negotiations to legitimize their presence in the region. They would welcome discussion about superpower spheres of influence, which would prompt Soviet assertions of primacy and the need for U.S. abstention on the Soviet periphery, in such places as Eastern Europe and Afghanistan. For the United States, however, such a concept of spheres of influence is unacceptable. Should the United States now accept that concept, the Soviet Union would reap substantial gains.

In sum, the United States cannot eliminate all Soviet political involvement and influence within Central America and the Caribbean. But we must curb Soviet military activity in the hemisphere. And we can reduce Soviet opportunities and increase the incentives for others to abstain from forging ties with Moscow that damage U.S. and regional interests....

Conclusion

We have concluded this exercise persuaded that Central America is both vital and vulnerable, and that whatever other crises may arise to claim the nation's attention the United States cannot afford to turn away from that threatened region. Central America's crisis is our crisis.

All too frequently, wars and threats of wars are what draw attention to one part of the world or another. So it has been in Central America. The military crisis there captured our attention, but in doing so it has also wakened us to many other needs of the region. However belatedly, it did "concentrate the mind."...

As we have studied these nations, we have become sharply aware of how great a mistake it would be to view them in one-dimensional terms. An exceptionally complex interplay of forces has shaped their history and continues to define their identities and to affect their destinies.

We have developed a great sympathy for those in Central America who are struggling to control those forces, and to bring their countries successfully through this period of political and social transformation. As a region, Central America is in mid-passage from the predominantly authoritarian patterns of the past to what can, with determination, with help, with luck, and with peace, become the predominantly democratic pluralism of the future. That transformation has been troubled, seldom smooth, and sometimes violent. In Nicaragua, we have seen the tragedy of a revolution betrayed; the same forces that stamped out the beginnings of democracy in Nicaragua now threaten El Salvador. In El Salvador itself, those seeking to establish democratic institutions are beset by violence from the extremists on both sides. But the spirit of freedom is strong throughout the region, and the determination persists to strengthen it where it exists and to achieve it where it does not.

Strategic Dimension

The use of Nicaragua as a base for Soviet and Cuban efforts to penetrate the rest of the Central American isthmus, with El Salvador the target of first opportunity, gives the conflict there a major strategic dimension. The direct involvement of aggressive external forces makes it a challenge to the system of hemispheric security, and, quite specifically, to the security interests of the United States. This is a challenge to which the United States must respond.

But beyond this, we are challenged to respond to the urgent human needs of the people of Central America. Central America is a region in crisis economically, socially and politically. Its nations are our neighbors, and they need our help. This is one of those instances in which the requirements of national interest and the commands of conscience coincide....

Secure Freedom

Our task now, as a nation, is to transform the crisis in Central America into an opportunity: to seize the impetus it provides, and to use this to help our neighbors not only to secure their freedom from aggression and violence, but also to set in place the policies, processes and institutions that will make them both prosperous and free. If, together, we succeed in this, then the sponsors of violence will have done the opposite of what they intended: they will have roused us not only to turn back the tide of totalitarianism but to bring a new birth of hope and of opportunity to the people of Central America.

Because this is our opportunity, in conscience it is also our responsibility.

The National Bipartisan Commission on Central America, chaired by former Secretary of State Henry Kissinger, was asked by Ronald Reagan to help formulate "a long-term United States policy that will best respond to the challenges of social, economic, and democratic development in the region, and to internal and external threats to its security and stability." The report was released in January 1984.

The Kissinger Report: A Critique

William M. LeoGrande

"I think it is imperative," said Henry Kissinger upon accepting the president's invitation to chair the National Bipartisan Commission on Central America, "that we avoid the bitter debate that characterized the Vietnam period." Kissinger understood immediately the task before him: to produce a report that would preempt the unfolding national debate over the wisdom of deepening U.S. military involvement in Central America and restore bipartisan support to the president's policies for the region.

The Report of the Commission is true to that purpose. Time and time again it reiterates that there is "no room for partisanship," that we must avoid the "agony of indecision" in meeting the challenge posed by our adversaries in the region, and that "we cannot afford paralysis in defending our national interests and in achieving our national purpose." If Ronald Reagan has his way, there will indeed be no national debate on Central America. The Kissinger Report will be the final word. Crafted by a master, it makes the best case that can be made for Reagan's policy toward the region.

At first glance, the Report appears to be no different from the reports of most other presidential commissions: a pastiche of compromises in which intellectual coherence and logical consistency are sacrificed to the expedient of satisfying people with diverse views. It reads, in fact, as if it were two documents interwoven: a liberal one calling for social reform and human rights improvements, and a conservative one calling for private-sector development and military aid to fight communism. But on closer examination, it becomes clear that the liberal agenda stands at odds with the underlying logic of the Report—mere gloss on a vintage Cold War brief for intervention.

William M. LeoGrande, "Through the Looking Glass: The Kissinger Report on Central America," *World Policy Journal*, Winter 1984. Reprinted by permission of the World Policy Institute, 777 United Nations Plaza, New York, NY 10017.

By making the case for intervention in Central America while U.S. involvement there is still relatively limited, Kissinger tries to do for the Reagan administration in Central America what he could not do for the Nixon administration in Vietnam: convince the American public that U.S. vital interests are threatened by revolution in the Third World. The Report makes its case not explicitly, of course, but by indirection, rewriting history and defining the terms of debate in a way that leads inexorably to the conclusion that the United States must be prepared to do whatever is necessary to prevail....

The essential outlines of the Commission's end product were predictable from the start. With Kissinger in charge, the Report would undoubtedly frame the crisis to accord with the administration's East-West vision of the security threat to the United States. Against this backdrop, a case would be made for increased military assistance. It was equally certain that the Report would recommend a "mini-Marshall Plan" designed to address the socioeconomic ills of the region, which liberals identify as the root cause of the crisis. Such a program would be essential to defuse liberal opposition and to recover moderate Congressional support for the administration. Even if never approved, it would serve as sugarcoating to induce the Congress to swallow the bitter pill of deeper U.S. military involvement....

The rationale for [the Reagan] policy has been based on four premises: first, that Cuba and the Soviet Union are behind the crisis and are posing a challenge to vital U.S. security interests; second, that the United States is supporting democrats and democracies in the region; third, that the United States supports social and economic reform to remedy historic injustices; and fourth, that the United States is seeking political rather than military solutions to the crisis. Much of the opposition to Reagan's policy has focused on whether one or another of these premises is true. The Kissinger Commission incorporates and elaborates on them all, giving the total package the imprimatur of bipartisan truth.

As objectives, meeting a Soviet challenge, supporting democracy and social reform, and seeking negotiated solutions are all unassailable. What Kissinger does, with great skill and sophistication, is to paint a picture of Central America that justifies recommendations ostensibly designed to achieve these goals. The Report begins by declaring that U.S. policy should be based upon the principles of democratic self-determination, development that benefits all, and mutual security. It then reviews the history of Central America, from which it proceeds to discuss its policy recommendations in the areas of economic and human development, security, and diplomacy.

Methodology Peculiar

Although its architecture is straightforward, one need not read far into the Report to realize that its methodology is peculiar. Its initial principles are not operative guides to policy, but symbols to be invoked and manipulated in order to rationalize a preordained set of recommendations. Notions of democracy, totalitarianism, and development are defined and controlled to make them serve a policy agenda that has nothing in common with the usual meanings of these words. Moreover, there is no effort to present an objective account of the region's history or its present agony. Instead, the history on which the Commission bases its recommendations is scandalously rewritten. Henry Kissinger, the modern-day Metternich, takes us on a trip through the looking glass, where words and history mean whatever Kissinger wants them to mean, nothing more, nothing less. At this he is a master. . . .

The heart of the Report begins with an historical overview of Central America that recounts the region's colonial legacy of poverty and inequality, the rise of oligarchic rule in the 1890s, and the post-depression development of the reformist challenge to the old order. This challenge took the form of two new political traditions that emerged in the 1930s in opposition to the authoritarianism of the landed elite—a "democratic" or, more properly, a liberal capitalist tradition; and a "socialist" tradition, which was sometimes "democratic," sometimes "Marxist."

The Report details how economic growth after World War II produced modernization without redistribution, raising popular expectations of better economic conditions without fulfilling them and stimulating demands for political change. Its account of how Central America's elite responded to these demands is uncompromising:

> In Nicaragua . . . (Somoza's) rule was characterized by greed and corruption so far beyond even the levels of the past that it might well be called a

kleptocracy. . . . And as opposition to his regime increased, repression became systematic and increasingly pervasive. In Guatemala, the more or less centrist and civilian regimes of the 1960s gave way in the 1970s to a succession of extremely repressive regimes . . . among the most repressive in the recent history of the hemisphere or in Guatemala's own often bloody past. . . . In El Salvador, the pattern was similar.

In light of this history, it is not difficult to understand how and why revolutionary movements arose in Central America. Long-term socioeconomic grievances aggravated by social and political mobilization, a reformist political movement smashed by repression—all the classic antecedents of revolution that have presaged every upheaval in the 20th century, from Mexico to China, were evident in Central America. After the "democratic" alternative there was defeated by state violence, it is little wonder that the initiative for change passed to the revolutionary socialists.

Communism and Revolution

Logically, one would expect this historical overview to trace the evolution of these revolutionary movements—the defection of the youth from the decimated reformist parties to the guerrillas, the growth of militant urban mass organizations, the role of the Church in organizing rural Christian Base Communities, to cite only a few developments. But that is not how the Report's history proceeds. It does discuss the growth of insurgency—"communist insurgency"—but not the development of Central America's revolutionary movements. Instead, the focus suddenly shifts to Cuba and its "effort to export revolution to Central America."

"Only the socioeconomic and political preconditions of revolution are defined as indigenous, whereas the revolutionary movements that emerged in the face of these injustices are labeled as foreign in origin."

The intent behind this strange progression is transparent: to blame Cuba for the growth of insurgency in Central America, thereby delegitimizing the region's revolutionary movements. To achieve this, many inconvenient facts must be omitted, so the Report rewrites history to remedy the inconvenience.

One inconvenient fact is that when guerrillas in Nicaragua, El Salvador, and Guatemala were developing into serious contenders for power during the mid-1970s, the Cubans were not engaged in Central America. The hiatus in Cuban involvement in Latin America, between 1968 and 1978, is too well established to deny, so the Report simply states that Castro once again became active in the "export of revolution" in 1978 because he saw "new opportunities" in Central America. With this sleight of hand, the Report erases ten years of history, ten years in which the Central American revolutionary movements grew indigenously, without the aid of Cuba or anyone else....

"The Report makes no effort to trace the independent growth of revolutionary movements in Central America."

There is more to the Report's rewriting of history than just an attempt to blame Cuba for the crisis in Central America. The argument the Commission makes is considerably more sophisticated. It acknowledges the existence of legitimate grievances against the oligarchic order. Moreover, it seeks to identify the United States with the recognized need for change in the region: "The United States is not threatened by indigenous change, even revolutionary change, in Central America." This theme, politically essential if the Report is to persuade Reagan's liberal critics, is a recurrent one. But it is always accompanied by this crucial caveat: "The United States must be concerned about the intrusion into Central America of aggressive external powers."

Indigenous and Foreign Distinction

Thus the Commission resolves the debate over whether the causes of revolution in Central America are internal or external by answering, "Both," and establishes the central premise upon which the logic of the entire Report hinges: "Indigenous" change is legitimate and hence acceptable, but change which is "foreign" in genesis is illegitimate and unacceptable.

All that remains is to define this distinction in a way that will allow the Commission to brand the revolutionary movements in Central America as "foreign," since it will later recommend measures to defeat them. If the Report granted that these movements are indigenous, it would be much more difficult to make such recommendations and still contend that the United States is not the guardian of an antiquated and unjust status quo. That is why the history of the Central American revolutionary movements had to be excluded, for it shows conclusively that these movements grew naturally out of the horrendous and brutal conditions the Report itself documents.

As the Report proceeds, the distinction between indigenous and foreign factors becomes increasingly clear; only the socioeconomic and political preconditions of revolution are defined as indigenous, whereas the revolutionary movements that emerged

in the face of these injustices are labeled foreign in origin.

> The roots of the crisis are both indigenous and foreign. Discontents are real, and for much of the population, conditions of life are miserable....But these conditions have been exploited by hostile outside forces....

> The crisis is the product of *both* indigenous and foreign factors....Poverty, repression, inequity were all there, breeding fear and hate...while outside forces have intervened to exacerbate the area's troubles and to exploit its anguish.

> The 1970s saw the sharpening of the social, economic and political crisis in Central America...which made the region an inviting target for insurgency.

The import of all this is that, had it not been for Cuba, there would be no insurgency in Central America—or at least none to speak of—no matter how ripe the conditions there might be. To use a medical analogy, the Report views the spread of revolution in Central America as a doctor would view the spread of infection in a patient whose ability to resist disease had been seriously weakened by malnutrition.

Central Americans thus are denied to have had any active role in determining their own destiny. As far as the Report is concerned, they remained passive in the face of injustice and did nothing effective to remedy it until foreign communists began pulling their strings. The absurdity of the argument does not lessen its insult....

Four Reasons Explained

All told, the Report gives four reasons that the revolutionary movements in Central America must be treated as foreign rather than as indigenous: first, they have a "foreign ideology"—Marxism; second, they have received aid from Cuba and the Soviet Union; third, wretched conditions do not, by themselves, produce revolution; and fourth, the movements have been able to survive for a protracted period.

The first argument is contradicted by the Report itself, which in its historical overview of the region identifies Marxism as one of two political traditions that emerged in the 1930s to challenge the oligarchies. This contradiction notwithstanding, to think that any revolution in the late 20th century would be free of all taint of Marxism is absurd. The ideology of the contemporary revolutionary movements in Central America, however, is not Comintern-vintage Marxism-Leninism, but an amalgam of Marxism and radical Christianity. This combination is unique to Central America—a product of the history of its revolutionary movements, a history the Commission ignores. Moreover, the very assertion that ideas—whether those of Marxism or of democratic liberalism—can ever be "foreign" is an affront to the concept of freedom of thought.

It makes equally little sense to define a revolution

as foreign in origin simply because the revolutionaries receive help from abroad, the second reason the Commission gives for treating revolution in Central America as foreign-inspired. Most revolutions attract some foreign involvement, either in support of or in opposition to their cause. The revolutions of Central America are hardly unique in this regard; the American Revolution received substantial assistance from France, but one could hardly deny its indigenous character on these grounds alone.

Guerilla Warfare and Revolt

The third and fourth arguments noted above are part of a treatise that purports to demonstrate that guerilla warfare "differs as much from indigenous revolts as it does from conventional war." In support of its claim that poverty and injustice alone cannot explain the outbreak of revolution in Central America, the Commission writes that "if wretched conditions were themselves enough to create such insurgencies, we would see them in many more countries in the world." Here, the artificiality of distinguishing between indigenous conditions and actual resistance blooms into a fallacy that is absurd on its face: Resistance must be externally generated, the Report claims, because otherwise it would spring up everywhere. According to this logic, there can be no such thing as an indigenous guerrilla war; the Mexican revolution, the Chinese revolution, and all the anti-colonial movements in Africa must be treated as foreign in origin.

The final argument against the indigenous character of these revolutionary movements holds that the survival of a guerrilla insurgency is, in itself, proof that it receives crucial aid from abroad because insurgencies can never prevail over established governments by their own devices. If an insurgency is successful, the Report reasons, it therefore cannot be indigenous.

The elegance of these arguments has to be envied; if one takes them seriously, "indigenous revolutionary movements" becomes a null set. Any assurance that the United States does not oppose such revolutions is thereby rendered vacuous, and Washington need have no fear that its bona fides will be put to the test. Despite the Commission's claims to the contrary, the position it lays out places the United States in opposition to *any* revolutionary change in Central America.

Judging an Authentic Revolution

It is, of course, possible to distinguish between authentic revolutionary movements and those that are the artificial creation of external powers engaged in subversion. The key to such a judgment lies in the history of the movement itself: Did the movement emerge and develop primarily out of the sociopolitical milieu of the nation? Does it have a significant degree

of popular support? Does it have autonomy from any external power in making decisions about its politics and strategy?

In short, if one is seriously interested in assessing whether a revolutionary movement is indigenous, the real question is whether outside aid is an adjunct that strengthens a preexisting movement, or whether it is a primary motivating force without which no such movement would exist. On this issue, the history of Central America leaves little doubt. The revolutionary movements of the region were well advanced before they received any significant outside aid from Cuba or anywhere else. By way of contrast, the counterrevolutionary forces fighting against Nicaragua did not exist before 1982, when the CIA, with the help of Argentina and Honduras, assembled and armed them. Thus if any insurgency in Central America is a product of external intervention, it is this one.

"In order to believe that a threat to the Caribbean sea lanes does exist, one must make a series of increasingly unlikely assumptions."

Similarly, if the Report had looked seriously at the history of Central America, it would have been compelled to note the broad ideological composition of the region's revolutionary movements, which include Christian Democrats, Social Democrats, devout Christians, Marxists, and Marxist-Leninists as well. This breadth of appeal has been a key factor in the movements' success. It has also been a major impediment to Reagan's efforts to rally domestic and international opinion—especially European opinion—behind the administration's policy of providing unlimited military support to the governments fighting these movements.

Movements Have Broad Appeal

The Commission portrays the broad appeal of these movements as nothing more than a communist ploy designed to "coopt some noncommunist leaders and to neutralize them as rival alternatives to the existing government . . . undermine the political center by sharpening the increasingly violent confrontation between left and right . . . (and) . . . disarm critics by posing as noncommunist democrats to obtain noncommunist international support. . . ." In this manner, noncommunists are reduced to useful fools, powerless pawns within a coalition dominated by communists. The communists, in turn, are charged with responsibility for the polarization of politics, as if the regime's repression of the peaceful reformist challenge had never taken place. Noncommunists elsewhere (read: Social Democrats) are assumed to have been duped, and behind it all stand the Cubans.

The mind reels at this conspiratorial fantasy of how the revolutionary coalitions in Central America were formed. Just as the Report makes no effort to trace the independent growth of revolutionary movements in Central America, it also makes no effort to determine the political weight wielded by various ideological elements of the revolutionary coalitions. In this envisioned conspiracy, the communists are omniscient and omnipotent, the noncommunists ignorant and impotent....

Good Guys, Bad Guys

This is the reality of Central America as defined by the Kissinger Commission Report: governments struggling toward democracy (good guys) and foreign-controlled revolutionary communists trying to stop them (bad guys). All that remains to set the stage for the policy prescriptions that follow is to review the role of the United States in the region.

"All the Commission has called for is a reinstitution of the certification process.... When this provision was in effect, the administration always managed to find enough dubious evidence... to certify that the requisite progress was being made."

That role, at least since the implementation of Roosevelt's Good Neighbor Policy, is portrayed as benevolent. The CIA's ouster of Jacobo Arbenz in 1954—arguably the critical event in the failure of reformism not just in Guatemala but throughout the region—goes unmentioned. The economic program of the Alliance for Progress receives plaudits. But nothing is said of its counterinsurgency programs, which gave guns to the military in Central America even when there were no guerrillas there—guns that later were turned against the reformers. Nothing is said of the U.S. indifference during the early 1970s, when Henry Kissinger ran foreign policy and the reformist movements of the region were being decimated by repression. Even the longstanding U.S. support for Somoza is portrayed as an illusion somehow created by Somoza himself "independent of the facts."

This rewriting of history, though heavyhanded, is essential to the argument the Report has under construction. Having conceded that the regimes of Central America were, until recently, corrupt brutal dictatorships that guaranteed the privilege of a few by exploiting the majority, the Report cannot further concede the unpleasant fact that the United States generally supported these regimes. For such an admission would invite impolite questions about what interests the United States was pursuing then that it somehow does not need to pursue any longer.

If the Report is to hold to its central premise—that indigenous change, even revolution, is acceptable and only foreign penetration is unacceptable—it can hardly allow history to record that the United States has been an armory for the preservation of the status quo in Central America. To do so would throw into question the sincerity of the soon-to-be unveiled policy recommendations, which will once again call upon the United States to support the region's existing regimes, this time in the name of "democracy."...

Security: The Cuban-Soviet Menace

Since Reagan's first weeks in office, national security claims have been a pivotal part of his administration's effort to justify its policy in Central America. They are equally pivotal to the argument of the Kissinger Commission Report. If its recommendations for economic development and social change are intended to remedy the social injustice that the Commission regards as the "indigenous" cause of revolution, its security recommendations are put forth to remedy the "external" cause—the revolutionaries.

The security chapter opens with an effort to disarm liberals who criticize Reagan for his emphasis on the military aspect of the crisis in Central America. Military measures, the Report tells us, are an essential adjunct to both reform and diplomacy—two liberal shibboleths. Without a military shield, reform is impossible; without military pressure, our adversaries will never negotiate seriously. Implicit in this scheme is the assumption that the regimes in Central America would be willing to undertake reforms and to negotiate peace if only they were not under attack—a dubious proposition given their records.

The core of the security chapter concerns the strategic threat posed by the revolutions in Central America to the United States. None of the Report's arguments, however, is new. All are variants on the familiar themes the Reagan administration has been advancing over the past three years: the danger of dominoes falling throughout the region and beyond; the threat to Caribbean sea lanes; the challenge to U.S. credibility; and the danger that revolution will send hordes of brown people streaming northward into the United States.

The Domino Theory

Not surprisingly, the Report refrains from mentioning the discredited domino theory explicity. But this does not stop it from couching the same argument in different—even more apocalyptic—terms. One of the key geostrategic advantages the United States has enjoyed, we are told, is the absence of any need to defend its land borders. This advantage has reportedly compensated our nation for its geostrategic disadvantage in other areas of the world, all far away, in which its interests are at stake. If the advantage of safe borders is lost, the Report implies, then the entire global position of the United States would be endangered.

> To the extent that a further Marxist-Leninist advance in Central America leading to progressive deterioration and a further projection of Soviet and Cuban power in the region required us to defend against security threats near our borders, we would face a difficult choice between unpalatable alternatives. We would either have to assume a permanently increased defense burden, or see our capacity to defend distant trouble-spots reduced, and as a result have to reduce important commitments elsewhere in the world.

This argument is essentially the domino theory in disguise. It rests upon the premise that the victory of revolutionary movements in Central America could lead, in turn, to the successful export of revolution beyond that region, principally to Mexico. This is the only contingency that would pose any conceivable threat to U.S. land borders.

The Report dares not say any of this explicitly, of course, because the Mexicans have been the most vocal opponents of U.S. policy in Central America and have rejected this scenario outright. Even to hint at its likelihood, therefore, is to imply that the United States knows better than Mexico what is in Mexico's best interest....

In making the oft-repeated argument that the Caribbean sea lanes must be kept secure, the Report begins by noting that a large portion of U.S. shipping, including military supplies for wars in other theatres, must traverse the Caribbean. If pro-Soviet regimes come to power in areas bordering the Caribbean, the Report warns, the Soviet Union could use basing facilities in these countries to interdict U.S. shipping, thereby weakening—perhaps fatally—the ability of the United States to prevail in a conflict in Europe, the Middle East, or Asia. A similar argument obtains for the strategic importance of the Panama Canal. Thus, according to the Report, a domino effect spreading south toward Panama would endanger U.S. security as much as one spreading north toward Mexico.

Sea Lanes Argument

The sea lanes argument is wholly contingent on what the Pentagon calls "war scenarios"—the military practice of envisioning all possible contingencies, no matter how bizarre or unlikely, and then planning to meet them. In order to believe that a threat to the Caribbean sea lanes does exist, one must make a series of increasingly unlikely assumptions.

First, one must assume that revolutionary governments in Central America will adopt a national security stance hostile to the United States and sympathetic to the Soviet Union. This is possible, of

course, as the example of Cuba demonstrates, but this outcome depends at least in part on the attitude the United States takes toward the revolutionary regimes.

Second, one must assume that a revolutionary government would grant the Soviet Union military basing facilities, or itself use facilities provided by the Soviet Union in accordance with Soviet global strategy. Because such an alliance would effectively close off to a regime all normal economic relations with the United States and much of the West, the Central Americans would presumably demand an economic quid pro quo of the Soviet Union. Therefore, one must further assume that the Soviet Union would be prepared to take on the economic burden of "another Cuba"—no small matter given the state of the Soviet economy and Soviet commitments in Afghanistan, Poland, Vietnam, Africa, and Cuba. In exchange for this investment, the Kremlin would acquire military assets that would give it only a marginal strategic advantage over what it already has in Cuba.

Third, any attack on U.S. shipping in international waters would be an act of war calling forth an appropriate U.S. military response. Such an attack makes no sense except in the context of a war between the United States and the Soviet Union, for only then are the sea lanes a strategic asset. Moreover, one must assume that such a war does not cross the nuclear threshold, since otherwise sea lanes would be irrelevant. Because the United States has the conventional forces needed to quickly destroy the ability of any Central American country to interdict the sea lanes, it would need to divert its forces only briefly to meet any such challenge. For the sea lanes to be threatened, one has to assume that a Central American government would be prepared to commit suicide in order to give the Soviet Union a marginal and fleeting advantage in a global war.

"In order to believe that a threat to the Caribbean sea lanes does exist, one must make a series of increasingly unlikely assumptions."

In detailing this hypothetical threat, the Commission neatly ignores two facts: that Nicaragua has shown no interest in allowing itself to be used as a Soviet forward base, and that the Soviet Union has shown no interest in paying the economic price of obtaining one. The Sandinistas have explicitly ruled out the establishment of any foreign military base on their territory. They have agreed to the Contadora principles of prohibiting such bases and of providing for a reduction of foreign military advisers on their soil. They have also offered to negotiate these issues directly with the United States to allay Washington's security concerns; the Reagan administration has rejected such negotiations. The Soviets, for their part, have refused to provide large-scale economic aid to Nicaragua, just as they refused to provide it to Allende's government in Chile or to Manley's in Jamaica.

US Credibility Argued

Like the domino theory and the sea lanes argument, the claim that U.S. credibility is at stake abroad, this time in Central America, is familiar. It was used to justify U.S. military involvement in Southeast Asia and Angola. But unlike the other two supposed dangers, a threat to credibility is intangible, depending entirely upon the perceptions of others. Thus the credibility doctrine is an expansive one; any local conflict can be seen as a challenge to U.S. credibility, and hence as a threat to national security, regardless of the importance of the region or what is actually happening there. This is the doctrine of the global policeman.

"The Commission grossly misunderstands the nature of state violence in El Salvador."

In Europe, credibility is held to be essential to the solidarity of the Western alliance. But in the last 20 years nothing has shaken the alliance more deeply than has the growing European perception that the United States lacks wisdom and prudence in its use of military force in the Third World. The "successor generation" in Europe recalls not the liberation from Nazism, but the war in Vietnam; it fears not the unwillingness of the United States to defend Europe, but that Washington's recklessness will drag Europe into war. Recently, even European leaders long identified as friends of the United States have begun to share this fear. U.S. credibility in Europe, properly understood, is more damaged than preserved by Washington's response to every brushfire war as if it were a global challenge.

In the Third World, many U.S. allies are dictators who would fall from power without the support of the United States. No doubt their faith in Washington's reliability would be shaken by a Central America policy that refused to defend the Salvadoran regime against the wrath of its own people. But this change would be all to the good. Dictators who believe they can depend upon the United States to keep them in power have no incentive to undertake the socioeconomic and political changes that are needed to build stable, legitimate political systems. Stability cannot be

guaranteed forever by force of arms.

In the end, the threat to U.S. credibility in Central America is self-inflicted. Credibility is at risk in direct proportion to how much of it is wagered. When Washington declares that U.S. vital interests are at stake in Central America, yet fails to control the outcome of events there, its credibility is damaged much more than it would have been had no such declaration been made. The inflated rhetoric of the Reagan administration, more than anything else, has raised the stakes of U.S. credibility in Central America. That much of this rhetoric was designed to extract greater support from a reluctant Congress does not lessen its escalatory effect. By declaring, as Secretary of State Alexander Haig did, that Central America is a "test case" in the struggle against international communism, the administration has made anything less than total victory equivalent to ignominious defeat.

US Must Defeat Revolutionaries

Having argued that the revolutionary movements in Central America are spearheads of Cuban-Soviet penetration whose success threatens U.S. vital security interests in the region, the Commission concludes that the United States must defeat these movements. This rationale serves to justify not only increasing amounts of U.S. military aid to "friendly" regimes, but also the pursuit of military victory by whatever means are required:

> Both the national interests of the United States and a genuine concern for the long-term welfare of Central America create powerful incentives to provide all necessary assistance to defeat totalitarian guerrillas.

For specific recommendations, the Report turns first to El Salvador, where the security problem is most acute. Again, it paints the best possible picture of the regime's efforts to build democracy. "Progress has been made in many fields," the Commission assures us. "(The government of El Salvador) allows debate, freedom of assembly, opposition and other aspects of democracy, however imperfect." The corpses of over 30,000 civilians killed by the Salvadoran regime in the past four years stand in mute testimony to the "imperfection" of Salvadoran "democracy."

The Commission tries to excuse these murders as the result of the primitiveness of the regime's counterinsurgency effort. If the armed forces of El Salvador had better training and more funds, we are advised, the government could pursue a "humane anti-guerrillas strategy," and the human rights problems of El Salvador could be reduced. The unwillingness of Congress to provide the necessary funds to aid the government in this effort, it is reasoned, has prevented the adoption of "enlightened counterinsurgency"; by implication, Congress is ultimately to blame for the mass murder of Salvadoran civilians because it is unwilling to give more money to their killers.

The Commission grossly misunderstands the nature of state violence in El Salvador. The regime's strategy of repression antedates the development of insurgency there by many years. It is not just a matter of backwardness in dealing with guerrilla war that explains the thousands of civilian deaths; in El Salvador that is the normal way of dealing with those who are believed to advocate significant social or political change. Nor is the violence there perpetuated by the regime and the death squads as indiscriminate as the Report implies. Victims are targeted by the intelligence branches of the military, and then systematically eliminated. Using this method, the regime successfully wiped out virtually the entire urban infrastructure of the popular organizations which served, until 1980, as the organized mass base of the opposition. The Commission reports the urban carnage of 1980-81 as one of the government's military successes.

The techniques used by the armed forces and the death squads in El Salvador are modeled after what was done, with equal efficacy, in Argentina during the Dirty War of the late 1970s—deeds for which the newly elected democratic government of Argentina is now trying military officers for war crimes. It is also eerily similar to the Phoenix Program used by the United States during the war in Vietnam.

The argument that with proper U.S. training the human rights practices of foreign nations can be improved was used throughout the 1960s and early 1970s to justify the continuation of U.S. military aid to repressive regimes. The strategy never worked. Weapons systems can be easily transferred, but value systems cannot be. The values a people hold are a product of the society in which they live. In Central America, the military has always stood outside the law and outside all norms of civilized behavior, accountable to no one. It regards anything done in defense of the status quo as acceptable.

Murderous US-Sponsored Troops

From 1965 to 1977, the United States trained over 1,000 Salvadoran military officers—probably a majority of the entire corps, which never numbered over 600 during this period. Yet between 1980 and 1982, these forces were responsible for the worst bloodletting in the history of Central America. The elite Atlactl battalion, trained by U.S. Special Forces advisers in 1981, has been responsible for at least one major civilian massacre (with victims numbering in the hundreds) every year since. The way the army treats its own citizens in El Salvador is viewed by the Commission as a technical problem, a matter of inadequate training, rather than a graphic symptom of a regime at war with its own people.

The Commission repeats the same error when it examines the deteriorating military situation in El Salvador and concludes that the army's failures are entirely the result of technical problems—poor training and inadequate equipment. No mention is made of the notoriously low morale of the troops, of the mass surrender or flight of entire units, or of the officers whose posts are political sinecures and who fight only from 9 to 5 or sell their U.S. equipment to the guerrillas.

"This scenario is, to say the least, highly unlikely—particularly because it is the guerrillas who are currently winning the war."

These problems go unmentioned because they raise embarrassing questions that can be answered only by examining the quality of Salvadoran society and the nature of the military institution defending it. To focus on such issues would take one to the heart of why there is a revolution in El Salvador to begin with, and why the guerrillas are winning it. It also would make it clear that these problems cannot be solved with more military aid, training, or helicopters. . . .

Aid and Human Rights

The Commission insists . . . that aid for El Salvador and eventually for Guatemala must be conditioned on improved human rights performance. It is this recommendation that caused Kissinger to lodge his only dissent, arguing that if the survival of these regimes is crucial to U.S. security the United States cannot let them fall no matter what their human rights records. When this recommendation was reported in the press, even before the finished report had been presented to the president, the White House announced that Reagan would be inclined to disregard it; he had just recently vetoed certification legislation that included a similar conditionality provision.

It is not entirely clear why the administration should be so upset over this provision. All the Commission has called for is a reinstitution of the certification process that existed from 1982 to 1983. When this provision was in effect, the administration always managed to find enough dubious evidence and tortured logic to certify that the requisite progress was being made. No doubt it could do so again.

The only other human rights recommendation the Commission makes calls for measures to be taken against Salvadoran exiles who are financing death squads from within the United States. This proposal is fully consistent with the announced intent of the administration, though no sanctions have yet been leveled against anyone.

In short, the Commission essentially ratifies the

Reagan administration's military agenda for the region, asking only that more consistent attention be paid to human rights.

Diplomacy: Winning Through Negotiations

If rhetoric is to be believed, everyone in Central America wants a peaceful diplomatic solution to the crisis. Even the contras in Honduras, who used to speak openly of their desire to overthrow the Sandinistas (even when they were supposed to be interdicting arms), now speak of their desire to restore democracy to Nicaragua by negotiating with the Sandinistas.

The Commission wants a negotiated solution to the crisis, too, of course. Yet its proposals for such a solution differ in no significant way from those the Reagan administration has been advocating for the past year—solutions which would allow the administration to gain at the negotiating table what it has been unable to win on the battlefield.

The Report argues that the overall objective of U.S. diplomatic efforts in the region should be to confine the Central American crisis to Central America. This goal seems reasonable enough. But it must be read in light of the Commission's earlier declaration that the revolutionary movements in Central America, including the Sandinistas, are instruments of foreign intervention, and that security measures to defeat them are therefore needed.

"The Commission is really interested in preserving the preponderant influence of the United States in Central America."

In El Salvador, the Commission poses the political alternatives as "elections" or "powersharing," and concludes that powersharing is "not a sensible or fair" solution. The Report rejects out of hand the FDR-FMLN's stated position that it does not oppose free elections in which everyone could participate, but that an interim government must be created to conduct them. The Report simply contends, without explanation or argument, that if the FDR-FMLN is allowed into a coalition government, it will take it over and establish a totalitarian regime—as if El Salvador were somehow equivalent to Eastern Europe circa 1947. If the Commission truly believes this is possible, how can it suggest that the FDR-FMLN be allowed to participate in *any* government, even one produced by free elections?

Instead of powersharing, the Commission recommends a negotiated solution that "amplifies" the Salvadoran government's proposal: The guerrillas must lay down their arms, entrusting their political future and their lives to the army they have been

fighting for four years. Elections will then be conducted under the existing regime, with its security forces intact.

Commission's Scenario Unlikely

This scenario is, to say the least, highly unlikely—particularly because it is the guerrillas who are currently winning the war. For refusing to surrender under this scheme, they are branded by the Report as enemies of free elections. In light of El Salvador's history of electoral fraud and political repression, however, they are simply being prudent. Who would guarantee the security of FDR-FMLN candidates, or, more to the point, their active supporters? The United States, despite three years of intense effort, has not been able to persuade the military to try any of its members for murdering U.S. citizens, let alone for murdering their own countrymen. It cannot convince them to stop the murders, even when Christian Democrats are the victims. And it is no longer clear that the armed forces would allow even the Christian Democrats back into power if they should win the elections scheduled for March 1984. The reality of El Salvador is inescapable: no one is secure as long as the armed forces remain structured as they are. That is why a restructuring of the military has always been a central element of the FDR-FMLN's negotiating posture.

The Commission portrays powersharing as giving the guerrillas something they do not have. But, in fact, powersharing already exists in El Salvador. The guerrillas control one third of the country or more and in some areas have established a civil administration. They have an army that is gradually gaining the upper hand against the regime's armed forces. And they enjoy considerable popular support, the Commission's denials of this fact notwithstanding. . . .

Negotiations and Communism

On the subject of negotiations in Nicaragua, the Report opens with a two-page explanation of why no negotiated solution that would leave the current "Marxist-Leninist" Sandinista regime intact is possible or acceptable. If "totalitarianism" is "consolidated," so the argument goes, Nicaragua will be a permanent threat to its neighbors; no international agreement it signs will be reliable, because communists cannot be trusted to keep such agreements. The Commission concludes this exposition by rejecting a policy of "static containment" toward Nicaragua. Instead, implying at least two alternatives, it advocates "first, an effort to arrange a comprehensive regional settlement," which, obviously, must include a fundamental change in the character of the Nicaraguan regime.

The Report insists that such a settlement must include guarantees of pluralism and free elections. But Nicaragua already maintains a degree of pluralism—at least as much as does Guatemala—and has scheduled elections for 1985. It is not clear, therefore, exactly what kind of internal change the Report expects the Sandinistas to undertake.

The Sandinistas have also offered to enter into bilateral negotiations with the United States regarding Washington's security concerns in the region, and with both Honduras and Costa Rica on the problem of border tensions. Honduras and the United States, however, have spurned these offers. Within the framework of the Contadora process, the Sandinistas have agreed to multilateral negotiations addressing many of the same security issues. All told, then, it is not Nicaragua that has been an obstacle to a peaceful solution to the conflict in Central America. One suspects, therefore, that it is neither the internal affairs of the Nicaraguan revolution nor its foreign policy that has engendered the wrath of the Reagan administration, but the very existence of the revolution itself.

The Commission never specifies the second alternative to "static containment," but it leaves little doubt as to what it is. If Nicaragua refuses to make the requisite changes in its internal affairs, it must be aware, the Report warns, "that force remains an ultimate recourse."

US Intervention and Freedom

One might think that a bald threat to intervene in Nicaragua to alter its internal politics would contradict the Commission's principle of self-determination (not to mention U.S. obligations under the Organization of American States and United Nations charters). Not at all. "Self-determination," like all the other symbols invoked by the Report, has its own special meaning for the Commission. The United States will respect the self-determination of Central American nations, the Report makes clear, as long as they "self-determine" themselves in ways consistent with Washington's vision for the region: "There is no self-determination when there is foreign compulsion or when nations make themselves tools of a strategy designed in other continents." A Sandinista Nicaragua, being a tool of the Soviet Union, has forfeited its right to self-determination; thus, the United States does no violence to the principle by interfering in Nicaragua's internal affairs by force or by threat of force. (Note the use of the word "continents" rather than "nations"—a necessary detail because Honduras has been embarrassingly eager to make itself a tool of U.S. regional strategy. But since the United States is of this continent, the principle remains inviolate.)

Such semantic gymnastics allow a majority of the Commissioners to endorse implicitly the CIA's secret war against Nicaragua and still proclaim their allegiance to the principles of self-determination and democracy. . . .

As it turns out, the Commission is really interested

in preserving the preponderant influence of the United States in Central America. What it recommends is nothing less than a full reassertion of the Monroe Doctrine: "The United States cannot accept Soviet military engagement in Central America and the Caribbean beyond what we reluctantly tolerate in Cuba." This doctrine is expansive in its implications. Revolutionary movements that include Marxist-Leninists or that receive aid from Cuba or the Soviet Union are intolerable, as are revolutionary governments that have any ideological affinity or security relationship with them. The Report has already argued that the Nicaraguan government is a Cuban-Soviet proxy that cannot be "statically contained," and that the other revolutionary movements in the region are spearheads of Cuban-Soviet penetration. It has already recommended measures to bring about the elimination of both, by negotiations if possible, by military measures if necessary.

"The United States retains a predominance of economic and military might in Central America."

After all this, the Commission has the audacity to declare that for the United States, unlike for the Soviet Union, "a concept of spheres of influence is unacceptable." But what else can it be called when a great power holds that its immediate periphery is closed to any significant influence by a competing great power, the national sovereignty of surrounding states notwithstanding?

Despite repeated denunciations of foreign interference in Central America, the Report is blind, ironically, to the most obvious and fundamental fact: no extra-regional power has been more directly or deeply involved in the Central American crisis than has the United States. This blindspot exemplifies a central underlying presumption of the Report, and likewise of current U.S. policy: Because Central America is close by, the United States has the exclusive right to interfere in its internal affairs. This right is somehow taken to be both natural and legitimate, whereas the involvement of other powers, particularly that of Cuba and the Soviet Union, is foreign and hence totally impermissible.

If either Cuba or the Soviet Union should violate this unilaterally declared prohibition—which both are already doing according to the Report—then the United States must be prepared to act, not just in the region itself, but at the "source" as well. Not-so-veiled threats of military action are leveled against both Cuba and the Soviet Union: "We must also bring home to Havana a due appreciation of the consequences of its actions," the Report says at one point, and later counsels, "If we do challenge directly any particular Soviet military activity in the region, we must be prepared to prevail."...

Letting Central America Alone

The alternative to the policy Reagan and Kissinger envision for Central America is one that would truly extend the right of self-determination to the people of the region, even if their choices are not always comfortable for Washington. The history of political polarization and violence in Central America has given rise to revolution; stability cannot be restored without incorporating the revolutionaries back into the political community. For the United States to allow the radical left to contend for power in Central America requires that we accept a degree of ideological diversity that historically has been unthinkable in "our own backyard." The potential security problems associated with this course are manageable; the affront to our pride ought to be.

The United States retains a predominance of economic and military might in Central America. We can expend vast resources to enforce our will, albeit at the cost of many Central American lives. The Kissinger Commission would have us believe that there is no conflict between such a course, based upon an expansive definition of national security and the moral authority of the United States. Nothing could be further from the truth.

The growth of popular opposition to Reagan's policy within the United States, much of it led by the religious community, demonstrates how acute the moral conflict is. People do not understand why the United States should act as the gendarme of Central America, arrogating to itself the responsibility to defeat revolutionary movements that have arisen against a morally indefensible status quo.

The central lesson of Vietnam, which the Kissinger Report has grasped only imperfectly, is that a democracy cannot fight a foreign war in defense of privilege and autocracy. The public will not stand for it. Kissinger has done his best with this Report to confuse, confound, and stifle discussion of the real issues at stake in Central America. For those who would sacrifice decency on the altar of realpolitik, an informed public debate is profoundly dangerous.

William M. LeoGrande is assistant professor of political science in the school of government and public administration at American University. He has written widely on US-Latin American relations.

The Kissinger Report Is Right

Penn Kemble

The Kissinger commission recognizes that there are two factors at work in the crisis in Central America. One is the attack being orchestrated and supported by Cuba and its patron, the Soviet Union. Democracy and political progress, the commission believes, cannot be attained until this security threat is met. But the commission is no less concerned with the second cause: the array of social, economic, and cultural difficulties that have so afflicted this region, and that have made it a prime target for Communist aggression and intrigue. The problem is that our political culture—especially as reflected in the media—cannot apprehend even this moderate order of complexity. In the favorite taunt of reports and editors in another election year, we seem to have trouble walking and chewing gum at the same time.

In trying to forge a consensus, the Kissinger commission has wholeheartedly embraced the liberal analysis of Central America's internal crisis: great inequality of income and property, illiteracy, bad health, weak and corrupt judicial systems, political repression, and the rest. But while this litany of maladies is usually recited to argue that the United States should avoid the quagmires in which they breed, the Kissinger commission actually proposes to do something about them. The estimated cost, over a five-year term, comes to some $8 billion.

The Great Society Advanced

More surprising, from what has been described as a "Reagan-dominated" commission, is the practical program for how these aid funds would be spent. It adds up to what could be described as a Central American version of the Mississippi Freedom Summer. Thousands of U.S. teachers, agrarian advisers, management counselors, legal-services

Penn Kemble, "The Democrats and the Kissinger Report." Reprinted from *Commentary*, March 1984, by permission; all rights reserved.

aides, health-care and even family-planning workers would be sent into the region, unloosing the Great Society on Central America. Boston University's President John Silber, a member of the commission, estimates that the number of U.S. personnel could go as high as 5,000. But he confidently predicts, on the basis of studies recently carried out by the Peace Corps, that such persons could be found—despite the laments of some conscience-keepers that this is a generation of self-seekers.

The emphasis of the report is emphatically against the traditional, top-heavy foreign-aid and technical-assistance programs. Like the Marshall Plan that serves as its model, this program would employ U.S. aid to build from the ground up. The stress is on aiding small business and entrepreneurs, on land reform, on projects such as housing construction and road building that would put numbers of people to work, and on fostering industries that would produce for local consumption. In combination with the considerable support offered to Central American trade unions, this strategy seeks to engender strong home markets in Central American countries. This approach was forcefully advocated by Lane Kirkland and it departs significantly from the earlier Caribbean Basin Initiative of the Reagan administration, which stressed foreign production for the U.S. market. Kirkland was concerned not only for U.S. jobs, but also for the independence and long-term strength of the Central American economies, and his approach was adopted only after much debate. (To the surprise of some, one of his most frequent allies was Republican Congressman Jack Kemp, a counselor to the commission.)

The mechanism proposed for implementing this aid program is as important a departure as the scope and character of the program itself. The commission proposes the creation of a new international body, a Central American Development Organization, which would administer a substantial portion of the aid.

Membership in this new body would be open to the seven countries of Central America—including Nicaragua—and to the United States. This organization, in the commission's words, "would do what no existing national or international body now does": it would require, as a condition for participation, that member states not only observe human rights, but also adopt a specific set of democratic practices, among them free elections, freedom of the press, free trade unions, and an independent judicial system.

Achieving Peace

The commission's report also deals in detail with the problems of achieving peace in Central America. Many critics of U.S. policy nowadays speak high-mindedly of negotiations and political settlements, as if these mechanisms were ends in themselves. When someone asks, Negotiations for what? or, What kind of political settlement?, he is belittled for quibbling or, more ominously, for promoting a "war plan." But a Democrat running for office in 1984 may be obliged to answer those questions. Someone may also remember to ask the candidate if he means negotiations and a political settlement like the ones we got in Vietnam.

"(The commission's) boldest stand . . . is its affirmation of the necessity of continuing to seek ways to fulfill the original democratic promise of the Nicaraguan revolution."

Henry Kissinger, understandably, recognizes that problem. The report of the commission is painstakingly clear on the objectives it proposes for negotiations and a settlement. It points out that the insurgents in El Salvador have—as if in contempt of wishful doves in the United States—stated their own position with Leninist truculence. In a document transmitted to Ambassador Richard Stone last year, they declared that "the Salvadoran people need a negotiated settlement between the government and the FMLN/FDR—to bring about peace; they do not need elections."

The insurgents' position paper also makes it quite specifically clear that their objectives in negotiations do not concern procedures and security measures which might assure all parties a fair and open election. Instead, as the Kissinger report describes it, they see negotiations "as a means of scrapping the existing elected governmental structure and armed forces and creating a provisional civil and military authority in their place in which the rebel leadership would have a major role. . . ." (It is notable that all

the Democratic members of the commission agreed in rejecting such terms for negotiations.)

As its alternative, the commission proposes the creation of an electoral committee, in which all political elements in El Salvador would be represented—including the FMLN/FDR. A cease-fire should then be arranged, and, with careful oversight by international observers, elections should be held.

Proposals for El Salvador

The commission by no means limits its proposals to efforts at strengthening democracy in El Salvador. Perhaps its boldest stand—again, but for one particular, evidently endorsed by all members of the commission—is its affirmation of the necessity of continuing to seek ways to fulfill the original democratic promise of the Nicaraguan revolution. "The consolidation of a Marxist-Leninist regime in Managua would be seen by its neighbors as constituting a permanent security threat. Because of its secretive nature, the existence of a political order on the Cuban model in Nicaragua would pose major difficulties in negotiating, implementing, and verifying any Sandinista commitment to refrain from supporting insurgency and subversion in other countries." Moreover, the commission argues, to prevent the export of revolution from such a country "would require a level of vigilance and sustained effort that would be difficult for Nicaragua's neighbors and even for the United States."

The commission affirms that all diplomatic efforts at persuading Nicaragua to modify its internal and foreign policies should be pursued. But it explicitly rejects the proposition that a strategy of "containment" can be applied if Nicaragua refuses. Therefore, ten of the twelve commissioners—those opposed are Mayor Henry G. Cisneros of San Antonio and Professor Carlos F. Diaz-Alejandro—endorse the continuation of some form of U.S. aid to the anti-Sandinista insurgents. These groups, the commission says, "represent one of the incentives working in favor of a negotiated settlement."

This conclusion, arrived at by a jury of distinguished American leaders, could be the most important event in the American foreign-policy debate in a decade. It is a rejection of the notion that a Communist state is a state like any other, accessible to the normal methods of diplomatic and economic persuasion. It is a sober reckoning derived from many hard experiences: the failure of the understanding John F. Kennedy and Nikita Khrushchev supposedly reached over Cuba's role in this hemisphere; the Soviet exploitation of a host of pacts and agreements; the unraveling of the Vietnam peace accords; the betrayal by the Sandinistas themselves of their promise to the OAS that they would hold free elections if helped in overthrowing Somoza. The commission is saying that peace plans which leave totalitarian states with the capacity to exploit our trust prove not to be peace plans, and that, where our vital interests are at stake, experience obliges the United States to require more than gestures or smiles before we lower our guard. No longer do *we* bear the sole burden of demonstrating good faith.

Contadora Nations Divided

That burden falls not only on the Communists. It also falls on those nations of the region who are making their own approaches to a negotiated solution: the so-called Contadora group consisting of Mexico, Venezuela, Colombia, and Panama. The Kissinger commission tactfully commends the efforts of the Contadora group to create a regional framework for setting the conflict, and to establish principles on which such a settlement can be founded. But the commission also recognizes some hard realities. The chief of these is that the Contadora nations themselves are seriously divided over the goals of their proposed negotiation.

On the one hand, Mexico and on occasion one or another of the Contadora states seem inclined to accept a ''Left'' solution. This would leave Nicaragua firmly in the hands of the Sandinistas, while obliging all foreign powers to withdraw their military troops and bases from the region. While this proposal would nominally discourage Nicaragua from supporting the insurgency in El Salvador, it would do nothing about the large body of intelligence and guerrilla advisers who have slipped into Central America from Cuba and the Eastern bloc. Nor does the ''Left'' approach provide for any means of verifying or enforcing a peace agreement.

On the other hand, Venezuela and four of the five Central American states themselves—Honduras, Guatemala, Costa Rica, and El Salvador—incline more toward the view held by the United States: there should be movement throughout the region toward more broadly democratic processes, with vigorous international supervision of agreements prohibiting aggression and subversion.

The Contadora process has a long way to go before these differences are reconciled and a regional consensus is developed that is strong enough to press for and enforce an end to the various conflicts. Mark Falcoff of the American Enterprise Institute, a consultant to the Kissinger commission, has likened the Contadora process to an airplane which can soar among the clouds, but is not capable of making a landing. It may some day discover how to land, but then, too, it could just as well crash. At this point it is an uncertain vehicle for the national interests of the United States or the Central American societies who are most threatened by the conflicts and who share our reservations.

The depth of the Central American crisis and the absence of any immediate or easy opening toward peace argue that the U.S. should expect to remain seriously involved in the region for some time to come. The Kissinger commission speaks strongly of the need for the U.S. to make no less than a five-year commitment, and to do it now. An aspect of that commitment entails unspecified but ''significantly increased'' levels of military aid to El Salvador, and additional training and equipment for the government of Honduras. The commission report, perhaps with a glance back at our experience in Vietnam, remarks that ''the worst possible policy for El Salvador is to provide just enough aid to keep the war going, but too little to wage it successfully.''

''We can still reasonably aim at fostering decent democratic regimes in Central America.''

This aspect of the report, predictably, has drawn the greatest attention and criticism, with some asserting that it reflects an emphasis on military matters over political and economic problems. Yet the commission does not recommend any specific levels of military assistance. It does note that the Department of Defense has asked for increases for El Salvador of up to $400 million over the next two years, with the expectation that the amounts would be significantly lower thereafter. If this request were met, it would in the worst circumstances add up to $1 billion in military assistance over five years, compared to the $8 billion the commission proposes for economic assistance—hardly an emphasis on the military.

But the numbers game misses the point. As Senator Jackson argued when he first proposed forming the commission, military assistance should be considered ''a shield behind which endangered nations can protect themselves from external threats while they go about the business of building democratic institutions.'' Commentators who never much agreed with Senator Jackson while he lived are now confidently insisting that even he would have quarreled with the Kissinger commission's recommendations on military assistance. But Jackson did have common sense, and it is plain that the amounts of military assistance now available to El Salvador are not enough to provide an adequate security shield. Guerrillas are able to destroy vital bridges, overrun garrisons, black out power systems, and in other ways foster chaos. Economic assistance alone is pointless in such circumstances, and anyone who proposes that we continue to make economic aid alone the centerpiece of our policy does not deserve to be taken seriously.

If we do give military assistance, how do we control it to prevent human-rights abuses by the security forces? The commission, as any newspaper reader knows, endorses the principle of "conditionality": that military aid to El Salvador be made contingent on progress toward democratization, the rule of law, and the prosecution of suspected offenders against human rights (for example, the murderers of the AFL-CIO land-reform workers and the American nuns). So far, the Reagan administration has swallowed its misgivings on this subject, leaving it to liberal Democrats, who won a great deal from the commission on this point, to assail the report that embodies their victory.

The commission evidently wrestled hard with the problem of how properly to condition military aid on human-rights progress. For the commission's mandate was not only to formulate a policy for Central America, but also to propose the means of fashioning a consensus to support that policy within the United States. There were many factors to take into account: partisan politics at home, labor politics (the AFL-CIO has a strong convention resolution on this question), the military situation in El Salvador, the national pride of the Salvadorans, and the commission's own abhorrence of the brutalities of some in the Salvadoran security forces. The outcome of its deliberations is more an effort at recasting the terms of debate about this matter than one of pressing a definitive answer.

"Anyone who proposes that we continue to make economic aid alone the centerpiece of our policy does not deserve to be taken seriously."

The report contains a thoughtful discussion of modern, humane counterinsurgency techniques. These must at once defend strategic installations and permit fast reaction and pursuit, while also avoiding high civilian casualties. Such tactics require well-trained troops, with expensive equipment like helicopters. They require well-organized local militias to provide defense against small-scale terrorist attacks or economic sabotage. All this means that the defense forces must outnumber the guerrillas by something like ten to one. (The Salvadoran armed forces have less than a four-to-one superiority over the guerrillas.)

A Vicious Cycle

The commission describes how tendencies in some quarters of the Salvadoran security forces produce "a vicious cycle...in which violence and denial of human rights spawn reductions in aid, and reductions in aid make more difficult the pursuit of an enlightened counterinsurgency effort." It believes we must use our aid to win progress in human rights. But it also recognizes that we cannot simply cut off

aid without hurting ourselves and, not incidentally, permitting a guerrilla movement to come to power which, as the Vietnam experience demonstrates, will bring far more repression than there is today. Try to punish the death squads by cutting off our military aid, and their patrons probably will end up living comfortably in foreign villas, while the people of El Salvador and our own security interests both will suffer the effects of a Communist victory.

But there are many ways to use our aid to encourage elements in El Salvador and elsewhere that will respect human rights. Funds can be channeled to provide more professional training for the security forces (currently prohibited by U.S. law) and to strengthen those who conduct themselves by decent standards while driving from power those who do not.

This is the reasoning that underlies the note appended to the report by Henry Kissinger himself and two other members of the commission, which urges that "neither the Congress nor the Executive Branch interpret conditionality in a manner that leads to a Marxist-Leninist victory in El Salvador, thereby damaging vital American interests and risking a larger war." This note is not, its authors have been at pains to explain, a dissent from the report. It is rather an attempt to emphasize that while the United States cannot wash its hands of human-rights violations in El Salvador—we must use our influence to end them—neither must we deal with these violations in a way that will lead to something much worse from the point of view of human rights themselves. This may not satisfy the likes of Congressman Barnes, who is like a nurse in a television movie standing by the bedside of a diseased patient, waiting for some blip on the fever chart that will justify pulling the plug. But if the plug is pulled, this patient will not die; he will be consumed by a more cruel and contagious disease.

Totalitarian Clique

The possibility that things could actually be worse in El Salvador and Central America is the point that divides the commission and its principal critics. According to a story in the *Wall Street Journal,* this judgment gained force during a visit the commission made to Nicaragua. Instead of a government of romantic revolutionaries, in Managua the commission encountered a callow and abusive totalitarian clique. A briefing on the military situation in Central America conducted by a key Sandinista official gave clear evidence that the Nicaraguans are thoroughly trained and informed by Soviet-bloc intelligence services, and possess military capabilities which genuinely threaten U.S. security interests. This new Nicaraguan reality is compounded by the enormous increase in Soviet and Cuban military capacities elsewhere in the Caribbean, and by the newly declared emphasis of the Soviets and their allies on the "armed road" to victory in the region. (Boris Ponomarev, who heads the international department of the Soviet Communist party, has openly urged his comrades to exploit "the seemingly quite reliable rear lines of American imperialism.")

Given all this, the consolidation of totalitarian power in Nicaragua and neighboring states poses an unmistakable threat to the international strategic balance. If that view is "doctrinal," as Senator Daniel P. Moynihan called it, the doctrine at issue is whether the United States should continue to be a world power capable of resisting the expansion of the Soviet empire.

Trujillo and Central America

In his account of the administration of President John F. Kennedy, Arthur Schlesinger, Jr. recalls approvingly how another liberal Democrat—in an even less threatening time—assessed the prospect of a revolution against the Trujillo regime in the Dominican Republic. "Kennedy examined the situation realistically. 'There are three possibilities,' he said, 'in descending order of preference: a decent democratic regime, a continuation of the Trujillo regime, or a Castro regime. We ought to aim at the first, but we really can't renounce the second until we are sure that we can avoid the third.'" This is not a bad summary of the strategy of the Kissinger commission.

But it is a measure of how much has changed within the Democratic party in a generation's time that Senator Edward M. Kennedy, the nominal heir to John F. Kennedy, scoffs at the scope of an economic program to implement a strategy squarely within the tradition of the Alliance for Progress. "Even under the best of conditions," he writes, "the countries of Central America would be in no position to absorb $8 billion of economic aid over five years. The only recipients capable of absorbing that much money are the oligarchs and the corrupt officials with their bank accounts and their booty piling up in Miami."

It is also a measure of how much liberals have changed that the idea of linking U.S. aid for the Third World to well-defined democratic practices should have provoked such remarkably candid opposition. Evidently it is one thing to condition our aid on "human rights"—a term that can have many meanings—but quite another to tie it to the practices of political democracy. So it is that the New York Times columnist Tom Wicker, a bellwether for liberals, informs the commission that "the American faith that fair elections define a democratic society is simplistic at best and often misplaced." He further explains that "economic and political progress may be possible if, on the other hand, the new aid is administered in accord with *Central American* political and economic dynamics. . . ." One naturally concludes that these "dynamics" encompass the ideas and practices of the Marxist revolutionaries in

Nicaragua and El Salvador, and that, in Wicker's view, we should not only stop resisting them, we should supply them with foreign aid.

Wicker's theme was even more clearly expressed in an op-ed piece in the *Times* by Daniel Oduber Quiros, the Costa Rican vice president of the Socialist International. Oduber lauded the commission's social and economic proposals. "But to force Central American countries to hold elections," he argued, "which in many cases would only be a cover for repression that denies freedom for the democratic process—might well further discredit democracy in countries where that word has historically meant cynicism and brutality."

"At this stage of the crisis, we can still reasonably aim at fostering decent democratic regimes in Central America."

The notion that there can be democratic processes without elections is not a new one—it is a stock item in the polemics of the "people's democracies." But it is another matter to see this idea taken so seriously in the pages of a liberal paper like the New York *Times.*

Democracy and Elections

This difference between the commission and its critics about the prospects of democracy in Central America may be as important as any differences over the advisability of U.S. military assistance to the region. In the past, rightly or wrongly, many Americans were dubious about prospects that democratic institutions would soon take root in Indochina. But the Kissinger commission may find greater acceptance among the American people for its more optimistic report from Central America that "Everywhere we found hope for a democratic future and a readiness to sacrifice toward that end." To one degree or another, democratic institutions are already established in Costa Rica, Honduras, and Panama, and in such other Latin American countries as Venezuela, Colombia, and Mexico. Important beginnings have also been made in El Salvador, soon to hold a second national election. The democratic opposition in Nicaguara has survived the depredations of the Sandinistas and the slander of their apologists. The hope for democracy in Central America thus does not appear to be some vestige of a far-fetched Wilsonian idealism.

It follows that, at this stage of the crisis, we can still reasonably aim at fostering decent democratic regimes in Central America. But that possibility depends in large part on the willingness of Democratic leaders now to join in a bipartisan program along the lines of the Kissinger report for the defense and development of the region. If they do so,

they can redeem the Democrats from the widely held
suspicion that they are the party of fear and retreat.
They can even claim, with considerable justice, that
the Democrats are more naturally the party of
international development and democratization than
the Republicans. If they do not, however, there will
be political profit to be reaped—but not for
Democrats, nor for democrats.

Penn Kemble is a frequent contributor to Commentary
*and chairman of the executive committee of the Coalition
for a Democratic Majority. He is also a board member of
the Institute on Religion and Democracy.*

"Every country has a right to its own Wars of the Roses."

The Kissinger Report Is Wrong

Arthur Schlesinger Jr. and Clark W. Reynolds

The following viewpoint is in two parts. Part I is by Arthur Schlesinger Jr. and Part II is by Clark W. Reynolds.

I

The Report of the National Bipartisan Commission on Central America is a serious document. It is literate, at times eloquent; it conveys much useful information; it is reasoned in analysis and humane in values; and it represents a valiant attempt to deal with intractable problems. It is also seriously deficient in its sense of political reality.

The Kissinger commission's thesis is that the exploitation of Central American unrest by the Soviet Union and Cuba threatens our security interests. The answer, the commission says, lies in offering pro-United States regimes military assistance to defeat externally supported insurgency and economic assistance to overcome the misery and depression that set off insurgency.

1. *The Soviet threat.*

Moscow unquestionably aims to benefit from Central American turmoil. But how? What goals are attainable? What risks is it prepared to run? What costs to pay? Instead of rigorous analysis, the commission rests its case for a dire Soviet threat on what Senator Daniel Patrick Moynihan correctly calls a "doctrinal position," dressed up with perfunctory military arguments.

The report broods about the danger to our Caribbean shipping lanes. But in what circumstances would Moscow try to "interdict" shipping? Only in the event of general war—and, with nuclear missiles flying, the sinking of oil tankers would be of small consequence, nor would Soviet military installations matter in Cuba or elsewhere. And Moscow knows it cannot establish nuclear missile bases in the Western Hemisphere in 1984 any more than it could in 1962. As for economic aid to pro-Marxist states, why, as the Latin Americans put it, would Moscow fatten a lamb in the jaws of a lion? For Moscow, Central America is a windfall, a target of opportunity, not of deep strategic purpose. The Kremlin will keep the revolutionary pot boiling, but it knows how vulnerable its investment will be.

The Domino Argument

The report also uses the domino argument: Guerrilla victory in El Salvador would spread Soviet influence through Central America. Actually, Communist success is quite as likely to galvanize anti-Communism and to move countries like Mexico to the right. In assessing the threat, Washington should listen to countries directly threatened, such as the Contadora group (Mexico, Panama, Venezuela, Colombia). It is too bad President Reagan did not assemble an *international* bipartisan commission, in which Latin American democrats might have joined in recommendations for multilateral action.

The commission's final argument is that failure in Central America will damage our worldwide "credibility." It may well be that the Administration's determination to inflate stakes and invest a civil war with global significance has made El Salvador a "test" of our "resolve." This does not, however, lead ineluctably to a military solution.

2. *The commission's program.*

The commission acknowledges the difficulty of combining military victory with social reform. Its answer is the military-shield concept—the idea that, if we help provide a military shield, we can persuade the regime taken under our protection to make the changes necessary to win popular support.

But regimes requiring military shields against their own people are under siege precisely because they don't give a damn about poverty and exploitation. The shield concept works when it helps governments already committed to agendas of democratic reform; but Romulo Betancourt (Venezuela) and Ramon Magsaysay (Philippines) were the exception, not the rule. Most of the time, the shield approach only nourishes the arrogance of the regime whose repression created the revolution. For, as soon as we insert the magic shield, we lost most of our leverage.

The guarantee of military protection means that we renounce the ultimate sanction—the withdrawal of support. Once we declare our commitment to a regime's survival, it becomes increasingly hard to make a beleaguered oligarchy do things it sees, probably correctly, as fatal to its privilege and power. The military shield turns into a blank check.

China and Vietnam

The report invokes history against alternative policies, like power-sharing. But when have we ever been able to force a right-wing regime, confident of our continuing support, to take action contrary to its own ideology and interests? We tried it in China, in Vietnam. When we bind ourselves to a client regime, we become the client's prisoner.

The report fails to note how skilled native elites manipulate their patrons. We are being manipulated by oligarchies in El Salvador, Honduras and Guatemala and by ex-oligarchs in flight from Nicaragua, using the "credibility" line to ensnare us into saving their property and power.

The men who run El Salvador do not believe in the splendid reforms urged by the commission—in civil liberties, in trade unions, in land reform, in redistribution of income. Vice President Bush rightly said of the death squads: "These right wing fanatics are the best friends the Soviets, the Cubans, the Sandinista *commandantes* and the Salvadoran guerrillas have." They are also the Salvadoran regime's best friends.

Does the commission really mean it when it conditions aid on "demonstrated progress" toward human rights? Does it expect Washington to end aid after the report's own vivid portrayal of guerrilla victory as a grave defeat for the United States? The Administration, once it deepens its military commitments, will certainly heed the footnote signed by the chairman and two other members and decline to "interpret conditionality in a manner that leads to a Marxist-Leninist victory."

Political Unreality

The commission's program is bathed in political unreality. Democratic economic development depends on restoration of peace and on a domestic will to reform. But militarism entrenches in power the people most opposed to social change. Peace restored by giving military victory to a crowd whose survival depends on the elimination of the democratic alternative—and who torture and murder their own democrats—will simply reproduce all the conditions that drove peasants and the middle class to revolution.

3. *The United States' role.*

The commission's program requires our "purposeful" leadership. But the report's sanitized historical review does not adequately suggest the credentials, or lack thereof, we bring to resolution of Central American problems. Distrust runs deep, understandably: Why should any Central American believe we have democratic interests at heart? Even Franklin D. Roosevelt's Good Neighbor Policy co-existed cheerfully with Somoza ("Our own S.O.B.") and other Central American dictators.

"Unless recovery is accompanied by social progress and political reform, added financial support will ultimately be wasted."

While there should be due consultation, the report says, "the United States cannot use the Contadora process as a substitute for its own policies." True enough; yet nothing has got us into more trouble through the long years than the delusion that we understand the interests of other countries better than they understand their own interests. The Contadora nations know the terrain far better than we do, are more directly threatened and are equally determined to protect themselves. If they do not see the threat as apocalyptically as we do, who is to say that they are wrong and we are right? If they still see possibilities in diplomacy, why should we put our chips on military power?

4. *And the alternative?*

Victory for the revolutionaries would be an international setback for us. And it would not lead to Central American regimes of sweetness and light.

Military Solutions

Still, if the military solution makes social change impossible, and if social change is impossible until peace is restored, what do we do? Negotiate. The commission insists that only the prospect of military defeat will bring the guerrillas to the table. "A successful counter-insurgency effort...is a necessary condition for a political solution." This may well be so, but it sends us down the military road again. The Contadora countries still work at negotiation. But if they fail, which seems all too possible, and if they refuse to endorse our military solution, do we go it alone and back our own S.O.B.'s? It is against the American grain to suppose there are problems we cannot lick with sufficient arms and money. Moreover, abstention would disturb those, like this writer, who feel an obligation to the many decent

Central American democrats who share our values and deserve our support. One can only say that a military solution is problematic as a way of saving them, since it confirms their enemies in power. And the international repercussions for us would be less if we pursued a policy of accommodation to the inevitable, like the French withdrawal from Algeria, than if we tried to enforce our will and failed, or succeeded at protracted and grievous cost.

Civil Wars

Civil war is a historical experience through which nations, including our own, achieve national identity. History takes its own time. Its ways are inscrutable and often tragic: People find their own paths to nationhood, and these paths often run with blood. Reflecting on the itch to save other lands from their own historical logic, a wise British Ambassador to Washington (Lord Harlech) said, "Every country has a right to its own Wars of the Roses."

Obviously, it would be wonderful to have in Central America a set of devoted, tranquil, prosperous, pro-United States countries. Equally, it would be unacceptable to let Central America become a Soviet base. Actually, both extremes are beyond the power of either the United States or the Soviet Union to achieve. We cannot attain the first, and we can prevent the second. We may well face an anguished time in Central America (Costa Rica always excepted) for a while to come. I believe we can live with that. It is conceivably better than trying to beat revolution by installing—and it would probably take G.I.'s to do it—a new generation of Somozas, who would only sow the seeds of later and fiercer revolutions.

II

The Kissinger Report on Central America offers something to everyone, but at a cost of fundamental inconsistency between its economic and political sections.

"When have we ever been able to force a right-wing regime, confident of our continuing support, to take action contrary to its own ideology and interests?"

In its political arithmetic, the commission's goals of social progress and political stability don't mesh with its economic means. For example, it correctly points to the desperate economic conditions of the region and requests $8 billion in U.S. support. Yet, the report admits, even if all that aid were forthcoming, plus an equal amount from private and international sources, the region could not be expected to more

than recover its 1980 level of per-capita income by 1990.

In short, the target is recovery, not growth. Output would increase to restore destroyed infrastructure, to recover the degree of capacity utilization in 1980 (which was below the peak years of the 1970s for all countries) and to match population growth. Yet the report also calls for fundamental social and political progress for the poorest segments of all the countries.

Recovery and Social Progress

However, as economists have repeatedly stressed, unless recovery is accompanied by social progress and political reform, added financial support will ultimately be wasted.

How can improvement in the lot of the masses take place in a zero-growth scenario without some loss of income and well-being for middle and upper classes? And what are the likely political consequences of such redistribution? The report is silent on this.

Even the modest economic performance called for by the commission requires assumptions about internal and external conditions that appear unduly optimistic: that the military conflict will quickly end with little added loss of life and property; that fiscal and financial stability will shortly be reestablished in all the countries, and political stability as well; that capital flight, which has more than offset previous borrowing, will be reversed; that the international economy will soon recover, restoring regional exports without increasing interest rates; that public and private investors' confidence in the region will be enough to more than match U.S. aid inflows; that the current debt of the region can be rolled over, and that the super-debt resulting from further borrowing, essential to meet the goals of the report, can be sustained. Yet the commission admits that "such an increased debt burden would permanently mortgage Central America's future, almost regardless of efforts to enhance export (and hence debt service) capacity."

The apparent inconsistencies might begin to be reconciled if military and security dimensions were reassessed in the light of economic and social goals. For example, the economic proposals appear to have been inserted as "carrots" to achieve political support for an approach to regional stabilization that is essentially military, not economic and social (except as needed to "win the hearts and minds of the people").

It is unclear whether any of the proposed $8 billion is to be for military-related expenditures in Central America—the "sticks" for achieving U.S. policy goals. These would include increasingly costly outlays for counterinsurgency in El Salvador, support for the *contras* in Nicaragua, restoration of aid to the Guatemalan military and massive military assistance to Honduras, not to mention infrastructure and other support to Costa Rica. If the commission figures do include at least part of such totals, this reduces the benefits of the purely economic assistance. If they do not, one may question whether the region could absorb such large additional inflows without severe inflation, increased dependence on imports from the United States and distortions in its domestic economies, such as happened in Vietnam.

Cost of the Carrot

The cost of the carrot rises with the application of the stick: Military and social expenditures are interdependent. The priority given to military, rather than negotiated, solutions, which is implicit in much of the report, would add to the destruction of the region and raise the economic and social costs of recovery.

There is no easy solution to the obvious security questions involved, but the countries of the region and the supporting Contadora Group have made a beginning. Cuba and ultimately the Soviet Union must be willing to play a role in regional demilitarization. (The essential question of Nicaragua's de facto participation in recovery of the regional economy is raised in the report, but not answered.)

Most important, while the Kissinger Commission mentioned the many steps taken elsewhere toward regional integration, it failed to take account of the differences. In the case of the Marshall Plan, the United States provided assistance for the recovery and growth of Europe based on a concept of regional economic interdependence, which was to be directed by Europeans (with initially important roles for U.S. management in occupied countries).

The Wheel of Economic Aid

In Central America, important representatives of every country—including Nicaragua—are committed to the goal of regional integration, notwithstanding the many difficulties and distortions that have marked that endeavor. The problem is that the Kissinger report sets up its economic-aid structure as a wheel, with each country linked to the United States as the hub, rather than to each other. This is quite different from the way in which the European Community was able to evolve—as a regional entity benefiting from, but not dominated by, economic and security relations with the United States.

Some practical proposals follow from the above. First, economic policies should not be proposed without examining their social and political consequences. Nor should military and security efforts be proposed without looking at their economic and social consequences. The sections of the report need to be put together in an analytical framework that tests their trade-offs and reveals their consistencies and inconsistencies.

Clearly, social progress is needed for the many. This implies some compensations for the few, if they are not to continue to destabilize through death squads, dictatorship, political repression and social ostracism. Since the United States does not want to open its doors much wider to exiles, the question of compensation for land and other property (and political power) must be addressed.

Security and Trade

Also, serious attention must be given to the caveat that trade incentives incorporated in the report aren't commensurate with the alleged "security importance" of Central America. As it stands, there are no fiscal incentives for U.S. investment in the region, and its proposed trade incentives are no greater than those in the broader Caribbean Basin Initiative. There is no "super CBI" for Central America, which would seem to be needed if the higher risks attendant to trade and investment for this subregion are to be covered. If, as commission member Carlos Diaz-Alejandro writes, the trade potential could do more than all the aid combined, it might be well for the United States to consider diverting the source of some of its imports from other regions of the world to Central America.

Social and economic security in the region, in the most fundamental sense, is the most important "national-security" aspect of development in the hemisphere. This means economic opportunity, social mobility and political democratization—though for much of the region the process will be long and painful.

Arthur Schlesinger Jr. is a historian and Schweitzer Professor in the Humanities at the City University of New York. Clark W. Reynolds is a professor of economics at the Food Research Institute at Stanford and the director of the Monticello West Foundation.

"The President's initiative reflects a long tradition of US leadership in the quest for peace. . . . Progress has been made."

The US Middle East Policy Is Succeeding

Nicholas A. Veliotes

As I and my predecessors have said to this subcommittee many times, peace, security, and well-being for the nations of the Middle East are critical to a broad range of American interests. That is why we continue to place such high priority on a comprehensive and balanced policy to protect these interests, which include:

• Meeting responsibilities we bear, because of our role in the world and our deep ties to the Middle East, to work for the settlement of conflicts there which stand in the way of progress and endanger international security, especially the Arab-Israeli dispute and the struggle for a fully sovereign Lebanon;

• Assuring the security and contributing to the welfare of friendly nations in the region;

• Prevention of wider Soviet influence in this strategic region;

• Supporting major U.S. economic interests, including access to oil and markets for U.S. goods and services, and assisting in meeting the economic development needs of the region; and

• Cooperating with the more well-endowed states of the area to maintain a healthy international financial and economic order.

In support of these broad interests, the policies of highest priority which we are currently working to advance are:

• A just and lasting solution to the longstanding and bitter Arab-Israeli conflict through negotiations, as proposed by President Reagan in his peace initiative of September 1, 1982;

• The restoration of a peaceful, independent, and fully sovereign Lebanon through full implementation of the agreement between Lebanon and Israel of May 17, 1983, and the withdrawal of all foreign forces;

Nicholas A. Veliotes, speech before the Subcommittee on Europe and the Middle East, the House Foreign Affairs Committee, June 2, 1983.

• Economic and military assistance to friendly nations of the region to enable them to defend themselves and deter threats from the Soviet Union and its proxies, as well as arrangements for strategic cooperation for access in times of threat; and

• We also continue to support a peaceful settlement of the tragic and costly war between Iran and Iraq.

The pursuit of these policies contributes to the fundamental goal of U.S. foreign policy: the promotion of U.S. national interests by working to create an international environment in which free and independent nations of the world, including those of the Middle East, can realize their rightful aspirations and the blessings of peace and progress.

I would like to discuss the situation in Lebanon, the peace process, and a few other matters in greater detail.

Agreement Between Lebanon and Israel

First, let me turn to Lebanon and our efforts to implement the agreement between Lebanon and Israel, concluded May 17 with the assistance of Secretary Shultz after many months of negotiations between the two states conducted with the good offices of Ambassadors Habib and Draper.

For many years Lebanon has endured much suffering and turmoil, riven by internal factionalism and beset by outside forces. The entry of Israeli troops into Lebanon last June added a new urgency to the need to resolve the Lebanese problem, and subsequent negotiations produced the May 17 agreement.

The agreement reinforces the policy which the United States has pursued toward Lebanon for many years: we support the restoration of Lebanon's sovereignty throughout its territory; a strong, stable Lebanese central government; and security for Israel's northern border. History has proved repeatedly that Lebanon can realize these goals and gain peace only if all foreign forces—Israeli, Syrian, and PLO (Palestine Liberation Organization), and others—withdraw from that beleaguered nation.

The agreement was an important step toward attainment of these goals for Lebanon, and we can be proud of this example of U.S. leadership and diplomacy. It proves again the point that we so urgently hope other states in the region will recognize: negotiations, if patiently and persistently pursued, can succeed in moving the area toward peace and stability.

The essential elements of the agreement are that Israel has agreed to withdraw all of its forces in the context of a simultaneous withdrawal of Syrian and PLO forces; the state of war is terminated; the border between the two countries is declared inviolable; and the territories of both states cannot be used for attacks on the territory of a third state.

By providing arrangements for withdrawal of Israeli forces from southern Lebanon in a way that will restore Lebanese sovereignty and protect the security of Israel's northern border, the agreement is a major step toward peace and national reintegration for Lebanon and, we hope, toward a wider process of reconciliation in the region. It is, therefore, vital that Syria and the PLO also agree to withdraw their forces soon, so that Israel will withdraw and Lebanon will finally have a chance to bind its wounds and run its own affairs.

"Negotiations, if patiently and persistently pursued, can succeed in moving the area toward peace and stability."

The Government of Syria has thus far opposed the agreement and has not yet agreed to withdraw the 50,000 troops it now has in Lebanon. This is disappointing, of course. Syria has stated publicly on several occasions in the past that it was willing to withdraw its forces when the Government of Lebanon indicated they were no longer needed. The Arab League summit at Fez last fall also addressed the matter of Syrian withdrawal in light of Israeli withdrawal. We hope that Syria, on reflection, will meet this commitment.

We recognize that Syria is a proud country and has legitimate security concerns in the area. But we are convinced that these can best be protected by withdrawal of Syrian and Israeli forces from Lebanon. The status quo leaves large scale Syrian and Israeli forces face-to-face in the Bekaa Valley and Israeli forces 25 miles from Damascus. The danger of confrontation and renewed hostilities in this dangerous and volatile situation, by miscalculation or otherwise, must not be underestimated. No one's

interest would be served by new tragedy.

We are encouraged that a large number of Arab states have either supported the Lebanon-Israel agreement or have supported Lebanon's right to decide for itself what is best for Lebanon. Only a few—like Libya—have joined Syria in rejecting the agreement. It is our strong hope that Syria will ultimately decide it does not wish to bear the onus for standing in the way of Israel's withdrawing from a neighboring Arab state and that Syria's interests will be served by supporting Lebanon's right to full sovereignty over its own country. The dialogue on these issues continues.

I realize that Americans are concerned about Lebanon, not only because the crisis there threatens the peace of the entire region but because U.S. Marines remain deployed in Beirut—together with French, Italian, and British forces—in the multinational force (MNF). The MNF, which is serving in response to Lebanon's request, is providing valuable backup to the efforts of the Lebanese Government to preserve peace and order in the Beirut area as it works to extend and assure its authority. We expect the MNF to continue this role in the near term. It is not possible to predict how long Lebanon will need the MNF for this valuable support role. Lebanon's request of some time ago for expansion of the MNF is still on the table, but all the troop contributors have agreed that no decision on the issue can be made until Israeli, Syrian, and PLO withdrawals are underway. The Lebanon-Israel agreement, which deals with the situation in southern Lebanon, makes no reference to the MNF.

The agreement does, however, envisage a continued role for UNIFIL [UN Interim Force in Lebanon], the UN peacekeeping force, when the agreement is implemented. It foresees that the presence of UNIFIL will assist the Government of Lebanon in reassuring Palestinian civilians located in the Sidon and Tyre areas in southern Lebanon of their safety. We believe this reassurance could be an inducement for the departure of PLO forces who remain in the northern and eastern parts of the country.

UNIFIL has performed an important service in Lebanon over the years in helping the Lebanese Government protect its sovereignty and territorial integrity. The United States supports a continued role for UNIFIL, not only in the south as envisaged in the agreement but elsewhere in Lebanon in response to the needs of the Lebanese Government. Of course, it will be up to Lebanon, working with the UN Security Council, to develop an appropriate mandate for UNIFIL in the future.

Before turning to another topic, let me say a word about the attack on our Embassy in Beirut on April 18 that shocked and outraged people everywhere and took the lives of 17 Americans and over 40 Lebanese employees and bystanders. I want to emphasize that we are thoroughly investigating that incident to ensure that we are doing all that we can to protect against recurrences of such savage acts against our diplomatic establishments. We have, over the years, devoted great efforts to securing our embassies against terrorism. However, we have learned to face the fact that drastic defensive measures to make our embassies invulnerable to attack would make it impossible for them to carry out the public functions they must perform. American embassies cannot be fortresses, and American officials abroad cannot be shielded from all danger if they are to do their jobs.

Middle East Peace Process

The focus of attention and diplomatic activity recently has been Lebanon. But the most fundamental and challenging issue in the Middle East remains the search for peace between Israel and the Arab states, including security and recognition for Israel and realization of the legitimate rights of the Palestinian people. I want to emphasize that although we have been intensely involved in the Lebanon question recently, we are determined to move forward in pursuit of President Reagan's peace initiative of September 1, 1982, which addresses the need for a just and lasting resolution of the Arab-Israeli conflict.

The President's initiative reflects a long tradition of U.S. leadership in the quest for peace in the Middle East. We have experienced many setbacks and frustrations over the years, but progress has been made, in part because of our determination and leadership.

We were instrumental in 1967 in the adoption of UN Security Council resolution 242 and subsequently Resolution 338, which laid down the concept of a simple trade-off: Israel would give up territory occupied in 1967 in return for peace, recognition, and guaranteed international boundaries; and Israel and its Arab neighbors would negotiate to this end. These resolutions remain the basis of U.S. policy in the Middle East today.

At Camp David in 1978, we brought Israel and Egypt together in negotiations that led to the historic peace treaty between those two former enemies. That treaty, based on principles of Resolutions 242 and 338, was a triumph of diplomacy over 30 years of war and hostility. These principles must be applied as well in achieving peace between Israel and Jordan and Israel and Syria.

President Reagan's peace initiative, which is based on Resolutions 242 and 338 and the Camp David accords, is an effort to reinvigorate the peace process. It offers incentives for other parties—most immediately Jordan and the Palestinians—to join the peace process. It represents a delicate balance of two principles essential for Middle East peace. It recognizes both Israel's right to exist behind safe and secure borders and the legitimate rights and just requirements of the Palestinians. In our view, these principles are best achieved by self-government for the Palestinians of the West Bank and Gaza in association with Jordan.

We are encouraged that the President's initiative has received wide bipartisan acclaim in the United States, and we are gratified by the support of our European friends, which we greatly value. We are also encouraged by support for the President's proposals we have received from moderate Arab leaders. In this connection, the communique of the Arab foreign ministers at Fez last fall indicated that the moderate Arab states now recognize that the question is not whether to make peace with Israel, but how best to do so.

"The most fundamental and challenging issue in the Middle East remains the search for peace between Israel and the Arab states."

In Israel, despite the government's rejection of the President's initiative, there is a longing for peace. Our proposal has sparked a lively dialogue and widespread new interest in a realistic, compromise solution to the Palestinian dilemma and Israel's security. These are positive signs.

We are keenly aware, on the other hand, of the obstacles that have thus far stood in the way of negotiations under the President's initiative. We understand and share King Hussein's frustrations with the lack to date of Arab support for Jordan's early entry into the peace process. King Hussein continues to support President Reagan's September 1 initiative, and he wants very much to join in the peace process based on the President's proposals. Other moderate Arabs have also told us they want time to help restore momentum to our efforts, and they want us to continue to support King Hussein. The door is still open. We stand ready to consult further with these Arab leaders. Our peace initiative remains on the table and will not be withdrawn. We will continue to work to move the process forward.

Iran-Iraq War

When I last met with the committee we were unable to address the Iran-Iraq issue because of lack of time. That devastating war is another conflict that endangers the peace and stability of the Middle East and Persian Gulf. I wish to reaffirm U.S. support for a prompt, just, and peaceful resolution of this terrible war, whose cost in human and economic terms is vast and tragic. Recently, a major oil spill in the gulf from wells damaged in the war has created a very serious threat to the marine and coastal environment as well.

We will continue to support a negotiated settlement of this war in accordance with the principles of international law, including support for the territorial integrity of both combatants and nonintervention in the internal affairs of another state. As in the past, we remain neutral in this conflict and stress the importance of independence and security for all states in the gulf region.

"This is a period of change and opportunity in the Middle East."

At the moment, it is difficult to assess the prospects for a negotiated end to the Iran-Iraq war, although there has been considerable activity in this area recently. A delegation from the Gulf Cooperation Council, composed of the foreign ministers of Kuwait and the United Arab Emirates, visited both Tehran and Baghdad in early May. They reported to the Gulf Cooperation Council in mid-May and are awaiting a further indication of intent by Iran before making a second visit to Tehran and Baghdad. The Prime Minister of Algeria visited Tehran in May and according to official Iranian statements, discussed the war with senior Iranian officials. Also, a team from the United Nations has been inspecting war damage to civilian areas in both Iran and Iraq at the invitation of both countries. Such contacts are encouraging, and we hope that they will help open the way to negotiations for a peaceful settlement. But we have no basis for predicting that this will happen soon.

Conclusion

Let me say in conclusion that this is a period of change and opportunity in the Middle East. The Lebanon-Israel agreement, the President's September 1 initiative, and signs of a growing recognition in the region that continued armed conflict is futile for all offer hope that peace is possible. As the President's peace initiative demonstrates, the United States remains committed to playing a central role in the search for peace and security in the Middle East. We are uniquely suited to this role because of our profound interests in the region and our strong ties to both Israel and the Arab states. We do not minimize the formidable barriers that still lie in the way, but we are determined to continue our efforts, working with our friends in the region, to surmount these obstacles.

Nicholas A. Veliotes is assistant secretary for Near Eastern and South Asian affairs. This viewpoint is an address delivered by the Secretary before the Subcommittee on Europe and the Middle East of the House Foreign Affairs Committee, June 2, 1983.

The US Middle East Policy Is Failing

Zbigniew Brzezinski

Five years after Camp David and one year after the Reagan Plan—both high-water marks of constructive United States engagement on behalf of peace in the Middle East—our Middle Eastern policy is in shambles.

Reacting to events tactically, the United States has been reduced to playing a subordinate role. Militarily, America is acting as an auxiliary to the Lebanese Army and, politically, as a proxy of Israeli foreign policy.

Most tragically, perhaps for the first time ever, uniformed Americans have been dying neither in defense of American national interest nor on behalf of any genuine American policy objectives. The longer-term beneficiary of this disastrous turn of events is likely to be the Soviet Union.

The other day, in justifying what is happening, Secretary of State George P. Shultz declared that "the crisis in Lebanon cannot be isolated from the larger Middle East crisis. . . . Progress toward a peaceful solution in Lebanon will contribute to the broader peace process; setbacks in Lebanon will make the broader effort that much harder." What was strikingly missing from his pronouncement was any acknowledgment of the critically important truth that the opposite connection is even more important: Lebanon cannot be restored without serious and tangible progress in the Arab-Israeli dispute. It was that dispute that destabilized Lebanon in the first place and produced the destructive chain of events of the last year.

The central fact is that Lebanon, as a multi-ethnic and religious compromise, became unstuck as a consequence of the Arab-Israeli dispute. First, the large-scale influx of Palestinians into Lebanon upset the fragile balance within that country between the Maronite Christians and the Moslems. The resulting strife then precipitated the entrance of the Syrians into Lebanon, in part to promote the Moslem cause and in larger part to restore Syrian domination that existed before the creation of the Lebanese entity under French rule. Finally, continued strife in Lebanon, the increased Syrian military presence and the use of Lebanon by the Palestine Liberation Organization for incursions against Israel precipitated the Israeli invasion last year, with its further destabilizing impact on the fragile fabric of Lebanese society. The cumulative effect has been the collapse of the Lebanese compromise and the resulting civil strife.

Lebanon and the Arab-Israeli Dispute

That strife cannot be undone by a political pastiche designed purely as a solution to the Lebanese problem. It is only a matter of time before the current cease-fire collapses. An enduring solution for Lebanon must somehow take into account the Palestinians' presence, which automatically intrudes the Arab-Israeli dispute into the Lebanese issue, and it must also deal satisfactorily with both Israel's and Syria's security problems. It is difficult to imagine the Syrians acquiescing in a permanent solution for Lebanon that results in a pre-eminent Israeli role, including the de facto incorporation of southern Lebanon into Israel, and that at the same time leaves the Golan Heights permanently in Israeli hands. In one way or another, the future of Lebanon is thus linked organically to the Arab-Israeli dispute.

Indeed, it was because of the United States effort to resolve that dispute that Menachem Begin and Ariel Sharon quite deliberately sought to preoccupy the United States with Lebanon. Diverting United States diplomatic efforts into Lebanon and involving the United States in a protracted diversionary crisis was the most effective way of derailing the Reagan Plan for a Jordanian-West Bank confederation. Moreover,

Zbigniew Brzezinski, "America's Mideast Policy Is in Shambles," *The New York Times*, October 9, 1983. Copyright © 1983 by The New York Times Company. Reprinted by permission.

the more the United States became engaged in Lebanon, the more likely it was that eventually the United States would become a protagonist in the conflict, pitted more directly against the Palestinians and the Syrians.

That is precisely what is now happening. The United States is on the brink of becoming plunged in military activity against the Palestinians and the Syrians. The result of such involvement is likely to enhance the standing of Syria in the Arab world as the authentic voice of Arab nationalism. Even moderate Arab governments unsympathetic to Syria would find themselves under popular pressures in the face of Syria's willingness to stand up to an America perceived by the Arabs as a military proxy of Israel.

Our prospective Presidential candidates, on both the Republican and the Democratic sides, are already beginning to compete in militant rhetoric, the effect of which is likely to further diminish the United States' ability to act as a mediator in the Middle East and to further transform America into a protagonist.

"The United States is on the brink of becoming plunged in military activity against the Palestinians."

The historically more farsighted Israeli statesmen probably realize that, in the longer run, Israel's security will not be enhanced by a Middle East that is further destabilized and radicalized. Indeed, not enough thought has been given to the extraordinary opportunities for Israel's prosperity in the event of a genuine Middle Eastern peace. However, the more militant leaders bent on incorporating the West Bank into Israel certainly welcome developments that have the effect of making the United States a direct military antagonist of the Arabs. This not only polarizes the Middle Eastern conflict in a manner that is welcome to them, but also it creates additional openings for the incorporation of the disputed territories.

The Soviets Can Benefit

From a geopolitical and strategic point of view, the most serious aspect of this development is that it is likely to redound to the Soviet Union's advantage. Without becoming directly engaged, but merely providing military assistance to Syria, the Soviet Union can reap the benefits of growing Arab resentment against the United States and of the continued absence of peace in the Middle East.

I have long held the view that the Soviet Union has no interest in a constructive settlement, and that is why it should not be a party to any American-sponsored effort to promote Arab-Israeli reconciliation.

The Russians' interests are best served by continued turmoil, and they are likely to be served best of all if American policy and military action create the pervasive impression of one-sided support for Israel's maximum objectives.

It is also only a matter of time before the United States is deserted by its European allies. None of them has any interest in duplicating America's willingness to take on the Arabs. Already some of them are placing obstacles to American military shipments in support of the Marines. Before too long, we will be alone in this strange adventure.

The situation has so deteriorated, and American options have so narrowed, that it is difficult to envision constructive alternatives. Yet what is happening is likely to produce the worst outcome of all: The United States will become gradually bogged down, the region is likely to be cast into greater turmoil and the Soviet Union, without too much exertion, will find itself increasingly influential. Under these circumstances, we have to consider alternatives, however difficult.

One is simply to withdraw, realizing that such a withdrawal may increase the chances of a head-on Israeli-Syrian collision. But the prospect of war may have a salutary effect on the minds of the leaders in Damascus and Tel Aviv. If war comes, the Syrians know that they risk a military defeat; the Israelis know that casualties will be high. An American withdrawal would have the effect of making the two sides confront the question of whether they prefer war or peace. And, if it is to be peace, both will then have to accommodate and accept some compromise.

Alternatively, the United States should more actively return to a determined pursuit of the Reagan Plan. In effect, what was missing from Secretary Shultz's statement would have to become the central focus of American policy: a concerted and determined effort to find a solution for the future of the West Bank and Gaza in the context of a larger peace settlement. This means using American leverage in the region—military assistance, economic aid, moral suasion—to press the parties toward serious negotiations and to be prepared to impose penalties on those who are not prepared to play ball with us.

If United States power is to be involved, and if American servicemen are to die, it should be on behalf of a desirable objective: a wider and more enduring peace in the Middle East. Focusing on Lebanon alone will never get us there.

Zbigniew Brzezinski was national security advisor under President Jimmy Carter. He is now professor of government at Columbia University and senior advisor at the Center for Strategic and International Studies at Georgetown University.

"Peace in the Middle East is not possible without resolution of the Palestine issue."

US Policy Must Focus on the Palestinians

Samid K. Farsoun

Peace in the Middle East is not possible without resolution of the Palestine issue.

While the Palestine Liberation Organization (PLO) and the 500,000 Palestinian civilians resident in Lebanon emerged center stage during the siege of Beirut, the real conflict is over the destiny of the West Bank and Gaza. These two areas, the remaining parts of historic Palestine, are under military occupation and have become the focus of the Palestine-Israeli conflict. For this reason Israel's assault on Lebanon was intended to deliver a knock-out blow to the PLO, the recognized leadership of the Palestinian people of the West Bank, Gaza and elsewhere. That the invasion had secondary political objectives is also true.

The West Bank and Gaza have become the locus of a Palestinian state in formation. This goal of a free, independent Palestinian state in only a part of historic Palestine is the minimal demand of the Palestinians which is necessary for an overall solution to the Middle East conflict. This minimalist Palestinian position was developed through extensive debates in the Palestine National Council (PNC), the parliament in exile of the Palestinian people. This position was diplomatically promoted by the PLO leadership, the elected executive committee of the PNC. An international consensus has emerged which recognizes the Palestinians as a people, their rights to self-determination and to statehood as well as to their representative, the PLO. Thus, the PLO came to be increasingly seen by Israel as a threat to its own legitimacy and an obstacle to the pursuit of its designs for incorporating the West Bank and Gaza into greater Israel (Eretz Yisrael).

In short, the purpose of the invasion was not simply to push the Palestinian guerrilla forces beyond

a 25-mile zone of the northern Israeli border. It was specifically to destroy the Palestinian *political* threat by decimating the Palestinian social, economic and political infrastructure located in Lebanon—the defacto headquarters of the PLO. The invasion was launched to shatter once and for all the mobilized and organized Palestinian collective structure. It seems that the Israeli intent was to destroy the PLO as an organized body and Palestine as an idea, leaving the Palestinians as atomized individuals, intimidated and controlled wherever they are—particularly in the West Bank and Gaza.

The successful Israeli invasion of Lebanon, occupation of half the country and liquidation of the PLO infrastructure there is a disaster for Palestinians second only to the destruction of their society in 1948. The establishment in 1948 of the State of Israel in a large part of historic Palestine was greeted in the United States with celebration. The creation of Israel was seen as the fulfillment of an idealistic dream by Zionists and a haven for European Jews. However, for the native Palestinians, the creation of Israel was an historic tragedy. It meant the destruction of Palestine, the dismemberment of the Palestinian homeland, the near annihilation of its culture and institutions, and the forced exile of nearly one million of its people. It was a traumatic experience of dispossession, destitution and dispersal.

The Palestinian People

Palestinians currently live in three major groupings under extremely varied and difficult conditions: (1) as second-class citizens in Israel, the so-called "Israeli-Arabs"; (2) under oppressive Israeli occupation in the West Bank and Gaza; and (3) dispersed in neighboring Arab countries under varying degrees of integration or suppression. The number of Palestinians is currently estimated to be four and one-half million, distributed in the following manner: 639,000 (12 percent) live in Israel; about 1,300,000

Samid K. Farsoun, "Palestinian People and Their Struggle for National Liberation," *CALC Report*, Vol. VIII, No. 8, November/December 1982. Reprinted by permission of the author.

(30 percent) live under Israeli occupation in the West Bank and Gaza; and another 2,500,000 (58 percent) in exile outside of Palestine. About 100,000 reside in the United States.

The socio-demographic changes of Palestinian communities since 1948 have been extensive. Massive loss of life—especially among civilians—and loss of property and of economic security have been the experience of Palestinians in wars in and around Palestine. These include the Israeli-Arab wars of 1948, 1956, 1967, 1973, the civil wars of Jordan (1970) and Lebanon (1975-76), and the Israeli invasions of Lebanon in 1978 and again in 1982. The horrendous suffering was accompanied by large-scale population movements, both forced and voluntary. Many Palestinians have become refugees four times over in their lifetimes as a result of military conflict. As stateless people, experiencing severe economic dislocations together with the natural pressure of population increase, Palestinians embarked on extensive voluntary emigration to the oil-producing Arabian peninsula and elsewhere in the world. The psychological, social, economic, and, of course, political consequences of these socio-demographic shifts of the Palestinian population have had a profound impact not only on the Palestinians themselves but on the whole Middle East region as well.

"Palestinians have become a nation of urban, skilled and highly educated people."

Regionally, the Palestine question in all its derivative aspects has become the central, dominating and pivotal issue which defines much of inter-Arab politics and sets the political parameters of the region. Indeed, in some states, the domestic social questions have become strongly intermeshed with the question of Palestine. For example, in Lebanon, the Lebanese National Movement (LNM), an oppositional social-political coalition of nationalist and leftist parties posed the issue of Palestinian rights as central in its struggle against the rightist parties in the protracted civil war there. Another example is the internal Egyptian opposition to Sadat and the successor regime. There too the Palestine question is intermeshed with social-economic issues. The formal "normalization" of state to state relations between Egypt and Israel has failed on the popular level. People boycott Israeli goods, unions and syndicates refuse to enter into relationships with their Israeli counterpart.

With respect to the Palestinians themselves, in one and a half generations (since 1948), Palestinian social structure has undergone deep-rooted and permanent

change. Its outlines are clearly visible; from a nation principally of small peasants, Palestinians have become a nation of urban, skilled and highly educated people. The Palestinians have now achieved the highest educational rates in the Middle East. From a nation divided (segmented) in its original homeland, it is now politically united in dispersal. From a nation of traditional institutions, they are now a people with modern rational organizations functioning internationally. In short, the Palestinians have transformed themselves from peasants to revolutionaries in the truest sense of the word. They have taken their affairs in their own hands in order to change their currently untenable status. This the Palestinians accomplished against extremely adverse conditions. The life of the Palestinian people since 1948 has not been stable, secure or free. They have been everywhere circumscribed socially, economically and politically.

Palestinians in Israel

In Israel, the Palestinians who remained in their villages persevered under extremely repressive conditions. Overnight they became a suppressed minority, strangers in their own land. Israel imposed upon them a system of control that included economic dependency, political cooptation and social segmentation. This produced a community, in contrast to Palestinians outside Israel, which has been quiescent, unskilled, rural, poor and with very low levels of education. The Palestinians in Israel have been turned into an exploited, segregated, internal colony. This situation is changing rapidly now—especially since 1967 when the isolation those Palestinians suffered was suddenly changed as Israel conquered the West Bank and Gaza and allowed movement in and out of those areas.

Palestinians in the West Bank and Gaza

In the West Bank and Gaza, Palestinians have resisted Israeli occupation through varied means. But Israel has imposed an increasingly repressive and bloody occupation which has stripped the native Palestinians of their freedoms. Even their livelihood and property have been violated. Israel expropriated about 60% of the land and a similar amount of the water resources, according to the former Israeli deputy mayor of Jerusalem, Meron Benvenisti. The West Bank and Gaza have been turned into an Israeli colony integrated into the Israeli economy. The Palestinian people there have few civil or political rights. Nevertheless, Palestinians under occupation have persevered and managed to build new institutions including four universities. Israel's occupation has continued to be met with unyielding, organized resistance.

Palestinians living in Arab countries have lived over the last thirty four years of exile in difficult and conflict-ridden situations. They have lived under varying degrees of integration. In general, Palestinians in Arab host countries have been integrated economically in occupations ranging from urban industrial workers to highly skilled workers, professionals, consultants, advisors, etc. Nevertheless, they remain circumscribed by local laws. Socially, the Palestinians have been segregated residentially either as refugees in camps or in specific urban neighborhoods. Nowhere in the Arab world do Palestinians have full freedom of action either as individuals or as a collectivity. Above all, they are circumscribed politically. The simplest way of describing the conditions of Palestinian life in Arab host countries is simultaneous "support and containment"—support for the cause and control of the people themselves.

Role of PLO

Against extremely difficult conditions, the Palestinians have succeeded in reorganizing themselves. Through the PLO, they rebuilt their institutions. These institutions include unions of workers, women, students, etc., and economic enterprises, hospitals, clinics, welfare and service organizations; also they set up research, planning, educational and cultural institutes as well as publishing, broadcasting and cinema centers. In short, the PLO is the central, autonomous organizing structure of the dispersed Palestinians. Its legitimacy and authority derive not only from its service to and employment of Palestinians, but also from the PNC, the Palestine National Council, the legislative congress in exile. Above all, the PLO in a short span of years built an extensive diplomatic and political network which led to its international recognition as the sole legitimate representative of the Palestinian people. 112 states recognize the PLO....

The PLO was created in 1964 by a decision of the Arab heads of state in the first Arab Summit Conference. It remained a tool of the Arab League and of the Arab states. As the militant Arab states became discredited in the 1967 defeat, the independent underground Palestine guerrilla organizations surfaced to gain control of the structure of the PLO. From 1968 on the PLO emerged as the organizing and mobilizing vehicle of the new, activist, militant and independent Palestinian movement. In 1974, at another Arab summit conference, the PLO was formally recognized as the sole legitimate representative of the Palestinian people. As such it was recognized internationally as well. The rapid rise in popularity and prestige of the PLO and its revolutionary platform threatened to shake the conservative and stagnant status quo in specific countries in the Middle East and the region. Thus, the PLO found itself fighting two civil wars, against an Arab army (in Jordan in 1970) and rightist (so-called Christian) militias (in Lebanon in 1975-76). It also fought twice directly against an invading Israeli army bent on its annihilation (in 1978 and 1982). While in 1982 the PLO was forced to withdraw from southern Lebanon and evacuate Beirut, it survived intact as a structure. The PLO continues to advance diplomatically.... It also continues to promote its policy for the peaceful settlement of the Middle East conflict.

PLO Peace Plan

The PLO peace policy has evolved from a general platform to greater specificity and clarity. In 1964 the PLO put forth a platform for the "liberation of Palestine" which was refined in 1968 into a policy of the "establishment of a free democratic society composed of Palestinian Muslims, Christians and Jews." This is the famous "secular democratic" state in all of Palestine which was greeted with total cynicism by Israel and the U.S. Responding to the material conditions internationally and regionally, the PLO evolved further its policy. In 1974 the new policy stated that the minimal goal for an overall settlement involved the liberation of... "Palestinian soil and the setting up on any part of it which is liberated the national authority of the people." This "national authority" means a sovereign, independent Palestinian state in the West Bank and Gaza.

> *"The PLO peace policy has evolved from a general platform to greater specificity and clarity."*

The recent American initiatives—the Camp David Accords and the Sept. 1, 1982 Reagan peace plan—has offered the Palestinians little but local "autonomy"—at worst a reservation to be exploited by Israel and at best a province of Jordan. Is it any wonder that these plans have been rejected by the Palestinians?

The Palestinians have long waged a determined struggle with a humane solution in view. Israel has offered little as a vision of the future except more exclusivity, more colonialism, more injustice and more expensive militarism. Sadly the U.S. government has adopted postures that allow a dependent Israel to continue such disastrous policies. Peace, however, can only emerge from the Palestinian vision of equal justice to all the people of Palestine: Muslims, Christians and Jews.

Samid K. Farsoun is chairman of the Sociology Department at the American University in Washington, D.C.

"A continuing obsession with the need to engineer a settlement of the Palestinian issue . . . is likely to be attended by failure."

US Policy Must Not Focus on the Palestinians

Robert W. Tucker

Conventional wisdom has it that American interests in the Middle East would be served above all by peace. Since the Arab-Israeli conflict is seen as the principal threat to peace in the region, a settlement of this conflict is considered to form the great objective of policy. A settlement of the Arab-Israeli conflict is taken to mean, in the first instance, a resolution of that part of the conflict that supposedly forms its core, or, to employ a familiar metaphor, its heart. Thus peace requires a settlement of the Palestinian issue, and indeed such a settlement is increasingly seen as roughly synonymous with peace. So strong is the persuasion that it has made a resolution of the Palestinian issue the Golden Grail of American policy in the Middle East.

The Reagan plan is but the latest manifestation on the level of high policy of what has become the received wisdom on America's Middle East policy. Although attention has been largely concentrated on the terms given in the President's proposal for settling the Palestinian issue, the real significance of the proposal is its assumption that a settlement not only responds to but is required by American interests in the region. Given this assumption, and the general view it reflects, the war in Lebanon was important in that it provided a new opportunity for achieving peace in the Middle East through a negotiated settlement of the Palestinian issue. "Triumphs of statecraft," Secretary of State George Shultz observed in the immediate wake of the war, "are decisions which join opportunity with action. If this opportunity is allowed to pass it may never come again." And the President, in announcing his peace plan, declared that the opportunity must not be allowed to pass. "Our involvement in the search for Mideast peace is not a matter of preference, it is a

moral imperative."

The view that peace is the great imperative of America's Middle East policy may be traced back to the 1967 war. It emerged full blown, however, only in the wake of the 1973 war. The October war had shown, it was argued, the very considerable danger held out by a continuation of the Arab-Israeli conflict. The war brought on something quite close to a superpower confrontation. It had provoked the Arab states to resort to an oil embargo of sorts. It opened the prospect of the displacement of moderate Arab governments by radical regimes. Another war, the argument ran, would almost surely raise these same dangers and very likely in a far more acute form. For another war would again provoke Arab states to look to the Soviet Union for support and to retaliate by use of the oil weapon.

Thus the great object of policy, it was concluded, must be the avoidance of a further round of hostilities. This required, in turn, such change of the status quo as would satisfy those who might otherwise again resort to war. America would have to preside over the process whereby the status quo was changed. Given its special relationship with Israel, it was in a position to help the Arab states in ways far less dangerous than the ways held out by Moscow. What Moscow could only do through war, Washington might do by virtue of Israel's dependence on American military and economic aid. . . .

There is little reason for concluding that this and other lessons of the war have been taken to heart. Quite the contrary, in the period that has followed the war in Lebanon, America's Middle East diplomacy has traced a thoroughly familiar course and reflected equally familiar assumptions. Although developments have occurred—of which the war, though signal in its importance, is only one—that should have prompted a far-reaching reappraisal of policy, Washington has acted with a striking, and depressing, consistency. It continues to respond to

Robert W. Tucker, "Our Obsolete Middle East Policy." Reprinted from *Commentary*, May 1983, by permission; all rights reserved.

the same stimuli, worry about the same dangers, retain the same obsessions. . . .

Today's Prospects

At present, we plainly have much less to fear from another round of war than we once did, or, at any rate, than we once thought we did. Even so, why should it be assumed that a failure to settle the Palestinian issue to the satisfaction of the interested parties—assuming for the moment that this is at all possible—will signal another round of war? Of Israel's once active military adversaries, none remains save Syria. Another war between Israel and Syria is a distinct possibility. But it strains the imagination to consider either party now entering upon war because of a failure to settle the Palestinian issue, whether on the basis of the Reagan plan or on the basis of any roughly comparable proposal. If anything, in Syria's case the temptation to threaten war would instead arise precisely because of the prospect that the Reagan plan might form the possible basis for a settlement. For then, Syria's interests, territorial and otherwise, might prove far more difficult to realize than they are today.

> "The peace between Egypt and Israel changed nearly all the equations of Middle East strategy."

The war in Lebanon demonstrated, if further demonstration were needed, that Syria will not sacrifice its blood and treasure to vindicate the cause of the Palestinians. The war demonstrated as well that what the Syrians will not do, no other Arab state will do. On the Arab side, the Palestinian issue can no longer form the effective cause of war with Israel; it can only be used as the pretext for a war entered into for other reasons. If these other reasons persist, they will do so quite apart from whether or not there is a settlement of the Palestinian issue. So, too, the opportunities for Soviet intervention in the region will have little relation to the status of the Palestinian issue. Syria apart, these opportunities must be seen in terms of developments in the Persian Gulf, and particularly in Iran. However they are assessed, it is very difficult to see why or how they would depend on the outcome of the Palestinian problem.

Who Achieved Peace?

The conclusion these considerations point to takes on added force when the obstacles attending a settlement of the Palestinian issue are again recalled. The point cannot be made too often that the Palestinian issue is not a normal diplomatic issue and the conflict it represents is not a conventional inter-state conflict. Even if it could be assimilated to such a

conflict, the prospects for its successful resolution today would not be promising. In this respect, we need to remind ourselves of the circumstances attending, and making possible, the peace settlement between Egypt and Israel.

The success achieved at Camp David was not primarily the result of American efforts. Although this government ultimately played a significant role in facilitating the outcome, it could do so only because the Egyptian and Israeli governments had already decided that the gains they could expect from peace outweighed the sacrifices entailed in making peace. Had this essential determination not been made by both governments prior to Camp David, there would have been no peace. Nor is it necessary to ask which party made the greater sacrifice and which received the greater gain. No conflict-settlement involves a precise symmetry of sacrifice and gain. What is required for such a settlement is not an equality of gain and loss, but the persuasion of both parties of a gain that outweighs the loss. Then, and only then, can a third party facilitate a settlement that otherwise might not have been achieved, or that might have been far more difficult to achieve. For even in these circumstances, the two parties will usually need a third party to whom "concessions" can be made that they are unable to make directly to each other.

Clearly, the circumstances that made the Egyptian-Israeli settlement possible do not at present exist with respect to the Palestinian issue. If they did, we might not unreasonably expect to play a role roughly comparable to the role we earlier played. Since circumstances rule this out, in the Palestinian case we can only choose between a relative passivity and an activism that has no easily definable limits. The Reagan administration, by virtue of the President's peace plan, has taken the latter course. The American government, in the person of the President, has committed its prestige to achieving a satisfactory settlement of the Palestinian issue and, since doing so this past September, has already invested a considerable amount of diplomatic capital in the enterprise.

In the Lebanese negotiations, the role and position taken by Washington can only serve to underscore further the importance that continues to be attached to a settlement of the Palestinian issue. The urgency that has attended our effort in Lebanon, the determination with which we have opposed initial Israeli efforts to conclude a separate peace with the government in Beirut, the insistence that we have shown in refusing to countenance an Israeli military presence in Lebanon, and the apparent willingness with which we have increasingly moved toward acceptance of the role of guarantor of the peace there, would be very difficult to explain were it not for our continuing obsession with the Palestinian issue and our conviction of the importance this issue retains for American interests. It is an effort to maintain, if not to restore, our credibility with the Arab states—and, above all, with Saudi Arabia—that must account for our position respecting a Lebanese peace settlement. In turn, the need for credibility is dictated by the need to obtain a greater measure of Arab support for the Reagan peace plan.

The Real Issue

It is against this general background that administration claims to an activism with very clear limits must be judged. From the outset, the American diplomatic initiative was explained by administration officials as one that placed upon the interested Arab parties the choice either of responding satisfactorily or of running the risk that we would simply cease to concern ourselves with the Palestinian problem, with all the consequences this might entail. If the Arabs responded satisfactorily, the onus would then be placed on the Israelis and it would presumably be a very heavy one. If the Arabs failed to respond, the onus would be theirs by election. In either event, the risks and price of failure would not be ours....

"We would simply cease to concern ourselves with the Palestinian problem."

A continuing obsession with the need to engineer a settlement of the Palestinian issue not only fails to respond to American interests and is likely to be attended by failure, it also diverts us from paying more attention to developments in the Persian Gulf. It is in the Gulf that our interests today, as in the past, are centered, and it is by virture of developments in the Gulf that these interests continue to be jeopardized.

Robert W. Tucker is professor of international relations at Johns Hopkins University. His books include The Purposes of American Power *and* The Fall of the First British Empire.

viewpoint **95**

The PLO Can Resolve the Arab-Israeli Conflict

R. Scott Kennedy

Recent developments in the Middle East suggest the great difficulties and weighty choices facing not only the Palestinian Liberation Organization's Chairman Yassir Arafat, but the Palestinian movement as a whole.

Oddly enough, over the past decade and a half the Palestinian national movement has increasingly patterned itself after its arch-nemesis—the successful Jewish Zionist movement of the first half of this century. After a series of unsuccessful Arab wars against Israel and the expulsion of larger numbers of Palestinians in the 1970 Civil War in Jordan, Lebanon became the last base from which the Palestinians could operate relatively openly and free of external constraint. In the wake of the 1975-76 Civil War in Lebanon, the Palestinians found themselves in de facto control of large areas of that fragmented country. From Beirut the PLO successfully pursued its foreign policy in the form of efforts to win recognition of their right to a national homeland. More nations now have diplomatic relations with the PLO than with Israel. The PLO also developed a domestic policy, building the social, political and economic infrastructure which they perceived to be the prerequisite for a Palestinian state. Palestinian hospitals; job training programs; factories, social welfare, academic and educational institutions; and quasi-governmental offices and agencies were established and functioned in Lebanon, to be transplanted to Palestine if and when such a state came into being. PLO officials spoke matter of factly about this phase of the Palestinian struggle being modeled after the Zionist movement.

The Israeli invasion of Lebanon in June of 1982 was determined to eliminate the PLO as a military threat, its stated goal. It was meant to destroy all of the Palestinian institutions in Lebanon, no matter how benign, and to destroy the PLO's claim to sole legitimate representation of the Palestinian people. Additionally, the invasion helped to distract world opinion from Israel's continued economic and social integration of the occupied West Bank and Gaza Strip into the Jewish State.

Ironically, Israel apparently sought to achieve these results without destroying the PLO per se, and without forcing Arafat out of his leadership role. The forced evacuation of Arafat and the PLO from Beirut was choreographed by the USA and Israel in such a fashion as to leave the PLO organizationally intact, though its power and influence had been drastically reduced, and with Arafat surviving as its symbolic leader. The Israelis could have removed Arafat at several points, but this would have created a power vacuum. The Israelis and Americans feared more extreme elements would replace Arafat, renewing terrorist action against Israeli, Jewish, American or other interests perceived to be hostile to the Palestinian cause.

With its base in Lebanon destroyed, the PLO and Arafat were expected to slide into oblivion. Resistance to Israel's annexation policies would be demoralized and the nationalist aspirations of the Palestinians dashed. Meanwhile, other Palestinians, more favorably disposed to Israeli plans for the region, would gradually surface and be cultivated. It is in light of these overarching strategies that the Israeli invasion of Lebanon must be viewed and this critical juncture in the evolution of the Palestinian movement assessed.

First the Moderates Go

The assassination of Dr. Issam Sartawi on April 10th of this year is but one indication of the corner into which Arafat and the PLO had been pushed.

Since the 1970s, Sartawi had served the PLO as roving ambassador to Europe. He had met frequently

R. Scott Kennedy, "What's Next for the PLO?", *Looking at the Middle East Puzzle*, ed. by Jim Wake, Deena Hurwitz and R. Scott Kennedy, Menlo Park, CA: Humanitas International, 1983. Reprinted by permission of Humanitas and the Resource Center for Nonviolence.

with Israeli Zionists and others while exploring possible grounds for a negotiated settlement to the Arab/Israeli conflict. As a close friend and aid to Arafat, Sartawi encouraged acceptance of a negotiated settlement based on mutual recognition of the Israeli Jewish State and a Palestinian State on the West Bank and Gaza Strip.

These discussions culminated in January of 1983 when Arafat, Sartawi and a PLO delegation met in Tunisia with the Israeli Council for Israel Palestinian Peace, headed by Major General (Retired) Mattiyahu Peled. This meeting signified the highwater mark of efforts at building dialogue between Palestinians and Israelis. The fact that Arafat publicly announced the meeting amounted to de facto recognition that negotiations with Israeli Zionists was not only possible but desirable.

But Arafat's decision to meet with Peled and the others in the wake of Israel's devastation of the Palestinians in Lebanon was not taken with the concurrence of others within the PLO and outside of it. In retrospect, the photographs of Arafat, Sartawi and the Israelis, broadcast widely in the Mideast and around the world, were not simply a sign of Issam Sartawi's success and Arafat's apparent tendencies towards a negotiated two-state solution. The photos also signaled that Sartawi's days were numbered and, even more significantly, that Arafat's domination of the PLO would soon face serious challenge.

"By his own estimate, Sartawi had survived no fewer than 27 attempts on his life."

The PLO is an umbrella organization including a **dozen guerrilla factions of different views and tendencies.** Fatah, founded and headed by Arafat, represents the mainstream Palestinian nationalist movement and is by far the strongest of the constitutive elements of the PLO. By most estimates, Fatah comprises 80% of the PLO's membership, military strength and financial resources.

A Two-State Solution

Fatah and Arafat generally accepted Sartawi's lead and the idea of a two-state solution. The PLO as a whole moved inexorably towards accepting Israel as a fact of life with which the Palestinians must eventually make their peace, whether they like it or not. The "Rejection" or Steadfast Front left the PLO in 1974 over Arafat's growing acceptance of coexistence with Israel. They argued "that it was better to retain *all* the rights to Palestine—even if it means losing the whole country—than to surrender *some* of those rights in order to recover *some* of the homeland." (R. Friedman, *Village Voice*, 6/7/83). But

even the so-called rejectionists had come finally to acquiesce to the Palestinian consensus in accepting a two-state solution. This position has been made obvious in recent Palestine National Council resolutions, Arab summit agreements and various PLO declarations in addition to statements by Arafat and his chief aides.

Nevertheless, because the PLO operates by a rough consensus process, progress towards a peaceful settlement along the lines suggested by Sartawi could be and was thwarted by relatively small and ideologically extreme factions within the PLO. Due to internal dissension over his contact with the Israelis, Sartawi twice offered his resignation from membership in the Palestine National Council, his only official position. Arafat and the PNC twice refused his resignation, as recently as February 1983.

Sartawi was killed in Portugal on April 10 by Abu Nidal, a notorious "gun for hire". Abu Nidal, who left the PLO because of Arafat's willingness to accept a negotiated settlement with Israel, has alternately been in the employ of arch-enemies Iraq and Syria. Abu Nidal has attacked Israeli officials and European Jews. He has since issued a death sentence against Arafat and, shortly before the slaying of Sartawi, publicly announced a similar fate for him. This was clearly no idle threat: by his own estimate, Sartawi had survived no fewer than 27 attempts on his life, and Abu Nidal publicly claimed responsibility for killing several other outspoken Palestinian moderates.

Abu Nidal defied the Palestinian consensus, even though the most extreme Arab states had gone on record in support of the two-state solution. When the PLO renounced international terrorism, and adopted diplomatic channels as the preferred method of pursuing their goal of a West Bank state, Abu Nidal targeted PLO officials as well as "Zionist enemies."

During the past several years, Issam Sartawi publicly warned that Abu Nidal served only the interests of Israel, a claim at least partially substantiated by columnist Jack Anderson. Israel capitalizes on such terrorism to shore up support at home and abroad for its military might. It exploits terrorism to justify military actions, such as the invasion of Lebanon which followed Abu Nidal's attempted assassination of an Israeli official in London. It seizes on international terrorism to claim there is no one in the PLO to talk with, even though the PLO has renounced Abu Nidal's gang for nearly a decade and Arafat himself is on their hit-list. And, finally, Israel has used international terrorism as an excuse to refuse negotiations while pursuing a policy of "de facto" annexation of the Occupied Territories, thereby making a Palestinian state a moot issue despite its support among moderate Palestinians.

The Lebanese Invasion

A sinister rationale thus envelops both Sartawi's killing and Israel's invasion of Lebanon. Both were aimed at silencing moderate Palestinians who favor coexistence and a two-state solution. As one Palestinian remarked, "Who but the Palestinians have more to lose by the murder of our leading moderates, and who more to gain than Israel?"

The more moderate stance of Arafat and the mainstream PLO may well have contributed to Israel's decision to invade Lebanon: an end to Arab rejectionism would force Israel's hand and soon reveal whether the Jewish State is in fact prepared to live peacefully with its Palestinian neighbors. Continued Israeli occupation of the West Bank and in Gaza suggests that historic roles may indeed have been reversed. Israel is now the "rejectionist" force dismissing the possibility of a negotiated settlement based on mutual recognition and partition of the land into a state of Israel and a state of Palestine. With Arafat crippled but not destroyed, PLO moderates would be muted, but would retain enough power to prevent the ascendency of extremist groups.

In the wake of the Israeli invasion of Lebanon and the virtual destruction of the PLO as a military, social and political force, rapprochement with the Palestinians as a political necessity is even more remote. The PLO may have been the primary military casualty of the invasion, but a major political casualty was the possibility of a two-state solution. The Israeli invasion strengthened those who deny the possibility of coexistence with the Jewish State. The timing of Arafat's meeting with the Israeli Peace Council in Tunis in the aftermath of Sabra and Chatilla seemed quixotic even to some moderates. To other Palestinians, it was a betrayal of their cause. At the Palestinian National Council meeting which followed Arafat's meeting with the Israeli Peace Council by a month, the PLO chief came under bitter attack and Sartawi was denied the opportunity to address the gathering. Optimists dismissed Sartawi's assassination two months later as a non-event within the PLO given Abu Nidal's isolation within the PLO. But Sartawi's death proved to be a harbinger of greater problems to come for both Arafat and the PLO.

The mutiny of PLO forces in the Bekaa valley is remarkable precisely because it originated within Arafat's Fatah faction of the PLO. It suggests that the dissension over a diplomatic rather than a military strategy cuts deeply through the PLO. It also spells the tenuousness of American and Israeli efforts to maintain Arafat as a unifying but neutered symbolic figure in the PLO. And it raises serious questions about whether the Palestinians could accept a two-state solution even were the Americans to brow-beat the Israelis into accepting such a compromise.

To date, Arafat and the PLO have issued ambiguous or even contradictory statements about their position on Israel's continued existence. Until Israel's invasion of Lebanon, Arafat leveraged this ambiguity to keep as many options open as possible at any one time. This enabled him to curry the favor of Arab states and other countries with different and often conflicting interests, those who provide him with arms, diplomatic support and financial resources.

Arafat and the Rejectionists

Until recently, Arafat's strategy avoided what he and others feared most—a divisive and potentially disastrous showdown with rejectionist forces within the PLO. But his approach also stymied efforts to change public opinion in Israel by peace forces there, where fear and hatred of the PLO remains one of the few unifying factors in Israeli society. It also preserved fertile ground in which extremism such as that of Abu Nidal and his kind flourishes.

"The Israeli invasion strengthened those who deny the possibility of coexistence with the Jewish State."

Issam Sartawi realized that the PLO must move decisively and unambiguously to embrace a two-state solution. He saw that Abu Nidal's particular brand of nihilism and the obstructionist posturing of the Rejection Front must be clearly and finally abrogated by Arafat and the PLO. The assassination of Sartawi and the fighting within the PLO strip away the romantic rhetoric of "armed struggle" and the false pretensions of ideological fanaticism. Do the mutineers and their benefactors truly believe that the Palestinians are better able to wage armed struggle against Israel in the wake of the recent war in Lebanon?

These events reveal the continued killing as cynical and futile gestures by spoilers who cannot determine events. Just as the continued Israeli presence in Lebanon demonstrates the inability of one of the world's half dozen strongest military powers to impose a solution by force on the region, so too, the violence among Palestinians in the PLO cannot, ultimately, shape future developments. Like Sharon's war against the Palestinians in Lebanon, Palestinian violence can only disrupt, postpone, and make more costly, but never destroy the necessity of the Israelis and the Palestinians coming to an end to the state of war and the establishment of coexistence based on mutual recognition.

A week before Sartawi's death, his Israeli counterpart Matti Peled commented, "the Palestinians have not yet reached their *Altalena*". In the 1930s and 1940s, the Jewish Hagganah, precursor to the Israeli Defense Forces, conducted a civil war against the Arabs of Palestine while waging a war of independence against British colonial rule. They tolerated an uneasy truce with those Zionists subscribing to the revisionist philosophy of Jabotinsky, who claimed all of Palestine as their own. (Jabotinsky's faction included the Irgun, a Jewish terror squad headed by Menachem Begin.) Only after the creation of the State of Israel did the dominant forces within Zionism square off against the extremists. The Israeli government forces sank a ship, the *Altalena,* off the coast of Israel. The ship was laden with arms, ammunition and volunteers destined for Begin's Irgun. The sinking of the *Altalena* was a symbolic response to the extremists who rejected the Zionist consensus to accept the United Nations' partition of the land into a Jewish State and a Palestinian State. It enforced the authority of the Zionist consensus on the Jewish "rejectionists" such as Begin who constituted a minority force in Israel from independence until 1976.

Sartawi's assassination and the PLO mutiny indicate that the PLO may indeed have reached its *Altalena*—that moment when a decision must be clearly made. Such a decision can only be done at risk to Arafat. But, as Sartawi told *New York Times* columnist Anthony Lewis last year, "Chairman Arafat will have to decide sooner or later."

PLO Is the Key

The Palestinian people have suffered greatly because its leadership has missed the boat on virtually every occasion when some concrete step could have been made towards realization of their dreams of a Palestinian state. The Palestinians can continue to seize on convenient pretexts for refusing to recognize or negotiate with Israel. Begin's settlement policy is only the latest in a series of excuses for not coming to terms with Israel.

"Recent events add new force and lend even greater urgency to the necessity of decision action by Arafat."

But recent events add new force and lend even greater urgency to the necessity of decisive action by Arafat and the dominant forces within the PLO; unambiguously declaring coexistence with Israel and creation of a Palestinian State on the West Bank and Gaza Strip as the grounds for resolution of the Arab-Israeli conflict.

Arafat should use his personal position and political power to persuade the Palestine National Council to revise its National Covenant to remove all references to liquidation of the State of Israel, passages which provide the seedbed for rejectionism. If the PNC will not act, Arafat should create a government-in-exile and declare his willingness to enter negotiations on behalf of the Palestinian people based on coexistence with Israel and the creation of a Palestinian State on the West Bank and Gaza Strip. A PLO cease-fire on military actions against Israel, including Israeli forces in Lebanon, should be enforced in the interests of creating an atmosphere conducive to negotiation.

Such actions look beyond the future of Arafat, Fatah or the PLO per se. The Palestinians are again at centerstage in the Arab/Israeli conflict. Their refugee camps and civilian residential areas in Lebanon have been subjected to massive artillery and aerial bombardment. Their social and political institutions have been decimated. Their political leadership has been dispersed and exiled. Any possibility of self-defense has been eliminated. They have become, as many have observed, "the Jews of the Middle East."

But they also offer the greatest hope for the Arab/Israeli conflict—a way out. Arafat and the PLO leadership are in the unique position to move the conflict decisively towards a political settlement, based on mutual recognition and coexistence of the Israelis and Palestinians. Perhaps their action alone will guarantee that the Palestinians do not also become the Armenians of the second half of this century.

R. Scott Kennedy is on the staff of the Resource Center for Nonviolence. He has been on ten fact-finding tours to the Middle East.

The PLO Cannot Resolve the Arab-Israeli Conflict

Daniel Pipes

I doubt that I was alone in being perplexed by the news from Lebanon in the summer of 1982. Even knowing the record of the Palestine Liberation Organization toward Israel had not prepared me to think that it terrorized Palestinians, too—yet such, it turned out, had been the case in South Lebanon from 1975 to 1982. This not only contradicted theories about the way in which guerrillas depend on the support of the local population among whom they live; it also made no sense that the PLO would alienate its own constituency.

Then, the PLO's military defeat highlighted another anomaly: why was it that an organization enjoying massive international acclaim failed to achieve even a single one of its military objectives against Israel? Why were political successes not translated into strength on the ground?

The continued fever pitch of PLO rhetoric in the aftermath of Lebanon raised other questions: were PLO leaders not aware of the Israeli bulldozers at work on the West Bank, and the short time left before that region became irreversibly part of Israel? Were they oblivious to the absurdity of planning to destroy "the Zionist entity" when their fighters were holed up in camps many hundreds of miles from Israel's borders?

Finally, in perhaps the strangest anomaly of all, the launching of the Reagan initiative in September 1982 turned the world's eyes once more on the PLO, as though *its* response were the key to a peace settlement in the Middle East. Could it really be that an organization of refugees had the power to dictate the position of twenty sovereign Arab states, including some of the richest countries on earth, on so large and important an issue as Arab relations with Israel?

On reflection I have reached the conclusion that these paradoxes all derive from one critical fact: support for the PLO comes much more from the Arab states than from the Palestinians themselves. It is Arab help that molds the PLO, that makes it unlike other irredentist movements, and that renders its role so elusive. To understand why the Arab rulers support the PLO, and what that support means, we must begin with pan-Arabism, the ideology that explains so much about political life in the Middle East.

The Muslim Legacy

Public life in the modern Middle East is dominated by a contest between two political systems, the traditional and the modern, the Muslim and the Western. While similar contests are taking place in China, India, and Africa, nowhere are the two sides so evenly matched, and nowhere do the contestants disagree on so many issues, as in the Middle East. During the period of colonialization Europeans often flattered themselves with the thought that Western ways had everywhere supplanted traditional attitudes and customs. But in most cases old practices had merely become less visible. Phrasing and appearances usually changed more than actual sentiments; despite the alteration of forms, feelings remained largely constant. What makes Middle East politics—including the politics of the PLO—perplexing to a Westerner is precisely the mix of these traditional Muslim elements with the more familiar Occidental ones.

For one thing, the Muslim legacy of a wide separation between ruler and ruled obstructed the adoption of democratic processes throughout the Middle East. In taking over European forms, most 20th-century Muslim states did in fact institute Western-style elections, but the difference in political background meant that Muslim leaders regarded citizen participation more as a way to prod the populace for support than as a means of creating

Daniel Pipes, "How Important is the PLO?" Reprinted from *Commentary*, June 1983, by permission; all rights reserved.

legitimacy or stability. Practices which came into being after independence betrayed this tendency: one-party elections in Syria, ballots for lesser officials but not for the head of government in Egypt, political parties representing religious groups in Lebanon, democracy alternating with military rule in Turkey, and manipulated elections in revolutionary Iran. Muslim populaces understood the authorities' purposes and responded warily; when they did show up at the polls, their expectations were modest.

As with elections, nationalism too underwent a metamorphosis in the Middle East. A product of special European circumstances, nationalism had developed out of the slow accumulation of common experience in England, France, Germany, and elsewhere. Shared language, religion, culture, territory, history, and racial characteristics all contributed to this process, with no single factor having decisive importance.

"The immense appeal of pan-Arabism helps explain many of the Middle East's most distinctive political qualities."

Nothing comparable to the nations of Europe existed in the Muslim world, especially not in the Middle East. There the guiding principle of political allegiance was pan-Islam, the doctrine that all Muslims should live together in one state under a single ruler, or, failing this, that all Muslim states live at peace with one another. Despite their inability historically to observe the ideals of pan-Islamic unity, Muslims always cherished this goal of brotherhood and emphasized the bonds of Islam. Differences of language, ethnic identity, and other traits did not prevent them from viewing one another as brethren in the faith (in contrast, non-Muslims usually appeared to them to be potential enemies). Muslims paid little attention to nations; loyalties tended to be directed either toward the whole brotherhood of Islam or toward the local community (village, tribe, city quarter, or religious order). Larger territorial units had little political meaning; even the most established of them, such as Egypt or Iran, were cultural abstractions like New England or Scandinavia, not political entities corresponding to existing boundaries.

Because Muslim and Western forms of allegiance were virtual opposites, nationalism was transmuted when it came into contact with pan-Islamic impulses. Whereas nationalism glorifies precisely that mixture of local qualities that makes every people unique, pan-Islam ignores such qualities as language and folk culture and urges instead the unity of believers within a single state.

Attracted to nationalism but wedded to pan-Islam, Muslims attempted to bridge the differences through compromise. Among Arabic-speaking Muslims, it was the drive to unify all Arabs within a single state, known as pan-Arabism, that won the greatest support. . . .

Believing that all Arabic-speakers form a single nation, pan-Arabists reject existing boundaries between Arabs as lines drawn by imperial powers to prevent the Arab nation from uniting and gainings its full strength. They hope some day to erase those lines and create a single Arab state reaching from Morocco to Iraq.

Pan-Arabism and Zionism

The immense appeal of pan-Arabism helps explain many of the Middle East's most distinctive political qualities, such as its volatility and the enduring predominance of local conflicts over the Soviet-American rivalry. It also accounts for the involvement of the Arab states in Palestinian affairs, and the special role of the PLO. In the early part of the 20th century Zionist efforts to build a Jewish community in Palestine, and eventually to establish a sovereign state in the area, stimulated the Arabs of the region to seek help from neighboring Arab states; their cry tapped the powerful vein of pan-Arabist feeling. (The support they received bore some resemblance to the support given by Diaspora Jews to the Zionists, for Jews and Muslims emphasize similar bonds of community.) Pan-Arabists then seized on the Palestine conflict and made it the centerpiece of their program; in part they did so because the prospect of losing to the Jews was particularly ignominious, in part because Palestine had strong Islamic associations, in part because the Zionist challenge looked so easy to defeat.

Pan-Arabism then transformed what would have been an obscure clash over territory into one of the greatest, most significant land conflicts of the 20th century. If not for the Arabs' impulse to engage in one another's affairs, the Palestinian cause would probably have remained as peripheral to world politics as that of the Armenians or the Eritreans. But the pan-Arabist focus on Zionism as the paramount enemy made the fate of the Palestinians a matter of direct concern to every government between Libya and Iraq. As the unifying element in pan-Arabism, the cause of the destruction of Israel acquired a symbolic importance out of proportion to the issues at hand. With time, it even took on independent existence, bearing its own mystique.

As the principal goal of pan-Arabist politics, the destruction of Israel also became a way for governments to assert their legitimacy; many rulers—Abdel Nasser of Egypt, the Syrian and Iraqi Ba'thists, and, especially, Qaddafi—made their involvement in the "Palestinian cause" a leading warrant of their worthiness to rule. . . .

The significance of anti-Zionism reached so far beyond Palestine that Palestinian Arabs themselves played for the most part a secondary, or lesser, role in it. It was the Arab states—Egypt, Syria, Jordan, Saudi Arabia, and Iraq—that led the struggle against the Jews. From the handful of independent Arab governments in the 1920's to the more than twenty members of the Arab League today, the Arab states have controlled the Palestinian movement by providing massive financial, military, and political support. Even before 1948, Palestinians relied heavily on the money, arms, and diplomatic pressure of the Arab states. From the declaration of Israeli independence until the 1967 war, the states so dominated anti-Zionism that they even suppressed Palestinian efforts to organize. After 1967, when the states retreated in defeat, the Palestinians reemerged as a distinctive force in the form of the PLO; but even then it was the states that contributed nearly all the resources.

The benefits to the PLO have been staggering. Financial statistics cannot be specified, for the PLO does not circulate its budget, but published reports indicate that in recent years the organization received about $250 million yearly from Saudi Arabia and smaller amounts from other oil states, including $60 million a year from Kuwait. At a summit conference in Baghdad in 1978, the Arab states promised another $100 million annually. Non-Arab governments (such as the Soviet bloc) also gave generously; and if these insisted on cash for arms, third parties might be induced to pick up the tab, as in April 1982 when the Saudis promised $250 million to pay for weapons from Bulgaria, Hungary, and East Germany. . . .

All in all, the PLO's annual budget in recent years has been estimated at about $1 billion, prompting *Time* (July 18, 1977) to call it "probably the richest, best-financed revolutionary-terrorist organization in history.". . .

The fact that support for the PLO derived mostly from governments had a price. To the extent that the Arab states strengthened the PLO materially, they distorted it politically. Because Arab rulers made the PLO richer and more visible than the scattered and divided Palestinians could have done, its behavior inevitably reflected inter-Arab policies more than Palestinian needs. When conflicts arose, the PLO leaders invariably gave priority to the wishes of Cairo, Amman, Riyadh, Damascus, Baghdad, and Tripoli over the interests of their ostensible constituency. The PLO flourished by becoming an organization answerable to rulers rather than refugees. Neither elected nor in some other manner chosen by the Palestinians at large, Yasir Arafat and his colleagues owed their power more to the interplay of Arab governments than to Palestinian approbation. Dependence on the favor of Arab rulers accounts for the paradoxes posed at the beginning of this inquiry: the illusion of power, extremist ideology, inefficacy, and brutality.

Thus support from the Arab states explains the anomaly of a refugee organization seeming to signal twenty-odd sovereign states what moves to make. It is true that the Arab states listen to the PLO and key their policies to its decisions; but its decisions, in turn, are little more than statements of the consensus of Arab states, however confused a position this may be. Far from formulating policies which the Arab states then adopt, the PLO reflects their will. PLO power is illusory; on its own, it no more influences Middle East politics than does the moon generate light.

The illusion of power is augmented by the fact that, as a symbol of pan-Arabism, the PLO enjoys a special prestige in inter-Arab politics. For this reason, Arab leaders do make efforts to have good relations with the PLO; but these efforts rarely extend to the point of being willing to change policy to accommodate it.

Dependent on kings and presidents, the PLO cannot afford to disobey; should it defy any of the six or seven most important Arab states, it can be punished in a variety of ways. The states can cut off funds and arms, deny it safe haven, promote certain member organizations of the PLO at the expense of others, found rival groups, or lobby against the PLO in inter-Arab councils. . . .

Extremist Philosophy

Were the PLO to give up the dream of destroying Israel, it would be putting parochial interests ahead of the good of the entire Arab nation. It is difficult enough for Arab states to take this step. Were the PLO to do so, against the wishes of the states, its position in inter-Arab politics would be destroyed. So long as influential states such as Syria and Libya demand total rejection of Israel by the PLO, the Palestinian leadership can hardly do otherwise.

Thus, to the extent that the cause of the military destruction of Israel provides the PLO with backing from the Arab states, extremism is inherent in its mission.

"So long as influential states such as Syria and Libya demand total rejection of Israel by the PLO, the Palestinian leadership can hardly do otherwise."

This means that for the PLO, satisfying the Arab demand for ideological purity counts more than satisfying the interests of Palestinians. The PLO does not pressure Arab governments to enfranchise Palestinian refugees in the various Arab countries in which they have been living since 1948, it does not work to win them citizenship or the right to own land, it does not take other practical steps to help them alleviate their plight. No wonder a 1980 poll revealed that only half of 1,200 Palestinian students in Kuwait considered the PLO to be their sole representative (*Al-Mustaqbal al-'Arabi*, November 1980).

As for the Palestinians on the West Bank, the leaders needed to promote their interests will not be found in the PLO. While a group of mayors on the West Bank prepared a document in December 1982 calling for the "peaceful settlement of the Palestine problem" through the "mutual and simultaneous recognition" of the PLO and Israel (*Al-Majalla*, December 25, 1982), and while in that same month four lecturers from Bir Zeit University stated that most of the students at their university favored territorial compromise with Israel (*Ma'ariv*, December 28, 1982), PLO leaders were reconfirming their intent to destroy Israel militarily. But what do mayors and students matter when heads of state give money, arms, and diplomatic support? Despite the fact that Israel enjoys complete military superiority over the Arabs and will for years to come, despite the daily advance of Israeli settlements on the West Bank, the PLO sticks to its hopeless irredentism. To do otherwise would jeopardize its standing and perhaps even its existence.

"The PLO can act as it does because it does not depend on support from below."

The involvement of the Arab states also explains PLO inefficacy; having to become party to inter-Arab disputes distracts attention from its anti-Zionist program. The more the Arab states disagree among themselves, the less power the PLO enjoys. An isolated Syria or a maverick Egypt reduces the pan-Arab consensus that makes the PLO prominent. Just as Israel would have the Arabs at odds, the PLO needs them brought together. But Arab rulers disagree so often that Arafat typically devotes more than half his time to patching up relations among them. Indeed, PLO relations with Arab states have at times soured so badly—armed wars with Jordan and Syria, spy wars with Iraq, cold wars with Egypt and Libya—that these have consumed all the energy intended for the conflict with Israel....

Finally, dependence on the Arab states also goes far to explain the paradox of PLO strength internationally and its wretched relations with ordinary Arabs and Palestinians. For the PLO is simultaneously the UN's most popular liberation front and the movement no Arab state wants to host; the toast of radical and Islamic groups around the world but widely resented throughout the Middle East. On the one hand, it enjoys a voice in Arab councils, wealth, vast military supplies, and a claim

to be the political voice of the Palestinians. On the other hand, it regularly murders opponents, relies on mercenaries and children to do its fighting, and uses civilians as military cover.

Of many examples (on the West Bank, in Gaza, Israel, and Jordan), the most dramatic is South Lebanon between 1975 and 1982, where the PLO enjoyed a nearly sovereign authority....

The People Suffer

Unable to fight the Israeli army on equal terms, the PLO protected itself with the lives of innocent Lebanese, using civilian facilities—homes, churches, schools, hospitals especially—as shields against Israeli retaliation. Even the Roman ruins at Tyre were converted into a military base, with weapons stored in the seats of the hippodrome. When PLO missiles hit the Galilee, civilians in South Lebanon paid the greatest price, for Israel responded with tenfold punishment. A bitter joke has it that a sheikh once went over to the PLO fighters camped near his village and requested that they fire their rockets at his village rather then into Israel. Mystified, the PLO leader asked the reason; the Lebanese replied, "Every time you shoot three rockets at Israel, they fire back twenty; so do us a favor and shoot at us directly!" In what came to be known as the "last massacre" during the Israeli advance of June 1982, PLO fighters deliberately brought down maximum destruction in South Lebanon, provoking the Israelis into bombing anti-PLO villages (such as Burg-Bahal) by taking up military positions as close to them as possible.

The Lebanese were also harmed economically. A backward region, South Lebanon could not cope with the large sums of money the PLO dispensed. Severe inflation which began in the mid-70's cut into the real earnings of laborers and reduced the value of savings. It also made working for the PLO, with its high wages, more attractive.

Even Palestinians, who should have benefited from the activities of the PLO, were victimized, as the PLO's constant problems with recruitment demonstrate. Any male Palestinian in Lebanon could receive $150 to $200 a month—as much as an agricultural worker—just for joining a PLO militia; then he had only to train briefly in the use of weapons, participate in parades, and show up for an occasional operation. In addition, his wife got $130 a month plus a small amount for each child. Yet these high wages were not enough, even in combination with a shortage of employment and ideological fervor. The PLO enjoyed the enthusiastic support of over twenty Arab states, two dozen other Muslim countries, most of Africa, and the Communist bloc, but it could not attract Palestinian men to fight for its cause. So alienated were Palestinians living in Lebanon from the PLO that it had to take active measures to recruit sufficient numbers of soldiers; characteristically, it resorted to coercion....

Assessments of the PLO are often confused by the fact that it provides services to Palestinians, employs them, and even sometimes protects them. Can an organization that performs all these functions really be so harmful to its own people?

Support from Above

To understand this better, it is helpful to view the PLO as a government rather than as a guerrilla organization, for its behavior resembles that of ''progressive'' regimes in the Middle East far more closely than that of other ''liberation movements.'' Certainly, PLO treatment of civilians in South Lebanon makes it unique among guerrilla groups: Robert Mugabe's Zimbabwean forces terrorized white Rhodesians but not the Zambians among whom for years they lived, and the Sandinistas did not harm Nicaragua's neighboring peoples. The Communist movement in China, the FLN in Algeria, and for that matter Menachem Begin's Irgun would have collapsed had they treated their own people as does the PLO.

The PLO can act as it does because it does not depend on support from below; so long as it satisfies the Arab rulers, it monopolizes the Palestinian national movement and can behave as an established government. The qualities it displays—disproportionate involvement in international politics, ideological extremism, grandiose ambitions, brutality—are the hallmarks of most Middle Eastern regimes; they are especially characteristic of the regimes which, like the PLO, live off money from outside sources—in this case, oil revenues. They, like the PLO, do provide basic services and do build economically—even as they base their contacts with their people on force and intimidation. The Syrian authorities conquered their own city of Hama in early 1982 at the expense of thousands of civilian lives (estimates of the death toll vary between 3,000 to 25,000). The Sunni rulers of Iraq wage war on the Kurds and repress the Shi'is. South Yemen lives in a darkness so complete the outside world knows almost nothing about it. Qaddafi has turned Libya into a maelstrom.

In short, the PLO's acts of violence against its own people—grenades against laborers seeking work in Israel, bullets for those on the West Bank and Gaza who disagree with its policies, truncheons for those living in the camps—closely resemble the policies of the governments that champion it most fervently. Remove the framework of a ''liberation movement,'' and what remains is the sort of dictatorial regime all too familiar in the Middle East. Only the fact that the PLO does not rule a territory endows it with the aura of romance lacking in ''progressive'' states already in power. But the PLO's record should make its character clear enough. Like other radical movements, this organization appeals to two groups primarily—the elite that it benefits and the distant admirers who stay far enough away to avoid the consequences.

No Political Power

Recognizing the critical role of Arab help has several implications for Middle East politics. First, the PLO has very little of the political power so often ascribed to it. It may appear to shape the policy of most Arab states, but in fact it reflects their wishes. It brings up the rear, echoing and rephrasing the weighted average of Arab sentiments. This implies that it will moderate only when its Arab patrons want it to; so long as the Arab consensus needs it to reject Israel, it must do so. Aspiring peacemakers in the Middle East must therefore not make settlement of the Arab-Israeli dispute contingent on PLO concurrence, for this is to give a veto to the organization least prone to compromise.

Second, while Arab rulers make the PLO rich and prominent, they also prevent it from becoming a representative body, an effective one, or a decent one. So long as it exists, the PLO will continue to ill-serve Palestinians by subordinating their interests to those of Qaddafi, Fahd, Assad, and Saddam Husayn. Do the Palestinians have an alternative to the PLO? Can they develop their own institutions, independent of the Arab states, which would cast off the PLO's illusory ambitions, discard its autocratic structure, accommodate Israel's existence, and promote practical interests? The ''New Palestinian Movement'' reportedly organized last fall in South Lebanon, the attempt of Palestinians living in the West to organize politically, or the efforts of West Bank mayors are moves in this direction. But their hopes of success must be slim, for no fledgling refugee organization has much chance against the weight of Arab consensus, which is still vested in the PLO.

Third, only the Arab states—and not Israel—can kill the PLO. By itself, Israeli force of arms, no matter how overwhelming, cannot crush this symbol of pan-Arabism; the PLO will last so long as it serves a purpose for the Arab states. The key Arab states (Syria, Iraq, Saudi Arabia) will join Egypt in recognizing Israel only when they have enough confidence in their own rule to dispense with hostility to Israel as a source of legitimacy; or when, as in Egypt, the endless futility of anti-Zionism makes it more of a political liability than a benefit. At that moment the PLO will lose both its support and its *raison d'etre*.

Daniel Pipes is a Council on Foreign Relations Fellow. He is the author of Slave Soldiers and Islam *and* In the Path of God: Islam and Political Power.

viewpoint 97

The US Threatens Middle East Peace

Robert Prince

The danger of a conventional war escalating into a nuclear war is real and often underestimated. This is especially true as the distinction between "nuclear" and "conventional" weaponry becomes technologically blurred by "tactical" nuclear weapons like the neutron bomb, which would be used in a so-called limited nuclear war, in response to a non-nuclear confrontation. With the increasing sophistication of modern weapons, the interchangeability of nuclear and non-nuclear components, and the accessibility of such weapons to all parts of the world, we have a situation where conventional arms sales directly increase the risk of nuclear war.

In no region of the world is the conventional arms race and military buildup as intense or as dangerous as in the Middle East. And no country has contributed to this military buildup, through arms sales, grants, and the buildup of its own forces in the region, as much as the United States. Partly to protect the interests of U.S. corporations in the region and partly to profit from lucrative arms sales, the United States is engaged in a Middle East arms buildup of dangerous proportions.

One indication of just how dangerous are the possibilities for nuclear war in the region is a recent observation in the *New York Times* that pointed out that the Pentagon considers the use of nuclear weapons in the Persian Gulf to be a "potentially effective expedient," a policy which some call "U.S. nuclear neocolonialism."

The rationale given by the Reagan Administration and its predecessors for this arms buildup is that it is necessary in order to protect the region from a Soviet threat. Yet, this presumed threat has no basis in reality. Besides the fact that the Soviet Union does

not make a profit from the labor of Middle East workers as U.S. and other multinational corporations do, the USSR is the largest oil producer and exporter in the world. At a time when its production and exports of oil are expanding, the notion that the Soviets have any reason to covet the oil of Saudi Arabia, Kuwait, and other Gulf states is nonsensical.

The main reason for the United States' arming of the Middle East has nothing to do with a Soviet threat, but rather is a response to indigenous national liberation movements in that region that aim to gain control of their own resources for the benefit of their own people.

The U.S. military buildup in the Middle East involves a "layered" policy. It includes arming a number of regional allies like Israel, Turkey, Egypt, and Pakistan, and making enormous arms sales to countries like Saudi Arabia and Kuwait. Since 1979, it also involves a new level of direct U.S. military presence through such mechanisms as the Rapid Deployment Force, the creation of a major U.S. military base with nuclear potential at Diego Garcia in the Indian Ocean, and the building of bases (or attaining the right to land and transfer troops and planes on existing bases) in Israel, Egypt, Morocco, Oman, Bahrein, Saudi Arabia, Pakistan, Somalia, and Kenya.

In a November 1982 interview in the British magazine *The Economist*, Henry Kissinger pointed toward what he considered the need for a "subtle but serious" U.S. military presence in the Persian Gulf region. Sensitive to the opposition of most Middle East countries to the presence of U.S. troops on their land, he explained the purpose of having large numbers of U.S. troops stationed *just off the coast* of the oil-producing region:

I think what we need is installations into which we could move rapidly; a physical presence near the Gulf that is plausible; and the demonstration of how we could reinforce the presence. And we must generate

Robert Prince, "War Danger in the Middle East," *Daily World*, August 11, 1983.

a credible capacity for rapid support against internal upheaval. The American embrace must be real and serious, but as subtle and non-public as possible.

Rapid Deployment Force

First created by Jimmy Carter through Presidential Directive 18, the Rapid Deployment Force became operational on March 1, 1980, with a combat unit of 100,000 poised for action in the Middle East and/or the Caribbean. Put under the command of the Joint Chiefs in October 1981, its combat force rose to 230,000. With the installation of a special Central Command in January 1983 whose purpose is to coordinate functions from Morocco to Pakistan and the Gulf Region, Diego Garcia, and the Horn of Africa, the proposed numerical strength of the RDF is now 400,000 (although some sources say 600,000).

The escalating pattern of RDF spending can be discerned from the following. The early FY 83 allocation for the RDF was $4 billion. After the British assault on the Malvinas, another $3 billion was added for the construction of 15 special floating arsenals capable of supplying three marine brigades of 16,000 men each. Now, projections for RDF budget allocations for 1984-88 range from $30 billion to $163 billion.

"U.S. arms sales...to Middle Eastern countries are escalating to a level that is nothing short of staggering."

According to Secretary of Defense Caspar Weinberger's report to the Congress on the 1984-88 military program, the U.S. Marine unit stationed in Lebanon as part of the "multinational peace-keeping force" and the U.S. contingent of "technicians" in the Sinai monitoring the Camp David Accords are actually forward units of the Rapid Deployment Force. Furthermore, the scope of the operations of the U.S.-RDF forces in Lebanon continues to increase. Its stated task is to keep the warring parties in Beirut at arms distance from each other. However, without Congressional approval U.S. troops began training the Lebanese army of Pierre Gemayel. In addition, President Reagan has hinted that U.S. troops could be deployed not only in the Beirut area, but also in Southern Lebanon in order to "guarantee the security of Israel's frontiers."

The RDF serves two purposes. It is a combat-ready intervention force, a strike force for corporate America. Its very presence, however, serves another function: political intimidation. In February 1983 the RDF was put on alert in connection with an imaginary threat to Sudan, a U.S. ally and one of the most repressive regimes in the region. The Reagan Administration was suggesting that it was willing to

fight for the survival of Jaafar Numeiri's dictatorship.

The likelihood of the RDF's use in the Middle East is heightened by statements from some Reagan Administration spokesmen that host country permission will not necessarily be required to launch an assault on what are considered "vital U.S. interests." This is an extension of the so-called Carter Doctrine, the Monroe Doctrine of the Middle East.

Just as the U.S. arms buildup in the Middle East is spiraling every year through the development of the RDF, so U.S. arms sales and grants to Middle Eastern countries are escalating to a level that is nothing short of staggering. From 1945 through 1982, the U.S. trained nearly 30,000 soldiers from the region and either sold or gave to them over $75 billion in U.S. armaments and spare parts, the bulk of these since 1973.

Arms sales as a whole from the United States to the region have risen dramatically. In the first half of the 1970s, U.S. arms sales in the Middle East averaged $3.2 billion annually, this being more than the total U.S. sales to the region ($2.3 billion) in the 15 previous years. From 1975-79, U.S. arms sales to the Middle East tripled again to average $8.9 billion annually.

US Military Hardware

U.S. military transfers to three countries—Israel, Egypt, and Saudi Arabia—are worth looking at in some detail. Of the three, the largest purchaser of U.S. weaponry is Saudi Arabia, whose ability to use the weaponry is perhaps the most limited of all Middle East nations. Its population is small, its political leadership unstable, its technical skills sorely weak. But this military buildup, which includes thousands of U.S. advisors and technicians to operate the equipment (a 1977 Congressional study estimated that one-third of the 30,000 Americans working in Saudi Arabia were involved in military-related activities; that estimate has certainly risen since) gives Saudi Arabia the appearance of much greater military strength than it actually possesses. This, in turn, permits the Saudis to play a critical role as a political broker for U.S. interests in the region.

The presence of U.S. military hardware in Saudi Arabia serves another purpose. When the Saudis received the controversial AWACs in 1981, they agreed to man them with U.S. crews. The information obtained with the AWACs is given to the Saudis on a selective basis. For instance, the AWACs detected the June 1981 Israeli attack on the Baghdad nuclear reactor, but the Saudis were not informed of it until the next day.

Egypt's role in U.S. plans for the region grew rapidly under the late Anwar Sadat. Sadat opened Egypt to foreign corporate investment, weakened its industrial infrastructure, and turned Egypt's military into a tool of U.S. corporate interests. Hosni Mubarek has proven to be an equally faithful servant of those interests.

With a military force of 350,000, a total population of 40,000,000, and the largest working class in the Arab world, Egypt is an extremely important country. Its political neutralization from the Arab liberation front was a change of the first magnitude, tipping the regional balance of power in the direction of U.S. imperialism by several important degrees. U.S. military aid to Egypt was literally non-existent until the 1970s. Since then it has jumped dramatically. Egypt now serves U.S. political interests not only in the Middle East, but in Africa as well, where Israel has almost completely lost its moral authority. Besides Egypt's role in destabilizing the Arab liberation movement, it has actively interfered in the revolutionary process in Ethiopia, Angola, Afghanistan, and Libya. (That Libya, with its army of 50,000, would present a threat to Egypt, with its army of 350,000 is something possible only in the creative world of U.S. journalism.)

"The Pentagon must have known that Israel was stockpiling at a massive and costly rate."

For such services to U.S. interests, the Egyptian comprador class has been richly rewarded. From 1978-1980, Egypt concluded over $3.5 billion in U.S. military sales agreements, much of it underwritten by U.S. aid. Taken together with the Israeli aid package, Egypt and Israel get almost 50% of all U.S. foreign aid at present, most of that military aid.

Carte Blanche for Israel

Despite its own lucrative arms industry with such unsavory clients as South Africa, the Philippines, Chile, Guatemala, and El Salvador, most of Israel's heavy and sophisticated weaponry is still supplied by the United States. If one includes the FY 83 projected budget allocation to Israel of $2.48 billion, Israel has become the highest all-time recipient of Congressionally approved foreign aid, topping even South Vietnam. Of the $25 billion allocated to Israel since World War II, $18.5 billion has been for military use.

These statistics, as high as they are, still do not reveal the whole picture. For example, of the $25 billion cited above, $5.95 billion has been "forgiven." This means that Israel need not pay this amount back. Furthermore, as Rep. Mervyn Dymally (D-Calif) has noted: "The remainder is loans with 10-year grace periods, 20-30 year amortization, and with interest rates below market levels."

A March 13, 1983, article in the *Detroit Free Press* notes that there are no strings attached to the economic aid the U.S. gives Israel. As a result, the Israelis can use that aid as they see fit. There is growing concern that a good chunk of the $6.5 billion non-military economic aid has been used to help the Israelis construct their illegal settlements in the West Bank, Gaza, Golan, and probably southern Lebanon.

But these statistics, which place U.S. aid to Israel at twice the amount the U.S. has given the entire continent of Africa, and 25% higher than all U.S. aid to Latin America, still do not complete the picture. According to a March 11, 1983, article in the *Philadelphia Inquirer,* an extensive General Accounting Office study of U.S. aid to Israel completed in February 1983 shows that U.S. aid to Israel is even higher than previously documented. Billed by the GAO as the most comprehensive study it has ever undertaken, the politically sensitive report shows that the total amount of aid to Israel is 30% higher than previously stated.

But there is more. Writing in Great Britain's *New Statesman* (August 20, 1982), Claudia Wright reported, "Pentagon figures just released in response to a Freedom of Information Act request reveal a massive surge of military supplies to Israel in the first three months of 1982 as Israel planned the invasion of Lebanon." Wright went on to point out:

At the very least, an extraordinary coincidence has occurred between U.S. weapons delivery schedules and Israeli military plans for Lebanon. Starting three months before the invasion commenced, the Pentagon must have known that Israel was stockpiling at a massive and costly rate. It is inconceivable that U.S. officials failed to anticipate what this stockpiling was for.

Wright's suggestion of U.S.-Israeli collaboration in the Israeli invasion of Lebanon is strongly reinforced by an article by Zeev Schiff in the Spring 1983 issue of *Foreign Policy* magazine. Schiff, defense and military editor of *Haaretz* (an Israeli newspaper considered the semi-official voice of the Begin administration), documents U.S.-Israeli contacts before the June invasion. The main point of the article is that Israel could not have conducted its war in Lebanon without full U.S. backing. It reveals high-level consultation—if not planning—between then Secretary of State Haig, Israel's then Defense Minister Ariel Sharon, and Chief of Israeli Military Intelligence Major-General Yehoshua Saguy.

Of course, nothing is more revealing of U.S. support of Begin's and Sharon's Lebanon war than the FY 83 allocation to Israel. The current proposal of $2.48 billion is actually a $300 million *increase* over the 1982 package—and the most unambiguous seal of approval possible of everything from Israel's bulldozing of the Rashidiyya and Ein al Helwa camps in the South to its encouragement of the Phalange massacres at Sabra and Chatilla.

US Goals

The goals of the U.S. military buildup in the Middle

East are concrete and visible: first, to destroy movements of national liberation like the PLO, which radicalize the region and stand in the front line against the interests of the multinationals; and second, to destabilize nationalist and anti-imperialist regimes. If the forces of national liberation should be in a position to strike a blow for their national independence in the oil-producing region, the U.S. stands ready to send the marines.

There is always the danger that conventional war will escalate into nuclear war. Today, the U.S. conventional military forces are equipped with nuclear potential. In the Middle East, they are backed up by nuclear weapons in the Mediterranean, Persian Gulf, and Indian Ocean.

A lasting and just Middle East peace is an essential requirement of our time if we are to avoid a nuclear catastrophe.

Robert Prince is the chairperson of the Middle East Task Force of the US Peace Council.

"The Soviet Union has encircled the Gulf with military strongholds and is biding its time for an opening in the center."

The USSR Threatens Middle East Peace

James A. Phillips

The recent upsurge in fighting in the Iran-Iraq war and Iran's threat to block the strategic Strait of Hormuz have focused attention on the Persian Gulf, an epicenter of world politics. Because it is the world's largest known storehouse of low-cost energy supplies, the Gulf region has acquired immense strategic value as one of the determining fulcrums of the global balance of power. The Gulf region's geopolitical importance, the kaleidoscopic nature of politics among Gulf states and the presence of volatile social and political forces within them, and the lengthening shadow of Soviet military power insure that the Gulf will remain a potentially explosive source of superpower tensions for years.

After centuries of southward expansion, Moscow is closer than ever to securing a land bridge to a warm water port. The advent of Soviet nuclear parity, the growth of Soviet power projection forces, the Iranian revolution, and the Soviet invasion of Afghanistan have altered fundamentally the strategic balance of the Gulf region. The fall of the Shah removed the American shield from Iran, sounded the death knell for the anti-Soviet CENTO alliance, and plunged Iran into chronic turmoil. This has afforded the Soviets increased opportunities to meddle in Iranian affairs and in the internal affairs of neighboring states threatened by the spillover of the Iranian revolution **The invasion of Afghanistan brought Soviet forces 400 miles closer to the Gulf, lengthened the Soviet-Iranian border by 400 miles, and gave Moscow well-positioned military and subversive bases that could** be used to intimidate, undermine, or dismember Iran and Pakistan.

In the near future, Iran is likely to be Moscow's prime target because of its proximity, relative diplomatic isolation, and internal instability. The

James A. Phillips, ''Moscow Stalks the Persian Gulf,'' *Backgrounder*, February 27, 1984. Reprinted by permission of The Heritage Foundation, 214 Massachusetts Ave. NE, Washington, DC 20002.

Soviet Union twice has attempted to swallow Iranian provinces—Gilan province in 1920 and Azerbaijan/Kurdistan in 1945-1946. Although it was forced to disgorge these occupied Iranian territories on both occasions, the story could be different today, given the marked pro-Soviet tilt in the global balance of power.

Moscow's ultimate target is Saudi Arabia. By gaining control of the kingdom's massive oil reserves, the Soviets could undermine the economic vitality of the West, split the Western alliance, and reforge the weakening energy links that help bind Eastern European satellites to the Kremlin. A pro-Soviet Saudi Arabia would be a grievous blow to Western Europe and Japan, which are dependent on Saudi oil, and to the smaller Gulf states that have looked to the Saudis for leadership in recent years.

The Soviet Union has encircled the Gulf with military bases in Afghanistan, Syria, South Yemen, and Ethiopia. A direct Soviet military thrust is unlikely, however, as long as regional trends continue to favor the Soviets and the American commitment to use force in defense of friendly Gulf states remains credible. Moscow is more likely to mount indirect threats to the Gulf in the form of opportunistic manipulation of ethnic separatist groups, local revolutionaries, and domestic political instability. In trying to deter the Soviet military threat to the Gulf, Washington should remain ready to defend its friends in the Gulf while taking care to avoid exacerbating the domestic problems of fragile Gulf polities. Washington also must stand ready to safeguard the continued flow of Gulf oil against the interference of Iran as well as the Soviet Union.

Soviet Goals

Russia was determined to push its frontiers southward for geopolitical reasons centuries before the Bolshevik revolution or the discovery of oil in the Gulf. In 1920, three years after seizing power, the

Bolsheviks organized a "Congress of the Peoples of the East" in Baku in a vain attempt to incite the Moslem world to launch a holy war against European colonial empires. The following year, however, weakened by civil war, Moscow signed a series of "friendship treaties" with Turkey, Iran, and Afghanistan, which ushered in a "period of armed truce" along its southern borders. Then, in 1940, Soviet Foreign Minister V.M. Molotov signed a secret protocol to the Hitler-Stalin pact that pledged "The area south of Batum and Baku in the general direction of the Persian Gulf is . . . the center of aspirations of the Soviet Union. . . ."

Emboldened by its military strength after World War II, Moscow prepared to carve up its southern neighbors. It demanded territorial concessions and control of the Bosphorus from Turkey and refused to withdraw from northern Iran, which it had occupied in 1941. Turkey and Iran rebuffed Soviet coercive diplomacy with the support of the United States and became key allies in the American effort to contain Soviet expansion. Having failed to subjugate the Northern Tier countries through intimidation, Moscow sought to lure them away from a strategic embrace with the West by implementing a good neighbor policy aimed at allaying their fears about Soviet imperialism.

The Soviets pursued a dual policy of cultivating good relations on the state-to-state level with its southern neighbors while backing local communist parties and other revolutionary groups. Economic development assistance was extended to buy good will and provide cover for subversion. The extensive Soviet military assistance program gave the Soviets entree into the armed forces of recipient states, an excellent position for recruiting potential coup leaders. Clandestine pro-Soviet elements in the armed forces staged an abortive coup in Sudan (1971), were purged from the armed forces of Iran (1977), Somalia (1978), and Iraq (1978), and staged successful coups in Afghanistan (1978) and South Yemen (1978).

In addition to strengthening its own influence in the Gulf region, Moscow has worked to erode U.S. influence there. It has sought to prevent local states from cooperating with Washington, pushed for the dissolution of existing alliances and agreements with the U.S., and tried to prevent new ones.

Soviet Union and Oil

The Soviet Union's long-term goals almost surely include control of the natural resources as well as the foreign policies of Gulf states. The Gulf region contains roughly 55 percent of the world's proven oil reserves, or about two-thirds of the non-communist world's oil supplies. Although Gulf oil production has fallen in recent years due to the world oil glut and the Iran-Iraq war, the Persian Gulf remains the center of gravity of the world oil trade. While the

United States has reduced significantly its dependence on Persian Gulf oil, its close allies in Europe and Japan remain vulnerable to disruptions in their supply line to the Gulf.

The establishment of Soviet hegemony over the Gulf could spell the end of the Western Alliance. Once astride the Gulf, the Soviet Union would be in a position to "Finlandize" Western Europe and Japan through economic blackmail. By becoming the arbiter of Gulf oil flows, the Soviet Union not only would gain influence over non-communist oil importers but would bolster its influence over its oil-thirsty satellites in Eastern Europe. The Kremlin has been unable to satisfy fully the oil import demands of East Germany, Poland, Czechoslovakia, Hungary, and Bulgaria over the last decade because the growth of Soviet oil production has failed to keep pace with either the growth of Soviet-bloc oil demand or the need to finance food and technology imports with foreign currency earned by selling oil to the West. If the Eastern Europeans are squeezed out of the world oil market, their economies will be hamstrung to the point where there might be an anti-Soviet political spillover. The Soviet Union probably will be forced to incur rising political, military, and economic costs to retain its East European satellites unless it can obtain adequate oil imports for them. And the Soviet Union itself may look to the Persian Gulf to fulfill its oil requirements as its own oil production reaches a plateau and declines in the late 1980s.

"The Soviet Union's long-term goals almost surely include control of the natural resources as well as the foreign policies of Gulf states."

Moscow's Indirect Strategy

Moscow so far has pursued an indirect strategy in the Gulf to avoid a direct confrontation with the United States. It has secured strongholds around the Gulf's rim in Afghanistan, Syria, South Yemen, and Ethiopia and retains residual influence in Iraq. Explains a leading expert on Soviet foreign policy: Moscow seeks to "subvert the center by radicalizing the periphery." East German and Cuban advisers safeguard the ardently pro-Soviet regime in South Yemen while the Yemenis support rebellions in neighboring Oman and North Yemen—back doors to Saudi Arabia. The communist Defense Minister of Afghanistan has indicated that the Afghan army would play a "significant role" in the future "like that played by the Cuban and Vietnamese armies."

A direct Soviet military thrust into the Gulf region cannot be ruled out and is probably more likely than a similar thrust into Western Europe. Such an operation, however, would be extremely risky because it could trigger a superpower confrontation. Moscow probably can afford to be patient, for trends in the Gulf appear to be running its way. The Iranian revolution has opened up new possibilities for Soviet probing, Saddam Hussein's Iraqi regime is tottering, and the traditional societies on the Arab side of the Gulf are beset by the destablilization born of too-rapid modernization. After demonstrating its ruthlessness in Afghanistan, Moscow does not actually have to use its military power in the Gulf to extract political benefits. The Soviet military machine casts a large political-psychological shadow that must be offset by countervailing Western power.

Soviet Threat to Iran

The opportunities for Soviet gains are highest and the risks lowest in Iran. As such, it probably will be the foremost target of Soviet meddling in the near future. The Iranian revolution has detached Iran from the U.S. security umbrella, weakened its military strength, unleashed political turbulence, and left the country internationally isolated. Soviet subjugation of Iran would inevitably lead the other Gulf states to reach an accomodation with the Kremlin.

Moscow's interest in fomenting a pro-Soviet revolution in Iran is longstanding. Communist ties to Iranian leftists predate the Bolshevik revolution. A Soviet writer speculated in 1918 that a revolution in Persia might become "the key to revolution in the whole east." In 1920, the Red Army invaded Gilan province on Iran's Caspian Sea coast and set up a Soviet Republic under Kuchek Khan. Soviet troops were withdrawn in 1921 only after Moscow had extracted a one-sided "Treaty of Friendship." Article VI of the treaty gave the Soviets the right to intervene if Iran were occupied by a third party or if Iranian territory were used as a base for "anti-Soviet aggression." A subsequent exchange of letters specified that Article VI referred only to anti-Bolshevik Russian forces, but the Soviets have constantly tried to widen the interpretation of the treaty to give themselves a pretext for intervention and to restrict the military activities of foreign powers in Iran. Although Iran has announced repeatedly the abrogation of the treaty, Moscow ominously insists that it remains in force.

In spite of a wary, correct relationship with the Shah, the Soviet Union welcomed the Iranian revolution because of its anti-American nature. Iranian opposition to Soviet imperialism, however, became a source of tension in Soviet-Iranian relations. Ayatollah Khomeini's government condemned the Soviet invasion of Afghanistan and shut down a natural gas pipeline to the Soviet Union when the Soviets refused to meet Iranian demands to raise the below market price they were paying for the gas. Moscow criticized the Iranian government for "artificially" restricting trade between the two countries but avoided criticizing Khomeini personally. The Soviets have staged troop maneuvers along the Iranian border on several occasions and maintain strong garrisons along the Afghan-Iranian border to deter Iranian "interference" in Afghanistan's "internal affairs." In early 1982, Iran shot down a Soviet helicopter that had pursued Afghan freedom fighters across the border into Iran.

Another source of tension in Soviet-Iranian relations is the ideological clash between Khomeini's militant Islamic fundamentalism and Soviet communism. Because the Soviet empire contains 40 to 45 million Moslems, Soviet leaders cannot ignore the possibility that this fast growing segment of the population will be caught up in the Islamic resurgence. Iran's Shia Moslem ideology, however, is unlikely to appeal to the predominantly Sunni Moslems in Soviet Central Asia. Even if the Iranian revolution should inspire Moslem restiveness in Central Asia, the massive Soviet police apparatus probably would have little trouble in isolating and crushing an Islamic rebellion. . . .

"Moscow's interest in fomenting a pro-Soviet revolution in Iran is longstanding."

An outright Soviet invasion of Iran cannot be ruled out, but it is unlikely as long as the military deadlock in Afghanistan persists, the U.S. Rapid Deployment Force becomes an increasingly credible deterrent, and Iranians remain unified and willing to sacrifice large numbers of lives to retain their independence.

If the Soviet Union should invade, the Iranian army and Revolutionary Guards, worn down by more than three years of war with Iraq, could not hope to repel the advance. The Soviet Army could mobilize 24 divisions along the Soviet-Iranian border with more than 200,000 men, 4,500 tanks, and 940 aircraft. Moscow could insert two of its seven airborne divisions into Iran in a matter of hours. Despite Iran's rugged terrain and limited road network, the invader's progress would undoubtedly be facilitated by the early use of paratroops, helicopter troops, and special forces to seize strategic chokepoints and transport links. Advance columns of the Soviet army could link up with air dropped elements in Tehran in one week and in Iran's oil province of Khuzistan in the upper Gulf area in as little as ten days, depending on the local opposition.

Such a bold move would be risky, given the U.S. commitment to use force to repel a Soviet attempt to gain control of the Gulf region. In addition, once they occupied the Iranian oil fields, the Soviets would be confronted with the difficult task of repairing oil production facilities and keeping them operating in the face of sabotage and aerial attack. They would be forced to occupy indefinitely a country with 35 million well-armed citizens—more than twice the population of Afghanistan—many of whom probably would be very willing to become martyrs for the Iranian revolution.

A more attractive option for Moscow would be a limited thrust into Iran, at the ''invitation'' of Iranian leftists or ethnic separatists who would collaborate with the Soviet army. Moscow could establish the military infrastructure in northern Iran that would facilitate later Soviet moves to the south. Although the Tudeh Party was decapitated in the 1983 crackdown, many of its cadres presumably escaped capture. In addition to the Tudeh, Moscow might be able to ally with some of the estimated 200,000 followers and sympathizers of various Iranian Marxist groups. . . .

Soviet Union and Iraq

Moscow and Baghdad have enjoyed a strategic marriage of convenience off and on since the 1958 Iraqi revolution. The 1969 rise to power of the Ba'ath (Renaissance) party tightened the Soviet-Iraqi strategic embrace and led to the 1972 Treaty of Friendship, which loosely affiliated Iraq with the Soviet scheme of collective security. Between 1974 and 1978, Iraq became Moscow's largest Third World arms customer, taking delivery of $3.6 billion of weapons. Soviet-Iraqi relations deteriorated after 1978 due to Iraqi displeasure over Soviet support of the April 1978 coup in Afghanistan, Soviet backing of Ethiopian attempts to ingratiate itself with Iran's revolutionary regime, and the subversive activities of the Iraqi Communist Party (ICP). In addition, the Soviets disapproved of Iraq's growing economic ties with the West, its suppression of the ICP, and its rapprochement with the moderate Arab Gulf states.

"Iraq received Soviet SS-12 ground-to-ground missiles capable of striking targets 500 miles away."

The Iran-Iraq war strained Soviet-Iraqi relations as it became clear that Moscow preferred cultivating its influence with Iran to helping Iraq. But after the Iranians crossed into Iraq in July 1982, the Soviet Union tilted toward Iraq by resuming direct arms shipments which had been halted when hostilities began. Most recently, Iraq received Soviet SS-12 ground-to-ground missiles capable of striking targets 500 miles away. Roughly 2,000 Soviet-bloc advisors work in Iraq. While Baghdad has diversified its sources of military equipment and is not as dependent on Moscow today as it was ten years ago,

the embattled Hussein regime will be hard pressed to beat back repeated Iranian offensives without strengthening its ties to the Soviets. . . .

The Arab Oil Kingdoms

After Britain announced in 1968 that its forces would withdraw from all outposts east of Suez, Moscow temporarily stopped supporting subversive activities in the Gulf for fear of delaying the British withdrawal or prompting an American buildup in the area. Once the British had withdrawn in 1971, however, it was back to business as usual. Moscow pursued its time-tested two-track strategy of trying to establish good state-to-state relations while covertly forming links with revolutionary groups. The traditional societies of the Arab Gulf states were resistant to both approaches. Most of the deeply religious ruling elites rejected diplomatic relations with Soviet atheists and the closely knit tribal social structures rendered revolutionary activities difficult.

Kuwait was the only Arab Gulf kingdom to establish diplomatic relations with the Soviet Union, probably to buy insurance against Iraqi territorial claims. The Soviet Embassy in Kuwait quickly became Moscow's listening post on the Arab side of the Gulf. Moscow persistently has courted Saudi Arabia in an effort to reestablish diplomatic links that were suspended before World War II, but Riyadh has not yet succumbed.

The steep climb of oil prices in the mid-1970s and the subsequent influx of wealth into the Gulf states ushered in a period of rapid modernization that has become intrinsically destabilizing. The authority and legitimacy of traditional political systems has been undermined by rapid urbanization, social change, and cultural disorientation. The quantum jumps in oil income fueled an economic boom that attracted several million foreign workers, which further disoriented the indigenous populations. This gave the USSR potential allies in fomenting revolution in the Gulf.

Because of these trends, Moscow believes that time is on its side in the Gulf. Almost any change in government in the Gulf would be an improvement from Moscow's standpoint. It is not known to what extent the Soviets have penetrated the armed forces of the Gulf states, but it is known that they have made serious efforts. For example, Saudi officers who served with the Arab peacekeeping force in Lebanon in the mid-1970s were approached by Syrian agents of the KGB seeking to build a ''Nasserist'' faction in the Saudi army. . . .

Kuwait and Bahrain are perhaps the Gulf states most vulnerable to subversion. More than half of Kuwait's inhabitants are non-Kuwaitis, 30 to 40 percent are Shiites who are disproportionately represented in the poorer economic strata, and roughly 20 percent are Palestinians. Close to 15 percent of Bahrain's population is non-Arab, mainly of Iranian descent. An abortive Iranian backed coup in December 1981 was believed to have been masterminded by an Iranian revolutionary thought to have connections with the KGB. Though the outlawed National Liberation Front of Bahrain is reluctant to proclaim itself a communist party, it is treated as one in Soviet-sponsored international conferences.

Soviet Union and South Yemen

The only self-avowed Marxist state in the Arab world is South Yemen, an important Soviet strategic outpost on the southern tip of the Arabian peninsula. Together with pro-Soviet Ethiopia, South Yemen dominates the mouth of the Red Sea. The South Yemenis have transformed their country into a military base, terrorist training ground, and staging area for Soviet-bloc forces. Moscow has been given a naval base in the Perim Islands, access to the port of Aden, and an anchorage off the island of Socotra. Soviet aerial reconnaissance planes conduct long-range surveillance missions in the Indian Ocean from bases in South Yemen. Two Soviet MiG-25 squadrons use Yemeni airfields and Cuban, North Korean, and East German pilots operate with the Yemeni Air Force.

"Approximately 5,000 Soviet-bloc advisors control the Yemeni armed forces."

Approximately 5,000 Soviet-bloc advisors control Yemeni armed forces and civil service bureaucracies. The East Germans run South Yemen's secret police, while the Cubans provide the backbone for a praetorian guard that shields the regime from its own people. Under Soviet guidance, South Yemen has become an international clearinghouse for terrorism. The Popular Front for the Liberation of Palestine (PFLP), a Marxist Palestinian splinter group, operates terrorist training bases in which Soviet-bloc advisors as well as Palestinians train a wide variety of terrorists from around the world.

South Yemen is Saudi Arabia's back door. The South Yemenis host leaders of the Communist Party of Saudi Arabia, Palestinian groups hostile to Riyadh's traditional leadership, and Saudi dissidents. According to Western European intelligence sources, 70 of the 500 men who seized the Grand Mosque in Mecca in 1979 were trained by Cubans with Soviet supervision at the PFLP camp in South Yemen. During the uprising, the South Yemeni army was mobilized along the Saudi border "apparently poised to intervene on the pretext of defending the Holy Places if the revolt showed signs of success."

South Yemen is also a threat to the stability of North Yemen, which it has battled time and again over the years. Saudi Arabia fears that the South Yemenis will succeed in realizing their long-standing goal of unifying the two Yemens under Marxist leadership. Such a state would have almost twice the population of Saudi Arabia and could foment instability within Saudi Arabia by harnessing its more than one million Yemeni guest workers. The Saudis also fear that a united Yemen, backed by Soviet military aid, would attempt to retake territories ceded to Saudi Arabia under the resented 1934 Taif Treaty....

U.S. Policy and the Soviet Threat

When the British withdrew from east of Suez in 1971, the United States came to depend on the two pillars of Iran and to a lesser extent Saudi Arabia to guard stability in the Persian Gulf. Skyrocketing oil prices enabled the Shah to undertake a massive military buildup, but rapid modernization triggered economic dislocations and an Islamic backlash that led to his downfall. The 1979 Soviet invasion of Afghanistan gave rise to the Carter Doctrine, which proclaimed U.S. willingness to resort to military force to protect the Persian Gulf.

The U.S. Rapid Deployment Force (RDF) was formed to give teeth to U.S. policy. Its purpose is to deter a Soviet intervention in the Gulf by raising the costs and risks of such a move. The RDF faces three problems: inadequate strength, mobility, and access to bases in the Gulf region. The first problem is a function of the second, which is in turn complicated by the third. The Persian Gulf is 7,000 miles from the United States and only 1,100 miles from the Soviet border. To offset this geographical disadvantage, the Pentagon has stockpiled military supplies in the area and is working to upgrade its long-range aircraft and rapid sealift capabilities....

The threat posed by the Soviet Union to the Persian Gulf region is greater than ever because of its improved power projection capabilities, the erosion of Northern Tier barriers to Soviet access to the region, and Moscow's many opportunities to exploit local instability. The Soviet Union has encircled the Gulf with military strongholds and is biding its time for an opening in the center. Given the prevailing trends, the Soviets have little reason to rely on brute military force to kick open Gulf doors—these doors may be opened for them from the inside.

In defending the various houses of the Persian Gulf, the United States must not only keep an eye on the approaches to the Gulf but also be aware of activities within Gulf states. Washington should work as hard to secure the basement windows of Gulf houses against Soviet trespassing as it does to bar the front doors.

James A. Phillips is a senior policy analyst for Middle Eastern affairs for The Heritage Foundation.

"The Administration's major mistake was to pull the Lebanese out of the Israeli embrace and dump them on the Syrian mercy."

US Failure in Lebanon: An American View

Lally Weymouth

Today the situation in Lebanon represents not only the Reagan Administration's worst foreign-policy defeat, but also a serious setback for American policy in the Middle East.

Yet a sizeable number of Lebanese, including at least one member of Gemayel's own government, as well as Israeli and American diplomats and policy-makers now insist that things might have turned out differently for the United States had Washington not intervened and offered Gemayel a way to avoid signing a separate peace treaty with Israel.

Abdallah Bouhabib, Lebanon's ambassador to the United States, put it this way: "The truth is that in the summer of '82, we did not have a choice. Israel was the only force on the ground, and if the United States had not come into Lebanon, it would have been difficult, if not impossible, not to have signed a peace treaty with Israel."

A high-ranking Israeli official who was intimately involved in the Lebanese negotiations claimed, "It could have been very different if they had gone along with us. It [a separate peace] could have worked. They could have gone for the May 17 type of thing, but enforced it. Syria was licking its wounds. I think all the Lebanese would have accepted it, including the Muslims. They don't want Syrian domination. They want Lebanese independence, which they won't have now. The Syrians have demanded the most fantastic things, cancelling all sorts of decisions that were taken over the past two years, firing various people in high office who are not pro-Syrian, saying who is going to be prime minister and who is going to represent the various communities at the Geneva conference. They are giving the orders."

But American intervention was not the only reason an Israeli-Lebanese treaty failed to materialize in

1982. Another was the assassination of then-Lebanese President Bashir Gemayel. His brother and successor, Amin, didn't have the long history of cooperation with the Israelis that Bashir had. Indeed, Amin had never had much sympathy for Israel.

Still, the United States played a crucial role in the treaty's demise, encouraging Gemayel, as one State Department expert said, "not to make a deal with the Israelis. Psychologically the Israelis were in bad odor [in Washington] because of the invasion. We were very irritated at them because they had invaded and made a mess of it."

The weight of this opinion was brought to bear on Gemayel in October, 1982, when he arrived in Washington for his first state visit.

He was visited in his suite at the Madison Hotel by Robert Basil, a Lebanese-American who had been friendly with his brother Bashir and who also had good contacts with the Israelis. Basil brought Gemayel a message from Moshe Arens, then Israeli ambassador to the United States.

As Basil recalled recently in his Washington office, Arens' message was blunt: "Israel wanted a peace treaty with Lebanon. If Israel did not achieve that treaty, then Israel could unilaterally initiate a course of events in Lebanon which could lead to the collapse of the Lebanese government." For example, Basil said, Arens pointed out that Israel would probably withdraw to the Zahrani River and would do nothing to help the Lebanese government hold the land it evacuated. According to other Lebanese sources, Arens also offered an incentive—an Israeli promise to expel the Syrians from Lebanon.

But the United States opposed an Israeli-Lebanese treaty. According to Bouhabib, "They, like many Lebanese, gave plenty of reasons why Lebanon should not sign a treaty with Israel: economic (the possibility of a boycott by other Arab states), sectarian divisions, Arab identity."

"A full peace treaty was too ambitious," explained

a former U.S. official, who at that time was one of the principal American negotiators. "It would have created a revolution in the Arab world against Gemayel." Another U.S. official, currently working on Lebanon, told me that in the fall of 1982, "a deal with Israel was not considered a prudent move. We were angry with the Israelis, angry over the invasion, angry over Chatilla and Sabra. We were in no mood to hand [then-Israeli Prime Minister Menachem] Begin the spoils of his victory. Undoubtedly, there could have been a separate peace but would that peace have resulted in an independent Lebanon?"

Diplomatic Moves

At Washington's Madison Hotel, Gemayel met with his advisers. They were worried by the Israeli threats Arens had conveyed, but pleased by the U.S. attention. Gemayel decided to reject the idea of a treaty with Israel and to put Lebanon's fate in American hands.

"By the time we got to negotiations, the Syrians were strong enough to be able not to withdraw."

At that moment, according to participants, then-American Middle East negotiator Philip Habib, rather than Secretary of State Shultz, was actually formulating and executing U.S. policy in the region. Habib refused to be interviewed either on or off the record and, therefore, this account of his activities is pieced together from conversations with others.

Habib and his assistant, Morris Draper, would send recommendations to the White House which would in turn be funneled back to them as orders from the State Department. "He had pretty much a free hand to do what he wanted to," said one government official, speaking of Habib.

Habib and Draper declared their priority was to get the Syrians and Israelis out of Lebanon. "Habib kept saying the Syrians are going to leave—don't worry about it," recalled one U.S. official. Believing he could trust Syrian statements and Saudi promises that Syria would withdraw, Habib felt secure in turning his full attention to getting the Israeli troops out of Lebanon.

Robin Raphel, an assistant to Under Secretary of State Lawrence S. Eagleburger, says she believes the crucial U.S. mistake was overlooking the problem of the Syrians: "The Syrians said they would withdraw, but they meant all other things being equal."

Habib and Draper, proud of their success in securing the evacuation of the Palestine Liberation Organization from Beirut, wanted another success. They were pleased that "Lebanon was ready to be the second Arab country to sit down with the

Israelis." They scheduled Israeli-Lebanese talks for Nov. 7, but weeks elapsed before the talks actually got under way.

By this time, Lebanon and the West Bank had become linked as issues and Jordan's King Hussein had made foreign troop withdrawals from Lebanon a precondition to action on the Reagan plan. As a result, while Habib, the Israelis and the Lebanese haggled over that issue, the Syrians had a chance to rearm and the Reagan plan dropped from view.

In December, then-Israeli Defense Minister Ariel Sharon let leak to the press that he had negotiated a secret agreement between Israel and Lebanon. "When Habib found out about it he went ballistic," Basil recalled. "He demanded President Gemayel not sign it."

Habib's Anger

Although one of Habib's close associates denies the story, a senior Israeli official also claimed that when Habib discovered the existence of the Sharon treaty, "he shouted his head off. He was furious and more or less said [to Gemayel], 'How do you dare do this behind our back? You're going to ruin yourself. You must not go with the Israelis that way.'"

However, Habib's associate claims that Sharon "stalled on the overt talks to make good on the covert talks. He tried to work a deal that would make him a great national hero."

But another American official disagreed. "Had Sharon not stupidly leaked, they might have gotten it [an Israeli-Lebanese treaty]."

Just how different in substance was the agreement Shultz got on May 17 from the one Sharon engineered in December? There were only slight differences between the two, according to one highly placed Israeli official, who added, "If Philip Habib had shut up, it would have saved five months of negotiations, and that would have given us and the Lebanese the possibility to go ahead. In those five months, the Syrians were able to strengthen themselves and the whole situation changed. That's the key. By the time we got to negotiations, the Syrians were strong enough to be able not to withdraw and to terrorize large sections of the population."

After Habib and Draper failed, Shultz took personal charge and pushed through the agreement that became known as the May 17 accord. But that agreement was unacceptable to Syrian President Assad, because, as he told *The Times* in an interview last summer, it ratified the Israelis' gains in Lebanon.

An American official admitted that "without American pressure, Amin Gemayel never would have signed the May 17 agreement which led to the position he's in today. Having persuaded him to sign it, we should have been better prepared to deliver and deal with the Syrians. We didn't do a good enough job, either diplomatically or militarily. Our promises had a hollow ring. We did not give enough attention when the groundwork was being laid for the agreement to parallel talks with Syria to see if they'd cooperate. Everyone agrees that Syria was important and we should do something, and no one did anything."

Arens' message to Gemayel had warned of a unilateral Israeli withdrawal, and by last July Israel was ready to pull its troops out of the Shouf Mountains and station them south of the Awwali River.

According to Bouhabib, "They withdrew after declining a request from the U.S. government to postpone their withdrawal for another week."

Israeli Delays

The Israelis had already delayed their withdrawal twice, but Bouhabib believes that negotiations then under way in Paris between Druze leader Walid Jumblatt and the government would have been successfully completed if the Israelis had remained in place one more week.

Moreover, according to a former U.S. official, David Kimche, the director of the Israeli Foreign Office, who was Israel's chief negotiator for the May 17 accord, came to Washington early last summer and offered to coordinate the withdrawal from the Shouf, using Draper as a middleman. "The Israelis offered to coordinate everything," said this official, who is not known to be especially sympathetic to Israel.

In the Israeli magazine *Koteret Rasheet,* Israeli negotiator Uri Lubrani was recently quoted as saying "Israel made every attempt to coordinate its withdrawal with the government of the U.S. and of Amin Gemayel." Lubrani described a visit by Arens to Beirut during which the defense minister had hoped that Gemayel would meet him to request that Israeli forces not withdraw from the Shouf. Lubrani says that Arens would have held up the redeployment if Gemayel had asked him to, but he remarked that "Travolta" or "the Hairdresser," as Gemayel is contemptuously known in some parts of Beirut, merely condemned the Arens visit. The Israelis withdrew, and, concludes Lubrani, "After that events happened like a Greek tragedy. One of the tragedies is that Amin Gemayel is president."

As American efforts faltered, a Lebanese diplomat wrote to Gemayel and reminded him that the late Egyptian President Anwar Sadat's first visit to Jerusalem had been undertaken in defiance of U.S. wishes. Therefore, the diplomat believes, the Israeli option was still open. In part, his letter to Gemayel read, "No U.S. Administration can oppose direct talks between Israel and any Arab government for the purpose of peace." The Israelis, he told Gemayel, still wanted direct relations. He blamed the Saudis for trying to block such a step, adding, "They probably dislike Israel more than the Palestinians. They always look sympathetic to Lebanon and tilt toward the Syrians."

Later, in an interview, this diplomat also questioned the motives of some members of the State Department's Near Eastern Affairs (NEA) section in blocking direct Israeli-Lebanese ties: "I don't know anyone at NEA who is sympathetic to Israel—a desk officer on his first assignment, maybe."

America's Role Changes

In September, 1983, during the battle at Souq el Gharb between Lebanese government and opposition forces, America's role in Lebanon decisively changed. The U.S. military commander received a message from the Lebanese army, saying that it would run out of ammunition in 20 minutes. He had to decide whether to resupply the army or not. His decision to go to the aid of the Lebanese put the United States in the position of defending the Christian-dominated government, thus incurring the wrath of opposition Muslim groups.

The State Department and National Security Council were in favor of using force to sustain the Gemayel government, whereas Defense Secretary Caspar W. Weinberger was never enthusiastic about an expanded U.S. role in Lebanon. "I thought our goals were the way to go," one supporter of the policy told me, adding bitterly, "But the Pentagon didn't seek to implement the policy and sought to subvert it."

The remaining key events in the Lebanese saga are well known—the terrorist bombing of the Marine headquarters and the fierce domestic political backlash that eventually lead to their pullout.

Among Reagan Administration policy-makers the whole affair has left a bitter residue of recrimination. At a National Security Council meeting held just after the decision to evacuate the Marines, the acrimony burst into the open when Shultz turned to Weinberger, the man he believed had undercut him in Lebanon, and said, "Remind me never, never, never to ask for the marines again."

"The American failure in Lebanon could have unpleasant long-term repercussions."

According to an account in the authoritative newsletter *Middle East Policy Survey*, Shultz continued, saying that in the future, if he wanted a policy to succeed, he would be sure to advocate the opposite position. That way, he could be sure the Pentagon would oppose him, and, in the end, he would get his own way.

One former high-ranking U.S. official said that in retrospect the Administration's major mistake was "to pull the Lebanese out of the Israeli embrace and dump them on the Syrian mercy."

Looking back over the last 18 months, Bouhabib said sadly, "We opted for what is called the American option—which is to have peace with Israel without calling it peace and remain a member of the Arab family. We thought it was done because a superpower had committed itself to the goal—our objective of liberating a small democracy from all foreign forces. We didn't see the limitations of the superpower. The option we opted for was a mirage, not an option," he said bitterly. "The U.S. can protect us from another superpower but not from a regional power like Israel or Syria. The U.S. is not ready to escalate the battle to the degree Syria is."

Syrian Hegemony

I got an example of this perception's impact when I spoke with a Maronite politician who had told me on several occasions during the last year that he favored an Israeli-Lebanese treaty. Last week, he was singing another tune: "We will coordinate very well with the Syrians," he said. "Syria trusts Amin Gemayel to be its main ally in Lebanon. They'll back Amin Gemayel. Syria has hegemony over our foreign policy."

The American failure in Lebanon could have unpleasant long-term repercussions. One former U.S. official who conducted many of the Lebanese negotiations said, "The people responsible for the terrorism against the Marines, the people who killed Malcolm Kerr [head of the American University in Beirut] must be overjoyed. Some of these guys are going after the American presence. They want to knock out the American presence in the Middle East. The next 10 years will be murder," he said, "a real escalation of terror."

Lally Weymouth is a free-lance writer who specializes in the Mideast.

US Failure in Lebanon: A Soviet View

Yuri Gudkov

Hearings in the House Appropriations Subcommittee on Foreign Operations are not usually top news. However, reports on a recent sitting of the subcommittee broke into front-page headlines. The reason: an unusual altercation between the Secretary of State and Congressmen.

The issue in dispute was not appropriations. George Shultz, ordinarily level-headed and imperturbable, lost his temper because of a remark about the need for talks among all the sides concerned in search of solutions to problems such as that of El Salvador. "I don't assume any special outcome to the negotiations, but I think there should be a willingness to talk," Representative David Obey observed. In the opinion of the Secretary of State such an approach was tantamount to "power-sharing" with forces not to Washington's taste and therefore inadmissible. This contention was angrily rebuffed by the legislators. If it is borne in mind that the heated exchange took place when several members of the subcommittee, David Obey among them, told the Secretary of State that U.S. policy in Lebanon had "failed because it was unrealistic," it will be seen that it was not a matter of secondary issues, but of principle, of a choice between negotiations and reliance on armed force.

Washington's Dilemma

Shultz's outburst not only showed how painful the topic of Lebanon is for members of the Reagan Administration. It also reflected the moods still prevalent in official Washington.

The redeployment of the U.S. Marines from the territory of the Beirut airport to ships 30 miles off the Lebanese coast was completed on March 18. The Marines should have been put on shipboard and the

Yuri Gudkov, "The Intervention in Lebanon: Anatomy of a Failure," *New Times*, March 1984. Reprinted by permission.

whole squadron sent to San Francisco, one Senator observed. But this, as is known, did not happen. More, immediately after the announcement of the withdrawal of the Marines on February 7, orders were issued for strikes from air and sea at the positions of the Druses, Shiites and the Syrian troops. On February 8 the battleship New Jersey fired 16-inch, one-ton shells for nearly ten hours straight. This was the most massive shelling since the U.S. "peacemakers" arrived in Lebanon. The casualty toll still remains to be counted up. Newsmen who went to the village of Btibyat 15 miles from the coast reported the inhabitants of the place had no weapons except a few shotguns. Nevertheless, the village suffered at least eight hits by the New Jersey shells.

In the opinion of the local press, the unprecedentedly heavy shelling was another attempt to impose a "settlement" in Lebanon on American terms. The idea was that Israel would join in the operation in conformity with its "strategic agreement" with the United States. On February 7, the U.S. Ambassador to Israel met with Prime Minister Itzhak Shamir and Defence Minister Moshe Arens. During the talk, which lasted an hour and a half, the Jerusalem correspondent of *Washington Post* reported, Israel made it plain that it was prepared to consider limited military operations in Lebanon, "but only if the United States acted first." A high-ranking Israeli spokesman said that "we are convinced that if the U.S. would shell the Druse and Shiite positions, it could change the mood in Lebanon."

Washington had claimed that the air force and naval guns were used exclusively to "protect" the Marines, and not to intervene in Lebanon's internal affairs. Now the Marines have been relieved of their "auxiliary role." U.S. Navy Secretary John Lehman hastened to dispel whatever doubts still remained on this score. "There very definitely has been a shift in emphasis to make it clear that we will be providing supporting fire to the Lebanese armed forces. That is not linked to specific incoming fire against the Marines at the airport." After it seized part of Lebanon's territory, Israel likewise repeatedly had recourse to air raids and artillery fire, but did not venture to launch operations on a larger scale. Open intervention, the *Washington Post* observed, turned out to be too risky an undertaking "because of the strong domestic pressure in both countries against becoming more deeply involved in Lebanon."

Marines in Lebanon

The U.S. press is trying to depict the withdrawal of the Marines from their land positions as a concession to public opinion in an election year. True enough, most Americans are opposed to military gambles in Lebanon, which is something the Administration is not happy about. But the trouble goes deeper than that. Two special commissions, one appointed by the House of Representatives and the other by the Administration, have called for a revision of policy. Moreover, one of the commissions, headed by retired Admiral Robert Long, has specially underscored the need for "a more vigorous and demanding approach to pursuing diplomatic alternatives." In the House of Representatives and the Senate draft resolutions demanding the immediate withdrawal of the Marines found wide support. The Administration's efforts to present the situation in Lebanon in a favourable light failed. Asked by a newsman whether the official optimism was credible, Congressman Augustus Hawkins replied: "It all depends on whether you believe in fairy tales." Senate Republican majority leader Howard Baker, known to be a loyal Reagan man, found it necessary to warn the White House that unless there was a change of policy a head-on clash with Congress was inevitable. Things came to a point when even the Pentagon figured among the dissenters. By that time 265 U.S. servicemen had been killed and 134 wounded, and the cost had run to $120 million. The war office evidently did not care to assume responsibility for obviously unjustifiable losses.

In this connection one Pentagon spokesman pointed out that for a "military solution" 1,800 Marines were not enough; at least 100,000 troops were needed. But who can guarantee what the consequences would be, and what to do about an openly hostile public opinion? In rebuttal of the "hot heads," the *New York Times* wrote: "Theoretically, the U.S. could occupy the country [this assumption led to the fiasco in Vietnam—Y.G.]. It took 100,000 Israeli troops to reach as far as Beirut and one third of the Bekaa Valley. But they haven't been able to pacify even the limited southern area they now patrol. Hundreds of thousands of Americans would have to be committed to a serious effort to impose peace, and the chance of success would be poor. Lebanon is not an island. That is no real choice."

The most persistent advocate of the use of armed force turned out to be Secretary of State Shultz, a fact which actually caused friction even with Defense Secretary Weinberger. The principle of using force or the threat of force is a tacit but integral element of the agreement between Israel and Lebanon, of which Shultz was one of the authors. The Secretary of State's bellicosity follows from, or, to be more exact, is a component of Washington diplomacy.

Aggressive Diplomacy

Lebanon became the direct target of this diplomacy after the Israeli intervention in summer 1982. Washington saw this aggression as creating the conditions for the continuation of the Camp David process—for the subordination of one more Arab country to U.S.-Israeli dictates by means of a separate deal. Needless to say, the Palestine problem remained, as before, the stumbling block. Reagan's "peace plan" which appeared in the autumn of that same year envisaged the imposition of the American "solution": no independent Palestinian state, but "association" of the Arab people of Palestine with Jordan, and the virtual perpetuation of the Israeli occupation of the West Bank and the Gaza Strip. The plan was obviously built on sand. It was left hanging in the air as soon as Jordan refused to be a party to the shameful deal. Whereupon Shultz went to the Middle East to make use of the "favourable situation" created by the Israeli invasion of Lebanon and to resuscitate the U.S. initiative.

"By that time 265 US servicemen had been killed and 134 wounded."

The agreement between Lebanon and Israel dictated by the latter and signed on May 17 last year was, according to Shultz, a "landmark" on the way to the "stabilization" of the situation in Lebanon. It recorded the commitment by the sides "to respect the sovereignty, political independence and territorial integrity of each other," and to "consider the existing international boundary between Lebanon and Israel inviolable." Further, the sides confirmed that the state of war between them had been "terminated." Washington's duplicity as an author of the agreement was glaringly revealed by the fact that Lebanon's "integrity and independence" were proclaimed when the country was occupied by the Israeli army and U.S. Navy guns were trained on it.

The American press burst into enthusiastic eulogies of both Shultz and the agreement. Two circumstances, however, gave rise to disquiet. First, most Lebanese and the leaders of such communities as the Druses, Shiites and even part of the Maronite Christians did not accept the "solution" forced on the country. Second, the status of the Syrian troops stationed in Lebanon remained unclear. The agreement provided for the simultaneous withdrawal of both the Syrian and Israeli forces. But Syria rejected the idea inasmuch as its troops were there at the invitation of the Lebanese government and equating them with the occupying army would have meant acceptance of Israel's aggression and expansionist policy. Shultz, however, counted on Israeli and U.S. military pressure being enough to bring things to a conclusion. So did the U.S. President, who said at his February 22 press conference that the idea of sending the Marines to Lebanon originated wholly with him.

Syria's Aims

Syria wants Lebanon to be a truly independent country with a really representative government because only such a Lebanon can stand up to Israel's expansionist policy, which threatens Syria as well. This rules out Lebanon accepting the role of a vassal of the United States and Israel. On the other hand, the U.S. attempts to install a "suitable" government in Lebanon in total disregard of the interests of all the sides concerned and to bolster it up with a hastily trained and armed army were doomed to fail. As one American newsman reported from Beirut, "Lebanon cannot be ruled by the whip alone for any length of time. This country is made up of 16 different religious communities and twice as many political trends. It has always been ruled by compromise. Lebanon has worked as a country only when a carefully balanced concensus has been achieved between all these different interests."

"I now realize that the principles mean nothing to the United States."

In the end Washington blamed its setbacks on Syria, and went over from intimidation and threats to open confrontation. Again there was war in the air. At a White House conference Shultz insisted that Syria would understand only the language of force and that the heavier the pressure on it the more pliable it would be at the negotiating table. U.S. Intelligence was actually instructed to keep an eye on the connection between Syria's diplomatic behaviour and the strikes from air and sea at the zone held by its troops. When no such connection was found, Shultz dismissed the findings as invalid. A massive air raid on Syrian positions in the Bekaa Valley was made as the first major move in exerting pressure on Syria. The loss of three aircraft, however, came as a complete surprise. It gave rise to criticism of the Pentagon and increased opposition to Administration policy among the public and in Congress. From that

moment the Washington design began to fall apart.

The decision to redeploy the Marines and intensify the shelling of Lebanese territory was contained in a National Security Council directive of January 26. On February 1, Reagan endorsed it "in principle." The official announcement came on February 7. In such cases the President usually addresses the nation over TV and radio. This time he okayed the text of the announcement enroute by air from Las Vegas to Port Mugu, from where, avoiding newsmen, he left by helicopter for his ranch. Shultz went to the Bahamas for a "short holiday." Other officials refused to comment. This was a tacit admission of the failure of a policy that for 18 months had been served up as the only way to "peace and stability" in Lebanon and that had taken a no small casualty toll.

US Miscalculations

On March 5, the Lebanese government officially denounced the agreement with Israel which only recently had been described as Shultz's main diplomatic accomplishment. "Progress towards a Mideast peace settlement probably is impossible without Syria's involvement," the *U.S. News and World Report* observed. Ten days later another blow fell. In an effort to revive Reagan's "peace plan," Washington had persistently worked to involve one more Arab country, Jordan, in talks with Israel. At the same time attempts were made to set up in Jordan with American participation an 8,000-man special duty corps for operations in the Persian Gulf area. But on March 14, King Hussein in an interview to the *New York Times* ruled out any talks with Israel in the immediate future. The U.S., he said, could not act as a mediator in the Middle East because of its one-sided support of Israel. "I am very concerned about the United States and its double standard everywhere," he said. "I have always believed values and courageous principles were an area that we shared. I now realize that the principles mean nothing to the United States."

Why has Washington miscalculated so badly? The history of U.S.-Israeli interference in Lebanon shows that the underlying reason is the blind faith in the omnipotence of armed force and the disregard for the realities of the present-day world that are so characteristic of the Reagan Administration. According to the New York news analyst Tom Wicker, the "real reason for keeping the Marines in Lebanon was to rebuff Syria, and hence, its powerful backer, the Soviet Union. This was in his [the President's] familiar pattern of 'standing tall' against the Russians and sending the world a 'signal' of military strength."

However, here is something that strikes the eye. Defence Secretary Weinberger has said that if need be the Marines could be used again in the same role as before. He has notified Congress that the Pentagon intends to ask for $250-$300 million for "military aid'' to Lebanon. The Administration also proposes to increase appropriations for the establishment and expansion of military bases in the Persian Gulf, the Indian Ocean, the Mediterranean, and the Caribbean by half as much again in the next fiscal year. Washington still banks on armed force, even though Lebanon has already gone down in history as ''Ronald Reagan's Bay of Pigs.''

Yuri Gudkov is a correspondent and staff analyst for New Times, *a Soviet weekly magazine of world affairs.*

organizations

Ad Hoc Group on US Policy Toward the UN
165 E. 56th St.,
New York, NY 10022
(212) 222-3776

The Group discusses and comments on US affairs, particularly in reference to US policy and its effects on the UN. It urges the US to reassess its policy toward the UN. The group acknowledges the usefulness of the UN as a forum for carrying out US foreign policy, but suggests the US turn to other nations or act independently when necessary, as in cases where "the United Nations sometimes heightened world tensions." The group publishes reports.

American Committee On Africa
198 Broadway
New York, NY 10038
(212) 962-1210

The Committee was formed to support actively the freedom of the African people and to stop all aid from the United States that would strengthen South African minority regimes. It publishes a semiannual report and other miscellaneous pamphlets.

Americanism Educational League
P.O. Box 5986
Buena Park, CA 90622
(714) 828-5040

The League, founded in 1927, campaigns on behalf of private ownership of property, strong national defense, strict crime control and limited government conducted within balanced budgets. It periodically publishes position papers and pamphlets on national defense issues.

American Enterprise Institute for Policy Research
1150 17th St. NW
Washington, DC 20036
(202) 862-5800

The Institute is a conservative think tank that researches a number of issues, including foreign policy and defense.

American Friends Service Committee
1501 Cherry St.
Philadelphia, PA 19102
(215) 241-7000

The Religious Society of Friends (Quakers) founded the Committee in 1917, but it is supported and staffed by individuals of all major denominations. Its purpose is to relieve human suffering and to find new approaches to world peace and nonviolent social change. It is a co-recipient of the Nobel Peace Prize.

American Security Council Foundation
Washington Communications Center
Box 8
Boston, VA 22713
(703) 547-1776

The Foundation is an educational institution created by several national organizations and private institutions as a specialized educational service center to further public understanding of the "basic foundations of American strength and freedom, the Communist challenge to American freedom and how a free society can meet the Communist challenge." It publishes the quarterly *International Security Review*, the *Quarterly Strategic Bibliography*, as well as handbooks, studies, and documentary films.

Americans for Democratic Action
1411 K St. NW, Suite 850
Washington, DC 20005
(202) 638-6447

ADA works in sustained political and legislative action to help formulate and achieve significant social change through government action. It promotes progressive legislation by being actively involved in politics and political campaigns.

America's Watch Committee
Fund for Free Expression
36 W. 44th St.
New York, NY 10036
(212) 840-9460

The Committee monitors and promotes the observance of human rights in the Western Hemisphere. It publishes the *America's Watch Report*, as well as reports on various Central American countries. Write for a list of publications.

Association on Third World Affairs
1740 R St. NW
Washington, DC 20009
(202) 265-7929

The association promotes cooperation between Americans and groups in developing countries. It publishes the bimonthly *Third World Forum*.

The Brookings Institution
1775 Massachusetts Ave. NW
Washington, DC 20036
(202) 797-6000

The Institution, founded in 1927, is an independent organization devoted to non-partisan research, education and publication in the fields of economics, government and foreign policy. It publishes the quarterly *Brookings Review*, the biannual, *Brookings Papers on Economic Activity*, and an annual report.

Campaign For UN Reform
600 Valley Rd.
Wayne, NJ 07470
(201) 694-6333

The purpose of the Campaign is to make UN reform a major political issue in the US by lobbying, electing congressional candidates committed to UN reform, and rating representatives and senators on their votes on elected "global statesman" issues. It supports a program to overcome existing weaknesses in the UN system. It publishes the quarterly, *UN Reform Campaigner.*

Cardinal Mindszenty Foundation
P.O. Box 11321
St. Louis, MO 63105
(314) 991-2939

This anti-communist organization was founded in 1958 to conduct educational and research activities concerning communist objectives, tactics and propaganda through study groups, speakers, conferences and films. It publishes the monthly *Mindszenty Report.*

The Center of Concern
3700 13th St. NE
Washington, DC 20017
(202) 635-2757

The Center is an independent, interdisciplinary team engaged in social analysis, religious reflection, and public education focusing on international social justice. It publishes the bimonthly newsletter *Center Focus* which is available free of charge by writing to the organization.

Center for Defense Information
600 Maryland Ave. SW, Suite 303 West
Washington, DC 20024
(202) 484-9490

The Center for Defense Information supports a strong defense but opposes excessive expenditures for weapons and policies that increase the danger of nuclear war. It believes that strong social, economic and political structures contribute equally to national security and are essential to the strength and welfare of our country.

Center for Information on America
P.O. Box 276
Washington, CT 06793
(203) 868-2602

The Center is devoted to furthering public understanding of America's self-governing process and the issues the country faces in continuing the successful operation of democracy. It publishes *Vital Issues.*

Center for International Policy
120 Maryland Ave. NE
Washington, DC
(202) 544-4666

The Center, founded in 1975, analyzes the impact of US foreign policies on human rights and social and economic conditions in the Third World. It publishes its research findings in *International Policy Report* and *Indochina Issues.*

Center for Philosophy and Public Policy
Woods Hall Room 0123
University of Maryland
College Park, MD 20742
(301) 454-4103

The Center examines topics expected to be important issues of public policy debate over the next decade. The research is conducted cooperatively by interdisciplinary working groups composed of philosophers, policymakers and analysts. This diversity permits comprehensive examination of the major aspects of the complex issues investigated. It publishes a monthly monograph.

Center for the Study of Foreign Affairs
1400 Key Blvd.
Arlington, VA 22209
(703) 235-8830

The Center's objectives are to coordinate and encourage foreign affairs research; to improve the relevance of such research to the Department of State; to conduct interdisciplinary studies on international democratic institutions. Write to the Center for a list of publications.

Central America Information Center
P.O. Box 4797
Berkeley, CA 94704
(415) 843-5041

The Center is dedicated to the study of US relations with El Salvador and Central America. Its objective is to contribute to the public understanding of the situation through publications and projects. It publishes the monthly *El Salvador Bulletin*, and has published the book *United States and El Salvador: Political and Military Involvement.*

Central America Resource Center
1701 Unversity Ave. SE
Minneapolis, MN 55414
(612) 379-8799

The Center is an organization dedicated to justice for the people of Central America. "We support their right to determine their own future, and we recognize the need for fundamental economic, political, and social change." They believe US policy must be changed to one which respects the basic rights and need of the Central American people.

Central Intelligence Agency
Office of Public Affairs
Washington, DC 20505
(703) 351-7676 Office

Write for a list of publications.

Christian Anti-Communist Crusade
P.O. Box 890
227 E. Sixth St.
Long Beach, CA 90801
(213) 437-0941

The Crusade, founded in 1953, sponsors anti-subversive seminars "to inform Americans of the philosophy, morality, organization, techniques and strategy of communism and associated forces." Its newsletter, published semi-monthly, is free.

Clergy and Laity Concerned
198 Broadway
New York, NY 10038
(212) 964-6730

The group is concerned with human rights and racial justice. It publishes the *CALC Report* and various books.

Coalition for a New Foreign and Military Policy
712 G St. SE
Washington, DC 20003
(202) 546-8400

The coalition of 40 national religious, labor, civic, peace and public interest organizations was founded in 1976 to promote the development of demilitarized, humanitarian and non-interventionist foreign policy. It wants to reduce military spending, protect human rights, and promote arms control and disarmament. A subscription to *Coalition Close-Up*, and other publications, is included in its annual $20 membership fee.

Commission on United States-Central American Relations
1826 18th St. NW
Washington, DC 20009
(202) 483-0022

The Commission was created out of a deep concern about the current course of American policy toward the countries of the Caribbean region. Their purpose is to focus public attention upon crucial issues in American policy toward Central America, provide reliable assessments of the impact of policies there, and produce alternatives that can be debated and adopted by public officials.

Committee for National Security
2000 P St. NW, Suite 515
Washington, DC 20036
(202) 833-3140

The Committee, founded in 1980, promotes change in the direction of national security policy through debate on alternatives to military confrontation and appropriate foreign policy. It publishes position papers, briefs and reports.

Committee On the Present Danger
905 16th St. NW, Suite 207
Washington, DC 20006
(202) 628-2409

The Committee, founded on 1976, describes its functions as directing attention to the unfavorable military balance between the United States and the Soviet Union. It publishes occasional papers dealing with this issue.

Council for the Defense of Freedom
P.O. Box 28526
Washington, DC 20038
(202) 229-1790

The Council is concerned about the mortal danger the US will face if it does not stop communist aggression. Its weekly paper, *The Washington Inquirer*, repeatedly deals with the arms race and US failure to take measures to overcome a lack of preparedness. It also publishes a monthly *Bulletin*, and monographs.

The Council On Foreign Relations
58 E. 68th St.
New York, NY 10021
(212) 734-0400

The Council is a group of individuals with specialized knowledge of and interest in international affairs. It was formed to "to study the international aspects of American political, economic and strategic problems." They publish *Foreign Affairs*, and the *Annual Report*.

The Council for International Understanding
136 East 64th St.
New York, New York 10021
(212) 832-2931

The goal of the Council is to influence political leadership towards sounder foreign policy formulation and execution, and to analyze, identify, articulate and introduce fresh insights into the media and the political process. Write for a list of publications.

Department of Defense
The Pentagon
Washington, DC 20301
(202) 545-6700

The Department of Defense is responsible for providing the military forces needed to deter war and protect the security of our country. It also plans policy on strategic international security matters. Write for a list of books and materials on foreign policy and an order form.

The Ethics and Public Policy Center
1030 15th St. NW, Suite 300
Washington, DC 20005
(202) 682-1200

The Center conducts a program of research, writing, publication, and conferences "to encourage debate on major domestic and foreign policy problems." It focuses on the role of organized religion in the public policy arena. It publishes original essays and reprints.

Foreign Policy Association
205 Lexington Ave.
New York, NY 10016
(212) 481-8450

The Association, founded in 1918, is a nonpartisan educational organization to stimulate interest in international relations, to assist in the development of greater understanding of foreign policy issues confronting the United States, and to encourage citizen expression of opinion on foreign policy. It publishes pamphlets entitled *Headline Series*, the annual report, *Great Decisions*, and a *Guide to Key Foreign Policy Issues*.

The Heritage Foundation
214 Massachusetts Ave. NE
Washington, DC 20002
(202) 546-4400

The Foundation, founded in 1974, is "dedicated to limited government, individual and economic freedom and a strong national defense." It supports US involvement in Central America to stop communist influence in the area. It publishes research in various formats on national defense. A subcription to the *National Security Record*, published monthly, costs $25 a year.

Humanitas/International
P.O. Box 818
Menlo Park, CA 94026
(415) 324-9077

The committee is a nonpartisan organization that works to identify and assist victims of human rights violations. It believes that respect for human rights is essential for the preservation of human dignity. It publishes the quarterly *Humanitas Newsletter*.

Human Rights Internet
1338 G St. SE
Washington, DC 20003
(202) 543-9200

The Internet, founded in 1976, is an international communications network and clearinghouse on human rights with universal coverage. It stimulates communication and coordination between and among scholars, activists and policymakers concerned with the promotion of internationally recognized human rights. It publishes the *Reporter*, the *North American Human Rights Directory*, the *Human Rights Directory: Latin America, Africa and Asia*, *Teaching Human Rights*, and *Human Rights Directory: Western Europe*.

Institute of American Relations
325 Constitutions Ave. NW
Washington, DC 20002
(202) 543-5120

The Institute seeks to encourage an adequate American foreign, defense, and security policy including a stronger posture for American defense. It has lobbied against SALT and for the B-1 bomber. They publish a monthly newsletter and pamphlets.

Institute for Contemporary Studies
785 Market St., Suite 750
San Francisco, CA 94103
(415) 543-6213

The Institute develops and publishes public policy studies and distributes them to leaders in government, the media and universities. It publishes the quarterly *Journal of Contemporary Studies*.

Institute For Policy Studies
1901 Q St. NW
Washington, DC 20009
(202) 234-9382

The Institute, founded in 1963, is a research and public education center which publishes a variety of books, reports, and issues papers on international affairs. Write for a catalog of its publications.

Inter-America Commission on Human Rights
Organization of American States
1889 F St. NW
Washington, DC 20006
(202) 789-6000

The Organization serves to promote cooperation among the American Republics and is a regional agency of the United Nations. The Commission's principal function is to promote the observance and protection of human rights. It monitors the human rights situation in the member-countries by examining denounced violations, on-site inspections and other procedures. They publish documents that are available upon request.

International Defense and Aid Fund for Southern Africa
P.O. Box 17
Cambridge, MA 02138
(617) 491-8343

Founded in 1972, the IDAF provides for the legal defense of the "victims of unjust laws and arbitrary procedures in South Africa and Namibia"; to aid and support their families and dependents; "to keep the conscience of the world alive to the issues at stake through the dissemination of information." It publishes the bimonthly *Focus on Political Repression in Southern Africa, Newsnotes,* and also publishes books and brochures about South Africa, Zimbabwe, Namibia, Angola and Mozambique.

Liberty Lobby
300 Independence Ave. SE
Washington, DC 20003
(202) 546-5611

The lobby, founded in 1955, is a group of "nationalists and populists interested in political action in behalf of 98 issues which are pro-individual liberty and pro-patriotic." They support less government spending, protective immigration laws, and withdrawal from the United Nations. They oppose federal aid to education, foreign aid, and "unfair" foreign competition, recognition of Red China, and world government. They publish the weekly, *Spotlight,* and the *Congressional Handbook* and *Liberty Ledger.*

National Committee on American Foreign Policy
200 Park Ave., Suite 303 East
New York, NY 10166
(212) 687-9332

The Committee's purpose is to stimulate citizen interest in American foreign policy with regard to the immediate and long-range national interest of the US and to support the enlightened interests of the US and non-communist world. It publishes a bimonthly newsletter as well as pamphlets and monographs.

National Network in Solidarity with the People of Guatemala
930 F St., NW, Suite 720
Washington, DC 20004
(202) 483-0050

The Network was founded in 1981 to educate the North American people about the current political, military, economic and human rights situation in Guatemala and to coordinate the efforts of support groups throughout the US. It publishes the monthly *Network News.*

Nicaraguan Embassy
1627 New Hampshire Ave. NW
Washington, DC 20009
(202) 387-4371

The embassy is against US covert activity in Nicaragua and unflinchingly defends its sovereignty, independence, and territorial integrity.

North American Congress on Latin America, Inc.
151 West 19th St.
New York, NY 10011
(212) 989-8890

The Congress is an independent research organization founded to document US corporate, military and political activities in Latin America and to related conditions in the US. It publishes an influential bimonthly newsletter that focuses on Central America, *Report on the Americas,* and pamphlets and books.

Overview Latin America
9 Sacramento St.
Cambridge, MA 02138
(617) 354-0576

A human rights education group dedicated to uncovering the social, political and economic roots of poverty and repression on Latin America. It mobilizes support and lobbies for US government policies for Latin America and publishes a variety of publications.

People's Anti-War Mobilization
19 West 21st St., 7th floor
New York, NY 10010
(212) 741-0633

The Mobilization is a national organization that educates and mobilizes against the US war drive. It plays a leading role in the growing movement against US intervention in the Middle East, as well as other areas. The organization publishes a monthly newsletter, pamphlets, and position papers, in conjunction with the All-People's Congress.

Policy Studies Organization
University of Illinois at Urbana-Champaign
361 Lincoln Hall, 706 S. Wright St.
Urbana, IL 61801
(217) 359-8541

The Organization promotes the application of political and social sciences to important policy problems. It publishes the quarterly *Policy Studies Journal,* the *Policy Studies Review,* and directories.

Religious Task Force on Central America
1747 Connecticut Ave. NW
Washington, DC 20009
(202) 387-7652

The task force's objectives are to stop US intervention in Central America and to educate people about circumstances there. It publishes a variety of newsletters and reports.

The Republican National Committee
310 First St. SE
Washington, DC 20003
(202) 484-6500

The RNC provides support activities to Republican administrations. It maintains a library of 6000 items including books, periodicals and newpapers.

The Resource Center
P.O. Box 4506
Albuquerque, NM 87196
(505) 266-5009

A non-profit organization, the Resource Center has produced educational materials on a variety of topics for the last five years. Many Center projects investigate the activities of US corporations and the US government abroad. It publishes a variety of books on foreign policy.

The Ripon Society
419 New Jersey Ave. SE
Washington, DC 20003
(202) 546-1292

The Society is the national progressive Republican research and policy organization. One of its goals is to develop an internationalist, not an interventionist, foreign policy. It publishes the *Ripon Forum.*

Socialist Workers Party
14 Charles Ln.
New York, NY 10014
(212) 242-5530

The Party's views include a call for an end to imperialist intervention abroad.

The Southern Africa Media Center
California Newsreel
630 Natoma St.
San Francisco, CA 94103
(415) 621-6196

The SAMC, a project of California Newsreel, brings together media specialists, educators, religious leaders, and concerned citizens to improve the effectiveness of film in church, community and academic education and action programs around Southern Africa. The Center distributes important anti-apartheid documentaries.

Unitarian Universalist Service Committee
78 Beacon St.
Boston, MA 02108
(617) 742-2120

The Committee is dedicated to promoting economic, social, civil and political rights of people throughout the world. It opposes US intervention in Central America. The UUSC publishes many newsletters and reports.

US-Helsinki Watch Committee
36 West 44th St.
New York, NY 10036
(212) 840-9460

The Committee monitors domestic and international compliance with the human rights provisions of the Helsinki accords. It is an independent, non-governmental organization. It publishes human rights critiques, and reports on all of the Helsinki accord's signatories as well as newspaper and magazine articles.

Washington Office on Latin America
110 Maryland Ave. NE
Washington, DC 20002
(202) 544-8045

The Washington Office on Latin America seeks to encourage US policies which promote human rights and to strengthen democratic trends in Latin America. It is committed to the belief the 1) the US and Latin America are tied by geography and history; 2) that US policy has a great impact on Latin America and 3) that the American public wants to know about and supports US policies which are conducive to the betterment of all people who live in Latin America. It publishes a monthly newsletter.

World Policy Institute
777 United Nations Plaza
New York, NY 10017
(212) 490-0010

The Institute, founded in 1948, is a pioneer in research and development of curriculum for the college and university level. It formulates practical alternatives to war, poverty, social injustice and ecological damage. It attempts to build understanding and public support for a just world order. The Institute publishes *Alternatives: A Journal of World Policy*, the quarterly *Bulletin of Peace Proposals*, and books and papers.

Women's International Resource Exchange
2700 Broadway, Room 7
New York, NY 10025
(212) 666-4622

WIRE functions as a clearinghouse and distribution center for the evaluation and dissemination of materials about women in the Third World. These materials range from previously published articles to unpublished pieces by unknown writers.

bibliography

The following bibliography of books, periodicals, and pamphlets is divided into chapter topics for the reader's convenience. The topics are in the same order as in the body of this Opposing Viewpoint *SOURCES*.

Basis and Goals of Foreign Policy

David Abshire	"No Nation Is an Island," *The American Legion*, September 1983.
George Ball	"Foreign Policy: A Tragedy of Errors," *Bulletin of the Atomic Scientists*, June/July 1984.
Richard J. Barnet	*Real Security: Restoring American Power in a Dangerous Decade.* New York: Simon and Schuster/A Touchstone Book, 1981.
Jeremiah Baruch	"Bye Bipartisanship," *Commonweal*, May 18, 1984.
Peter L. Berger	"Indochina and the American Conscience," *Commentary*, February 1980.
Seyom Brown	*The Faces of Power: Constancy and Change in United States Foreign Policy from Truman to Reagan.* New York: Columbia University Press, 1984.
Patrick Callahan	"Bipartisan Foreign Policy," *America*, November 12, 1983.
Nicholas Capaldi	"Moral Absolutes and Foreign Policy," *Free Inquiry*, Spring 1984.
Harlan Cleveland	"U.S. Foreign Policy: The Illusion of Impotence," *East-West Perspectives*, Summer 1982.
Eliot Cohen	"When Policy Outstrips Power—American Strategy and Statecraft," *Public Interest*, Spring 1984.
Henry Steele Commager	"Of Virtue and Foreign Policy," *Worldview*, October 1982.
Kenneth W. Dam	*Extraterritoriality and Conflicts of Jurisdiction*, April 15, 1983. Pamphlet available from the United States Department of State, Bureau of Public Affairs, Washington, DC 20520.
Department of State Bulletin	All issues.
Alexander M. Haig	"American Power," *Vital Speeches of the Day*, June 15, 1982.
Stanley Hoffman	*Duties Beyond Borders: On the Limits and Possibilities of Ethical International Politics.* Syracuse, NY: Syracuse University Press 1981.
Jacob K. Javits	"Who Decides on War?" *The New York Times Magazine*, October 23, 1983.
Jeane J. Kirkpatrick	"Dictatorships and Double Standards," *Commentary*, November 1979.
Jeane J. Kirkpatrick	"Gaining Strength and Respect in the World," *Vital Speeches of the Day*, March 1, 1984.
Langhorne A. Motley	"Democracy as a Problem-Solving Mechanism," *Department of State Bulletin*, February 1984.
Robert J. Myers	"The Moral High Ground," *Worldview*, August 1983.
Kenneth A. Oye, Robert J. Lieber, & Donald Rothchild	*Eagle Defiant: United States Foreign Policy in the 1980s.* Toronto: Little, Brown & Company (Canada) Limited, 1983.
George Shultz	*Project Democracy*, February 23, 1983. Pamphlet available from the United States Department of State, Bureau of Public Affairs, Washington, DC 20520.
George Shultz	"American Principles and Foreign Policy," *Department of State Bulletin*, April 1983.
Joel M. Skousen	"A Winning Strategy for Hemispheric Foreign Policy," *Conservative Digest*, June 1983.
Howard Trivers	*Three Crises in American Foreign Affairs and a Continuing Revolution.* London: Feffer and Simon, Inc., 1972.
Margaret D. Wilde	"Jeane Kirkpatrick: Utilitarianism as U.S. Foreign Policy," *The Christian Century*, March 4, 1981.

Defense and Foreign Policy

Dennis Bark	"United States Security and World Peace," *Vital Speeches of the Day*, April 15, 1984.
Glen Fisher	"International Negotiation: Cross-Cultural Perception," *The Humanist*, November/December 1983.
Ken Hancock	"Canadians Refuse the Cruise," *WIN*, October 1983.
Harvard Nuclear Study Group	"A Primer on Arms Control," *Current*, September 1983.
Robert C. Johansen	"Numerical Insecurity," *The Atlantic Monthly*, August 1983.
Henry Kissinger	"A New Approach to Arms Control," *Time*, March 21, 1983.

Sidney Lens	"The Deterrence Myth," *The Progressive*, 1984.
Cord Meyer	"Are the Dominoes Leaning Our Way?" *Conservative Digest*, December 1983.
Charles Mohr	"Cruise Missile Passes Tests but It's Critics Score Too," *The New York Times*, July 17, 1983.
Christopher E. Paine	"Arms Control Poker," *Inquiry*, June 1984.
Ronald Reagan	"Building Peace Through Strength," *Department of State Bulletin*, October 1983.
Republican National Committee	*Rebuilding Our Defenses: The Reagan Administration's Record on Defense Issues.* Pamphlet available from the Communications Division Review, Department of the Republican National Committee, 310 First St. SE, Washington, DC, 20003.
US Department of State	*U.S. National Security.* Pamphlet available from the US Department of State, Bureau of Public Affairs, Washington, DC, 20520.
Jim Wake	*The International Arms Trade.* Fall 1982. Pamphlet available from Humanitas International, PO Box 818, Menlo Park, CA 94026.
Francis J. West Jr.	"Defense and Security Beyond Europe," *Defense*, May 1983.
R. James Woolsey	"Defense and Arms Control," *The New Republic*, March 31, 1982.

Trade and Foreign Policy

John Block	"As U.S. Farmers Struggle for Foreign Markets" *U.S. News & World Report*, March 14, 1983.
Carol Brookins	"Carrots & Sticks," *Foreign Service Journal*, April 1983.
Peter G. Brown and Henry Shue	"Exporting Hazards," *Report from the Center for Philosophy and Public Policy*, Fall 1981.
Nick Butler	"The US Grain Weapon: Could it Boomerang?" *The World Today*, February 1983.
Kenneth W. Dam	"U.S. Foreign Policy and Agricultural Trade," *Department of State Bulletin*, February 1984.
Thomas R. Graham	"War & Peace," *Foreign Policy*, Spring 1983.
Monroe W. Karmin	"Industrial Policy: What Is It? Do We Need One?" *U.S. News & World Report*, October 3, 1983.
Edward Lamb	"A Frank Look at Today's Soviet Union," *The Churchman*, December 1983.
David R. Macdonald	"Rethinking U.S. Trade Policy," *Context*, 1984.
Nicholas Mavroules	"Denying Moscow High-Tech," *The New York Times*, October 10, 1983.
Tom G. Palmer	"Chipping Away at Free Trade," *Inquiry*, November 1983.
Joel M. Skousen	"A Boycott in the Works," *Conservative Digest*, October 1983.
Daniel Southerland	"The Inscrutable Secretary," *Foreign Service Journal*, April 1983.
Robert E. Wood	"The World Bank and the Third World: Toward a Politics of Aid," *Socialist Review*, January/February 1984.

| Benjamin Zycher | "A U.S. Department of Trade—or Protection," *The Backgrounder*, December 9, 1983. Available from The Heritage Foundation, 214 Massachusetts Ave. NE, Washington, DC 20002 |

Foreign Aid

James Bednar	"Foreign Aid," *Agenda*, December 1980.
Grace Goodell	"Conservatism and Foreign Aid," *Policy Review*, Winter 1982.
Billy Graham	"The Black Horse Is Coming," *Eternity*, January 1984.
Maclean's	"Guilt by Association," March 10, 1980.
Larry Marton	"American Farmers and Foreign Aid," *Agenda*, December 1980.
Edmund F. McCaffrey	"Why Foreign Aid Is Our Moral Obligation," *Catholic Twin Circle*, February 21, 1982.
David Rockefeller	"Foolish Attacks on False Issues," *The Wall Street Journal*, April 30, 1980.
Michael J. Schultheis	"National Security and Economic Assistance," *Center Focus*, September 1983.
Theodore W. Schultz	"The Economics of U.S. Foreign Aid," *Bulletin of the Atomic Scientists*, October 1983.
Allen Wallis	*Economics and Politics: The Quandary of Foreign Aid*, March 3, 1983. Pamphlet available from the US Department of State, Bureau of Public Affairs, Washington, DC 20520.

Human Rights

Elliott Abrams	"Human Rights and the Reagan Administration: Another View," *America*, June 4, 1983.
America's Watch	*Review of the Department of State's Country Reports on Human Rights Practices for 1982*, February 1983. Pamphlet available from America's Watch, 36 West 44th St., New York, NY 10036.
Peter G. Brown and Douglas MacLean, editors	*Human Rights and U.S. Foreign Policy*, Lexington, MA: D.C. Heath, 1979.
Center for Philosophy and Public Policy	*Human Rights and the 'National Interest': Which Takes Priority?* Pamphlet available from the Center for Philosophy and Public Policy, College Park, MD 20742.
Commentary	"Human Rights and American Foreign Policy," A Symposium, November 1981.
Arthur Goldberg	"The Perilous State of Human Rights, Then and Now," *The Center Magazine*, January/February 1984.
Jeane J. Kirkpatrick	"Why Not Abolish Ignorance?" *National Review*, July 9, 1982.
Theodore H. Von Laue	"Human Rights Imperialism," *Bulletin of the Atomic Scientists*, September 1982.
Michael Levin	"The Case for Torture," *Newsweek*, June 7, 1982.
Adam Meyerson	"A Conservative Philosophy for Advancing the Cause of Freedom," *Policy Review*, Winter 1984.
The New Republic	"Friendly Fire," February 17, 1982.
The New Republic	"Rights and Regimes," May 9, 1983.
Michael J. Perry	*The Constitution, The Courts, and Human Rights*. New Haven, CT: Yale University Press, 1982.

Juliana Geran Pilon	"The U.N. and Human Rights: The Double Standard," *Backgrounder*, May 11, 1982. Available from The Heritage Foundation, 214 Massachusetts Ave. NE, Washington, DC 20002.
Henry Shue	*Playing Hardball with Human Rights*, Fall 1983. Pamphlet available from the Center for Philosophy and Public Policy, College Park, MD.
George Shultz	*Human Rights and the Moral Dimension of U.S. Foreign Policy*, February 22, 1984. Pamphlet available from the United States Department of State, Bureau of Public Affairs, Washington, DC 20520.
US Department of State	*1983 Human Rights Report*, February 1984. Pamphlet available from the United States Department of State, Bureau of Public Affairs, Washington, DC 20520.
US Department of State	*Report on the Situation in El Salvador*, January 16, 1984. Pamphlet available from the United States Department of State, Bureau of Public Affairs, Washington, DC 20520.
US Department of State	*1983 Human Rights Report*, February 1984. Pamphlet available from the United States Department of State, Bureau of Public Affairs, Washington, DC 20520.

Intervention

Eqbal Ahmad	"Political Culture and Foreign Policy: Notes on American Interventions in the Third World," Institute for Policy Studies 1982.
T.D. Allman	"The Doctrine that Never Was," *Harper's*, January 1984.
Richard J. Barnet	*Intervention and Revolution: The United States in the Third World*. New York: New American Library, 1972.
Charles R. Beitz	"Should All Countries Be Democracies?" *Report from the Center for Philosophy and Public Policy*, Winter 1982.
Robert Blum	*Drawing the Line: The Origin of the American Containment Policy in East Asia*. New York: WW Norton and Co., 1982.
Jack Child	"Abstention or Intervention," *ORBIS: A Journal of World Affairs*, Summer 1982.
Michael T. Klare	*Beyond the 'Vietnam Syndrome'*. Washington, DC: Institute for Policy Studies, 1981.
Tibor R. Machan	"Fighting Isolationism," *Reason*, February 1984.
The Nation	"Awacs of August," August 20, 1983.
Sheldon Richman	"The Culture of Intervention," *Inquiry*, March/April 1984.
Emily Rosenberg	*Spreading the American Dream*. New York: Hill and Wang, 1982.
Murray N. Rothbard	"Where the Left Goes Wrong on Foreign Policy," *Inquiry*, July 1982.
Jerry W. Sanders	"Breaking Out of the Containment Syndrome," *World Policy Journal*, Fall 1983.
James C. Thomson Jr., Peter W. Stanley & John Curtis Perry	*Sentimental Imperialist: The American Experience in East Asia*. New York: Harper & Row/Collophon Books, 1981.

Intervention Case Study: Grenada 1983

Elliott Abrams	"Human Rights Implications for U.S. Action in Grenada," *Department of State Bulletin*, February 1984.
Marvin Alisky	"Grenada's Importance," *Vital Speeches of the Day*, December 15, 1983.
Richard J. Barnet	"The Empire Strikes Back," *The Progressive*, January 1984.
Alexander Baryshev	"Operation 'Urgent Fury'," *New Times* December 1983.
Jan Knippers Black	"The Selling of the Invasion of Grenada," *USA Today*, May 1984.
The Christian Century	"We Got There Just in Time," November 9, 1983.
Commonweal	"Grenada's Gain, Our Loss," November 18, 1983.
Barbara Crossette	"The Caribbean After Grenada," *The New York Times Magazine*, March 18, 1984.
Department of State	"Grenada: A Preliminary Report," December 16, 1983.
Yuri Deporov	"The Rape of Grenada and International Law," *New Times*, December 1983.
Marc Edelman	"Costa Rica Next?" *The Nation*, May 21, 1983.
Joseph Gonda	"Morality and Politics: The Case of Grenada," *Catholicism in Crisis*, May 1984.
Christopher Hitchens	"Grenada: The Menacing Runway," *The Nation*, May 29, 1982.
Jonathan Kwitny	"Oh, What a Lovely War," *Mother Jones*, June 1984.
Michael Massing	"Grenada: Before and After," *The Atlantic Monthly*, February 1984. Letter responses: June 1984.
Richard McSorley	"Is the Grenada Invasion Moral?" *The Churchman*, December 1983.
Langhorne A. Motley	"The Decision To Assist Grenada," Current Policy No. 541, January 24, 1984. Available from Bureau of Public Affairs, US Department of State, Washington, DC 20520.
V. S. Naipaul	"An Island Betrayed," *Harper's*, March 1984.
The New Republic	"Anatomy of a Little War," November 21, 1983.
Virginia Prewett	"Grenada Move Thwarts Soviet Expansion Bid," *Conservative Digest*, November 1983.
The Progressive	"Tomorrow the World," December 1983.
Ellen Ray and Bill Schaap	"US Crushes Caribbean Jewel," *Covert Action Information Bulletin*, Winter 1984.
John Rees	"An Interview with Conservative Representative Dan L. Burton about What He Discovered in Grenada," *The Review of the News*, November 23, 1983.
William Steif	"Reagan's Island," *The Progressive*, January 1984.
Stephen Zunes	"A Revolution That Could Have Worked," *The Progressive*, January 1984.

Covert Operations, Terrorism

Philip Agee	*White Paper? Whitewash*, New York: Sheridan Square Publications, Inc., 1983.

Ray Cline — "National Intelligence: A Moral Imperative," *Values in Conflict*. New York: Macmillan, 1981.

Congressional Digest — "Controversy over Legislative Limitations on Covert US Intelligence Operations," Special Issue, May 1980.

John Dinges and Saul Landau — "Follow-Up on the Letelier Case: The CIA's Link to Chile's Plot," *The Nation*, June 12, 1982.

Allen W. Dulles — *The Craft of Intelligence*. New York: Harper and Row, 1963.

V. Dmitriyev — "Terrorism: An Instrument of US Policy," *Soviet Military Review*, October 1983.

Edward Jay Epstein — "Disinformation: Or, Why the CIA Cannot Verify an Arms-Control Agreement," *Commentary*, July 1982.

Don Feder — "Tracking Terrorists Won't Abridge Civil Liberties," *Conservative Digest*, February 1984.

Tom Gervasi — "Black Ops, 1963 to 1983," *Harper's*, April 1984.

Inquiry — "Bad Neighbor Policy...War on the Sly," January 1984.

Noel C. Koch — "Special Operations Forces," *Defense*, July 1983.

Saul Landau and Craig Nelson — "Destabilizing Nicaragua—The CIA Rides Again," *The Nation*, March 6, 1982.

Walter Laqueur — "Reagan and the Russians," *Commentary* January 1982.

Ernest Lefever — "Can Covert Action Be Just?" *Policy Review*, Spring 1983.

Guenter Lewy — "Can Democracy Keep Secrets?" *Policy Review*, Fall 1983.

Angus Mackenzie — "The Operational Files Exemption," *The Nation*, September 24, 1983.

Angus Mackenzie — "A CIA-ACLU Deal? The Operational Files Exemption," *The Nation*, September 24, 1983.

National Security Record — "What to Do about Terrorism in America," April 1984. Report available from The Heritage Foundation 214 Massachusetts Ave. NE, Washington, DC 20002.

Keenen Peck — "A Court that Never Says No," *The Progressive*, April 1984.

Jay Peterzell — *Reagan's Secret Wars*. 1983. Pamphlet available from the Center for National Security Studies, 122 Maryland Ave. NE, Washington, DC 20002.

Herman Schwartz — "A Constitutional Disaster: Agents Protection Act," *The Nation*, July 3, 1982.

Peer de Silva — *Sub-Rosa: The CIA and the Uses of Intelligence*. New York: New York Times Books Co. Inc., 1978.

US Congress, House Committee on Foreign Affairs, Subcommittee on International Security and Scientific Affairs — *The Role of Intelligence in the Foreign Policy Process*. Washington, DC: Government Printing Office, 1980.

Murray Waas — "The CIA and Page Airways: The Case of the Flying Spies," *The Nation*, February 20, 1982.

Russell Watson and David C. Martin — "Is Covert Action Necessary?" *Newsweek*, November 8, 1982.

Francis M. Wilhoit — "The Morality of National Intelligence: A Rejoinder," *Values in Conflict*. New York: Macmillan, 1981.

George Wittman, editor — *The Role of American Intelligence Organizations*. New York: The H.W. Wilson Co./The Reference Shelf, 1976.

Nikolai Yokovlev — "Cold War Kamikazes," *New Times*, September 1983.

US and Europe

Meg Beresford — "A European 'Declaration of Independence,'" *WIN*, January 1, 1982.

David Cooper — "Effective Armaments Cooperation: NATO's New Long-Term Planning Procedures," *NATO Review*, March 3, 1983.

David Corn — "Euromissiles in Home Stretch," *Nuclear Times*, October 1983.

Jonathan Dean — "Federal Germany after the Euromissiles," *Bulletin of the Atomic Scientists*, December 1983.

Kate Donnelly — "Women Resist Euromissiles," *WIN*, October 1983.

Ed Hedemann — "The Rise of Civil Defense In West Germany," *WIN*, October 1983.

Helmut Kohl — "Our Mandate: A Europe," *Vital Speeches of the Day*, September 1, 1983.

Pierre Lellouche — "France and the Euromissiles: The Limits of Immunity," *Foreign Affairs*, Winter 1983/1984.

Jonathan Marshall — "The Missiles of December," *Inquiry*, December 1983.

Joseph S. Nye Jr. — "Deploy Missiles: Cut Arms," *The New York Times*, October 21, 1983.

George Shultz — "North Atlantic Council Meets in Paris," *Department of State Bulletin*, August 1983.

Pierre E. Trudeau — "Reflections on Peace and Security," *Vital Speeches of the Day*, December 1, 1983.

The US and Asia

Asian Studies — *Taiwan: Facing Mounting Threats*, 1984. Pamphlet available from The Heritage Foundation, 214 Massachusetts Ave. NE, Washington, DC 20002.

Asian Studies — *President Reagan's Trip to the People's Republic of China*. April 1984. Pamphlet available from The Heritage Foundation, 214 Massachusetts Ave. NE, Washington, DC 20002.

Robert W. Barnett — "In Defense of Japan," *Worldview*, March 1984.

Walden Bello — "Springboards for Intervention, Instruments for Nuclear War," *Southeast Asia Chronicle*, April 1983.

William A. Brown — "The Soviet Role in Asia," *Department of State Bulletin*, December 1983.

Francisco F. Claver — "Free Even in Enslavement," *Commonweal*, March 1984.

John F. Copper — "Sino-American Relations: Reaching a Plateau," *Current History*, September 1982.

Defense Monitor — "The Defense of Japan: Should the Rising Sun Rise Again?," 1984.

Edwin J. Feulner Jr., Hideaki Kase, editors — *U.S.-Japan Mutual Security*. Washington, DC: The Heritage Foundation, 1981.

Haruhiro Fukui — "Japan Sees No Security in Increased Militarization," *The Center Magazine*, May/June 1982.

Maeda Hisao	"The Free-Rider Myth," *Japan Quarterly*, April/June 1982.
Paul H. Kreisverg	"Military Ties With China," *The New York Times*, December 23, 1983.
Amaya Naohiro	"The Millenium of Armageddon Japan May Hold the Key," *Japan Quarterly*, October/December 1983.
David Osborne	"Lobbying for Japan Inc." *The New York Times*, December 4, 1983.
Peter Tarr	"The Economic Threat to Marcos," *The Nation*, March 24, 1984.
Time	"Japan: A Nation in Search of Itself," Special issue, August 1, 1983.
Theodore H. White	"Banishing Mao's Ghost," *Time*, September 26, 1983.
Christopher S. Wren	"China's Courtship of Capitalism," *The New York Times*, December 25, 1983.

The US and the Third World

Douglas J. Bennet Jr.	"U.S. Opportunities in a Fast-Changing Third World," *USA Today*, January 1981.
Arnaud de Borchgrave and Michael Ledeen	"An Interview with Alexander Haig," *The New Republic*, February 7, 1981.
Peter L. Berger	"Speaking to the Third World," *Commentary*, October 1981.
Cesar A. Chelala	"Argentina, Prosecute All Officers," *The New York Times*, March 6, 1984.
John Jefferson Davis	"First-World Wealth and Third-World Poverty," *The Freeman*, November 1982.
George Shultz	"The U.S. and the Developing World: Our Joint Stake in the World Economy," *Department of State Bulletin*, July 1983.
Dan Dickinson	"Free Enterprise: The Salvation of Many Third World Countries," *Human Events*, January 21, 1984.
Dan Dickinson	"Capitalism in the Third World," *Conservative Digest*, April 1984.
Richard E. Feinberg and Kenneth A. Oye	"After the Fall: U.S. Policy Toward Radical Regimes," *World Policy*, Fall 1983.
Malcolm Fraser	"The Third World and the West," *Vital Speeches of the Day*, August 15, 1981.
Frances Moore Lappe and Joseph Collins	*World Hunger: 10 Myths.* San Francisco: Institute for Food and Development Policy, 1982.
Judith Moore	"Justice and Economics: A Third World View," *Lutheran Woman*, March 1984.
Thomas Sowell	"Second Thoughts about the Third World," *Harper's*, November 1983.
William Steif	"Murder on the Mountaintop," *The Progressive*, April 1984.

The US and Africa

Ian Butterfield	"U.S. Exports to South Africa: The Tough Choice," *Backgrounder*, March 1, 1982. Available from The Heritage Foundation, 214 Massachusetts Ave. NE, Washington, DC 20002.
Danny Collum	"No Apologetics for Apartheid," *Sojourners*, October 1982.
Thomas Conrad	"Legal Arms for South Africa," *The Nation*, January 21, 1984.

Chester A. Crocker	*The Search for Regional Security in South Africa*, March 3, 1983. Pamphlet available from the US Department of State, Bureau of Public Affairs, Washington, DC 20520.
Chester A. Crocker	*Our Development Dialogue with Africa*, March 3, 1983. Pamphlet available from the US Department of State, Bureau of Public Affairs, Washington, DC 20520.
Current History	"Africa South of the Sahara, 1984," a collection of articles, March 1984.
Justine De Lacy	"Western Investors Now Welcome," *The Atlantic Monthly*, January 1984.
Economic Notes	"U.S. Coal and South Africa," November/December 1983.
Gail Hovey	*Apartheid's New Clothes*, Pamphlet available from *The Africa Fund*, 198 Broadway, New York, NY 10038.
I.D.A.F. News Notes	*South Africa's Bomb*, August 1983. Pamphlet available from the International Defense and Aid Fund for Southern Africa, PO Box 17, Cambridge, MA 02138.
Charles Krauthammer	"Rich Nations, Poor Nations," *The New Republic*, April 11, 1981.
Carol Lancaster	"Africa's Economic Crisis," *Foreign Policy*, Fall 1983.
Scholastic Update	Special issue on Africa, January 20, 1984.
Richard E. Sincere Jr.	"The Churches and Investment In South Africa," *America*, March 3, 1984.
Southern Africa Project	*South Africa 1983: Reorganizing Apartheid.* Pamphlet available from Lawyers' Committee for Civil Rights, 1400 'Eye' St. NW, Suite 400, Washington, DC 20005.
U.S. News & World Report	"Will North Africa Be Next Hot Spot for US?" March 12, 1984.
Ted Weiss	"American Policy and African Refugees," *Africa Report*, January/February 1984.
Geoffrey Wheatcroft	"The Anguish of Africa," *New Republic*, January 1984.
World Press Review	"The Africa Challenge," August 1983.

The US and Central America

Robert Armstrong and Janet Shenk	*El Salvador: The Face of Revolution.* Boston: South End Press, 1982.
Phillip Berryman	*The Religious Roots of Rebellion* Maryknoll: New York, 1984.
Phillip Berryman	*What's Wrong in Central America and What to Do about It.* Philadelphia: American Friends Service Committee, 1983.
Cole Blasier	*The Giant's Rival: The U.S.S.R. in Latin America.* University of Pittsburgh Press, 1983.
John A. Booth	*The End and the Beginning: The Nicaraguan Revolution.* New York: Westview Press, 1982.
The Cardinal Mindzenty Report	"Some Questions and Answers on Central America," March 1984.
Raymond K. DeHainut	"Reagan's War on Central America," *The Churchman*, April/May 1983.

Bernard Diedrich	*Somoza and the Legacy of U.S. Involvement in Central America.* New York: E.P. Dutton, 1981.
Marvin Diskin	*Trouble in Our Backyard.* New York: Pantheon Books, 1983.
Marlene Dixon and Susanne Jonas	*Revolution and Intervention in Central America.* San Francisco: Synthesis Publications, 1983.
Michael Erisman	*Colossus Challenged: The Caribbean Struggle for Influence,* Boulder CO: Westview Press, 1982.
Mark Falcoff	*Crisis and Opportunity, U.S. Policy in Central American and the Caribbean.* Washington, DC: Ethics and Public Policy Center, 1984.
Marvin E. Gettleman, et al.	*El Salvador: Central America in the New Cold War.* New York: Grove Press, 1981.
Eric Jorstad	"Sanctuary for Refugees: A Statement of Public Policy," *The Christian Century,* March 14, 1984.
Joanne Kenen	"Practically Neutral," *The Atlantic Monthly,* June 1983.
Nancy Komisar	"The Case of Honduras," *National Review,* August 15/22, 1983.
Peter R. Kornbluh	"U.S. Involvement in Central America: A Historical Lesson," *USA Today,* September 1983.
Robert S. Leiken	*Central America: Anatomy of a Conflict,* Pergamon Press, 1983.
Barry B. Levine	*The New Cuban Presence in the Caribbean,* Boulder, CO: Westview Press, 1982.
Los Angeles Times	"On the Verge of Disaster in El Salvador," January 8, 1984.
Jonathan Evan Maslow	"Honduras, Regional Pawn," *Harper's,* June 1984.
The New Republic	"Nicaraguan Nettle," May 9, 1983.
The People	"U.S. 'Aid' Will Make Things Worse," March 3, 1984.
Policy Alternatives for the Caribbean and Central America	*Changing Course: Blueprint for Peace in Central America and the Caribbean* Washington, DC: Institute for Policy Studies, 1984.
Ernesto Rivas-Gallont	"El Salvador: The Principle of Non-Intervention," *Vital Speeches of the Day,* October 15, 1981.
Carla Anne Robbins	*The Cuban Threat.* New York: McGraw Hill Book Co., 1983.
Max Singer	"The Record in Latin America," *Commentary,* December 1982.
Thomas W. Walker	*Nicaragua in Revolution.* New York: Prager, 1982.
The Washington Spectator	"The Not-So-Secret War in Central America," March 15, 1983.
Robert Wesson	*Communism in Central America and the Caribbean.* Stanford, CA: Hoover Institution Press, 1982.
Richard Alan White	*The Morass: United States Intervention in Central America.* New York: Harper and Row, 1984.

The Kissinger Report

America	"The Kissinger Report," January 28, 1984.
Coalition Close-Up	*No Consensus on Kissinger Commission.* Pamphlet available from The Coalition for a New Foreign and Military Policy, 120 Maryland Ave. NE, Washington, DC 20002.

John H. Coatsworth	"Central America," *Bulletin of the Atomic Scientists,* January 1984.
Enrique Dominguez	"The Great Commission," *NACLA Report,* January/February 1984.
Francis X. Gannon	"Central America," *Vital Speeches of the Day,* November 1, 1983.
Phil Land	*The Kissinger Report.* Newsletter available from the Center of Concern, 3700 13th St. NE, Washington, DC 20017.
The Nation	"Contra Kissinger," January 28, 1984.
The New Republic	"The Truth Is Sometimes Banal," January 30, 1984.
Clark Reynolds	"Guns and Butter Still Don't Mix," *The Los Angeles Times,* January 30, 1984.
Eugene Stockwell	"What Kissinger Really Thinks About Nicaragua," *Christianity and Crisis,* January 23, 1984.

The US and the Middle East

Leonard Binder	"The Middle East," *Bulletin of the Atomic Scientists,* January 1984.
William R. Brown	"The Dying Arab Nation," *Foreign Policy,* Spring 1984.
Noam Chomsky	*The Fateful Triangle: The United States, Israel and the Palestinians.* Boston: South End Press, 1984.
Noam Chomsky	"The Middle East and the Probability of Nuclear War," *Socialist Review,* July/August 1983.
Sam Cohen	"Wall Against War," *Reason,* March 1984.
Thomas Draper, editor	*Israel and the Middle East.* New York: The H.W. Wilson Company, 1983.
Foreign Policy Association	"The Palestinians: History, Politics and Conflict," *Great Decisions '82,* 1982.
Max Holland	*The Militarization of the Middle East.* Philadelphia: American Friends Service Committee, 1983.
Ian S. Lustick	"Israeli Politics and American Foreign Policy," *Foreign Affairs,* Winter 1982/83.
Robert G. Neumann	"Assad and the Future of the Middle East," *Foreign Affairs,* Winter 1983/84.
Robert G. Neumann	"United States Policy in the Middle East," *Current History,* January 1984.
The New Republic	"The 'Peacekeeping' Fraud," November 14, 1983.
Walter Reich	"A Stranger in My House: Jews and Arabs in the West Bank," *The Atlantic Monthly,* June 1984.
Amnon Rubinstein	*The Zionist Dream Revisited: from Herzl to Gush Emunim and back.* New York: Schocken, 1984.
Nikola B. Schahgaldian	"Prospects for a Unified Lebanon," *Current History,* January 1984.
Scholastic Update	"The Middle East: Region at War with Itself," March 16, 1984.
George Shultz	"Promoting Peace in the Middle East," *Department of State Bulletin,* January 1984.
U.S. News & World Report	"We Can Still Rebuild Influence in Mideast," February 20, 1984.

index